BARRY SALT

MOVING INTO

PICTURES

MORE ON FILM HISTORY, STYLE, AND ANALYSIS

* STARWORD *

To the memory of Francis Robert Salt and Margaret Jaffray Incoll

Notice to librarians

This book is primarily a work on the history of film style.

Catalogue records relating to it can be obtained from
the British Library and the Library of Congress

Published in 2006 by

STARWORD

5 Tadmor Street
London W12 8AH

Printed by Hobbs the Printers,
Totton, Hampshire

Made in England

ISBN 978 0 9509066 4 5

CONTENTS

MOVING INTO
PICTURES

My first contact with the movies was being taken, along with a long crocodile of other small children, to see *Babes in Toyland* (1934) at a special screening arranged by the local Protestant churches. The only images which stayed with me from this film were the scenes that disturbed me, and these were the punishment of Oliver Hardy by submerging him on a ducking stool, and much more strongly, the march of the giant toy wooden soldiers later in the film. Re-seeing the film over sixty years later, all these things seemed pretty feeble. The one image of the marching wooden soldiers that had been burned into my brain I could now see was a low angle shot from in front of the soldiers taken with a wide angle lens. This must have had its effect because I was sitting down near the front of the cinema when I first saw the film, and with the big high screens used in cinemas in the 'thirties, the magically marching soldiers would have towered over me.

This experience took place in the Empress cinema, one of the two cinemas in Williamstown at the time. The Empress was a large wooden barn of a building, down near the beach and the other entertainment facilities for the summer traffic, like the sea baths, the bandstand and the small amusement park. The Empress had originally been a roller skating rink, built at the beginning of the twentieth century when roller skating was a major pastime, but it had been converted into a cinema in the 'twenties. A feeble attempt was made to give it the style of the "atmospheric" cinemas fashionable at the time, but this amounted to little more than hanging lamps in the auditorium with shades decorated with camels and pyramids. The point of this touch was a bit of a puzzle to us children. We delighted in using the cinema's nickname, "the Bughouse", instead of its real name, as often as possible. It was claimed that it was infested with fleas and vermin, and boastful boys in the school playground alleged they had seen rats running round in the dark there, and had even knocked them out with thrown marbles. I never saw any myself on the rare occasions I was allowed to go to the movies, though I kept a sharp lookout for them. The Empress was certainly a cheap operation, for the management "bicycled" (actually motor-bicycled) the two halves of the bill back and forth alternately every evening between the Empress and the Plaza, the other cinema they owned at Newport, two miles up the railway line towards Melbourne.

The other cinema in Williamstown was new and modern, being purpose-built around the beginning of the 'thirties for the major Hoyts chain of cinemas in Australia. The Hoyts chain, though originally of Australian ownership, was now controlled by Twentieth Century-Fox. It was there that I saw the only other film I remember from so early in my life, Disney's *Snow White and the Seven Dwarfs*, on its first release. Again, the only lasting visual impression for me was the scene in which the wicked queen fell to her death over a precipice near the end of the film. I was told years later that I had hidden under the seat of the cinema when the wicked queen was at work earlier in the film, with the request, 'Tell me when she's gone', but clearly I had got up enough courage by the end to watch the climax.

Two years later, and two years older, I coped rather better with *Pinocchio*, and after that there was a new Disney feature-length cartoon every year. In those days everyone considered this a natural part of life, like Christmas. Unlike my schoolmates at State Primary School No. 1183, who went to the movies once or twice a week, I was allowed to go to the cinema only rarely, and the latest Disney feature was one of these occasions. I think my parents considered the movies a low form of entertainment that stultified the mind. I did feel deprived, as the talk from the other little boys in the school playground was often about what they had seen the previous night at the movies. Such as garbled ravings about actresses like Veronica Lake who aroused their immature lust. All I was allowed to go to were the monthly 'Cartoon Carnivals' on Saturday afternoon at the Hoyts theatre. I enjoyed most of this, particularly the 'Tom and Jerry' films and most of the Disney cartoons, though I disliked Donald Duck's characteristic rages. I was a shy and somewhat sensitive child, and there was no shouting or loud public disagreements in front of the children by the adults in our family. Indeed I disliked loud noise in general, as I do still, so I also hated the continuous uproar between the films from the children packing the cinema.

Williamstown had been the port for Melbourne back in the early days of the colony, and it was there that my great-grandfather William Henry Salt had ended up in 1870, on the crew of the lightship moored off the shore to guide ships into the Williamstown docks. He had jumped ship at Queenscliff, down near the entrance to Port Philip Bay, around 1852,

from a clipper out of Fowey in Cornwall. There were many sailor Salts from Cornwall on ships in the nineteenth century, though mostly they went right back home after their voyages. Much later in my life, I met Brian Salt, the author of two standard works on rostrum camera operating, who claimed that all the Salts originally came from Cornwall in the distant past, though by the nineteenth century there were more of them around Lancashire. In the twentieth century, liners and warships docked at Port Melbourne on the other side of Hobson's Bay. Nevertheless, there were always smaller steamers and sailing ships alongside the piers at the Williamstown docks, and during the war, as well as the frigates and destroyers docked there, cargo ships were being built as part of the war effort. From the docks to the rifle range at the other end of Williamstown, the city was a giant adventure playground for a boy on a bike.

Being a shy child, and with no other respectable children in my immediate neighbourhood, I mostly played with my cousins, particularly Richard White, who lived fairly close by, on the way down to the beach. This had its advantages, as Richard had more toys than me, and also comic books,

The Salt family fathers and children in front of one of the peppercorn trees in the "shop yard" behind my grandmother's house, one Christmas day early in the war. The boys have wooden "Tommy" guns made by their fathers. The guns are painted with camouflage for jungle fighting against the Japanese. The mothers always insisted on being left out of the picture.

which I was not allowed to have. His father also had a 9.5 mm. projector, and films to go with it, so another special treat was seeing old Felix cartoons. Another film favourite with the junior members of the family was a little live action interest film showing a fight between a Mexican Roadrunner bird and a snake.

In the 'thirties my father, who had left school at fifteen, was just a clerk working for the Shell Oil company, so we did not have much money at all. But he was passing his accountancy exams at night, and this got him slowly moving up the management ladder by the nineteen-forties. Both my parents came from large families, and so I have getting on for thirty first cousins. The Salts in particular were a close family, and often visited one another, and every Christmas everyone gathered to have the traditional dinner at my grandparents home, which was just across the other side of the railway line (and Williamstown Beach station) from our house. Grandfather Salt had once had a substantial painting and decorating business, with workshops for mixing paint and for carpentry and so on in a gigantic backyard behind their house. This derelict "shop yard", with several large peppercorn trees for climbing, and all sorts of interesting debris, was another major playground of my youth.

By co-incidence, my maternal grandfather Incoll had been a coach painter for part of his life. Early in the twentieth century there still a lot of work to be had painting fine decorative lines and patterns around the edges of the bodies of horse-drawn carriages, and indeed motor cars as well. Motor cars in those days were still mostly black all over, and could do with the individual touch, if you could afford it. The Incolls were of Scottish origin, and were rather more widely distributed, with schoolteachers and Forestry Commission officials scattered round the state. Nevertheless, there were also lots of holidays to stay with them, and vice versa. So I spent a fair amount of my childhood in the country, and in particular down on a dairy farm in the Western District of Victoria owned by my great-uncle and aunt Kinghorn. There were to be found second cousins with a barnyard attitude to life, outdoor privies, horses, dogs, and wild animals to be hunted with them. There was even a wooden bridge where the road crossed the Main Drain (most of the land around the farm was swampy), and on it one could play Poohsticks. Some farm work in the cowshed and elsewhere was expected of the visitors, too. I was fascinated with how things worked, and cars and other machinery were always being mended on the farm. The Kinghorns naturally came to stay with us during Show Week, when the yearly Royal Agricultural Show was on in the immense dedicated showgrounds outside Melbourne. This was another small boy's paradise, with working agricultural machinery on show, and sample bags being handed out by the confectionery manufacturers in the produce halls. And there were sheep dog trials and wood-cutting competitions and trotting races in the arena.

A special part of the Salt family ethos was that talking about other people (i.e. gossip) was wrong, as were boasting and showing-off. The discussion of money, and what people earn, was also forbidden to the children.

Early in World War II there was another long crocodile, this time from State School No. 1183 to the Empress cinema, to see *The Foreman Went To France* (Charles Frend, 1942). I was now capable of taking all of this in, including German planes strafing refugees on the road, though the moment that really stayed with me was when Tommy Trinder retrieved his cherished beer bottle from under the machine about to be lowered onto it. *The Foreman Went To France* would have been chosen for its patriotic thrust, burnished by the contribution of famous playwright J.B. Priestley to the script. Likewise Laurence Olivier's *Henry V* (1944), which moved along well enough to hold the adolescent attention, not to mention being in colour, which was a very rare thing at the time. Another Technicolor film with cultural connections, *A Song to Remember* (1945), also got the school children out. Chopin coughing consumptive red blood onto the black and white keys of the piano is something that stayed with me, too.

But in those days, what I really wanted to be was a Spitfire pilot, or a racing car driver. After the war my fantasies moved on to being an engineer building bridges, then an astronomer discovering what The Mysterious Universe means, then an organic chemist inventing new plastics. My temple was Hall's big used book store in the centre of Melbourne. At school my main concern was my rivalry with Margaret Ashworth for top of the class in the yearly exams. The excuse proffered in my family for my failure to beat her was that her mother was a former school teacher who coached her. She always did better than me all the way through primary school and then through High School, until she left to do a vocational course in radiography after the fourth form. Being a clever boy did not endear me to the other children, or to the teachers, partly because I was inclined to correct them once in a while, since I knew more about some aspects of science and maths than they did. The boys admired by the staff were those who were good at sport, and hence had a certain power over the other school children. Success at sport was what mattered most at that time and place.

Amongst the usual school classes, an important part of the English Expression course was a component called "Clear Thinking". This was concerned with valid and invalid arguments, and the tricks used by politicians and advertisers to deceive us about their wares. It extended as far as the traditional logic of the syllogism. I don't think they had an immensely valuable course like this in English schools, then or later, though the text-book used, R.H. Thouless' *Straight and Crooked Thinking*, was English. Exposure to this book might have prevented most of the faulty reasoning that I have had to criticize in the writings by other people about film. *Straight and Crooked Thinking* also advocated clarity in writing, and the précis writing component of the English Expression course encouraged me to seek concision in my writing as well. Since then my aim has always been clarity, accuracy, simplicity, and brevity in everything I write.

Books like this, plus the exposure to the arguments of thinkers like Bertrand Russell, combined with a general resistance to authority, had removed any religious belief I had by the time I was fifteen, though I kept up church attendance to keep my parents happy, and also so that I could continue playing in the church cricket and badminton teams. On the other hand, I had already acquired the belief that what mattered was what one accomplished, not how much money one had, or what one's social standing was, and my parents would have been very happy with that.

And ART had started creeping up on me around the age of fourteen. My parents wanted to take me to a production of *Die Fledermaus* in one of the big theatres in Melbourne. Naturally it was being done in English, and under the title *Gay Rosalinda*. I remember holding forth to a small assembly of my younger cousins in the back yard of one of their homes, boasting that my parents would have to put me in chains to get me to it, since art was of no importance next to the glory of science. But I *was* taken, and I loved it! Actually, I had been softened up by taking piano lessons at my own insistence, to be like my best friend at State School No. 1183. My first experience of performing in public was at the yearly shows that my piano teacher put on for her pupils' proud parents in the Williamstown Town Hall. The first one was terrifying, but I got a little more used to them after that, though not to the piano exams up at the State Conservatoire in Melbourne that we were also entered in. The worst part of these were the ear tests, with which I had difficulty, since my sense of pitch is not particularly good. My mother's good musical ear by-passed me, and went straight to my younger sister.

There were also amateur performances of Gilbert and Sullivan operettas put on in the theatre in the Williamstown Mechanics Institute. All this might have had something to do with my joining the Dramatic Group at Williamstown High School, though I was not aware of any connection at the time. It was just another incident in the flux of my adolescent life, along with swimming down at the beach, playing cricket and badminton, and reading, reading, reading. The first play the Dramatic Group did was *Lord Richard in the Pantry*, an antique English farce. I played the hero's friend, Captain 'Tubby' Bannister. Not that I was tubby. Hardly anyone was in those days. I suffered from stage fright on my first performance, due to fear of forgetting my lines, despite my excellent memory, and I did not get to feel really at ease before the production's run was over.

I was still not allowed to go to films as a regular thing, and I did not get enough pocket money to go without permission. I don't think I particularly wanted to, at that point, because science was still my god. Nevertheless, there were occasional films that were considered worthy or important that came along once in a while, such as *The Overlanders* (1946) and *Odd Man Out* (1947). The story and the expressive flourishes in the latter really took me inside the film and shook me about. Then in 1948 *Oliver Twist* and *Hamlet* and *The Queen of Spades* and *The Red Shoes* all came out. This was the period just after the second World War when the British cinema seemed to be at the beginning of a new era of success, for as well as these films the Ealing comedies were just starting to appear, and all were being shown around the world.

So it is not very surprising that I started getting seriously interested in film. The Williamstown High School Ex-Students Association had been created by energetic young people from the school who had recently left it, and were now mostly at Melbourne University. Their self-imposed mission was to make the cultural desert that was Williamstown flower, and they began putting on revues, and also formed a film society, led by Lindsay Tassie. It put on small 16 mm. shows in the High School once a week in the evenings, and I got sucked into all this, probably with some encouragement from my parents. Indeed my father came along to some of the film shows, and I remember him convulsing a high-minded after-screening discussion which was considering the significance of Georges Méliès' *le Voyage dans la lune*, by suggesting it had too much emphasis on sex. He tended to be the life of the party, if given a clear field.

The Ex-Students also started making their own films, on 9.5 mm. The first was a thriller shot on a week-end group holiday down at a distant beach. I remember being sent off to shoot the titles by filming words scratched in the sand being washed out by the advancing waves. The filming was done with the camera upside down, and when the resulting shot was spliced into the finished film with the end of it first and the beginning last, the words appeared to be revealed in the sand by the retreating waves. This was the reverse-motion trick first done by G.A. Smith in 1899 for *The House That Jack Built*. The older ex-students who were behind this production wouldn't have seen that film, but probably learned the trick from some book on amateur film-making.

They gave me the rushes of the film to edit, because I could use my uncle "Pinky" White's 9.5 mm. projector to check the work. The selection of cutting points had to be done by holding the film strip over a light box and examining the frame with a magnifying glass. My editing was slow and clumsy, and the others took it away from me and finished it themselves. The next project was a psychological drama inspired partly by a mixture of Cocteau's and *The Cabinet of Dr. Caligari* and other arty German films from the 'twenties. I played the protagonist – not at my suggestion, and with a fair amount of resistance. I would have rather been behind the camera. My character was a sensitive young lame hunchback, rejected by society, who in the end cuts his own throat in his sordid room with a knife supplied by a death figure with a mirror face, right out of Maya Deren's *Meshes of the Afternoon* (1943), the other source of inspiration for Lindsay Tassie and the rest who had dreamed it up. They, and we, were seeing lots of recent arty films from the more advanced parts of the world, and another of their cribs was an abstract film painted directly onto film in the manner of Norman McLaren's *Begone Dull Care* (1949). Like Maya Deren's films, this had got through to the 16 mm. library of the Victoria State Film Centre very quickly.

Inevitably, I was now having fantasies about making my own film, and I began to plan out a version of the myth of Prometheus (Hello, Cocteau again) shot in the style of Eisenstein, with abstract sets inspired by the theatre designs of Edward Gordon Craig. The latter got into the mix because I had recently spent my pocket money on the little 1948 King Penguin book of his stage designs. Nothing came of it, nor of my pressing my nose against the window of the camera shop in Melbourne that sometimes had second-hand 16 mm. movie cameras for sale.

The British high priest of film art in those days was Roger Manvell, and naturally I devoured his book *Film*, and then the Penguin Film Reviews that he edited from 1947 to 1950. These strove to be international in scope, with much the least part of them being about American cinema, reflecting the atmosphere in Britain just after World War II. I also read all the rest of the very limited number of books on film available in those days, such as *The Art of the Film* (Ernest Lindgren), Béla Balázs' *Theory of Film*, Pudovkin's *Film Technique*, and Eisenstein's *Film Form* and *The Film Sense*. It is noteworthy that all of these except the Lindgren, which did not interest me, were written by film-makers, and indeed partly based on their practical experience. The aesthetic notions about film that they expounded were those of practising film-makers. In particular, Pudovkin's book sets forth the basics of film technique as visible in *American* films of the middle 'twenties, when it was written, and what Balázs has to say is likewise inspired by what film-makers were doing at the beginning of the sound period. Eisenstein was describing what he did, which was not the same as what other film-makers did, and inventing theories to justify it. And of course he was also bringing in lots of fascinating cultural references.

Following the Penguin Parade

By the time I was sixteen my voracious reading included modern poetry as well as science. So when the English teacher made us write a poem for homework, something I had never contemplated before, I sat down with *Why Smash Atoms?*, one of my favourite Pelican paperbacks, and a copy of *Contemporary Verse* edited by Kenneth Allott for Penguin Books, another recent acquisition, and whipped up the poem above right, as subsequently published in the school magazine.

A characteristic Australian attitude, still surviving from the pioneer days of less than a hundred years before, was that anyone can do anything if they put their mind to it. This is exemplified by a local anecdote from early in the twentieth century told to me by my father. A famous visiting musician, let us say Paderewski, was staying at Menzies Hotel, which was the very exclusive and expensive equivalent in Melbourne of Claridge's in London. He asked the manager if he could have the broken lock on his wooden music case repaired, and the manager said he would take care of it. A couple of days later, Paderewski asked if had been repaired. The manager apologized, saying that the hotel carpenter had been too busy to do it. When asked how that could be, the manager said,

The Man-God

Here is the laboratory.

The curved metal gleams in the diffused light of the sun.
Seated before the glowing window is the scientist. One
who in his mind arranges the destinies of electrons
that surge in a wire. He, god-like, controls their reactions.
His thoughts appear on the paper, blackening
the white, empty sheets of ignorance. Awakening
men's minds to visions of the future, possibilities
coming from this new source of power. Liabilities
do not appear to daunt the spirits of men who
are to know of this new achievement, too.

But he is also a man, he must see it again.
He turns to the room where, children of his brain,
the strange electrical machines towering stand.
This one, more beautiful, can wield a brand
of one million volts. Its surfaces are curve upon curve,
forming ellipsoids, cylinders, and each corner is a curve
to foil the leaping power of the spark.
He looks to one whose dials are eyes in the half-dark,
flicks several switches, valves glow, hears the answering hum.
He places the radio-active metal, sees the beam of neutrons come.
The green circle of the cathode ray tube lights the walls.
The luminous line leaps. Uranium fission. Darkness falls.

"Well, the hotel chef is off sick, and the carpenter is doing the cooking."

Another basic notion that I had acquired by this time, was that what mattered, in art as well as science, was originality. I had now moved on from the tiny library in the Williamstown Mechanic's Institute to going the eight miles into Melbourne by the FAST ELECTRIC TRAINS to the central public lending library, to borrow books by the armful. All the way from *Paul et Virginie* to Alfred Wegener's *The Origins of Continents and Oceans* (about his continental drift theory), to Stefan Themerson's *Professor Mmaa's Lecture,* to Sacheverell Sitwell's fantasias about obscure works of art in *The Hunters and the Hunted*. Nowadays I am only embarrassed about falling for the show-off pretentiousness of the last of these. More important was Bertrand Russell's *History of Western Philosophy*, which I ploughed through. Reading Russell's successive analyses of the theories of the great philosophers of the last two thousand years, with his isolations of the various weaknesses in *all* of their thinking, suggested to me that the philosophy of the present that he admired was probably vulnerable to similar demolition.

After doing my sixth form matriculation year at Melbourne High School, I went on to Melbourne University to do a science degree with a specialisation in chemistry. The Ex-

Student's film society was still functioning, and one evening the programme included a fairly new documentary film, *Steps of the Ballet* (1948). It may have been put in because Powell and Pressburger's *The Tales of Hoffman* had just come out, or because it was a successor to the famous documentary *The Instruments of the Orchestra* (1946), for which Benjamin Britten had written his *Variations and Fugue on a Theme of Purcell*. It was likewise directed by Muir Mathieson, the noted conductor of hundreds of British film scores, and likewise made for the Central Office of Information film unit. In it, the chorus of male dancers did quite a bit of vigorous jumping stuff, including an enchainement that featured *cabrioles à la seconde*, and on the way home down the street alone in the dark I tried this step out, and I could do it!

I had long been searching for some physical activity I could be really good at, and was currently trying fencing at the Melbourne University Fencing Club, but this dancing thing was artistic as well as physical. The only Melbourne ballet company that was doing anything at that moment was Ballet Guild, so I went to see one of their performances, liked what I saw, and the next week enrolled as a student in their evening classes. The other alternative was trying the ballet school attached to the Borovansky Ballet, which was the only big ballet company in Australia, but I felt that was out of my league. The Borovansky Ballet was run by a dancer of that name who had been in the Russian ballet companies managed by Colonel de Basil that toured the world, including Australia, in the 'thirties. One of de Basil's companies was called the Ballet Russe de Monte Carlo, which had a home base in the opera house at Monte Carlo. The De Basil companies were part of the inspiration for Powell and Pressburger's *The Red Shoes*, though the director of the company in that film is more based on Serge Diaghilev, of the original Ballet Russe. If you look carefully at *The Red Shoes*, there is actually no evidence that the period is 1947, when the film was shot, and indeed the whole environment could well be the late 'thirties, when the first version of the script was written by Emeric Pressburger.

Borovansky restaged the Fokine and Massine ballets from the repertoire of the de Basil companies for his company

(without bothering to pay for the rights), and they would play for months in the big cities of Australia, till the audience was exhausted, and then the company would go into recess for a year or so. I had been bowled over by their performances of *Petrouchka*, *The Polovstian Dances*, and the like. After doing ballet classes in the evenings at Ballet Guild for a couple of months I was put into a costume and pitched onto stage in a walk-on part in *Giselle*, and this time I was really lost to the greasepaint. Ballet Guild also only functioned intermittently in its little way, with weekend seasons of performances every few months, so I could keep on going to my university lectures.

I was also keeping up with the culturally certified films getting into Australia, and now we were getting sex in the dish. Arne Mattsson's *Hon dansade en Sommar* (*One Summer of Happiness* in the English speaking world) gave me my first sight of naked bodies in warm embrace, and Max Ophuls' *la Ronde* got me heavily steamed-up in the "Young Man and Chambermaid" episode, apart from impressing me with the film's stylized presentation and the Oscar Straus theme song.

The last hurrah of the Williamstown High School Ex-Students Association Film Society came in 1952, when the leaders of the gang arranged to get free entry to the second Melbourne Film Festival in exchange for blacking out the building in which it was to be held. The first Melbourne Film Festival the year before was a very small scale affair held in a country town called Fern Tree Gully outside Melbourne. The venue now was to be in Melbourne in the Exhibition Buildings, an immense set of halls built in imitation of the nineteenth century exhibition buildings in the big cities of the Northern Hemisphere, and in particular the Alexandra Palace in London. However, unlike its models, it was built entirely of wood, which made it a major fire hazard, and hence generally unused. Walking around on a two foot wide ledge twenty feet up in the air while stapling sheets of cardboard over the clerestory windows of the halls seemed a pretty good deal at the time, though in the end I was no longer passionate enough about film to force my way into most of the heavily attended shows. I made do with a sideshow of short films involving art and music, and was particular impressed by Halas and Batchelor's semi-abstract animated film *The Magic Canvas*, to music by Matyas Seiber.

As my ballet technique advanced, and as I worked my way up to more prominent parts, my absorption in ballet had the inevitable result that I failed my second year exams for the B.Sc. I had not tried that hard, as I was spending much of my spare time at the university working my way through the stacks of the university library, reading irrelevant books like the works of Ronald Firbank and Sigmund Freud. I retook the year again, but by this point I was beginning to dance leading roles such as The Bloke, in our ballet based on C.J. Dennis's famous (in Australia) vernacular narrative poem *The Sentimental Bloke*. (I was now performing under the stage name of Robert Jaffray.) So despite changing my major from chemistry to physics, in which I was doing rather better, I failed the exams again, and was chucked out of the university.

At this point there was no prospect of a full-time professional job as a dancer in Melbourne, so I made a try for film work. Unfortunately things were just as bad in this area. There had been quite a lot of Australian feature films made in the nineteen-twenties and 'thirties, but in the 'forties the industry had almost completely collapsed, and the drought continued through the 'fifties. What little there was happened in Sydney, which was five hundred miles away. The only professional film-making in Melbourne was a tiny company making cinema commercials, and they did not have a place for me when I asked. I filled in with a few months teaching maths and science in a suburban secondary school before I was rescued by Ballet Guild obtaining a contract for a full-time professional tour of New South Wales from the N.S.W. division of the Australian Arts Council. There were no real ballet companies based in New South Wales at that time.

The tour was a marathon affair, lasting almost five months. We gave 110 performances all across the country towns of New South Wales and the south of Queensland, covering thousands of miles in the Arts council's giant semi-trailer van, which contained a large passenger compartment as well as the wardrobe and scenery. The usual drill was to travel a hundred miles or so in the morning to the next town, get set up, do a class, then give a matinee performance in the afternoon and another in the evening, and so on. We performed on the stages of town halls and schools, and even on a stage built of duckboards supported on 44-gallon oil drums in the showgrounds in Wagga Wagga. My big numbers were the Sentimental Bloke and the Prince in our shortened version of *The Nutcracker*.

At the beginning of the tour, all of us youngsters were off the leash for the first time in our lives, and we got really drunk at the first country hotel we stayed in out west in the back-blocks. The girls when off duty had adopted the latest female summer fashion in the big cities, which was wearing brightly coloured cotton "pedal-pusher" pants with high-heeled wedgie sandals and Caribbean-style front-tied shirts revealing a bare midriff. In West Wyalong, all the stockmen and shearers and what-have-you were in town on Saturday afternoon, and some of them took two of the leading dancers for prostitutes, and propositioned them. The girls fled in tears, and after that the director of the company enforced more sober dress for the women. But our adventures on tour don't really have anything to do with me and the movies.

After the tour of New South Wales there was no immediate prospect of further professional engagements for the Ballet Guild company, so one of the young leading dancers with whom I was infatuated decided to go to England to further her career. She was taking along another lesser female dancer from the company, and asked me to come as well. I think she just wanted me along to protect them and carry their bags, as she did not return my feelings. But still being a naive youth, I agreed to come like a shot. I had to make some money to pay for the passage and to support myself when we arrived, so I looked around for a job.

I Was the Last Computer

Being a computer was still something one could be in 1955. There was a long tradition of human computers who did calculations for technical and scientific purposes with pencil and paper, and in the twentieth century with desk-top calculating machines. The recent invention of *electronic* computers, as they were called, had barely reached Australia. I think there were only four in the country at that time. The Physics Department at Melbourne University had built themselves one by hand out of large amounts of electronic valves and stuff, as had the people at Sydney University, while the Australian Atomic Energy Commission had an imported commercially produced one, as did the main establishment of the Commonwealth Aeronautical Research Laboratories (CARL) in Canberra. Insofar as the Australian government needed calculations for new planes, it was mostly taken care of by that machine. When I arrived at the CARL establishment at Fisherman's Bend on the mud flats of the mouth of the Yarra river, the facility there was run down from its glory days during World War II, when it was the factory making Australia's own contribution to the war in the air, the Wackett Trainer and the Wirraway (which was actually a version of an outdated American 'fighter', the North American BC-1).

I was put on trial repeating the aerodynamic calculations that had already been made of the profiles for a propellor blade, in a very large deserted room with rows and rows of desks laden with rows of shrouded and now unused *electric* calculating machines. (You can see one of these being used to impress a war-time civil servant in Powell and Pressburger's film of 1949, *The Small Back Room*.) I could do the calculations satisfactorily, so I was moved to what they really wanted me for, which was to be little more than a machine minder, running a big calculation for one of the few aeronautical engineers still working there. He was working out the best dimensions for a jet engine intake. This was tricky at the time, as it was feared supersonic shock waves could form inside a jet engine intake and blow the flame out, or worse. To get the appropriate dimensions for the intake, he had to solve a fluid flow equation. This equation had no analytical (algebraic) solution, so it had to be done numerically. This means putting actual numbers over and over again into the variables of the equation, and calculating the result until the particular value that solved it was hit upon. Thousands and thousands of values, each given to several significant figures.

Since the equation was complicated, separate parts of it had to be calculated separately, and then put together to give the result for any of these values. This whole process was automated to an extra degree beyond the kind of thing I had done for my test calculation, by using an IBM machine called a Multiplier. This was a giant version of the desktop calculating machines, and instead of the operator putting in the figures by hitting keys, the Multiplier was fed the numbers automatically by reading them from IBM punched cards. After doing the additions, subtractions, and multiplication required by the stage of the calculation in question, the machine punched out the numerical result on a blank IBM card, then did the same for the next card and the value on it, and so on. Division was done by multiplying with the reciprocal of the number in question, which had to be selected from a sequence of pre-calculated reciprocals selected and fed in on an interleaved series of punched cards.

The Multiplier was really a successful modern realisation of Charles Babbage's Difference Engine, conceived a hundred years before. It could carry out a simple repetitive programme of arithmetical operations that was set up by plugging wires from one hole to another in a plug board attached to it, but unlike a real computer, it could not modify this pre-set

"programme" itself. My job was to sort the punch cards into appropriate orders between stages of the calculation, and then keep feeding packs of them into the machine. Periodically the cards would tear and jam, and then the machine had to be stopped and reloaded. The relays, gears and cams inside it made a continuous loud grinding noise as they did the calculations, interspersed with an occasional machine-gun like ratatattat as it punched out an new answer for each calculation. The more complicated the calculation it was performing, the longer the cycle for each number took, which gave it a semblance of something straining to perform a mental process. Of course, this sensation can be felt with modern computers too, but in a far weaker way, since they don't make so much noise about what they are doing, or take so long over it. After several weeks, all the calculations had been done, and the moment came to compare both sides of the equation for all the values of the variable that was being tested, to find the unique value that would give the perfect jet engine intake. Both sides of the equation matched for every value! In other words, any value could be used, the calculation had been futile, and the months of work were wasted. Was that engineer's face red!

I am telling this story to make the important point that in research, both of the applied kind, but also in more purely theoretical work, this sort of thing frequently happens, although the general public is not aware of it. EVERY scientist, even an Einstein, will spend a certain amount of time barking up the wrong tree during their careers. Several years later on, I too was to go down a number of dead ends, though not in such a colourful way, before getting a fairly satisfactory conclusion to my own research.

In the Home Country

So with my fare paid, the MV *Fairsea* pulled away from the pier at Port Melbourne with streamers breaking, music playing, and friends and relations crying, just as in the old movies. When the ship was halfway across the Indian Ocean, the Suez war of 1956 broke out, and we were rerouted round the Cape, so that the trip took six weeks. While we were in passage, the dancer with whom I was infatuated had an affair with a middle-aged minor writer who was on the ship. This broke my tender little heart, and made the rest of the long passage to England a nightmare for me. Once arrived in England, I got myself a room in Bayswater and started doing ballet classes. I only had £700 to support myself till I got a dancing job, so I was living on porridge for breakfast and whale steak at night, cooked on a gas ring in my tiny room. I could not afford much of the cultural delights of London, so I read my way through the books in the public library round the corner in my spare time.

At least I was living my own life, as I had long wanted. After several months luck turned my way again, and a ballet with me in it that a would-be choreographer had put together for school lecture-demonstrations was picked up by a newly formed small ballet company called Western Theatre Ballet. This was based in Bristol, and had got Arts Council funding to commission new works and tour them round the west country of England. For initial rehearsals we took up residence in the legendary Dance building at Dartington Hall. Dartington Hall is a 14th. century manor house complex that was turned into a private residential arts centre in the 'thirties. The Dance School itself is a Modernist creation from that period, specially built to house the famous Kurt Jooss modern dance company when it fled Germany after the Nazis came to power.

This was the high point of my career as a dancer, when I created the role of Baudin, the younger of two prisoners who escape from jail, but end up trapped in another virtual prison by a sexually predatory woman. Once again, the choreographer Peter Darrell saw me as a naive and sensitive youth for the purposes of his work, called *The Prisoners*, which is still sometimes performed. I got some good notices in the part. The tour ended in a short London season at the Arts Theatre, and then the company went into hibernation. The management let me know that they did not want me back if the company restarted, on the grounds that I was not good enough. However, I think that some personal comments I made about them while tipsy may have had something to do with it.

A Logical Step

I was in trouble again, as not only was I out of work, but the British government were threatening to put me in the army. Britain still had conscription, and since like all Australians I was a British subject, and had been in the country for two years, I was liable for one year and five months of years of military service. My spell of conscription in the Australian Army only counted for seven months, since that was the total time I had spent in uniform, even though it had been spread over two years. I could get this postponed if I went back to university, so that is what I did. To support myself while I did a university degree part-time at night, I needed a job, and my father came to my rescue once more, by pulling the strings of a former office-boy of his, who was now an executive employment consultant in London. He got me an interview for a job as a computer programmer with International Computers and Tabulators (ICT), one of a handful of British computer-making firms in 1958.

The computer industry was still getting under way at this point, and the typical computer was still constructed, with considerable labour, from valve circuits wired together for the logic elements, while storage of the digits that made up the programme and the data inside the machine was done in mercury acoustic delay lines or core stores, which were a matrix of wires connected together by tiny ring magnets. Computers at this time were still big enough to fill a whole house. However, the first "small" computers using transistors wired together to form the logic elements were just starting to be designed, and ICT, which sought to rival IBM, was following their lead in this direction. However, ICT's P3 (later 1301) computer, which was still in the prototype stage, and which I was to work on, was still big enough to fill a

whole room. I was employed in a newly created department of ICT called "Forward Planning", which a low-level executive had got set up to build a little empire for himself. The idea was that this department would discover the speed and efficiency of the firm's new computers in carrying out typical office calculations, while they were still in the design stage, and this information could be used for sales purposes. The un-admitted obstacle to this was that most of the time required in typical office computations like payroll calculations would be spent in the data input and output stages, and we would not know the speed of that until the building of the first machine was actually complete.

Although the first high-level computer programming languages like FORTRAN had just been created, we had to write the programmes for our machine in what is now called "machine code", in which the numbers have to be programmed to move out of specific storage locations and into the arithmetic registers where the basic calculations are carried out, and then out again to another specific memory location, and so on. Programmes that do this still exist in computers, but they are hidden far below the level of ordinary programming done in BASIC or C or whatever. Fortunately, I managed to get away with only writing one complete programme, for the PAYE tax module of a payroll programme.

Our office was in a mansion in Mayfair, and the four Forward Planning programmers sat at desks facing each other from the four corners of a large and grand first floor front room panelled with wood. With nothing that we could do most of the time, we spent the mornings and afternoons in wide ranging intellectual conversation. I took very long lunch hours, mostly going round the art galleries to look at the new art that was coming out. At this time all the commercial art galleries in London were in Mayfair, clustered around Bond Street. I discovered that the key to understanding the latest advanced art was seeing a lot of examples of an artist's work together at the one time. This illumination came to me when studying a show by Alan Davie, the point of whose abstractions had evaded me when I had seen single examples before. Later illuminations included the discovery that Frank Stella's shaped-canvas abstract paintings, like *Grave Light*, which were merely interesting in reproduction, rang like a visual gong when seen in actuality at full size. And now I could afford to go to concerts and the theatre. England was finally starting to catch up with real modern music, with performances of the work of the Second Viennese school, and even more importantly, the contemporary music of people like Karl-Heinz Stockausen. Besides concert performances, I had a record of his electronic works, including the impressive *Gesang der Jünglinge*, but my most prized possession was a box of Robert Craft's performances of the complete works of Anton Webern. Despite the more recent performances and recordings of Webern by Boulez and others, I still prefer the readings of the vocal works by Craft's performers. I was also catching the latest European art films at the National Film Theatre and elsewhere. Like many people, I was bowled over by Antonioni's *l'Avventura* and his subsequent films, and also Alain Resnais' *Hiroshima, mon amour* and *l'Année dernière à Marienbad*. Eventually I got onto Jean-Luc Godard's wavelength, and his work became my main inspiration.

After doing the first couple of years of a B.Sc. at night at Birkbeck College, one of the colleges of the University of London, I quit International Computers Limited (ICL), as it now was, and did the last two years of the course full-time, with the help of my savings and a government bursary. My degree was an honours degree with a specialization in theoretical physics, and so besides physics courses, it also required mathematics to the level of a mathematics degree. I had decided to try to realise my youthful dream of solving the riddle of the universe after all.

A Tribute to Genius

Despite a lot of emotional turmoil just before the final exams over my rejection by another dancing girl (I never did learn), I scored an Upper Second in 1962, so I was able to go on to do a Ph.D. Birkeck College seemed to be the place to do it, since David Bohm had taken the post of Professor of Theoretical Physics there in 1961. Bohm was a brilliant American theoretical physicist of the same generation as Richard Feynman. After World War II he created a version of quantum theory without the quantum uncertainties, by adding a new variable, later called a quantum potential, to the existing variables that figured in the basic quantum equations. This alternative description produced exactly the same results as existing quantum theory, though it did also suggest some new physical phenomena that were subsequently observed. Since Bohm's theory cannot predict anything that is not describable by standard quantum theory, it has been largely ignored by physicists, who have preferred to go on working with the existing formalism in quantum mechanics. In 1962 I was only vaguely aware of this, and at this time Bohm was concerned with looking for clues from the rapidly developing particle physics of that date which might lead to a new version of his theories.

The nineteen-sixties were a carnival time for physics, as new fundamental particles were being discovered every month with the new giant particle accelerators, and then their behaviour was being explained by the application of new mathematical theories. These families of particles, together with the already known fundamental particles, such as neutrons and electrons, were being classified and predicted with mathematical group theory, and their interaction in collisions calculated using what was called "S-matrix" theory. The notion that it might be possible to get a unified physical theory of everything, including gravity, had arrived, and Bohm's current idea was that it might be constructed by using mathematical objects called "simplices". These include triangles in two dimensions, tetrahedra in three dimensions, and their analogues in higher dimensions. It was fairly obvious that the unification of all the forces — electromagnetic, weak, strong, and gravitational, would take place at what is called the Planck length, which

is about 10^{-33} cm., so what mattered was the structure of space-time at that scale. As it turned out, he could not get it put together, though at the end of his life others constructed a quite different unified theory involving objects called "superstrings" existing and interacting in ten dimensions at the Planck length.

David Bohm was the only person with an intelligence in the genius category that I have ever known, and it was awe-inspiring in seminars to experience his mind looking down on whole areas of physics like an eagle, and then diving down onto a significant detail whose importance was crucial, and then analysing it in relation to the whole. Equally humbling were the post-graduate lectures I attended at Imperial College, which were given by some of the stars of the new wave of particle theory, the most important of whom was Abdus Salam. He later got a Nobel prize for his work on the creation of a quantum theory giving a unified treatment of the electromagnetic and the weak interactions between particles.

I had great difficulty keeping up with these new theories, and my own theoretical work was in an area of quantum mechanics that was not quite so advanced. This was to do with the theory of superfluid helium. When cooled to below 2.18 degrees above the absolute zero of temperature, helium is a liquid displaying bizarre new properties, such as zero viscosity when flowing, and immensely increased heat conductivity. These are the result of quantum effects, uniquely manifesting themselves at the macroscopic level instead of working invisibly at the atomic level, as is usual. Bohm had actually wanted me to work on explaining the properties of another form of liquid helium, that of the isotope He^3, instead of the ordinary He^2, but I misunderstood his suggestion. Nevertheless, he got interested in what I was doing, and made helpful suggestions about methods that I might use to give a theoretical description of the key aspects of the behaviour of superfluid helium.

The basic point about theoretical physics is that its purpose is to give explanations of phenomena in the real world, so it is continually interacting with experimental physics, as new unexpected phenomena are observed, and the predictions arising from theories are checked against observation. How this process works has been described, to the satisfaction of most scientists, by Karl Popper, in his book *The Logic of Scientific Discovery*, whose English translation was published in 1959. I was aware of his ideas in the first place from his *Conjectures and Refutations* (1963), which came out while I was doing my Ph.D. Popper's falsifiability criterion for .a theory to be regarded as scientific rules out systems of ideas dear to many literary intellectuals, such as Freudianism and Marxism.

The key experimental result to be described by any theory of superfluid Helium was the way energy excitations in superfluid Helium varied with their wavelength. These excitations behaved like virtual quantum mechanical particles, which had been called "phonons", at long wavelength, and at higher energies like another virtual particle referred to as the "roton". The graph representing all this had been established by bombarding liquid Helium with slow neutrons, and the problem was to calculate this theoretically. Various attempts had been made to do this by various methods, and Richard Feynman and M. Cohen had come fairly close to it. Bohm suggested using a favourite mathematical technique of his for redescribing the equations for the energy of the system of atoms making up liquid Helium, by changing the co-ordinate system used in the equations. When I did this, various features of previous theoretical descriptions by others emerged from the new equations, but I could only calculate parts of the energy spectrum. The difficulty arose mostly because the terms in the transformed equations formed an infinite series, and to do full calculations with them, one had to prove that after a certain point one could neglect these higher terms as being too small to matter. One could make arguments why this was probable, but an exact mathematical proof that it was so was impossible. This is a common problem in this sort of work.

Although my work was judged good enough to warrant a doctorate in 1965, it showed me that I was not going to be able to compete with the great minds in this area. However, getting a Ph.D. did reinforce my confidence, since though I had always felt I was worth something, I had nothing concrete to demonstrate it, which was very galling. Even an unremarkable Ph.D. in theoretical physics is not exactly easy to get. I could have gone on being a mediocre theoretical physicist for the rest of my life, and indeed I immediately got a job as a lecturer at Sir John Cass College in the City of London teaching physics and maths for their degree course, but I had already decided to abandon physics and have a go at being a film-maker. A couple of years later David Bohm rewrote the work that I had done under his guidance, and published it as *Collective Treatment of Liquid Helium* in the *Review of Modern Physics* v 39 n 4 1967 by D. Bohm and B. Salt, which was only right.

Two-Timing

Although I had enough theoretical knowledge, and also practical experience of photography, to make films right away, I thought it would be a good idea to do a course in film-making first. The only film school in Britain at the time was the London School of Film Technique, so I set out to save as much money as possible for a year, and also if possible to get an educational grant from the Greater London Council for the purpose.

All these years, I had continued doing two or three ballet classes a week, not to mention jazz dance classes, and a bit of modern dance as well. The main ballet teacher I was going to was Errol Addison, and he was a very colourful character as ballet teachers go. His dancing career had begun in the 'twenties, and ranged from a solo act in variety theatres, to being a soloist with the Diaghilev ballet. To support my application to the film school, I decided to make a film about him to be quite certain that I qualified for admission.

I hired a Bolex 16 mm. camera for a day, bought several 100 foot rolls of Kodak XX reversal film, and whipped off a hand-held record of one of Errol Addison's classes. This was of course shot wild (without synchronised sound), but I also took a wild recording of the sound from the class with a microphone and recorder hung at the front. As it turned out, the footage shot with the wide angle 10 mm. lens, which was a good part of the film, was all slightly out of focus, as the rental company had given me an incompatible lens for the camera. So I made them loan me a Beaulieu camera for free, and I did retakes at a later class. I also recorded an interview with Errol Addison. I bought a cheap amateur editing viewer and edited the reversal master, then edited the sound by cutting the 1/4 inch tape into a vague correspondence with the picture. I took the cut picture, with a magnetic edge stripe now coated onto

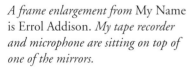

A frame enlargement from My Name is Errol Addison. *My tape recorder and microphone are sitting on top of one of the mirrors.*

it, along with the two sound tracks to the Central Office of Information editing rooms (Yes, they were still in business!) and paid them for a quick and primitive dub, which involved re-recording the tape at a slightly changed speed to make it the same duration as the film, adding the interview track over it, and then transferring the result to the magnetic stripe. The lack of synchronism between the live sound of the ballet class and the movement in the picture seemed to me surprisingly unimportant, perhaps because they were both really a "wallpaper" background to Errol Addison's reminiscences on the soundtrack.

Towards the end of the academic year of 1965-66, while I was still teaching at Sir John Cass, to make as much money as possible, in case I didn't get a grant to go to the film school, I secretly got a job with another very small ballet company. Ballet Minerva was based in Wembley. They had just got Arts Council money to expand to do tours of outer London and the home counties, so I was once more engaged in bringing ballet to the parts other companies could not reach. On tour we got as far west as Fowey in Cornwall. And I was holding down two full-time jobs simultaneously for several months, without either of my employers being aware of this. This was the big moment for my sneaky side, which had been lurking in the background most of my life.

When I heard that I had been given a grant to go to the film school, I threw a fake tantrum and stamped out of Ballet Suburbia, as I called it. I enjoyed that. The film I had made was all wasted effort as far as getting a place at the London School of Film Technique was concerned, since they didn't even want to look at it. The fact that I had the money for the fees was enough for Robert and Tanya Dunbar, who ran the school at that time.

I mostly didn't enjoy the film school, as I knew a lot of what they were teaching already, and the school was housed in an old warehouse in Covent Garden which was cold, and dirty from its previous industrial tenants. The course did have its moments, naturally. One was when Charles Frend came in as a visiting teacher of directing, and I impressed him with my exercise, which had two actors playing a text I had constructed by cutting lines out of stories in women's romance magazines, and then shuffling them around. Oh, yes, I had been keeping up with William Burroughs and other avant-garde literary doings.

Other visitors who gave talks at the school included Jean Renoir, though I couldn't get into that one, there were so many people present. More importantly for me, there was Raoul Coutard explaining how he did it. There were also film history classes given by Roger Manvell, but in Close Up I could see my former idol's feet of clay. His understanding of film was clearly shallow, and had not advanced over the previous twenty years. Most of the basic technical teaching at the school was done by Phil Mottram, and his way of analysing existing films by running them backwards and forwards on a projector to pick out technical details probably had some influence over my later methods of analysing films.

At the end of the first year of the course, I did not bother to complete the intermediate exams, and resolved to hazard some of my savings on making a film outside the course. With the help of two other students, I made a documentary over the summer holidays called *Pop Up into a New World*. This project started out as a survey of some of the exciting things that were going on in Britain in the middle of the 'sixties. My original idea was to cover, besides pop music, which everyone thinks of in this context, kinetic audio-visual art, new ideas in city planning, the latest visionary architecture by the Archigram group, and the nuclear fusion research going on at the Culham laboratories. All this would be presented in a Chinese box structure, with each section in two parts forming a frame for the next one to appear inside it. In the end, some of these subjects did not work out, so the film was mostly about the Archigram group. This was a mistake, as the BBC had made a film about the Archigram people the year before, and although I think my film was quite good, I could not get a sale to television.

By this time, the next academic year at the film school was about to begin, and since the management seemed to be ignoring my failure to complete the exams (they were still getting my fees paid by the Greater London Council, after all), I went back and did the second year of the course. I did learn more, particularly about film lighting, as I did a good deal of the photography for the other student's films. In fact I and Tak Fujimoto, who was in the same intake as me, lit more of the films than anyone else. I also directed and photographed my own production for my sixth term graduation film. This was a one reel science fiction film in 35 mm. colour and Techniscope. It involved humans in the future messing around with people in the present, and had various would-be clever notions in it. One was doing the future against a set of pure burned-out white. This was years before George Lucas made *THX 1138*, and I think I did it better. I also tipped my hat to Godard and William Burroughs with a scene with two people reading alternate sections of *The Ticket that Exploded* and Hume's *A Treatise of Human Nature* at each other.

When it came to editing my film, I had to deal for the first time with cutting dialogue exchanges. We had not been taught any rules about how to do this, nor were there any published in books about film-making. So I went down to the Commodore cinema in Hammersmith, which was a repertory house at that time. A double bill of *The Big Sleep* and *Helen of Troy* (Robert Wise, 1955) showed me that the best point (in general) to make a cut in the picture from a shot of one speaker to a shot of the other speaker in a dialogue is during the last word of the first speaker's speech. This was apparent to me because *The Big Sleep* was in general cut like that, and *Helen of Troy* was not, and the dialogue scenes in *The Big Sleep* seemed to flow better.

I had to edit my film, *The Future Perfect*, "in the hand". That is, by examining the place to make the cut on the positive with the film held over a light panel, with the occasional assistance of a magnifying glass. This was because the Cineola editing machines used by the school were notorious film butchers. They were an inferior imitation of the industry standard Hollywood Moviolas. I was not aware at the time that I was making a journey back into the past of film editing, for as I found out later, silent films were in general also "cut in the hand". Actually, most of the rest of the LSFT's equipment was also outdated. For the third term film exercise, we used Newman-Sinclair spring-driven 35 mm. cameras, which everyone else had stopped using decades before, and so on. Some of the students had got the agreement of Jonathan Miller to let them film him rehearsing a play, and they used this to bludgeon the management into hiring a new Eclair NPR 16 mm. synch. sound camera for a week for their fourth term documentary exercise. John Barnes and Harley Cokeliss then grabbed it for their documentary about Georgie Fame recording an album, which I photographed. I was to use the Eclair NPR a great deal after I finished at the film school.

At the end of the course, as part of the requirements for gaining the school's diploma, students had to write a thesis on a film subject. Andrew Sarris' *The American Cinema: 1928-1968* had just come out, and I was mightily impressed by his insights. Given my scientific background, I thought that his assertions about the formal style used by particular directors could do with more solid and detailed empirical support, and it seemed to me that this might be provided by an adapted version of recent work on the statistical style analysis of music. I had been following the latest developments in advanced music, which at that date mostly meant the Darmstadt school. People connected with this started a very short-lived magazine called *Die Reihe*, which was put out from 1955 by Universal Edition, the principal publishers of advanced music. The first number of this contained, besides articles by Stockhausen, Boulez, Pousseur, etc. on electronic music, which was what had originally attracted my attention, another article by Werner Meyer-Eppler on some of the mathematical principles that underlay the electronic generation of music. This article also contained a few brief lines on the statistical analysis of existing conventional music, and it was from here that some of my ideas came. However, in other respects my approach to the problem was my own. Here it is, as pounded out on the cheap portable typewriter I had recently bought, and on which I had taught myself touch-typing, sort of.

THE ANALYSIS OF STYLE IN THE CINEMA

In this essay I make a proposal for a quantitative stylistic analysis of cinema films, and apply these considerations to a description of the development of normal style in the American sound cinema.

Style in literature and music have already been analysed quantitatively in certain instances (1), and the same procedure could be applied to cinema films. Basically, the method depends on the assumption that films, just as language, are made up of single definable elements which can be nominated and described, i.e. they are not structureless continua. This granted, the compositional elements of films can be taken to be shots, and what is next needed is a record of the characteristics of each shot of the film under consideration.

Selectivity is obviously need in this recording owing to the complexity and magnitude of the information contained in each shot, but without attempting to justify my choice, I suggest that the most usefully significant characteristics with respect to style are the following:

1.) The length of the shot.
2.) The type of the shot, i.e. Close-up, Medium Shot, etc.
3.) Camera movement during the shot, including as a sub-division camera angle.
    e.g. camera at eye-level, tilted 10 deg. down -- pan left 90 degrees -- track 15 ft.
4.) Objective or subjective with respect to the characters.
5.) Objects, including people, important with respect to the action of the film shown in the shot at its beginning and end.
6.) Type of shot transition. i.e. cut, dissolve, fade, etc.

There are undoubtedly other elements of stylistic significance, such as pictorial composition, but these do not lend themselves easily to analysis or are not so important as those above. In any case it is my opinion that interesting and important results can be obtained while ignoring these other elements, and even while using a reduced list of characteristics, as will subsequently become apparent.

I suggest that a straightforward tabulation of these quantities with a determination of their average values and distribution about the average will provide criteria for a formal distinction between the works of many different directors. Even some directors not ordinarily considered to have any individuality. However, at any period there are a large number of film directors whose works approach the average with respect to the values of these variable characteristics. It must also be noted that the average of these stylistic characteristics also changes with time under the influence of changes in fashion and technical development.

The results of an analysis of the relation of adjoining shots with respect to each class of characteristics listed can also be expected to contribute to these stylistic distinctions, but analysis of the higher order relations between more distant shots (2nd. order Markov chains in terms of information theory) is not worth pursuing, as organization of film shots hardly ever reaches such a high level.

For the way that this net would catch the stylish fish I can only give some indicative examples; full proof would depend on the complete application of the program. For simplicity I restrict myself to the American sound cinema, and proceed historically.

In the early 'thirties, the difficulty of editing the sound track produced on the average greater length of takes than later became customary. (Incidentally, the same difficulty produced a refreshing absence of background music.) The difference between the masters and the mediocre at this period consisted in what was done despite this limitation; the accomplished director using camera movement and extensive tracks (e.g. Mamoulian) in a positive way, the rest using static camera with at best tiny pans to keep the action in frame.

In the first category interesting, but slightly less notable directors like Cukor and Victor Fleming would appear, and more importantly, Sternberg being distinguished by his use of more Close-ups than average, Hawks by a great preponderance of pans amongst his moving camera shots (a difference that became even more marked as others followed subsequently changing fashions), John Ford by a rather larger number of Long Shots and Very Long Shots than average.

As the 'thirties wore on and sound editing problems were overcome, shots tended to become shorter, but many directors resisted this tendency. Mitchell Leisen retained his long takes all his career, as did Mamoulian and George Cukor. One of the few notable directors whom the new style suited was Raoul Walsh, and he took advantage of faster cutting, particularly back and forth between characters, to keep his films moving along in a uniquely brisk way.

Of the new directors appearing in the early 'forties, most did not have any distinctive style (e.g. John Huston, Preston Sturges, Billy Wilder), but they adopted the style of the studio in which they found themselves, for there were slight differences between studios by this time. For instance, at Paramount rather longer takes than average were usual, due to the influence of the senior director, Mitchell Leisen.

Of course there was also Orson Welles, with a style based on an excessive number of low-angle shots, and Vincente Minnelli, whose style, particularly (but not only) in the musicals, is marked by long takes usually starting on a static set-up, then tracking to another static set-up at the end of the shot. At this time Hitchcock became an American director, but without change in his style; i.e. much back and forth with fairly short shots, and many more subjective shots than usual.

Of the post-war newcomers Otto Preminger had the most distinctive style, with no subjective shots, and based on mostly short tracking shots with pans either at the beginning or the end; a style that was ideally suited to the wide-screen systems that arrived in the 'fifties.

These wide-screen systems called forth a general shift in style; increasing the average length of shots again, reducing the number of Close-ups, and the amount of camera movement; effects which were most marked in the new directors of this period. Of these, we might mention Robert Aldrich, who tends to use a succession of unusual angles to cover a script scene; for instance low angle to overhead shot to eye level, and so on. If his films were storyboarded they would tend to look like a comic strip. There is something of the same element in Samuel Fuller's choice of angles, but he had a weakness also for long, elaborate, non-functional crane shots at this period.

More recently, in the 'sixties, there has been a change in the way script scenes are linked together, with a steep reduction in the use of fades and dissolves under the influence of the new French cinema. This would show in an analysis of the connection between adjoining shots as I proposed at the outset.

It is not to be supposed that I think that this is the only way, or the best way in all cases, to determine the style of a film or its director, but the importance of these suggestions is that they have not even been considered before, either in themselves, or in the observations I have made about their application.

30 October 1968

You may notice that I recommend collecting the percentage of Point of View (POV) shots as a principal stylistic variable, but not the amount of Reverse Angles. This was because I suspected that only the amount of POV shots used would distinguish Alfred Hitchcock's style from that of some other directors. Looking back, I now think that this emphasis was probably right, as Point of View shots are a more fundamental feature of film construction than reverse angles.

London School of Film Technique theses were supposed to be at least 5,000 words long, but the above piece was less than half of that. Nevertheless, I was given the school's diploma without any arguments. For several years I didn't do anything further about the programme of research I had put forward in the essay, as my principal concern was to get into the film industry at a fairly high level, and then direct my own films. I got a certain amount of work around the fringes of the business as a lighting cameraman, basically through fellow graduates of the school and their connections. This included photographing about a dozen short fictional films and industrial documentaries, and *The Great Wall of China* (Joel Tuber, 1969), an independent feature film very much derived from the recent work of Jean-Luc Godard. This was right down my alley, as my lighting style — not that I thought of it in such a pretentious way — was heavily influenced by Raoul Coutard's work for Godard.

I was also still going to the more notable ballet and dance performances, and even wrote some dance reviews in 1969 and 1970 for *The Morning Star*, the national daily newspaper funded with concealed support from Communist Russia. Not that I was inclined towards Communism, but the offer of free seats was too good to miss.

Learning More Lessons

I was not making enough money as a cameraman to live on, so I had to take a job as a supply teacher for the Inner London Education Authority. This was the last time in my life that I have had to wear a suit and tie. I was not interested in teaching maths and science in a London secondary school, and so I was bad at it. My most important experience was a discussion with the sixth form students after the exams, in which their interest in what they might do after graduating was solely restricted to how much they could earn in different jobs. This shocked me, because in the isolated world of my own life, what had always mattered was accomplishing something worthwhile, not how much money one might get for it. Over subsequent decades it has become clear that this experience was an early sign of the continuous increase in greed and selfishness throughout the populations in the developed countries of the world, right up to the present.

In 1970 I made a film called *Six Reels of Film to Be Shown in Any Order* over three weekends. This was exactly what the title says, and its variable structure was inspired by the use of chance operations that had been going on in the composition of some advanced music over the previous decade by people like John Cage and Karlheinz Stockhausen. However, in the case of my film, each reel contained two scenes involving the relationships between four people: three women and a man. The content of these scenes was worked out so that a different story would be created over the length of the film for each order the reels were shown in. For instance, a suicide attempt by drug overdose in one reel would be either taken as a consequence of what had happened involving the character in a reel shown previously, or as a failed suicide attempt, which was referred to by the character in another reel which happened to be shown subsequently.

As originally conceived and made, the film was actually seven 1000 foot reels of 35 mm. film, and so there were 720 different stories, since one reel was neutral in a narrative sense. I checked that this would work before shooting by writing the essence of the incidents on each reel on cards, which I shuffled into different orders. To keep the cost of shooting down, the film was shot in Techniscope, and each reel consisted of only two shots, one running 8 minutes, and the other running 2 minutes. This meant that any faulty takes could be thrown away without incurring the cost of having them developed and printed. Also, I shot the film on rolls of recanned negative and short ends of film stock, which were fairly easy to get hold of cheaply, or even free, in those days. The actors were paid the minimum union rate for extras for the actual shooting, though everyone involved owned a piece of the picture in the event of any notional profit. The rushes constituted the final print, which was possible since I got the exposures bang on the button, as I always did with my cinematography, and the sound was later put onto a magnetic stripe applied to the sound track area.

Most of the film had only direct sound, but there was one reel that had a complex double stream of consciousness voice over. I created this by doing a mix from the original tapes recorded by the two actors played back on two Nagra recorders through a portable mixer onto another Nagra while I manipulated their volumes. The final mix for the whole film in a proper dubbing theatre took three hours, which is undoubtedly the fastest mix there has ever been for a feature film. All these tricks meant that the total cost of the film was very close to £1,000, which makes it the cheapest 35 mm. feature film that had ever been made, or indeed ever will be made.

Although I paid for the film, and photographed it as well as writing and directing it, I had some important support on the production from other contemporaries from the London School of Film Technique, particularly Mark Forstater, who was producer, also Terry Bedford, who was my camera operator most of the time, and Harley Cokeliss, who was assistant director, and Julian Doyle who was my gaffer. Besides them, Tony Hide was a brilliant sound recordist, despite his steady intake of drugs on the shoot. That was the whole crew. We lugged the Elemack dolly up to upstairs flats on our own, and on one weekend I even cooked up vast quantities of curry and rice to feed everyone. Several of the locations were in people's flats; including Harley's, and Mark got the use of a room in Terry Gilliam's penthouse flat for two days. Gilliam went right

Barry Salt about to film a two-minute take of actress Felicity Oliver having a nervous breakdown along the front of Marshall & Snell-grove's store in Oxford Street for Six Reels of Film to be Shown in Any Order.

on drawing and airbrushing away at his animations in another room while we knocked out ten minutes of film.

The film only got a few screenings, including one at the National Film Theatre, as the sound track was on a magnetic stripe on the sole print, and so could only be projected in a theatre with "Fox penthouses" on its projectors. These are the special blocks of four magnetic heads added to a 35 mm.

projector above the film gate to play 'Scope type films with the four magnetic tracks on the print, as introduced by Twentieth Century-Fox with their CinemaScope process. Most large commercial cinemas still had these in 1971, but such cinemas were not going to show a rather far-out "art movie". My big surprise was that the serious film critics who reviewed it were not interested in the basic idea of my film. As one put it in

The final frame of the shot as she collapses after negotiating the crowds and 50 metres of flashy merchandise in the windows.

his review in the *Monthly Film Bulletin* (Vol. 40 No. 476 September 1973), audiences want to recompose films in their own minds, and so my cleverness was pointless. I very much doubt that this is true of most audiences, but what my film certainly did was prevent film critics from creating their own interpretations of it. This is all that highbrow critics live for, as you can easily check. Another objection from George Melly, who was at that time writing film reviews, instead of imitating Bessie Smith in front of a trad jazz band, was that the events in the film could be seen as a flashback structure, whatever the order it was shown in. This had not occurred to me when I made certain that the scenes could be understood as being in chronological order, whatever their sequence. It began to look as though there was not much of an audience for the kind of films that I wanted to make.

Parts of *Six Reels of Film* were shot in University College London, and this was one of the reasons I was offered a part-time job teaching film-making at the Slade School in 1971. This offer was extended by Thorold Dickinson, who was now teaching there, and I very reluctantly took it. The excuse I made to myself was that it would leave me some time to pursue my own film-making ambitions. The Slade is an old and important art school which exists as a department of University College London, which in its turn is the original and biggest individual college of the University of London. Dickinson ran a small post-graduate diploma course in film studies in the Slade. This was rather an anomalous place for it to be, but the existence of this course was due to Sir William Coldstream, the head of the Slade, who in his younger days had been a significant part of the famous GPO Film Unit, before returning to his career as painter, and later art teacher as well. The course of film studies at the Slade was the first of its kind in a university in Britain, and was set up in 1960 after Dickinson left the United Nations, where he had been running the Film Section of the UN Office of Information. Before that he had a long career in the British film industry, starting as an editor, and after that directing a number of notable features from the nineteen-thirties through the 'forties, including *The Queen of Spades*.

Thorold Dickinson believed that people studying the history and aesthetics of film should have a practical knowledge of the subject, which was a novel idea at the time. The usual notion was that all you needed to be a film critic was a reasonable command of English and the ability to see the screen. A important part of the course were about a hundred and twenty screenings a year, which were mostly of 35 mm. prints which Thorold had persuaded some of the major film distributors and the National Film Archive to let the course use rent-free. He had one of the Physics Department lecture theatres outfitted to show the films, including a 'Scope screen, and also with the extra safety features required to show nitrate prints.

At the Slade my job was to teach a basic film-making course to both the diploma students on the film studies course, and also to those regular art students at the Slade who wanted to try film making, using the Film Unit's 16 mm. equipment.

After I had been there for several months, Thorold Dickinson retired, and James Leahy was appointed as a Senior Lecturer to head the course at the Slade. He got me to give classes of technical analysis of some of the films shown in these screenings, which quickly evolved into a course entitled "The History of Film Style, Technique, and Technology". One of the many things I did in my spare time was what proved to be my last work as a lighting cameraman, firstly on a couple of documentaries Lutz Becker made for the Arts Council. These were based on two major exhibitions at the Hayward Gallery on the South Bank that Lutz was involved in staging. They were *Art in Revolution* and *Kinetics*, both from 1972, and the films are still in distribution. Around the same time I did most of the photography on *Clockmaker*, a 30 minute documentary that Richard Gayer made on 35 mm. Any time the film distributors in Britain needed something to go with a shorter than usual feature they put it round the circuits as a supporting film, right through the 'seventies, and it was nominated for an Academy Award in 1974.

At the Slade, James Leahy had me promoted to a full-time lecturer in 1973, and, as well as the film-making classes I had already been teaching, there was the course on Film Style, Technique and Technology just mentioned, and later I also taught a new course on avant-garde cinema. This last was possible because I had been keeping up with what was going on amongst local and international avant-garde film-makers through screenings at the London Film Makers Co-operative and elsewhere. The numbers of films screened for our courses at the Slade was also increased further, and one of the college porters was engaged more or less full-time in ferrying the films in and out of the Slade in taxis. It was quite a show.

In the early 'seventies, rising prosperity meant increases in the funding of the arts as well as the universities, and one of the beneficiaries of this was the Society for Education in Film and Television, an organization of people teaching about film in secondary schools. These people all had a literary background, as was always the case with those eager to write about the movies. It was funded by the British Film Institute, whose Education Department had been taken over by Marxists, and started to publish a magazine called *Screen*. From 1971 the journal was taken over by more Marxists, who began to publish articles inspired by French literary intellectuals who were trying to apply a mélange of new ideas about semiotics, psychoanalysis, and Marxism from French "thinkers" like Saussure, Metz, Althusser, and Lacan. James Leahy and Liz-Anne Bawden, the other full-time lecturer in the Film Unit, became interested in these ideas, and began to introduce them into their seminars. At first glance, all this stuff seemed very dubious to me, and indeed more careful investigation showed that pretty well all of it was illogical and based on a neglect of the relevant facts. You can read my reasoned demolition of some key examples of it in *Film Style and Technology: History and Analysis*. However, my immediate reaction was to put forward a more sensible theory of film, which I did in the following article published in *Sight & Sound* (Vol 43 No 2, 1974).

LET A HUNDRED FLOWERS BLOOM:
FILM FORM, STYLE, AND AESTHETICS

An extensive theoretical framework for the audio–visual medium still seems to be needed, particularly to help with the description of what particular films actually look like (as opposed to what they are about), but also for considering the relation of finished films to their production process, and yet further to give an all-inclusive basis for film teaching. V. F. Perkins' recent *Film as Film: Understanding and Judging Movies,* (Penguin Books, 1972). makes a good job of clearing the ground of unsatisfactory earlier theories, but his original proposals, after a corner-of-the-eye glimpse of a new possibility, are finally and admittedly both restricted and restrictive. A theory of film which excludes a Godard film (or any other film) must be defective.

Most attempts at a theory of film have always been vitiated by an excessive eagerness to say just what sort of films are good and what sort are bad; by an unconscious desire to justify personal preferences. To make a new start, suitable stages of analysis should be distinguished. These are firstly of the nature of the medium, secondly the possible set of forms, next the style possibilities, and only finally the possible systems of aesthetics that might deal with these forms and styles.

Form

The first crude holographic films have already been made, and we can anticipate a complete, all-surrounding audio-visual representation of reality being possible at some time in the future. So the most useful basic way of regarding the medium (and this includes television) is as a more or less faithful reproduction of audio-visual reality. One extreme that is technically possible at this moment would be a pair of 70 mm. colour stereoscopic films with multichannel sound taken of an unstaged event and projected hemispherically so as to fill the complete area of possible vision; while the other extreme would be some kind of small screen abstract film with synthetic sound, or no sound at all.

All films can be considered from a formal point of view to lie on a spectrum between these two extremes, with a greater or lesser degree of distortion or transformation of reality being introduced in various ways: by making cuts between shots rather than running the camera continuously, using zooms and camera movement within shots, shooting in black and white rather than in colour, using various degrees of non-natural sound, filming acted events rather than actual events, and so obviously on. The amount of distortion of reality introduced in the separate dimensions of the medium (cutting, photography, sound, acting, the events represented, etc.) is not necessarily parallel between these dimensions and the general effect of the film itself, though there is usually not a great divergence.

These dimensions can even be considered semi-quantitatively in many cases; for instance 'strength' of a CU or other shot transition can be defined in terms of the amount of discontinuity in space and time introduced into the action by the cut. Another possibility is a precise analysis of numbers of shots in a film with various shot lengths, and with the various types of shot and camera movements. This approach has produced some interesting preliminary results. It might be claimed that this is a rather arid approach; but considerations of how long a shot is to be, where the camera is to go, and so on, are what the director of a film is principally concerned with. (Remember that acting style has been included as a dimension of the medium as well.)

Style

Questions of style arise when we consider films in relation to film-makers. If an analysis along the lines just mentioned has been carried out, then the distributions of these quantities (shot length, etc.) for a particular film-maker, when compared with the average for all directors at a certain place and time, gives a sure indication of the existence of a personal style; in fact this is what formal style is. (Analogous analyses have long ago been successfully and usefully carried out for the style of literary and musical works, see *The Computer and Music*, ed. H. B. Lincoln, Cornell, 1970 and *Statistics and Style*, ed. Dolezel and Bailey, Elsevier, 1969.)

It could be argued that often the individuality of a director lies in the verbally expressible content of his films, and indeed it often does partly, but this individuality of content will mostly be found allied to formal individuality if the analysis is carried far enough. (That is, by going as far as considering the relation of the type of shot to the type of the succeeding shot—Markov chain analysis.)

The importance of this type of approach is beginning to be recognised, but it still does not go much further than remarking things like the fact that Howard Hawks keeps the camera at eye level and doesn't move it if possible. But in fact there are other directors of his vintage who do this too; for instance, Henry Hathaway. (The first of these peculiarities makes for efficient shooting because the actors can be kept well-framed at all distances without tilting the camera up. If the camera were tilted, the lighting set-up would sometimes have to be changed to keep the back-lights out of the shot.) The real style distinction is that, further than this, Hawks uses more panning shots than average, and keeps his average shot length rather longer than normal.

Some recent attempts at style analysis have unfortunately been conducted in spurious terms which ignore conditions imposed on the director, and also the relation between the approach of a particular director and that generally prevailing at the period in question. For instance, the style of Douglas Sirk cannot be simply pinned down by talk about mirrors and flat shiny surfaces. Mirror shots are quite common in dramas made by ordinary Hollywood directors from the 1930s onward (it makes shooting a studio scene more interesting for the director); and in so far as Sirk's films have flat, glossy surfaces, this is due to the art directors at Universal Studios and to the deficiencies of CinemaScope lenses. (Their squeeze ratio varied with object distance, so emphasising the existence of the picture plane.) Actually, Sirk's formal style is distinguished by a so far unremarked excess of low angle shots over the norm. To judge by an unprompted statement, this results from his seeking after expressiveness.

The formal spectrum which was described in the first section, when translated into terms of style, becomes a spectrum stretching from extreme naturalism to extreme expressionism.

If one looks back to statements made by Hollywood directors in past times, it is apparent that they saw their task as one of expressing the material in the script—'putting the story across'—in the most effective way; and a point at issue between them was just how much expression to use—or conversely how much realism. The general desire was to affect the audience in the appropriate way, and this called for the application of unmentioned supplementary principles, unmentioned because obvious, such as internal consistency in all aspects of the film to maintain suspension of disbelief. This is closely related to Victor Perkins' principle of internal coherence. Incidentally, many of the examples discussed in *Film as Film* are cases of the expression of the script content through formal devices. Indeed, discussion of detail in a film in these terms is not new, but it has always taken place within a framework that unfortunately assigned aesthetic values to particular styles and content.

Of course, nearly all commercial films occupy a fairly small central region of the style and form spectra, but the extremes are increasingly taken up by films of the avant garde and 'underground'. These last are still denied extensive discussion, partly because the terms for this are lacking, partly for less creditable reasons.

At this stage questions of value, of aesthetics, are still excluded, but there are still lots of things that can be said about films, even in a more general way. For instance, we can say that Bergman's stated preference for filming in black and white rather than colour was because he wished to make films that were more expressionist than the norm; that Preminger used to prefer 'Scope and colour because his intentions were to be more objective (naturalistic) than the average film-maker. We can talk about how the degree of naturalism of the average entertainment film has changed over the years, and about many other interesting matters. And we can talk about films like Godard's, which contain different styles within a single film.

Nothing has been said about the interaction between style and content, but these second order effects can obviously be dealt with after the first approximation in the analysis has been satisfactorily carried out.

Aesthetics

Once form and style have been considered, value judgments can be introduced without creating confusion. We may have a preference for a certain degree of realism, and say that films are good in so far as they approach that degree; or we may say that completely abstract films are intrinsically best; or we may use some content-based criterion such as moral worth or political content, or some combinations of these criteria. But the exclusiveness of such positions should be acknowledged.

It seems to be more reasonable to accept the style of a film as given, to say that one film is a good direct cinema-type documentary or that another film is a bad expressionist drama, and so on. One part of the criteria for value can be determined by the degree to which the maker's intentions are realised in the film. This criterion is generally rejected out of hand in discussions of general aesthetics, with a certain amount of justification when the example in mind is fine art of the past. But because of the film's short and recent history, interview material from film-makers is fairly easily available, and so their intentions can be found out with sufficient exactness when they are not otherwise obvious.

Another criterion for the worth of a film resides in the difficulty of the task the filmmaker sets himself. Making a successful formula picture is less demanding than creating variations within a genre, and much less demanding than successfully tackling a unique type of picture. This approach seems to be followed in a partial and unconscious way in some week by week reviewing of individual films, and more general explicit recognition of it would be all to the good. What we are talking about here is the degree of originality of the work, a fundamental matter, since the continuing occurrence of the exceptional is essential to the existence of art; a fact which makes any more absolute criteria impossible. (Originality is also closely related to the amount of personal expression achieved in a film by its maker; the basic standard of auteur theory in the Sarris form.)

A final criterion is the influence a film has on other films; and this of course depends on the estimation other film-makers have for the work in question. This is more important in pure film terms than what audiences or critics think of a film.

These three criteria, the most objective possible, need to be taken into consideration together, not separately, when evaluating a film.

The whole approach to the film outlined here is oriented towards the way film-makers in general see films, and to the realities of film-making, rather than to the point of view of single or collective spectators, as has usually been the case.

It is not suggested that this is the only possible way to look at films, but just that it is a widely embracing and powerful approach, and useful too.

The reference to Victor Perkins' book at the beginning of this article was not absolutely necessary, but it had not been reviewed in *Sight & Sound*, and I felt this was an injustice, whatever its faults. I think *Sight & Sound*'s failure to review it was the result of a long-running feud between the *Movie* magazine people, including Victor Perkins, and Penelope Houston, the editor of *Sight & Sound*. I believe it was started by some very disparaging, even insulting, remarks made in *Movie* about Penelope Houston and *Sight & Sound*, so her refusal to review Perkins' book was explicable, if not justifiable.

I had been thinking seriously about these ideas from the point at which I started teaching film-making at the Slade. In a general kind of way, some of the ways of looking at film in this article had appeared before in the writings about film by people who had some acquaintance with film-making, but I think I was the first person to present a consistent framework that was free of illogicalities and personal preferences. Since my article was written, the possibility of a form of cinema that reproduces the world in a way fairly closely corresponding to human vision has been realised in the OMNIMAX system, though holographic cinema has got no further forward. The title of the piece was an ironic reference to Chairman Mao's dictum about allowing free discussion of alternatives to the Communist Party's official line. I was aware that this was a cruel hoax, and likewise it began to appear that the Marxists in control *Screen* were of similar totalitarian inclination. They were actively discussing how they could take control of all film education in Britain, and got some way towards achieving this in subsequent years by means of new university posts created with money from the BFI Education Department, who made sure that the right sort of left-thinking people got the jobs.

The program of research indicated in my article was already underway, and I offered Penelope Houston another piece with my first results shortly afterwards. She didn't want to publish it, having an aversion to numbers and graphs, like many people. I think there was only one graph ever included in an article published in *Sight & Sound* during the many years she was editor. I then tried the article on *Screen*. This was when I found out that they didn't want to publish anything that not only didn't support the party line, but also showed up the total lack of original thinking (as opposed to the reproduction of French stuff), by their own people. However, I then sent *Statistical Style Analysis of Motion Pictures* to *Film Quarterly* in the United States, and Ernest Callenbach, its editor, published it in v 28 n 1 Fall 1974. Callenbach was sympathetic to my approach because he had a scientific education before he moved into writing about film. Since then my work in this area has been greatly expanded and improved for *Film Style and Technology: History and Analysis*, so there is no point in reproducing the original article here.

However, it is worth remarking that in it, I recommended that the ideal way to establish general stylistic norms was to take a random selection of films from the period being considered. This notion was adopted by David Bordwell for the re-search leading to his book *Classical Hollywood Cinema*, though he neither said where he got it from, nor carried it through properly. The obvious difficulty with getting a random sample from the films produced in the distant past is that a large proportion of the films made before the Second World War no longer exist, and those that do survive are not a random sample of the original population. This is a result of the different policies of different production companies towards preserving their old films, and after that, of the whims of collectors and preservers of old films. MGM was fairly assiduous in preserving its films, but Paramount was not, and so on. Hence a random sample taken from surviving films cannot represent with any degree of accuracy what once existed. There are measures that could be taken to get a reasonably representative sample from the surviving films, in the same way that political pollsters get a representative sample of voters, but nobody has tried that yet for motion pictures.

In all my researches, I was consciously following the principle of avoiding areas that I considered had been adequately covered by other people, and concentrating on those where I could bring to bear knowledge that was not available to anyone else. So I resolved to leave the discussion of the content of films to those people with a literary background who weren't interested in anything else. And as it happened, circumstances seemed to favour my approach.

As a result of researching the early silent films available on 16 mm. from the BFI for use in my film history course at the Slade, I began to realise that the story of the development of the basics of film construction that was printed in all the books was seriously mistaken. It so happened that at this time the National Film Archive (NFA) was accelerating its program of preservation of the original nitrate copies of old films that it held, and so viewing copies of them on acetate film were being produced in increasing numbers. Although nobody was particularly interested in them at the time, the NFA had copies of thousands of films made before 1915 in its collection. In fact it was the largest collection in the world giving a representative survey of film developments up to 1920. Of the other large collections, the Library of Congress of the USA has copyright deposits on paper prints of a highly unrepresentative selection of American films, and the collections of Gaumont and of Pathé films in France were not accessible at that time. In 1975, after I had seen a sample of the films in the NFA from before World War I, I felt compelled to write an article correcting the errors of the existing film histories. When Tony Harrild, who had been an MA student on our course, set up a new film magazine called *Film Form*, he asked me if I had something for it, and I offered him the choice between *The Early Development of Film Form* and *White Slaves and Circuses*, a piece on early Danish cinema resulting from my recent trip to the Danish Film Museum. He chose the former. In this re-publication I have set it in Univers 55, as the nearest approximation to the type used in the cheap type-setting which was all that the magazine could afford.

THE EARLY DEVELOPMENT OF FILM FORM

The years from 1903 to 1917 are the most obscure part of film history, as far as nearly everyone is concerned occupied only by the films of Griffith and Chaplin and a vague intimation of Ince. Although sufficient films from the early years of this century have been available for a number of years to anyone determined to seek them out and view them, it seems that no one has bothered, and the superficial and false commonplaces current for many decades about the early development of film technique have continued to be repeated up to the latest film histories published in English. These mistaken ideas, as far as they go, centre on attributing to D. W. Griffith the complete invention of "film language." Griffith may have been the best director working in the years from 1908 to 1915, but that does not prove he invented everything. An outline of the true situation as it developed from 1903 to 1917 follows, based on the examination of hundreds of films of the period, and hopefully to be expanded when more film material comes to light.

INTRODUCTION

There is little to be added to the best accounts of developments up to 1903, for instance that in Jean Mitry's *Histoire du cinéma* (though even this book is not adequate after that date), but there is one minor new point to be made about George Méliès' *L'affaire Dreyfus* (1899). This concerns an early form of staging in depth in the courtroom scene and in one of the street scenes. In these scenes, apparently unique in Méliès' work and indeed in fictional films of the period, bystanders and observers of the action fill the space between the principal actors, far in the upper background, to the bottom of the frame as seen from a slightly elevated camera position, in a way that copies a common framing occurring in actuality footage of the period. This could be considered to be the first occurrence of a purely "cinematographic" angle in fictional film, but this kind of feature had to wait several years before really being developed in the films of the Vitagraph Co.

At approximately the same time the first "chase" films appeared in England, though the earliest still available seems to be Williamson's *Stop Thief!* of 1901, and as is well known, the possibility of continuous action passing from shot to shot directly cut together without intervening titles was realized. (Strictly speaking there was a small space-time ellipse at each cut already in these first examples.) The other well-known development of this year was in *Grandma's Reading Glass* made by G. A. Smith, in which long shots of children looking at various objects with a magnifying glass alternate with close shots of these same objects (inside a circular mask). This film and others similar by G. A. Smith were widely imitated in France and elsewhere, e.g. *Scenes from My Balcony* (Zecca, 1901).

1903-1907

1903 saw the application of the "Grandma's Reading Glass" device to film narration in *A Search for Evidence* (American Mutoscope and Biograph). In this film, a wife searching for her erring husband peers through a series of hotel bedroom keyholes and the long shot of this scene is cut directly to a shot of her point of view through the keyhole (vignetted by a keyhole-shaped matte). When her husband is finally located the shot of wife and detective breaking through the door is directly cut to a long shot of the inside of the bedroom shot at 90 degrees to the angle on the corridor action, and also showing action matching to the shot in the corridor. However, the device of the subjective shot took a number of years to be generalized, as did another development noticeable in the same year, the close-up cut directly into an action scene. In *Gay Shoe Clerk* (Edwin S. Porter, 1903) made for the Edison Co., a true close-up of a ladies' shoe being fitted is cut directly into a long shot of a shoe store scene in which a salesman is fitting the lady with shoes under the eye of her chaperone. The angle of the close-up is the same as that of the master shot, and the matching at the cuts is fairly good, which was not always the case in similar examples in succeeding years.

(Porter may well have been anticipated in the use of this device by G. A. Smith if one believes Georges Sadoul, but many of the dates he gives for other films are too early by a year or two, and the earliest film made by Smith we have using a close shot cut into the course of the action is *The Sick Kitten* of 1903. The instant plagiarism which was such a feature of the early years of the cinema means that absolute priority is rather difficult to establish, but that is no reason for historians not trying to do so.)

The use of a close shot, not integrated into the action, either to open or close a film, seems to have been quite common around this time. Apart from the well known instance of *The Great Train Robbery* (Porter, 1903), similarly emblematic close-ups begin the British films *Raid on a Coiner's Den* and *The Eviction* (both Alfred Collins, 1904), and also *The Widow and the Only Man* (McCutcheon, 1904, for American Mutoscope and Biograph). The first shows the hands of three individuals coming into frame, one with fist clenched, another pointing a pistol in the opposite direction, and that of a policeman holding a pair of handcuffs; the second film begins with an eviction notice; and the last begins with shots of the widow and the only man. *The Widow and the Only Man* also contains a medium close shot cut into the course of the action, as did a number of subsequent films from other makers before 1908.

Lighting Effects

It was around 1905 that the major film producing companies, Edison, Vitagraph, and Biograph, began to use artificial lighting in their studios. In general this did not make much difference to the appearance of their films because the banks of mercury vapour tubes (Cooper-Hewitts) were used sparingly to supplement the main lighting from the diffuse sunlight coming through the studio roofs, and the light they produced was very nearly equally diffuse. They were not used to mimic the effect of light coming from a real source of soft light such as a window, as modern soft lights are sometimes used. However, there was also from this time some extremely rare use of theatrical type arc floodlight, and one striking instance is in *The Seven Ages* (Edwin S. Porter, 1905). In one scene in this film the light from a fire falling on two old people sitting in front of a fireplace is simulated by an arc floodlight in the position of the fire and out of shot to the side. This is the sole source of light in this scene, and is possibly the first appearance of such a usage.

It does not seem to have been noticed that the well-known *Rescued by Rover* (1905) contains a lighting innovation usually credited to Bitzer and Griffith. The light coming through the window of the set representing the kidnapper's garret room is produced by a pair of arc floodlights simulating the fall of daylight in an almost identical arrangement to that in Griffith's *Edgar Allen Poe* of 1909.

However some innovative camera work was being done at this time by Billy Bitzer and F. A. Dobson at Biograph. 1906 saw the appearance of *The Paymaster*, photographed on location by Bitzer and featuring an available light interior scene in a watermill in which sunlight coming though windows from the side produces a strong chiaroscuro effect. In the same year F. A. Dobson produced *The Silver Wedding* and *The Tunnel Workers*, doubling as director and cameraman, as was quite usual at this period, and in these films, more by the nature of the sets he had constructed than by the exact sources of light used, created scenes with illuminated backgrounds and dark foregrounds showing silhouette figures of actors, scenes of a type that were not extensively exploited till a decade later. Dobson mixed studio sets and real locations in the way that was quite standard by this time, but his choice of locations was more enterprising than most. In *The Skyscrapers* scenes of actual skyscrapers under construction are filmed from slightly higher and lower angles as appropriate, these non-eye-level angles appearing possibly for the first time in a fiction film.

Cross-Cutting

The earliest recorded appearance of cross-cutting between parallel actions appears to be in *Her First Adventure*, directed by Wallace McCutcheon for American Mutoscope and Biograph in March 1908, which is after D. W. Griffith joined Biograph as an actor, but before he started directing. In this film scenes of the flight of kidnappers are intercut with scenes of a faithful dog searching for a stolen child. It would appear that Griffith took over this established usage as well as others already mentioned and has been granted credit for them ever since. And this is not the end of the story.

1908-1913

In 1908 nearly all films, with very rare exceptions, were at the most one reel in length — that is, 1000 feet running for 15 minutes. Whatever the subsequent form, they commenced with a long explanatory title setting the scene for the action to follow. A fair portion of the production was still made up of "tableau films," in which each scene of the action was shown in one shot invariably preceded by an explanatory title. The scene itself might be staged in long shot in front of a theatre type set of painted canvas to take one possible extreme, or a realistic constructed set might be used, or at the other extreme an actual place might form the location. It was also possible that the camera might be placed closer to the scene to take either what was called a "French foreground" shot with the bottom of the frame cutting the actors off at the shins, or an "American foreground" in which the actors were only visible from the knees up. Not surprisingly, the use of shots with closer camera tended to be associated with greater naturalism in other elements of the film. Indeed about the beginning of this period the Vitagraph company had arrived at using what was then called "the nine-foot line," that is using actor positions up to nine feet from the camera to play a scene, and so giving what would now be referred to as a medium shot, with the actors only visible from the hips up. In this major group of film types the story told was usually one that in other media would occupy a full-length play or novel, so the series of shot-scenes served the purpose of illustrating the titles which preceded them, and which by themselves almost conveyed the story. The range of possibilities alluded to can be illustrated by *La Dame aux camelias* (Pouctal) with Sarah Bernhardt of 1910 at the theatrical extreme, and two aspects of the Vitagraph Company's production to represent the centre and naturalistic extreme of the spectrum: namely J. Stuart Blackton's *Romeo and Juliet* of 1908 and *The Romance of an Umbrella* of 1909.

The category of one-reel films which proved more important for the development of film narration includes Griffith's work at Biograph, but it is really a development of the "chase" type of film widely established before 1908. This type of film had a specially written story involving two or three connected incidents covering a short span of real time and particularly suited to being conveyed without titles before every shot-scene. In other words, the action could appear to move directly from one shot to the next, though usually in fact with a small space-time discontinuity. Virtually all Griffith's Biograph films illustrate this tendency, but it also characterised the Westerns and other action subjects made by the smaller American production companies such as Lubin, Selig, Essanay, etc., around 1909.

In Biograph films scenes were shot exclusively with fixed camera, and the actors were framed in either long shot or medium long shot ("American foreground") with a very limited number of big close-ups of objects important to the action cut into the middle of shots in some films only. These shots would be described in later terminology as "inserts," whereas true close-ups (which at that period were referred to as "busts") are entirely absent from Griffith's films at the beginning of his career. He did, on occasion at this period, use the already well-established device of a medium shot of the actors to conclude the film. His use of a true close-up cut into the body of the action did not occur till around 1911.

As far as camera movements are concerned, Griffith took up the "parallel track" in which the camera moves a fixed distance ahead of actors in a car or on horseback, etc., and which had already been used on occasion in the previous period, but he seems to have had an aesthetic objection to the use of panning shots. This attitude was quite common till well into the twenties, the idea being that panning shots drew attention to the mechanics of filming. That this was the case with Griffith can be seen from those odd occasions when a cameraman supplied him with a pan, such as in *The Massacre* (1913), and it is cut off in the editing just as it starts. An earlier instance of this occurs in *Drive for a Life* (1909), in which a scene involving interplay between actors in two cars, filmed with a car-mounted camera as a parallel track, clearly was shot by the cameraman with a pan at the conclusion of the shot to follow one of the cars diverging from the main road. Again this panning shot was removed in the editing, though even without it the scene has a remarkable intricacy of staging.

Throughout his whole career Griffith never really mastered the use of the angle-reverse angle cut between two actors in a scene, and it remained to others to develop this in interior scenes from 1912 onwards. The lack of this feature, and also the related one of cutting on action, is intimately connected with the way in which he shot scenes for his films. According to Karl Brown's description in his book, *Adventures with D. W. Griffith* (London: Secker and Warburg, 1974), it was Griffith's practice to create variations in the action of each shot in each take he made of it; so with all takes different in movement, there was no way for the actors or anyone to remember the exact movements they made if it was decided to shoot a closer shot to insert in the master shot. On the other hand, if he decided beforehand to use a close-up at some point, which of course he did on a relatively limited number of occasions, he could not allow as much in the way of acting variations as he customarily preferred to do. Another aspect of Griffith's style that persisted throughout his career and which could already be regarded as conservative by 1910 is that all the actors in his scenes tend to play toward the camera as though to a theatre audience, and on the limited

LOVE'S AWAKENING (1910)

Cinematographic angle and modelling from arc floodlights and general diffuse light.

occasions when a closer shot is cut into the scene, it is almost always shot from the same frontal direction. In contrast, the Vitagraph company directors were already using an arrangement of actors in the shot in which one or more of them could be in the foreground with their backs more or less turned to the camera in medium shot and the others deeper in the shot, an arrangement that gave the appearance of a natural scene unawares, and which was to become the usual practice in later film-making. (See for instance *Love's Awakening* [1910].) Other compositional features found in Vitagraph films alone at this time could be classed together with the foregoing as the discovery of the "cinematographic angle"; for instance the use of skew angles to architectural features, and shooting through doorways from dark interiors in a way that was not done in still photography. In general the

LOVE'S AWAKENING (1910)

The development of the cinematographic angle.

THE LOAFER (Essanay 1911)

Just-off-eyeline angle-reverse angle pair of shots. Note the reflector fill light.

Vitagraph films have an elegance of composition and, where appropriate, of setting and costuming, that is absent from Griffith's work.

Despite what has been said above about Griffith's failure to recognize the importance of cutting on action and "angle-reverse angle cuts" for film construction, there are very rare appearances of these techniques in his films and they should be mentioned. In *The Squaw's Love* (1911), the squaw jumps from a bluff into the river to escape a pursuer, and a downward angle of her fall from the point of view of her attacker cuts to a long shot of the scene from the other side of the river at the instant the splash of the water forms. This particular instance occurs because the scene was shot with two cameras. And in *The Coming of Angelo* (1913), a climactic confrontation between two leading characters on the seashore is presented with an "angle-reverse angle" pair of medium shots. But there is no question that Griffith did not develop these forms, and on innumerable subsequent occasions in his films when they would have been appropriate he does not use them.

A technique that D. W. Griffith did popularize, though he did not originate, that of cross-cutting between parallel actions can be studied in his early films such as *Drive for a Life* (1909). It must be pointed out that although we now call this cross-cutting, at that time it was referred to as the "flash-back" or "cut-back" technique, and flashbacks as we understand the term did not exist before 1912. It was the extensive use of cross-cutting that enabled Griffith to do without the use of cutting on action and matching cuts in general as a means of creating filmic movement.

An aspect of film construction that came to

be understood in the period we are concerned with was the spatial orientation perceived by the film spectator between the scenes represented in the different shots. To give an example, in all films made around 1908, if an actor exited out of frame right in one shot, and then the next shot showed a different scene, the actor was quite likely to make an entrance from the same (that is right) side of the frame. Although this conforms to the theatrical convention for entrances and exits in succeeding scenes, it is confusing to the unconscious expectations of the film audience, who naturally think of the character as continuing to walk in the same direction for the few seconds before he appears in the next shot from the left side. This latter convention established itself by 1913, at least with the more intelligent directors, and its application called for the continuity record procedures described by Karl Brown. Of course more complicated problems of apparent orientation can arise than this particularly when some reasonable relative orientation of the different scene locations can be deduced by the audience, but these problems can be dealt with by extension of the principle mentioned. A well-known Griffith film that demonstrates lack of awareness of this scene orientation problem at Biograph in 1911 is *The Lonedale Operator*, whereas just about any good film of two years later shows the problem conquered.

The Importance of the Western

The development of Western and other outdoor action subject films in these years is rather difficult to fix precisely at the present time, but it is clear that the physical conditions involved in making Westerns in the countryside predisposed cameramen to make small panning movements of the camera to keep the actors within the frame or even further to keep the picture well composed, despite the difficulty of turning both the camera crank handle and the pan head crank handle simultaneously and in different directions. This can be seen sometimes in G. M. Anderson's films from 1909, and the natural elaboration of these framing movements into definite pans following the actors about the scene has become common in the films Essanay, Kalem, and The American Film Manufacturing Co. made in 1911. Examples can be seen in *The Poisoned Flume* (Allan Dwan, 1911) and *Rory O'Moore* (Sidney Olcott, 1911), and an attempt at the ultimate virtuosic elaboration, a series of combined pans and tilts to follow a group of horsemen on a zigzag path down a hillside, appears in one shot in Dwan's *The Fear* (1912).

But prior to this had occurred the capital innovation in this stream of filmmaking, the use of off-eye-line angle-reverse angle combinations of shots, when two people are conversing or otherwise interacting in a film. Obviously it is much easier to get into the use of this device on location than when shooting on sets that lack the side opposite to the principal direction of filming. The earliest example that can be quoted occurs in *The Loafer* (Essanay, 1911) where the shots in question are true close-ups, but the usage must have developed before that date. (It is really necessary to distinguish between the different varieties of angle reverse angle cuts—the cut from a watcher to his point of view, which was the first to appear as already described; the cut from one long shot of a scene to another more or less oppositely angled long shot which must have happened somewhat later, (the first example that can be quoted is in *Røverens Brud* [Viggo Larsen, 1907]); and the cut between just-off-eye-line angle-reverse angle shots of two people interacting, which is what is under consideration at the moment. The distinction between the first case and the last case can be rather difficult to make in these early years, and indicates the way the last must have developed.)

Titling

During these years a great contribution to narrative speed, economy, and construction was made by the gradual replacement of descriptive or narrative titles by dialogue titles. This development presumably arose in films based on literary classics of one kind or another such as *Romeo and Juliet* (1908) where there was an obvious compulsion to include celebrated lines of dialogue from the original. In keeping with the somewhat conservative attitude to filmmaking at Vitagraph this procedure was very slow to be generalized to their other productions, and in fact it caught on much faster in the Western/action stream of filmmaking elsewhere. For instance in G. M. Anderson's films as early as 1909 there sometimes appear spoken dialogue titles, but like all early occurrences these dialogue titles are not cut into a shot at the moment when they are spoken, but either at the beginning or the end of the relevant shot. By 1911 the use of dialogue titles was fairly common, though not in Griffith's films, but although some are at the point between shots when they would be heard, most are not, and it is doubtful if the principle had yet been realized. (One can see examples in *The Loafer* and *A Tale of Two Cities* by J. S. Blackton.) The dialogue title was generally used by 1913, but in any particular film narrative titles still predominated.

Lighting Techniques

As already remarked, the standard lighting in the better studios was now a mixture of diffuse daylight and diffuse mercury vapour lamp light, but around 1910 supplementary light from arc floodlights on floor stands began to be mixed in, either from the front or sometimes solely from the side. Examples of this latter use can be seen in *Oliver Twist* (1909). Since arc floods are effectively point sources they produce much more definite figure modelling than diffuse light, but for the full benefit of this to be realized the general set lighting has to be reduced in intensity first, and this happened rather more quickly in Denmark than in the United States. Nevertheless, by 1912 entirely arc lit interiors had appeared in American films, for instance in *An Ill Wind* (Weber and Smalley) and *Conscience* (Vitagraph Co.). In the first the key light in a series of office scenes is provided by sets of arc floodlights at one or both sides of the set to give a moderately naturalistic fall of light, and in the second there is heavy chiaroscuro effect lighting from one side source in a waxworks-at-night scene, not to mention general use of arc light for figure modelling. By 1913 arc floodlights were being used on location, as in *Coronets and Hearts*, in which scenes in a real bank and its vault are lit solely with a couple of arcs in what had become the usual disposition: angled at 45 degrees to the scene from either side of the camera. It must be emphasized that this sort of thing was fairly rare

CONSCIENCE (Vitagraph 1912)

*Scene lit by a pair of arc floods
in the bays at the front right
and left back of the picture,
plus a single weak arc flood
out of frame at the left front.*

in American films at this time, the mass of them still using the earlier diffuse light arrangements. The technique of simulating lamplight by an arc floodlight just out of frame on the side where the oil lamp was standing was finally established by 1913, years after this happened in Danish films.

As far as exterior photography was concerned, the only important development was the introduction of reflector fill light, and this is one

of the few cases where the claim for Griffith-Bitzer priority may be correct. Significantly this first occurred after 1910 (e.g., *Faithful*, 1910) when the move to filmmaking in California had begun. The harsh middle-of-the-day light in that area produces much less attractive results when used frontally on faces than the more diffuse light usually found in the New York area, so the discovery of back-lighting of figures with direct sunlight plus the reflecting of

CONSCIENCE (Vitagraph 1912)

*Good figure modelling from
pairs of arc floods left and
right, plus weak fill diffuse fill
light. Note shadow positions
and reflection of lights in the
milk bottle.*

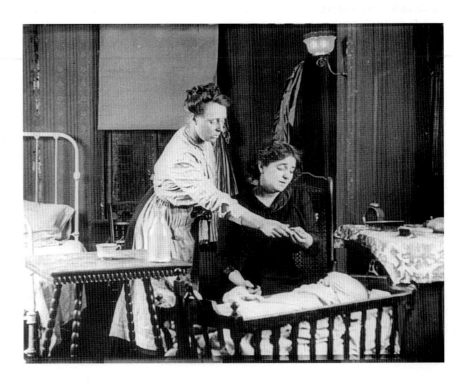

scattered sunlight onto the front from matte white surfaces was probably inevitable.

Flashbacks

Flashbacks evolved out of the earlier representation of dreams and memories by a subsidiary scene inset within the frame containing the scene showing the dreamer. This technique goes back of course to Zecca's *Histoire d'un crime* (1901), but is slightly troublesome to produce photographically, requiring as it does a double exposure with accurately positioned masks and counter-masks in front of the lens. The easier option of total area superimposition of the present and dreamed scene of past events had appeared by 1911 (*After One Hundred Years*) and probably earlier, but the full-blown flashback needed something more than a title to indicate where it started and ended. The fade-out, which had just arrived as a means of concluding a film, was the device pressed into service. For instance in *A Wasted Sacrifice* (Vitagraph, 1912) there is a fade-out on the shot of the rememberer, a cut to the remembered scene, a cut away from it, and a fade-in on the rememberer again. By 1913 the device was well established, but the earlier convention of matting in the remembered scene in one area of the frame was still being used, e.g., in *Atlantis* (August Blom).

In the same year one can see time-lapse within a flashback indicated by the same means as the flashback was entered and left, namely a fade-out and fade-in. This happens in *The Tiger*, made by Frederick Thompson for the Vitagraph Company.

The Missing Link

When we consider, together with the film *The Loafer* already mentioned, such films from 1914 as *Bad Buck of Santa Ynez* (Reginald Barker), which contains scenes cut up into a number of shots taken from many different angles, and when we consider that earlier Ince produced films such as *An Apache Father's Vengeance* made in 1912 contain no cutting around at all, then the simplest deduction is that when Ince took over the Reliance company at the end of 1912 he also took over the director who knew how to do this. Reginald Barker was one of the directors for Reliance; he had directed at Essanay in 1910, and when we add in the fact that a fragment of *Wheels of Destiny* (Reliance-Broncho, 1911) shows very advanced cutting around for that year, it rather looks as though Barker is the man who developed the technique

of off-eye-line angle-reverse angle cutting, and indeed of cutting around a scene in general. In any case that technique was certainly developed along a path leading through the production companies mentioned.

1914-1917

By 1914 an "Ince style" was a definite option being taken up by a number of directors, though for the reasons already mentioned it is doubtful that the formal aspects of this style were of Thomas Ince's creation, and indeed it may be suspected that the more retarded features of *Civilization* were due to his personal intervention in the direction. In this style angle-reverse angle combinations of shots are freely applied at appropriate climactic points, though it must be noted that the idea of "not crossing the eye line" had not been established when using this device. (There is an example of this lack in *Bad Buck of Santa Ynez*, in the scene where W. S. Hart meets the widow and the child.) The possibility of following the characters with panning shots is also present, not only in exteriors but also in interiors, e.g., *Typhoon* (Barker, 1914). In 1915 these tendencies were definitely established in such films as *Between Men* (Barker), and another characteristic feature of Ince studio films had also appeared, namely the use of arc spotlights to give backlighting of the figures in interior scenes. However in these films diffuse overhead light still tends to form an important component of the general set lighting. This was not the case in some other places for example in the work of Alvin Wyckoff (*The Cheat, The Golden Chance*) for Cecil B. DeMille.

DeMille was the leading exponent of a new style of filming that he himself did not develop, but which he adopted with great address. The emergence of this style is apparent in films made in 1914 such as *The Hour and the Man* (Essanay) and *Weights and Measures* (Victor), in which there is a heavy concentration on camera closeness to the action of around medium shot. (This is almost the exact inverse of D. W. Griffith's practice of avoiding medium shots and conducting most of the film in longer shots relieved by a proportion of close shots.) This newly emerging style also tends to involve framing movements, and demands cutting on action with good matching as the actors move from one shot into another as they move about the set. Although it uses close-ups on occasion, this style did not at first include the use of angle-reverse angle close-ups, but these were included by the style's exponents and converts in the next year or two. One instance of this was Ralph Ince, who had recently become a director for the Vitagraph Company.

To some extent allied with these developments was the device of starting a scene with a close shot, rather than showing the whole location in a long shot before cutting in closer, and examples can be seen in *Elsa's Brother* (Van Dyke Brooke for Vitagraph, 1915), and other examples exist in the contemporary works of Maurice Tourneur and Allan Dwan.

Another aspect of shot continuity had reached its definitive formulation by 1914. This was the handling of the movement of actors from one shot to another shot taken in a different location. Previous to this date this transition was dealt with by having the actors walk out of one shot and then walk into another and merely having the directions match. (Though for years after 1914 there were a number of directors active who still could not manage even that much.) But in *Detective Burton's Triumph* (Reliance) the actor is placed in such a position while still within the frame and his direction of movement is so arranged that when the cut is made to the same actor in another different location his movement seems quite continuous to the casual eye, and the space-time ellipse between the shots is concealed. So thoroughgoing is the demonstration of mastery of these weak shot transitions in this film that one is tempted to take it as a consciously virtuoso performance by the unknown director. Strangely, this film, so exceptionally advanced for 1914 in this respect (and also quite forward in most other respects except lighting), entirely lacks dialogue titles, the story being carried by a limited number of narrative titles. Anomalies of sophistication between the handling of the different dimensions of the film medium are not uncommon during this period; for instance crude acting sometimes occurs in a film with good shot dissection, but this is the most singular example noted so far. (Most films make considerable use of dialogue titles by 1914-15, though Griffith was already slipping behind in the proportion he used.)

Generally, compared with the films we have been discussing, D.W. Griffith's *Birth of a Nation* is technically retarded, though of course other qualities outside our concern at the moment compensate as far as its absolute aesthetic value is in question. In the two hours of this film's duration there is not one use of a subjective shot or more generally of the angle-reverse angle combination, even in scenes crying out for these devices such as Flora Cameron's pursuit by the negro and leap

from the cliff. Always the camera moves straight in from the established "audience" side for closer shots. And there are not very many closer shots compared to the usage in the films previously mentioned. Cuts on action are almost completely absent as well, and of course all this still stems from Griffith's technique of using varied improvisation on each take. These features would tend to produce a slow moving film but for the well-known feature of Griffith's style, the cross-cutting between parallel actions. This produces a series of very strong cuts between shots which propel the film forward and compensates for the relatively static nature of the individual shots due to the distance of the actors from the camera and hence the small amount of movement within the frame. Also the cutting in *Birth of a Nation* is slightly faster (average shot length—8 seconds) than the Ince school films, which all have an average shot length of about 10 seconds.

Watching a film such as *His Phantom Sweetheart* (Ralph Ince), one has the subjective impression that it is moving very fast, and this clearly happens because of the relatively large amount of movement within the frame due to the close camera placement which overrides the effect of the somewhat longer shots and "weak" cuts. When one adds in the camera movements used by the Ince school, both a limited number of framing movements and true pans and tilts, one has the direction that the mainstream of cinema was to follow eventually. But not immediately, for a proportion of American films were being made in a style closer to that of Griffith at this time, though usually without his well-planned use of parallel action to give drive to them.

One can indeed point to such films as James Kirkwood's *The Eagle's Mate* of 1914 which show these features, but Kirkwood and anyone else who persisted in this style in America went to the wall even faster than Griffith. (The development of a style depending on quasi-static shots joined by strong fast cuts led away from the mainstream to the avant-garde through Gance and Eisenstein.)

More About Flashbacks

In 1914 a new method of entering and leaving flashbacks through a dissolve began to appear, and for a while coexisted with the earlier fade-out fade-in convention sometimes even in the same film, as in *The Man That Might Have Been* (William Humphrey for Vitagraph 1914). This one-reeler has a remarkable complexity of construction, being a series of memories and reveries that contrast the imaginer's real passage through life with what might have been if his son had not died. The use of the dissolve had become practical at this time owing to the addition of frame counters to movie cameras. (Standard on the new Bell & Howell, and then added personally by enterprising cameramen with older Pathés etc.) The dissolve was not restricted to introducing flashbacks; it also began to be used to cover a suspected mismatch in actor position when making a transition from a longer shot to a closer shot, or indeed even when there was no possibility of mismatch on moving from long shot to close-up. This usage, which continued to be a standard possibility till the latter part of the twenties, can be seen in Ince's *Civilization* (1916) as well as in numerous other films. The dissolve was not used to indicate a short time lapse.

Before long other ways of getting into a flashback appeared, for example matting in the past scenes into the centre of an insert shot of the letter that inspired their recollection, as in *The On-the-Square Girl* (F. J. Ireland, 1917). But these did not displace the dissolve convention.

Lighting Developments

Even in the small number of dramatic films still available from the time of the First World War one can see important developments taking place in the lighting of both interior and exterior scenes. The earliest detected use of "night-for-night" filming with artificial light occurs in *Their One Love* (Thanhouser, 1915), where an extended night battle sequence is lit with arc floods; sometimes picking out foreground areas with frontal light, in other shots producing silhouette effects with back-lighting alone. (The short "burning of Atlanta" sequence in the earlier *Birth of a Nation* is lit with flares.) However "night for night' shooting did not really become much used until a few years had passed, as was also the case with the use of underexposure on "day-for-night" exteriors. This latter technique can be seen in *The On-the-Square Girl* (1917), but only occasionally thereafter for a number of years.

The main thrust in the development of the lighting of interior scenes in American films was the change to the overall use of directional artificial light and the application of this lighting separately to the actors and to the sets. This was a gradual process and has already been alluded to in part. The cameraman who led the way in combining all these elements seems to have been Alvin Wyckoff. By the time he lit *The Cheat* and *The Golden Chance*

he was using stronger and weaker arc floodlights from the front to provide key and fill light from the appropriate angles to give good modelling on the faces, and at least some of the time using a back spotlight for more modelling and figure separation from the background. Figure separation is also aided by arranging that the light intensity be lower on the walls of the set than on the figures. Also included in these films are strong chiaroscuro and low-key lighting effects where appropriate, these being produced by lighting limited areas of the scene from the side with a single arc light and not using any fill light at all. This chiaroscuro lighting was applied from above or below eye level as seemed fitting. Of course all these techniques had been applied to lighting isolated scenes in various films before this, but Wyckoff was the first to use them throughout a film with consistency.

In contemporary European lighting practice back-lighting was not used, and it was quite possible to produce good-looking results without it, as the lighting some American films made later than *The Golden Chance* shows, for instance that of *The On-the-Square Girl*. Although not using true back-lighting, this last film does use cross-back figure lighting from arc floods in closer shots. The cameraman, Morris E. Hair, also manages to add the features of the lighting of large sets entirely with directional light, and the use of diffusion on floodlights for figure lighting, to those already appearing in Wyckoff's work. Diffusion on floodlights was a notable advance, as it softens the shadow line around the curves of the face, though the original reason for putting glass diffusers in front of arc floodlights may have been an attempt to prevent the "klieg-eye" condition of eye inflammation prevalent among film actors.

Tracking Shots

Inspired by the well-known example of *Cabiria* in 1914, the more adventurous directors in Scandinavia and America took up the occasional use of tracking shots on quasi-static scenes (the "Cabiria movement") in the following years, for example in *David Harum* (A. Dwan), *Civilization* (Ince), *Terje Vigen* (Sjöström), *Himmelskibet* (Holger-Madsen), etc. At the moment it appears that the last use for a number of years was in *The Blue Bird* (Maurice Tourneur, 1918), but who knows what will turn up as more and more films from the early twenties come to light. During the First World War period the parallel tracking shot also continued to be used on occasion, as it had been earlier.

CONCLUSION

When one looks at a film like *The On-the-Square Girl* made in 1917 one can see all the main features of what was to be the mainstream of cinema in place and working beautifully, and hopefully it has been made clear how this has much less to do with D. W. Griffith and Thomas Ince than is usually supposed.

The other important point that comes out very strongly from a comparative study of films from the 1903 to 1917 period is the lack of fixed meaning in the devices that constitute their form. At one particular date in those years a fade-out could indicate a time-lapse, a flashback, or simply the end of the film, and the same sort of consideration applies to other devices such as dissolves and even camera angles. And yet people then and now appear to have been able to understand the meaning of these films quite easily. The converse situation, in which the same meaning is conveyed by different devices, is illustrated by the telephone conversation problem. Seen from the viewpoint of those early years this was the difficulty of making clear that the two people using the phone are in fact speaking to each other, remembering that before 1910 the two participants in a conversation were always simultaneously visible in the same shot. The first solution offered was simple superimposition of shots of the telephone users, as in *The Story the Biograph Told* (1904), and some time after that the idea of using a split screen showing the speakers in the two halves must have appeared,

certainly before 1910 (*Den Hvide Slave-Handel*). Once the idea of cross-cutting between parallel action was established it became possible to cut directly from one phone speaker to another, but the earlier conventions persisted, as can be seen in *Ved Fængslets Port* (1911), in which a phone conversation is first treated by superimposition, and then on a second occasion by simple cutting. Later, in 1913, when cutting between the speakers had become the usual way of treating a phone conversation, it was still possible to use the triptych screen device in the American film *Suspense* (Weber and Smalley). In other words, in 1911 these three conventions for treating the subject matter of a phone conversation existed simultaneously.

This lack of regularity in the significance of style features, which was to become even more marked with the emergence of the avant-garde in the twenties, is one of the main reasons for the failure of attempts to create a science of film considered as a language system. The more film is an art, the less it is a language system. (Consider the treatment of a flashback in *The On-the-Square Girl* described earlier, which is probably a unique case of that handling of the device.) This is not to say that aspects of film cannot be studied by scientific methods, or that there are no regularities in the forms of films at all, just that these regularities are insufficient to be usefully considered as a language system.

The above version is in the form I actually wrote it, but when Tony Harrild published this piece, he put sections of it into footnotes, presumably to make it look more "academic". My initial statement in the article that developments up to 1903 had been adequately treated in previous work soon proved to be wrong. At the time, I was thinking of not only the Jean Mitry book mentioned, but also *The History of the British Film 1896-1906* by Rachel Low and Roger Manvell, and *British Creators of Film Technique* by George Sadoul, on which Mitry's ideas were based, and which I had also read. The completely misleading concept of an "Ince style", so dear to Jean-Luc Godard and other Frenchmen, also came from Mitry. The other major error in it is the importance accorded to Reginald Barker. This arose from a number of errors in the film catalogues and books I was using for production information about these films. The date *Bad Buck of Santa Ynez* was made and released was 1915, not 1914, and it was directed by W.S. Hart himself, not Reginald Barker. The information given about Barker's career, which I had got from Mitry, is also not correct. However, I *was* right to emphasise the importance of the Western in the development of reverse-angle cutting, as became clear later as I saw more films from the period, and as you can read in *Film Style and Technology*. I subsequently worked out that *The Loafer* was directed by Arthur Mackley, and Ben Brewster found out that the original American titles of *Love's Awakening* and *Detective Burton's Triumph* were *A Friendly Marriage* and *The Bank Burglar's Fate* respectively. This piece shows, as does the previous one, that I rejected the term commonly used to describe the basics of film construction, "film language". Indeed, it was obvious to me that the standard filmic devices did not constitute anything like a language, and so I was already consistently using the term "film form" to describe the subject under investigation. It also introduces some useful particular terminology that has since been taken up by others, and specifically the phrase "emblematic shot". Noël Burch, who was a frequent visiting lecturer on the course at the Slade, and read my article in draft in 1975, frenchified it as *plan emblematique*, and others who subsequently became interested in early film adopted the term as well.

The pictorial illustrations of the points I was making were all from frame enlargements I took from prints of the films. The use of frame enlargements in books about film had been very rare up to this point, though Kevin Brownlow had used some in his essential book, *The Parade's Gone By*. I took them with a special rig I made, which in its first form involved putting extension tubes on a Pentax K-1000 single lens reflex camera, with an ordinary lens clamped onto the end of the extension tubes in the reversed position, using a special fitting, and then a slide copier holder clamped on the back end of the lens. The Pentax K-1000 SLR camera is one of the very few cameras whose through-the-lens exposure meter averages the light from the subject across the whole frame. This makes it easier to make an extra mental correction to the exposure meter reading when photographing frames that are

brighter or darker than the norm. Shortly afterwards, I bought a proper macro lens, and then this could be used attached in the normal way to the extension tubes. I had to modify the slide copier holder internally to get the required enlargement of the smaller film frame, so that it filled the height of the still camera frame, as the slide copying attachment was only intended for making same-size copies of 35 mm. still slides. (It is possible to make frame enlargements with an off-the-shelf extension bellows, plus a bellows-type slide holder, but these are much more expensive, and also much bulkier and heavier.) I always use Ilford Pan F negative for making black and white frame enlargements, and its slow speed is not a problem, as the original film and the negative in the still camera are held rigidly with respect to each other by the rig. This means that longer exposures than normal are possible. In any case, I put a bit more light behind the original film, by replacing the ordinary 80 watt bulb found in the anglepoise lamp attachment on the Steenbecks used for viewing films in archives with a 100 watt reflector spot bulb. With this apparatus I can take up to a hundred frame enlargements a day, and so I now have many thousands of frame enlargements from films in the National Film and Television Archive, and also from films from foreign archives.

Meeting a Challenge

My investigation into the history of film technology as well as film style came about because James Leahy showed me a recent French piece by Comolli claiming that film technology had an important influence on the nature of movies. James was a bit dubious about some of the things in it, and I could see at a glance that many of the facts and arguments in it were mistaken, and I said so. The challenge then was to do better, so I began to crash through the complete files of the major film technology journals, the *American Cinematographer* and the *Proceedings of the Society of Motion Picture Engineers*, alongside the empirical research I was doing into the development of film style. This led to further articles published in *Film Quarterly* in 1976 and 1977 on film style and technology in the 'thirties and 'forties. When Liz-Anne Bawden congratulated me on one of these being really scholarly, I could feel the skin crawling up my backbone, but I forced out a polite "thank-you" with great difficulty.

I have complete contempt for the way the words "scholar" and "scholarly" are constantly used by people in the humanities as a badge of value, and to distinguish themselves and their doings from other people who are actually doing the same work, but don't put lots of pointless references and footnotes on their articles. Scientists don't constantly use the words "scientist" and "scientific" about themselves to validate their work in the same sort of way. In the real sciences, the important thing is how good your work is, and in general this is fairly obvious to all other scientists working in the same field. Insofar as I think about myself in relation to what I do, which is not very much, I think of myself as a researcher or historian.

Besides Noël Burch, some of the prominent proponents of French ideas invited themselves in to give seminars in the Film Unit. The most notable of these was Raymond Bellour, who gave a lecture (in French) on various applications of psychoanalysis, which the French had just discovered, to various films. Bellour had adopted the artificial style of dress favoured by charlatans through the ages seeking to impress their audience; in his case it was riding breeches and boots and a slim cigar. The films he was talking about included *Battleship Potemkin* and *The Birds*. In the subsequent discussion, I pointed out the non-specificity of the psychoanalytical interpretation of any individual feature of a film, but this point escaped him, as did my critical analysis of what he was saying about the crop-dusting sequence in *The Birds*. Later he published this as an article, and you can read my dissection of the muddled thinking in it in *Film Style and Technology*. (Pp. 16-19).

Stephen Heath, whose act involved dressing entirely in black, and wearing dark glasses indoors as well as outdoors, also came in, and in his case I can't remember what he was talking about. I do remember that in the middle of his seminar I pointed out that he had contradicted what he had said about a minute before, and he acknowledged this. But half an hour later, he was still appealing to the same contradictory ideas. Afterwards, he sidled up to me, and said he admired my work, and he saw my role as providing him with facts to drape his theories over. I was struck dumb at his conceit. Here was someone who knew little about film, and was clearly incapable, in that seminar and elsewhere, of sustained logical thought, and was offering to do my thinking for me.

Noël Burch was a different matter. Although not completely free of affectation, he at least was an intelligent film-maker, and so could see some of the things about film development that others missed. He obviously felt the need to compete with them with his own "theory", which was more traditionally Marxist. Hence his invention of new descriptive terms, such as the "Institutional Mode of Representation" or the IMR, and the "Primitive Mode of Representation" or PMR. These sort of concepts, together with their capital letter abbreviations, were inspired by Althusser, but they were just dressing up an idea that was oversimplified, and which exaggerated the already existing false notion that there was a complete break between "primitive cinema" and "classical cinema", or whatever you called it.

These ideas of Noël Burch have died out, but they have been replaced by the equally false and crude idea due to Tom Gunning, of a "Cinema of Attractions" being replaced by "classical cinema". At the time, Noël Burch was pushing the idea that his "Primitive Mode of Representation" gave a vision of an alternative form of working-class cinema that was suppressed by the middle class. This ignored a whole raft of facts, in particular the middle-class origins of many of the people who created cinema before 1903. One of his particular points about film technology was that the "double acting" projector shutter, which removed the flicker from the projected movie image, was invented just at the beginning of the nickelodeon boom. This bothered me, and I shortly found out that the first "double acting" shutter was patented in 1900 by Oskar Messter and Ludwig Petzold. Noël Burch was also much exercised by the two versions of Edwin Porter's *The Life of an American Fireman* which were known at the time. These were the copy rephotographed from the copyright paper print deposited in the Library of Congress archive in 1903, and the 35 mm. print held in the Museum of Modern Art archive. The first of these shows some of the action in the story twice, as seen from both inside and outside the burning building, and there are dissolves between every shot, whereas in the MOMA print there are cuts on action from inside to outside twice, and the shots have been recut to remove repeated action and the dissolves eliminated. I felt this was making a lot out of something which should be obvious, since I had read the Edison catalogue description of the film from 1903, which accurately and completely described the Library of Congress version. This was clearly the authentic version. I had already come across other early films which had been faked to give the impression that the makers were the first to discover various basic features of film construction, specifically Skladanowsky's *Eine Fliegenjagd* and *A Maiden's Distress*, an Australian film shot sometime in the 'twenties or later, which the makers pretended was made in 1902. So it seemed obvious to me that the MOMA version of *The Life of an American Fireman* had been improved by someone at a later date. Since then, another version of this film has been found which has the shots in the same order as the Library of Congress version, and this has been accepted by many as authentic. But they have ignored that it too has been "improved" at some point, by having all the dissolves between all the shots removed. But anyway, one could get on with Noël, unlike the other conceited and ignorant "theorists".

Digging in the Celluloid Mines

At this time I was also making trips to foreign film archives at my own expense, for as a temporary lecturer without tenure, I was not eligible for research grants. I preferred those archives that were well organized, with proper catalogues of their holdings, and viewing machines to watch the films on. This last was important, as my method was to watch much of any film at double speed or higher. This is particularly suitable for most early cinema, where the shots tend to be long, and the narrative pace slow. An experienced viewer can pick up all the significant features of a film at high speed, and another important consequence is that one can get through vastly more films in a given time. Of course I slow down from time to time to check specific points and to get the full flavour of the film. Seeing lots of films from any period is the only way to get a grasp on the comparative stylistics, and the lack of this has bedevilled the work other writers on film in the past, and indeed is still frequently the case nowadays.

The first of these trips was to the Danish Film Museum (det Danske Filmmuseum), which was the Danish equivalent of the British Film Institute, combining a national film archive, film book library, and film theatre. I was very well looked after there by Karen Jones, who, despite her name, was a true Dane, and who worked for the Danish Film Museum, after having spent some time working at the British Film Institute. In a few days I shot all the surviving Danish films made before 1920 through a Steenbeck, and had time for the usual cultural excursions as well. The Danish national gallery in Copenhagen does not have an outstanding collection of old paintings, and the only local artist whose work struck my eye was Wilhelm Hammershøj, the Master of Murk (or Mørk, if you like). I toyed with the idea of trying to make a connection between his work and the low-key visual effects in early Danish cinema which are described in the following article, but really the compositions and lighting in his paintings are quite different to those in the films. The most unexpected pleasure came from a visit to the Glyptothek, a sculpture museum created by Carl Jacobsen, the founder of the Carlsberg brewery, in a specially designed building. In Copenhagen, I also met Russell

Merrit, who was on a long term visit studying early Danish cinema. His big idea at the time was that early Danish films had influenced D.W. Griffith. I couldn't see this myself, and still don't. Apart from the lack of visual evidence for this in the surviving films, my impression is that by 1910, Griffith was so convinced of his own brilliance that he largely ignored what other film-makers were doing. The reverse effect, that of American films on Danish films, which might be expected since American films were technically more advanced by around 1912, and were being shown in Denmark, is not particularly evident either. But then this is true for the whole European film industry prior to the first World War. Of course, American faster cutting and closer shooting did have some influence, but it was much slower in having an effect than one might expect.

When I came back to London, I wrote up my observations on the films, and then arranged to put on a season of early Danish films at the National Film Theatre, which finally happened in 1979. I then offered the article I had written about them to Penelope Houston at *Sight & Sound*. However, she turned it down, as being of not enough interest to most people, and it did not appear till 1986, and in Italian, in *Schiave bianchi allo specchio*, edited by Paolo Cherchi Usai, and published by Edizioni Tesi. This publication followed the Pordenone *Giornate* on early Scandinavian cinema in 1985. Paolo was taken with my white slave angle on early Danish cinema, and combined it with Noël Burch's fascination with mirrors to give the title of the book, but he also changed the title of my piece, to *Schiave bianchi e tende a strice - la ricerca del "sensazionale"*. I have an uneasy feeling that it may have been published in English subsequently somewhere, but if so, I cannot remember where. Anyway, here is my original version, set in Simoncini Garamond as it was in the Italian publication.

WHITE SLAVES AND CIRCUSES:
THE PURSUIT OF THE SENSATIONAL

It was all Ole Olsen's fault. The fairground showman who set up the Nordisk Film Company wanted his films to be built around at least one "sensation", just like the shows he had presented at fairs in Denmark and at his Malmö Tivoli amusement park. As his company's instructions to scriptwriters put it in 1913, "Each film should have some effective — and original — trick that can create the climax of the piece." Ebbe Neergard and Ove Brusendorf have already told most of what happened in *The Story of Danish Film* and *Filmen* – Vol.3, but there is still a little more to be added about the consequences of Olsen's approach to making movies.

As in other countries, such as Italy, which entered as the second growth of the world film business, Olsen started his company in 1906 on the foundation of the world-wide expansion in film production that followed on from the Nickelodeon boom in the United States. The first fictional films he made were inevitably modelled, both in form and in subject matter, on those from the three major film producing countries of the time, France, Britain, and America, and the "sensations" they contained made no stylistic contribution at first. So *Konfirmanden* (1906) was a direct imitation of those Pathé films about youths smoking their first cigar and getting sick, which had started in 1902, and went on being elaborated up to 1905 with *La premiere sortie du collégien*. Similarly with *Heksen og Cyklisten* (The Witch and the Cyclist) of 1909, which is a late contribution to a series of trick films that involve the magical transformations of a means of transport to the confusion of a traveller, starting with the British *The Jonah Man – or; The Traveller Bewitched* (Hepworth, 1904) and continuing through *Voyaqe irréalisable* (Pathé, 1905). In the case of the famous *Løvejagten* (Lion Hunt, 1907), the "sensation" was that a real lion was shot in front of the camera (or appeared to be), but the film itself is a variant of a widely dispersed and long established series of fiction films built around the exploitation of the Point of View shot. *Løvejagten* uses this filmic device to integrate shots of wild animals which were actually photographed in a zoo into its narrative of African hunting, by establishing them with the hunters looking offscreen in the shot before, as had been done in number of previous films such as *Tour du monde d'un policier* (Pathé, 1906), which had also used exotic actuality material that had been shot separately.

Like a true showman, Ole Olsen had no compunction about exploiting other people's sensational efforts, as in the Nordisk company's instantaneous response to Victorin Jasset's series *Nick Carter – le Roi des Detectives* which began in mid-1908, and which dealt with the fight of a master-detective against a master-criminal. Nordisk imitated this immediately with a *Sherlock Holmes* series started at the end of the year by their principal film director of the first few years, Viggo Larsen. When the series ran out of steam in 1910, it was realised that every Sherlock Holmes has his Moriarty, and so the Nordisk company struck out on its own with the novel (and more sensational) idea of a series of films developing the master-criminal, Dr. Gar-El-Hama, as the centre of interest, rather than the master detective who opposed him. The first of these films, *Dødsflugten* and *Gar-El-Hamas Flugt* (Edouard Schnedler-Sørensen, 1911 - 1912) preceded the other better known series of films about the exploits of master-criminals made in France by Jasset (Zigomar), and later Feuillade (Les Vampires). The Gar-El-Hama series was very successful, and continued till 1916, but even more importantly it was at this point that the pursuit of sensations led to some interesting stylistic developments in lighting effects.

Prior to 1911, there is no sign of an interest in the use of lighting to create special effects in the surviving Danish films, but in that year we suddenly have a number of notable instances of this technique. The most remarkable is *Den sorte Drøm* (The Dark Dream), made by Urban Gad for the Fotorama company, and photographed by Adam Johansen. The interior scenes in this picture were lit, in the usual manner of the period, by diffuse daylight through the glass studio walls, supplemented by arc floodlights on floorstands to sharpen the modelling of the figures. (At this time European studios tended to use arc floodlights alone for supplementary lighting on studio sets rather than the mixture of mercury vapour tubes and arcs that were usual in American studios.) However, for the scene which forms the anguished emotional climax of the film, the arc floodlights were taken off their stands and placed at floor level, so that as the actors moved forward towards the camera their shadows loomed high on the walls. This effect, which was presumably inspired by its use in the same way in Max Reinhardt's 1906 stage production of Ibsen's *Ghosts*, is not quite as striking in actual execution as it sounds when described, for the overall diffuse daylighting weakens the shadows to grey rather than a heavy black. As far as the Gar-El-Hama films are concerned, they contain the first use of lighting to enhance sinister scenes. In a scene in which Dr. Gar-El-Hama appears through a secret

Low key scene in Dr. Gar-el-Hama II *(Schnedler-Sørensen, 1912) done purely with controlled daylight.*

panel in the wall to drop a drug into a glass, the scene is in general darkly lit by diffuse daylight at a low level, while his face and arm are fully lit by a patch of direct sunlight delimited by a hole in the thin cotton blinds across the studio walls which keep the light off the rest of the scene. And in another scene in which the victim of the drug is disinterred from a coffin in a vault, the same method is used to create another low-key scene, with only the unconscious body picked out by a patch of light. The use of a hand-held light carried through a dark scene to light

it up as it was pointed here and there by the actor carrying it was another popular device in Danish thrillers from 1914 onwards, and particularly striking examples can be seen in *Dr. Gar-El-Hama III -- Slangoen* (Robert Dinesen, 1914) and *Verdens Undergang* (The End of the World) (August Blom, 1916). Yet another lighting feature already established elsewhere which was pushed to greater lengths in the Danish cinema was the trick of having a character come into a fairly dark room and switch the lights on. (The standard way this was already being done for film

Another low key scene in Dr. Gar-el-Hama II *(Schnedler-Sørensen, 1912) done purely with controlled daylight.*

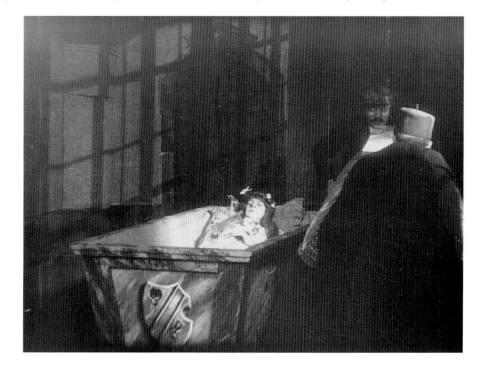

Semi-silhouette effect on location interior in Ekspeditricen *(August Blom, 1911).*

purposes was to stop the camera as the actor switched on a domestic light that appeared within the frame, change the film lighting falling on the set so that it simulated that which would come from the apparent light source in the room set, and then starting the camera again.) This trick came to be used more and more in Danish films, to the point where scenes in the story seem to exist for no other reason, as in *Hævnens Nat* (The Night of Revenge, Benjamin Christensen, 1916).

Another kind of lighting that occurs for the first time in Danish films in 1911, and which I have not seen in earlier films from elsewhere, is the kind of semi-silhouette effect that is created by shooting from inside a room on location out through a doorway, so that the people standing in the opening are seen half-silhouetted against the correctly exposed outdoor scene behind them. Examples of this occur in *Ungdommens Ret* (The Rights of Youth) and *Ekspeditricen* (The Shop Girl), both directed by August

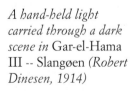

A hand-held light carried through a dark scene in Gar-el-Hama III -- Slangøen *(Robert Dinesen, 1914)*

*Harem scene from
Holger-Madsen's*
Opiumsdrømmen (1914)

Blom for Nordisk. The other kinds of special lighting effects which begin to appear in quantity in Danish films in this year, such as that of a lamp lighting up its immediate surroundings, though they are well carried out, are less remarkable, since they had already existed in American films for several years.

The development by Nordisk of other new and sensational subject matter in the series of films about the white slave trade from *Den Hvide Slavinde* (The White Slave, 1907) to *Den Hvide Slavehandel* (The White Slave Trade, 1910), and then onwards through a series of further films to *Slavehandlerens Sidste Bedrift* (The Slave Trader's Last Stand, 1915), did not lead to any formal innovations, but it did make its contribution to the increasingly frank handling of sexuality in the Danish cinema, as did the famous *Afgrunden* (The Abyss) directed by Urban Gad in 1910 for Kosmorama. (This last film was yet another instance of a major Danish work coming from outside the Nordisk company.) In Danish films from this point onwards adultery and what led up to it was often depicted directly in a way that was unknown in American cinema, and slightly surpassed even the French cinema. I know of nothing in films made elsewhere before the war to match the depiction of the unfocussed sensuality of a hot day affecting a group of young people in *Ungdommens Ret* (August Blom, 1911), and other notable contributions in the same direction include scenes in *Ved Fængslets Port* (Blom, 1911) and *De fire Djaevle* (1911). Apart from launching Asta Nielsen, *Afgrunden* also seems to have initiated a series of films in which the things performers are doing on stage intersect and reflect their off-stage life" relationships, as in

Desdemona (1911) and *Vampyrdanserinden* (The Vampire Dancer, 1912), and others. In *Vampyrdanserinden*, the leading lady does a stage dance which directly parallels, in a stylized way, her off-stage behaviour as a "vampire"; i.e. a highly alluring woman who leads men to their doom through their infatuation with her. From somewhere about this point the "vampire" film was a developing European genre, with contributions from Italy also, before the famous *A Fool There Was* (1915) introduced the "vampire" to the United States. A mention of the first Danish sex farce must be added here, in the shape of one section of Holger-Madsen's episode film *Opiumsdrømmen* (Opium Dreams, 1914). This film may quite possibly be derived from the Pathé *le Fumeur d'opium* of 1911, but I doubt that the latter went as far as the surviving episode of *Opiumsdrømmen*, in which the hen-pecked hero gets off through a pipe-full of the poppy into a harem scene with a veiled houri chasing him into a poolful of naked handmaidens, etc., etc. The whole fantasy was denoted as such by being shown inset within a ring of smoke bordering the film frame.

De fire Djaevle (The Four Devils) was the initiator of a circus film genre, which was again an almost exclusive speciality of the Danish cinema, and it also began a new line of formal development. This film was made by Robert Dinesen, Alfred Lind, and Carl Rosenbaum working in collaboration for Kinografen, one of the small companies which sprang up in Denmark from 1909 onwards. These companies were trying to cash in on the immense success of the Nordisk company, and naturally many of them tried to outbid its films in sensationalism. *De fire Djaevle* was

Low angle shot in De Fire Djævle *(1911), which precedes the high angle shot shown right to form an off-eyeline reverse angle pair.*

High angle shot in De Fire Djævle *(1911), which completes the off-eyeline reverse angle pair with the low angle shown left.*

based on a story by the Danish writer famous at the time, Herman Bang, and it dealt with the passions of a group of trapeze artists, and inevitably also with gripping events above the circus ring. These trapeze scenes were exploited by shooting them with the use of high and low angle shots at the appropriate points in the narrative, which was the first time such extreme angles had been used anywhere in fictional films. After the great success of this film (300 copies sold world-wide), Nordisk rushed to make their own films of this type, such as *Dødspringet til Hest fra Cirkuskuplen* (Deadly Leap on Horseback from the Big Top) and *Den Staerkeste* (both Schnedler-Sørensen, 1912), which repeat the use of extreme angles, but now they are even more effectively presented as being from the point of view of the characters involved in the vertiginous situations. These two latter films cross the circus film genre with another favourite theme at the Nordisk studios,

the frivolous behaviour and emotional entanglements of the aristocracy. Whether the creation of this genre was encouraged by Ole Olsen's social pretensions, or by the fact that Denmark had more nobility per head and per hectare than the rest of Scandinavia is not clear.

Another piece of idle virtuosity used in some Danish films was to have the reflection of a character who was somewhere off-screen in the scene appear in a mirror visible within the shot, which can be seen used in *Ved Fængslets Port* and *Desdemona*, and also some later films. There does not seem to any expressive purpose in the surviving examples of this practice, but it could be considered that it avoids cutting the film scene up into more shots, a procedure with which the Danish film-makers were still not completely at ease.

For apart from the exceptional features of extreme high- and low-angles which I have described earlier, the

Low angle shot in Dødspringet til Hest fra Cirkuskuplen *(1912), which precedes the high angle shot shown right.*

High angle shot in Dødspringet til Hest fra Cirkuskuplen *(1912), which in context can be taken to be a reverse angle Point of View shot.*

Ved Fœngslets Port (1911)
The light from the table lamp left is simulated by an arc floodlight off-screen left, and a woman in part of the set out of frame is reflected in the mirror centre-right.

staging and *découpage* of scenes in general in Danish films of the pre-war period otherwise adheres to the standard European model of the time, which was French in origin. Before 1914 nearly all scenes are staged with the actors coming no closer to the camera than four metres (called the "French foreground" in America), which cuts the actors off at the shins when they are at their closest to the camera. Cuts to a closer shot within a scene are rare, other than to an insert shot of an object, and reverse-angle cuts to actors confronting each other at fairly close range are unknown, as they were elsewhere in Europe at the time. Fully developed crosscutting between parallel actions was also unknown. This is despite the fact that American films *were* being shown in Copenhagen before 1914, along with the ubiquitous French output, and also a sprinkling of Italian films. As might be expected, given the Vitagraph factory outside Paris making prints for European distribution from a second negative, by far the largest number of American films shown in Denmark came from that company, but there was also a certain number of Biograph films being exhibited, including some made by D.W. Griffith. Nevertheless, no Danish

An outdoor scene staged in depth in Ungdommens Ret (1911)

Staging in depth in a studio interior in Dr. Gar-El-Hama II (1912)

film-makers took up the very characteristic naturalistic Vitagraph way of staging scenes, with actors only nine feet away from the camera in the foreground turning their backs to it while playing towards other actors more distant in the background. In fact there is only a small amount of conscious use of depth in the staging of scenes in Danish films, just as in French films, but a couple of extreme examples are worth noticing in *Ungdommens Ret* and *Dr. Gar-El-Hama II* (illustration). It is only in 1914 and later that some of the new features such as tracking shots, flashback construction, and cross-cutting between parallel actions, which were developed in American films a couple of years before begin to make their appearance in Danish films. Continuity from scene to scene was also a weakness in Danish films when compared to contemporary practice in the U.S. and France. It is very common to find a transition from a scene with an actor in one place cut straight onto a scene with the actor already in frame at another place at a later time, without either having them walk out of shot at the end of the first scene, or inserting

An evening silhouette scene in Det hemmelighedsfulde X (1914)

A contre-jour shot staight into the setting sun in Det hemmelighedsfulde X (1914)

an explanatory narrative title, as was already the practice elsewhere to smooth over such a transition. And the shots in Danish films go on for a long time by the American standards of the time.

A graphic demonstration of the way that Danish films were influenced by French cinema before the First World War is given by one of the most famous, *Det hemmelighedsfulde X* (The Mysterious X, Benjamin Christensen, 1914). Not only is the plot of this film fairly closely based on those of two films made earlier in 1913

by Leonce Perret, *L' Enfant de Paris* (The Child of Paris) and *Roman d'un mousse* (The Story of a Cabin-Boy), but it also takes over the full silhouette effects that are such a striking feature of *Roman d'un Mousse*. However, in *Det hemmelighedsfulde X* Benjamin Christensen pushes these silhouette effects further, and adds to them all the other striking low-key lighting effects already in use in Danish films, as well as other more original ideas. For instance, when a woman in the story begins to realise the significance of a drawing of an elephant seen earlier in

The outline of an elephant superimposed on a sleeping woman to suggest a mental image in Det hemmelighedsfulde X

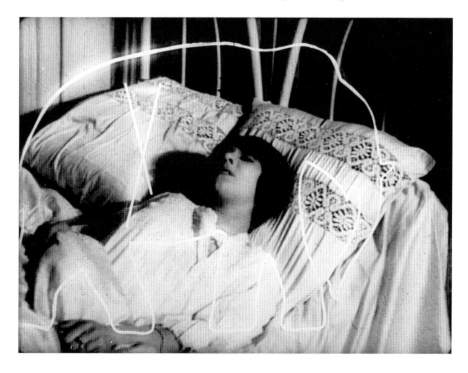

the film, the image growing in her mind is represented by the superimposition of the glowing outline of the elephant being gradually traced out over her.

In their turn, Danish films had some influence on films made elsewhere in northern Europe. When the first Swedish company, Svenska Biografteatern, began large-scale continuous production in 1912, the first films Mauritz Stiller made for them included *De svarta Maskerna* (The Black Masks) and *Vampyren*, which were closely derived from the preceding examples of circus films and "vampire" films that had just been made in Denmark. In fact *De svarta Maskerna,* which was about a troupe of circus performers of that name, was described in its publicity as "...the world's greatest sensation-film...", and Svenska Bio even made a *Dödsritten under cirkuskupolen* (Deadly Ride under the Big Top) a couple of months after the Danish film of nearly the same title had been filmed. The early films of Stiller and Sjöström were slightly less advanced technically than the contemporary Danish product, which remained the case throughout the war years, but over the next couple of years they developed their own distinctive direction as far as subject matter and its dramatic treatment was concerned, and there is nothing in the surviving Danish films from 1915 to approach the commanding way balanced visual and narrative repetitions and mirrorings are used in the dramatic structure of Sjöström's *Havsgamar* (The Sea Vultures). (A little boy is in a dark cabin lit only by the light creeping through a porthole when he sees the customs officer being killed by smugglers, and then twenty years later he is in a dark attic lit in the same way when he finds the gun that was used in the crime, and then when finally the chief criminal is trapped in a cave the lighting is again similar, while the evil-doer is suffocated by the burning of his contraband goods that were behind the crime in the first place.)

Danish films were also extremely successful in the Russian market before the revolution, to the point where an alternative conclusion was sometimes shot for Danish films to satisfy the Russian love of unhappy endings. (In many other cases the films could be simply adapted to Russian taste by cutting off the obligatory final scene in which the hero or heroine happily recovers from what had been an apparently fatal illness.) But owing to the lack of a sufficient number of examples of pre-revolutionary Russian cinema, it is impossible to say whether Danish movies had any effect on Russian production.

However, the most important market for the Nordisk company was Germany, at least up until 1917 when their German subsidiary was expropriated by the German government. There the company made so much profit that they owned a large chain of cinemas, as well as having a number of distribution exchanges in various German cities. It is in the relation of the earlier Danish cinema to the German cinema of the 'twenties that the most interesting speculations arise. I have already noted the way

in which such expressivist features as extreme angles and low-key lighting, which are often thought to stem from post-war German cinema, were already used dramatically in Danish films made before 1914, and as well as the master criminal theme, there are even such specific features as the overhead shot of a spiritualist seance which turn up in Fritz Lang's films of the 'twenties. (First to be seen in Holger-Madsen's *Spiritisten* (1914)).

Concentrating on one particular example, I note that the Nordisk company's *Verdens Undergang* (The End of the World, 1916), was the first of the large-scale spectaculars with an apocalyptic theme which were made in many countries during the First World War, since it was actually filmed in 1915, and so precedes Thomas Ince's *Civilization*. In *Verdens Undergang* a comet is discovered heading straight for collision with the earth (the ultimate sensation), and a general breakdown of society ensues, with the rich indulging themselves in an orgy of pleasure, and the workers rising in massed revolt. Along the way, we are shown the usual low-key lighting effects, with silhouettes and a lamp-lit chase down subterranean passages. In fact, if we combine the content of this film with the earlier Danish master-criminal genre, we get something that is not very far away from Otto Rippert's *Homunculus* made later in 1916 in Germany, which is often described as the precursor of the German Expressionist cinema of the 'twenties. It might be added that *Verdens Undergang* is better made than *Homunculus* from a technical point of view, being shot from closer in on the average, with more cuts within scenes, and with more use of varied direction of shot, including reverse-angle cutting, not to mention the lighting effects. (The limited attempts at low-key lighting effects in *Homunculus* are carried out in a very crude way.) Of course expressivist effects were also being developed in America at this same time, but in a Danish film like *Verdens Undergang* they were tied into a much more dramatically exaggerated story, and indeed to something very much closer to those famous films that followed in the early 'twenties in Germany.

Because of the economic collapse of the Danish film industry at the end of the First World War, the Danish film-makers were in no position to make further significant contributions to the development of the cinema, but even in more recent times a late lingering influence of early Danish films can be detected in Ingmar Bergman's *Gycklarnas Afton* (Twilight of a Strolling Player, 1953). Around 1950 Bergman had been seeing prints of films from the Danish Film Museum, and in *Gycklarnas Afton* he uses the same opening of the circus rolling into town in the dusk of a dirty day as in *Den flyvende Cirkus* (Lind, 1912) and *Klovnen* (Sandberg, 1917), and then builds the core of his film around the humiliation of clowns in love which also forms the main subject of *Klovnen*. And reflections in mirrors play a considerable part in Bergman's film as well, just as they do in *Klovnen*.

Besides going to the Danish Film Museum in 1975, I also made trips to the Library of Congress, the Museum of Modern Art, and Eastman House in the United States, the Cinématheque Royale de Belgique in Brussels, and the Dutch National Film Archive. I avoided those, like the Cinémathèque Francaise, where access to films depends on hanging around the place and ingratiating oneself with the keepers. I have always had extreme difficulty in sucking up to people, or "networking", as it is known nowadays, and this is no doubt one thing that has prevented me from having a career in university film studies.

I began to present my historical discoveries in seasons of films shown at the National Film Theatre in London, starting with one on "The Early Development of Film Form" in 1976, and continuing with one on early Danish cinema the next year. After that, these seasons on film history topics continued about once a year or so up to 1993, when I ran out of important new discoveries.

One positive result of the creation of film studies courses in British universities in the 'seventies was that some of the people who got the new lecturer posts put on conferences to mark the establishment of their courses. The first of these was organized by Victor Perkins at the University of Warwick in 1978 on the subject of Max Ophuls. Victor Perkins was one of the group of young film critics who had set up the magazine *Movie* in the 'sixties. He had been teaching on a film studies course for school teachers at Bulmershe College of Higher Education before getting the post at Warwick, which was a new university built fairly recently, just outside Birmingham. The *Movie* critics had propounded their own version of the "auteur" policy back in the late 'sixties, and naturally, like the *Cahiers du Cinéma* critics who had invented the idea in the first place, Max Ophuls was one of their fave raves. After the conference was set up, James Leahy persuaded Perkins to include me amongst the speakers. I ran through the Ophuls films that were available in England at that time, and got the statistics out of them, made up the graphs, and shot slides of them. I also took frame enlargements that I used to show how the lighting was done in *Liebelei*, *Letter from an Unknown Woman*, and *The Reckless Moment*. I collected James Leahy, and three of the students who wanted a free trip, into my old Citroën DS, and hurled it up the motorway towards the Midlands. Night fell, and a snowstorm developed, but James and the students were embroiled in intense discussion. As we turned off into the local road, I observed that we were doing 100 mph. (as we had been for quite a while), and there was quite a fearful clamour from the back seat. I bounced off a snow drift, and then gave them the right to it. The ride in the Citroën DS was very smooth, because of its aerodynamic shape, its very large wheels, and its hydropneumatic suspension. It was a bit scary to drive at high speed, because the power-assisted steering and the aerofoil lift from its body shape made you feel as though you were not in complete control of the car, but you were. There was nothing like it before, and there has been nothing like it since.

There were a lot of people at the conference, and after sarcastically acknowledging that I was a "Johnny come lately", who had not been part of Vincent Perkins' scheme of things, I gave them both barrels. It did not make that much impression, as most of the people present were still under the sway of the notion that the inspired taste and intuition of the critic were enough, as exemplified in *Movie* and the other film magazines. When there was a season of Ophuls films at the National Film Theatre the next year, I got hold of the prints of his early films, and added them to my statistical collection. The results of this form an appendix to *Film Style and Technology*, and you can read my analysis of the lighting of some of the Ophuls films later in this book.

My activities in researching early film meant that David Francis, the head of the National Film Archive, asked me to collaborate on the symposium on the years 1900-1906 which was part of the 1978 congress of the Fedération Internationale des Archives du Film (FIAF), to be held in Brighton. The big expert on British cinema around 1900 was John Barnes, but for some reason he did not want to be concerned in the organization of the event, though he did take part in the actual congress. David Francis' idea was to show every fiction film made between 1900 and 1906 that still survived to the participants in the congress, and also to have presentations by invited experts on topics relating to the films. The various film archives sent the films they held from the period to the National Film Archive in advance of the congress, and so I was able to view them all beforehand. The exception to this was the Library of Congress paper print collection of films from the period, which were being examined by a group of American film historians organized by Eileen Bowser, the curator of the Museum of Modern Art film archive. I was not particularly impressed with this, since I had seen a lot of the Library of Congress paper prints already, and knew what was in the ones I hadn't seen from the published catalogue of the collection. The films in the Library of Congress collection seemed to me to offer little new information on the subject that mattered most, the development of film form. These group viewings and discussions being carried out in the United States were given the title of "The Brighton Project" by Eileen Bowser. A notion that the FIAF viewings and subsequent symposium at Brighton were called "The Brighton Project" has subsequently arisen amongst American academics who weren't there. It seems to me that this has been associated with a tendency to give the impression that only Americans were present at the event.

My survey of the main developments in film construction up to 1906, entitled *Film Form: 1900-1906*, was written and accepted by *Sight & Sound* for publication before the congress, though the issue it appeared in did not come out till just afterwards; the Summer number of 1978 (Vol. 47, No. 3). It was also included with the papers written by the other participants in one of two volumes published by FIAF in 1982 under the title of *Cinema 1900-1906: An Analytical Study*. This volume was edited by Roger Holman, and also includes a transcription from audio tape of the addresses and interventions at the symposium. I was involved in transcribing some of these tapes, and I insisted that their contents be transcribed verbatim, which is not usually done. Usually such speeches are heavily edited in transcription to make them as much like a correctly written essay as possible, but I believe that my approach gave a better feeling of the occasion. The published proceedings used cheap electric typewriter setting, using the now-vanished Cubic typeface. I have reproduced an approximation to the effect of this here.

My presentation at Brighton was impromptu, as were all my lectures on other occasions, unless I was prevented from doing this. It was anchored by the films I was showing as illustration, but even these were subject to alteration under pressure of events, as you can see below in an extract from my presentation. I gave the first address at the symposium, and on David Francis' suggestion I made a conscious effort to have interaction from the participants in the congress.

... I'd like to press on with a short example that illustrates the way that what would seem to us to be an obvious improvement in film construction was not taken up at the time, not recognised. It's a case of in evolutionary terms a mutation, a new occurrence which didn't become the beginning of a line of development in a way that all the examples which I've presented to you did become the beginning of a line of development of film form immediately. This is a British film of 1902, again of unknown maker and of unknown title, which for the sake of convenience we have called *Interfering Lovers*. Would you run that please?

Well, there are lots of other things about these films that I don't need to tell you about, which I see you appreciate, which is a very good thing. They are not all as entertaining as that - a lot of them are, but not all of them. You notice that with the cut the camera position has changed from three-quarters to front, and it is moved in at the same time, and this covers the mis-match of actors' positions because there is indeed, as there is in all the other examples I've shown you, when there is a cut within a scene there is a mis-match in the actor's position in one, (demonstrates) and then a cut, on the other side of the cut it's there, but you don't notice it particularly - it looks quite smooth because of the change of angle and the change of scale to a different view of the scene and if you look closely you can see it (but I think most people don't), and that has become a standard way of course of joining scenes together. But despite this particular example, this is a unique example, for a number of years

as far as I know, certainly amongst the several hundred films that we've viewed, it's unique before 1903, I'd say. And even after 1905 the idea of producing a smooth transition in our terms quite clearly didn't exist. All cuts to closer shots (and that is indeed a cut to a closer shot, the camera's moved closer as well as around) are done in the way that you saw them done in *Gay Shoe Clerk* and *The Sick Kitten* by moving the camera to the new position for the second shot straight down the camera axis. The idea of changing to different camera angles within a scene (not different camera positions) didn't become well established until after 1912 of so; even then it was rather slow in being established. By 1914 it was becoming well established. But the idea of cutting into a closer shot was very well established indeed by the end of the period we are considering, 1906. So, any comments on this point? Yes?

Question: Denis Gifford (not clear)
(Denis Gifford says that the actor in *Interfering Lovers* is Alf Collins, and hence that he probably directed the film.)

Answer: Barry Salt
Ah, excellent, superb. Looks like him, yes. If you could tell one of our cataloguers, Roger Holman or someone, he'll probably know about it, it would be most helpful. It sounds very encouraging indeed, thanks very much. Possible positive identification, yes. Noël?

Question: Noël Burch:
(Beginning incomprehensible) ... to link shots together in some way or another, to link the stronger and more

successive shots which are the mode of construction of films at that time from let us say the first Passion film, which are successive quite autonomous tableaux linked together simply by the knowledge which the audience has of the story of the Passion, for example. The chase obviously does provide an element of successiveness and continuity, so that even without the existence or consciousness of, for example, the fact that people are chasing out of one shot calls for the appearance of another shot in another place which will continue this pursuit and at the same time, which I will talk about on Wednesday, has a certain historical structure which you find on the symbolic -- on these films extremely important that we go into that on Wednesday,

Barry Salt:
That's a good point about the security of continuity that the chase gives, very good point indeed. So ...

Question:
Could you just repeat what you said about entrances and exits and the screen, I didn't understand.

Barry Salt:
I'm sorry, I was rather rushing. The point is that in *Stop Thief!* (I may not get this exactly right, but I'll get it sufficiently right to make the point), in the first shot the thief runs out right of the frame, then, no, sorry, he runs out of the frame left in the first shot, and then in the second shot he runs in from the left and then he runs out right, and in the third shot he runs in that way if I remember rightly. The convention gradually developed that when you run out of frame right to

a shot representing another scene the smooth continuity is given by appearing from frame left. In a way this method of entrance and exit of frame differs from the theatrical convention in successive scenes in a play. There, if someone exits right, curtain comes down, new scene - he'll enter from the same side, but this is a rather tricky point. Nevertheless, the convention I've no doubt whatsoever exists, and if you look at the films on successive days for this I think you'll see some examples of it. The fact that around 1904 the convention of exiting right and entering left into the next scene establishes itself, is evident in Méliès films around 1904, and it's also visible in a film that I'm going to show you, with any luck, of 1905 (interruption) It begins to establish itself as a convention that not everybody got into. In fact, large numbers of people didn't get on to it for several years. You can still see a lot of Griffith's films that this convention is not formulated. I think they began to formulate it as far as Griffith and Biograph are concerned probably around 1911/12, somewhere around there, but that again is another matter. But the convention begins to establish itself in sufficient films in which it appears around 1904/1905 at least with some film-makers if not all; some had got this idea, otherwise the entrance to exit would be random, sometimes they did it rightly, sometimes wrongly, speaking in our present day terms. Does that make it clear? Right, let's proceed to another film based on the mode of overall construction already established, or not established I should say, but used in *Fire!*; that is of going from a person appearing in one place and then in another place, and back to the other place, the first place. This is a British film of 1903 from the Sheffield Photo Company called *Daring Daylight Burglary*; it was made early in 1903 and it was distributed in America by Edison, that is Edwin S. Porter's company, several months before Porter made *The Great Train Robbery* which also uses some of these features that appear in this film. Well, let's run the film. A particular feature which has some more general relevance to films of this period is that it's not fully intelligible. What happens in the last couple of shots is not intelligible without a commentary. If I remember rightly, the catalogue description says that when the burglar leaps on the train the police telegraph ahead to the next station, which of course you don't see them doing, and I think the film is more or less complete. This suggests that as was probably the case in Britain at any rate, earlier than this that some of these films, longer films, were presented with a commentary, just as the earlier slide shows were presented with a commentary by a speaker. But we're entering a period now in 1903 where films seem meant to be intelligible without any commentary, although this again is a complex matter. It certainly is a point worth consideration. Returning to any possible influence of this film on Porter and the American cinema - the point is that before this I think that Porter had not made any films with cuts of this general sort; certainly, he was still using dissolves in 1902 to join all the shots together in his films, whereas with *The Great Train Robbery* he changed over to using cuts and of course, *Jack and the Beanstalk* (what year was that Charles, 1902?),

which is again joined together with dissolves, has a pretty continuous story - is quite true, but I don't think Porter produced anything quite of this nature, but this is something the Americans might like to or might not like to speak about ... tomorrow, the session tomorrow. Before I proceed, any comments? That chap behind Charles ...

Question; (not heard)

Answer: Barry Salt;
I can't quite follow you, could you elaborate that point slightly?

Question:
The first shot of this film we've just seen opens with seeing the burglar going through the window and in the interim the boy has gone for the police, the boy who had seen him going through, so there was a kind of ...

Barry Salt:
Yes . . .

Question:
... It looks as though they just shot the scene straight through and then just cut, made a physical cut in the shot at that point, them moved the two parts apart then put in the scene of the boy going to the police station, that's what you're getting at.

Barry Salt:
Yes.

Question:
It's interesting to observe that ...

Barry Salt:
Yes it is, indeed. Off-hand, I would

say that is the likeliest thing, but it could do with some closer examination of the film to get this point out, certainly. I think Charles had his hand up next, actually.

Question; Charles Musser
... to say that in Porter's films well he did use dissolves throughout this period, 1901 very beginning of 1903. There are just as many films in which he did not use dissolves, and it's really hard to say that he ... had something to do with the genre he was working with. When he was working in the genre that had its traditional magic moments slides, he tended to use dissolves and other circumstances he used straight cuts, -and there are two films, from the years 1901 and 1902, where this can be shown. (What were some of the examples actually?)

A film like *By Telephone*, which was early 1902, and *The Tramp's Dream*, roughly early 1901, *The Finish of Bridget McKeen*, also 1901, they are the three that come to mind.

Barry Salt:
Yes, most of those are pretty short films, not *the Tramp's Dream*, but *Bridget Mackeen*, is two shots, the other one has three shots. Yes, I would think, you know, because there is an English film of 1903 which unfortunately we can't show you called *Alice in Wonderland* which is again entirely executed with dissolves, that there is possibly some idea that if you are making a fairy-tale type film, like in the case of Porter's *Jack and the Beanstalk*, you follow Méliès' model - yes, is that what you are saying really?

Many of the films shown at the 1978 FIAF conference are now available on the DVD *Early Cinema — Primitives and Pioneers* from the British Film Institute.

There were about 200 people in the auditorium, and so I could not recognize some of the people who posed questions, but in this extract the significant commentators included, besides Noël Burch, Charles Musser, an American expert on Edwin Porter and the Edison company, and Denis Gifford, who showed his grasp of the detail of the British film-makers of the period. Denis Gifford was a cartoonist who had a special interest in old comics and comedy films, and also researched and published *The British Film Catalogue*, a list of all the British films ever made. Like many other film historians in this country, such as Kevin Brownlow, he worked outside the academic establishment, which was not interested in film history, and he pursued his researches at his own expense, just because he thought it ought to be done.

Another person who was present at the congress was Audrey Wadowska. She was an old lady who was the daughter of Arthur Melbourne-Cooper, one of the early British film-makers. She had been pestering the people at the NFA and elsewhere with her claim that her father had actually made lots of the films long ascribed to the better known British film-makers of the period. Indeed, they let her include a list of her claims in the volume recording the Brighton congress to keep her quiet. Her list of films that she claimed Melbourne-Cooper had made included *Grandma's Reading Glass*, *The House That Jack Built*, *The Sick Kitten*, *Stop Thief!*, *Desperate Poaching Affray*, as well as dozens of others. To get over the difficulty that the first three were included in the section dedicated to undisputed films by G.A. Smith in the Warwick Trading Company catalogue, Wadowska claimed that Smith was a booking manager for the Warwick Trading Company. Of course this was not so, and Smith was busy down in Brighton making his own films. The people concerned with early cinema in England did not take Audrey Wadowska seriously, as they had experienced her in action. For instance, Jeremy Boulton of the NFA reported to me that she did things like sitting in front of a Steenbeck pointing to a little dog in the background of some street scene, and claiming that this was her family's dog, and that this proved that her father had made the film. Regardless of the fact that she was only a babe in arms when the films in question were made. Her other proofs of his authorship were of a similar nature, and a 1958 taped interview with Melbourne-Cooper that she claimed to have, in which he describes the films in question, has never been produced up to the present day. The dates she gave for some of these films were also unbelievably early.

One of her claims was that an unidentified animation film possessed by the National Film Archive, and given the "supply title", *(Matches Appeal Film)*, had been made by Arthur Melbourne-Cooper about 1901. This showed matchsticks moving around by single-frame animation to spell out an appeal for help for "… our British soldiers…". Although there was no specific information in the film that established the connection, Audrey Wadowska claimed that it related to the Boer War. For a short period I believed this claim, and unfortunately included it in my *Film Form 1900-1906* article,

which launched it on the wider world. A little further thought showed that a single frame animation film made in 1901 would have created a big stir and been noticed at the time, as a mighty innovation. And if Melbourne-Cooper had been the only person to possess the secret of single-frame animation as early as 1901, he would undoubtedly have made more animated films to exploit this. When the secret of animation finally got to Europe in 1908, Melbourne-Cooper was indeed one of those who tried it in a couple of his authentic productions. Obviously the *(Matches Appeal Film)* was really related to the First World War, when such things were fairly commonplace.

I believe the truth about Arthur Melbourne-Cooper's activities is that he only got into film-making in 1904, when he made imitations of some of the most famous British films of the previous years, as well as original subjects. In fact his imitation of Williamson's *Stop Thief!* has since turned up. Called *Lost, a Leg of Mutton*, it was undoubtedly released in 1904.

The other volume published as a result of the 1978 congress was a filmography created by André Gaudreault of the 548 films shown at Brighton. A number of films sent by the various archives were in fact of later date than 1906, and in particular there were a lot of Pathé films from 1907 and even 1908 that got screened. The quality and nature of these Pathé films was the big revelation of the congress for everyone concerned. They showed the basic features of film construction which had appeared at the beginning of the century in the work of the British film-makers being polished and given higher production values. The Pathé films of 1905 to 1908 were the bridge and springboard to the further development of film form in the United States. As it happens, the French had not been very interested in exploring their film legacy up to this point, and indeed there were no native French historians at the congress.

Meanwhile, things were unravelling at the Slade. Through the 'sixties into the 'seventies, universities in Britain had been expanding, and spending more and more money. They would build up a deficit during the year, and then the Universities Funding Council would cover the deficit, and then ask for more money from the Government, which they then received. However in the middle 'seventies, the Government got tired of this, and attention inside the universities turned to cutting costs. The Slade film course was very expensive to run, with the cost of getting all the films in and out, and using a technician to project the films three nights a week at overtime rates. And we no longer had Bill Coldstream to protect us. He had retired, and been replaced by Lawrence Gowing, a slimy creep of the first order. The course was shut down in 1978, and I was reduced to a part-time lecturer, teaching film-making to the ordinary Slade art students. I could easily survive on this, as I had spent most of my adult life living on very little money. At least it gave me more time for my research and writing. I did pick up a small amount of work as a visiting lecturer over the next few years at the National Film School, which had recently been established, and at the London College of Printing, and at Goldsmiths College.

My next published article was again in *Sight & Sound*, in Vol. 48, No 2. 1979, and was the result of a large season of German films of the nineteen-twenties at the National Film Theatre and the Goethe Institute, together with an associated show of Neue Sachlichkeit paintings at the Hayward Gallery. The most significant part of this was that many German films of the 'twenties that no-one had seen were shown, and that is what gave me the initial information for my revision of received ideas about the period, as is indicated at the beginning of this piece.

FROM CALIGARI TO WHO?

After months pursuing the trail of the German 'twenties through a hundred films, by way of the associated literature and the show of Neue Sachlichkeit painting, a solitary figure was wandering the streets somewhere between the National Film Theatre, the Goethe Institute, and the Hayward Gallery, and could be overheard talking to himself...

Why bother to go over all those questions again?

Because the answers may come out rather differently, and also in an attempt to salvage the concept of Expressionism so that it may be of further use. Expressionism is well on the way to having so many vague meanings attached to it that it could become meaningless, and also useless as an analytical tool, as has happened with "realism".

So what was Expressionism?

An artistic movement in German painting and literature that was well under way before the First World War started. It had nothing to do with Hitler, who only got under way ten years later, after the war. Expressionist plays written by Fritz von Unruh, Georg Kaiser and others were performed with settings in the style of Expressionist painting during the last year of the war and the first year of peace (1918-1919) at a number of theatres in Germany. For a couple of years after this a small minority continued to be interested in manifestations of this movement, but by 1922 this interest was evaporating, and the number of periodicals devoted to Expressionist art and the number of performances of Expressionist plays were already in sharp decline, as was the production of this art. (The details can be read in John Willet's *Expressionism*, World University Press, 1970.) In other words, the Expressionist movement was in decline before the end of the period of German inflation and the beginning of the period of stabilisation in 1924, so there is no connection between these two things. Unless someone is suggesting that the decline of Expressionism caused the end of German inflation.

What was Expressionist cinema?

Six films made between 1919 and 1924: namely *Das Cabinet des Dr. Caligari* (Robert Wiene, 1920), *Genuine* (Wiene, 1920), *Von Morgens bis Mitternacht* (K.H. Martin, 1920), *Torgus* (H. Kobe, 1921), *Raskolnikov* (Wiene, 1923), and *Das Wachsfigurenkabinett* (Paul Leni, 1924). These are the only films in which most of the features are indebted to Expressionist painting and drama. The only arguable addition to this list is Fritz Lang's *Metropolis* (1926).

Is that all?

There are a fairly small number of other films that have one or two features derived from Expressionist art and drama, in particular Expressionist acting from the leading player. But does one raisin turn a suet dumpling into a Christmas pudding?

Well, no. But there are other things besides acting and set design that are special ...

No doubt you are thinking of things like extreme angles and looming shadows. But these things would be better described as "expressivist" features, since they had already begun to develop well before the 'twenties in American and Danish cinema, and had no real connection with the rise of Expressionist art.

The use of high- and low-angle shots, and low-key and silhouette effects done with arc-lights was developed in Danish films before and during the war, when the German industry was still small and feeble and its products less advanced in style. Although most people have nowadays heard of Benjamin Christensen's *Det Hemmelighedsfulde X* (1914), it is still not realized that that film is but one example in a line of development from the film industry that dominated the German market up to 1917, and which included amongst many other films Holger-Madsen's *Spiritisten* (1915) with its spiritualist seance round a table (yes, you've seen that same high-angle shot in Lang's 1922 *Dr. Mabuse der Spieler*), and August Blom's *Verdens Undergang* (1916), in which the rich divert themselves with spectacular stage shows while society collapses into chaos outside, and there are violent chases in black tunnels lit only by the light of a hand-held lamp, and so on and on. Expressivist effects such as atmospheric montage sequences of empty landscapes, and also superimpositions to denote subjective states had simultaneously begun to appear in American films made by Maurice Tourneur and

Det hemmelighedsfulde X
(Benjamin Christensen 1914)
*Low-key villainy with pat-
terns on the walls of the set.*

Cecil B. DeMille in 1917-1918; and both also made use of shadow effects. No doubt some of these films, which were celebrated at the time, were shown in Germany after the war. All this seems to be unknown to everyone who has written on German cinema of the 'twenties.

This comes close to denying that there was anything special about the German films at all.

Oh no. Just that there was less than people who have looked at them out of context think. There were just a few films which pushed the expressivist features remarked on further than before: a longer series of dissolving superimpositions than anyone had used before to indicate a subjective mental state in Karl Grune's *Die Strasse* (1923); more looming shadows than ever before in *Schatten* (Arthur Robison, 1923); and more low-angle shots in *Das Wachsfigurenkabinett*. The first two of these have sets in the normal realistic style of the period, and even the illuminated signs that the protagonist of *Die Strasse* apparently feels menaced by, were an actual feature of Berlin streets at the time. The performance of Eugen Klöpfer in the role is only slightly exaggerated, those surrounding him work right on the acting norms of the time, and the plot of the film, though derived from that of *Von Morgens bis Mitternacht*, has also been normalized by dropping the episodic construction and increasing the internal interconnections and naturalistic motivation of the action. The same sort of remarks could be made even more strongly about other films often described as Expressionist, namely *Vanina* (Arthur von

Gerlach, 1921), *Hintertreppe* (Leopold Jessner, 1921), and *Scherben* (Lupu Pick, 1921). As a matter of fact, Lupu Pick, like Fritz Lang, explicitly rejected the association of his work with Expressionism. There are also a few other films whose only substantial connection with Expressionism is Expressionist-style acting from one or two of the leads, as already mentioned.

But what was Expressionist acting?

At first glance Expressionist acting seems no more than bad old-style melodramatic acting done *very* slowly; and indeed that is what it is at second glance too, if one happens to be looking at any but the handful of first-rank German actors of the period. There was in fact an explicit theory of Expressionist acting, according to which broad and slow gestures amplified the emotions communicated to the audience, and also gave them time to think about the emotions being felt by the characters in the play. This conception was probably erroneous even at the time, and is certainly so today. Owing to the elementary nature of Expressionist plots, the emotions the characters are likely to be feeling are only too simple and obvious, and can be guessed even in advance of the moment. But whatever kind of acting went on around them, great players like Conrad Veidt and Werner Krauss came up with an original twist to the physical details of their characterisations. A major theme on which variations were played by Expressionist actors was the use of the shoulders: held raised a little throughout by Werner Krauss in *Caligari*, held pushed forward by Ernst

Paul Wegener with his shoulders pushed up around his ears in Vanina; oder die Galgenhochzeit *(1922).*

Asta Nielsen tops her despairing gesture in Vanina *by fluttering her hands.*

Deutsch in *Von Morgens bis Mitternacht*, pushed up around the ears by Paul Wegener in *Vanina*, and so on.

A favourite despairing pose deriving from the acting in Expressionist theatre can be seen in a number of films from *Torgus* to *Hintertreppe*: standing erect but slackly

Henny Porten strikes a despairing pose in a production still from Hintertreppe *(Leopold Jessner, 1921)*

with back against a wall, and allowing the head to drop and turn to one side. This was usually the high point of a female Expressionist role. The only actress who could meet the great male actors on their own ground was Asta Nielsen, though she never appeared in a true Expressionist film. Asta Nielsen had developed her own stylized and individual form of acting well before the First World War, and a moment from *Vanina* can show the way that original invention in the detail of highly stylized physical acting, even if not from an Expressionist actor, can redeem the lowest common denominator of the style. She is in a conventional pleading and anguished pose, leaning backwards with her arms stretched forwards parallel and close to each other, but just when one has had time to think that this pose was a cliché, her anguish rises to a peak and she *flutters her hands*.

There is not much about Expressionist theatre in books on German cinema.

No, indeed. Even Lotte Eisner's *The Haunted Screen*, which has a deal of pertinent information on the influence of Max Reinhardt on the German cinema, says nothing on this point. A glance at photographs of scenes and designs from the plays *Der Sohn* by Walter Hasenclever designed by Otto Reigbert, and *Die Wandlung* by Ernst Toller designed by Robert Neppach for productions staged in 1919 (before *Caligari* was made at the end of the year) show the connection. In fact Robert Neppach also designed the film of *Von morgens bis Mitternacht*, which was directed by Karl-Heinz Martin, who had directed it on the stage in 1917. Since the early years of the century, the cinema had taken over plays that had recently been successful on the stage, but what was unusual about Expressionist cinema was that the plays it turned into films were more avant-garde than had been the case before.

The exclamatory, telegraphic speech characteristic of Expressionist writing is of course missing from these films, which mostly have no intertitles. Admittedly Carl Mayer, the co-writer of *Caligari*, came to adopt the Expressionist style of writing in his scripts, but only after he had turned to writing what came out as non-Expressionist films with no visual correlatives to that jerky literary style. Though no doubt it impressed film producers. As we have now had an opportunity to see, the original script of *Caligari* is written in a perfectly conventional manner.

And some of the leading actors who appeared in Expressionist plays before 1919 — Conrad Veidt, Werner Krauss, Ernst Deutsch, Paul Wegener, Emil Jannings, and Heinrich George — took the acting style used in these plays into the films they appeared in during the early 'twenties.

Is that all?

Not quite. One later film has strong connections with the Expressionist theatre of the end-of-the-war years that no one seems to have noticed. This is Fritz Lang's *Metropolis*, and the connections lie in the narrative rather than the visual forms. *Metropolis* derives a large part of its major plot features from Georg Kaiser's trilogy of plays *Die Koralle, Gas I*, and *Gas II*, produced in 1917, 1918, and 1920. These plays, which are set in the distant future, take place around a gigantic factory which provides power for the whole world. The leading characters in the first play are the Billionaire, owner of the factory, and his Secretary, who comes from the working class, and is his identical physical double. In the course of the play the Billionaire kills the Secretary and takes his place, and his son rebels against his father and sides with the workers, taking a job as a stoker. In the second play the billionaire's son is now operating the factory on a co-operative basis, but there is an explosion which destroys it ..., and so on. Take all that, add touches from *Der Golem* and the future society of H.G. Wells' *The Time Machine* and *When the Sleeper Awakes*, add a dash of sentimental religiosity, stir, and you have *Metropolis*. In fact, *Metropolis* could be substituted for the first half of Kaiser's trilogy, which then could proceed on its existing course; and since this has been certified as anti-capitalist and "progressive", it could be taken to confer the same distinction on *Metropolis* in prospective retrospect. If you insist on seeing things in those terms.

Well, no. But there still seems to be something distinctive about all those other films by Lang, and Murnau, and ...

There is, indeed, in the same way that there is something special about earlier American films by Maurice Tourneur. Someone has imposed a strong control over the total look of the film. In other countries at the beginning of the 'twenties there were at best one or two directors who could do this on the set. In Germany it quickly became the standard procedure in expensive films that all, or many, of the shots should be completely pre-designed by the art director, in some cases with the collaboration of the director.

Although *Caligari* is one of the first films for which this happened, the visual style of this pre-designing was not restricted to a derivation from Expressionist painting. *Der müde Tod* has among its sources low-grade Art Nouveau and other early and late 19th century German painting (and also touches from Lubitsch's earlier costume films), as does *Die Nibelungen*; Lubitsch's *Die Puppe* (1919) uses "Toy Town" stylization of the sets; *Carlos und Elisabeth* (Richard Oswald, 1924) uses a balanced geometrical simplification of the details of its period décor, and so on. None of these films has any connection with the visual forms of Expressionist art; and they have no connection in any other way with the nebulous "spirit" of Expressionism.

As for Murnau, it is a nice question as to what extent he was responsible for the very distinctive "look" of his most famous films, *Der Letzte Mann, Faust*, and *Tartüff*. As one can see from the pre-shooting sketches by Herlth and Rohrig reproduced in Lotte Eisner's *Murnau* (Secker and Warburg, 1973), the compositions of these films are fully realized down to the strange smudgy patches of lighter and darker greys scattered over the surface of the

Production design by Robert Herlth for **Der letzte Mann** *with dark smudgy patches already in place.*

Production still shot under daylight showing the dark smudgy patches painted onto the walls of the tenement sets for Der lezte Mann.

image. These smudgy patches, which came to be used on the sets of other German quality productions, may have been an invention of Herlth and Röhrig, for they first appear in embryonic form on the walls of the sets of *Der müde Tod* which they designed in 1921. By the time we reach *Tartüff* (1926), this phenomenon had become much more marked in their work, and completely dominated the image, rather than being incidental to its general pattern.

At a casual glance one might think that the patterns of light and dark in these later films are true *chiaroscuro* (i.e. caused by by the fall of light or its absence), but this is not so, as one can see from photographs of the sets taken under flat daylight. But the smudges painted onto the sets *are* intensified by soft-edged ellipses and circles of bright light cast on them in the actual shots in the later films. This was not the case in 1921, because the spotlights to do this were not readily available in Germany. A third layer of dark smudges is added to the images in *Der letzte Mann*, *Faust*, and *Tartüff* by an edging of fuzzy black gauze out of focus in front of the camera lens which integrates almost perfectly with the other dark areas. This fuzzy black edging to nearly every shot in *Tartüff* prevents any camera movement, and also prevents the joining of the shots by having a character

walk out of the edge of the frame from one shot into the next. The characters are literally trapped inside the shot.

But isn't camera movement supposed to be a major feature of Murnau's style?

So say people who haven't really looked at the films, and who just copy ideas from one another's books. In fact there is hardly any camera movement of any kind in most of Murnau's films, and really only a very limited quantity in *Der letzte Mann* and *Sunrise*. In the context of their various times, only *The Last Laugh* is the least remarkable in respect of camera movement.

You have been describing the kind of visual patterning that...

Smudgy dark patches do not occur in Expressionist painting.

What about the supernatural element in German films of the 'twenties?

It is surprising how little there was, and most of that was fathered by just two men, Henrik Galeen and Paul Wegener. Mostly working together, they were responsible for the conceptions, direction, or scripts of *Der Golem* (1914 and 1919 versions), *Der Student von Prag* (1913 and 1926), *Nosferatu* (1922), *Peter Schlemil* (1919), *Das Wachsfigurenkabinett* (1924), *Alraune* (1928), and a couple of other less well-known films with supernatural stories. That is almost a clean sweep of German silent

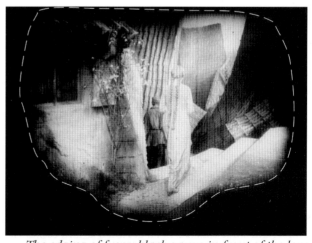

The edging of fuzzy black gauze in front of the lens which merges with the other dark patches on the set is indicated by the dotted line in this frame enlargement from Murnau's Faust.

films with a supernatural element, except for *Galigari* and *Orlacs Hände* (1925). In the first of these two films the supernormal and horror elements are due to Hans Janowitz; and the second is a last desperate attempt by Robert Wiene to hit the jackpot again with some of the same ingredient which he fortuitously came to direct in *Das Cabinet des Dr. Caligari*. But note that *Orlacs Hände* takes nothing from Expressionism in its set design, and most of it is quite conventional in its look, and also in the acting by everyone except Conrad Veidt.

Do ten films with a leaning to the supernatural out of a couple of thousand constitute a significant trend? (German production was well over two hundred films a year right through the nineteen-twenties.) To be fair, these supernatural films were more successful with the public than the Expressionist films which, with the exception of *Caligari*, nobody wanted to see at the time.

So that is why there were not more Expressionist films.

That is undoubtedly the main reason, but surely a subsidiary reason was that their basic form, which entailed filming a pre-designed set of compositions against painted flats arranged perpendicular to the camera, left little to the initiative of the cameraman and director on the set. For such sets had to be flatly lit in the main, or the painted patterns on them would be lost. Also it was almost impossible to change the camera angle, for that would have meant shooting out through the gaps between the flats at the side. What enterprising film-maker wants to be stuck in the position where all

he has to do is guide the actors from one pre-designed place to another? And what can films that hardly anyone wanted to make, and hardly anyone wanted to see, tell us about the society they came from? However good they might be, do the films of the recent avant-garde British structuralist film-makers give us access to the depths of national psychology?

Siegfried Kracauer says that the path leads *From Caligari to Hitler*.

.... !!!

Control yourself!

From Caligari to Hitler is a strong runner in two crowded competitions: for the most worthless piece of "culture criticism" ever written, and for the worst piece of film history. It was written in a state of understandable hysteria during the Second World War by someone who had clearly seen no films made before 1919, and very few after that until the latter part of the nineteen-twenties, as is shown by the numerous errors in descriptions and plot synopses. *From Caligari to Hitler* has all the usual faults of "culture criticism" or "cultural history" writ large – and often. Kracauer suppresses information that spoils his case; for instance that Expressionist films derive from Expressionist plays of the war years, and that hardly anyone wanted to see the group of truly Expressionist films. But worse than that, over hundreds of pages he repeatedly commits the irrationalities and

Der letzte Mann. *The third layer of dark smudges again merges into the heavy masking.*

The fuzzy masking effect has been adjusted here for the close shot.

illogicalities that invalidate all culture criticism. First of all there is the error of using similar films to support opposite conclusions. To take just one example from amongst scores, Kracauer claims that Ruttman's *Berlin – Die Symphonie der Grosstadt* (1927) testifies to "inner discontent with the system", but that *Melodie der Welt*, his completely similar film made two years later, indicates "a desire to believe that all was well". This is because Kracauer is intent on relating both films to the change in the economic situation that had taken place in that period, even if there was no visible evidence in these two films for this.

Secondly, there is the error of claiming that entirely different films demonstrate the same features of the mass psychology of their time. Again to take one example from amongst dozens, two utterly diverse films of 1926, *Die Unehelichen (The Illegitimate)*, by Gerhard Lamprecht, and Paul Czinner's *Der Geiger von Florenz (The Florentine Violinist)* are both claimed to be "dreams" indicating the paralysis of the collective mind, though the first straightforwardly depicts brutalities inflicted on slum children, and the second is a typical ingeniously upholstered vehicle for Elizabeth Bergner, showing her wandering round picture-postcard Italy in boy's clothing, and falling in love with an artist.

Surely Kracauer gets something right?

Yes, the titles of the films, who directed them, and most of their release dates. But his comments on stylistic aspects of film history are entirely wide of the mark. As I have already said, he is unaware of the way that the Germans only developed trends that were already well underway elsewhere. Even after 1919 the Americans were still in the lead in the development of continuous heavy chiaroscuro, with films like Maurice Tourneur's *Victory* (1919) and Albert Parker's *Sherlock Holmes* (1922), and in both these this is carried out with a polish that the Germans could not match at those dates. At the same time, the French avant-garde of Delluc, Epstein, L'Herbier and others was independently developing expressivist devices such as soft-focus and superimposition, and the use of non-narrative shots of landscapes for mood effects, if anything ahead of the German film-makers (i.e. before 1922). The best that Siegfried Kracauer can do is to suggest that high-angle shots were inspired by war photographs!

And as far as subject matter is concerned, Lang's *Dr. Mabuse* (1921-22) is nothing more than a vastly expanded version of the Danish and French master-criminal thrillers which flooded the German market in pre-war days. All its features, except for a passing joke about Expressionism, can already be found in those tales of Dr.

Gar-El-Hama made at Nordisk, and of Zigomar directed by Victorin Jasset for Eclair. Lang's film is not even much of an improvement in craftsmanship, despite the several years of development there had been in film technique elsewhere.

Also, the oriental themes in German films of the early 'twenties that Kracauer makes much of had their precursors in some earlier American adventure films and in the Danish series of thrillers about the Maharajah's favourite wife and associated oriental skullduggery.

What happened in the later 'twenties?

The kind of gritty naturalistic detail that is beginning to develop in *Die Strasse*, and is fully under way in Dupont's *Varieté* (though somewhat obscured in the truncated American distribution print which most people see nowadays), has its parallel in Stroheim's *Greed* (1924), but it must be said that there were slightly more films made in Germany in the late 'twenties with this inclination than elsewhere. In fact, when one takes into account Gerhard Lamprecht's series of films from the 1925 *Die Verrufenen* (Disreputable People) onwards, as well as other little-known films such as *Die letzte Droschke von Berlin* (Carl Boese, 1926), one finds a continuous and well-filled line of naturalistic development towards *Menschen am Sonntag* (Siodmak and Ulmer, 1929). This is slighted in the history books, either because the authors want to relate everything to Expressionism if possible, or because they insist on looking at a few favourite and better-known films in isolation or in relation to a director's career, as is the case with Pabst's films.

The point about these more naturalistic depictions of life in the lower strata of German society is that they surely demonstrate some degree of social concern peculiar to that country, which is incompatible with the "psychological paralysis" that Kracauer dreamed up. He manages to conceal this realistic line of development, which runs counter to his thesis, by fastening his interpretations on just a few plot points in a few of these films, and ignoring the rest.

So does this line of naturalistic development relate to *Die Neue Sachlichkeit* in painting?

Die Neue Sachlichkeit was not a coherent, organized and conscious movement in the way that German Expressionism was; indeed the application of the label was one of the earlier examples of the kind of cultural generalship by an art gallery director or similar person that has since become more common. As everyone in Berlin, Paris, and London has had a chance to see in recent years, the artists usually included under this description are a rather varied group, and many of them produced paintings nearly as unnaturalistic as those of the Expressionists. Most of those who produced the more naturalistic work show connections with Surrealism in their painting, and all this takes such art far away from the group of realistic films considered above, which just carry naturalism a bit further than was usual in the average mainstream film of the late 'twenties. If they relate to anything in painting, it is to the kind of slightly sentimental realism which had been around for a long time before.

It seems that this group of films was more popular with the German audiences than the Expressionist films, though hardly a box-office smash, being merely on the edge of profitability.

What did the German audiences want to see?

In the early 'twenties, apart from American films, which were No.1 as everywhere, they wanted to see obvious things like crime thrillers, Harry Piel adventure films, comedies of varying degrees of crudeness, and of course Lubitsch films. Lubitsch was in fact the only German film-maker who had much idea about applying the contemporary American style of faster cutting to varied angles with free use of closer shots. Everybody else stuck to a more or less retarded style for years, using long takes shot from far back, and with the few cut-ins being done straight down the camera axis. This was one of the principal reasons why German films were unsaleable in America, and also why Lubitsch and his films got to Hollywood as early as 1923. By 1925 other German directors were beginning to catch up, but the kinds of films German audiences wanted remained the same. They got them, but Kracauer refuses to investigate them.

There was just one group of films very popular with all levels of society which was unique to Germany, and which indicated the way popular feeling was going. This was the series of films about Frederick the Great of Prussia. Kracauer first notes it with *Fridericus Rex* of 1923, but in fact it goes back earlier, at least to 1921 and *Die Tänzerin Barberina* by Carl Boese. Kracauer does devote a couple of scattered pages to a few of

these films, but of course spends them on convolutions of "psychological" interpretation of plot details, when in fact the films speak loud and clear directly. They show Prussia ringed by hostile and scheming nations, and always include long scenes of Frederick reviewing his goose-stepping troops, banners flying. But that was all obvious to the meanest intelligence in Germany at the time, and not worthy of a fully-fledged German literary intellectual's ink.

In any case, the question that lies behind *From Caligari to Hitler* is rather different. It is: "Why did the Germans, and in particular a large part of the working class, vote for Hitler and not for the Communist Party?" To a committed member of the left this is so inexplicable that it requires the irrational mental convolutions which Kracauer's book exemplifies.

But there must be a reason.

A short and simplified answer, to which the Frederick the Great films are a testimony, is that Hitler promised the Germans of all classes material progress and recovery of national pride. (Remember that the French held the Rhineland from 1923 till 1930, something Kracauer ignores.) The Communists offered the working class material progress, the middle classes material regress, and everyone absorption into the Communist International.

A historian interested in this question would not only go thoroughly into the Frederick the Great films, but also investigate other films that indicate attitudes to the French fairly explicitly. For such films, though not famous, existed in the 'twenties.

And the moral of the story?

Don't make generalizations about film history or history in films without taking into account all the films, and also without seeing a representative and sizeable sample of them. It also helps for the historian not to have a large axe to grind.

Thank you National Film Theatre, Goethe Institute, National Film Archive, and Arts Council of Great Britain (not forgetting the Blaue Reiter show of 1960 at the Tate Gallery) for this enlightenment.

Like the previous two articles that were published in *Sight & Sound*, I have set this in ITC Garamond. In the 'seventies, *Sight & Sound* was using a version of Garamond as standard for body text, but exactly which version is difficult to ascertain for sure. The best way of identifying a font is by looking at the letter capital Q, and then comparing it with known fonts, after which one may have to look at other features of the typeface. The problem is that capital Q is a rare letter in ordinary text, and also that one needs samples of all the fonts that have ever been used in recent times for comparison. There are more versions of the Garamond typeface than of any other font, but fortunately most of them differ significantly from one another. Adobe Garamond, which is used for all the previously unpublished material in this book, like these "Moving into Pictures" sections, is particularly distinctive.

From this point onwards, most of the articles I wrote were commissioned by various people for special occasions and publications. The first of these was asked for by Peter Baxter, who had been a student at the Slade, and was now teaching film in Canada. He was editing a book about Josef von Sternberg for the British Film Institute, which was a collection of existing articles on the subject, except for my piece. The book was mostly set in Berthold Baskerville, I think, and so I have used that here.

STERNBERG'S HEART BEATS IN BLACK AND WHITE

Where does it beat?

In the centre of the frame.

How does it beat?

Slowly.

Is this just rhetorical hyperbole?

No, – I will explain.

Here are four sequences of frame enlargements taken from *The Scarlet Empress*. If you look carefully at those in sequence I, taken at a fixed interval of 160 frames (6.7 seconds), you can see that they show a regular alternation between mainly light and dark tones in the centre of the frame, from one frame to the next. This slow pulsing or flow of light and dark through the centre of the frame is achieved in a number of different ways in this and other films made by von Sternberg in the 'thirties. Sometimes the simple change from one shot to the next reverses the basic tonality in the central area, as in the first eight frames illustrated, which make up a montage sequence following the title "Across a huge soft carpet of snow ..." and also frames 24, 25, 26 which intersect more or less static shots. But mostly these large changes in the tonality of the image in the central area are produced by movements within the frame resulting from camera and/or actor movements. In frames 9-14, which all fall within the length of one longish take lasting 33 seconds, the changes from light to dark are produced by groups of horsemen in alternately light and dark coats riding up through the frame from the bottom to the top. This use of the movement of actors either in very light or very dark costumes through the centre of the frame is in fact the principal way the pulsation from light to dark is achieved in Sternberg's 'thirties films, and many other examples of it can be seen in the other sequences illustrated (e.g. the shots illustrated by the groups of frames 1-4 and 17-22 in Sequence II, and 2-6 and 7-10 in Sequence III).

After the shot just described in Sequence I come three short shots, only one of which is intersected by the 160 frame division being used (15), and then another longish take running over frames 16-20 in which the dark chandelier forms one of the dark patches flowing through the frame. (Here and elsewhere Sternberg is the first and only director to get any use out of dark chandeliers and lamps.) Subsequent shots in this sequence are covered by the groups of frames 21-23, 24, 25, 26-27, 28,29, 30-31, 32, 33, 34-35, 36.

Sequence I

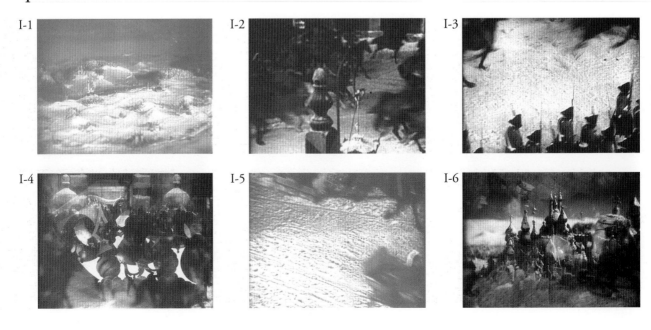

I-1 I-2 I-3

I-4 I-5 I-6

I-25 I-26 I-27
I-28 I-29 I-30
I-31 I-32 I-33
I-34 I-35 I-36

The steady rhythmic pattern I have described continues through several more shots which are not reproduced, until a very short dissolve introduces what is more or less a direct continuation of the same scene, and at this point I resume the illustrations, as Sequence II, with the same 160 frame interval between them. Straightaway we have another long take covered by the first four frame enlargements which show a miniature procession through a doorway by characters attired in alternately light and dark clothes who appear in succession in the centre of the frame. After 9 more frames, corresponding to 7 shots through which the processes already described continue, the tempo of the rhythmic pulsation of light and dark in the centre of the frame doubles, and to show this the frame illustrations from number 14 onwards are taken once every 80 frames.

It is also in this sequence that actual shadow (as opposed to naturally dark costumes and objects), plays a part in producing the dark patches passing through the centre of the frame. This can be seen for instance at frame number 34 in the illustrations. In general actual shadow plays a small part compared with the darkness of black costumes and objects in generating the apparent strong chiaroscuro of Sternberg's images, and indeed many of his scenes that appear to be made up of strong contrasts of light and dark areas are actually lit with high-key lighting -- the lighting is fairly uniformly bright over the whole picture area -- as can be seen by careful examination of all the frame stills collected here. This feature of Sternberg's approach to the static image, which was quite conscious, became more pronounced as the 'thirties wore on, but it was

apparently not understood by his associates. For instance, Lee Garmes has posthumously rebuked him for not understanding the "necessity" to have an equal distribution of light and shadow in the image – meaning of course actual shadow, which is what cameramen are ordinarily concerned in producing and manipulating to get photographic effects.

It might be wondered if these regular rhythms in the picture have some connection with regularities in the music track, but this cannot be, for the scenes illustrated by the frame enlargements are largely unaccompanied by music. In the first section shown, the background music which accompanies the initial montage sequence stops shortly after the beginning of next scene illustrated, which is the arrival at the Russian court, and similarly for Sequence III following the title 'From the very start...' In fact if we examine carefully the musical accompaniment to the montage sequence after 'Across a huge soft carpet of snow ...' we find that it is just a succession of popular classical themes with no particular *musical* connection with one another; a kind of crude collage without the kind of musically smooth transitions we usually find in like cases in other Hollywood films.

Mea Culpa; I had not left much for others to do, even being bold enough to conduct members of the Los Angeles Symphony Orchestra in playing the background music.
Josef von Sternberg

Just so. And even in the wedding scene, which has a continuous music track alone, the relation of the musical phrases to the action is very slight except at the very beginning and end of the scene, and it has none at all that I can see to the regular pulsation of light and dark at centre frame.

In the wedding scene the period of pulsation is again 160 frames, and something similar seems to apply to most of the film, though Sequence III which covers the two earlier scenes following the title "From the very start ..." has a basic pulsation of 127 frames (5.3 seconds). Consequently the frame enlargements are taken at that interval throughout the two scenes which end with the title "After weeks of hard riding ...".

There are no sections of double tempo pulsation in these two scenes.

Sequence III

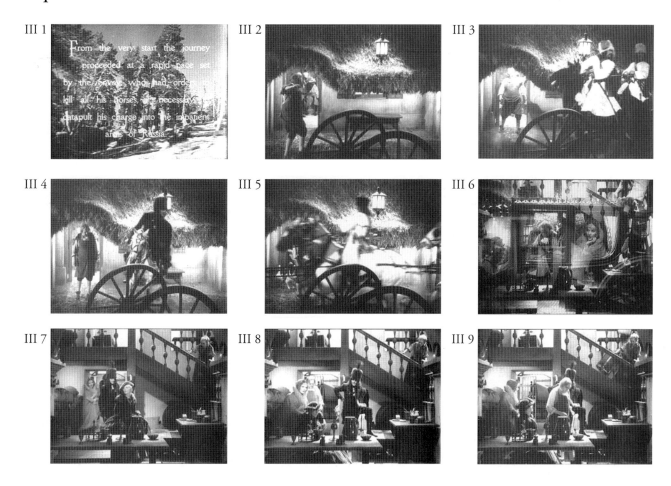

After weeks of hard riding the Russian border was reached, where the populace hid behind closed shutters — — out of the way of the feared Cossacks, who with reckless fury protected their nobles from even a glance of the enslaved people.

Another point of some interest is raised by Sequence III at frame enlargements 20 and 25, in which the replacement of a light area by a dark area in the centre of the image is produced by Count Alexei leaning in front of Sophia Frederica and kissing her. This is one of the rare points where the visual process I have been describing can be reasonably considered to have some degree of expressive function, namely underlining visually the submission of Sophia Frederica to Count Alexei. At a few other places in this film, and also in other films by Sternberg, he makes a characteristic expressive use of shadow over the face or eyes of one of his characters when they might be assumed to be feeling confused or unhappy or uncertain. Just such an instance is illustrated from near the beginning of the film when Sophia Frederica first meets Count Alexei

IV 5

IV 6

(Sequence IV). However, in even these limited number of cases -- several per film -- the information available usually makes it slightly uncertain exactly which of these emotions the character might be feeling, and again there is a further ambiguity of meaning from case to case. After all, unhappiness is not the same as uncertainty. Beyond these few cases, as far as I can see the flow of dark and light in Sternberg's films has no meaning in any real sense of the word, though those hell-bent on producing interpretations at any cost could no doubt invent some. Just as one can see camels in the clouds and continents in cracks on the wall if one wants to.

As if I were a computing machine, I built scene after scene to form an exact pattern ...
                                          Josef von Sternberg

So this statement is the literal truth rather than rhetorical exaggeration as one might at first (or even at second) sight think? Well, not quite, for my analysis has simplified what is actually going on in *The Scarlet Empress* a little. The sharp-eyed will have noted that there are one or two stutters in the rhythm of the pulsation of black and white as I have illustrated it here, and beyond that the period of the pulsation is not quite completely steady at 160 frames or 127 frames, as the case might be. In fact the period of alternation fluctuates around these values, but hardly ever gets far enough away for successive black phases and white phases to escape the grid I have laid upon them. Even this much is in itself quite remarkable and unique.

Then of course there are the short sections of double tempo pulsations in some scenes which I have already mentioned, and finally it must be said that there are a few short scenes, forming a very minor part of its length, in which the process is totally in abeyance, and the centre of the frame remains light in tone throughout. One such is the scene in which the Grand Duchess makes the servants take the places of the court at the dinner table.

But the best way to appreciate this temporo-visual structure in *The Scarlet Empress* and the other Sternberg-Dietrich films is to run them backwards and forwards at high speed on a viewing machine with the central circular area marked on the screen. Or failing that, the next time one of the films is shown on television, draw a circle with a felt-tipped pen on the tube, sit back, and marvel.

A few people have had intimations of the kinetic-visual effect you will see, but they have never grasped it in its completeness. For instance Aeneas Mackenzie in his celebrated article "Leonardo of the Lenses" has it that Sternberg obtains his effects purely by movement within the shot, and that this alone propels the drama, whereas I have shown that cutting from one shot to the next also plays its part at times in the pulsation of light and dark, and also that in the main all this proceeds quite independently of the dramatic developments, and indeed is anti-dramatic in its regular alternation.

... a film is built out of a succession of images, each replacing the last, though their cumulative effect can be as powerful as a single canvas, providing that the shifting values are controlled to produce a homogeneous entity.
                                          Josef von Sternberg

True indeed, and we have just seen the major way that the shifting values produce the homogeneous entity, but some other visual shifts remain to be noted.

Although most of Sternberg's compositions have strong central organization, as is usually the case in mainstream cinema, he does vary this occasionally with a diptych type of static composition. Mostly this vertical central division of the frame is only implied, as in Sequence III, frame 12, which has a light coloured vertical figure filling the left half of the frame, and a dark one filling the right half, but on rare occasions some foreground object in the set produces an actual vertical line dividing the screen into two halves. There are no examples of this in the illustrations here, but the

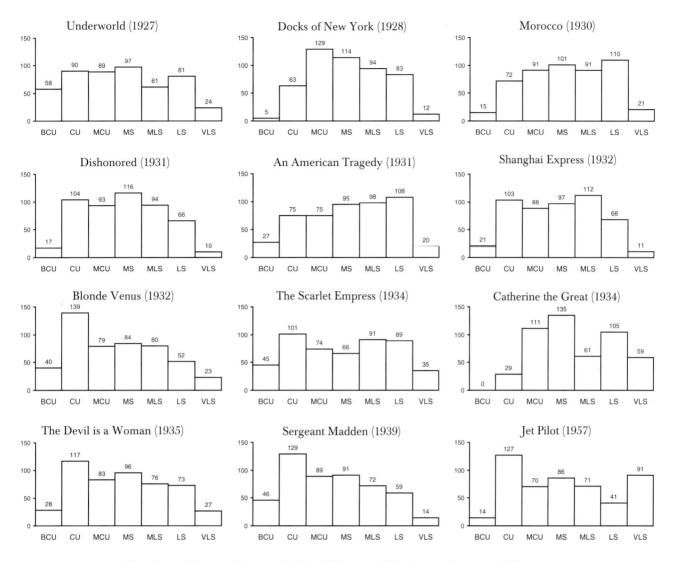

Number of shots with given Scale of Shot per 500 shots in the named films

shadowed statue holding up a crucifix in frame 21 of Sequence I goes halfway to dividing the frame in this way. Incidentally, this distorted Russian Orthodox cross is a recurring element at the centre of the frame in this film, and it increases in height throughout, until at the end it rises to the full height of the frame, while Tsar Peter is strangled behind it. This image is simultaneously another of the continuing series in Sternberg's work that owes something to the drawings of Felicien Rops, as does the earlier one of a man hung by his feet from the clapper of a bell, and the later one of Catherine signalling her assumption of power by pulling on a bell rope. (compare Rops' *Le Vrille*) But this side of Sternberg's films does not concern me at the moment, fascinating though it is. I must return to the abstract patterns of visual organization in The Scarlet Empress and the other films.

Although *The Scarlet Empress* and *The Devil is a Woman*

show this regular pulsation of light and dark in the centre of the frame in its most fully developed form, it is already well established in *Der blaue Engel*, occurring in about half the scenes, while in *Morocco* it is nearly continuous, though with the middle grey of the legionnaires' uniforms sometimes forming a third term in the alternation along with the usual black and white. Before that the process is still struggling to reveal itself, and when one goes back to *Underworld* it only exists inside single shots, and obviously has no rhythmic regularity. At that initial stage Sternberg was experimenting with the looming shadows of moving people passing across brightly lit wall areas, and it is doubtful if he had discovered what could be done with the alternation of light and dark costumes, but *Underworld* certainly contains one instance of the control of light by painting the décor. When Bull Weed escapes from prison his dark figure creeps past a fairly brightly lit wall at the centre of a darkish image, and the brightness of the centre is accentuated by having an irregular splodge of white paint slapped on it. A certain connection with the practices of the German set designers of *Der müde Tod, Der letzte Mann*, etc. springs to mind at this point.

And also like those earlier Murnau films which were so dominated by pre-production design of the shots, Sternberg's films rarely repeat a camera set-up in the chain of shots as edited. In the process of making a considerable change of the image from one shot to the next, he nearly always changed the closeness or scale of shot from one shot to the next, moving continuously back and forth equally over nearly the whole range of possible scale of shot.

Throughout his career, Sternberg made fairly equal use of closenesses or scale of shot from Close-Up (showing head and shoulders) to Medium Close Shot (with the figure from waist to head reaching the height of the frame) through Medium Shot (hips upward) and Medium Long Shot (knees to head reaching the full height of the frame) to Long Shot (showing the full height of the body). Big Close-Ups (which show just the head) and Very Long Shots always played a much smaller part in the scheme of his shots. This would seem to be because it is much more difficult to produce variety in the patterns of light and dark in the image at these two extremes by the methods Sternberg ordinarily used. The degree of constancy Sternberg achieved in respect of his use of the different scales of shot throughout his career is best illustrated with histograms showing the number of shots for each scale of shot or closeness of shot within 500 shots for each of his Paramount Dietrich films. For comparative purposes the like figures are illustrated for Paul Czinner's *Catherine the Great* (1934).

The distinctiveness of the distribution of shots amongst the different possible scales of shots in von Sternberg's films can be seen by comparison with those for other varied films I have given elsewhere. Suffice it to say that Czinner's film on the same subject as *The Scarlet Empress* has considerably greater emphasis on the use of more distant shots, while some other directors of the 'thirties stayed even further back from the action, and then again yet others used a far greater proportion of close shots than Sternberg. One can see from the bar charts that at the beginning of the 'thirties Sternberg himself was very slightly more inclined to use more distant shots than he was in the silent period or from 1933 onwards. This deviation is a result of the technical constraints on the shooting of early sound films; of either having to use cameras in large sound-proofed booths, as in *Der blaue Engel*, or with inadequately soundproofed blimps and inefficient microphones as in *Morocco*. Although the restriction on close shooting was not absolute, both kinds of technical shortcomings produced a mild pressure to keep the camera back from the actors which

you see reflected in these shot distributions. When these difficulties were overcome, von Sternberg was free to return to something very close to his silent period approach in this respect.

Another manifestation of technical pressures on the early sound film can be seen in the differing types of transitions Sternberg used between scenes in his early 'thirties films. This feature is the subject of a statistical analysis by Lawrence Benaquist given in a paper, "A Syntagmatic and Punctuational Analysis of Josef von Sternberg's Films, 1928-1941", delivered at the Purdue Film Conference in 1978. Benaquist found that between *Thunderbolt* and *The Scarlet Empress* the number of scene transitions made with fades decreased from 12 to 1 or 2, while at the same time the number of dissolves rose from 3 to nearly 100.

This is a reflection of the fact that a dissolve between shots taken with synchronous sound mostly requires an accompanying mix (cross-fade) on the sound track to be made after editing, with another consequent stage of sound re-recording. Up until the middle of 1931 this re-recording of the sound onto a new optical sound film audibly increased the level of noise and distortion on the new combined sound track, so this procedure was avoided if possible, and hence the use of dissolves in the picture was avoided too. In Sternberg's films the transition to the free use of dissolves occurs between *Dishonored* and *An American Tragedy*. Once it became easy and convenient to make dissolves at the editing stage, Sternberg occasionally used them to make small adjustments to the rhythm within a shot or to juxtapose two shots that he had not originally planned to use in that way, and an example of this can be seen in the actual film of *The Scarlet Empress* immediately before the title "Across a huge soft carpet of snow ...". His pre-planning of his films was not perfect, merely almost perfect.

... I paid a final tribute to the lady I had seen lean against the wings of a Berlin stage.
Josef von Sternberg

Can the value of such a tribute be counted? In this case, the answer is yes. If we count the shots of Marlene Dietrich in *The Scarlet Empress* in which it can be seen, both in the shot itself, and from the two surrounding shots, that no one is definitely looking at her, and compare this with the number of shots in which it is clear that someone in the film is looking at her, we find that there are 40 of the former and 72 of the latter.

The point of these figures only becomes clear when we compare them with those for an almost contemporary film on the same subject, *Catherine the Great*, which was created by Paul Czinner as a star vehicle for his wife, Elizabeth Bergner, in the same name part. In this film there are 93 shots of the Empress in which it is clear that people are looking at her, and only 17 in which they are not. The significance of this manner of presentation of Dietrich in the Sternberg film is fully established if we look back at the earlier films in the series. In *Morocco* there are 54 shots of Dietrich in which it is apparent that people are looking at her, and 32 in which they are not, while in *Der Blaue Engel* the respective figures are 34 and 16. However, if we look back past the Dietrich films to *Underworld*, in which Evelyn Brent plays the female lead, we find that there is a marked change in the proportions of these two kinds of shots, towards values that seem more characteristic of the conventional treatment of a female star, for there are 52 shots of her when someone is looking at her, and only 14 for which no one is. But if we look at the shots in which the male lead, George Bancroft, is alone in the frame, with people looking at him or not looking at him, as the case may be, we find 62 of the former and 52 of the latter. This high proportion immediately suggests that in this film George Bancroft in some sense takes the Dietrich role, and although specific figures are not at the moment available for the other Sternberg films from before 1930, memory suggests that the presentation of the male lead in isolation is characteristic of them as well. In other words, the presentation of a protagonist in this unusual way, isolated from the gaze of the other characters, was done by von Sternberg without regard for the sex of the character in which he was most interested.

So my conclusion is that the pre-Dietrich films are structurally different from those with Dietrich in the manner of presentation of the female lead, as well as in the kinetic treatment of light and dark, and that there is strong objective evidence for this, although some writers such as Andrew Sarris have suggested the contrary. Sternberg's "filtered feminine mystique" took a back seat in his films before the advent of Marlene Dietrich. (Nevertheless, Andrew Sarris's comments on the general thematics of von Sternberg's work are in a class of their own, in part because they are based on the known facts about von Sternberg and his opinions and ideas of what he was doing, rather than being the usual baseless speculations of interpretation.)

The work of an artist communicates the calibre of his thinking, not the calibre of his emotions, though the latter does not interfere when under control.

Josef von Sternberg

And what are we to say of the artist who organized the details I have described, not to mention the hundreds of more obvious ones in each of his films? Might not some special descriptive category be useful to contain him? Could we call it "genius", or is that word too offensive to the untalented?

The field of art is vast ... and no scale, calibration, or test-tube can aid in its analysis.

Josef von Sternberg

Even a genius can be wrong sometimes.

A genius is also likely to be misunderstood by his lesser associates. I am sure that pieces of direction like the staging of the scene in I-2 here must have irritated the production crew. Although this is not visible in the frame illustrated, along the lower edge of the mass of horses galloping through the frame, every third horse is a white horse between the other dark horses. The rehearsal necessary to get this apparently pointless feature right must have been staggering. In the scene in *Morocco* in which the Adjutant interrogates Gary Cooper about his actions the previous night, you will notice that some of the characters are made to squeeze themselves between his back and the wall to make their entrances and exits in an unnatural way, when there is tons of space in front of his desk available for passage. This is, of course, to create alternations of tonality in the centre of the frame as someone in a dark costume is obscured by someone in a light costume, or vice-versa. I am amused by the instant in a scene in Sternberg's *Sergeant Madden* when a child actor flinches as he realises he has started off in the wrong direction for exiting the scene, before going in the unnatural direction Sternberg had demanded, round the back of his father's table.

I had first noticed the process I describe in this article when screening *The Scarlet Empress* at the Slade, and discovered its regularity when running the film at high speed on a Steenbeck, and then picked it up the process in *Morocco* in the same way. There are lots of things which show up when running a film at high speed, and this is merely the most important of them.

The strange way in which no-one is shown looking at

Le pendu, *an engraving by Felicien Rops*

Dietrich in adjoining shots is not quite unique. Exactly the same sort of thing happens in Eisenstein's *Ivan Grozny*, where Tsar Ivan is presented with no-one looking at him in adjoining shots in the scene. Indeed, in that film it is even more marked. This may be more because in most of Eisenstein's films the scene dissection in general does not give the impression of a unified space, as ordinary films do. It is also quite likely that Eisenstein saw *The Scarlet Empress*.

Sternberg himself mentioned the drawings of Felicien Rops in connection with *Der blaue Engel*, but, as I indicated, they also played a part in the iconography of *The Scarlet Empress*. I was not able to show what I was talking about when my piece was first published, but here one of them is now.

Subsequently, I came across reproductions of the furniture that Catherine the Great's lover Count Gregory Orlov had in the sex room in one of his palaces. These illustrations have obviously been rephotographed many times, from one book to another, and hence their poor quality. Sternberg was interested in this sort of thing, as you can read in his autobiography, and I suspect that these photographs may have been reproduced in one of the scabrous fake memoirs of Catherine the Great which inspired the screenplay of his film. Hence Peter Ballbusch's weird chairs sculpted in the form of human figures in Catherine the Great's council chamber.

FANTASIES OF FLYING

Through the clouds with Hughes, Hawks, and Sternberg;
from *Hell's Angels* to *Jet Pilot*.

A Fantasist

Having a close involvement with aviation is no guarantee that the films a person makes about it will have much to do with reality. Take Howard Hughes, for instance. Those who have seen *Hell's Angels* (1930) don't need to be told that it includes surprisingly little flying footage, or indeed that what flying there is in it is silly in a very juvenile way. It only contains two sequences of air action, and the second of these doesn't go much beyond standard flying film foolishness in the way a giant bomber manages to fight off simultaneous attack by a dozen fighter planes. But the central sequence showing a Zeppelin attack on London exceeds even the wildest imaginings of *The Boy's Own Paper*, with the villainous Hun commander ordering all his crew to jump to their death to lighten the airship and speed his escape. The school-boy obsession with giganticism — giant bomber, giant airship — that is common to both episodes

reappears later in Howard Hughes' career with the giant unflyable flying-boat that he built during World War II, and only finally reaches realistic scale with the Convair B-36 sequence stuck into *Jet Pilot* for no good reason other than to show the biggest plane available at that date.

The other major element contributing to the success of *Hell's Angels* was the display of overt sexuality, that Jean Harlow was encouraged to give in it. Her part in the story presents other adolescent male daydreams, that of easily available sex. In later years Hughes looked at the same goal from a slightly different angle in *The Outlaw* (1944), and some touches of similar coarseness near the beginning of his production *Jet Pilot* were no doubt imposed on its director, Josef von Sternberg, from above. Nevertheless, in *Jet Pilot* Sternberg's handling of Janet Leigh's muscular outdoor-girl presence is something of a relief from what had gone before, so that taking

Sternberg gets Janet Leigh into an elegant and beguiling knot in Jet Pilot.

into account the realism of the flying it includes, it could be considered to represent some kind of psychological development. One might say that Hughes matured all the way from early to late adolescence. But what are we to say about Hughes' occasional associate Howard Hawks?

Another Fantasist

As is well known, the resemblances between these two men goes well beyond the similarity of their names. Although not a pampered only child like Hughes, Howard Hawks was also born into a wealthy family who seem to have treated him with some indulgence, buying him racing cars and flying instruction before he had finished his proper education. Although he and his fans have contrived to give the impression that he fought in the First World War, in fact his service was in the useful but unglamorous occupation of flying instructor at a United States base. Although the American Army records for his service were destroyed, I strongly suspect that he was only a technical instructor on the ground, not a real flying instructor. Indeed, if one looks at Hawks' various interview statements with a critical eye, a picture emerges of his essentially dilletantish involvement with flying and motor-racing, and one deduces that he was a young man wanting to be part of the group of men who *had* to fly, fight, and drive dangerously to go on living, because they didn't have much alternative. Hawks could always sleep between clean sheets at night. His experience of being a real insider in a professional group was in fact limited to his lifelong career in Hollywood, a somewhat different world. With this in mind it becomes easier to understand the almost total lack of authenticity in the

air warfare in Hawk's *The Dawn Patrol* (1930) — the general situation of German air superiority belonged to 1915, not 1918 as depicted in the film, the planes are bogus, etc. — and equally in *Air Force* (1943), another comic-strip version of war in the air. This is just one part of the way that in Hawks' films as a whole, there is no interest whatever in the manner in which real things are really done. If one wants that (within the limits that were possible in Hollywood) one has to turn elsewhere, for instance to William Wellman's films as far as war and flying are concerned. Even Clarence Brown's *To Please a Lady* (1950) shows more interest in the practicalities of motor racing than any of Howard Hawks' films on the subject. Likewise when it comes to what Action Men do between bouts of action, the standard Wellman scene of a line of silent tough guys just standing there looking tough, and the locker-room rowdiness in some of Walsh's films such as *Manpower*, were both nearer reality than anything by Howard Hawks, though not necessarily more attractive to the various kinds of film audience. It may well be said that some of the points I have been making about the films of Howard Hawks have been noticed before, for instance by David Thomson with respect to *Red River*, but I am hunting bigger game. I am really concerned with certain conclusions that follow from these observations, but which have not so far been confronted by other writers.

A Touch of Seriousness

Many critics still apparently consider that a suitable general criterion for judging the worth of films (and indeed of literature) is the extent to which they can be considered to represent emotional and psychological maturity, and also be morally improving for their audience. It has been claimed by Robin Wood that by taking all of the films of Howard Hawks together, including the comedies, as well as the dramas I have been talking about, that they can then be considered to satisfy this criterion. Apart from the questionable legitimacy of this tactic, I would suggest that another dispassionate look at *Bringing Up Baby, Ball of Fire,* and *Monkey Business,* all of which include the destruction and/or ridiculing of a scientist's work, will show that they hardly support the required conclusion. The films of Howard Hawks directly show themselves to be the films of someone who has fled the ordinary workaday world, the world that provides the comforts of living for film critics.

So the alternatives are either that the films of Howard Hawks are valuable for other reasons, and the promotion of maturity and moral improvement is not an adequate general aesthetic criterion, or that the films of Hawks are not very valuable. If you are prepared to face this dilemma and adopt the second alternative I will note that similar points can also be made about the films of many directors who figure in most critical pantheons of the last few decades. For instance, both the films and life of Max Ophuls follow the sexual "double standard", and so I could go on. Another favourite critical criterion, that good films must be "a coherent comment on the human condition" is vulnerable to the same sort of observations, so my suggestion is that these ideas should be dropped as general criteria for aesthetic evaluation, and only applied to those films whose directors can be reasonably assumed to have wanted them applied. Satyajit Ray, for instance. Howard Hawks only claimed that his films were meant to be entertaining, which indeed they are, and more importantly they use original approaches to that goal. And Josef von Sternberg was one director who explicitly rejected the application of moral criteria in judging his films, as you can read in his memoirs.

The Flying

The large number of fighter planes briefly used in *Hell's Angels* are all fairly authentic for 1918, assuming that is the supposed date of the action, but the giant bomber already mentioned (giant in World War I terms, that is) dates from some years after the end of the war. Hughes' fighters are in fact more authentic than the machines used in Howard Hawks *The Dawn Patrol* a year later, and as well as that, most of the close shots of their pilots were taken in mid-air even while they were doing loops and other stunts, whereas the close shots in *The Dawn Patrol* were taken in front of a background projection screen, with the result that while the view below goes through the appropriate evolutions, the shadows cast by the plane's structure on itself do not move. When *The Dawn Patrol* was remade in 1938 the

Very Long Shots of aerial action from the earlier version were reused, but new planes of improved authenticity were acquired for the closer shots and ground scenes. These latter planes have engine cowlings that are now much more like those of 1918 Sopwiths for instance, though still not being exactly like any real model. I mention this just for the record, for after all, "It's only a movie, Ingrid". But a more important point about *Hell's Angels* is that the directorial credit for the film should, by the usual rules, be given to James Whale, who directed the dialogue scenes shot as synch. which make up exactly three-quarters of the length of the film. Howard Hughes' credit should just be as a very "creative" producer.

Moving forward to *Jet Pilot,* consideration of the planes involved leads to some interesting conclusions as to when various parts of it were shot, and hence which parts were made with Josef von Sternberg present as director. Starting at the beginning, Janet Leigh as a Russian pilot defects to the United States in what is first identified as a "Yak-12", but later described as ". . . like our T-33.". The plane in question is indeed so like a Lockheed T-33 jet trainer that it *is* one, while in fact the real Yak-12 was an old piston-engined plane that looked quite different. John Wayne is, at this stage in the film, ostensibly flying a North American F-86 Sabre belonging to the 94th. Squadron of the U.S. Air Force. These planes had been in service for about a year when shooting on *Jet Pilot* started in early 1950, and a good deal of the aerial footage in the film involves these planes alone, with Janet Leigh later being shown flying one up there in aerial flirtation with John Wayne. These sequences, like all the aerial scenes, are very elegantly shot, but it is difficult to show this with black and white stills.

The next stage in the air-borne romance of Leigh and Wayne takes place when they fly together in a radar-guided night interceptor. As the film exists now they fly in a Lockheed F-94A Starfire to an aerial rendezvous with a Convair B-36B, but it seems highly probable

The North American F-82 Twin Mustang

that as the film was originally shot they were ostensibly flying in a North American F-82 Twin Mustang. In early 1950 the F-82 was the only radar-guided night fighter in regular service with the U.S.A.F., but it was replaced by the Starfire from June of that year onwards. The amount of footage that would have had to be replaced by this change was minimal, and it was done in part by combining a model shot (the only one in this film) of a Starfire with some of the original B-36 footage projected onto a background screen. Apart from that, all that would have been necessary was the re-shooting of a few cockpit Close Ups, and this might have been done by Sternberg, since he was still working on *Macao* at R.K.O. till the end of 1950. It can be deduced that this new material was not shot in 1951 or later, since by that date the 94B variant was superseding the 94A Starfire, and in any case the other participant in the scene, the B-36B was already being replaced by its B-36D variant with 4 extra jet engines by the end of 1950. And what red-blooded American boy would be able to resist putting that in his movie?

A PLANE WITH TEN ENGINES! WOW!

In a way it is a pity that the twin Mustang footage was replaced, since that aircraft's construction out of two plane bodies fused together would have represented an amusing intermediate stage in the simultaneous earthly and heavenly union of John Wayne and Janet Leigh. But we still have the next scene after their return to earth, undoubtedly shot by Sternberg, in which coloured airfield lights cast an alternate warm and cold glow on Janet Leigh's face to accompany the ebb and flow of the couple's conversational sparring. Admittedly this use of colour is just slightly to the conventional side, as is a subtle touch of green light sneaked onto Leigh when Wayne discovers that she has continued to secretly spy for the Russians, but it shows that von Sternberg was still alert for anything that could be done with the material available to him.

After a couple more twists in the plot, the pair of them are in Russia, and the prospect of John Wayne's mind being reduced to mush by Commie drugs leads Janet Leigh to turn again and escape with him. At this point in the film we come to the only substantial sequence which may have been helmed by someone other than Josef von Sternberg. This escape sequence involves a number of planes, all purporting to be Russian types, but all of course played by well-known American models. The situation in the film is that John Wayne is supposed to be demonstrating to the Russians how the U.S.A.F. manages to hook a parasite fighter carried by a large bomber back underneath it in mid-air. It may have been the original intention to use U.S.A.F. film of the single unsuccessful attempt in 1948 to hook the McDonnell XF-85 Goblin back under a B-29, as is suggested by some dialogue still in the film about the difficulties of this procedure. But what we actually see is the Bell X-1 experimental rocket plane, ostensibly flown by John Wayne, being dropped from beneath a B-29, while Janet Leigh in a T-33, and also an escort F-86

A model of a Lockheed F-94-A Starfire makes rendezvous with a Convair B-36B on a background projection screen.

The McDonnell XF-85 experimental satellite fighter with hook for dropping from a B-29.

The Bell X-1 experimental rocket plane dropping from a B-29

Janet Leigh shapes up to a Northrop P-89 Scorpion

Sabre(!), both painted in Russian colours, fly alongside. Clearly this film is now nuttier than Screwy Squirrel, but that shouldn't spoil the pleasure of any reasonable sophisticated person. And actually the presence of the B-29 at least was realistic, since the Russians had made large numbers of (nearly) perfect B-29 replicas after the war, and called them the Tupolev Tu-4. (No, they didn't make any exact copies of any other American planes.) Now that the Bell X-1 had been dropped, it was in fact impossible for it to hook on beneath the B-29 again, and it doesn't try, but after a little bit of air action it glides down to a certain dry lake bed, as was its habit. (Yes, boys, it's the famous Muroc air research base, made up as Siberia with a ton of synthetic snow.)

All this could easily have been staged specially for the film in 1950, since by that date the Bell X-1 had been superseded by the X-1A in the American experimental rocket plane programme, but this material was certainly not part of the original shooting, since the T-33 used is painted differently to that appearing in the early scenes

A T-33 (left) and a F-86 (right) painted in Russian colours accompany the Bell X-1 rocket plane (below).

in the film. This means that it may have been shot later in 1950 under Sternberg's direction, or perhaps in 1951 without his participation. A relevant point is that on the pretended Russian airfield at the beginning of this sequence there is a Northrop P-89 Scorpion, playing the part of yet another imaginary Russian plane, and also playing a role in the plot which I will not reveal for fear of spoiling your enjoyment if you have not seen *Jet Pilot* already. The F-89 Scorpion did not enter regular service till July 1951, but there were a number of prototypes around for years before that, which the owner of the Hughes Aircraft Company (supplier of weapon systems to the U.S. Government) would surely have been able to borrow for a day or two. The Scorpion in the film is certainly an early but non-standard model. This scene is unlikely to have been shot in 1953 or later, as by that time the F-89C and later variants had become operational, and these visibly differed in certain small ways from the one actually used.

Taking everything I have noted about *Jet Pilot* into account, it seems impossible that it contains any material added to it in 1953 or later, as has often been claimed, and more than that, the film now exists pretty much as Josef von Sternberg made it, with just some small doubt hanging over the details of the final escape from Russia. The impression that the contrary was the case no doubt stems, as so often, from believing studio publicity releases, which are never to be trusted.

The Mechanics of a Fantasy

When he directed *Jet Pilot,* Josef von Sternberg did not have the total control over the conception and execution of the film that he had enjoyed while creating his masterworks of the nineteen-thirties. Nevertheless he managed to decorate it with some of the visual devices he used in those former days, and even sneaked in one or two new ideas as well. The "Sternberg process" — the regular alternation of light and dark tones in the central area of the frame as a scene progresses — is still present in some scenes; achieved as it was before by moving actors around within the frame, having taken care that some are covered in light costumes, and some in dark. This process is in operation throughout the scene at the beginning of the film in which Janet Leigh is interrogated by John Wayne and another Air Force officer, as is shown in the accompanying sequence of frame enlargements In the section illustrated most of the changes from light to dark in the central area of the frame are done by cutting, but frames 4 and 5 are part of one panning shot which starts with Wayne in his dark uniform centered, then has him walk behind Janet Leigh's white figure (frame 4), and finally centered again in frame 5. The big black stove visible in this picture is not there just to heat an Alaskan office, but really so someone dressed in white can walk behind it and in front of it to generate the same kind of effect later in the scene. Sternberg's characteristic way of throwing a shadow over the eyes of someone worried or uncertain can also be seen at work in frames 8 and 10, and later in the scene shadows play a minor part in the "Sternberg process", as they always had. (Contrary to popular impression, actual shadows always played a small part in Sternberg's armoury of effects. The light and dark areas he habitually worked with were mostly built into the costumes and decor, and the lighting in his films was often fairly uniform over the whole frame, as in this scene. If the reader is inclined, on the basis of the limited evidence presented here, to think that this process is not real but the product of a delirium of interpretation, close attention should be

directed to *The Scarlet Empress,* where the pulsation of light and dark in the centre of the franc occurs throughout nearly the whole length of the film, and with quite remarkable regularity.)

In a later scene in *Jet Pilot* showing a visit by Janet Leigh and John Wayne to a dress shop, Sternberg extended this process to the carefully controlled moving of coloured areas round within the frame, but you will have to see the film yourself to appreciate the subtleties of this. However there are other sorts of visual wit in this scene that I can hint at with more frame enlargements.

AND THERE'S MORE I TELL YOU, MORE!

Jet Pilot cannot equal the layers of incredible organization in both static and dynamic staging and visuals that Josef von Sternberg achieved in his Dietrich vehicles, but with two talents like Sternberg and Jules Furthman on the job, the result had to be very diverting even after tribute had been paid to Howard Hughes' obsessions.

The previous piece dates from 1981, and after I had finished it, I offered it to Penelope Houston at *Sight & Sound* as usual. She rejected it as having to much esoteric aviation detail in it for the magazine. She was probably right, but I think it is still worth your attention. The frame enlargements in it were made from a 16 mm. print of the film, showing Sternberg's original compositions for the Academy aperture frame. The wide-screen version of this film loses a fair amount of the elegance of the compositions, and also weakens some of the visual jokes, unfortunately. I have set it in 11 point Adobe Garamond instead of the 10 point face usually used for the new material in this book, so that the content of the text aligns better with the illustrations to which it refers. This is one possible solution to a perennial problem

My part-time job teaching film-making at the Slade was now terminated, but again fortune smiled on me. Two of the art students whom I had taught film-making at the Slade had decided to switch from making avant-garde movies to conventional film-making, and had got into the Royal College of Art film school. They recommended me to the head of the school, who took me on, again part-time, as a tutor there. At the same time, I was invited to come back to the London School of Film Technique to teach film history. After graduating from their course in 1968, I had sworn to myself that I would never enter its doors again, because I had so disliked being there, and I had lived up to that vow. Actually, the school as it was had gone bankrupt in 1974, and had been reformed as a limited company registered as a charity, and was now effectively owned by its students and staff. It was now called the London International Film School, though the course was still pretty much the same. Fortunately the building had been cleaned up and improved a little, and the film equipment was a few less years out of date. John Fletcher, the head of the school in 1982, had tried to get Kevin Brownlow to teach the film history course, but he did not want to do it, and suggested me. I needed the money, so now to keep my self-respect I had to do better than Roger Manvell had done in the old days.

Most of the text of what was to become the first edition of *Film Style and Technology: History and Analysis* was now complete. The presentation of the central material in it had taken a certain amount of thought, because of the multiple inter-relations and inter-connections between the material it contained. The division of the time span into sections followed approximately from the major developments in film style during the silent period, but for the sound period I just gave up and covered the period in decades. With a history covering multiple themes, and in which there are few instantaneous developments, it is impossible to make a single clear cut and obvious periodization of the subject, and only a fool and ignoramus would think otherwise. Inside the chapters I followed an obvious order of the material, starting with film stock and what is done to it, and working my way through cameras and their movements, and so on to editing. It was obvious enough, I thought, though not easy to carry out. During the process of writing it, I sometimes felt the need for

some multi-dimensional presentation of the material, in fact for what came to be known as hyper-text. Strictly speaking the idea of hyper-text had already been put forward in 1965 by Ted Nelson, but it was not practically realised till the middle of the 'eighties. Nowadays the hypertext idea is even more extensively realised in the use of hyper-links on the World Wide Web.

I sent the finished work out to publishers of serious books on cinema, naturally starting with the University of California Press, since they were the publishers of *Film Quarterly*, in which preliminary versions of some of the material had appeared. Their anonymous readers wrote reports saying that although most of it was just fine, it should not be published while it included the opening chapters criticizing recent film theory. Actually the real problem was my irrefutable criticism of psychoanalysis, as a theory whose practical application for curing neuroses did not work. Hence it must be of no value for producing interpretations of movies. Ernest Callenbach, who was the editor of film books for the University of California Press as well as being the editor of *Film Quarterly*, pointed out to me that psychoanalysis was an subject of blind faith, not just for American film academics, but the whole of the American middle class. I had no intention of removing those critical chapters, since they were an attack on a series of major intellectual frauds. Trying other publishers in England as well as in the United States produced a pile of reports from their readers an inch thick saying the same thing. I was not going to be silenced by the academic Thought Police, so I set out to publish it myself.

In 1982 the day of the microcomputer had arrived. So after quickly researching the field, I bought myself a Sirius 1 computer, a daisy-wheel printer, and a copy of the Wordstar word processing programme. This last suggested a name for the imprint under which the book would be published, namely "Starword". The Sirius was a competitor to the original IBM personal computer, and it was available in Britain before the IBM PC. It was in fact a superior machine, but like all the other competing microcomputers of that time, it was incompatible with the IBM PC, and they were all incompatible with each other. As we know, the IBM PC came out on top, but that was because IBM did not patent its basic architecture, and others eventually realized they could copy it. Anyway, I typed away like mad and got the text of my book into the computer. The thing now was to get it out again in typeset form. This was long before the invention of desk-top publishing programmes, and so far there was only one man in England who was enough ahead of the game to typeset from all the various incompatible brands of microcomputers that existed. Tom Graves did it by having rows of microcomputers of the various makes all linked in to a standard phototypesetter. I chose the typeface from those few he had available, settling on Melior. Because Hermann Zapf, the great type designer, had based the forms of Melior on Piet Hein's super-ellipse, it had a squareness about it led the eye along its parallel tracks, which was good for the large line length I had chosen. However, the italic face of the

Melior font was little more than the ordinary face slanted, so it was not suited to making the titles of the many films I mentioned stand out well from the text. Fortunately Tom Graves had Palatino, another Zapf typeface, and by trying the italic of this with the regular face of Melior, I could see that they looked good together. This somewhat unusual approach was endorsed by Tom Graves when he saw the result. Although Palatino has been used a lot for American books, I find that whole pages of it set as body text look a bit like a thorn hedge, because of the heaviness and prominence of its serifs.

The possibilities of formatting the text were limited, so I had to get it output from the photo-typesetter as one long strip of bromide paper per chapter. I then had to cut this into page lengths, and do a paste-up page by page in the old-fashioned way, with the page headings stuck in separately. Although I had written a programme to display the graphs on my computer screen, there was no way to get them off the screen onto paper, so I had to draw all the graphs for the distributions by hand. It didn't take me as long as you might think. I reduced all the graphics to the correct size with the process camera in the graphic design department of the Royal College of Art. When the position of the illustrations had been marked in and the percentage reduction from my frame enlargement prints worked out to fit them into the right sized space, it was ready for the printers. I have always been annoyed by illustrated books that have been printed on thin paper to save money, which means that the illustrations show through behind the text on the other side of the leaf. So I had it printed on very heavy 130 gm/sq. cm. paper, which was rather excessive, and contributed to the slightly old-fashioned look of the book. Flashy modern book design depends on using lots of white space on the page, but this means the text and pictures need more pages to encompass the content, and

hence greater cost for me and the purchaser.

I handled the distribution myself, of course. The first edition eventually sold in thousands, which was quite good for this sort of book, I gather. It possibly could have sold more if I had been able to get an American distributor, but the academic advisors to American publishers that handle serious film books vetoed even its distribution by them.

The printers got it finished in time for me to pick up the first copies on my way to another film studies conference dedicated to various aspects of the silent cinema, and in particular the films of Ernst Lubitsch, this time held at the University of East Anglia at the end of 1983. This conference was organized by Charles Barr and Thomas Elsaesser, and had some international contribution. I gave two presentations: one on statistical comparisons of the style of films from different countries, and the other on the roots of many of Ernst Lubitsch's films in French and German operettas. I had also just discovered how much Lubitsch's films owed to the set designs Ernst Stern had done for Max Reinhardt, but I didn't speak about that. I also sold some copies of my book to the participants, including David Bordwell.

Now the interest in re-evaluating early cinema began to widen out to Europe, and I was asked for a piece for a new magazine called *Iris*, published in France, but with most contributions in English. This struck me at the time as a French effort to get access to the well-endowed American academic world. Nevertheless, I took the opportunity to make my objection to the notion that there was a "discontinuous style" existing in the early years of cinema at slightly greater length than I had before, and with some extra examples in proof of it. Although the idea of a consciously created "discontinuous style" existing in early cinema is still being promoted, I am not aware of anyone trying to rebut my criticisms of the notion.

WHAT WE CAN LEARN FROM THE FIRST TWENTY YEARS OF CINEMA

The period covered by the first twenty years of the cinema provides an excellent laboratory for the testing of general ideas about films, as well as having its own intrinsic and peculiar interests. Because the majority of films made in this period are one reel or less in length, it is fairly easy to see a large number of them in a short space of time if one wants to, and also to remember and compare their distinctive features, and in fact the comments I shall make in this article are based on the viewing of about 2000 films of dates spread fairly evenly over the years 1895 to 1915. My comments all relate in a connected way to some of the main features of the standard forms of films which have remained constant from the end of the period in question down to the present day.

One particular feature of a small number of films made before 1906 which has been commented on recently by several observers (Tom Gunning, Charles Musser, and André Gaudreault in *Cinema 1900-1906* FIAF, 1982) is that they contain repetitions of the same action in successive shots. The best known example of this is Edwin S. Porter's *The Life of an American Fireman* (1903), in which several people in succession are shown leaving a room through a window in a shot taken from inside the room, and then in the next shot they are again shown coming through the window in succession in a camera angle from outside the window. A few other similar examples exist from this year and the next couple of years such as *Next!* (Biograph, 1903), and *The Firebug* (Biograph, 1905), but these coexist with other films, some even from the same studios, where the passage of several people through a doorway or window from one shot to the next is handled with fairly accurate action continuity in the manner we nowadays expect. One example is *A Search for Evidence*, made at Biograph several months later in 1903 than *Next!*, and others can be found amongst European films of these years.

If one thinks twice about this phenomenon, its occurrence is not particularly surprising, since the artistic media which pre-existed the cinema gave no guidance as to how to handle the situation of action moving from one delimited space to a contiguous but also delimited one. For instance, the most striking feature of narrative lantern-slide sequences was their narrative *discontinuity*. Most of them are only fully comprehensible with the verbal narration in prose or verse supplied with them, and in the most famous of them, *Bob, the Fireman*, it is quite obvious that a different man is named by the text as "Bob" in each slide, and also that the allegedly continuous events take place at different times of the day and night. In fact it is more surprising that most film-makers only took a couple of years to adopt what is the logical solution to continuity in the case of several people going through a doorway in succession. I would say that at that point in time there was no possibility of repeated action across cuts being adopted by film-makers as an *intentional* artistic strategy, and its occurrence was on the contrary the result of an absence of thought.

It is clear that at the same time other film-makers were consciously creating static position matches on cuts to a closer shot *within* scenes, as the actors in *Mary Jane's*

The frame before the first cut in to a Close Shot in Mary Jane's Mishap (1903). *The actresss holds this position for 11 frames in an attempt to match with the following shot.*

Mary Jane's Mishap *The following frame with the cut in to a closer shot.*

Mishap (G.A. Smith, 1903) and *Ursus et son taureau lutteur* (Pathé, 1904) can be seen moving into the matching position within a couple of frames after the cuts in question. Most (though not all) film-makers were smart enough to make the generalization from this situation, in which the logic of continuity is even more apparent, over the next couple of years.

If we are really interested in finding a meaning in this phenomenon, then from a film-historical point of view, which is the only way to deal satisfactorily with this subject, then the opinions of audiences, critics, and film-makers of the period could be considered to have various degrees of relevance to the matter. The ideal would be that we had documentary evidence as to exactly what film-makers thought they were doing with respect to this problem at the time, and indeed this evidence should be sought for if one thinks that this is an important issue. I have to admit that I myself have not done this, but I want to warn against the easy assumption that what is written in the trade journals of the period provides a good guide to the thinking of the actual film-makers. To make this clear I will consider a stylistic matter from a few years later, to do with the closeness of the camera to the actors.

In an article in the American trade journal, *The Moving Picture World* of 25 March, 1911 (Vol. 8, No. 12), an anonymous staff writer advocated the avoidance in films of close shots showing less than the whole bodies of the actors, and this was reiterated in the same magazine a year later. If one considered these articles alone, one might draw the conclusion that this use of a close camera was a recent development, whereas in fact in the films made by the Vitagraph company, the largest American producer, the use

of the "nine foot line" as a standard limit to actor closeness to the camera had begun in 1909, and by 1910 a sizeable proportion of the framings in Vitagraph films cut the actors off at the thighs. Many of the other American film-makers, including D.W. Griffith at Biograph, had begun to respond to this trend by 1910, so that by 1912 this feature was solidly established in American films. Likewise with the general case of smooth continuity of action from scene to scene, which an article in *The New York Dramatic Mirror* (13 March 1909, p.16) claims to have been achieved for the first time in an American film in D.W. Griffith's *A Fool's Revenge*, whereas in fact in this respect this and other Griffith films of 1909 are no improvement on such earlier Vitagraph films as *The Mill Girl* (1907).

My final point which has to do with accepting a journal reference as an accurate guide to filmic practices relates to the employment of commentators or lecturers to describe and explain films to the audience as they were being shown. On the basis of a couple 1908 references to the desirability of having a commentator at a film show it has been suggested that this was still the usual practice in the United States at that date. But when we consider that 1907 articles in *The Moving Picture World* (Vol. 1, No. 9, May 4) and *The Saturday Evening Post* (Vol. 180, No. 21, November 23) both omit the commentator from a list of staff required to run a Nickelodeon, but do include a piano as being necessary, then taking this together with the fact that all films made after 1906 are comprehensible on their own, whereas some made before 1906 are not, then the obvious conclusion is that the commentator was at least well on the way to disappearing by 1908, and the expressed desire of a couple of writers for his continuance was a futile

The Vitagraph company "nine foot line" framing in The Spirit of Christmas (William Humphrey & Tefft Johnson (1913)

rearguard action which was of no interest to the film-makers and exhibitors, just as in the case of the "cutting off the feet" mentioned above.

The most significant lesson to be learnt about the importance of considering the facts when one is formulating theories about the cinema can also be illustrated from the films of the first twenty years. If we consider the use of the dissolve between shots in the surviving films from this period, we find that at first it was merely a way of joining *all* the shots in a film together, regardless of their temporal relation to each other. This can be observed in the films of Georges Méliès, who was presumably the inventor of the device, from *Cendrillon* (1899) onwards. It is quite clear that in the case of Méliès' films the dissolve did not indicate a time lapse, since in some cases it occurs between shots even though there is absolute action continuity across it. Examples can be quoted in *Barbe-Bleue* (1901), in which there is a dissolve as his last wife goes through a door seen from one side, to the next shot as she appears through the door in the other room, and similarly in *Le voyage dans la Lune* (1902), just to start at the beginning. Exactly the same observations can be made about the use of the dissolve in some Pathé films such as *Histoire d'un Crime* (1901), and in most of the films made up to 1903 by Edwin S. Porter for the Edison company. From 1903 onwards all film-makers except Méliès dropped the use of the dissolve as a general method of joining all the shots in a film together, and took up the use of the cut for this purpose, in the same way as it was already being used by G.A. Smith and other British film-makers from 1900 onwards.

However, simultaneously with all this, there was also a group of films in which the dissolve was exclusively used as a means of indicating the transition from real events happening to a character in a film to events that he dreamed, or vice-versa. The film that initiated this usage was probably *Rêve et réalité*, made at Pathé in 1901, and other early examples include *Hooligan's Christmas Dream* (Biograph, 1903). From 1903 to about 1911 this was the *only* thing the dissolve was used for (except in the films of Georges Méliès), and then with the development of the true flashback (as we now understand the term), the use of the dissolve was generalized to cover that kind of transition as well. In fact from 1913 onwards the dissolve was principally used to indicate a transition into and out of a flashback shot or sequence, though its use as a transition into and out of a dream also continued. With the full development of "continuity cinema" in America from 1914 onwards, yet another use for the dissolve appeared. This was in the transition, with intended strict continuity, from a distant shot to a closer shot of an actor in a scene, when it was suspected that there had arisen a mismatch in the actor's position when he repeated the action he had been engaged in at the end of the distant shot after the camera had been moved to take the continuing closer shot. Because American film-makers (except D.W. Griffith and a few others who

The flash-back scenes in The On-the-Square Girl (Frederick J. Ireland, 1917) *done as scenes inset with an Insert Shot of the letter which recalled them.*

were quickly out of work) rapidly came to understand the technique of action matching across cuts within a scene, there are not a great many examples of this in American films of the years 1914 to 1920, but enough exist to prove the point. It is rather easier to find examples in the work of European film-makers well into the 'twenties, and even in the United States one can still find occasional examples of the use of the dissolve in this way in the sound period (e.g. near the beginning of *The Private Lives of Elizabeth and Essex* (1939)).

From this brief survey, which is however based on the viewing of the larger part of the surviving fictional films of those years (and more on this and other related matters can be read in *Film Style and Technology: History and Analysis* (Starword, 1983)), it should be clear that in the short period between 1900 and 1915, not only was the dissolve being used with different significances at any point in time, but also those significances were changing quite quickly. This applied not only to the case of the dissolve, but also to other filmic devices. For instance, although fades came to be mostly used to indicate a time lapse after 1910, there are a number of cases where the transition to a flashback is done with a fade (e.g. *The Two Columbines* (Harold Shaw, 1914) and *The Vengeance of Durand* (Vitagraph, 1913)). And the fade could be, and was, used both to indicate the passage into and out of a flashback and also to indicate a time lapse within the length of a one-reel film, as in *The Quality of Mercy* (Vitagraph, 1915). Yet despite the evident fact that individual formal devices had no fixed meaning in themselves, and also that a particular narrative function could be served by more than one formal device, there is no reason to suppose that audiences in those days could not follow the films using them. Certainly there are no complaints on this score to be found in any of the records. Not only that, but one can point to unique formal devices that apparently only occurred once, but which can be readily understood by audiences now, and presumably could be understood by audiences then. One such is the introduction of a flashback in *The On-The-Square Girl* (1917) by representing the events in the past as a series of scenes inset into the middle of an insert shot of a letter one of the characters involved is reading.

These examples, together with many others from later periods of film history, show the impossibility of treating the specific features of cinema as constituting a language system in any useful sense, and they constitute one of the reasons, though not the only one, for the now obvious failure of attempts such as that of Christian Metz to create a theory of film semiotics. If one has been content to know no more than a handful of famous films from the first twenty years, then one could not realize the inadequacy of simple general theories about the movies. The moral to be learnt is that trying to theorize without solid empirical knowledge of the subject in question is doomed to failure. After all, it is only in physics, the only one of the established sciences that has hundreds of years of history behind it, that separate groups of theoreticians and experimentalists have quite recently come to exist, and even so they continually depend on each others work. On the other hand, in biology, despite its remarkable achievements in this century, there is still no real separation into experimental and theoretical branches. I see no reason why the new and undeveloped discipline (if it is one) of film studies should be an exception to this law.

Book designers mostly avoid using Times Roman, but *Iris* was printed in it, so I have reproduced that here with Times New Roman.

A conference on early French cinema organized by l'Institut Jean Vigo at Perpignan in 1984 was the next important event to which I was invited. This gave me the opportunity to see more French films from the early years, and also to sample authentic southern French cuisine. One of the films that struck me was a shot taken sideways from a boat going up the Grand Canal in Venice. This was presented as the film that Alexandre Promio claimed to have shot in this way in 1897, and hence it was the first tracking shot. However, most early films did not have any titles or other obvious feature identifying them uniquely, and so the attribution must remain doubtful. The only way that one can be certain about the identity of an early film is if there is a watertight provenance trail for the copy, or a frame enlargement made when it was released, which often happened, that identifies it absolutely. There is no way this last will suffice for a film showing a fuzzy distant shot of one side of the Grand Canal.

The conference was quite a study in the different ways of speaking French, for there were a number of Italian and French-Canadian participants as well as a small number of native English speakers. Even the actual French people had a number of different speaking styles, ranging from the old-fashioned rolling oratorical style used by some of the older speakers, to modern flat colloquialism. One of the older Italians, who prided himself on his French delivery, made some nasty remarks about the French of one of the Canadians. The speaker in question did indeed have a truly barbarous way of speaking French, though it was hardly polite to mention it. So I refused to deliver my presentation in French, though a translation had been prepared. I was not going to have my accent sneered at. Of course my piece came out in French as *L'espace d'à côté*, in the proceedings of the conference published in 1985 as *Les Premiers Ans du Cinéma Francais*, edited by Pierre Guibbert for l'Institut Jean Vigo. I identified the font used as Simoncini Garamond.

THE SPACE NEXT DOOR

For the first decade of the cinema it is impossible to discuss stylistic developments in France, Britain, and the United States separately, so intimate are the connections between them. But during the world-wide film boom after 1906 British film-making lost its innovative drive, and left the field to the French and American producers. For the next few years the French cinema still had a formal contribution to make to American film-making before falling behind the newest American developments, and it is this period from 1907 to 1910 that I want to discuss.

In 1907 the Pathé company was still the major force in the American market, and at this time the film-makers of Vitagraph and Biograph derived some major stylistic features from their example. It has now become quite clear that the development of lines of parallel action as used in film narratives for suspense purposes was well under way before D.W. Griffith appeared on the scene, starting with a single alternation between scenes in two different places in James Williamson's *Fire!*, and proceeding through many versions on this structure to the Vitagraph Company's *The Hundred to One Shot* (1906) which shows the actual race to the rescue in two shots alternating with two shots of the people in danger. So far, no other American films taking this technique further during the next two years have been identified, but it now seems that the Pathé company continued this development. Titles to mention include *Je vais chercher le pain* (1907) and another Pathé film also of 1907, *Ruse de mari*. Even more interesting is *A Narrow Escape* released in the United States in March 1908. (This

film was distributed in Britain as *The Physician of the Castle*. Its original French title is unknown.) As you can see, there are now more alternations between shots of the parallel actions, including both sides of a telephone conversation. Even more interestingly, this film also includes the villains having to break through two doors in adjoining rooms in succession to get to their victims, as D.W. Griffith was later to use so often in his films. *A Narrow Escape* also includes a cut in to a closer shot in the middle of a scene, like many others such occurring in French films of around this date. Curiously enough, although there are also many American films made up to 1906 including this sort of cutting in to a closer shot, I have never seen any with cuts into a closer shot of a person which were made during 1907 and the first half of 1908. (I am excepting here films that include a cut into a closer shot of a detail of an object other than a person's face, as all the evidence suggests that these sort of close shots were regarded quite differently by film-makers at this period.) In other words, I am suggesting that French films carried on the use of cutting within a scene during a couple of years when this technique had been abandoned by American film-makers.

Taking one of the most popular Pathé films of late 1907 distributed in America, *le Cheval emballé*, we can see cross-cutting developed even further. There is no doubt that D.W. Griffith saw this film, as his film *The Curtain Pole* made in late 1908 is definitely based on it, and in particular accurately reproduces the business of the backwards movement of the horse. However, there is also no

The delivery man leaves his horse and cart outside a grain shop in le Cheval emballé, *before going inside to make a delivery.*

The delivery man going up the Pathé staircase.

A cut back outside to his horse devouring a bag of oats.

Back inside the delivery man makes conversation with one of the families to whom he makes a delivery. And so on.

question but that the French film-makers (and indeed American film-makers other than D.W. Griffith) were unable to fully develop the use of cross-cutting between parallel action further, so I will leave this aspect of *le Cheval emballé* and turn to the way the delivery-man is shown moving round the house while the horse is simultaneously devouring the bag of oats. This use of what I think of as the "Pathé staircase set" (actually there was more than one of these staircase sets over the years) began about 1902, with the series of "Peeping Tom" films (*Un coup d'oeil par étage*, etc.), where the staircase was basically somewhere to put as many keyholes as possible for someone to peep through. But having established this staircase activity as a crude way of making longer films, the Pathé people kept the staircase and foyer sets and used them in other sorts of dramatic films.

In America, the Vitagraph people took note of the way the Pathé film-makers had been using extra shots of the comings and goings of their actors on the Pathé staircase to increase the length of their films. As Albert E. Smith, one of the directors and founders of the Vitagraph company put it in his autobiography, *Two Reels and a Crank* (1952), "No one complained about this until it became evident that Pathé was using its goings and comings over and over again. The stories varied, but sandwiched in would be the same goings and comings. This aroused a two-horned complaint: the audiences were getting tired of the same goings and comings, often having little relation to the story, and secondly the buyers weren't going to pay fifteen cents a foot for this surplusage. They said the story was better without the goings and comings, and so they began to scissor them out of the picture, paying Pathé only for what was left."

Now although this anecdote is rather exaggerated in its details, there is no doubt that many Vitagraph films made after 1907 lack transitional scenes showing the movement of the actors from place to place, and some even omit

the less important dramatic scenes in their stories, which are merely reported in the narrative titles bridging the shots, as in *A Brother's Devotion* (1910). Although the Pathé example had a largely negative effect on Vitagraph practice, this does not mean that the flow of movement from scene to scene is not well handled in Vitagraph films on the occasions when it was judged appropriate. It is just that there is less of it than in most of the other American companies' films.

On the other hand, D.W. Griffith at Biograph derived quite the opposite lesson from these "goings and comings" in Pathé films. In his films he developed the practice of transferring part of the action of a scene into adjoining hallways and rooms even when this was not strictly necessary, although in his case what the actors were doing was always relevant to the development of the story, as we can see in *Simple Charity (1910)*. What this practice gave Griffith was the same amount of action split up into a greater number of shots, and this greater number of shots within the same length of film was undoubtedly the major feature of the dynamics of his films, with the extra cuts giving a visual impulse at each transition. The other way that Griffith used what we might call "the space next door" was to provide an extra delaying stage in the advance of the villains on his helpless heroines in his suspense films — the next room had one more door they had to break down while the rescuers got closer in a cross-cut scene of parallel action, just as in the earlier Pathé film, *A Narrow Escape*.

As is well known, D.W. Griffith saw the famous *Assassination of the Duc de Guise* early in his career, and as you can see, it also features, in a more positive way, in fact rather in the manner that became obsessive with Griffith, the spreading of the main action backwards and forwards over a number of rooms. But as well as that, it seems to me that Vitagraph, the other major American studio, also learnt something from *l'Assassinat du Duc de Guise* and similar *Films d'Art*. (And can somebody tell me why this copy — obviously from an early print, and given to the National Film Archive by Charles Pathé in 1940 — says "*la Mort du Duc de Guise*" when everyone insists on referring to the film as "*L'Assassinat du Duc de Guise*"?). One of the noticeable features of *La Mort du Duc de Guise* when compared with other French and American films of the period up to 1908 is that the camera is set at somewhere about waist height instead of being set at the more usual and convenient eye-level. This is only noticeable because the actors in the foreground fill most of the height of the frame and there is simultaneously a small degree of staging in depth. This kind of camera height is also used in many of the subsequent French films in the *"Film d'Art"* genre, and also subsequently in Pathé films in general, many of which you have seen at this conference, and it was also taken up in a weaker form by the Vitagraph company in America from 1909.

As you know, the Vitagraph company was the major American film company in the European market, and the only one which produced prints for European distribution in their factory outside Paris from a second negative sent over from New York. As you can see in *A Brother's Devotion*, the Vitagraph company used the a chest-height camera fairly consistently from 1910 onwards, but they combined it with a greater camera closeness than was used at that date in European films, with the actors performing up to the "nine-foot line". (This is the source of the *"plan Americain"*). This consistent camera closeness, together with the fact that the Vitagraph actors were allowed to turn their backs to the camera when appropriate to the action, gives the Vitagraph films made between 1910 and 1913 an instantly recognizable look. Actually, if you look at *la Mort du Duc de Guise* again, you will see that the actors in that film also do a small amount of acting with their backs to the camera, but in subsequent French films this feature was not developed as it was by the Vitagraph film-makers. In fact in French films of the period 1910 to 1914 in general there was a far greater tendency for the actors to play directly towards the camera than there was in American films. The extreme of this is to be found in French comedies such as the Rigadin series and the Léonce series, where the protagonists address long speeches directly to the camera. Although the principal actors in American comedies sometimes acknowledge the presence of the camera and the cinema audience with a brief look in films made during this period, they never go so far as to talk to it at length. Likewise, in dramatic subjects, there is nothing to be found in American films of this date like the extensive acting straight to the camera employed by the principal figure in Gérard Bourgeois' *Les Victimes de l'alcool* (1912), and many other French dramas. For instance the films made by Feuillade include occasional looks cast by the principal actors straight towards the camera in a way long abandoned in American dramatic

films. It could also be considered that the tendency in the Vitagraph films to ignore the camera direction when arranging the staging of the scenes opened up the possibility of using true reverse-angle cutting as was developed in American films from 1911 onwards, but not at all in French cinema up to 1914. (This is really the other side of the coin from the point already made by Ben Brewster that a reverse-angle shot is difficult to conceive if the principal actor in a scene directs their playing straight at the camera).

The use of acting with the back to the camera was just one element of the increasing naturalness in some American films which, though noticed by some French film-makers such as Victorin Jasset, only had a limited and belated effect on French cinema. This delayed effect of American film-making practice during the 1910-1914 period is typified by the limited adoption of the "nine-foot line" in France. It is only in a few Pathé films made from 1911 onwards such as *Nick Winter et le banquier* and *les Victimes de l'alcool* that a substantial proportion of the shots are as close as nine feet to the actors, whereas in the majority of French films, the regular closeness of camera is four metres. (This scale of shot was referred to by the American film-makers at the time as the "French foreground"). I must make it clear at this point that I am talking about the standard staging of the master shot of the script scenes, and not the rare use of a closer shot cut into the middle of a scene, which existed to some extent in French films just as it did in American films at this time. In other words, it is a matter of the <u>average</u> closeness of the camera to the actors, for frequent use of the "nine-foot line" was common in films from other American companies besides Vitagraph by 1913.

After 1909, nothing that happened in the French cinema had any influence on the American cinema until we come to recent times, though within continental Europe one can still see some effect from French films in other countries: for instance there are certain complex interactions between the subjects of Danish films and those of French films up until 1914 which was not just confined to the series of "master criminal" thrillers. For instance, Holger-Madsen's *Opiumsdrömmen* (1914) was apparently inspired by the Pathé film *le Fumeur d'opium* (1911), and Benjamin Christensen's *Det Hemmelighedsfulde X* (1914) (The Mysterious X), not only has its plot based on the plots of Léonce Perret's 1913 films, *Roman d'un mousse* and *l'Enfant de Paris*, but also takes over and develops the silhouette effects used in those films as well.

All in all, I have been telling you a story of how American film-makers developed stylistic features that were embryonically present in French films in 1907 and 1908, whereas the French film-makers proved unable to develop these features themselves. And with the exploitation of these features, along with others such as the use of faster cutting (more shots per reel), which was unique to the American cinema, the American films took over the French home market even before the First World War. The figures proving this are in Sadoul's *Histoire Générale du Cinéma (Tome 3, Vol. 2, Le Cinéma devient un Art)*, but this fact still does not seem to have registered with most writers on film history, let alone why it happened.

An amusing footnote to the story of Pathé's "goings and comings" is that when the Pathé company reissued *Le Cheval emballé* in 9.5 mm. format as *Boireau et le cheval emballé* they themselves cut out the "goings and comings" at the front of the film, so also removing the cross-cutting between parallel actions, and thus the film's principal claim on our attention.

Music Forward! *made by Pathé in 1908, using a second distant set inside the shot to get the appearance of miniature figures.*

My presentation was illustrated by the screening of the films from the National Film Archive mentioned in it. I am not sure now why I included the Pathé *Music Forward!*, which is a much more polished and elaborated version of George Méliès' *L'homme-orchestre* (1900), featuring the most charming of Pathé's female magicians. It may be because I hoped that the French participants could tell us the original title of it, which the Archive did not know, because of the lack of Pathé catalogues after 1907. The French could not. Eventually, I worked out that it must have been called *Musique en tête*, which was the standard French military command for the band to lead off at the head of a column of troops, and a clever play on words as well, given the subject matter.

In my piece, I refer to the question of camera height, which can have a significant effect on the look of a film if there any staging in depth with the actors. At that point I thought Pathé's standard waist level camera came in about 1908, but

Ben Brewster suggested to me that it started even earlier, and I quickly came to agree with him. I illustrate an example from 1906 in *Un drame à Venise*. Since there is no staging in depth here, you have to look at the shots quite carefully to see that the camera is indeed about waist height.

I actually made these frame enlargements from the two shots on either side of a cut in to a close shot to illustrate an editing trick that still works. This is to cover up a mismatch of actor position across a cut by making the cut the frame before the end position of a movement when you do not have the movement itself recorded in both takes so that you can cut in the middle of the movement. This preferred option will of course cover up all sorts of discontinuities elsewhere between the two shots. There is a reference in this piece to the presentation that Ben Brewster gave at the conference on staging in depth. Besides discussing examples of this in French and American cinema before World War I, it also analyses the general implications of staging in depth for the film form of the period. It can be found in English in *Early Cinema: Space – Frame – Narrative*, edited by Thomas Elsaesser for BFI Publishing in 1990.

There is also a reference in my article to a recent discovery, *The Physician of the Castle*. The National Film Archive viewing service continued to be very keen for researchers to look at the new viewing copies of early films that they were churning out, and Elaine Burrows pointed out to me that they had other incomplete copies of *The Physician of the Castle* besides the English distribution copy that I had seen, so naturally I looked at them. The consequence was the series of events described in the following article. Unlike other people, the editor of *Sight & Sound* never commissioned me to write pieces, but I realised that as it was the fiftieth anniversary of the National Film Archive, she would have difficulty in refusing a piece that not only celebrated the anniversary, but made some very important new points as well.

The actor's left hand has not quite come to rest on the paper when the cut is made to the next shot in Pathé's Un drame à Venise (1906). *Both shots have waist level camera height.*

The frame after the cut from the shot on the left. Cutting just before the static position is reached covers up the mismatch in the position of the right hand when the film is actually seen.

THE PHYSICIAN OF THE CASTLE

THE PHYSICIAN OF THE CASTLE

1. TITLE: The False Telegram

2. Two men order drinks, then write a telegram at a table outside a café

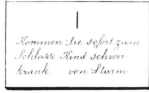

3. TELEGRAM INSERT: 'Come straight away to the castle. Child very sick. von Sturm'

The most striking thing about *The Physician of the Castle*, a Pathé film from early 1908, is the extent to which it anticipates many of D. W. Griffith's methods of film construction, such as the cutting back and forth during a race to the rescue, and also the use of movement from room to room, not only as a thing in itself but also to give the criminals a series of suspenseful doors to break down to get to their prey. To a few people already in the know, however, *The Physician of the Castle* will only be a small surprise, because they have seen other films made between 1906 and 1908, mostly by the Pathé company, which show earlier stages in the development of cross-cutting between parallel actions. In fact, we know that Griffith saw at least one of these Pathé films, *Le Cheval Emballé (The Runaway Horse)*, which cuts back and forth four pairs of times between separate events inside and outside a house, because his 1908 film The Curtain Pole is fairly closely based on it.

So where has *The Physician of the Castle* been hiding, unknown and unsung, all these years? The answer is that it was not hidden at all, but waiting, almost fully catalogued, in the National Film Archive to be looked at by anyone curious enough to do so. The original print had been given to the Archive around 1942, by a Mr H. R. James. It then stayed in the vaults, with periodic testing until the first signs of chemical instability appeared in 1956, when the appropriate committee ordered its duplication on to acetate-based safety stock. Harold Brown, Film Preservation Officer of the Archive, made the duplicate negative on

4. The men pay for their drinks and leave.

5. One man sends the other into a post office.

6. The men loiter outside the gateway to a house. They watch a postman enter with a telegram.

7. Outside the house, the postman gives the telegram to the maid.

8. *The maid gives the telegram to the doctor, who is with his wife and son in the living room. The doctor leaves the room.*

9. *The doctor comes into his office and gets his equipment.*

10. *Coming back into the living room, the doctor says goodbye to his family.*

11. *He drives out of the front gate watched by the two men.*

his legendary home-made printing machine used for shrunken and delicate films, and he also made an initial approximate dating of the film when its title was still unknown, using his knowledge of the small changes year by year in the print stock used by the major early film-makers. From this lead, precise identification was made by the Archive's cataloguing department with the help of the plot summaries in the Bioscope, the British film trade paper of the time, which listed *The Physician of the Castle* as being released in Britain on 7 May 1908.

There the matter rested until, moved by the new spirit in film history which requires that the historian see all the relevant films available, Ben Brewster and I were viewing a group of films to top up our knowledge of the first twenty years of French cinema before going to a conference on the subject at Perpignan last year. After we had seen *The Physician of the Castle*, Ben Brewster established from the American trade journal the Moving Picture World that it had been released in New York as *A Narrow Escape* on 28 March 1908, which is just at the point when D. W. Griffith had started writing film scripts for the Biograph company, but before he began directing. (This is the kind of helpful extra information which film archives are glad to get, hard pressed as their staff are by the mass of material in their care. And anyone can join in such film history research, though it must be realised that one gets no material reward for it. Indeed it usually costs one money.) Despite all that we know about the English and American releases of *The Physician of the Castle*, we still do not know either its original French release date, or indeed its original French title. This is part of a

12. *The doctor's car going down the raod into the distance.*

13. *The two criminals put on masks and enter the grounds of the house.*

14. *The men ring the doorbell and stab the maid when she comes out, but they are seen by the doctor's wife watching through the window.*

15. *Inside the living room, the wife and son barricade the door.*

16. TITLE: Arriving at the castle.

17: The doctor drives through the front gates.

18. In the living room of the castle, the owner and his family are surprised by the doctor's visit, but let him examine one of the children.

19. Back at the doctor's house, his wife and son enter the study and barricade the door to that as well.

rather general problem with French films made after the middle of 1907, for there are no French catalogues or trade papers available outside France, and possibly even inside France, for dates between 1907 and 1910.

Like the surviving prints of many early films, *The Physician of the Castle* had lost some footage at the beginning and end, where the wear and tear are greatest on prints, and both the main-and end-titles were missing, as is often the case. Indeed, it seemed probable to me that the whole first scene was missing, and enquiry showed that the Archive had other incomplete versions of the same film, one with Spanish titles from the Uruguayan archive in Montevideo, and a German-language version acquired in the Joseph Joye collection from Switzerland. The Spanish version, *El Medico del Castillo*, had been obtained by the Archive as a result of making safety copies of a group of early films sent by the Montevideo archive for the 1978 Brighton conference of the International Federation of Film Archives (FIAF) on Cinema 1900-1906. (The National Film Archive sometimes provides this kind of service for the smaller members of FIAF, which do not have full technical facilities for film preservation.) *Der Arzt des Schlosses,* the version with German titles, came from the large collection of early films assembled by a Swiss monk, Joseph Joye, for teaching purposes around the time of the First World War.

Like most of the films in this collection, *Der Arzt des Schlosses* was on the verge of decomposing when it was acquired in 1977. Not only that, but sections of the film had already been cut out at some earlier date, presumably .because those sections already showed

20. The criminals break through the barricade into the living room.

21. The doctor's wife looks up the phone number of the castle and rings it.

22. At the castle, the doctor is given the telephone call.

23. Medium close Shot of the doctor's wife talking on the telephone.

24. *Medium Close Shot of the doctor talking on the telephone.*

25. *Long Shot of the doctor talking on the telephone.*

26. *The doctor leaving the through the castle gates in his car.*

27. *The doctor's car going down a stretch of road.*

signs of deterioration. Exactly the same applied to the version from Montevideo, which also had visibly sticky emulsion and missing sections. Both these copies had been duplicated on to safety stock shortly after being received by the Archive, and then catalogued by Anne Burton and Don Swift respectively, who identified them as the same film as *The Physician of the Castle* already held by the Archive. This was done, as is usual in such cases, not by actual physical comparison of the prints, but by using the story description entered in the Archive catalogue for the copy acquired earlier.

Once the importance of the film was recognised, a physical comparison of the viewing copies of all the versions was made, and it was found that the German and Spanish versions, though much less complete than the English one, contained the sections missing from it. Elaine Burrows, the Archive Viewings Officer, who is never slow to action, took a splicer, and a complete viewing copy was assembled from duplicate prints of the three versions. It is this which is described above. The first three shots of this complete version came from the German print, and the last shot half from the German version and half from the Spanish version. Quite remarkably, those two incomplete half shots, which were all that the Spanish and German versions contained of the last shot, fitted together perfectly, to the very single frame, to make up the complete final scene of the film. This was an event that gave a slightly eerie feeling, suggesting either that Somebody Up There Likes Us or that the creators of Tlön, Uqbar and Orbis Tertius are still at work.

Happy 50th birthday, National Film Archive.

28. *The doctor's car stops to pick up two armed policemen.*

29. *The doctor's car stops outside the gates to his house, and all run inside.*

30. *The criminals burst through the second barricade, but as they seize his wife and child, the doctor and police rush in and overpower them.*

31. *Outside the front gate, the criminals are led away by the police, leaving the doctor there in triumph.*

Because this article was meant to celebrate the Archive, I wrote myself out of the story, but actually, I was the person who recognized that the three prints could be put together to make a complete copy. And I showed Elaine Burrows where to make the joins, though she did indeed wield the splicer. After this, when I discovered disordered prints and incomplete copies in the Archive, I did not bother to tell anyone, but just corrected them myself on the spot.

After I went to the Royal College of Art, I got to know Raymond Durgnat, who had been the first film studies student at the Slade under Thorold Dickinson, before he became a script editor in the movie industry, and then a well-known as a writer on film. We had a number of interesting and pleasant meetings, and he later passed some book reviewing assignments on to me. Some of these were for the *British Journal of Aesthetics*, and after writing a few of them that dug into the low standard of thinking in this area, I was emboldened to submit an article expounding my own view of film aesthetics (and indeed general aesthetics). These ideas have mostly been reproduced above in my *Sight & Sound* piece entitled "Let a Hundred Flowers Bloom", but I was sure the academics at whom the *British Journal of Aesthetics* was directed would not have read it. I also added a brief section on what should be called art, which I had not published before. The main idea in this was that art is whatever an artist does that he says is art. According to me, an art work includes the actions of the artist in designating as art the things concerned, as well as the things themselves.

Although I invented it independently, this definition does have some resemblance to George Dickie's institutional theory of art, as put forward in his book *Art and the Aesthetic: An Institutional Analysis*(Cornell University Press, Ithaca, 1974), but it removes the power he gives to art critics, etc. to prescribe what is art and what isn't.

After submitting this, I heard again the tinny sound of one tiny mind slamming shut. The editor rejected it purely on the grounds of it being too short. This was quite specious, as although the journal had a maximum length limitation on articles, it had no such explicit minimum length requirement. Of course, the problem my proposal creates for the kind of people who go in for philosophical aesthetics is that it closes the subject down, except for the discussion of the ideas of past philosophers about aesthetics. But in any case, the subject is closing itself down without my help, as it is quite obvious now that all the past philosophical theories about art are useless in dealing with the advanced art of the last fifty years.

So that was the end of my relation with academic aestheticians. The same thing happened after I had written a series of book reviews for the Times Higher Educational Supplement. In this case, I dared to submit a piece about the nature of teaching in the humanities departments of universities.

WHAT WENT WRONG WITH MEDIA STUDIES?

Many people feel there is something very unsatisfactory about the academic discipline (if it is one) of Media Studies. This feeling has even worried some of the practitioners of that activity occasionally, but of course they are unlikely to see what the problem really is, and where it comes from. To see the truth one has to go back to a time before the subject existed. Way back to when there were only film studies courses in universities, and even further. And it is time for someone who has seen things from outside as well as inside the business to be allowed a few words about the matter.

The first film studies course in an English university was set up in 1960 at University College, London, in the Department of Fine Art, or to give it its usual name, the Slade School. This is in the first place a famous art school, but the head of it at that time, William Coldstream, as well as being a well-known painter, had also been a significant member of the GPO Film Unit for some years during the 'thirties. The man who was brought in to run this new course in film studies was Thorold Dickinson, who had himself been an important British film director during the nineteen-forties. Thorold Dickinson believed that people studying the history and aesthetics of film should have a practical knowledge of the subject, which was a novel idea at the time, as it still is. (The usual notion is that all you need to be write about film is an elementary command of English and the ability to see the screen.) Dickinson also believed that students of the subject should also see as many films as possible, and during the course large numbers of films a year were screened for the students, and also anyone else in University College who was interested.

Courses for secondary school teachers who wanted to introduce film study into their schools also came to exist in the 'sixties, but outside the universities. The people who taught these courses, as well as the students, came with degrees in English literature and similar humanities subjects, and of course had no direct experience, and little knowledge, of film-making. What the teachers taught in these courses was interpretation of the "meaning" of films, just in the way that the teaching of literature had come to be mainly the teaching of the invention of interpretations of the "meaning" of poems, etc. This was the side of things that contributed to the initial growth of film studies in the nineteen-seventies, as part of the general expansion of higher education going on at that time.

I became involved in all this at the very beginning of the 'seventies, when Thorold Dickinson asked me to take over the teaching of practical film-making at the Slade part-time. (I had been working as a lighting cameraman for the

previous few years around the edges of the film business, after having been a theoretical physicist, amongst other things.) After Thorold Dickinson retired, James Leahy became Senior Lecturer in Film, and the Slade Film Unit itself benefited from the general university expansion then going on. The amount of teaching was increased, now including classes in the history of film style and technology, and also in avant-garde cinema, which were both given by myself, and the number of films shown increased to around 200 per year. There were also classes and seminars on the latest ideas about film theory imported from France, and some of these were given by some of the fashionable figures of the time. It was quite a show, but the cut-backs in university funding that began in the late 'seventies (under Labour governments, you had better know), and the retirement of Sir William Coldstream eventually did for the course. And that was the end of having film studies in universities related closely to the practicalities of film.

If anyone was capable of thinking about the matter, they would realise that there is a strange division within universities. On the science side, all the teaching is done by people who actually work at and contribute to the subject they are teaching, but in arts subjects this is mostly not the case. The people teaching literature do not in general create any real literature, nor are most of them capable of doing so; the people teaching about art have never painted, and so on. The one major exception in the arts is music, insofar as it is taught in universities. Everyone who teaches music can perform it, and write it too. So it is no wonder that the media industries despise university media studies. Its products are of no practical use to them.

Elsewhere in the late 'seventies new posts in film studies were set up, and this process was strongly influenced by the Education Department of the British Film Institute, which helped to make certain that the teachers appointed had the right (i.e. left) political credentials. What was taught in these new courses was a mixture of the old literary-based criticism and the new theories about film recently imported from France. These ideas, which were all derived from mixtures of French linguistics, Marxism, and psychoanalysis, moved out of film studies into the other humanities, where they still are. Although these ideas have since been widely discussed, what is always been ignored is that the further application of these "basic" ideas in the areas for which they were first dreamed up has completely failed over the last thirty years. Linguistics on the Saussure model has failed to develop any further, and Marxism as an applied social system has almost vanished from the earth because it can't deliver the goods. And as for psychoanalysis, even

Woody Allen now admits it hasn't done anything to cure his neuroses. In fact, the experimental demonstration of the failure of psychoanalysis to do better than no therapy at all is quite widely accepted, even by many of the people who still, against all reason, continue to believe in it as a tool for inventing interpretations of art and society. It is well past 1984, and the age of "double-think" is well and truly with us inside the universities.

Even more than this, some of the principal originators of these ideas such as Althusser and Lacan admitted towards the end of their lives that they were indeed charlatans. Literally: in that they did not actually understand the concepts purloined from logic and mathematics and real science that they used to justify their own ideas to their dupes. And the late Christian Metz, a major figure in creating French film theory, also admitted in private that his semiotic system of film analysis did not work properly, although he never did so in public. And he never did anything to stop his disciples teaching those admittedly defective ideas, as they still do. That is academic integrity for you. The logical and factual defects of these theories were demonstrated in print in considerable detail already in the nineteen-seventies by people like Brian Henderson and myself, and more recently Noël Carroll and others, but that hasn't stopped naive and ignorant undergraduates still being stuffed with them in film and media courses.

There was one positive development starting from the end of the 'seventies, which was a new wave of interest in film history, but this was led by people outside the universities, who also did most of the new research in this area — the most famous of whom is Kevin Brownlow. The prime impulse behind this new film history was the large numbers of prints of old films that became available through the 'seventies from the major world film archives, particularly our own National Film Archive. These films made it evident that the tired old stories about what happened in film history were not only inadequate, but downright wrong, particularly with respect to the first twenty-five years. In the 'eighties, some of the people filling the new academic posts in film studies became interested in working in film history, and real film history secured a place on the curriculum in some university courses. (Real history is different to cultural history, in which the false or banal generalities about past society that the perpetrator already believes are supported by mentioning a few specially chosen facts from past art.) But by the 'nineties this first flush of film history as a real part of film courses began to fade, as the teachers concerned (Ben Brewster, John Fullerton, Thomas Elsaesser, etc.) left the country for more congenial posts elsewhere. The trouble with film history is that it is too much like hard work. The only way you can get a proper grip on what really happened is by looking at large numbers of old documents or old films in film archives, and you really *do* get your hands dirty taking lots of old films out of cans and putting them on a Steenbeck. Reading a few recent books and articles,

seeing the odd film, and then dreaming up notions about cinema in the comfort of an armchair is *so* much easier.

The major event in the nineteen-nineties, as far as higher education is concerned, was the renaming of the polytechnics and other similar institutions as universities. Media studies had initially come into being in polytechnics in the nineteen-seventies, with a central orientation towards showing students that the cinema was a tool of capitalism for brainwashing the masses into accepting its evils. (Animistic thinking in terms of the personalization of abstract entities is a major continuing feature of this strain in humanities education.) This crude aim was conveniently concealed by the superimposition of the new notions and jargon first introduced through university film studies. Given that polytechnics were supposed to be principally devoted to education in practical technical subjects, they also already contained a small number of practical courses in film and television production. When both media studies and practical media training were present in the same institution, the two courses had little connection with each other in subject matter. This is inevitable, because the "theoretical" part of film and media studies has hardly any basis in the way films and television are actually put together, and what film and television makers think they are doing.

How something as irrational and uninterested in any solid connection with reality as all this could get started can only be properly explained by going much further back, to when English Literature became established as a subject in universities. It was developed from the style of literary criticism that already existed, but the difference was that the people who previously wrote about novels and poems themselves produced published literature, so there was a good chance that what they had to say about another writer's prose or poetry might be of some interest, even if not of any general truth. The first wave of literary critics with university posts included some such as I.A. Richards and William Empson who were practising poets on the side, but as the subject grew more, then more of the new teachers were like F.R. Leavis, who only had their subjective taste to work with, plus a desire to lay down what society should be like, backed up in his case by an impressive pose as a rebel guru. (And it worked only too well: one of his many students, who later became a well-known academic film critic, abandoned for a time his essential homosexuality and got married, because Leavis preached that homosexuality was wrong.)

A few academics in the new literature departments in universities in the 'thirties realised that interpretation of works of literature needed limiting by something outside the work and the critic. Something better than the famous Leavis technique of pointing to a feature in a poem or story, proposing an interpretation of it, and justifying this by saying "It's like that, isn't it?", and then relying on the force of their personality to convince their students. Unfortunately the students never said, "No, I don't see that, or feel that." What should have been demanded was the continuation of the justification, which can actually be done when it has some validity, by saying, "It is like that because...", and then in a chain of argument appealing to known facts about the creator of the work and his ideas, and the context in which the work was produced. A few people like René Wellek, F.W. Bateson, and more recently E.D. Hirsch have advocated this kind of much more objective approach, but unfortunately they did not follow through with it strongly enough. The pull towards expressing their own subjective intuitions was too strong for them.

Wanting to express one's passionate feelings about things, including works of art, is a natural human disposition, and there is nothing wrong with doing it in writing, but pretending that it is a proper academic activity, however decorated with valueless jargon, is surely wrong.

The solution to the problem should be obvious from what I have said above, but what about all those untalented and unskilled people teaching in university humanities departments? Time for a new Modest Proposal?

Now there were lots of film history conferences going on. Susan Hayward put one on at Aston University in Sheffield in 1986, for which I did a paper making a general stylistic comparison between French, German, and American films of the nineteen-thirties. It can be read in **European Cinema Conference Papers** (AMLC Publication – Aston University) 1984-5, edited by Susan Hayward. It does not make any important points that are not included in *Film Style and Technology*, so I will not reproduce it. Actually, the most interesting paper at this conference was by Bob Pester. He analysed statistically the occurrence of particular words in the dialogue of *Ma nuit chez Maude* by Eric Rohmer, and identified the major concerns of this film from these results. Although this sort of thing had been going on for some time in literary studies, it could probably give some interesting results for films too, particularly those with a more literary tendency.

A major force in the study of silent cinema had emerged in north Italy. This was the *Giornate del cinema muto* held every year in the small city of Pordenone, about fifty miles north of Venice on the way to the Austrian border. The festival had started in 1982 in a very small local way, but it grew rapidly into an international event. The driving force behind it were a group of young Italian film enthusiasts, Livio Jacob, Paolo Cherchi Usai, and Lorenzo Codelli, but there were many others assisting them in putting it on. The first of the *Giornate* that I went to was in 1986, which had Scandinavian silent cinema as its principal subject. The *Giornate* were not conferences, though there were a few brief symposia as part of the events. The principal aim was to show lots of silent films that had not been seen in modern times. On this occasion, the major discovery were the films directed by Georg af Klercker at the Swedish Hasselblad studios during World War I. The original negatives of these films had been preserved, so the prints were of a sharpness and clarity that few people had experienced. Most silent films one sees are duplicates from worn positives at best. At their worst, prints of old films, even sound films, can be many generations removed from the original negative. Some people got quite excited about af Klercker's films, but in my opinion they are not as interestingas all that. They are very slow as narratives, with hardly any scene dissection, like Swedish films made at Svenska Biografteatern years before, but without the same dramatic power.

At the *Giornate* papers by the principal guests were circulated, and these got published afterwards one way or another. Either in numbers of *Griffithiana*, a magazine on silent cinema edited by Davide Turconi, or in special volumes published by local specialist publishers such as Studio Tesi. My piece on early Danish cinema, originally written in 1975, and reproduced earlier in this book, came out in 1986 in the volume *Schiave bianchi allo specchio*, edited by Paolo Cherchi Usai, and published by Edizioni Tesi in 1986. The next year, the principal subject of the *Giornate* was American Vitagraph, and of course I had something to say about that, given the hundreds of Vitagraph films in the National Film Archive I had seen. In fact, I had so much to say that I wrote two articles, published in *Vitagraph Co. of America*, edited by Paolo Cherchi Usai (Edizioni Studio Tesi, 1987), under the titles of *Vitagraph, un tocco di classe* and *Ralph Ince, un fratello "minore"*?

Although the original English versions of these were immediately circulated to the participants in xeroxed form, the first of them was only published in English much, much later, in *Screen Culture: History and Textuality*, edited by John Fullerton for John Libbey in 2004. The paper by Ben Brewster mentioned in my article is fortunately also in included in English in the same volume.

VITAGRAPH FILMS — A TOUCH OF REAL CLASS

The films of the Vitagraph Company of America are distinctive in a number of ways, and some of these ways can be related right back to the variety act involving lightning sketches and conjuring that James Stuart Blackton and Albert Edward Smith, the founders of the company, performed in white tie and tails on the "Lyceum" circuit in New York before they moved into motion pictures. They were presenting entertainment, but it was entertainment with class. And when they eventually undertook serious large scale film production after 1905, they were particularly proud of the number of Shakespeare adaptations they produced, more than those by any other producer before 1914, not to mention a large number of other "culturally worthy" films on historical and biblical subjects. Compared to other American companies, their films had slightly more of a tendency to deal with the upper classes, which was not surprising given that, when he gained the opportunity, James Stuart Blackton showed a marked taste for social climbing. Contrariwise, Vitagraph was slower to move into the wild and woolly west than other American producers, both by keeping most of their production in New York, and also by a reluctance to make a large number of film Westerns. And the company's product truly reflected the taste of its founders, for Blackton and Smith always chose the scripts to be produced from amongst those passed up to them from the scenario department.

But in the early years of their company's existence before 1905, when film was mainly just a part of their variety act, their limited production of films had little significance on the international scene in comparison with the products of other film companies in France and Britain. This situation changed when Vitagraph undertook expansion, with the building of a proper studio, and the sale of their films on the open market in the middle of 1905, just before the nickelodeon boom in film exhibition in the United States started. The reasons for them taking this fortunate step is just one of

Studio scene in Uncle Tom's Cabin (1910)

the many things about the company that have yet to be discovered, but once the rapidly increasing demand for films became apparent in 1906, Smith and Blackton increased the number of films they were making even further, and put more care into the productions themselves. In doing this, their model had to be the French Pathé company, the largest film producer in the world, and the only one working on a truly industrialized basis at this date. At Pathé in 1906 film production was already organized with specialized departments for scenery, scripting, and so on, and the filming was done in more than one studio with more than one production team, and with specialized directors, cameramen, etc. Starting with two units with Smith and Blackton undertaking multiple production functions themselves, Vitagraph moved to a similar organization over the next two years, with a specially staffed scenario department and so on. By 1914, the company had 400 people on the daily payroll, 4 studios, and 14 separate departments taking care of scenario, reference, scenery, property, costume, ornamental, cabinet and upholstering, carpentering, developing, joining, negative, mechanical, publicity, and executive. With these resources, the company mounted occasional large-scale productions from 1909 onwards, which were of a size, and with the kind of realistic detail in the sets and costumes, that other American companies could not match. In the context of their time the exterior scenes constructed in the studio for *Uncle Tom's Cabin* (1910) are striking, and the reconstructions of the battle of Balaclava, with artificial snow driving across a general shot of the camp in *The Victoria Cross* (1912) even more so. Vitagraph was simply the biggest film company in America before World War I.

Apart from the tendencies mentioned above, the subject matter and attitudes displayed in the Vitagraph films were not so very different from those of other American film companies of the time, but the way it was presented in style and form on the screen *was* different in some significant respects, and it is these with which I will mostly be dealing here. However, this did not happen till about 1909, and at first the films themselves were just a part of the general stylistic interaction between the movies from other producers in the U.S., France and Britain.

Single Frame Animation

There was just one area where Smith and Blackton made a noticeably individual contribution in the early period, and this was in the development of true single frame animation. Here Smith's background as a conjuror who depended on clever mechanical devices for his act, and Blackton's skill as a "lightning" sketch artist played their part, but more important was that J.S. Blackton had done drawings in 1896 which were filmed by the Edison company so as to give a semblance of movement. This was done by taking a short section of the film in the normal way, then stopping the camera and making an alteration to the drawing, and then filming a further short section, and so on. To do this, the Edison film-makers were drawing on the "stop camera" trick effect that they had invented for *The Execution of Mary, Queen of Scots* in 1895 — in fact the effect on which Méliès later based most of his trick films. True single frame animation, in which one frame is shot, then the scene changed very slightly, then another frame shot, the scene changed again, and so on, dates from Edwin Porter's *The Whole Dam Family and the Dam Dog* of 1904, in which cut-out letters are moved about the screen continuously by single frame animation. However, Porter restricted himself in this and subsequent films of this kind to the animation of objects, and it is Blackton's *Humorous Phases of Funny Faces* of April 1906 which contains a section of the first true fully animated drawings, though most of it is done in the more primitive "stop camera" mode. (It is not impossible

that the developments in animation between 1900 and 1906 involved some more interaction between Blackton and Porter which are at present unknown.) Subsequently, Blackton did little more with drawn animation himself, but moved over to polishing the technique of object animation to a fine finish in *Work Made Easy* and *The Haunted Hotel* of 1907. All European efforts in true animation, such as those by Segundo de Chomon and Arthur Melbourne-Cooper, were inspired by the films mentioned, and done subsequently to seeing them, though there have been attempts in recent times to pretend otherwise. And of course the Vitagraph company produced Winsor McCay's first demonstration of his total mastery of drawn animation in *Winsor McCay the famous cartoonist of the New York Herald and his moving comics*. However, Vitagraph did also sometimes make use of ideas derived from the basic animation concept in their later films, by using a machine that produced a fairly convincing simulation of rain falling on the film scene by scratching very fine slanting parallel lines into the emulsion of the negative. Amongst other less common tricks in this area used by the Vitagraph film-makers I can also mention a swarm of midges bothering some campers in *The Men-Hater's Club* (1910), which are likewise created directly on the negative with animated black dots.

In a related area, *Liquid Electricity; or, The Inventor's Galvanic Fluid*, also produced by Vitagraph in 1907, shows a fine understanding and control of accelerated motion produced by cranking the camera more slowly than usual, though this was not the first appearance of this technique. Some shots in this film contain actors moving much faster than normal under the influence of the inventor's galvanic fluid, while the inventor himself appears to move at normal speed within the same shot; an effect achieved by having the latter move much slower than normal when the film was actually shot at reduced speed.

Narrative Constructional Devices

As I have said, once Vitagraph went into serious expanded production in 1906, their films became part of the process of continual and rapid interaction between the film-makers in Britain, France, and the United States, as can be seen in a chase film like *The Jail-Bird, and How He Flew* (1906), which steals its two basic gags of a man pretending to be a scarecrow, and another man taken for a convict because he gets stripes on his suit from wet paint, from earlier film-makers. Likewise, *The Hundred to One Shot* (1906), which was based on the stage melodrama of the same title, opens with an example of the "emblematic shot", which was a shot independent of the narrative which was sometimes put at the beginning or end of the film in those days to sum up the main point of interest of the film in one striking image. In this case it was a close shot of a hand with a fistful of money and a betting ticket, which was rather similar to the opening shot of the British film *Raid On a Coiner's Den* of 1904. But on the other hand, *The Hundred to One Shot* (1906) adds its own contribution to the early development of cross-cutting between parallel actions for suspense purposes. The sequence of shots in this film moves from house interior with a family threatened with eviction, to a racecourse where the son wins a bet that will pay off the debt, and then to a shot of him racing towards home in a car. This is followed by another shot of the house interior with the family in the process of being evicted, followed by an exterior shot of the son driving up to the house in the car, and finally another shot of the inside of the house into which the son enters and saves the day. In the next two years the Pathé film-makers in their turn added a couple of extra switches to this plot and structure in *Terrible Angoisse* (1907) and *The Physician of the Castle* (1908), so producing the egg that D.W. Griffith immediately hatched, and then made a meal of. Vitagraph did not let the idea of cross-cutting between parallel actions completely alone either, but in *Get Me a Step Ladder* (released 7 July 1908) added literal to metaphorical suspense. In this film a husband falls off a chair while fixing the curtain rail, and dangles suspended from it while his wife rushes through the rooms of the house trying to find a ladder. The scene of the husband hanging from the rail was shot in one long take which was then cut into three parts in the editing of the film, and these were interspersed with shots taken of the wife's comic mishaps in sets representing other rooms of the house. When we combine this sort of thing with other quite different novel ideas in other Vitagraph films such as *The Story the Boots Told* (released in June 1908), which are described by Ben Brewster, and add in what was going on in Pathé and other imported films, we have a rich ferment of filmic development on the New York screens which could only nourish the work of D.W. Griffith when he became a film-maker later in the year.

However, like all other film-makers, both in France and America, the Vitagraph people were unable to develop cross-cutting between parallel actions any further, and D.W. Griffith alone pushed it on into a basic and highly developed method of construction. Even in 1910, when Griffith had already shown in scores of films what could be done with many cuts between parallel lines of action, one can only

find limited use of a few such "cut-backs" in a few Vitagraph films such as *The Telephone* and *Society and the Man* which happen to have plots that definitely call for the use of the device. (A woman trapped by fire in an apartment telephones for help in the first, and a husband contemplating suicide is saved by his wife who has received a message alerting her when she is away from home in the second.) Even four years after this the use of cross-cutting is still very rare in the surviving Vitagraph films.

Flashbacks

Besides cross-cutting between parallel actions, another alternative to simple linear narration in films developed over these years, and here the Vitagraph film-makers made an original contribution. This was in the use of what we now call flashbacks, meaning the inclusion of a scene or scenes which are understood to have taken place earlier than the scene in the film which they follow. There is unfortunately the possibility of confusion here, for Griffith referred to his use of cross-cutting between parallel actions indifferently as "cutbacks", or "switchbacks", or "flashbacks", but he certainly did not mean what we understand by the last term, for he did not use "flashbacks" in the modern sense in his films. True flashbacks developed out of the representation of past scenes as dreams, which were used in one way and another in films from the beginning of the century, either by showing the dream memory as a scene inset within the film frame of the main scene which pictured the dreamer sleeping, or slightly later by a dissolve from the scene with the sleeper to the scene he dreams shown as a full-frame scene continuing on afterwards. There are hardly any surviving films in which the person remembering is awake; the only one I am aware of being *The Old Chorister* (James Williamson, 1904), and here the memory is shown as a brief inset scene. The Vitagraph film-makers moved on beyond this in *Napoleon — Man of Destiny* (1909), in which Napoleon is shown after the battle of Waterloo in the late Empress Josephine's bedroom remembering the past, which is then shown in a series of scenes, each of which is announced by superimposed titles in the main scene, before there is a direct cut to the past scene. One of these past episodes takes place over a number of shots and more than one scene, though most of them are done in just one shot. This series of flashbacks concludes with a "flashforward", as Napoleon has a vision of his future exile on Saint Helena. There was probably further development of the true flashback idea in America in 1910, before the famous instance of Luigi Maggi's *Nozze d'oro* of in Italy in 1911, but in any case it became an increasingly used way of producing a more complex narrative structure at Vitagraph and elsewhere from 1912 onwards. By 1914 it was possible for William Humphrey at Vitagraph to create, in *The Man That Might Have Been*, a really complex structure of reveries and flashbacks which contrast the protagonist's real passage through life with what might have been, if his son had not died. In this film dissolves were used to enter and leave the flashbacks and wishful reveries, as was now standard, and also to represent a time-lapse inside one of the flashback sequences.

The French Influence

Vitagraph set up a Paris office to handle the distribution of their films in Europe in 1908, and their drive to conquer this market may have led them to take even more careful note of exactly what was being done in French films at this date. Here is what Albert E. Smith said of the Pathé films on page 135 of his autobiography, *Two Reels and a Crank* (1952):

> 'Each one showed what we came to call "goings and comings". Here is a typical example of a goings and comings: a man enters a house through a front door, crosses the hall, enters a room, leaves the room through another door, goes upstairs, walks along a hall, enters another room. Then follows a scene with another character, in which, let us say, they shake hands. Then the man leaves the room, following the same devious route which he had just travelled. No one complained about this until it became evident that Pathé was using its goings and comings over and over again. The stories varied, but sandwiched in would be the same goings and comings. This aroused a two-horned complaint: the audiences were getting tired of the same goings and comings, often having little relation to the story, and secondly the buyers weren't going to pay fifteen cents a foot for this surplusage. They said the story was better without the goings and comings, and so they began to scissor them out of the picture, paying Pathé only for what was left.'

Anyone who has seen a large number of Pathé films made before 1909 will recognize that this is a not very exaggerated description of the action in quite a lot of them, and there is also no doubt that many Vitagraph films made after 1907 lack transitional scenes showing the movement of the actors from place to place, and that many even omit the less important dramatic scenes in their stories, which are merely reported in the narrative titles bridging the shots. Although the Pathé example in this respect was largely negative, this does not mean that the flow of movement from scene to scene is not well handled in Vitagraph films on the occasions when it was judged appropriate. It is just that there is less of it than in most of the other American companies' films.

Intertitles

As the Vitagraph company, like all other film producers, wished to cram ever more complicated stories into one reel of film from 1907 onwards, and more particularly given their predilection for adapting the classics, they had to place even more dependence on intertitles to explain not only the action that was to follow in the next scene, but also those parts of the story which had been left out of the picturization. There was another approach to film narration, and this was to make sure that the story chosen had been adapted to play in continuous action as nearly as possible, and hence to be directly represented on the screen in its entirety. This was the approach that D.W. Griffith gradually came to adopt after he started making films in the middle of June 1908, but since his approach was not clearly preferred by audiences, it was not generally taken up for some years. And even Griffith had some difficulty with what now seems the next logical step, which was to report the important lines of dialogue spoken by the characters in the scene in intertitles, rather than narrating the general trend of the conversation indirectly, as part of the purely narrative intertitle preceding the scene. Such "spoken" titles, as they were called, had appeared in the early years of the century, but they were extremely rare, and continued to be so until 1909, when one or two dialogue intertitles began to appear in a certain number of American films, and a few European films as well. Vitagraph may have played an important part in this development, since their *Julius Caesar*, released on 1 December 1908, includes a well-known dialogue quotation in an intertitle. Since there were a number of other Vitagraph films from 1908 based on classic stories which are now lost, it is quite possible that some of these also contained other famous lines of dialogue in their intertitles. In any case, starting from late 1909, Vitagraph films, like those of other American companies, slowly progressed from putting these dialogue titles before the scene in which they were spoken, to cutting them into the middle of the shot at the point at which they were understood to be actually spoken by the characters. This happened

Decorated intertitle in Daisies (1910)

The scene referred to in the intertitle in Daisies.

approximately between 1910 and 1913. By 1915 quite a number of American films had more of the narrative information conveyed by the image action in combination with dialogue titles than by narrative titles, but there were many exceptions to this, including the films of D.W. Griffith, not to mention European films, which were slow to catch up with this development, as they were with most others that had taken place in the United States just before World War I.

Although they were fairly typical of American companies in the way they handled this aspect of film form, Vitagraph did toy with a novel idea in the presentation of intertitles in 1910 and 1911. In 1910, perhaps in response to the new striving after "art" in film-making which had just begun, they made a few films which had special illustrated borders

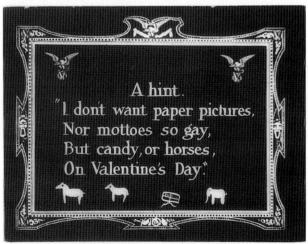

Intertitle with illustrations in Consuming Love: or St. Valentine's Day in Greenaway Land (1911)

round the intertitles. The most striking example in 1910 was *Daisies*, in which the whole plot turned on that flower, which was present in most of the film scenes in various forms. Here the intertitles had a border of daisies, instead of having the standard Vitagraph "picture frame" style decorative border. A few weeks before this the company presented *Hako's Sacrifice*, a Japanese subject, in which the intertitles had a border made of bamboo rods, though this plant played no part in the story. Another surviving example is *Auld Robin Grey* of a couple of months later, and it is quite likely that there were a few more Vitagraph films with illustrated title borders from this period.

In 1911, the Vitagraph film-makers made a small extra step forward, in *Consuming Love; or, St. Valentine's Day in Greenaway Land*, which told a story of school infant love and gingerbread hearts in slightly stylized settings reminiscent of the paintings by the famous children's book illustrator. (The costumes of the children followed the Kate Greenaway style closely, too.) In this case, the borders of the intertitles were not exactly the same throughout the film, but included toys and other things which changed in accordance with the course of the narrative. This was a remarkable anticipation of the vogue for illustrated intertitles which only started properly in American films in 1916, and lasted into the early 'twenties, but there are no other early examples of this feature among the surviving Vitagraph films. The most likely explanation for this was that by 1911 the larger part of Vitagraph's film sales were overseas, and the difficulty of reconstituting these illustrated intertitles for the title cards for every foreign language, which had to be remade at their Paris factory, was not considered worthwhile. This last point probably also explains why the idea was only taken up generally in American films in 1916, when it was clear that most of the foreign market was cut off by the Great War, and also why the practice died out again after the war.

The Vitagraph Angle

The most important influence of French film practice on Vitagraph films made from 1909 onwards was in the development of a certain standard kind of staging of the action with respect to the camera position. Ben Brewster has noted that for some years before this date it can be seen that many scenes in Pathé films were shot with the camera at waist height, whereas American films were usually shot with the camera at eye level, which was more convenient for the operator. In both cases, the lens axis was kept horizontal when shooting on studio sets, so that the vertical lines in the sets stayed parallel to the sides of the film frame and did not slant, as "correct" still photographic technique had long required. When the actors are distant from the camera, as was mostly the case for films made before 1908, the camera height makes no visible difference to the look of the image. But if the camera is close enough for the actors to fill most of height of the frame, and if they are also disposed in depth within the scene, the waist level camera position gives a very distinctive look to the image, with the actors in the foreground markedly overtopping the actors in the background. The key film that demonstrates this development is the famous *L'Assassinat du Duc de Guise* (Calmettes & Le Bargy, 1908), and Vitagraph signalled that they had taken note of it by giving two of their films made just after *L'Assassinat du Duc de Guise* had appeared in New York, namely *The Judgement of Solomon* and *Oliver Twist*, the extra descriptive subsidiary title "A Vitagraph High Art Film". *L'Assassinat du Duc de Guise* also introduced into films another stylistic component which was gradually taken over as part of the characteristic Vitagraph "look" from 1909 onwards. This involves allowing the actors in the foreground of a group to turn their backs to the camera if it is appropriate to the action of the scene, as with a group of people in a real scene caught unawares. Whereas in the vast majority of French and American films it was, and continued to be, the practice to keep the central foreground clear of actors, and also to allow any actors in the foreground to angle themselves at least side-on to the camera. The extreme case in the way actors were placed within the shot in films made up to 1914 was to allow them to play directly to the camera lens, and this can frequently be seen in

European dramas, though much less so in American films. (In comedies address to the camera has always been permitted, though here again, the Americans quickly dropped the practice of actually talking to it and the putative cinema audience, while the Europeans did not.) Amongst American film-makers, D.W. Griffith was notable for the way he persisted with a frontal organization of his stagings right through into the 'twenties, even when everyone else had followed the Vitagraph example.

The final component producing the distinctive appearance of Vitagraph films made after 1909 was what the film-makers there called the "nine foot line". This was a line, or in the case of studio scenes, a plank, laid down nine feet in front of the camera lens, and at right angles to the lens axis, and it represented the closest the actors were allowed to come forwards towards the camera. With the usual studio lens aperture setting of f5.6 to f8 a standard 50 mm. lens would give sharp focus from nine feet to about 50 feet if the focus was set at 15 feet. There are some Vitagraph films made in 1909 that begin to show the effects of this practice, such as *Romance of an Umbrella*, but the stagings in them do not take the actors quite as far forward as the nine foot line, though sometimes they get to within 11 feet of the camera. At this distance the bottom of the film frame cuts the actors off at the thighs, and the top of the frame is about a foot above their heads. (The exact height included within the frame for the silent aperture when a standard 50 mm. lens is used is 3 foot 9 inches at 10 feet, since of course the actors would not stand right on the nine-foot line, particularly when it was a plank of wood, and in the case of the usual European forward limit at 4 metres the height with the frame would be 5 foot 2 inches high at that distance.) Over the next few years more and more of the Vitagraph films show stagings that make use of this "nine foot line" set-up, but it is not until 1913 that one finds some shots that have the actors standing right on the nine foot line, at which distance they are cut off at the hips. Other American film producing companies quickly followed the Vitagraph example as far as closeness of camera was concerned when shooting standard scenes, though no other company made as much use of actors positioned with their backs to the camera. Despite the fact that this kind of natural staging with some of the actors having their backs to the camera had first appeared in a French film, French and other European film-makers proved unable to develop the idea, and they also kept their limit on actor closeness at 4 metres, though they did respond to the closer camera placement in Vitagraph films over the next couple of years after 1909 by sometimes moving the

The space behind, with extras dancing, revealed by this final camera position in a scene in The Inherited Taint (1911).

actors right up to the 4 metre line. When French films finally began to use a true Medium Shot or nine foot camera closeness in a few rare shots cut into the course of a more distant shot about 1913, they referred to this as the *"plan américain"*, and in the United States the distinction was made by the terms "French foreground" for the 4 metre line and "American foreground" for the effect of the full use of the nine foot line.

The Space Behind

Although the use of a room visible in the shot behind the main set was only a passing feature in *L'Assassinat du Duc de Guise*, so to speak, and in any case it was entered by a cut to the other camera position, this kind of stage setting, with a room or other space visible behind through an opening at the back of the main acting area, became fairly common in European films after 1909, but in them the space behind was never afterwards entered by a cut to the opposite direction. This kind of set design is to be found much more frequently in European films than in American films made before the First World War, and sometimes in them part of the main action of the scene takes place in this space. True to their status as a company which bridged the Atlantic, Vitagraph began to use this kind of set occasionally from 1911 onwards, but almost entirely for scenes at grand parties, of which they were quite fond. (Not very surprisingly, given J.S. Blackton's taste for social climbing in his private life.) However, in such cases,

the room visible behind was only used to contain extras dancing, or the like, and not to contain part of the main action. (This could really be considered to be an indoor variant of the Red Indians or fisher folk going about their colourful business behind the main action, which D.W. Griffith introduced into his outdoor subjects from 1909 onwards.) A particularly fine early Vitagraph example is in *The Inherited Taint* (1911), in which the camera steps back twice during the course of the scene as the actors move forwards, so revealing more and more depth in the set. During the war the simpler form of this sort of set design and staging for big party scenes spread to other American companies.

Vitagraph Acting

Another major feature of many Vitagraph films from 1909 onwards was the restrained naturalism of the acting, to an extent that *on the average* exceeded that in any other films of the same date, and this generalization certainly includes the work of D.W. Griffith, despite the claims later made on his behalf that he introduced restrained acting. It must be understood that in this and every other stylistic matter that I have been discussing, there is a certain amount of variation amongst Vitagraph films made in the same period, which is hardly surprising given that by 1910 the company already had seven different directors making films for it. It is possible that Charles Kent and Van Dyke Brooke were the directors most skilled at obtaining very restrained

An example of the "cinematographic angle" in A Friendly Marriage (1911).

and natural performances from the actors, but owing to uncertainty about who directed what at Vitagraph before 1911, I cannot be sure of this. Although most actors in the Vitagraph stock company were capable of very restrained acting, one can sometimes see quite a variation in their performances, presumably depending on who was in charge of the film. For instance, Maurice Costello, the first established male star of the company, had a tendency to exaggerated acting at climactic moments, and different directors restrained him to a greater or lesser extent, or sometimes not at all, as in *Through the Darkness* (1910), whereas the performances of Florence Turner, the other major early star of the company, were much more consistently part of the restrained house style. And some of the younger actresses such as Edith Storey and Lilian Walker managed to project emotions very strongly while making hardly any physical movement at all.

The exact origin of this interest in naturalism is at present obscure, owing to lack of information, but it is reasonable to think that it was introduced from the top of the company; by Blackton and/or Smith. In any case the company was capitalizing on this aspect of its production in its publicity by 1910, describing its films in its publicity magazine, *The Vitagraph Bulletin* (issue of 15 March) thus: "They are more than motion pictures, as you have noticed. They have the vital spark of life itself. The characters you see in Vitagraph dramas and comedies are not artificial and stagey. They act like real people doing the things that real people would do in the way that real people would do them." And in 1910 the Vitagraph actors were doing their acting like real

people in sets that were slightly more solid-looking and detailed than those of any other film company, as continued to be the case up to 1915. All this pursuit of naturalistic detail was not necessarily an advantage as far as the achievement of art was concerned, and many might find more exciting the world that D.W. Griffith put on film, which was much more made up from what was in his own head, even down to the details of the actor's performances, than from observation of the real world.

The Cinematographic Angle

Vitagraph also pioneered what Jean Mitry has called the "cinematographic angle" in his *Histoire du Cinéma*, although they did this earlier than the 1914 date which he gives for the introduction of this feature into the movies. By this term is meant those shots which are taken from such an angle that they give an image of the kind that was not to be found in still photography of the same date, and this basically results from shooting people from high or low angles. This is particularly striking if the shot concerned is not presented as the Point of View (POV) of an actor in the preceding or following shot, and one of the earliest examples is to be found in *Back to Nature* (1910). Although this film contains an example of a high angle POV shot, it also contains another separate high angle shot which is purely objective. Also into this category come such matter-of-fact silhouette shots as that in *A Friendly Marriage* (1911), though these were preceded by two occurrences of a more "artistic" use of skyline silhouettes in films by D.W. Griffith.

Lighting and Photography at Vitagraph

As far as photographic technique goes, the early Vitagraph films made before the opening of their first studio in late 1906 were shot under direct sunlight, with no use of diffusing screens to soften it, and no use of additional artificial light, as can be seen in the interior scenes of *The 100 to 1 Shot; or, A Run of Luck* (September 1906), and a number of other films made before this date. The new studio, which was of dimensions about 25 feet by 40 feet, had a roof and walls made of prismatic diffusing glass on two sides following what had become the standard pattern at Pathé and elsewhere. However, presumably because Smith and Blackton had not had a chance to study the few large-scale film studios already existing in France, their studio had a serious design flaw, in that it was crossed by large, thick horizontal beams spaced quite closely together. These were intended to act as supports for arc lights hanging over the set, but they were so thick and so low that under bright daylight, when the arcs were not needed, the light coming through the glass ceiling cast their visible shadows onto the set, as has been noted by Ben Brewster in his study of the early copyright fragments of Vitagraph films in the Library of Congress. In other studios, including the much larger one Vitagraph built around the beginning of 1910, this problem did not arise, as when overhead arcs were needed they were hung in on a movable light temporary beam of wood. The overhead arcs used were of the standard kind used for street lighting, which had the arc enclosed inside a hanging glass bell cover, and they shone their light equally in all downwards directions. They were fitted with improvised metal reflector sheets on one side of them to block off light heading horizontally back towards the camera, and seem to have only been used when the diffuse daylight through the studio ceiling and walls was weak, and needed boosting. For dates before 1912 they did not make much difference to the look of the lighting, and there is no discernible pattern as to which kind of scenes they were used on in general. For instance, these overhead arcs contribute a large part of the light to a number of varied scenes – a low dive, some factory interiors – in *The Mill Girl* (1907), though always without any attempt to simulate the effect of actual light in the real situations.

Another kind of arc floodlight was mounted on floorstands, and this had the arc in a metal box with the front open on the pattern of theatrical flood-lights. At Vitagraph these were used mostly for special effects at first, though at Pathé and Gaumont in France such lights were already being used by 1906 to produce a large part of the ordinary set

lighting on some occasions. To give an example of effect lighting at Vitagraph, *Foul Play* (1906) has the effect of light from a table lamp within shot simulated rather well by an arc floodlight just out of shot on the same side of the frame. This seems to have been an innovative idea in movie-making, and the Vitagraph cameramen returned to it from time to time, though not very frequently, and it spread to films made elsewhere after a few years. Not quite so novel was the use of a small arc light placed inside a domestic light, such as a table lamp, which formed part of the decor of the set. In *After Midnight* (1908), the dominant lighting of a night interior scene is provided by a small arc light concealed in a hanging lamp over a table, and throwing light onto the actors. In this and other similar lighting set-ups in *Cupid's Realm* and *For He's a Jolly Good Fellow*, which were also made early in 1908, there is always a much weaker general diffuse light over the scene, but this in no way detracts from the strikingly natural effect. Also, in *After Midnight*, one of the actors carries a hand lamp round the darkened set, lighting it up with the small arc concealed inside it, in a subtler repeat of a similar usage in *Falsely Accused*, a British film of 1905. Exactly who was responsible for introducing such lighting effects is not known, but it is possible that it was Smith and Blackton themselves, since they habitually operated the camera on the films they personally directed, at least up to 1908. The orgy of lighting effects tried out at Vitagraph in early 1908 also includes a studio scene in *"True Hearts are More Than Coronets"*, in which people stand at an open door lit from a constructed exterior scene beyond it by horizontal artificial light simulating the sunset. (For more details on these lighting effects see Ben Brewster's article.) Vitagraph films also used the standard effect of light from a fireplace, done by hiding an arc light inside it, after the model of Porter's *The Five Ages* (1905), but none of the early Vitagraph examples has the expressive force of the device as it was used in D.W. Griffith's *The Drunkard's Reformation* (1909). However, Vitagraph may well have been the first to give a flicker to the arc light to better simulate the effect of flames, as they did in *Washington Under the American Flag* (1909).

In *Washington Under the British Flag*, which was made, like the previous film, in the middle of 1909, and released on June 27, another important lighting innovation appears for what seems to be the first time. This is the use on exterior scenes of reflectors to bounce the sunlight back onto the front of the actors when it is actually shining directly onto their backs when seen from the camera direction, or "backlighting with reflector fill", as it has come to be known. In this film, the scenes in question were shot

Fill light reflected up onto the actors faces from a white surface at their feet in Washington under the British Flag (1909).

Extra fill light put onto the figures from an arc flood-light out of shot to the right in an exterior scene in Betty's Choice (1909).

near noon, with the sun almost directly overhead, and only slightly behind the actors, but the effect is the same as when the technique became standard in outdoor filming in American films a year or so later, when such scenes were usually taken with the sun somewhat lower down from the zenith. (The first D.W. Griffith film in which there is any possible backlighting is *The Message*, which was shot after the Vitagraph film and released a month later.) This fact appears to substantiate the later claims by Norma Talmadge and Marian Blackton on J.S. Blackton's behalf that he invented backlighting. However, as far as can be told from the surviving films, Vitagraph did not adapt true backlighting to interior studio scenes, but instead took up a compromise form a couple of years later in 1912. This can best be described as "three-quarter back lighting", and involved putting arc floodlights on floor stands out to one side of the frame and shining onto the backs of the actors from one side, as in *Coronets and Hearts* (1912). In 1913 there begin to be films in which a weak kind of backlighting was produced by a combination of the reduction of the amount of diffuse daylight light falling on the set, together with a move to hanging some of the overhead arclights at the back of the set, rather than in front of the actors, as had been usual up to then.

However, as far as the lighting of exterior scenes was concerned, Vitagraph seem to have introduced another even more advanced technique in 1909. In *Betty's Choice*, a garden scene shot under dullish daylight has the light on the figures boosted and sharpened by the light from an arc floodlight just out of shot.

These sorts of specialized lighting were not used

regularly on most films at Vitagraph prior to 1915, and usually only in one scene in the small number of films in which they *were* used, and this was just as true for other film companies when they also took up these techniques. As far as the further develop-ment of the *expressive* use of lighting effects was concerned, Vitagraph made a few early contributions in 1909. In *The Life Drama of Napoleon Bonaparte and the Empress Josephine*, Napoleon is singled out by rather stronger lighting in his area of the scene during the proceedings of his divorce from Josephine. This film was released on 6 April 1909, on which date Griffith's *A Baby's Shoe* was being shot, which is the first of his films to contain a similar device of lighting which isolates the principal in a scene. Admittedly the Griffith film develops the idea further, in that the area lighting is more strongly distinguished, and is produced by lowering the lighting on the surrounding area during the course of the scene. *Napoleon Bonaparte and the Empress Joesphine* also uses an incomplete fade-out on the scene of Napoleon's leave-taking from Josephine, four months before the first use by Griffith of the fade-out in his *Fools of Fate*. But all this was exceptional, and even in 1910, in Vitagraph's *Auld Lang Syne*, which has two carefully arranged low-key scenes showing two different totally dark cottage rooms, each lit only by the light from a fire and from a small window, and which are much better handled than anything Billy Bitzer ever did, the lighting has no expressive function in the narrative, and must be taken as purely decorative or naturalistic. However by 1912 there was finally a definite move towards a more expressive use of lighting effects in Vitagraph films, as in *Conscience; or, the Chamber of Horrors*, where the eponymous

Low key scene in Auld Lang Syne (1911)*, lit solely by articial firelight at the rear, and window light in the foreground.*

Scene in Conscience; or, The Chamber of Horrors (1912)*, lit by arc floodlights in the alcoves, plus a weaker one from the left on the foreground figure.*

scene is mostly dark, and lit almost entirely by lights concealed in the deep alcoves around its edges, with just a tiny bit of fill light on the guilty party who is about to be terrified to death.

Other areas of lighting in which the Vitagraph cameramen led the way were in location filming with available light, beginning with interiors in a real police station in *Clancy* (1910), and also in *The Telephone* in the same year, in which one scene takes place in a large New York telephone exchange. They also took shots inside actual railway carriages on the move, as in *Coronets and Hearts* (1912), and a number of other films, but this was less exceptional, as other American and European companies did this too by this date. However, the Vitagraph cameramen seem to have had the edge when it came to putting film lights into real locations which were too dark for filming with the available light, and a prime instance of this is again *Coronets and Hearts*, though this is not the only example from Vitagraph. In *Coronets and Hearts* there are three scenes shot in a real bank, two of which are down in the bank vault, and in these the action is entirely lit by sets of arc floodlights specially brought in. I have seen nothing like this anywhere else amongst about a couple of thousand films made between 1906 and 1914. As can be seen from looking at a large number of Vitagraph films, (and also those from other American studios), the general movement in set lighting towards 1912 was that the contribution of the diffused daylight through the studio walls was slightly reduced, and the contribution of arc floodlights on floorstands increased. Since the light from overhead lamps when mingled with the overhead diffuse daylight did not

alter its general effect very much, the increasing importance of the horizontal light from the arc floodlights on floor stands made a real change to the look of the lighting, moving it towards the standard form it achieved in the early 'twenties. The intensity of the light from floodlights on floorstands fell off rapidly from the foreground to the background, so producing a certain amount of separation of the brighter figures of the actors from the more dimly lit background scenery, even without backlighting. Also the modelling of the figures became much sharper as a result of these two new groups of very directional light sources, with one group on either side of the actors, and shining onto them from slightly to the front.

Scene Dissection

Although most American film-makers had experimented with the use of close shots of people cut into the middle of a scene before 1906, they seem to have then turned against using this as a standard and common practice, and this was just as true of the people at Vitagraph. So around 1908, and for three years after that, the film-makers there almost entirely restricted their use of close shots cut into the middle of a scene to shots of objects which had to be shown clearly because they were essential to the plot. In other words, to what would now be called "insert shots", though at the time the word "insert" was used to describe not just shots of objects, but every sort of interruption of a continuous script scene, including close shots of people and also intertitles. But there are a few exceptions to this

Low angle shot of a ship on location in Back to Nature; or, The Best Man Wins (1910)

High angle Point of View shot in Back to Nature; or, The Best Man Wins (1910). *A rain effect has been scratched directly onto the negative, and a lightning flash painted on as well in this frame.*

generalization in Vitagraph films, such as *Solomon's Judgement* and *The Life Drama of Napoleon Bonaparte* made in the earlier part of 1909, which contain cuts straight down the lens axis from Long Shot to Full Shot or Medium Long Shot. Even after 1911, when a few Vitagraph directors began to occasionally use cuts to different camera angles within a scene, the general house style largely avoided this up to 1915, by which time cutting within a scene was common practice at other American film companies. A striking exception to these generalizations was *Over the Chafing Dish*, made by Larry Trimble in 1911. This film, which apparently no longer exists, has been described independently by two people present at the time as being made up entirely of close shots of hands and feet, which nevertheless contrived to tell a "boy meets girl" story, with the main participants only fully revealed in the final shot of the film.

Point of View Shots

Although very infrequent, the most usual way of breaking a scene down into more than one shot at Vitagraph was the use of the "Point of View" (POV) shot, in which there is a cut to a shot taken with the camera positioned at a point roughly in the direction of the sight of one of the characters in the scene. In the early years this was usually only done when the character was looking at something through a telescope or binoculars, as in *The Hundred to One Shot* (1906), and then the character's view was shown surrounded with a black vignette mask cut out to simulate the actual appearance of things seen through such a device, but after a few more years

there come to be rare appearances of unvignetted POV shots in films to represent the unaided vision of a character in the film. A particularly interesting case in a Vitagraph film is in *C.Q.D.; or, Saved by Wireless* (1909), in which a title describing the pleasure that the crew of the damaged ship involved in the collision have in reaching New York harbour is followed by a series of three shots taken forwards from the bow of an unseen ship sailing into the harbour. This is followed directly by a Long Shot of sailors on the deck of the actual ship looking out to one side of the frame and pointing, which implies, not entirely convincingly, that the previous shots were their Point of View. This kind of "revealed" POV structure, in which the shot of the looker does not precede the POV shot, but only comes after it, was extremely rare in the beginning, and has remained so to this day, for obvious reasons. The more conventional presentation of the Point of View shot, as the unvignetted view seen by one of the characters we have seen looking at something in the previous shot, becomes rather more frequent, though still rare, from 1910 onwards. An example of this is *Back to Nature*, in which we see a Long Shot of people looking down over the rail of a ship taken from below, followed by a shot of the lifeboat they are looking at taken from their position. However, the Vitagraph film-makers continued to be a little uneasy with the device, as a true POV shot is introduced by an explanatory intertitle, "What they saw in the house across the court" in Larry Trimble's *Jean and the Waif*, made at the end of 1910. However, a few months later, Trimble made *Jean Rescues*, which has POV shots introduced at an appropriate point

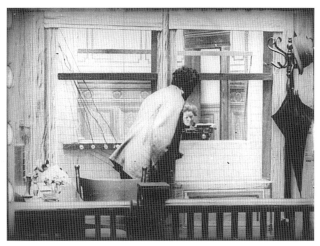

"Reverse scene" setup in a studio scene in Romance of an Umbrella (1909). *The actress is about four metres from the camera.*

The opposite angle from the previous frame across the intervening street on the set of Romance of an Umbrella.

without explanation. After this, unvignetted POV shots continued to occur occasionally in Vitagraph films, in fact in five more titles released in 1911 among 26 surviving prints, as compared with only two films from the same year among 68 prints from other American companies that I have so far seen. These latter are *The Corporation and the Ranch Girl* from Essanay, and Edison's *The Switchman's Tower* of 4 August 1911, which is still using a "What he saw" intertitle to explain the nature of the following POV shot.

It is not until 1912 that such shots come to be used more freely, and more importantly, always used at the point in the narrative that will have the maximum dramatic impact. Such films are still not very frequent, but William V. Ranous' *Poet and Peasant* (1912) is one striking example. Here the story is about a country hunchback who secretly loves a beautiful girl, and the shots in question are cut in from his POV when he sees the girl with a visitor from the city with whom she has fallen in love.

Also in 1912, the earlier way of using POV shots with a binocular mask could still be exploited at length in *The Victoria Cross*, in which a nurse standing on the side lines sees the entire charge of the Light Brigade at Balaclava exclusively through cuts to a long series of POV shots with binocular masking. In this particular film, the shot of the watcher was taken from the front, instead of from the more usual side or back, as occurs in *Jean Rescues* (1911), *Cardinal Wolsey* (1912). But we are now at the point where the emerging use of the Point of View shot as a standard constructional device (outside the theatrical situation) blended with the new reverse angle idea, so that the shots of watcher and their Point of

View could also form a angle -- reverse angle pair of shots from closer in. A much more polished example of the combination of the two techniques occurs in *Out of the Shadows*, made by Rollin S. Sturgeon late in 1912. In this film the watcher is shown from the front looking out past the camera in a series of shots which cut in closer to her as she becomes more disturbed by what she is watching unobserved. This use of cutting to a closer shot to increase the intensity of emotional expression in a scene, rather than just to show something more clearly, dates back to about 1904, and though early examples are extremely rare, one finds a good example in *The Physician of the Castle* (1908). After this, D.W. Griffith was the person who used the device most effectively, though still quite infrequently before 1910. However, because of his inability to handle the general form of reverse-angle cutting outside a theatrical audience situation, he was not able to develop the device further, as was done by other film-makers in films such as *Out of the Shadows*.

Reverse Scenes and Reverse Angles

To cover the development of reverse angle cutting properly, I have to return to the crucial case of *L'Assassinat du Duc de Guise* yet again. For this film contains yet another novel feature that proved to be much more significant for American than for European film-making. This is in the final pair of shots in the sequence showing the Duke's progress through various antechambers in the Royal palace to a waiting room crowded with conspirators. In the first of these two shots the Duke is seen walking away from the camera up to an open doorway

First of a pair of reverse angle Point of View shots in Out of the Shadows *(1912).*

through which can be seen the final room and some of the conspirators in it, and then there is a cut to a continuation of the action as he walks through the doorway, which is shot from the opposite direction, so that the conspirators are now in the foreground and the doorway and the room the Duke is leaving is in the background. To obtain these two shots, both sets had to be specially constructed with movable back walls to enable the camera to get far enough back to cover the figures seen in each in the foreground in Full Shot. This is something no film-makers had thought worth the bother of doing before this date. Although shots taken from opposite directions to a scene had been put together well before this date, as far as I know this very infrequent practice had always been in scenes shot outdoors on real locations, as in one of the earliest examples, *The Runaway Match* (Alf Collins, 1903), where the use of the device created no set-building problems. After *L'Assassinat du Duc de Guise* had appeared, Vitagraph used the idea from time to time, as in *Romance of an Umbrella* (1909) and *Uncle Tom's Cabin* (1910), and so did a few other people, and by 1912 the device was commonly referred to as a "reverse scene" in the United States. By late 1910 the reverse scene had begun to move outdoors, in the Yankee company's *The Monogrammed Cigarette*. However, in all these cases, the camera is well back from the actors, who are in Medium Long Shot at the closest, at about 12 feet distance.

In modern terms, this sort of cut to an opposite direction at a fair distance from the actors is only one variety of "reverse angle", and the least common at that, whereas the most common nowadays is a cut from a fairly frontal close shot of a person to a similar shot in roughly the opposite direction of the other person with whom they are interacting. This kind of cutting seems to have been developed in outdoor filming in California in 1911, though definitely not by D.W. Griffith, and the classic surviving early example of this is in *The Loafer*. This film was made by Essanay at the end of 1911, and contains a series of alternating Medium Shots of two men exchanging angry words, which are taken from almost opposite directions just off their eyeline. The available evidence now suggests that watcher-Point of View shot pairs which also happened to be reverse angles provide part of the developmental link, for there are some films amongst surviving copies from 1911 and 1912 which show this construction. As far as Vitagraph was concerned, it seems that Rollin S. Sturgeon, who directed the films made by their California company, was the director who took up the usage first. Most of the examples in his films made in the latter part of 1912 are of POV -- reverse angle pairs of shots, with the camera moderately distant from the watcher and what he or she sees, but in *Out of the Shadows*, which was released on 7 November of that year, there are two scenes in which reverse angle cutting is extensively used. One has already been mentioned in connection with Point of View shots, but in the second one, which occurs earlier in the actual film, we are shown a stranger coming to a garden gate in a shot taken

The reverse angle to the previous shot in Out of the Shadows. *This is a Medium Shot with the actress at the nine foot line.*

from outside the garden. He notices a young woman in the garden, and then the next shot is of the man from the opposite angle inside the garden shooting towards the garden gate, followed by a close shot of the young woman looking at him, taken from the opposite direction to that. Neither of this last pair of set-ups, which are immediately repeated, is a POV shot, as both participants are close enough to the camera to be seen to be looking slightly off the lens axis. Unlike *The Loafer*, the two participants exchange looks rather than words, but this is still the second earliest known instance of the most common modern form of this technique.

Rollin Sturgeon seems not to have developed the use of reverse angle cutting further, and the only Vitagraph film-maker who quickly picked up on its possibilities was Ralph Ince, who had recently been promoted from actor to director. Other Vitagraph directors, like all other film-makers for a couple of years, had difficulty in fully taking up the use of reverse angle cuts, *unless* they were between a set of watcher--POV shots as well. As late as 1915, the only non-POV reverse angle cuts in surviving Vitagraph films by directors other than Ralph Ince is in C. Jay William's *She Took a Chance*, and here the device is rather clumsily used. Indeed, cutting within a scene of any kind at all was still not that frequent in Vitagraph films at this date, and most of those few cuts which were used were still mostly straight down the lens axis to a closer or more distant shot, or alternatively were cuts to a Point of View shot.

Needless to say, all this was just as true of the films produced at other American companies.

Continuity Cutting

Besides reverse angle cutting, the development of other major formal features of what I dubbed "mainstream continuity cinema" in 1976 (or "classical cinema" if you prefer that rather vaguer designation), such as using a "cut on action" to smooth over the move to another angle on a scene, can also be traced through the Vitagraph films. The general tendency, at Vitagraph as elsewhere, was to make the cut to another angle on a static position of the actors, and this continued to be the case till about 1914, but as early as 1910 one can find examples of the intentional use of the cut on action. One such is in *The Telephone*, in which a shot of a woman falling away from a window back into the room inside, which was taken from outside the house on a location exterior, cuts to the same action filmed from inside the room on a studio set, the cut matching the action perfectly to the frame, and the actress's restaged movements being identical. Although rare, what has to be a similarly conscious use of this device by directors and editors can also be seen in a few other later Vitagraph films such as *Billy's Burglar* (1912). Small framing pans and tilts of the camera to keep the actors well placed in the frame when they made small changes in position are also to be found in Vitagraph films with increasing frequency after 1910, and together with the features already mentioned, such as the use of dialogue titles, the "Vitagraph angle", etc., the ground was prepared in 1912 for someone at Vitagraph to work at putting all this together in the final polished form that most people unthinkingly accept as the normal way films are constructed. This someone turned out to be Ralph Ince, and he did it in the films he made between 1912 and 1916.

Also as it turned out, the management of Vitagraph appreciated what they had got in Ralph Ince, but they were not able to take full advantage of it, for like the other biggest film companies elsewhere in the world, particularly Nordisk and Pathé, the Vitagraph company was placed in serious financial difficulties by being cut off from most of their foreign markets by the beginning of World War I. This meant that, unlike the other American companies, which did not yet depend on the foreign market, their productions were now too expensive to get their money back in the United States alone. The management's response was a drastic cut-back in 1916, with the dismissal of a large part of the established production teams. They kept Ralph Ince, and gave him all the facilities he might need, but within the next year he left, along with some of the other major talents they had retained, and after that nothing was ever the same again, even though the company continued to function, sometimes quite profitably, until 1924.

SOURCES

This article is based on the study of about 250 viewing copies of Vitagraph films, mostly in the National Film Archive, London, but also elsewhere, including the Library of Congress, Washington, The Australian National Archive, Canberra, and The Cinema Museum, London, and the staffs at all these institutions deserve my special thanks for their help. Ben Brewster generously let me see his frame enlargements from the pre-1910 Vitagraph fragments in the Library of Congress, and Ben and I shared viewings and discussions on a number of occasions at the National Film Archive, with his contributions acknowledged above in the text, though not the occasions when he corrected my careless slips. As far as written sources go prior to the Pordenone "Giornate" of 1987, the starting point for orientation and basic information about the Vitagraph organization has to be Anthony Slide's *The Big V* (Scarecrow Press, 1976), and Marion Blackton Trimble's *J. Stuart Blackton* (Scarecrow Press, 1985), plus Charles Musser's thorough 1980 study of Vitagraph during the years 1894 to 1902, which is reprinted in *Film Before Griffith*, edited by John Fell for The University of California Press (1983). Although nearly every event before 1914 mentioned in A.E. Smith's autobiography, *Two Reels and a Crank* (Doubleday, 1952), even those not directly connected with Vitagraph, is given a date two or three years before it actually happened, this book contains much useful information if used with due care, knowledge, and cross-checking. As well as the above, I have also consulted the leading film trade paper of the time, *The Moving Picture World*, and the locally available issues of *Vitagraph Life Portrayals*.

The placement of Vitagraph films within the general stylistic background of the period up to 1916 can be studied further in my *Film Style and Technology: History and Analysis* (Starword, 1992). More background on staging in depth in European and American cinema before 1915 can be found in Ben Brewster's *La mise en scène en profondeur dans les films français de 1900 à 1914* in *Les premiers ans du cinéma français* published by L'Institut Jean Vigo (1985). This is now available in English in *Early Cinema: Space - Frame - Narrative*, edited by Thomas Elsaesser, and published by the BFI in 1990.

The journal this article was published in used Melior for the body text, and I have reproduced this here, but I have replaced the Melior italic by Palatino italic, just as I did in the first edition of *Film Style and Technology*, for old time's sake. However, you can see Melior italic in the captions for the illustrations here.

The other article relating to Vitagraph films that I mentioned, about Ralph Ince, was published in English in *Sight & Sound*, v 57 n 4 1988. Penelope Houston changed my original title, which ruined my attempt at a play on words, so here I have restored it. In the 'eighties *Sight & Sound* had a couple of design revamps, and at this date it was using ITC Century for body text, which is what you see here in the following pages.

WAS RALPH INCE MINOR?

Well, if one wants to be English Public School about it, it was really Thomas who was Ince Minor, whereas John was Ince Major, and Ralph was Ince Minimus, but in the world of movies the arrangement was somewhat different. Now Jean Mitry knew that there was more than one Ince brother, as you can see in his *Histoire du Cinéma*, and so does Ephraim Katz, if you look up his *Film Encyclopaedia*, and naturally Anthony Slide, author of the first book on the Vitagraph company, does too, but most people interested in film history have still to recognize the existence, let alone the importance, of Ralph Ince, the first master of mainstream continuity cinema, or "classical cinema", or whatever one wants to call the

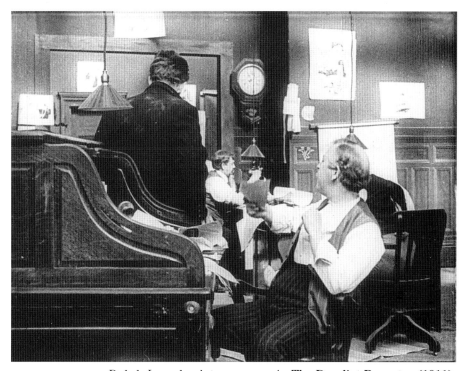

Ralph Ince, back to camera, in The Derelict Reporter (1911).

standard form of cinema which everyone accepts as normal without thinking about it. Actually, when one looks closely at the workings of the highly organized Vitagraph studio before 1914, the largest in America, most of the usual claims made for the famous Thomas Ince, as being the man who created the American system of studio production, begin to seem feeble. They just boil down to no more than that he insisted on his directors sticking to the shooting script, and that he was the first studio head with such a talent for self-publicity that he succeeded in taking all the credit for his studio's products. Not a lot to boast about.

Briefly, there were three Ince brothers, the sons of a pair of American travelling actors of no particular importance, and as was fairly inevitable in that milieu at the turn of the century, their children too acted from their early years, also without making any great mark on the theatrical scene. Ralph was the youngest, born in 1887, and after several not very successful years in the theatre, he became a commercial artist. He then joined Vitagraph in 1907, before his elder brothers had had anything to do with the cinema. He apparently started at the bottom of the organization acting as a prop boy, amongst other jobs. Taking account of the way a large

studio of those days was organized, his job was in part equivalent to being a Second Assistant Director on a feature film nowadays. From this position he progressed in the next couple of years to appearing in small parts in Vitagraph movies, so small in fact that even if you know what he looked like it is hard to detect him. For instance, in *C.Q.D.; or, Saved by Wireless* (1909), he is one of two men who are called in to hear the news of the distress signal from the maritime accident, but he wears a hat pulled down over his eyes, is on screen for such a brief time, and keeps moving so fast, that even his mother would have difficulty in recognizing him. And he is there somewhere in the background under costumes, whiskers, and whatever in about a hundred Vitagraph films before he pulled himself out of the ruck, possibly by the classic move of writing a story for the studio that was designed to feature himself in a leading part. Certainly in the surviving films from Vitagraph, the first one that features Ralph Ince in a leading part without whiskers, etc. is *The Derelict Reporter* (1911), and his role in this seems to present his favourite self-image as a demoralized, defeated drunkard at the end of his tether, who pulls himself together when the crucial testing moment comes, and then saves the day. There are two variants to this role, in one of which our anti-hero survives and gets the girl, as in *The Derelict Reporter*, and in the other he dies nobly at the end, as in *His Last Fight* of 1913, which Ralph Ince directed as well as playing the leading role. In this film especially, the image of Humphrey Bogart springs to mind, particularly since there was some physical resemblance between the two men. However, Bogart was not the only person who made a career out of this sort of role, for before him Hans Albers became a star playing similar parts from *F.P.1 antwortet nicht* (1932) onwards, and no doubt the original idea stems from somewhere in the mists of nineteenth century drama. In the Ralph Ince version a part of the characterization involves playing the scene where he is really right at the emotional bottom with his back to the camera, which is the kind of thing that Emil Jannings became famous for in the 'twenties, but this approach was less outstanding at Vitagraph, given the form of staging with actors playing with their backs to the camera that became standard there from 1910 onwards.

After *The Derelict Reporter*, Ralph Ince began the series of Abraham Lincoln impersonations for which he gained most public renown, starting with *The Battle Hymn of the Republic* in 1911. (Vitagraph had already picturized George Washington, so they just had to do Lincoln too.) Then in the middle of 1912 he was given a chance to direct, and here it is just possible that the fact that his elder brother Thomas was beginning to make a name for himself at other minor studios as a director and producer helped to turn the trick for Ralph, even though there was no direct connection between their careers.

The earliest extant picture which it is likely that Ralph Ince directed is *A Double Danger*, and this is what the anonymous *Moving Picture World* reviewer said about it:

'One sees, before the picture is finished, why it was called "Double Danger"; but the two sides of the situation are not woven together in a very dramatic way. A little crippled girl is being operated on at home. Her father, who is in charge of an express car and is carrying a very large invoice of money, is fighting a convict at the same time. This half of the picture is the only truly dramatic side. All that is dramatic on the other side is expressed by the mother; but the complex emotions in the mother that, if means had been found to make them very plain, would have united the two parts into one whole, were not clear enough. It would be very difficult to make them clear. Also the matter of fact way in which the father responded to the call to duty and left the wife and child hampered the real meaning of the picture. Perhaps, if more time had been given to this scene, it would have been a stronger production. But there is good material in it, and it will give good entertainment.'

(7 Sept. 1912. Vol. 13, No.10.)

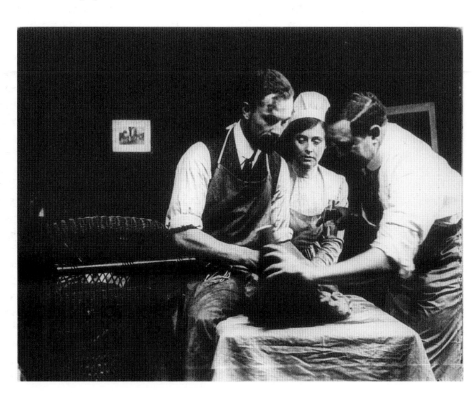

Ralph Ince on the left in A Double Danger (1912).

In my opinion this review is quite just in its estimate of this film, and quite penetrating about its weaknesses. *A Double Danger* is quite clearly an ambitious attempt to realise a Griffith-type arrangement of three strands of parallel action, but the construction is rather contrived, since, as the review notes, it was not very natural in 1912 America that the father would *have* to go to work while his child was operated on (on the living room table!) by a "famous European surgeon" (Ralph Ince in a chin beard). The third strand of the parallel action is created, again in a rather forced way, by having the mother confined to the kitchen next to the living room during the operation, listening to its progress through the door, and registering anguish the while. The cross-cutting between the strands of action is not as rapid as it would be in a comparable Griffith film of the same date, but by Vitagraph standards it is quite striking. The review does not mention some of the more technical features of the film, which include a clever transition from the interior of a real guard's van of a train shot with available light on location, to closer shots of its interior done on a good studio set, and also cuts to closer shots with angle change at two other points in the film. The second of these, in the express car (i.e. guard's van) is not really necessary, since the usual Vitagraph "nine foot line" staging makes everything clearly visible already, but seems to be done purely for its own sake. The way in which the guard nails the re-captured convict up in the box in which he was hiding, and addresses it to San Quentin prison, where it duly arrives, suggests the same sense of humour displayed in other Ralph Ince films.

Ralph Ince was successful enough with his first films to be allowed to direct one of the three-reel features which Vitagraph was starting to produce fairly regularly in 1912. This was *The Mills of the Gods*, released on the 4th. of November, and it was this film which really drew attention to his talent as a director. At the beginning of 1913, amongst many other films now lost, Ralph Ince made another larger-scale feature film, which *has* survived, the two reel *Strength of Men*, based on one of James Oliver Curwood's stories of the rugged north, where Men are Men. Apart from saving me having to tell the story, the *Moving Picture World* review is worth quoting as a demonstration of the extent to which the best American film criticism had progressed by this date, with acute attention to the technical side of film-making, as well as dealing accurately with more general features of the film and with its aesthetic value. On stylistic and other grounds I would guess that it was written by George Blaisdell, the most capable and perceptive staff writer of the journal.

'A two-reel feature subject that will probably stir enthusiasm. It is a picture of Alaska and deals with two men and a girl. The tale is cleverly introduced and leads up to a race between the two men for a rich gold claim. This is a long gruelling contest in which the two, each in their canoes and each with an Indian helper, follow a rough line down a torrent half blocked by huge bowlders, and through a wild pine forest. To complicate matters the forest gets on fire, and this is used to bring out

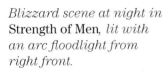
Blizzard scene at night in **Strength of Men**, *lit with an arc floodlight from right front.*

A low angle shot in
Strength of Men.

the human quality of the men, for it turns out that neither can save himself without the other's help. The picture is full of elemental vigor, and then has this human ending. There is a marked freshness in it, and in the production of this the photography and the angle at which the scenes are taken play a very important part. All the camera work deserves high praise. Those blizzard scenes are unusual, and the water and the water and the fire views are as good. The acting holds all through, and Miss Story (the girl) shows especially clear insight in one scene -- that in which the first man comes back and finds her in her father's cabin with the stranger she doesn't really love. It's a big picture, a true feature.'

(5 April 1913; Vol.16, No.1)

The key word here is "vigor", for Ralph Ince's films tend to have more of it than the rest of the Vitagraph productions, and that quality is also evident in the scene of Ralph Ince directing a film scene which is shown in the 1914 *How Cissy Made Good*, a Vitagraph comedy which features a tour of the studio, and shows most of the Vitagraph directors at work. In *Strength of Men* the real sense of scale is achieved, despite the small cast of actors, purely by camera placement in suitable locations. In the core of this film, which is the race between the two miners to the disputed claim, the shots of the canoes shooting the rapids are topped by

further shots of the canoes taken from a distant high angle from up on the mountain side, with giant burning pine trees falling between them and the camera. Then on to the big fight, with two bare-chested muscular men slugging it out amongst the smoke and flames from the burning trees. The reviewer speaks of the camera angles (for the first time in any review I have read), and besides the high angle shots I have just mentioned, earlier in the film the protagonists are shot from low angles close in at Medium Shot, and framed so that they reach to the same height as the mountains and tall trees behind them. Big Mountains, Big Trees, Big Men. The earlier Griffith films which introduced the use of distant views of large-scale scenery only inserted these as picturesque punctuation and decoration, whereas in *Strength of Men* the giant landscape is much more part of the action, in the way that was to become the ideal in later film-making. The film opens, at any rate in the surviving print presently available, with a striking night scene, also mentioned in the review, in which a man is struggling through a blizzard up to a log cabin. This scene is actually shot at night, and the man is picked out in the foreground against the blackness by the light from an arc lamp, with the lighted window of the cabin showing in the distance. As he comes up to the cabin and its window there is a cut to a closer shot, and he is picked out again by a little well-judged fill-light. There just isn't anything else comparable to this film in all these respects, which had been made up to the beginning of 1913.

In between making multi-reel features, Ralph Ince continued to knock out many one-reelers, and even split-reel comedies, like *Two is Company, Three is a Crowd*, also made earlier in 1913. It is a lively piece of work, though without any great distinction, but it does contain a demonstration in the last scene that Ince was still working at perfecting the technique of cutting to different angles within a scene, at a date when this was still very rare. The film is concerned with trickery amongst the male office staff about who should get to take the office typist to the theatre, and the object of their desire is played by Anita Stewart, who was a rising new star at Vitagraph. She was the sister of Lucille Lee Stewart, another Vitagraph actress whom Ralph Ince had earlier married, and after he started directing in the middle of 1912, he introduced Anita into the company, and thereafter directed all her films up to 1916. As well as being a very beautiful woman, she proved under Ralph Ince's direction to have a personality that came across strongly in films, and a fairly wide acting range as well, playing all the way from society women to country girls, and being particularly adept at comedy.

During his first year directing, Ralph Ince quickly absorbed all the latest technical developments in film construction, like the use of high and low camera angles just mentioned, which was just one part of the newly emerging practice of breaking a scene down into a greater number of shots taken from different angles, and even more importantly, the specific device of reverse-angle cutting. By the end of 1913, Ralph Ince had pushed reverse-angle cutting further than anyone else had up to this point. *His Last Fight*, released in November 1913, contains 75 shots altogether within its total length of 731 feet, which is indicative of the way he and other American directors were following the speed-up in cutting rate led by D.W. Griffith, and of those 74 cuts, no less than 25 were from one angle on a scene to the reverse angle. But this latter feature was something that one definitely did *not* find in Griffith's films, except in the very rare scene showing theatre and audience, when in any case he took the shots from a greater distance. In *His Last Fight* the interchange of looks and words are covered by reverse angle shots taken at the nine foot line, and closer, and Ince also uses the technique of cutting in closest at the emotional peak of the scene. All this takes place in the long climactic scene on the deck of a schooner, which of course as an exterior scene makes the reverse angle cutting easier to use, but no-one else did anything like it at this date in any film I have been able to find, and that includes the films made at his brother Thomas Ince's company.

At the beginning of 1914 Ralph Ince made the first of the five-reel features released by Vitagraph, *A Million*

Bid, and this film was used for the opening season of a large Broadway theatre which the company had bought and renamed the Vitagraph Theatre. The more or less accurate details of this event can be read in Albert Smith's memoirs (pages 253 to 258), but the film itself, which was very well received at the time, is now lost. In fact the only Ralph Ince film available from about a dozen he made in 1914 is the one reel *Midst Woodland Shadows*, released on the 12th. of October. This shows no technical advance on the earlier films I have mentioned, for although smoothly cut together with suitable use of Point of View shots, it does not otherwise use cutting within scenes. (This phenomenon, in which a director who has mastered new technical means does not always exploit them in all his films, is commonly to be found elsewhere amongst the film-makers of the first couple of decades of the cinema, however puzzling it may now appear.) But when we move on to the surviving films he made in 1915, it is apparent that Ralph Ince must have been doing further work on his technique throughout 1914.

To start at the beginning of the year, *The Right Girl(?)*, which was released on January 20th. 1915, now has all the basic features of mainstream continuity cinema in place and working properly. It has many reverse-angle cuts within scenes, and indeed the main visual joke at the end of the film depends for its existence on reverse-angle cutting. *The Right Girl* is an example of domestic comedy, which at this date was just reaching a degree of sophistication that we would nowadays accept as normal, and it begins in the way it is going to go on, with an introductory Medium Close Up of the backs of the heads of a young couple with their arms around each other's shoulders. Then there is a cut to the opposite angle to reveal "Mr. and Mrs. Newly-Wed" at the breakfast table, as the title puts it, and also to reveal that they are played by Anita Stewart and Earle Williams, the permanent centre of the Ralph Ince team. (Starting a scene on a close shot, and then cutting back to reveal the whole of the setting, rather than doing it in the reverse order, was a very new idea in 1915, and although Ralph Ince did not necessarily invent it, he was certainly already doing it well.) The reluctant farewell and parting on the front steps of the Newly-Weds as he departs for the office is filmed with a series reverse-angle cuts with perfect position and action matching that seems a conscious demonstration of mastery of the technique, for they are not strictly necessary to the staging. Here as elsewhere in this film, small and smooth framing tilts and pans are used by the cameraman to keep the actors well framed as they move about; a technique that had been developing for some years at Vitagraph, but which was still not common at this date, and indeed did not become standard till the late 'twenties. The very great

Repeated reverse angle cuts in The Right Girl(?) —

— as the "Newly-Weds" take a protracted farewell.

emphasis on close shooting in this film, which makes framing pans desirable, was yet another feature that was quite exceptional, and helps to make it look very modern. As does the fact that nearly all the intertitles are dialogue titles, and they are all cut in at the moment the character starts to speak the words they record, and then back to him or her when they are just finishing the line. The first encounter of Mrs. Newly-Wed with the bachelor looking for the "right girl" takes place in a street outside a surgical goods store, and this looks like another piece of sly humour from Ralph Ince, at any rate to older people who remember which piece of equipment of interest to bachelors-about-town could only be bought in a surgical goods shop, once upon a time.

Some White Hope(?), released a month later, continues the Ince in-joke tradition with a moment when the principal character, starting to undress for bed, looks towards the camera as though suddenly recognizing its presence. He then walks up towards it and pulls down a blind in front of it, as though the camera were peering through a window, which we do not see, into the room. The blind is only lifted when he has finished changing into his nightshirt, and then the comedy proceeds, as it had started, in the standard American way, with no further acknowledgement of the existence of the camera. The story of the film revolves round the comic potential of hypnotism, a popular idea in films of this period, both at Vitagraph and elsewhere, and it is a rather coarser piece of work than *The Right Girl(?)*. Nevertheless, it does display an equal amount of cutting within scenes, though there are some more obvious directional mis-matches than in the previous films, and when compared to the Vitagraph John Bunny "comedies" of earlier years, it is still a masterpiece of humour.

From several weeks later (14 April) we still have

Ince's *His Phantom Sweetheart*, another one-reel vehicle for Earle Williams and Anita Stewart. This depends on a narrative constructional trick that only works properly in films, and that indeed had done fairly continuous service since the beginning of the century, but *His Phantom Sweetheart* is the best realisation of it up to 1915. It also shows that the command of all the basic features of continuity cinema evident in *The Right Girl(?)* was no accident, as it has further extensive use of dialogue titles and close shooting, and also has more demonstrations of what reverse-angle cutting can do to increase the impact of glances exchanged between characters, and how it can also be used to speed the action, by making it possible to leave out undetectably the boring and unnecessary depiction of the travel of a character from one side of a room to another, and indeed from one side of a street to another. The way cutting on action can be used to smooth over the transition to a closer shot of an actor is also on show, as it is in Ralph Ince's other 1915 films, and the whole is topped off by an almost perfect display of low-key lighting used for mood purposes. Indeed the lighting is some of the best produced up to this date, even though a number of the scenes were made under the handicap of being shot on location in a real theatre auditorium and foyer, with arc floodlights brought in specially for the filming. And it also contains what seems to be the earliest example of "soft focus" photography, for the beautiful mysterious woman of the title first appears behind rows of people in the foreground, with the focus set so that they are sharp and she is slightly out of focus, a point which is proved by the identical set up on the reverse angle showing the hero behind a similar row of people, but having sharp focus covering everything in the picture. When there is a cut to a closer shot of the woman alone, the focus on her stays slightly soft. *His Phantom Sweetheart* is so far in advance of all the other films that I have seen of this date, that when I first came across it I was rather troubled by the fear that it had been wrongly dated, and had been made several years later than 1915. Amongst all the other films made at other studios in 1915 that might be compared with Ralph Ince's work, there is nothing else that I have seen that is so advanced in all these respects. In particular, the best of the films made at the Thomas Ince studio in 1915, which are those directed by Reginald Barker, such as *The Coward* and *The Italian*, largely lack the features I have been describing, and where they are present in minimal form, the handling is much clumsier. In fact Barker's 1914 films show that he had not yet then discovered the reverse-angle idea. It should be hardly necessary to say that D.W. Griffith was still working in an entirely frontal way at this date, with any transitions to closer shots being done down the lens axis, rather than with angle change. As well as that, most of the shots in his films had an iris-in and iris-out at their beginning and end, which introduced extra discontinuity into his movies, not to mention the positional mismatches when he did do a direct cut to a closer shot. He also made minimal use of dialogue titles. In fact Griffith never properly caught up with the new style of continuity cinema (or "classical cinema", if you insist), but over the next few years most of the American directors who stayed in the business followed in the direction in which Ralph Ince had led.

His Phantom Sweetheart was immediately followed by the five-reel feature *The Juggernaut*, which was Ralph Ince's biggest public success. The evaluation of this film awaits the rediscovery of all of its reels, as at the moment only one containing one of its massive train smash climaxes is available. After this, Ince was occupied for the rest of the year with directing the 15 episodes of *The Goddess*, Vitagraph's first true serial. From the plot summary, this sounds a bizarre enterprise, but no doubt it was further proof that our hero was the only director employed by the company who could drive through the production of a big film, and produce a vigorous result. The management of Vitagraph certainly appreciated Ralph Ince's work, for when they sacked most of the contract directors and actors at the end of 1915, they kept Ince, and even built him a special new studio on Long Island exclusively for his productions. But something went wrong, for Ince left Vitagraph at the end of 1916, and then set up as an independent producer with his oldest brother, John, who had taken up film directing a couple of years before. Ince remained an independent producer-director for the rest of the silent period, but clearly nothing he did thereafter was as striking as his achievements at Vitagraph. The only one of these films that I have so far been able to see is *The Woman Eternal* made in 1918 as a vehicle for Elaine Hammerstein (who?), of

which the only really striking feature in the context of other films of this date is a gunfight at night between people trapped inside a house with their enemies in the surrounding forest. As before, he had no connection with the activities of his brother Thomas until the latter's sudden death in 1924 required Ralph to take charge of his studio to see through the productions already under way. (For what it is worth, I record the information, told to me by one of his colleagues from the 'thirties, that Ralph Ince was one of those who believed that Thomas Ince was murdered by William Randolph Hearst, and that the latter bought off all the potential witnesses to his crime.) Throughout the 'twenties, Ralph also continued to play leading parts in some of his productions, which although not common, was more frequent then than in the following decades. Then in the transition to sound, which created many difficulties for silent film people, particularly the independents like Ralph Ince, he was reduced to acting in character parts for a couple of years, but he managed to return to direction in England for Warner Brothers at their Teddington studio. The only two of his films that survive from this period are in fact solidly made, very good-looking productions, appreciably better

than the usual idea of British "quota quickies". *Crime Unlimited* of 1935 has a number of vividly staged action scenes, and in *Perfect Crime* (1937), Ralph Ince introduces himself in a leading role with his back to the camera, in the good old style. His career would seem to have been set to continue fairly successfully, but he was killed in a motor-car crash later in 1937. He was drunk, but his wife was driving, they say.

But for a few years round 1915, Ralph had certainly been Ince Major.

Ralph Ince surprised with his back to the camera (above), and standing in the centre of a shot (left) in his **Perfect Crime** *of 1937.*

I was wrong with my guess that Ralph Ince directed *Double Danger*, and I was also wrong about him directing *The Woman Eternal*. I found that credit given to him in a trade publication of the period, but after I had written this piece, I found that Ralph Ince himself attributed the direction to his elder brother John, with whom he had a production company at the time. And it was only some time after this article was published that I discovered that Ralph Ince had returned to directing in the sound period with three films at RKO in the period when David O. Selznick was in charge of production. And that these films were still in distribution in 16 mm. in England. They were *Men of America* (1932), *Lucky Devils* (1933), and *Flaming Gold* (1933). They were all action subjects starring Bill Boyd just before his Hopalong Cassidy days, and like many RKO films from this period, they have broken-backed scripts, with plots that fall into two halves with little connection between them. The first of them, *Men of America*, is a rather peculiar concoction, in which the villain, played by Ralph Ince, leads a gang of escaped convict gangsters in an attempt to take over a Western town. He dreams of being a new Napoleon setting up a criminal empire in the Wild West, but of course Bill Boyd and the locals come out on top. The best of the series is *Lucky Devils*, which deals with the trials and tribulations of a group of film studio stuntmen. It is obviously an attempt by the studio at a cheap cash-in on the formula they had created with *The Lost Squadron* the year before. *Flaming Gold* is another of those stories about wild-catting oilmen trying to get the better of each other. All three are vigorously handled by Ince, with novel touches in the way some of their scenes are staged. This new demonstration of Ralph Ince's ability seems to have led to his engagement by Irving Asher for his operation at the Warner Bros. Teddington studios.

The information at the end of this piece about Ralph Ince's views on the death of his brother, and on Ralph Ince's own death were told to me by Peter Proud. In 1987 Peter Proud came in as head of the production design department at the London International Film School, where I was still teaching film history. I had seen and admired the brilliance of his work on the Ralph Ince films made at the Warner Bros. Studios at Teddington, and noted his individual style, which involved ceiling beams, murals, and his signature flattened arches, amongst other distinctive features. His great talent, skill and facility were still evident in the work he did with the students. I interviewed him on tape, and after his death put together this piece, which supplements what he said to me with other bits of his reminiscences recorded later in interviews conducted by Sidney Cole for the Oral History programme carried out by the Association of Cinema and Television Technicians. I tried it out on Penelope Houston, but she turned it down as being too far from the interests of most *Sight & Sound* readers, though interesting in its information on the period. She was probably right, unfortunately, but here it is for you.

PETER PROUD – ART DIRECTOR

First of all, I've always been a draughtsman. I've never been taught by anybody. I was always automatically top in my class, and my drawings were always on the wall, either hospital ward, or prison, or whatever I was in.

I was born in 1913. My father and mother were separated. My father was a fine art dealer in Glasgow, and I ran away with mother when I was about five. It was decided that I should be a bank clerk at about six, and I went back to Glasgow to my father. His business failed and he became progressively alcoholic, so that mother and the rest of the family, including the dog, left him, except for me, and I stayed on. I don't know if I'm self-reliant, but I had to look after him at the age of eleven, and cook and shop and all that sort of thing. I also had to work the main fine art shop — where what had been a picture gallery had become a bit of a second-hand furniture shop. Anyway, I had this period in Glasgow, very seldom seeing my mother except when she came up with dress collections. She was a dress-designer, and I think to see us she would undertake to travel these collections round the country. That went on until my father became quite ill, and it was agreed that I should come down to mother to go to school, to a boarding school. I went to Queen Elizabeth Grammar School at Wimborne in Dorset, and I stayed there for a few terms, and then father died.

I had about £500 from him, and I thought that would take me through Dulwich College and on to Oxford, but what actually happened was, I had five terms of paying my own way, to a certain extent, at Dulwich, starting on the Modern side, and then, because I had decided to be an architect, going over to the Engineering side, which seemed the closest thing to it. (I was wrong about this, but I saw their drawing boards.) And then when I got over to the engineering side, this is the beginning of my film story. I am not enormously practical, I am more of an inventing man, not a bench man, you know, and many of my colleagues in the class-room were wonderful mechanics, making two-stroke engines, and so on. I didn't know how to join two bits of metal together, but I wandered around the engineering block at Dulwich, and I found a thing called a ripple tank, and a certain apparatus used for locating the wave length of a vibration. I found those fascinating and within my scope, so I found myself studying sound. Well, the £500 very quickly ran out, so that at 15 I was out. My mother was in St. George's Hospital at Hyde Park Corner, and I went and saw the Master of Dulwich and told him I could not pay my fees, and I must go. He said, "If the housemaster agrees, you can go.", so I went.

Now at the time, sound pictures had just started, and the sound department at Elstree was run by a rather comical silhouette with a cigarette holder called R. E. Jeffreys. It was

also run by a man whose name I have forgotten – the second partner of the headship, of course, who had a restaurant in Leicester Square, and the third partner was Atkins, who went to prison (he was from the BBC). The middle one with the restaurant in Leicester Square had a girl-friend called Anna Newman who was very beautiful, had "Horse Guard's Red" sofas, and lived in a mews round the corner from where my mother lived, with whom she was friendly. Anna Newman put her finger on it, and sent me to the man who had the restaurant in Leicester Square, so I went down to what was then called BIP studios, at Elstree (before it became all the things it became, ending with Cannon), and I talked about this apparatus that you used for detecting vibrations. They thought I was a genius, because they had just discovered the value of this. I added a few years to my age, I was actually 15. A few other things that I threw up gave the impression that I was a highly trained sound engineer, and I started as a sound cameraman in the Central Recording Unit.

The Central Recording Unit had been set up for criminal reasons by this man Atkins, so that he could have a shadow company sending in boxes with nothing inside to build up the Central Monitor Room, which was quite unnecessary, but was a good sort of cover plan for his robbery. Anyway, I was very disappointed, because I wanted to be on the studio stage, and I was sitting there with the sound recording camera like a telephone operating girl, shouting "Over Shot", Over Shot", "Over Shot", and at the end of the day I was released from my headphones. I would be recording four or five productions at a time on the same piece of film. (I don't know how they worked it out afterwards from the length of film with scene number, etcetera.) The sound people were kings of course at this time. One of the things we were trying to do was to make *Blackmail* (of Alfred Hitchcock) into a sound film. I think I was in on the recording of the famous "knife, knife, knife" track, and so on.   So, starved of what I had hoped for, I used to work at night for nothing with the Art Department, doing what I still like doing, which is set dressing. This is a literary job, where you are really expressing something else, not just the architectural ambiance of a person's life but the sort of person they were, (a slut, or very neat), and so I did this, and later, when I got the sack from the sound department, which was inevitable, it became a transfer. That takes me back to the antique shop, because the directorate of the studio was at the time slightly Glaswegian. Which hadn't helped me to get in, but it was now going to help me to get the transfer, because the supervising art director was Clarence Elder, who aimed to be head of the studio. When I approached him about having me as a runner in his department, he said "Are ye any relation of R.H. Proud in Gordon Street, Glasgow?" I said "Yes, I'm his younger son." He said, "You're on, you start Monday". And so I was part of the nepotism of Glasgow.

I then had a very, very informative time, because everybody in the department was an art director, except me, and everybody in the department, all five of them, thought I was his personal assistant. So I was running around morning, noon, and night. I lived in a bell tent on the lot, and I did all the blue-printing. I did the call sheets for Elder, who wanted to be head of the studio. I did most of the building on the lot, which was quite a senior sort of job, because everyone was so frantic. I built streets at this early age, usually converting existing streets. I worked as a dresser – a set dresser with Hitch, and he saw me drawing one day, so the two things which, to this day I feel attached to were brought about, about this time. Dressing and its importance, even more so with the close camera shooting of today, but also storyboarding. I know sometimes a director can be bugged by storyboarding because he feels pre-empted, specially if he hasn't had any part in doing them. But storyboards of that sort are not worth having. But if you can get a director to start his homework as early as possible, briefing the man who is doing the drawing, preferably doing it himself, like Kurosawa or Hitchcock. Hitch just did the little sketches, and I blew them up for him. He always was tremendously well organized, Hitch. He said that life was a bit boring because he sat down on his seat on the first day of shooting and said, "Now it's all done, I've just got to implement it", and his hands went right back like this -- he had child-like lashes. He was an awful man. Very cruel. But like most clever men, a natural teacher. And so I thought that all directors were like this, I didn't realise how bloody lucky I was being. He not only told me what to do, but why I should do it. Why he was going to do what he was going to do. So right from the beginning I didn't see sets as plywood boxes, but bits and pieces following the line, the flow of the editorial streams of the production. Always. There are times when you build four walls, and walk away, but not for the more interesting type of motion picture. So I had two or three years there.

Norman Arnold, the elder brother, and Wilfred, the younger, had been monarchs of the Art Department, but they were playing bowls one day, and the mural painter called Clarence Elder, to whom I had referred previously, when there was a hold-up, he said, "– the Arnold brothers are always down at the pond at Elstree", and they were both fired. Wilfred Arnold was eventually brought back by Hitchcock, much to the embarrassment of the new supervising Art Director, who was the ex-mural painter Clarence Elder, later to be the managing director of the studios. Wilfred was unwell during most of the shooting of *Rich and Strange* (1931).

The great calamity was that I had looked forward to this with enormous excitement, for we were going to travel the world. The story is how an uncle of Harry Kendall, the star, gives him the money he is going to get under his will in order to see what he will do with it. What he does with it is to wreck his life and that of his wife, and they travel all over the world and take lovers, and have lots of adventures, and so on. I was looking forward to it very much, and the studio cancelled the whole location shooting, and we had to do it at Elstree. And with Wilfred rather ill, and mostly away, little me, aged about 16 or 17, perhaps 18, I can't really remember, had to do Shanghai streets, Hong Kong, Cairo, – I thought Cairo was probably sort of a North African village, but I didn't know quite. So I thought of making it very sophisticated. I had a donkey tram, which I improvised, but it didn't much matter because it was a sort of travelogue really, by then. I do remember, we had to do a sinking vessel, which we did, by sinking one section. We had a spill-over from the studio tank, about one hundred and fifty feet length of water, which was quite a lot, but only a small part of it was deep, the rest was nine inches deep. And lying in sinking mode was this liner in which they had taken the trip, and we tracked in from a shot holding the whole length of it, into the middle part which then detached itself off-screen, and finally sank. Which I thought was very clever. And then there was a Chinese junk, full of Chinese buccaneers. And that had to come sailing out of the fog, and hijack what was left of the liner. This was done by tracking in to the junk, which of course was static. We built a bit of ship's rail, with Harry Kendall and his wife on it, at the angle of sinking, and tracked in to this thing. This sort of thing was going on all the time with Hitch, so that one was never daunted to get that sort of cinematic feeling. You're never daunted by script requirements, just naturally do it.

Anyway, this of course, without my at all realising it, was awfully good training. And then I was painting a big cloth, and a page boy came towards me, and I swore at him, for walking on my cloth, and he swore back, and eventually handed me an envelope, which was the sack. I mean ten years later, I would probably have accepted it, but being young and everything, I just went straight up to the managing director, and said I can't go on Monday, I've got at least a week's work on this backcloth. He said, "Who are you, boy?" He again was a Glaswegian. And I said, "But I'm Peter Proud." "Who's that". I said, "Well, Art Department". "Oh, aye, I'll speak to Mr. Elder. Go back and finish your backcloth." That was passed over. The next time I got a note, they meant it. That was the slump, you see, it was then about '31. And I couldn't leave this, you know. How could they make pictures without me? And so I went through a very dismal time foot-loose, and far from fancy-free, around London, and eventually I got into selling silk stockings, from door to door. For Real Silk Hosiery Mills, and I broke the sales record. Funnily enough their factory was at Boreham Wood, so I went down to the film studios there, and I earned four pounds. You see with the deposit they paid on the stockings, the shilling per pair deposit, that was your commission, so you could start off in need of breakfast, and without any money, and be eating well by the evening. That was a big day, because it took in the studio I suppose. But I did have high record right through.

Suddenly I got a job back with Elder at an increase, having already art directed *The Black Hand Gang* (1930) at seventeen, now he really made me up to art director with another chap, who was new to it all, a West-End interior decorator, and I had to sort of groom him into cinema ways. Then we did the film, by Cecil Lewis, called *Eve's New Year* (1932), (as opposed to "New Year's Eve"), and we had singing statues and things, and I would love to see it again, or hear about it. He was delighted with me, and when the film was over, he gave me all sorts of letters and things.

Anyway after that, I tried again with Alfred Junge, who was very important in my career. Among other things at BIP I had seen Junge handling the scenery for E.A. Dupont, the *Cape Forlorn* (1931) light house, wonderful the way he did it, and other things. And perhaps I helped him with the dressing. I had worked on *Dreyfus* (1931) with Walter Reimann, another German. I was offered a job by Alfred Junge at the new Gaumont-British Lime Grove studios, which were not yet finished, and they had shot *After the Ball* (1932), which I missed, because being young, I had wanted to scrub the tin-tack that I had suffered at the hands of the people before, BIP, and get that cleared up, before moving on. And at Gaumont-British I found myself very nobly treated by Alfred Junge, and made senior assistant, on the strength of my portfolio, you know, my good drawings, which were always not too bad, and we had this international art department, Alfred Junge, and Peter Proud, just around the corner, with my own office. Frank Bush, who went to Technicolor, was my draughtsman, and later Arthur Lawson who won an Oscar on *The Red Shoes*, and he was with me thereafter for eight or nine years. Then there was Oskar Werndoff from Vienna, designer of the famous German fairy-tales, then Shamoon Badir, from Bombay. Alexander Vetchinsky was from the East End, and a great chap, and then Bowden, and another man who became art director for Wilcox, but I was next to Junge. Some of these men were far beyond my experience, but I had cinema feeling, you know. Well, with Alfred I worked on *Good Companions* (1933), *Waltz Time* (1933), I did quite a lot on *Evergreen* (1934). And so did Michael Relph, who had now joined me at five shillings a week, from school. I was still adding to my age, but we were more or less the same age, but I had the advantage of having to leave school much earlier. My relationship with

Michael Relph was long, and extensive, and close. Michael was my associate, really. For the moment he was a schoolboy, and I said, "Will you go and get me a cup of tea?", and he said, "Go and get your own f---ing tea, you conceited little ego." I said, "Alright." And when I came back after tea, I said, "Do come and have a drink with me." So we became close friends on that basis.   I was getting seven pounds a week. And when I got married, they raised me to nine. And then after a few years there, the man who put a nail in my shoe was a man called John Croydon. Phil Samuels was the manager at Lime Grove, bit more than manager, and Croydon was this Grey Eminence, behind him, with this great big board of directors, always having meetings.

What happened was, Sinclair Hill asked if I would like to come on to his film being made at Islington, at the Gainsborough studios, which were part of Gaumont-British. Now he already had a famous art director belonging to Pabst, called Ernö Metzner, and he said, "Well, I thought you ought to come and help Metzner, because it's a very cockney English film, called *My Old Dutch* (1934), and I don't think Metzner is familiar with the sort of ambiance that we expect on this film. Perhaps you could guide him." And I said, "In what capacity? Art director?" And he said, "No, he would be the Art Director." So my capacity was the lowest of the low when I got there, because he could see that I was drawing. He was a very competitive man and he put all the other members of the Gainsborough art department onto blowing up his film. He couldn't draw, you see. You don't have to draw, to be a designer. And he was a very clever man, he was wonderful with camera tricks. The rest of the staff were doing blow-ups -- big sketches, from his lousy drawings, and I was doing break-downs -- a snuff box on a mantelpiece, you know? A practical light switch, and all that. That's the boy's job, you know. I mean, I had been left alone at this stage by Junge, who was building a house in Berlin, and I had been alone with quite big pictures, as senior member of the art department. So I had a little office there, in my flat in Belsize Park, a drawing office, with T-squares, and so on, rather dusty, because I never used it. I went back and I did the whole bloody film again. You know, right from scratch, if they were going to treat me like that. So then Sinclair Hill asked me to come with Ern, to see Mick Balcon, and to talk about the production. So Ern had to take me, for that was official. I had my roll of drawings. He looked at them in the car rather like this, on the road to Shepherd's Bush. And we went in, and without any briefing from me, or any rigging of the situation, his stuff was thrown out, by Sinclair. He said, "You have something, haven't you, Peter, to show us?" I said, "Yes", going slightly pink. I opened my drawings. "This is what we want," he said. "Yes, this is it." It was, perhaps a shitty thing, but Metzner was being shitty to me. So he was brought to Lime Grove, to work for Alfred, in Alfred's department, at least recognizing, for the first time, which they should have done long since, that he wasn't an art director, he was the supervising art director. So Ern was put in a subordinate position to Alfred at Lime Grove, and

A Peter Proud set in
Crime Unlimited
(1935).

I was made boss at Islington. We used to call it Siberia, you know. Anyone who got in trouble was sent to Siberia, which was Islington. And so I stayed there for a while, and then this Croydon figure reappeared. He was the manager at Islington, and he seemed to dislike me very much. I couldn't understand that, of course. Anyway, I started casting round, and I found — I had been working on *The Fireraisers* (at Shepherds Bush, 1933), based on that insurance man who went to prison. And when Jerry Jackson the producer came up to me, and shouted at me, and I said, "If you stick your chin out at me, I'll hit the f---ing thing", and a he gave a great big grin. He loved that. And he took me with Micky Powell to the Warner Brothers studios at Teddington to make *Something Always Happens* (1934), and then I became head art director at Teddington. One of the first things I did was Monty Banks in *So You Won't Talk?* (1935). He had to pretend to be dumb. And there were a lot of Monty Banks films there. And films directed by Ralph Ince, William Beaudine, Micky Powell, Arthur Woods.

And Micky, as you know, did several more films there, but the next one for me was *Some Day*, which had Esmond Knight, and another newer star, called Margaret Lockwood. They were servants in a block of flats, in the story, and they went to Southend. And, I always remember, Micky asking me how I thought they could accommodate themselves, as they were penniless, in Southend. And I said, "Well, they sleep on the beach, that's what I would do." And he said, "Oh, that's good, can you give us a beach?" And I said, "Yes, of course." So we built a very acceptable breakwater, which acted as the ground row, and we put down a tarpaulin, and then against the sea-wall, the break-water abutted that, and the two of them straddled the tarpaulin, and we had a yard or two of sand and pebbles against that, with the two children sleeping side by side. But for the rest, I put "four by two" all round, to

make a pond of it, and I stood with the other corner, the black tarpaulin corner, making the water run up the beach, and I remember Micky being awfully pleased with that. Oh, yes, of course, over the top of the breakwater was the pier. Beautifully painted, with great sensitivity and tremendous speed, by George Gresty, who had also joined me from Lime Grove. He came to Lime Grove with me, from Elstree, and then again on to Teddington. And he really was the most splendid scenic painter. Lawson came, and Relph came, too. There was an interesting man, who had been the art director, called Wardie. And Wardie was a very old man, or so he seemed to us, and he hadn't been told that he had been replaced by me. It was an awful, embarrassing morning. We went next door, to "The Anglers", which sorts things out fairly well, and had a drink or two. I said, "What can you do?" He said, "Nothing, I can't do anything." I said, "You wouldn't like to stay on as a sort of secretary, would you. The art department assistant, and researcher." And he said he would love to. So without being art director, he stayed on, and he died after two or three years. But he was an affectionate figure for us. Lawson, and Relph, and myself.

Irving Asher was in charge of the studio, but he seemed to lean on me, I suppose I was already fairly knowledgeable, with my movements so far, and as a sort of Assistant Producer was Jerry Jackson. It went on quite happily ... Bert Bates, who was my doing, Les Norman, the film editor, my doing, John Sloane the studio manager was my fault, again. And the whole thing tightened up in two ways. One of them was, John Sloane was sent out to Jack Warner to be processed at Burbank, and there he learned the very essential thing, to have a meeting every day of heads of departments. And John came back and introduced that. And on the other hand, I rebuilt the studio. It is the only thing I have ever built that was permanent, and so I can

A gambling club set in Crime Unlimited *with mural and ceiling featuring modern type I-beams with lights.*

say, although it is much changed, I could say I built Thames Television, which now uses it. We built the other stage. We had only one stage, you see, and we built another one. And there were one or two innovations. The front was usable as the exterior of The Dorchester, or something, and the carpenter's shop had a classical colonnade at the end, and down the side of the carpenter's shop there was a street based on a charming Georgian street up at Hampstead – Holly Hill, and so on. And there were wooden sockets all round on the pavement, so that one could move the lamp-posts about, to fit. So we were converting sets all the time. I have some name, I am well known, at least with the art department, for my converting, you know. I learnt from Alfred Junge also, about the system of what you should call solid geometry, but he called arithmetic. Where anything that was built at Teddington, at Warner Brothers, was related arithmetically to everything else that we had. We always had six inch risers, even if we wanted five and a half. But everything could be fitted together. And we also used to run over-budget deliberately, to an exact amount. So that we could gradually screw them in to giving us a reasonable budget, over the years. And I had a quite large amount of money on my hip, at all times. I had demolition trucks arriving

The Teddington stock I-beams and lights used in a different way in one of the ocean liner sets in The Perfect Crime (1937).

The standing "Holly Hill" street set on the Teddington backlot being used in They Drive By Night *(1939).*

with all sorts of things. Someone with doors would come up, and they would say, "Where is Peter?" They'd say, "He is in 'The Anglers'" So they would go to 'The Anglers', and say, "I've got a truck load for you, Governor." And I would give them a couple of quid, or something. I had a fairly good time at Teddington, because now they allowed me to have certain policies. Such as I have described. Having money to buy. I also had an overall job number, where something that was going to become stock, I could charge it to that job number, it had money appropriated to it, which was spread over all the other productions of the year, so everything was made rather well, and of wood. Very little plaster. Although I got the head of the plaster shop at Lime Grove over, as well, Arthur Napman. But I had this policy of everything being made of timber, as far as possible. All the mouldings, and overmantels, and things. We also bought an entire mansion out of Park Lane, and I still see bits of it appearing on television. We had a system of building up a vast stock by purchases, as described, and also by making things really well. And when we had some panelling to do, we would probably extend the panelling we had got. We were very possessive, you know, we were fond of all these things. Gradually building up the Stuart Room. And Michael Relph would come dancing into my room, and say, "I'm going to do a beautiful fireplace for the Stuart Room." These were our props. And of course we were very successful.

We had a large high platform down one end of the studio for a long time, and we built sets on it with stairs going up to them for a number of films. Those statues outside the window in *The Man of the Moment* (1935) were modelled on the spot in wet clay, and then painted, and filmed before the clay dried out. For *The Man of the Moment* we also got a good matte artist, and back-projection, and we reproduced the big Monte Carlo hotel and casino interiors and exteriors. In the final

scene when Laura La Plante was out on the window ledge, she was only a several inches above the studio floor. For *They Drive by Night* (1939) we built 37 sets. Michael Relph did the roadhouses and the Palais de Danse. Basil Emmott, the principal studio cameraman, said my sets made him do more interesting lighting.

And then for 1939, Asher, with my help (and others), planned a whole programme of double quota films, but the double quotas had to be treble budget to qualify for double quota under the new rules. They were £45,000, instead of £30,000. And we had a whole succession of these planned. I was so excited about this year of '39, then we were all fired. Out. Everybody. Les Norman, Bert Bates, Irving Asher. What happened was that in the winter of '38 I went skiing, and I came back, (by this time they had rebuilt the studio), and I walked into a terrazzo corridor which I had personally supervised, so that I considered it to be my floor, too. And I stood there talking to the Chief Sergeant, the commissionaire. And he said, "How did you get on, on holiday? Did you have a good holiday? I said, "Yes, fine, done some skiing," and I said, "Is John Sloane back from Africa?" He said, "Yes, but he left the company this morning." I said, "Good gracious me. What about Jerry Jackson?" "He's not coming back anymore." Now in addition to this, Irving had already left off his own bat, to go to Alexander Korda, but having stopped me from going to Vincent Korda. Vincent wanted me to design all the pictures except the ones he wanted to do, so they could save money. I said, "I save the money, and you spend it?" He said, "That's right". Irving had told me that I was in with Warners for life. Then he himself went to Korda. And now Jerry was the head at Teddington, but he was finished. I said, "Good gracious me, what on earth has happened?" And he said, "And they are waiting for you in the boardroom." So I

An office set in Man of the Moment (1935), *with the window inside a flattened arch, and clay statuary visible outside it.*

went up, and I had a little bit left before my option came up, and they offered me that money. And they said, "We're taking on Norman Arnold". I also had a divorce on my hands. I was living at the Richmond Hill Hotel, and I had two nannies, and my mother there. A terrible hotel bill. So I drove back to Richmond, cleared things up, put the kids in the car, and I drove to Paris. Then we moved slowly down to St. Tropez, where we settled down with what was left of my money, for a few months. My wife was with her lover along at Monte. The kids were with me, anyway. And then I came back and joined the Army. I volunteered. And they said, "Go home and wait War Office instructions."

Laura la Plante out on the ledge of the Monte Carlo Hotel set for Man of the Moment, *with matte painting below her and out to the right.*

What this piece needed was some examples of Peter Proud's actual set designs from the thirties, but he had not kept any of them, unfortunately. I think the only surviving material there is relates to the post-war period of his career. You can see some of his designs for *Green for Danger* in Edward Carrick's *Art and Design in the British Film*.

As is often the case, some of the details in these reminiscences are not quite correct. Peter Proud's description of the boat business in Hitchock's *Rich and Strange* does not tally with what is in the film as we have it. Part of the section of sinking liner built in the studio tank does not break off, nor is there a track in on it later on.

Peter Proud's wartime activities inevitably derailed his film career, and after he came back to movies as art director on *Green for Danger* (1947), he tried to enlarge his role by acting as producer and co-director as well as art director on *Esther Waters* (1948). I think he was trying to emulate Michael Relph, previously his junior partner at Teddington, who during the war stayed at Ealing Studios designing their films, and then moved over into producing there in 1946. The attempt at producing and directing by Peter Proud was not a success, and he then went into television, and designed the long running *Robin Hood* series in the 'fifties, and later a few other films, plus more television.

Sometime in the early nineteen-eighties, I came across an old issue of *Film Comment* (Vol. 11 No 1, January-February 1975) dedicated to the Hollywood Cartoon. This contained a number of interviews with some of the great names of animation, and also various critical articles on the subject. One of these was by Jonathan Rosenbaum on Walt Disney. When discussing the question of "authorship" (in the *politique des auteurs* sense) of the Disney films, Rosenbaum claimed that "No one has ever been able to tackle the slippery matter of assigning Disney precise authorship. On the one hand, the cartoon features exhibit a style that is both unmistakable and all-pervasive: a tree in a Disney film is a Disney tree, a doorknob is a Disney doorknob." I was aware that this was not completely true from studying the illustrations in some recent picture books on *Snow White*, so I put together the following piece about the matter, although I did not specifically name Rosenbaum's article in *Film Comment* which was part of its inspiration. I offered it to Penelope Houston for *Sight & Sound*, but she turned it down. Because she had the usual literary orientation, I don't think she had a sufficient developed visual sense to recognize the importance of what I was saying, any more than she could recognize the point about Fritz Lang's style in the piece on that subject elsewhere in this book.

A few years later, in 1987, David Jefferson published it in his magazine *Animator* (No 21, Oct/Dec 1987). This journal did rather well by film animation in the 'eighties, helped by the strong local animation industry, and a bit of Arts Council backing.

SNOW WHITE MEETS GIOVANNI MORELLI

"But the study of drawings is not only indispensable to our knowledge of the different masters; it also serves to impress more sharply on our minds the distinguishing characteristics of the several schools. Much more clearly than in painting we recognize in drawings the family features, both intellectual and material, of the different masters and schools, for instance their manner of arranging drapery, the way they indicate light and shadow, ... the forms of the human body (especially the shape of the hand and also the ear), and of the harmony of colours, so different in the works of these artists."

Giovanni Morelli, *Italian Masters in German Galleries* (1883)

Cosimo Tura's Shape of Ear.

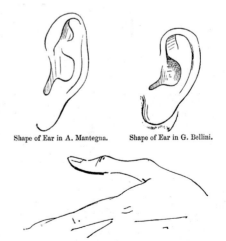

Shape of Ear in A. Mantegna.   Shape of Ear in G. Bellini.

Shape of Hand in G. Bellini during his so-called Mantegnesque period (about 1460-1475).

Giovanni Morelli hoped that his method of examining the minor and subsidiary parts of old paintings and drawings for characteristically idiosyncratic ways of handling would put connoisseurship (the art of attributing paintings to their correct author) on a more scientific basis. Although his approach has undoubtedly made a contribution to this aspect of art history, it has not been as overwhelmingly successful as he hoped it would be. In fact Morelli recognized the principal difficulty, even if he underestimated it. The problem is that a fairly large run of known examples of a particular artist's work is needed to establish for certain just what *is* the habitual way he draws or paints ears, or just how long and thin he habitually draws fingers, and so on. Curiously enough, (and this is also the case for other methods of stylistic analysis), Morelli's approach works much better with some forms of Twentieth century popular art than with the high art of the Renaissance for which it was invented. This is because in such things as comic strip art the large numbers of drawings by the one hand necessary to the method are readily available, and so it is easy to recognize when a continuing comic strip is taken over by another artist. It might be thought that the artist's signature would be sufficient, but in the nineteen-forties and -fifties such changes in the draughtsmanship of comic strips were not acknowledged as they are now, and the standard signature of the originator of the strip was often forged. Of course with twentieth century popular art it is often possible by other means to find just who drew the cartoon in question, but there are still occasions when this can be either very difficult, or even impossible. Since animated cartoons are a closely related medium, all this may well have something new to tell us about them.

1. When I saw *Snow White and the Seven Dwarfs* again some time ago (and I had to assure the box-office that was the film I really wanted to see), I was struck by the way that Snow White's appearance and movement changed from sequence to sequence.

2. Two books that appeared a few years ago relating the story of Snow White as it is told in the Walt Disney film make possible a closer study of these differences. One of these books is published by Penguin Books in England and is illustrated by frame enlargements made from a print of the film; the other is published by Viking Books in the United States, and is illustrated with very large numbers of reproductions of the art work used in producing the film, particularly story sketches and animation layouts.

3. The various sequences of Snow White and the Seven Dwarfs were produced by different units within the studio, as is the case for all feature-length animated films. The first stage in the production of the visuals starts with the story sketches.

4. Then come animation layouts which are more precise and show the exact positions of the frame within shots. These first two stages are largely the creation of the Sequence Directors and Art Directors, though there is a certain fluidity in the organization of the process.

5. Afterwards come all the stages of the actual animation drawing, the tracing and painting of the cels, and then photography to give the final film frame, which is illustrated here.

6. In the story sketches and animation layouts the drawing styles of the different artists are quite evident. This artist draws Snow White as a tall, slim young woman, whose total height is nearly seven times the height of her head.

7. These body proportions largely carry through into the same section of the finished film, for here Snow White is about six heads tall, whereas in most of the other sequences of the finished film she is between five and five and a half heads tall.

8. Of course, producers of animated films had long been aware of this problem, and used "model sheets" with correct proportions of the figures to try to control any variation in the drawing from one animation artist to another, but this just didn't work fully with Snow White.

9. The proportions and shape of the face are where the different styles of the artists show through most readily. In this animation layout showing Snow White talking to the animals, her eyes are very large and very widely separated.

10. And this has been carried through
to the actual painting on the cel, as have
those peculiar 'S'-shaped eyebrows
that some (but not all) of her creators
favoured.

11. Another derivation from the norm
has Snow White's eyes small and widely
separated, and her cheeks exceptionally
chubby.

12. This too has been carried through to the
final frame, despite the many intervening
stages of the actual animation process.

13. Yet another stylistic theme is the
shape of the face in profile. One main
variant has flat brow and pointed tip
of nose.

14. While another shows curved brow and rounded tip of nose. And then there is the case of Snow White's eyelashes. When her eyes are shut everyone drew her eyelashes all the way across her top eyelid.

15. But when here eyes are open, some artists still drew them all the way across the lid, while others drew them only on the outer part of the lid, as here.

16. And still others drew them only on the inner part of the lid. Actually, it was only in close shots like this one that the head animator supervising Snow White, and the animators who drew her in different sequences were able to achieve a fair degree of uniformity throughout the film. This is partly because the close shots were those most influenced by the use of rotoscope drawings.

17. For instance, live-action footage of young Marjorie Belcher registering shock was projected frame by frame on the rotoscope, and tracings made of selected frames. In this case frames 1, 19, and 26 of her recoil have been traced, with the artist concerned supplying his own stylization of the eyes and mouth.

18. When these rotoscope drawings had served as a basis for an animation layout, a quite different simplified stylization of the eyes emerged. None of the drawing of Snow White is *very* close to a real girl in live action, and some is quite far removed.

19. Although the lesser creatures in *Snow White and the Seven Dwarfs* were designed with the kind of very rounded and simplified forms that tend to more readily conceal the different hands that worked on them, characteristic distinctions could still emerge. Ordinarily the boundary between the white area and the darker area on the heads of the squirrels was drawn with a sharp cusp behind their eyes.

20. But when the squirrels turn their backs to the camera, one of the animators, but not the others, changes this line into a smooth flowing curve without the point. (Yes, Giovanni, he also draws their ears differently as well.) So a squirrel in a Walt Disney film is not simply a standard Walt Disney squirrel, but visibly a squirrel drawn by a particular artist. And the same goes for trees and other objects.

21. Looking beyond the static design of Snow White and the Seven Dwarfs, I also detect idiosyncratic differences in the way our heroine moves in different sequences. The way her shoulders give little jerks upward with excitement when she discovers the dwarfs' cottage does not occur anywhere else in the film, and the swooping trajectories separated by poised holds as she runs through the forest led by the animals is likewise unique. But that is another story, for access to an actual print of the film is required to demonstrate it.

With the help of more recent books on the production of the film Snow White, I have now been able to deduce the names of some of the artists concerned in producing the drawings above. The artist who drew the inspirational sketch No. 6 was Gustave Tengrenn, and the source of the pointed tip of the nose on Snow White in No. 12 was probably either Albert Hurter or Grim Natwick, both of whom were involved in the early stages of the evolution of the film, and both of whom favoured pointed noses on their sketches of women.

Actually, now that it is possible to examine many of the early Disney sound cartoons on DVD, it can be seen that there are noticeable differences between them, depending on who was the director. The earliest Disney sound cartoons were all largely or even wholly animated by Ub Iwerks, as is indicated by the credit "by Ub Iwerks" under the title of most of them. After he left the studio, Burt Gillet and Wilfred Jackson directed most of them for the next several years, without getting explicit credit on the title cards, nor did David Hand when he was promoted to direction in 1932. Jackson's work is recognizable by his fondness for including bi-laterally symmetrical compositions involving large numbers of active figures of one kind or another. An early example where there is a lot of this is *Busy Beavers* of 1931.

builds to a delirious climax of contrary motion across bands of the friezes that is well on the way to the brain-spinning glory of the Pink Elephant sequence in *Dumbo*. A later Jackson spectacular is *Woodland Café* (1937). In this, besides some of his trademark symmetrical frames, the whimsical fantasy includes a pair of earthworms who become a biped through love of jive.

There is a labour-saving angle to this, because half the figures can be traced onto the cels by flipping over the animations drawings for those on the other half of the frame, but clearly Wilfred Jackson liked the effect, which is intrinsically lightly humorous in itself. The other aspect of Jackson's work is an extra degree of fantasy that appears quite frequently in his films. Another example from 1931 is *Egyptian Melodies*, in which a spider investigates a subterranean Egyptian tomb, and after proceedings are warmed up by a chorus line of dancing mummies, we find the wall friezes coming to life with lines of warriors cheering on a chariot race. After gags based on what two-dimensional figures on a surface can and cannot do, it

On the other hand, Burt Gillett's work is more pedestrian in the visual sense, and sticks with the more traditional vulgar slapstick gags, and has rather greater violence in its content. And David Hand is bland.

Back in the 'seventies while teaching at the Slade, long before writing the previous article, I had conceived of a new measure for use in the stylistic analysis of animation, namely the area of the shot swept by the animation, and recently I tried this out on a number of animated cartoons. While looking closely at these films, it also occurred to me that another technical feature of animator's work might give yet another stylistic indicator. The result was the following article, which has not been published anywhere before.

COUNTING IN ONES & TWOS

In traditional motion picture animation not every successive drawing photographed to make up the film is different to the one before it. When part of an animated scene does have a new drawing for every frame, this is called "animating it on ones", and when a part of the scene has each drawing filmed twice before going on to the next one, this is called "animating it on twos". Just how much of a film is done on twos is fundamental to the quality of the result.

As Richard Williams put it on pages 57 and 58 of his book *The Animator's Survival Kit* (Faber & Faber, 2001),

"But when to use ones and when to use twos?
The rule of thumb is - use twos for normal actions and ones for very fast actions. For instance, runs always have to be on ones - normal 'acting' on twos.
Walks can function nicely on twos, but they're going to look better on ones.

Obviously, life is on ones (or whatever speed we film it on), but twos work well for most actions and, of course, it's half as much work as doing it on ones. And half as expensive! Working on ones is twice as much work and expense all the way down the production line.

Apparently, in the early 1930s as Disney's animators got better and better, costs were skyrocketing, and since twos work for most things, they tried to stay on twos whenever they could.

A lot of great animators even say that twos are really better than ones, that ones lead to a mushy result, that broad, fast actions on twos 'sparkle' and adding ones diminishes that vitality. Well, yes, this is true if the ones are just dumb, mechanical inbetweens.

My experience is different. I've found that if you *plan* for ones, the result is usually superior to twos.

I feel that twos are an economic answer to an artistic question. With twos being half the work, everybody gets to go home on time, and why would *I* make a case for ones? Hell, I was a studio *owner*.

When I was re-learning all this stuff, I would wait till my animation on ones was traced and painted, then I'd shoot it on ones as planned and then I'd take out every other cel and shoot the rest on twos to see if it 'sparkled' and was better.

In all but one case, ones worked better. The time the twos worked better was when I had an old lady pulling out a doctor's stethoscope from her pocket. The ones produced a very smooth movement.

It worked just fine, but then I removed every other painted inbetween and shot it on twos. It was better on twos! I cannot figure out why - it just was better.

So they're partly right, I guess. But I became addicted to using ones whenever I could - ones seem to make for compulsive viewing and that's what we're after.

Art Babbitt used to nag at me for using ones. 'That's too realistic - one of the things about animation is that it's *not* like life!' But I would often add ones to Art's work when he wasn't looking and it came out better - and *he* liked it better.

And twos tire the eye after a few minutes. I feel that ones are twice as much work, but the result is three times as good. Compulsive viewing, easy to watch.

I think my co-animator Neil Boyle said it best: 'Twos work - ones *fly.*'

And Ken Harris, who spent most of his life working on twos, would say to me when I'd be putting ones into his stuff, 'Oh, it's *always* better on ones.'"

So who are these people?

Richard Williams is a Canadian who is best known nowadays for directing the animation sequences in *Who Framed Roger Rabbit?* (1988). He started out at Disney and UPA in the late forties, then moved to England where he made his name with the animated fable *The Little Island* in 1958. He went on to build an animation studio in London that made money from commercials and title sequences for feature films, which he then used to fund his own personal projects like *The Cobbler and the Thief*. Williams' early work relied as much on graphic design as on animation style, but he was well aware of this, and sought to improve his own animation technique, as well as that of his staff. After his studio had made the animation sequences for *The Charge of the Light Brigade* in 1967, he invited some to the top American animators of the 'thirties and 'forties to give classes in traditional animation technique to himself and his employees. These old masters included Ken Harris, Milt Kahl, Grim Natwick, and Art Babbitt.

Ken Harris was the leading animator in the Chuck Jones unit at the Warner Bros. animation studio during the 'forties.

Milt Kahl was a long-time leading animator at the Disney Studio from the early thirties onwards.

Art Babbit was an animator for Paul Terry's Terrytoons at the end of the 'twenties, then moved to Disney early in the thirties, staying there through the forties, before going to UPA in the nineteen-fifties.

Grim Natwick's extremely lengthy career as an animator began in 1921 at Hearst Film Services, then went through the Fleischer studios, where he created Betty Boop, on to the Ub Iwerks studio, and then to Disney in 1935. He went back to Fleischer for *Gulliver's Travels* (1939), and various other places later, including UPA.

And what did they really do?

As usual, the story is more complicated than suggested in Richard William's summary history quoted above. Just for a start, there are in fact no American animated cartoons made for the cinema through the nineteen-thirties, 'forties, and 'fifties that are animated exclusively on twos, not even those worked on by Ken Harris. The mixture of both methods was standard.

Going back to the very beginnings of animated films, we find that Vitagraph's *Humorous Phases of Funny Faces* of 1906 is entirely done on twos, except for a few short sections in which James Stuart Blackton's hand can be seen drawing in continuous filming. As is well known, most of this film is done by the movement of cut-out figures between the exposures, but there is a tiny amount of drawn animation in it, at the point when the drawing of a man blows smoke in the face of the drawing of a woman. For some reason the second exposure of each position of the jointed cutout figures that are mostly used in this film is slightly less than that of the first exposure. It would appear that the repeated frames were not filmed with a "one turn" exposure for each frame, but with a camera exposing two frames in succession from the same drawing with one turn. On the other hand, the animated section of the Edison Company's *The Teddy Bears* of 1907 is entirely done on ones, with the toy teddy bears moved slightly between every exposure to create the illusion of movement. This film also introduces the idea of "holds" in the midst of continuous movement, in which the figures stay completely still for several frames. Ever afterwards the "hold" has been used to make a comic or dramatic point in animated films, or as in the case of *The Teddy*

Bears, as a rhythmic device. But the labour-saving usefulness of animating entirely on twos was established definitively by Emile Cohl in his drawn animations from 1908 onwards. The first of these, *Fantasmagorie*, is entirely done on twos: in fact there are only about 700 individual drawings for the 1,872 frames making up the length of the film, according to Donald Crafton on page 121 of his book *Emile Cohl, Caricature and Film* (Princeton University Press, 1990).

I have examined Cohl's second surviving film, *Un drame chez les fantoches*, and find that the technique is similar. To be specific, most of this film is done on twos, but there are some sections where frames are repeated three or four times before proceeding to the next different frame. There are also a couple of short sections which are actually done on ones. These involve firstly a character tipping liquid out of a window onto the head of another below, and secondly one of the stick figures sharpens a knife on a foot-treadle grindstone, which then disintegrates explosively. To judge by the letters quoted in Crafton's book, Cohl found the labour of producing his animated cartoons tedious from the beginning, and this must have encouraged him to follow Blackton in giving two exposures to each drawing to reduce the work to be done in creating a given length of film. On the other hand, some of the people who took up model animation followed the example of Edwin Porter's *The Teddy Bears*. Arthur Melbourne-Cooper's first animated film, *Dreams of Toyland*, made in 1908, is a manic creation showing a model toy-town square filled with a dozen different figures and vehicles moving independently through re-adjustment of their positions for every single frame exposed.

The next development in drawn animation, Winsor McCay's animation of figures from his *Little Nemo* comic strip, is contained in the Vitagraph film of 1911 called *Winsor McCay*. McCay did this entirely on ones, as he did also for his subsequent masterpieces, *Gertie the Dinosaur* (1914), and *The Sinking of the Lusitania* (1918). The people producing regular series of animated cartoons during the First World War stuck with basically working on twos.

A typical example from 1919 is one of Earl Hurd's "Bobby Bumps" series, *Their Master's Voice*. Earl Hurd was one of the holders of the patents for the "cel" method of animation, and also was apparently the first to do animation on a background of still photographs, as part of his approach of depicting the interaction of cartoon characters with live humans. He was doing this at least as early as 1918. His "Bobby Bumps" character was the best drawn of the contemporary cartoon series during the First World War, and also the most inventive, and it was almost completely done on twos, even when the shortcomings of this technique were evident, such as when a figure falls from a height. (See page 163)

However, as the amount of animated film made in the United States increased after the First World War years, and became more sophisticated, some animators did do short sections of their films on ones. For instance, the illustration on page 160 below from the animated cartoon *Feline Follies*, contained in an issue of the Paramount Magazine released to cinemas on 9 November 1919, is located in part of a scene where the white cat dances to the banjo of the proto-Felix. The movement here is animated on ones, though most of the cartoon is not. As this character became the real Felix in the next month under the pen of Otto Messmer, most of the scenes

of rapid movement in his films were done on ones. The horde of running cats in *Felix Revolts* of 1923, for instance, which is illustrated here, is likewise done on ones, with a four positions for the cats repeated in a cycle. However, such sections form a small part of the total running time of a typical Felix cartoon of that date.

On the other hand, the Fleischer's *Out of the Inkwell* series is almost entirely done on ones. From 1919, when they began, these cartoons were a mixture of live action and animation, on the model of Earl Hurd's "Bobby Bumps" cartoons. The innovation in the Fleischer films was that most of the movement of their cartoon clown (later called Koko) was rotoscoped from live action film of Dave Fleischer jumping around in a clown suit. The rotoscoping technique, which was invented and patented by Max Fleischer, involved tracing around the outline of the live action figure projected one frame at a time onto a ground glass screen from behind. Obviously, this method can provide a different drawing for every frame of film if it is desired, and this is the way the Fleischers operated the system. The resulting animation was smoother than that of anyone else who was in regular production at the time, and this was

the Fleischer's Unique Selling Point. Even when the movement of the clown was drawn without the guide of rotoscope images in their early films, as for instance when he emerged from, or re-entered, the inkwell, the action was still drawn on ones. Although the clown tended to interact mostly with live action figures, from at least as early as *The Chinaman* (1919), he sometimes got into extensive tussles with other drawn figures, and these were *not* drawn from rotoscope images. Nevertheless, their movement was also done on ones. Occasionally there would be Big Close Ups of the clown and other characters cut into a scene, and these were also not rotoscoped, but drawn from scratch, and in a much more caricatural or "cartoony" style. Such shots also tended to contain more holds than the basic action, which was all done in Long Shot, as it was in everybody's animated cartoons at the time.

In The Chinaman (1919), *the clown has human proportions resulting from rotoscoping, but the Chinaman, who is drawn from scratch, does not.*

Chemical Koko (1929) *shows the greater threee dimensionality of the figures, and the more caricatural drawing of the clown.*

How Animated is it?

One way to measure the amount of full animation is to count the number of drawings (i.e. frames where the image changes) against the total number of frames in a cartoon, omitting the intertitles. Calculating this as a ratio gives 0.37 for *Their Master's Voice*. If *Their Master's Voice* had just been animated completely on twos all the way through, the animation ratio would have been 0.50, but the lower figure results from the large number of holds in the film. *Feline Follies* has an animation ratio of 0.43, and *Felix Revolts*, 0.50. The latter figure does not mean that *Felix Revolts* is entirely done on twos, just that the sections done on ones are compensated for by the frames spent in holds, during which absolutely nothing moves. At this time cartoons were still produced by a handful of people, so animators were very keen to exploit long holds whenever possible, to make their task easier.

As has already been indicated, the Fleischer films at the beginning had an animation ratio approaching 1 in their animated sections. To be specific, *The Tantalizing Fly*, has an animation ratio of 0.95, the shortfall representing quite a number of appreciable holds scattered throughout the film. The total amount of actual work for the Fleischer artists involved in the number of drawings per cartoon was not too different from the competition, who were mostly working on twos, since at this time about half of any issue of the *Out of the Inkwell* series was live action. The rotoscoping of the clown was gradually abandoned, starting from 1921, and Koko, as he came to be, was completely drawn from scratch all the time. He, and Fitz, his new dog sidekick, were drawn in a very cartoony style in the latter part of the 'twenties, with Koko's legs and hands exaggerated in size compared to his torso. His head and features were also no longer naturalistic. An interesting minor stylistic feature of the drawing of the figures in the Fleischer cartoons in the late 'twenties was that they were slightly more three-dimensional in appearance than the competition because of extra lines delineating their shape.

And along with this, the clown and other human figures in the Fleischer cartoons were drawn with five fingers on their hands all through the 'twenties. In the late 'twenties the Fleischer artists made less use of the large areas of undifferentiated black fill to make up the figures, which is what gave the characters from the other studios (including Disney) the flat "cookie cutter" look so typical of the period.

As far as the fullness of the animation was concerned, the Fleischer animators did not cut back very much from doing it on ones in the late 'twenties, but instead made more use of repetition in the action, with repeated cycles of drawings. *Koko the Kid* from 1927 is typical of the Inkwell Studios output of the period in that the animation ratio is 0.91. The remaining 0.09 represents a small amount of action done on twos, but is mostly made up of lots of holds. The proportion of the whole film that is handled purely in live action is 16%, which is similar to the other Fleischer films of the late 'twenties.

At the end of the nineteen-twenties, the Disney studio films were also very fully animated. For instance, *Plane Crazy* (1928), the first of the Mickey Mouse films to be made, has an animation ratio of 0.90, and of course has no live action sections to make things a bit easier for the animator, Ub Iwerks. As most everyone knows, *Plane Crazy* was produced without any intention of it being a sound film, but was held back and post-synchronized after *Steamboat Willie* showed that sound was the way to go. *Skeleton Dance* (1929), the first of the Silly Symphonies, which was completely conceived as a sound film, is still almost entirely done on ones, with an animation ratio of 0.91. This was also animated completely by Ub Iwerks, without the assistants usual by this date. *Skeleton Dance* makes a great deal of use of repetition and cycling in the animation.

Contrary to the claims of the old hands, things didn't change appreciably through the 'thirties in the amount of full animation in the Disney Silly Symphonies. *Busy Beavers* of

1931 shows the animals dancing around while they work, and has a animation proportion of 0.95, though this involves large amounts of movement on repeated cycles. In fact the basis of the Silly Symphonies was repeated rhythmical movement, and they relied on the tunes in the music to add variety to what was otherwise going on in them in a repetitious visual way. Things had not changed much by 1937, so that *Woodland Café*, with insects jiving through the night, and also directed by Wilfred Jackson, has an animation ratio of 0.88. In the other side of Disney animation, the Mickey Mouse series, which were not so music dependent, we find that *Mickey's Trailer* of 1938 has an animation ratio 0.91. This film is at the peak of the complexity in Disney animation, with the scenes inside the caravan having the walls of the trailer moving in a rubbery way independently of the characters as the trailer careers out of control down a mountain path, plus a scrolling background visible through the windows. Curiously enough, the shaking walls of the caravan are almost entirely done on ones, but some sections of the movement of the characters going on in front of them is done on twos, at any rate in the earlier, more slow moving part of the film. (In these sections I take my measure from the animation of the movement of the caravan.) There is a certain amount of use of cycles in this film, but the cycles are longer and more irregular in content than those in the earlier films mentioned previously.

For the magnum opus that all this was leading up to, namely *Snow White and the Seven Dwarfs* (1938), the amount of animation done on twos is rather greater than in the films just mentioned, though I don't have an exact figure. (I can't spare a couple of weeks to count through 100,000 frames.) But curiously, the scenes most dependent on the rotoscoping of human figures, which are those between Snow White and the Prince, are mostly done on twos, which I have always felt gives them a slightly stiff and jerky character. It seems that accurate human shapes show up the lack of movement on every second frame more than simplified cartoon figures do.

One might expect the Warner Bros. cartoon studio, being a cheaper operation, to have made more use of animation on twos, but in one of their music-based cartoons from 1938, *Katnip Kollege*, which has cartoon hep-kittens relentlessly swinging to the beat while in class and out of it, the animation ratio is 0.90. Though in this film the amount of repetitious movement created by cycling the drawings is horrendous.

It was in the nineteen-forties that the reduction in the use of animating on ones really set in. The Disney studio showed what you could get away with in the "Baby Weems" sequence in *The Reluctant Dragon* of 1941, which could be considered to be not much more than 171 holds stretched over its 8 minutes length. Actually, some of the static story-board shots making it up do have a little simple animation, mostly overlays of falling rain and paper showers and explosions and the like, which bring the animation ratio up to about 0.10, if you count them. Disney confirmed the viability of very limited animation at feature length with *Victory through Air Power* (1943). In a more ordinary Disney cartoon, *How To*

Ride a Horse, and also included in *The Reluctant Dragon*, the animation ratio was 0.64, with much less than half (in fact 36% of the length of the film) being done on ones, and hence the larger part of it on twos. To explain this point clearly, a film that is made up of exactly half its length done on ones, and the other half completely on twos, will have an animation ratio of 0.75, by the measure I am using. In *How To Ride a Horse* holds make up 3% of the running time in total.

The economic squeeze was equally obvious at Warner Bros. *Long-Haired Hare*, which was made in 1949 by the Chuck Jones unit, with Ken Harris one of the animators, is very similar to the Disney example, with an animation ratio of 0.66. This again means that less than half the picture was done on ones. And there was also much use of holds in *Long-Haired Hare*, in fact about 5% of the footage.

From here, it was downhill all the way as the effect of television was felt by the animation industry.

"Disney-type animation is economically unfeasible for television, and we discovered we could get away with less." – William Hanna, on p.338 of *Of Mice and Magic* (Leonard Maltin, 1980)

Take an episode of the Hanna-Barbera studio's *The Jetsons* series, *Elroy's TV Show* from 1962. If we ignore static figures being slid across the frame on the infantile "futuristic" personal conveyor belts, or being jet-packed across the sky, the animation ratio is 0.41, and none of it is on ones. And most of it is made up characters standing there with only their lips moving, while they emit the yak-yak-yak. The illustration below represents three seconds of screen time — or more strictly 80 consecutive frames at 25 frames per second, and was created by superimposing 5 frames taken at 16 frame intervals from a videotape of the show. As you can just make out, the only thing moving in this scene is the lips of one of the characters, and also a couple of tilts of his head. This shot goes on for another 4 seconds like this, and is succeeded

Nothing but lip movement and a small nod of the head by one character over seven seconds of screen time in The Jetsons.

A look in the opposite direction in The Jetsons *done by flipping the head position without any body movement, to the sound of scores of great animators turning in their graves.*

by more shots of characters standing there with their lips flapping up and down. The resemblance to cartoons from the primitive period is quite striking. (This is just as true for *The Flintstones*.)

So how to get at the amount of movement inside the frame, which clearly affects one's sense of the fullness of the animation?

Filling the Frame

To measure the degree to which the animation fills the frame, the obvious possibility is to measure the amount of the screen swept by the drawn movement over a time period. Looking at that early triumph of full animation, McCay's *Gertie the Dinosaur*, if we superimpose a series of 5 frames taken at 10 frame intervals, we get the compound picture illustrated. Then drawing an outline around the area of the film frame swept by Gertie's movement over about 2 seconds of the scene, we can measure the proportion between this area and the total area of the frame. It is 49%. The area in the

upper left quadrant of the frame is included in the swept area as the tree trunk sweeps through it after Gertie bites through it at the beginning of the action covered. (To get this figure, I delimited the relevant area with the lasso tool in Adobe Photoshop, and then used the pixel count in the Photoshop histogram function, but there are probably other ways to do it.)

But when we look at a more typical cartoon from the early years, *Feline Follies*, and the illustration below showing the same thing done to 10 drawings at 10 frame intervals, we find that the swept area is only 6.8%. Making the obvious comparison with *The Jetsons*, in that case the ratio between the swept area and the whole frame is only 2.8%, which is

about as low as you can go and still call the result "animation" at all.

Returning to the rise of full animation in the 'twenties, one of the easy ways that animators found to increase the swept area was by repetitive mass movement, as in *Felix Revolts* of 1923, where hordes of cats gallop to join the insurrection led by Felix. The running cats are animated on ones on a 4 frame cycle, in a way that was standard for Felix cartoons of the time. Superimposing the 4 frames of one cycle, which are illustrated

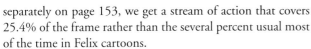

separately on page 153, we get a stream of action that covers 25.4% of the frame rather than the several percent usual most of the time in Felix cartoons.

Another occasional trick from the end of the 'thirties that enabled action to completely cover the frame was to have a character move straight towards the "camera", till their mouth swallowed it. I don't know who started this in the late 'twenties, but I illustrate an example from *Skeleton Dance*.

In the 'thirties, the Disney studio pushed the area of

the frame swept by the movement to the limit. In the two illustrations above and below of shots from *Mickey's Trailer*, we have action from scenes in the second half of the film, where the caravan trailer runs out of control. In the first example, the action sweeps 77.8% of the frame (5 drawings at 10 frame intervals superimposed) and in the second example, where Mickey and Donald are bouncing around inside the caravan, 100% of the frame (6 drawings at 10 frame intervals). So the rise and fall of full animation over history shows a parallel between the greater use of "ones" and the animation of a greater area of the frame.

Scene Dissection

Animated cartoons depict a basically flat world, as in the cartoon strips which were their origin, and also the origin of most of the animators who drew them too. No-one has managed to find precursors in comic strips to those basic features of film construction that are made possible by the depiction of the real three-dimensional world on a two-dimensional surface in live action movies. I mean reverse-angles and Point-of-View shots. And in early animated cartoons, everything went on in Long Shot as well. As late as 1919, in the cartoons *Their Master's Voice* and *Feline Follies* mentioned earlier, there are no closer

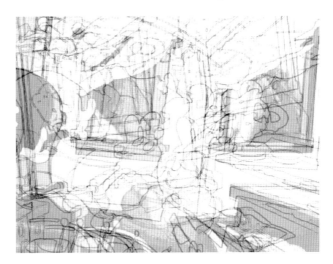

shots cut into the scenes which are being exclusively carried on in Long Shot. But before long we do find a very few close shots cut in to the master scenes in *Felix Revolts* (1923) and *Koko the Kid* (1927). However, when these occur, the contents of the Close Up are always shown inside a hard circular black vignette or mask. This style for the treatment of Close Up shots was vanishing through the early 'twenties in American live action filming, and on those rare occasions when it was used in live action films, the mask always had a soft edge. But even in *Plane Crazy* in 1928, the Close Ups are still all inside hard-edged vignettes, and this is quite typical. As for Point of View shots, there are none in *Feline Follies* and *Their Master's Voice*, but the object of a character's attention is indicated by a dotted line drawn from his eyes to whatever he is looking at. This device lasted all the way through the nineteen-twenties in animated cartoons, and the use of real reverse angle cutting is lacking as well. It is as though for cartoon directors the development of film form had stopped with D.W. Griffith.

As far as cutting rate is concerned, the Average Shot Length for early 'twenties cartoons was around 10 seconds, which is a appreciably longer than for American live-action films of the same period, and again indicates a stylistic backwardness. But

in the 'thirties things began to move forward, particularly at the Disney studios. *Mickey's Trailer* of 1938 has an ASL of 5.5 seconds, and also uses some Point of View (POV) and reverse angle (RA) shots, amounting to 11.5% and 8% respectively. So it wasn't just *Snow White* that was cut like a live-action film, as the Disney people correctly boasted at the time. In fact *Snow White* has an ASL of 6.1 seconds, which is actually faster than the norm for American live-action features of that date, while the usage of true RAs and POVs is comparable with the norms in those areas of scene dissection in live-action films. In contrast, the Warner Bros. cartoon *Katnip Kollege* of 1938 has an ASL of 7.6 seconds and 27% reverse angles. There are no POV shots in it, but they were not called for, since the film has no plot to speak of.

I append the figures for some later animation features for comparison. Once past *Hoppity Goes to Town*, which is a bit retarded in scene dissection in comparison with the Disney product, the more recent films become much closer to the norm for their period (see *The Shape of 1999* in this volume).

Recent Times

The fullness of animation used on Disney features has not changed much since the 'forties, but the competition from other companies very frequently drags along the bottoms of TV style animation. For instance, the famous Japanese animated feature, *Akira* (1988), is entirely done on twos, even in the many scenes of fast action, and uses a lot of holds as well. A more recent film that also uses hand-drawn animation exclusively on twos is *Titan AE* (1999). This is interesting as it also has many scenes with 3D CGI backgrounds going on behind the hand-drawn characters. These, as is the way with CGI 3D animation, all proceed on ones, and of course draw attention to the low-grade animation going on in front of them.

The distinction between full animation and TV animation can be graphically illustrated by a comparison of six consecutive superimposed frames from *Titan AE*, showing one of the evil alien Drej energy beings jumping off a space ship, with six

TITLE	YEAR	DIRECTOR	ASL	RA	POV	INSERTS
Snow White and the Seven Dwarfs	1938	Hand, David	6.1	21	7	6
Hoppity Goes to Town	1941	Fleischer, Dave	7	7	3	
Akira	1988	Otomo Katsuhiro	4.7	29	11	
My Neighbour Totoro	1988	Miyazaki Hayao	5.4	27	13	13
Antz	1998	Darnell, E. & Johnson, T.	3.9	27	4	
Bug's Life, A	1998	Lasseter, J. & Stanton, A	3.3	26	5	
Titan A.E.	1999	Bluth, Don & Goldman, G.	3.4	22	6	24
Final Fantasy	2001	Sakaguchi & Sakakibara	4.3	29	14	
Shrek	2001	Adamson & Jensen	3.5	43	8	4

Six consecutive frames from Titan AE *superimposed. Animated on twos, they show one of the Drej dropping down without any change of body position, and a severe impression of jerkiness in the animation.*

Six consecutive frames superimposed showing Jiminy Cricket jumping down onto a vibrating saw blade in Pinocchio *done on ones. There is also animation of pose and expression as he falls.*

consecutive superimposed frames from Disney's *Pinocchio,* showing Jiminy Cricket jumping down onto a saw blade.

Japanese animation of recent times is also done entirely on twos, or very frequently with even more frames of repeated drawings before the next new one. The most admired work in the last twenty years has come from Hayao Miyazaki and his Ghibli Studio, but even he works in this way. This is not very surprising, as he began his career working in Japanese made-for-TV animation through the 'sixties and 'seventies. For instance, in his *My Neighbour Totoro* (1988), many of the runs are done on fours, and the moving vehicles are also animated on fours. This is pixillation, not animation. You can study the effect of this by running his films at double speed, when the animation becomes very smooth, and incidentally the pace of the story is increased, which helps the less inspired sections of films like *Princess Mononoke* (1997). However, Miyazaki more than compensates for this shortcoming by the beauty of his static images and the completely distinctive imagination

of his stories. On the formal style side, Miyazaki's films are marked by a tendency to go back, often very far back, from the action.

3D Computer Animation

Computer animation has up until recently sensibly stuck with non-realistic characters. Sensibly, because with the standard 3D animation computer programmes, the figures are created on a jointed armature, a schematic skeleton with flexible joints – called "bones" – that has fixed dimensions. Standard CGI figures are in fact essentially puppets which are moved both as a whole, and by their connected elements, over trajectories in space. And their internal volume remains constant, although their outer surface can move. All this precludes the use of the "squash" and "stretch" that were a basic part of the animator's armoury.

Bobby Bumps may be falling on twos in 1919, but at least Earl Hurd changed his body position as he fell.

Felix is squashed to a cat-puddle by the force of his ejection from a beanery. I have superimposed frames from Felix Revolts *(1923).*

Koko's dog Fitz stretches out as he leaves the frame with a purloined beard in Koko the Kid *shown in two superimposed frames.*

("Squash" and "stretch" mean treating the drawn figure as though it were made of rubber, so that, for instance, when a character lands heavily, their body shortens, and when they shoot forward at high speed, their body stretches out.)

Hence the use of rigid toys as characters in the first 3D CGI animated feature, *Toy Story* (1995), followed by rigid insects in *Antz* and *A Bug's Life* in 1998. 3D CGI computer animation programmes have been developed to handle the appearance of movement of skin and flesh around the bones of living creatures, and eventually an attempt at the realistic depiction of humans in movement was made in *Final Fantasy* (2001). It failed. The stumbling block was the appearance of the human face, particularly when moving to express feeling. The complicated network of facial muscles, and what they can do to the fine detail and imperfections of the skin in movement, is still far beyond the capabilities of computer programmes. Here is a close shot of one of the characters in

Final Fantasy failing to react to the violent and gruesome end of her companion.

And the leading character in the film, Dr. Aki Ross, on whom the most care was lavished by the animators, doesn't do any better than this in reacting to her even more astounding experiences. The possibility of interesting human interaction with this level of computer animation technique is zero.

However, strong facial expressions *can* be created on simplified faces without realistic detail, as had been demonstrated with insects in *Antz* and *A Bug's Life*, and more recently for simplified quasi-humans in *Shrek*. The makers of these films seem to be clear about what is the best way to use the computer technology available at the moment, whereas the makers of *Final Fantasy* are not. More recently, the confusion about what to do at the intersection of 3D computer graphics animation and live action filming is illustrated by *Sky Captain and the World of Tomorrow* (2004), in which live actors with the detail of their features smoothed out are inserted into computer generated scenes, and *The Polar Express* (2004), which achieves the same sort of effect in a more extreme form by using Tom Hanks' performance incompletely recorded by motion capture as the model for the computer generated figures. This last has a kind of parallel in the technique devised by Bob Sabiston and used in Richard Linklater's *Waking Life* (2001), and subsequent films, to flatten live action film footage into the appearance of drawn graphic art, again removing the interesting detail of the human face and body in action.

But all this is a far cry from drawn animation, where the idiosyncrasies of an artist's line can give a special kind of beauty to the movement of imagined beings. That's really what it was all about.

The frame illustrations for this article were grabbed from the appropriate VHS tapes and DVD recordings, which means that they lack the sharpness of my usual frame enlargements taken from film prints, but I judge that they are adequate to make my points. I get them by feeding an analogue signal from the VHS or DVD player into Adobe Premiere through a digitizing card with minimum compression, and then selecting the frame inside Premiere, and grabbing it as a TIFF file. There may be other ways to do this, but I doubt that they will produce appreciably better results.

Richard Abel's valuable researches into French cinema of the 'twenties resulted in a book, *French Cinema: The First Wave, 1915-1929* (Princeton University Press, 1984), and eventually a season of films to illustrate it at the National Film Theatre. Most of them had not been seen outside France, at any rate since the nineteen-twenties. The main revelation was the many French films with rural themes, which were referred to a "*plein air* films" at the time. Although Richard Abel had looked at most of the films in the French archives before he wrote about them, he had missed André Antoine's *L'Arlésienne*. After seeing it, I felt that it would be useful to make some important points about Antoine's film-making, based on what he actually did in his films. It appeared in *Sight & Sound* in the Spring 1988 number (v 57 n 2).

WHAT IS WRONG WITH
THIS PICTURE?

Or, why were there no more André Antoine films after L'Arlésienne?

This is certainly a good-looking picture, like most of the images in Antoine's films, for the man had long experience as a photographer, having taken immense numbers of stills as reference material for his stage productions. But then we have to ask how this picture fits into the flow of shots in the film.

It is actually the first shot from a scene almost at the beginning of the *L'Arlésienne*, and it is the point at which the narrative gets under way, just after the main characters have been introduced. Fréderi, the protagonist, has just been given an errand by his widowed mother (standing foreground) as he rides off from the stables (middle distance) of their farm. By 1920 most French film-makers would have used some cutting to closer shots in the exchange between mother and son, but Antoine, whose 1919 film *La Terre*, was still constructed on the primitive "one scene -- one shot" basis, had only just learned about this, and tended to relapse into the older style of covering all the action in one shot taken from a distance, as he does here. Then he suddenly remembers what he has been told about cutting to different angles, or someone on the crew reminds him, and we get a shot of Fréderi's simple-minded little brother, "L'Innocent",

calling out "Take me with you, Fréderi." But where is L'Innocent standing? He cannot be recognized anywhere in the first shot of the scene, and it is impossible to tell where he is from any reaction given by the tiny figure of Fréderi as he rides away after a cut back to the first set-up. In fact it was only after careful repeated examination of the print of the film that I could work out that the little brother *is* actually in the frame in the first shot, as a tiny, nearly invisible dot, sitting on a rock under a tree at the top right of the main shot, rather than somewhere behind the wall at the left of the picture, as I assumed with puzzlement on first seeing the film. Not a good beginning to a major film production, even in France back in 1921.

Antoine had established himself as one of the most important figures in French theatre from 1887 when he set up the Théâtre Libre, and he made his name by following two principles. The first was the staging of large numbers of new plays, and the second was the thorough-going application of the ideas that Zola had put forward in his essay *le Naturalisme au théâtre* (1881) and other writings, and indeed had also demonstrated when collaborating in the stagings of versions of his novels *L'assomoir* and *Nana* in 1879 and 1881. But after long success pursuing these ideas, in 1914 Antoine was forced into film-making in an attempt to recoup the large sums of money that his productions at the Théâtre National de l'Odéon had lost in the preceding several years. He quickly became fascinated by the medium, and in a letter to a friend in 1916 he wrote:

> "For some weeks I have been up to my neck in the cinema. It is not as horrible as one thinks, and is even probably a new art that is rising up, which will regale our children, but there is not enough time to adapt myself to it, and I will be satisfied to draw from it some resources which basically the theatre could not provide me."

What he meant by this was that film made possible an even more detailed realism (or naturalism) than he had been exploiting in the theatre, and this led to his determination to shoot as much as possible of his films on location. This is the feature of *L'Arlésienne* and his other films that makes them more interesting now than they were at the time, for they reproduce for us the look of a world that has vanished for ever. But on the other hand, Antoine did not really understand the true nature of editing in the cinema, tending to think of it as just something that could make instantaneous scene changes in a way that was impossible in the theatre; "The cinema can do everything! It is a magician! It is at the same time the theatre and the novel, conversation and painting! And nature, old man! The cinema satisfies all our curiosities, all our taste for speed, and this desire for changes that the fastest revolving stages cannot give us. At the cinema, you are in Paris; one second later, in San Francisco."

Although by the time he made *L'Arlésienne* Antoine had heard about editing, he did not properly understand the way it worked, and that the real power of cutting in the standard form of cinema ("mainstream continuity cinema" or "classical cinema") which had been recently developed in America, and which was just beginning to be assimilated by the French film industry at the end of World War I, lay in the way it made possible the omission of the boring bits of action

within scenes that did not contribute to the story, and also the way it was able to emphasize the emotional interplay between characters by careful control of the camera placement. Close examination of *L'arlésienne* shows that Antoine covered every inch of his actors movements over the ground within the scenes when he shot the film, whereas any experienced French film-maker, even at that date, would have been able to arrange camera set-ups, and exits and entrances from the frame, to get a character from A to B quickly. This frequently put the editor of *L'Arlésienne* in an impossible position when trying to speed up the action by cutting out the bits completely irrelevant to the narrative, and at one point he even had to resort to producing an actual version of the legendary joke of film-makers with continuity problems "oh, well, we will just have to cut to the cat" -- in this case, a totally pointless insert shot of a rooster put in to shorten the non-functional travel of the hero from background to foreground in a scene near the end of the film. Even after his film career had ended in 1923, Antoine was still insisting that the only best way to film would be to use multiple camera filming -- "It must be possible to shoot the scenes with five or six operators. To make the actors work under the cross-fire of the lenses, and know how to select successively the best gestures, the truest expressions. This is elementary, this is logical." But of course, this practice, if it had been carried out, would not only have forced the whole scene to run in real time, but would also have limited the possible angles chosen, through the necessity of keeping the cameras out of each other's field of view, as everyone found out several years later at the beginning of the sound cinema, when they were forced into it by technical constraints. Antoine's collaborators in the cinema had a dim realisation of what was wrong with his approach, but they were obviously unable to explain it properly to him, presumably because they had not yet fully understood the newly developed standard form of cinema themselves.

Although Antoine had two cameramen on *L'arlésienne*, it seems that they were not used to get

L'ARLESIENNE, prise de vue de la farandole devant la ferme du Castelet.

_ Le voilà donc encore,
ce vieux Castelet que
je n'ai pas vu depuis
tant d'années!

two angles simultaneously on the scenes, but just to shoot side by side to get a second negative for foreign distribution, as the Americans had been doing for several years. (There is a contemporary sketch of one scene of the film being shot to prove this.) However, it is possible that some scenes of *L'hirondelle et la mésange*, which Antoine made after *L'Arlésienne*, but which was never released by Pathé, (see *Sight & Sound*, Summer 1984, page 163) may have been shot with two cameras simultaneously. This would explain the strange cuts from one angle to another angle at 90 degrees to the first, but at the same camera distance, on some of the group scenes in the former film. Unfortunately, these cuts in *L'hirondelle et la mésange* show nothing that was not equally visible from the first angle, and so forcibly disprove the mistaken theory of film-making that Antoine clung to. Likewise, in *L'Arlésienne*, Antoine's literal-minded attitude to the reproduction of reality by the cinema is surely behind the clumsiness of his scene dissection. In a later scene in that film, in which an old relative makes an emotional return to the farm after many years, she is placed with her back to the farm, looking out away from it as she recognizes it. And when she names the buildings – sheep-folds, silk-worm shed, barns -- we are not shown them, nor do we get a frontal view of her face to show her emotion clearly. (In the same scene in Daudet's stage play, on which the film is based, both she and the buildings are all in view to the audience at the same time.)

In fact the adaptation André Antoine made of Alphonse Daudet's play for the film is a rather clumsy piece of work, and is basically carried out by putting onto the screen the events that are related in the play as having taken place before the action started, or that take place off-scene during it. Daudet had carefully carpentered the stage play *L'Arlésienne* after the standard nineteenth century model of the "well-made play", using material from stories in his *Lettres de mon moulin*, principally from the one also called *L'arlésienne*. In the play, this brief story of the infatuation of the son

_ Je le crois bien!...
Ici, les bergeries....
là-bas, la magnanerie
et les hangars

of a farm with the girl from Arles, the discovery that she was already another man's mistress, and his eventual suicide, was contrasted with the effects resulting from the way the old shepherd Balthazar had long ago forsworn an illicit love, and was also paralleled with the struggle of M. Seguin's goat against her fated death, which is referred to at various points in the action of the play by L'innocent and Balthazar. Antoine retains the final ironic quotation from *le Chèvre de M. Seguin* in the film, but he eliminates the telling of the significant part of the story near the beginning of the play, so completely destroying Daudet's effect. In the play the comic relief derived from *Tartarin de Tarascon* is also cleverly integrated, and the indeed the whole vehicle held the stage in France for several decades. But in the film these parallel themes are partially lost, and what is left of them does more to hold up the action than illuminate it. Even the dramatic effects of Daudet's stage directions are ignored. The first half of the second act of the play, in which Fréderi is emotionally devastated and adrift, is described in the play text as being set on the flat marshy Camargue plain by the lake of Vaccarès, with its "immense, empty horizon", but this paralleling of Nature and dramatic action of the best Zolaesque variety is thrown away entirely in the film, despite Antoine having insisted on shooting the film on the real locations.

As well as the exteriors, some of the interior scenes of *L'Arlésienne* were shot on location, with both positive and negative results. The positive results are that we can still see what a few rooms in a few buildings in the Arles region looked like in 1921, and the negative result is that these interiors are rather crudely lit with the extra lights put in by L-H. Burel to get an exposure: in one case making nonsense of the important fact that the scene was supposed to be taking place in the middle of the night. At this date Burel was far from being the master cameraman he eventually became, as is also shown by the major scene in the film that was shot in the studio, and not on location. Here the lighting is much rougher than the best film lighting of the period, as can be seen in the illustration, which shows the final moment of the scene which had ended the second act of the play. Fréderi has just announced that he will renounce the girl from Arles, and marry the farm girl his parents had wanted him to marry all along, and then we get the old-fashioned theatrical posed "tableau -- Curtain!" (Sorry, "Fade-out!"). And consider also the cheap look of the set. It might be added that such faults as these are common enough in other French films of the period, and are just some of the reasons that French films could not break into the American market in the 'twenties.

We are always told that Antoine introduced a new realism and restraint in acting into the theatre, which

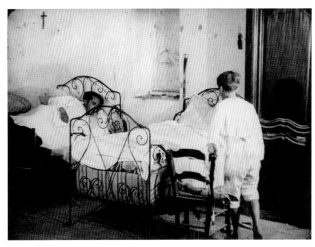

Night location interior overlit by L.-H. Burel with arc floodlights so that it looks like day.

Studio interior with cheap set, crude lighting, and theatrical tableau staging.

Gabriel de Gravonne upstaging a horse.

Lucienne Breval and Gabriel de Gravonne giving it all they've got.

may be true, but a glance at a couple of frames from *L'Arlésienne* should suggest that he was far from being up to date with the point film acting had reached in 1921. Gabriel de Gravonne, in the leading role of Fréderi, gives a grotesquely exaggerated performance, which has a certain interest as an indication of what was presumably still acceptable at that date from a *jeune premier* on the European stage (and rather similar to the embarrassing performance of Gustav Frölich in Fritz Lang's *Metropolis*), and Lucienne Breval, the opera singer, in the other main part of his mother, periodically lives down to the traditional idea of opera acting. The rest of the cast do fairly well by the standards of Continental film acting of the time, but was Antoine directing the actors, or wasn't he? Altogether, it is not surprising that Pathé took his camera away from him after they had given him one more chance on *L'hirondelle et la mésange*.

Despite these faults, enough of the strong original material from Daudet's play survives in passable form to make Antoine's film of *L'Arlésienne* bear re-seeing, but it seems to me that his truly valuable legacy to the cinema was a man he had employed to direct stage productions at his theatres earlier in the century; namely, Maurice Tourneur. For it was actually Tourneur, in the films he made during World War I in America, who pushed restraint and the precise control of the detail in film acting into regions that were inaccessible to Antoine himself.

The film school at the Royal College of Art was in an annexe that was behind the Natural History Museum in South Kensington, and a quarter of a mile away from the main buildings of the college, which are next to the Albert Hall. This suited me very well, because I found the atmosphere of conceit and snobbery at the RCA rather unpleasant. It can be epitomised by the fact that the lecturers boasted about their Senior Common Room, with its expensive silver cutlery, fine wines on sale for lunch, and paintings by famous modern artists on the walls. University College was not like that. They also continuously boasted about the accomplishments of their departments and themselves in a way that repelled me as well. All this was largely due to the special nature and status of the Royal College of Art, which is not a full part of the system of higher education in Britain. It is funded directly and lavishly by the Government, and not through the University Funding Council like all the other institutions. It is solely a postgraduate college, unlike all the other art colleges in Britain, and so could select the cream of the graduates from the other schools of art and design to do its higher degrees. So it was actually quite small, with only a few hundred students. The RCA did have some advantages for me, like access to its technical facilities, as I have already mentioned. The film students also already had degrees, mostly from art schools, and had already made films or videos. Each year we were in a position to select only the most talented handful from hundreds of applicants. This meant that the students did not need that much teaching, which made the job less interesting for me. Also, the head of the school, Dick Ross, tried to sideline me as much as possible. He had no experience in film, having been an editor (in the newspaper sense) in television news before he got the job. He played favourites amongst the students, who were those who sat at his feet in his office while he told them self-glorifying anecdotes about his past life. He fitted right in to the Royal College of Art. Eventually he proposed to throw out one of the more talented and idiosyncratic students who did not worship at his court, on the bogus grounds that his work was no good. I had to speak up against this, which did

not endear me to Dick Ross. So he looked for someone more compliant to replace me.

After I had been sacked from the RCA at the end of 1987, another part-time job teaching film making at Goldsmiths College was passed on to me by Yossi Bal, who wanted to take up a better job running the film course at another London college. Yossi was another graduate of the Slade film course: the most talented and intelligent of them, I would say. The film-making course at Goldsmiths was very small scale, and rather like the film-making course at the Slade. I did all the teaching, as I had done at the Slade. This job only lasted a term, as the possibility of a full-time job came up at the London International Film School, where I was still teaching film history. There I was put in charge of the film-making in the fourth and fifth terms, where the film exercises were now shot on 35 mm., and mostly in the school's studios. I supervised the production of these student films, which were 10 to 15 minutes in length, from the script stage through to the final creation of their mixed sound tracks in the dubbing studio. The instruction in the various craft areas of film-making was done by the teachers in the school's camera department, sound department, editing department, and so on, but given my own technical expertise and experience, I also contributed technical as well as aesthetic advice along the way. I would say that since 1988 I have supervised about 70 hours of finished 35 mm. film; equivalent to 40 or so full-length features, which is quite a bit more 35 mm. production than anyone else in the British film industry has handled over these years.

Teaching at the London International Film School was not like teaching at a university, where one is given plenty of time outside a limited amount of classroom teaching to do one's own research. Nevertheless I still managed to get more work done in the evenings and holidays. One piece that I wrote at this time was about Cecil B. DeMille's early films, which was a consequence of seeing a season of them at the National Film Theatre. I did not try to get it published when I wrote it, because I felt it needed something extra to wrap it up in a satisfactory and striking way. It could still do with a better finish.

THE WORLD INSIDE
CECIL B. DeMILLE

Long ago Kevin Brownlow put forward the idea that the best Cecil B. DeMille films date from before 1919, and I am not going to disagree with him. However there is quite a lot more to be said on this subject, and some of it follows here. Not only are the early films DeMille's best, but there are also more of them, for half his films were made before 1919. Although DeMille himself ascribed the sharp slow-down in his productivity from 1920 onwards to the need to take more care with each production, the case was probably not that simple. As early as 1918, DeMille had diverted part of his attention to flying and to his aviation company, and even after he sold it in 1921 he continued to alternate mildly adventurous trips by land, sea, and air with his film-making, and sometimes combined the two. I see this effect as a newly rich and successful man enjoying himself after twenty years of hard work and struggle. Then too, there was the fact that from 1920 DeMille felt that he was not getting a share of the profits of the Lasky company commensurate with his contribution to its success, which seems to have dampened his enthusiasm for making films for them, and led to him setting up his own production company in that year, and then eventually to his quitting Lasky altogether. (The details can be found in his autobiography and also the subsequent biography of him written by Charles Higham.)

Apart from there being less of them, the Cecil B. DeMille films of the nineteen-twenties also differ from the earlier ones in that they mostly contain explicit moral preachment, both in their intertitles, and also in the way the story is written to present a moral, or indeed sometimes a totally religious subject. DeMille himself was quite conscious of this shift, and described his *Something to Think About* of 1920 as "... the first of my pictures to embody a religious theme." The earlier films do often contain central moral dilemmas for their characters, but these are implicit, just another part of the workings of the plot, and not baldly stated in the titles. For instance, in the best-known film of the early period, *The Cheat*, the heroine makes improper use of money with which she has been entrusted to get herself out of a difficulty, and this activates the plot.

The same is true of other early DeMille films that have re-emerged from the archives. In *The Golden Chance* the heroine, who is raised from the lower depths by an upper-class couple, is persuaded by them to pretend to be a society woman to further their financial schemes, and is then entrapped

The destitute father and daughter struggle across country in What's-His-Name (1914)

in a complex of further dishonest concealment, and in *The Warrens of Virginia* the heroine is torn between her obligations to her family and to her sweetheart. Although the earliest productions of the Lasky Feature Play Company were true melodramas, in which any improbable event could to be used to set up a situation which would produce a strong emotional reaction in the audience, these moral cruces in the DeMille films of the next years move them some very real steps away from melodrama and towards Ibsen.

These early films are also the most directly related to DeMille's own life in some of their details — the 1914 *What's-His-Name* includes a sequence in which a penniless father takes his little daughter on a long journey home across country while living rough, and this is shown in uncontrived-looking scenes with the breath of the real open air in them. The daughter is played by Cecilia, DeMille's own daughter, and at this date he frequently took her around with him to work at the still fairly primitive and casual Lasky studios in Hollywood, sometimes riding across country to locations. In fact the parts of both the father and daughter in this film are filled out with much observant detail, in a way that becomes much less marked in DeMille's direction of actors over the decades. Lively invention abounds elsewhere in this film, starting from the introductory cameos which show the two leading characters as posters which come to life and josh the poster-hanger who has just stuck them up. This beginning is cleverly integrated with the theatrical subject of the film later, because the plot spring of the film is activated by the heroine seeing the poster for a travelling vaudeville company being hung. The subsequent separation of husband and wife, as she becomes a vaudeville star, and he is left at home with the baby, could also be connected, with a reverse twist, to the end of DeMille's sexual relationship with his wife at this time.

The DeMille films in the war years often deal with poverty, and this is represented in them in a more convincing way than in other contemporary American films, partly due to the excellent sets created and dressed by Wilfred Buckland and his team, but also because it was only a decade since DeMille and his wife had themselves been poor, and knew what it was like. Ten years later, and the erosion of time and wealth left DeMille's films no closer to reality than the average Hollywood film.

In 1914 DeMille was still largely filming on the basis of one shot to each scene, with the camera at the "French foreground" distance of 12 feet, but over the next few years he absorbed some of the new ideas about film construction which were already standard in the work of other directors who had been in the business longer than he had. He first seized on Griffith's use of cross-cutting between parallel actions, which Griffith used mostly for suspense and similar purposes, whereas DeMille developed it to emphasize the contrast between the two separate actions. In *What's-His-Name*, as the destitute father and daughter starve in the countryside, the mother lives in luxury and is courted by a millionaire, and in *The Warrens of Virginia* (1915), a young couple have their first kiss as a

battle rages elsewhere. The peak of DeMille's efforts in this direction was the sequence in *The Whispering Chorus* (1918), in which a supposedly dead husband is having a liaison with a Chinese prostitute in an opium den, while his unknowing wife is being remarried in church.

Another important technique that Griffith had developed was the use of the Insert shot — an object (other than a person's face) in the main scene shown in a separate close shot. With Griffith Inserts were basically used to emphasize a dramatic point, and though DeMille used them for this function too, he also got striking and original sensual effects from them. In *The Golden Chance* (1915), a brutish petty criminal breaks into a woman's bedroom in a rich home, and examines the silken and lacy underwear by the light of a torch. DeMille lingers on a series of inserts of his large rough hands moving inside transparent lacy stockings, etc.

The climax of Cecil B. DeMille's efforts in this period is *Old Wives for New* (1918), which integrates all this personal form and substance — his relations with the women around him, and new devices of film construction — in a way that stands up very well and deserves repeated viewing.

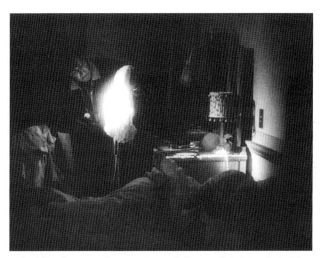

A burglar fingers a sleeping woman's flimsies lubriciously in The Golden Chance (1915)

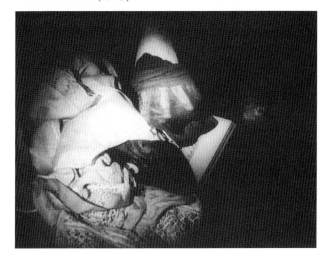

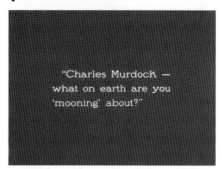

"Charles Murdock — what on earth are you 'mooning' about?"

DeMille claimed that he was pressured into making this film by the New York office, and it is indeed possible that the material in it follows a trend that was emerging on the East coast in the previous couple of years, as in *The On-the-Square Girl* (1917), but this claim might also be the result of hindsight, after having realised that he had, consciously or unconsciously, let a little too much of himself get into the film. In any case, he had himself broached sophisticated cosmopolitan depravity in the first place in 1915 with *The Cheat* and *The Golden Chance*.

In *Old Wives for New*, the wife of the protagonist, a successful business man, has grown fat and slovenly over the years, and this is presented with gruesome vividness in the opening scenes of the film. Then the husband, looking at a picture of her when she was young, slim, and beautiful, has a flashback to their first meeting. The dissolve through the shot of the husband looking at the picture takes us to a series of shots showing the young man fishing in a country stream. He accidentally hooks the skirt of a young country girl paddling in the stream, and reels her in, thinking he has a bite. This scene is shot with DeMille's customary visual elegance, combined with a touch of humour in the detail of the staging. He shares his lunch with her, and she eagerly hoes into it, in a way which presages her future grossness and gluttony. At this point there is a straight cut to a close shot of his wife, as she now is in the present, entering a door and looking off camera in a way that gives the impression that she is looking at the scene we have been watching, and to which we cut straight back, so reinforcing the effect. Now the husband kisses her younger self in the past scene, and there is another cut straight back to the same shot of the present fat, sluttish wife looking off screen, continuing the Point of View effect, and she says, "Charles Murdock — what on earth are you 'mooning' about?". We cut back yet again to the past scene, in which the embracing couple spring apart, and only now is there a dissolve back to

the wife as she is now, standing behind her husband's chair. A simultaneity of past and present the equal of anything in Resnais, and also sharply directed to the immediate point. The husband goes off on a hunting trip with some other men, just like C.B. often did at the time, and he meets another woman, who like himself (and C.B.) wears leather leggings or tight high boots in the wild. (Oh, yes, Jeanie Macpherson, DeMille's scriptwriter and lover from 1915 took to copying his characteristic footwear on location, and she accompanied him on some of his extra-filmic adventures, too.)

DeMille's mildly fetishistic fascination with feet and footwear continues to play its part in the symmetries of this film, for after the husband has rejected the possibility of an affair with the other woman, because his wife will not give him a divorce, he meets her again by recognizing her feet at the dress shop which she manages. The hopelessness of his situation leads him to accept an invitation from some loose-living society types to go to a smart night-club. There follows a brilliantly worked out scene of interplay between several people — the husband, his elderly roué friend, the latter's mistress, and two other women, one of whom has eyes for the roué, and the other for the husband. As a natural part of night-club behaviour of the period, the mistress of the

roué draws a funny face on a balloon with her lipstick, and holds it next to his head. He laughs, and accidentally bursts it with his cigar, so presaging what is to shortly happen to him. The other woman who is out to snare the husband writes "Memory" on her balloon, shows it to the husband and then bursts it to suggest that he forget his sorrows. But he smells the perfume on her handkerchief, which is the same as that used by the woman loves. This is conveyed by a matted-in image of flowers sliding over the frame about her head — a striking composition, as usual with DeMille — in the same way that the perfume had been introduced visually in the hunting scene. Now a woman sitting at another table makes a play for the roué by impressing her lips on a balloon while giving him the eye, and then throwing it at him. When he invites her over and makes up to her, his mistress stalks out in anger. She goes home, broods over her wrongs, notices her silver revolver nestling among a pile of silk ribbons in a drawer, picks it up and puts it in a white fur muff, all of this being shown off in a series of yet more Inserts of great visual sensuality. The mistress, who is played by Julia Faye, DeMille's own new inamorata since 1917, bribes her way into her lover's apartment where he is entertaining his pick-up, has a hair-tearing fight with her, and then lets him have it

with the revolver. While the pickup becomes hysterical and crawls into a corner clutching a toy dog, the roué collapses with surprise, investigating the fatal hole in his shirt, and the seduction music he has playing on the gramophone grinds into the centre of the record — "You're Here, and I'm Here", from *The Laughing Husband*, by Jerome Kern.

There's more, but I'll leave you to find it for yourselves, just pausing to note a scene a little later, when our hero, to protect the name of his friend, threatens the mistress in case she should reveal what really happened, with nice looming shadows up the wall to emphasize his point, provided by cameraman Alvin Wyckoff. To keep your head spinning, I also note that the script of this film had been written by Jeanie McPherson, who had been superseded in DeMille's affections by Julia Faye. With this film the reality and fantasy inside DeMille's heart reached its most intense statement on screen,

and also its most perfect formal expression. *Old Wives for New* was a film he couldn't help making, whereas after this, his films became increasingly those he *thought* he should make.

This was the point in his career when the fantasy life of DeMille's films was the most continuous with the life he created around himself off screen. Of course, he was not the only successful film-maker to do this, for later on there were other Hollywood directors who did it in their own different ways, most notably John Ford.

Nevertheless, the later films still contain a fair deposit of DeMille's inner self, all connected with his innate sensuality (in the general sense of the term), his liking for the splendour and feel of rich fabrics, fur, leather, and metal, as attested by the way he surrounded himself with them in his home and estate, where he kept weapons, costumes, and props from his films, and wore Russian silk blouses when relaxing.

At the London Film School, I did get a few days off on a few occasions to go to a few silent film conferences and festivals, although I was never able to be there for the full duration of these events. A series of these occasions brought forth some pieces on German cinema, starting with one on the origin of many of Lubitsch's films in operetta plots, which I had sketched several years earlier at the University of East Anglia conference in 1982. This work was presented at a small conference on German silent cinema held in Luxembourg in 1989, which was organized by Walter Schatzberg, with the assistance of Uli Jung. The organizers looked after us well, and the high point as far as I was concerned was reclining on a garden lounger in the grounds of the residence of the German ambassador to Luxembourg at a reception in the evening, looking out over the city with a drink in my hand. Once in a while little extra pleasures come along for film researchers.

THE WORLD INSIDE
ERNST LUBITSCH

It is always said that the basic substance of Ernst Lubitsch's German films was formed by the local Jewish comedy of Berlin and the theatre of Max Reinhardt, but is this really true? On the first count, it is true that in his two earliest surviving films some of the characters have Jewish names, but in other respects I find it hard to see any of the specific features of Jewishness that might well have been present, either in the home life of the characters, in their gestures, or in their speech as rendered in dialogue intertitles, given that all of these indications of Jewishness can be seen reproduced elsewhere in other German silent films made by other directors. In fact, *Der Stolz der Firma* and *Schuhpalast Pinkus*, the names of the characters apart, could just as well have been based on the nineteenth-century Viennese shopkeeper comedies of Nestroy. Even if we turn to the films that Lubitsch made before 1920 which are now lost, there is only *Meyer aus Berlin*, *Die Firma heiratet*, and *Der Blusenkönig*, making just three films out of forty, that give any indication of relating to the Jewish shopkeeper milieu, and there is no reason to think that these other three films were any more specifically Jewish than *Der Stolz der Firma* and *Schuhpalast Pinkus*. As for the influence of Max Reinhardt, that is rather more difficult to decide, as we have to rely on rather vague verbal accounts of his productions that do not tell us their exact nature, plus just a little help from the surviving photographs of scenes from them.

But if we look at what was playing in Berlin when the 15 year-old Lubitsch became so infatuated with the theatre that he left his father's business, we find that although Max Reinhardt had been an important part of the theatre scene for a few years, there were also, and I suggest far more exciting and glamorous to a teen-ager, no less than five theatres presenting operetta and *opéra comique*. To take the completely typical week of 14 April 1907, as recorded in the *Berliner Tageblatt*, the Theater des Westens was showing Franz Lehar's *Die lustige Witwe*, which was premièred in 1905, and restarted the operetta craze in this period before World War I, and also *Der Zigeunerbaron* (Johann Strauss II, 1885), while the Central Theater had *Die Fledermaus* (J. Strauss II, 1874) and *Wiener Blut* (J. Strauss II, 1899), the Deutsch-Amerikanische Theater *Mamzelle Nitouche* (Hervé, 1883), the Komische Oper *Carmen* (Bizet, 1875) and *Hoffmans Erzählungen* (J. Offenbach, 1881), while the Apollo had Paul Lincke's *Der Triumph des Weibes* (Première unknown, but recent). For a city of three million people, that is a lot of operetta. In fact, from before the first world war up to the nineteen-thirties, operetta

was a major part of central European theatre, to a much greater extent than musical comedy was in America or England, and throughout the same period it had a glamour at least equalling that of the cinema. By the end of 1908 two theatres, the Berliner Operettentheater and the Neue Operettentheater had been named as exclusively dedicated to the operetta form, and the latter of these was showing *Die Dollarprinzessin* (Leo Fall, 1907) and *Der tapfere Soldat* (Oscar Straus, 1908). The amount of operetta showing in the Berlin theatre continued constant through until the beginning of the 'twenties, and in 1919 most of these operettas, such as *Die Dollarprinzessin*, were still appearing in repertory.

Given all this, it is no surprise that when Ernst Lubitsch was able to move on to more ambitious film projects, he and his script collaborators should turn to the musical theatre for inspiration. Of course, wherever they could possibly get away with it, Lubitsch and his collaborators did not give credit to their sources in the lyric theatre, since most of them were still in copyright, and I very much doubt that they paid for any film rights to the story details they "borrowed". This was much easier to do in the Germany at the end of World War I than it was in Hollywood a decade or so later, when litigation by authors who imagined the slightest resemblance of a film to their own work became the order of the day. So in 1917 we have Lubitsch's film *Ein fideles Gefängnis*, which is a fairly straight version of *Die Fledermaus*, in 1918 *Carmen*, with the scenario source credited to Prosper Merimée's novel, which *was* out of copyright, and then in 1919 at least three films derived from operetta. The first of these was *Die Austernprinzessin*, which takes its departure, as might be guessed from its title, from *Die Dollarprinzessin*. The opening scene of the film is almost identical to that of the operetta, with a chorus of typists working in unison under the supervision of the American tycoon John Quaker, whereas in the operetta they are working under the supervision of his daughter, and the tycoon's name is John Couder. In the operetta, his daughter says, "If I should ever want a man, I'd buy one – you might have to pay a bit more for a Baron or an Earl. I regard a man as much a plaything as a monkey on a stick", and the sense of this speech is reproduced in the film, as is the general attitude of the millionaire's daughter. Two of the male principals, an impoverished German aristocrat and his friend, are also taken over into the film, but after the first scene the plots of the operetta and the film diverge. However, a little later in *Die Austernprinzessin*, ideas from other operettas are laid under tribute, for the jokingly improvised enthronement of the impoverished nobleman irresistibly recalls that of the similarly impoverished Count of Luxembourg at the end of the first act of the operetta of the same name by Lehar which was a smash hit in 1909, and there is also more than a hint of *Die Fledermaus* in the things the men in Lubitsch's film get up to.

Lubitsch's second operetta-based film of 1919 was *Madame Dubarry*, the first hour of which follows the narrative of Carl Millöcker's operetta *Gräfin Dubarry* quite closely. (I am referring here to the original 1897 version of *Gräfin Dubarry*, and not the Theo Mackeben revision of 1931, which was called *Die Dubarry*). Both operetta and film start with Jeanne Bécu working in the hat shop of the tyrannical Madame Labille, both have her getting into trouble over the loss of hats, and then escaping to an assignation with her lover, a young poet. After a scene unique to the film, the Count Dubarry sees and desires Jeanne, and then in both operetta and film there is introduced an intrigue to make the sister of the Duc de Choiseuil the King's mistress. Next both contain a gambling party at which use is made of Jeanne's sexuality, though in the film Jeanne has already become the Count Dubarry's mistress at this stage, whereas in the operetta she is the lover of other men. In both operetta and film Dubarry introduces Jeanne to the King to further his political ambitions, in both she is married off to Count Dubarry's brother to satisfy convention, and in both her former poet lover finds her in the King's presence in a compromising situation. Jeanne now becomes the King's mistress, which is the "happy end" of the operetta. However the film continues on from this point with more plot, presumably as an excuse to include the spectacle of the French Revolution, and it finishes with the decapitation of Madame Dubarry shown in detail, though this gruesome scene is missing from some surviving prints.

Finally in 1919, Ernst Lubitsch made *Die Puppe*, which follows Edmond Audran's operetta *La Poupée* (1896) so closely in characters and action that I will not bother to detail the correspondences, except to say that the sexual suggestiveness of the film is already present in the operetta, as is the cheeky

doll-maker's assistant and his antics. In fact the only significant narrative addition Lubitsch made was to add an introductory scene in which he himself was shown taking dolls representing the two principal characters out of a toybox, and setting them up on a miniature set which becomes, by a trick cut, real actors performing the beginning of the story in doll-like manner on a full-sized version of the same stylized set. The whole of *Die Puppe* is played out in this manner against sets flatly simplified and stylized in the "Toy Town" style, and it is worth noting that it was released on 4 December 1919, one month before shooting started on *Das Cabinet des Dr. Caligari* (see *Der Film*, 4 January 1920, page 38), and so it could well have been one of the reasons that the makers of *Caligari* also adopted flatly stylized sets. It is also possible that the introductory scene which Lubitsch added to *La Poupée* may have been suggested in its turn by the beginning of Benjamin Christensen's *Hævnens Nat* (The Night of Revenge, 1916), which was possibly shown in Berlin, like most other Danish films, at this time. At the beginning of *Hævnens Nat* Benjamin Christensen shows his leading actress a model of the house in which most of the action of his film will take place, the camera tracks in to it,

Lubitsch starting off Die Puppe *in the same way Christensen did* Hævnens Nat *in 1916, as shown on the right.*

*A set design by Ernst
Stern for Max Reinhardt's
1916 production of*
Sumurun.

and there is a dissolve to the narrative proper starting on the
equivalent part of the full-sized set.

In 1920 I do not recognize any operetta influences on
Lubitsch's films, but there was of course the clearest connection
with the theatre of Max Reinhardt in his film version of
Sumurun. Except that the written descriptions of the original
Reinhardt production of *Sumurun* emphasize its stylized
qualities, with actors in brightly coloured costumes disposed
against extremely simplified and colourless sets, whereas the
Lubitsch version is fairly realistic in settings and performances.
As a further digression on Reinhardt and stylized sets, I would
like to note that the use of flats with the major features of the
set painted on them in stylized form occurs at least as early
as Reinhardt's 1916 production of the Mozart/Hoffmansthal

pantomime *Die grüne Flöte*, as described on page 119 of
the designer Ernst Stern's *Bühnenbilder bei Max Reinhardt*
(Aufbau-Verlag, Berlin 1955).

Moving on to 1921, we come to Lubitsch's film *Die
Bergkatze*, and this is in essence a version of Offenbach's *Les
Brigands* (1869) which has suffered a glancing collision with
Oscar Straus' *Der tapfere Soldat*, which in its turn is George
Bernard Shaw's *Arms and the Man* (1894) with music. *Les
Brigands* has always been one of the most popular Offenbach
operettas in Germany (as *Die Banditen*), although this is not
so elsewhere, and in fact the only complete recording of *Les
Brigands* up to the present (i.e. 1989) is in German. Taking
the major correspondences in order of appearances, in both
Die Bergkatze and *Les Brigands* the second major scene has

Ernst Stern design for Die Grüne Flöte, *and on the right, a shot
from* Die Bergkatze.

a gang of comic bandits who are complaining that business is bad, and the heroine of both is the tough daughter of the bandit chief, who is loved by a less forceful bandit man. In both works the daughter of the bandit chief captures a noble traveller who is passing, and in both the daughter takes a portrait from him and then lets him go. At this point we find a part of *Der tapfere Soldat* embedded in *Die Bergkatze*, the connection being that the hero is caught without his pants in both, and the role of the photograph is reversed, from being one of the hero to one of the heroine, and going into, rather than out of, the lost clothes. *Der tapfere Soldat*, which takes place in the Balkans, and like all three works satirizes comically inept soldiery, presumably supplies the reason for the shift of the action of *Die Bergkatze* to the Balkans from the Italy of *Les Brigands*, though it is noticeable that one or two Italian names have survived among the bandits in Lubitsch's film. The next event in *Les Brigands* and *Die Bergkatze* is that ineffectual soldiery are sent against the bandits, but their later false claim to heroism in *Die Bergkatze* is again a reminiscence of a key part of *Der tapfere Soldat*, though in that work the inept battle is described in song, rather than visually represented, as it is in the film. When the bandits invade the fort in *Die Bergkatze* and get partly dressed in the clothes of the soldiery during a celebration, this is a straight transposition of a major part of the action of the Second Act of *Les Brigands*, but after being so close to each other in all these respects, the conclusions of the film and operetta are quite different. However, the points I have been making about what has been taken over into *Die Bergkatze* from the two operettas neglects all the extra novel invention brought to it by Lubitsch and his scenarist Hans Kräly, and there is more of that in this case than in the other films Lubitsch derived from the musical theatre of his day. Perhaps the most distinctive thing about *Die Bergkatze* is that the robber chief's daughter is the only strong active character, whereas the main men set opposite her are all weak and silly. This is not something that one ordinarily finds in operetta, or indeed in any other popular dramatic work of the period of which I know, with the possible exception of the "vampire" films of several years before. The "silly ass" characterization of Prince Alexis in *Die Bergkatze* is however something which is used for the hero's friend in some operettas, and it is also anticipated in a less extreme form in Count Danilo, the leading male character in *Die lustige Witwe*. This last point is of some importance, since the suave leading man who is sufficiently secure to brush aside reverses and rejections without shifting his smile is one of the most obviously distinctive features of Ernst Lubitsch's American films. The standard view of this character sees him as derived from the part Adolphe Menjou played in Chaplin's *A Woman of Paris* (1923), but the mould had cast him before that in the person of Count Danilo.

There is one last connection with the operetta world that I know about (though there could well be still more) in Lubitsch's German films, and this is that his last film made there, *Die Flamme*, is based on a play by Hans Müller, who was also totally involved in the world of the lyric theatre, having written a number of operetta libretti, and who also provided the story source for Oscar Straus' *Ein Walzertraum*, another big operetta hit of 1907, which was filmed by Lubitsch in 1931 as *The Smiling Lieutenant*. The record of the direct operetta influence on Lubitsch's American films can be read in any complete filmography, so I will just note that the six such films stretch all the way to the end of his career. (Yes, there are six, since *Monte Carlo* is based partly on a story by Hans Müller (again) and partly on André Messager's *Monsieur Beaucaire*, which was an operetta version, popular from 1919 in England, France and the U.S., of the 1907 straight play derived by Booth Tarkington from his original story.)

Although Lubitsch always carried the operetta world round inside him, it must be admitted that there was a real change in the story sources for the majority of his American films; a change from operetta to contemporary Central European boulevard comedy. This can be looked at in two ways: firstly as a move up-market yet again, to sources having a couple of millimetres more intellectual respectability, as a result of the big American studios being able to pay for the film rights to such plays, and secondly because these plays were more easily changed into the genuinely "American" product which Lubitsch said he wanted to make when he went to the United States, as recorded in an interview with Herbert Howe published in *Photoplay* (December 1922, page 28). This interview is an extended record of Lubitsch's desire to immerse himself in America and things truly American, and confirms that while the operetta world was a large part of the world inside Ernst Lubitsch, in the world outside him he was part of Jewish assimilation, and hence the political misjudgement of his *To Be or Not to Be* (1942).

SOURCES and ACKNOWLEDGEMENTS

The story content of the operettas referred to above has been taken from the vocal scores published by Joseph Weinberger (Vienna and London) in the case of *Der tapfere Soldat* and *Die Dollarprinzessin*, and in the other cases from both *Gänzl's Book of the Musical Theatre* by Kurt Gänzl and Andrew Lamb (The Bodley Head, 1988), and from *The Complete Book of Light Opera* by Mark Lubbock (Putnam, 1962). I also gathered confirming information from gramophone records and their accompanying libretti (which are licensed from the original publishers) for nearly all of the operettas mentioned. I would particularly like to thank Uli Jung and Walter Schatzberg for finding and passing on to me the information on the shooting date of *Das Cabinet des Dr. Caligari*, which confirm what I had long suspected, that its makers had the opportunity to see not only the September 1919 stage première of Ernst Toller's *Die Wandlung* with its Expressionist sets, but also that of Lubitsch's *Die Puppe*, with its equally stylized (but non-Expressionist) sets.

In this piece I missed out another couple of examples of Jewish humour in Lubitsch's early films. In *Die Austernprinzessin* there is a marriage-broker who is played as Jewish, with a couple of characteristic Yiddish lines of dialogue, but I don't think this enough to controvert my general point about Lubitsch's psychology. The piece itself was published as

Die innere Welt von Ernst Lubitsch in *Filmkultur zur Zeit der Weimarer Republik*, edited by Uli Jung and Walter Schatzberg K.G. (Saur, 1992).

The Pordenone *Giornate del cinema muto* took up the subject of German silent cinema in 1990, and I put together the following piece based on my researches.

FROM GERMAN STAGE
TO
GERMAN SCREEN

Straightening out Caligari...

The most specific reference I have seen to when *Das Cabinet des Dr. Caligari* was shot is in a statement made by Hermann Warm towards the end of his life, and collected in *Caligari und Caligarismus* (ed. Walter Kaul, Deutsche Kinemathek, 1970), where he says it "... was shot in 1919 in the late summer,". But, as I mentioned above, the Issue No. 1 of the German film trade paper *Der Film* for 4 January 1920 contains this note amongst the studio information about current production on page 38:-

'The preparations are completed for the new major Decla-Film "Das Cabinett des Dr. Caligaris", script by Hans Yanow and Karl Mayer. The direction is in the hands of Dr. Robert Wiene.
Conrad Veidt has been secured by Decla-Film Gesellschaft for the role of Caesare in the film "Das Cabinett des Dr. Caligaris".'

A set for Ernst Toller's Die Wandlung *by Robert Neppach in 1919.*

The next issue, a week later, contains the assignation of most of the rest of the cast, and the issue of 18 January notes that Hermann Warm, Walter Reimann, and Walter Röhrig will do the sets, and also changes the spelling of the title to "Das Kabinett des Dr. Kaligari", as does a full page advertisement in the same issue, though this title was of course changed back again to *Das Cabinet des Dr. Caligari* for the premiere and subsequent showings. The second of the two notes in *Der Film* also implies that shooting has not yet started, though not as definitely as the note in Issue No. 1 of 1920. Even if the note of 4 January 1920 had been in the press for a week, this implies that the shooting of *Caligari* could not have started before the end of

December 1919, long after the premiere of Toller's *Die Wandlung* at the Die Tribüne theatre on 30 September 1919, with sets by Robert Neppach in the style of Expressionist painting. This was the first stage production of an Expressionist play with sets unarguably in the style of Expressionist easel painting, though more were to follow in the next year. This premiere was an event of such significance in every way that all Berlin set designers, including Warm, Reimann, and Röhrig, would have known about it, and fairly certainly seen it in the flesh as well. However, a few months before the premiere of *Die Wandlung*, Max Reinhardt put on a production of Else Lasker-Schüler's non-Expressionist play written in 1909, *Die Wupper*, at the

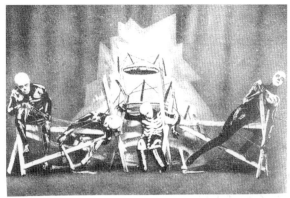

TOLLER, ERNST: *The Conversion* (Die Wandlung)

More photographs of the December 1919 production of Ernst Toller's Die Wandlung *above and right.*

NEPPACH, ROBERT: Sets for *The Conversion* (Die Wandlung) by Ernst Toller, production by Karl Heinz Martin

Deutsches Theater. For this production, which opened on 27 April 1919, Ernst Stern designed sets that were naturalistically rectilinear in shape, but covered with painted patterning like a weak version of the early type of "dazzle" camouflage used in World War I. These sets look like a very reluctant dip of the toe in the Expressionist waters by Stern, and indeed this was as far as he ever went in that direction. It also seems that Piscator's production of Hasenclever's *Der Sohn* at Königsberg sometime in late 1919 also had truly Expressionist sets by Otto Reigbert, but unlike the Berlin production of *Die Wandlung*, it is doubtful if Berlin's professional set designers knew what it looked like.

It is of course quite possible that the decision by Decla to produce Janowitz and Mayer's script for *Caligari* was

taken in "the late summer of 1919", but I very much doubt that any decision about the set design was made before the premiere of *Die Wandlung*. In any case, the six weeks from mid-January 1920 to the premiere on 27 February 1920 gives quite enough time to design, build, and shoot such a small-scale production as *Caligari*. Indeed, Hermann Warm himself says that it took four and a half weeks to build the sets and shoot the film. All of my deductions also square with Pommer's 1935 claim to have initiated the production of Janowitz and Mayer's script four or five months before it was actually shot, in other words in the middle of 1919, while he was still in charge of production at Decla, and with his statement that Janowitz and Mayer wanted the sets done by Alfred Kubin. Although Kubin had exhibited in the second *Blaue Reiter* show in Berlin

A model set by Ernst Stern for a fairground scene in the 1919 production of Die Wupper.

THE FAIR

The model for the set designed by Ernst Stern for a street scene in Die Wupper.

in 1912, he was older than most of the other participants, having been born in 1877, and his style and subject matter had long been formed, being a combination of the styles of the earlier Symbolist artists Odilon Redon and Max Klinger. That the idea of design in the style of Kubin per-

sisted some way into the production process of *Caligari* is suggested by a sketch by Walter Reimann for it which is reproduced on page 108 of Kurtz's *Expressionismus und Film*. This looks rather like something by Redon, but has no relation to the design of the finished film.

A set design by Otto Reigbert for a production of Hasenclever's Der Sohn *at Königsberg in 1919.*

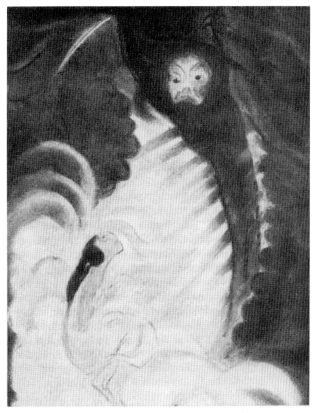

Preliminary sketch by Walter Reimann for Caligari

we find that...

All the above also agrees with Fritz Lang's repeated assertion that he was assigned to direct *Caligari*, but then was switched to making the second part of *Die Spinnen* when the first part proved so successful after its premiere on 3 October 1919. Thus part 2 of *Die Spinnen* and *Caligari* were shooting at the same time, and were also premiered close together in February 1920. This would also mean that Wiene was assigned to the production in December 1919, and the set designers Warm and Röhrig, who worked regularly for Decla, were assigned some time after that. Reimann, who had just designed the costumes for Lubitsch's immensely successful *Madame Dubarry* at UFA, was also brought in to do the same again. Following on from my reconstruction of events, the only discrepancy in all the accounts by the participants then remains the lie by Warm that the film was shot in the late summer of 1919.

On this last point, I feel slightly embarrassed to have to say what seems so obvious, at least to someone who has been inside the world of show business in general, and also the film industry in particular, which is that making "a good story" out of events, boastful exaggeration, and even downright lying to enhance one's own reputation, are standard procedure everywhere, with Germany no exception. Although in 1920 most people in Berlin seriously interested in new art would have been well aware of the relation of the design of *Caligari* to that of *Die Wandlung*, within a few decades the fame of *Caligari* had so eclipsed that of every Expressionist stage work that they barely existed any longer in people's minds. By then, for everyone who worked on the production except Carl Mayer, *Das Cabinet des Dr. Caligari* was by far the most successful and renowned thing they had ever been associated with, and hence their main claim to fame, and they had no interest in admitting that its creation was to a large extent a piece of casual entertainment industry opportunism involving no deep thought and intentions. And by the nineteen-sixties everyone who might have been interested in giving the lie to Hermann Warm was dead.

there is nothing much behind the painted flats,...

Although Hans Janowitz, who had the original idea for *Caligari*, had writing published before the war in *Arkadia* (Kurt Wolff Verlag, 1913), edited by Max Brod, which contained work by some of the new Expressionist writers as well as by others, this was because he was a friend of the editor and likewise from Prague, rather than because there was anything really Expressionist about his writing. Janowitz's writing was just a dilute Nietzchean denunciation of those aspects of modern society, such as prostitution, which were of little concern to the actual Expressionist writers. The final script of *Caligari*, written by Carl Mayer in collaboration with Janowitz, is of course just a mystery thriller with some supernatural or super-normal elements, and has nothing to do with Expressionist drama, as it lacks all the distinctive features of such literature; for instance the un-named characters, the telegraph-style syntax, and the simple and explicit revolt of a son against his family, or alternatively of the protagonist against authority.

(And I don't want to hear about any figurative or metaphorical interpretations of these features, because Expressionist plays did not depend on them, but only contained the *actual, literal* features just mentioned. In Fritz von Unruh's *Ein Geschlecht* a son tries to strangle his mother and rape his sister, and then kills himself; in Walter Hasenclever's *Der Sohn* the son threatens his strict father with a revolver, which brings on a fatal heart attack in the latter; in Sorge's *Der Bettler* the son poisons his father on purpose and his mother by accident; and in Kornfeldt's *Die Verführung* the son is against everyone, gratuitously kills a stranger, and dies poisoned and abusing God. And so on. And none of the canon of Expressionist plays is a mystery thriller, or contains supernatural elements in the plot. As for deeper themes, what these writers *said* they were concerned with was "the renewal of mankind" – Kaiser, "working for peace" – Toller, "this play was meant to change the world" – Hasenclever, and so on, which also has nothing whatever to do with any discernible theme in *Der Golem*, *Dr. Mabuse*, or *Nosferatu*, etc. Nor does the widely accepted characterization of the Expressionist dramatic literature at the time, as "a theatre of ecstasy".)

But unfortunately, because of the thriller and fantastic elements in *Caligari*, every German film made before or after it that also has these plot elements is labelled "Expressionist" by mindless writers.

When *Das Cabinet des Dr. Caligari* proved to be a success, the people concerned moved to cash in on it, and Decla and Wiene immediately put *Genuine* into production. The script of this film had no more connection with Expressionist drama than that of *Caligari*, but the sets by César Klein were in a slightly more thorough-going Expressionist style. The box-office failure of this film was enough for the production company, but Robert Wiene on his own had one last try with *Raskolnikov* (1923). Also, the producer and designer of Toller's *Die Wandlung* on the stage, Karl-Heinz Martin and Robert Neppach, who had their thunder stolen by the much greater stir created by *Caligari*, undertook an independent film production of Georg Kaiser's *Von Morgens bis Mitternacht*, and produced, as well as another box-office disaster, the only film that was totally Expressionist, in both design and content. There remains only to pass quickly over *Verlogene Moral* (1920), usually referred to as *Torgus*, which is weakly Expressionist in design and content, but is also a monstrously incompetent and tedious piece of film-making.

but elsewhere...

One might well ask, which of the other major works of Expressionist drama besides *Von Morgens bis Mitternacht* were filmed? What of such frequently performed plays as Sorge's *Der Bettler*, Hasenclever's *Der Sohn*, Kornfeld's *Die Verführung*, Unruh's *Ein Geschecht*, and Reinhard Goering's *Seeschlacht*? Not one of them were filmed, nor any other work by their authors or any other recognized Expressionist writer. There is just one partial exception to this generalization, and that is that the plot of Fritz Lang's *Metropolis* is heavily indebted to various features of the first half of Kaiser's trilogy of plays *Die Koralle, Gas*, and *Gas – Part II*, which were first performed from 1917 to 1920, and many times thereafter in the 'twenties.

In *Die Koralle* the protagonist is the Millionaire who operates a large number of mines and factories. His secretary is his identical double, and stands in for him at unpleasant moments. The Millionaire also has a son who rebels against his father's exploitation of the oppressed workers who labour in his mines and factories, and takes a job as a stoker on a tramp steamer, rather than leading the life of idle luxury that his father wants him and his sister to follow, far from the Millionaire's factories. The son then turns his sister against his father as well, and when there is a disaster in one of the Millionaire's mines followed by a rebellion of the workers, the Secretary puts it down while impersonating the Millionaire. His daughter hears of the disaster, despite the Millionaire's attempts to keep it secret, and wants to go to help "...my sisters and brothers." The Son who has been present at the disaster returns to plead with his father to succour "the pale thousands" of workers, but his father orders the mine to be closed down, leaving the surviving workers unemployed and doomed to starvation. After this confrontation and rejection by his children, the Millionaire shoots his secretary and takes his place, and is tried for his own murder and condemned unresistingly to death. However, this last part of *Die Koralle* (which was savagely mocked after its premiere in 1919 by the famous Berlin critic Walter Kerr), contributes nothing to the plot of Fritz Lang's *Metropolis*.

But the next play in the trilogy supplied more usable material to Lang and von Harbou. *Gas* begins in an immense gas factory which supplies power for the whole world, and has been set up on a co-operative basis with the workers by the Millionaire-son, as he is now called. At the beginning of the play the gas production process runs out of control and there is a gigantic explosion. The details of this disastrous runaway, though only reported indirectly in the play, have a fair correspondence to how this incident was later handled in Fritz Lang's film, even though none of the leading characters is involved on the factory floor itself in the play. Then most of the rest of *Gas* deals with the struggle between the Millionaire-son, the Engineer, and the Workers over what should be done

in the future about rebuilding the factory and the world power supply. Eventually a reconciliation between the Workers and the Millionaire-son is achieved after the Engineer resigns. In *Gas – Part II*, the central figure has become the Millionaire-worker, who struggles against the decision by the Super-Engineer and the Workers to turn production over to poison gas, as part of the war against another country. This part of Kaiser's trilogy mostly has nothing to do with the plot of *Metropolis*, except for the way the Millionaire-worker is presented as a kind of modern secular saint, bare-footed in simple work clothes. He urges the workers to turn the other cheek to the enemy, and to build a new kingdom that replaces gas with hard work. The climax of one of his last speeches is the cry "The Kingdom is not of this world." This role can obviously be considered to be changed in sex and folded back into the earlier events to give the figure of the "good Maria" in the film, who also takes on some of the aspects of the Millionaire's daughter in *Die Koralle*. However, the Millionaire-worker's final speeches are as close as Kaiser's plays get to the more conventional religiosity that appears at a number of points in Lang and von Harbou's film. As can be seen from my brief summary, other major parts of the plot of *Metropolis* are created by combining other parts of the characters and action of the Kaiser trilogy, and then shifting their place in the narrative. The major features of *Metropolis* which I have not dealt with, the creation of the robot "false Maria", and the project of replacing all the workers by robots, are taken from Karel Capek's *R.U.R.*, as has been noted by previous observers, though the character of Rotwang in *Metropolis* also owes something to the Super-Engineer in *Gas - Part II*.

It is interesting to note that the sets designed by Johannes Schröder for Erich Engel's 1920 production of *Gas* in Hamburg, which have accurately been described as "constructivist", anticipate, on a smaller scale, and with greater elegance, some of those done for Lang's *Metropolis*, and that in its turn Lang's film seems to have influenced the designs for the 1928 productions of the play by Leopold Jessner in Berlin and Hamburg.

other major artistic developments contributed...

Another source of the design for Fritz Lang's *Siegfried* (1923) that Lotte Eisner did not pick up in her limited discussion of the subject in her book *Fritz Lang* (Secker & Warburg, 1976) are the sets, some with broad simple geometrical patterning on the walls, done by Carl Czeschka for Max Reinhardt's production of *King Lear* at the Deutsches Theater premiered on 16 September 1908. The source of this style was the sort of design promoted by the Wiener Sezession movement guided by Josef Hoffmann and Joseph Olbricht. This style dominated the advanced art scene in Vienna when Fritz Lang studied architecture at the Technische Hochschule für Architektur, and then

Design by Johannes Schröder for Erich Engel's production of Gas I *at the Kammerspiele, Hamburg in 1920.*

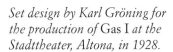

Set design by Karl Gröning for the production of Gas I *at the Stadttheater, Altona, in 1928.*

art at the Wiener Akademie der graphische Künste around 1910. This general look of Jugendstil moving into modern architectural design is evident also in the sculpture Fritz Lang did in his spare time while serving with the German Army in the Balkans during the Great War, though after *Siegfried* Lang finally shook himself free of this early twentieth century Viennese artistic influence, and moved on to film images composed in the manner of truly modern geo-

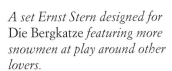

An Ernst Stern sketch for the 1915 Reinhardt production of Ferdinand Raimund's Rappelkopf.

metrical abstract art. All of which has nothing whatever to do with Expressionism, of course.

Nor do the things Lubitsch took from Reinhardt's stage productions to give extra class to his post-war films. I have previously mentioned one scene in Ernst Lubitsch's *Die Bergkatze* (1921) which takes something from the 1916

Reinhardt production of *Die grüne Flöte*, and Lubitsch in collaboration with Ernst Stern also re-cycled the scene of the live snow-men from the 1915 Reinhardt production of Ferdinand Raimund's *Rappelkopf* for the irrelevant but very charming dream sequence stuck into the middle of *Die Bergkatze*. Although the design by Kurt Richter and

A set Ernst Stern designed for Die Bergkatze *featuring more snowmen at play around other lovers.*

Above, a scene in the film of Sumurun, *and on the right a design by Ernst Stern for the 1911 Reinhardt stage production.*

Ernö Metzner for Ernst Lubitsch's film version of *Sumurun* was far more realistically detailed in general than Ernst Stern's settings for Reinhardt's original 1911 stage production, the design and staging of at least one scene was copied for the film. This was the scene outside the harem, though in the film the scale of it is expanded, and the row of rythmically nodding eunuchs who squat blocking the door increased from four to ten. Another recurrent design feature of Max Reinhardt sets by Emil Orlik, Karl Walser, and Ernst Stern from 1906 onwards, which is the narrow crooked alley with a little bridge joining the houses across it at first floor level, became part of the small change of German set design, and can also be seen in Lubitsch's *Madame Dubarry* as well as in *Sumurun*. The basic point to note about the staging ideas which Lubitsch borrowed from Max Reinhardt is that they come mostly from the more superficial and purely entertainment-oriented end of the latter's output. The other important point to make is that after Lubitsch went to America, his films almost immediately lost the high visual interest that is so characteristic of his German films made between 1918 and 1923. There is probably more of this borrowing by Lubitsch from Max Reinhardt's stagings and set designs than I have been able to find so far, and the next major suspect to be investigated is the uncredited relation of Reinhardt's 1915 production of Ludwig Anzengruber's Austrian peasant farce *Doppelselbstmord* to Lubitsch's *Romeo und Julia im Schnee* (1920), both in plot and staging.

Besides Ernst Stern, quite a number of German designers worked for both stage and screen in the silent period, and one of the best was Rochus Gliese. He was born in 1891, and so was almost the same age as Fritz Lang when he studied art and architecture, though this was in Berlin in Gliese's case, rather than Fritz Lang's Vienna. But in Berlin too the reigning influences in art school and outside it at the time were Jugendstil and Symbolism. Modern Art as we think of it was still a dream known only to a few in 1910. From art school Gliese went straight into professional stage design, and from there quickly moved into designing films for Paul Wegener, specifically the first version of *Der Golem* (1914), and *Der Rattenfänger von Hameln* (1916), amongst others. Although he continued to work for the stage, and indeed designed the German premiere of *Der Sohn* at Dresden in 1916, his sets for this were fairly straightforwardly naturalistic, which is indeed what seems called for by the stage directions of the play itself. (However, Hasenclever was not fully satisfied by any production of his play, nor with the designs used, until Weichert's Mannheim production of 1918, which had severely simplified and abstracted sets by Ludwig Sievert.) Gliese's later cinema work for Wegener, *Der verlorene Schatten* (1921), etc. and also for Murnau during the 'twenties (*Der Brennender Acker*, *Die Finanzen des Grossherzogs*, *Sunrise*, etc.), was entirely in a vein of standard film cinema naturalism, and only very slightly stylised by simplification occasionally, and then not in any Expressionist manner.

to manifestations of...

Ideas about what true Expressionist acting should be like were held by many of the leading playwrights and directors, and quite typical of this is Paul Kornfeld's *Afterword to the Actor* printed with the 1916 publication of the text of his *Die Verführung*, which contains a description of his ideal actor including:- "Let him abstract from the attributes of reality, and be nothing but representative of thought, feeling, or Fate. The melody of a large gesture says more than the highest fulfillment of what is called naturalness can ever do." The problem with this approach was that, divorced from a likewise stylized delivery of the text, it resulted in something visually indistinguishable from old-fashioned melodramatic acting of the worst kind. Thus the distinction between the two styles is particularly difficult to make in silent films. This difficulty is reinforced by the fact that before it became customary to break a film scene down into many shots, some of them taken close in, it was quite common for a leading actor to act more broadly than the supporting cast, who could be quite natural in what they did. On top of this, it was also quite usual for the principal player to increase the broadness of their acting towards the climax of the film. This can frequently be seen in American films made before 1914, including those by D.W. Griffith, and given the relative lack of scene dissection still usual in European films in the early 'twenties, the phenomenon is still quite common there in the period under consideration.

The two men considered the quintessential Expressionist stage actors at the time, Ernst Deutsch and Fritz Kortner, acted almost entirely in the more ordinary commercial films during the Expressionist years; the only exceptions to this being *Hintertreppe* (1921), in which Kortner certainly gave what could be described as an Expressionist performance; slow, with plenty of grimacing at peak moments, even though this was entirely out of keeping with the story and the performances of the other leads, Dieterle and Porten, and in *Schatten* (1923) he did likewise.

Ernst Deutsch played the lead in appropriate style in the unarguably Expressionist film, *Von morgens bis Mitternacht* (Karlheinz Martin, 1920), and in *Der Golem, wie er in die Welt kam*, which has the kind of fairly broad acting from all the leads usual at that time in all films dealing with the distant past, Deutsch did likewise. But then Deutsch usually just fitted right into the reigning style of the films he acted in, as is the case for instance in *Das alte Gesetz* (1923), where his performance is just a good standard film performance, and gives no reason to guess that he was also one of the ornaments of the Expressionist theatre.

Paul Wegener gave some highly un-naturalistic performances on stage before any of the Expressionist plays had been written, let alone before the end of 1916, when the first of them was put on in Berlin. One of Wegener's pre-Expressionist turns is repeated in *Vanina; oder die Galgenhochzeit* (1922), where his rather extravagant use of a pair of high crutches in the part of the evil prison governor takes over from the performance he gave in the role of Director Hummell in Reinhardt's October 1916 production of Strindberg 's *The Ghost Sonata*. But in films his acting was mostly well within the norms of ordinary European film acting of the period.

As for Werner Krauss, although like most of the best younger actors of the time he appeared in leading roles in a few Expressionist plays, his major career was in the cinema during the 'twenties, and what he did there was also varied in style to suit his surroundings.

Paul Wegener in Vanina *repeating the crutches routine that he had developed for Max Reinhardt's 1916 production of* The Ghost Sonata.

other expressive techniques that...

All the features of film style that lazy critics call "expressionist" predate any possible influence from any part of German Expressionism. These are such things as sinister shadows cast by an actor on the walls, which can be found in Cecil B. De Mille's *Maria Rosa* as early as 1915, and were taken up by other American directors in the next couple of years; low-key lighting to create a sinister mood as early as 1912 (Vitagraph's *Conscience*), light shining up into the face from below for the same purpose in *Going Straight* (Sidney Franklin, 1916), anamorphically distorted images in *La Folie du Dr. Tube* (Abel Gance, 1916) and *Till the Clouds Roll By* (Victor Fleming, 1919), and low angle Close Ups to create an imposing effect in Gance's *Barberousse* (1915), and as we look at more and more of the films from the early period, more and more examples like these come to light. For instance, there is a series of now well-known films by Benjamin Christensen made between 1913 and 1921 which build on an embryonic Danish film tradition of chiaroscuro applied to dirty doings. By the beginning of the 'twenties, before anyone in American film-making had seen any Expressionist art, expressive effects like these were being put into use, not just in isolated scenes, but in whole films like Al Parker's 1922 *Sherlock Holmes*, in which low-key lighting is used to reinforce the mystery atmosphere throughout the film, and Charles Giblyn's *The Dark Mirror* of 1920, which lives up to its title with a delirium of confused identities played out in dark night rooms and streets. (For more on all this see my *Film Style and Technology: History and Analysis* (Starword, 1983)). Then Christensen came to the United States in 1925, and without needing to bother about what was in German films, went right on doing his own thing in films like *The Devil's Circus* (1926) and *Mockery* (1927), which contributed to the purely native American tradition of horror films, then already under way.

But despite all this, we still get endless waffle published about the derivation of American horror films of the thirties and thrillers of the forties from German Expressionism, with "expressionist", poured like a strong sauce over everything, so obscuring the varied and interesting constituents of film history.

call for better analysis than...

Books like *Passion and Rebellion -- The Expressionist Heritage* (edited by S.E. Bronner and Douglas Kellner, Croom Helm, 1983), which is smugly introduced by its editors as being "...interdisciplinary, uniting scholars from a variety of academic fields.", but contains statements like:-

> "Even today's films owe a serious debt to Decla's 1919 production, since the appropriate setting and garb for many a Hammer studio horror film is the nineteenth century, with its heavy clothing and deceptively polite manner -- just the atmosphere for Caligari."

I suspect the writer of that is not the only person who is unaware that *Caligari* is set in the period in which it was made. The clothes people are wearing are those of a North German town around the time of the First World War, and even those peculiar truncated conical hats that some of the extras are wearing were still standard for North German farmers at the beginning of the twentieth century, however odd they make look now.

The increase of knowledge demands not just making generalizations, as most people with a literary education seem to think, but also in making distinctions, and when a word is used in the incredibly wide and fuzzy way that "expressionist" is used, it loses all power to discriminate amongst things.

We have the advantage that we can stand away from these works from the now distant past, and see them without unthinking preconceptions about their description. Of course one has to have some mental categories to describe art-works, but the least subjective, and also the most valid from a historical point of view, are those used by the artists when they were creating the works in question. In the case of Expressionism, all the major writers (Hasenclever, Toller, Kaiser, Unruh, Johst, etc.) and artists (Kokoschka, Schmidt-Rotluff, Kirchner, Franz Marc, etc.) who were so labelled at the time, accepted the label. But in the case of Paul Wegener, one of the major instigators of German films of the fantastic (*Der Student von Prag* (1913), *Der Golem, wie er in die Welt kam* (1921), etc., he explicitly refused the label of "expressionist" for these films. And he knew

what he was talking about, because he had acted leading parts in a number of early major productions of Expressionist plays such as *Der Bettler* (1917), *Der Sohn* (1918), and *Die Koralle* (1918). Likewise, Paul Leni rejected the "expressionist" label for his films such as *Scherben* (1921), and *Sylvester* (1923), and as is well known, Fritz Lang also repeatedly rejected the appellation for his films.

But so typically, on page 398 of the book just mentioned, which is no doubt on the reading lists for hundreds of university courses, E. Ann Kaplan insists that *Dr. Mabuse, der Spieler* is an Expressionist film, despite Fritz Lang's repeated explicit denials, which she describes as "ambiguous statements". She knows better, because she has a Ph.D. in film studies and a university professorship, and is a "scholar" who puts footnotes on what she writes.

most sources.

Even when they are fairly reliable about most aspects of Expressionism, the most well-informed writers cannot resist sometimes trying to draw in more works under this label to increase their subject matter, however little sense it makes. *The Revolution in German Theatre 1900-1933* by Michael Patterson, has a good summary in English of many of the general points about German theatre dealt with above, but he is determined to drag Leopold Jessner's productions under the Expressionist banner, even though Jessner did not use sets, costumes, and actor blockings that created any visual appearance akin to Expressionist art, except for his 1923 production of *Romeo and Juliet*, nor indeed did he stage an actual Expressionist play until the late 'twenties when the movement was long over.

The only good general treatment of Expressionism in English is John Willett's *Expressionism*, published by Weidenfeld & Nicholson in 1970, though even this weakens in his last chapter, when presumably the publishers told him that not enough people were going to buy the book unless he suggested that Expressionism had something to do with the art subsequently produced in their own countries.

Play texts by Toller, Hasenclever, and other Expressionist playwrights, together with statements about their intentions and how their works should be performed, can be found reprinted in *Zeit und Theater 1913-1925, Vol. II*, edited by Günther Rühle (Ullstein, 1973), and key documents are also reprinted in other places, such as Paul Pörtner's *Literatur-Revolution 1910-1925* (Luchterhand, 1960). Georg Kaiser's plays are all in his collected works published by Propyläen Verlag (1971). Pictures and fragments of information about Reinhardt's productions are scattered over a large number of books, and indeed more than I have been able to get my hands on, but I give special thanks to Alan Bernstein for drawing to my attention, and then loaning me, *Reinhardt und seine Bühne* edited by Ernst Stern and Heinz Herald (Verlag Dr. Eysler & Co.)

I have added some extra illustrations that were not included when this piece was published in 1990 in *Prima di Caligari*, edited by Paolo Cherchi Usai for Edizioni Studio Tesi. It is set in Simoncini Garamond once more.

These books resulting from the Pordenone *Giornate* were now being published in bilingual editions, with the Italian translation facing the English text of most of the articles. The Italians were brilliant at getting books published fast, as you may notice from the date of this publication. There is nothing to stop such speed of publication in the English speaking world, except for the talentless parasites leeching onto the editorial process these days, and the pursuit of as much profit as possible by the publishing companies.

Another short article I wrote in 1982 about Fritz Lang's visual style fits in here very well. I offered it to Penelope Houston at that time, but she turned it down. This was another occasion on which she was wrong, as I believe I make several very important points in it. When I set up the Starword web site a few years ago, I put it on there, where it is still available, so this is not strictly its first publication.

FRITZ LANG'S DIAGONAL SYMPHONY

You and Me

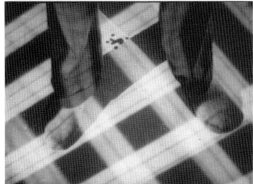

You Only Live Once

Secret Beyond the Door

Human Desire

'**Master of the Lens** — is Fritz Lang, Paramount producer-director, who is here shown looking through a finder with Kenny De Land, camera technician, on the set of "You and Me", Sylvia Sidney-George Raft prison parole drama. Lang works with the precision of a physicist before he is satisfied with a camera set-up. One of his innovations is the subjective camera which records impressions of one player from the viewpoint of the listening player, and vice versa.'

(Paramount Photo by Malcolm Bulloch)

1. The Visual Signature of the Auteur

The visual motif of strong diagonal lines crossing the frame that appears from time to time in Fritz Lang's films is clearly no accident. For instance, to get the pattern of shadows on the floor shown in the frame from *You Only Live Once* (1937), the shot had to be specially re-lit, since in the other shots that surround it in the film it can be seen that the shadows lie in quite different positions. In the other examples illustrated the compostion has been created by putting the camera in a somewhat unusual position, or a shot has been taken that is not at all necessary or helpful to the action of the film, as in the shot of the suitcases from *The Secret Beyond the Door* (1948), and also in the shot of the rails from *Human Desire* (1954). And in the case of *The Woman in the Window* (1944), the production designer's photograph of the real toll-gate on which he based his studio set is taken from a much more banal angle than the composition that Lang finally got from the set when he shot the film. Most of these characteristic shots from Fritz Lang's films are associated with a typical camera position -- at eye-level or above, tilted slightly down, and with the lens direction at about 45 degrees to the walls of the buildings in the horizontal plane. At the beginning of Lang's career there are only a few clear-cut examples of this characteristic angle to the decor, but by the time he made *Beyond a Reasonable Doubt* in 1956 this approach to composition had become quite relentless.

It must be emphasized that what I am describing is a matter of flat pattern, for I believe that this was what interested Lang, rather than the concern with architectural space so often postulated in interpretations of his work. In fact his brush with architectural training was very brief and reluctant, whereas he followed the calling of artist by choice for several years before World War I. According to his own testimony and the available evidence, his favoured masters in art were Klimt and Schiele, but it is obvious that their styles could be of no help when it came to film composition. The only possible source that I can see for Fritz Lang's most characteristic compositions is the style of abstract painting using regular geometrical shapes that was just beginning to consolidate after World War I.

The first abstract painting involving regular arrangements of parallelograms (and hence of diagonal lines) by Frantisek Kupka date back to 1913, but by the end of the War a number of artists such as Lazlo Moholy-Nagy and Theo van Doesburg had taken up the motif of regular shapes arranged on the diagonal, and even Mondrian had a brief flirtation with the regular diagonal line in 1919. The parallelogram motif also began to appear in applied art, and Moholy-Nagy transferred this kind of composition to his photographic work as well in 1924. But whatever the exact source of this patterning in Fritz Lang's films, there is no question but that firstly it had nothing to do with Expressionism, and secondly that Lang quickly made it his own as far as films were concerned. Besides using this sort of composition in its purest form in a few shots in each film, sometimes before or after the actors have been permitted to enter or leave the frame, he also used it to form the diagonal grid across which he disposed the figures of the actors in a far larger number of shots.

Lang's pride in his mastery of this approach is surely responsible for the many different of portraits

The Woman in the Window

Painting by Frantisek Kupka, 1913

Painting by Laszlo Moholy-Nagy, 1921

Photograph by Laszlo Moholy-Nagy, 1924

Spione

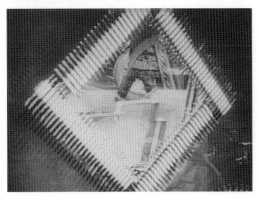

M

of himself that he had taken looking through a camera viewfinder, and it is also the reason that he detested CinemaScope, for such compositions are impossible within the proportions of the 'Scope frame.

2. The Things Take Over

As you can see, many of the shots reproduced here are inserts; that is, they are shots of objects or parts of the human body other than the face. Now particular cases of Fritz Lang's use of inserts have often been commented upon, but an interesting point that has not been brought out is the amount of inserts he used. When he started directing after World War I, the best American directors, following on from D.W. Griffith's example, were already making use of a fair number of insert shots in their films to make dramatic and expressive points. In fact at the beginning of the nineteen-twenties it was quite common for 5 percent of the shots in an American film to be inserts, and in some films even up to 10 percent. Some of the bright young European directors immediately caught on to the possibilities of the use of the insert and followed the American lead. Fritz Lang was among them, and there was nothing special from a dramatic point of view in his use of insert shots, or in the amount he used, at any rate until the last two years of the decade.

However, by the latter part of the 'twenties a new trend towards even greater use of inserts had developed, this time led by the so-called European avant-garde. (Actually, in present-day terms, the kind of films in question, typified by Kirsanov's *Ménilmontant* (1926), would be referred to as "art films", as opposed to the truly avant-garde efforts of say Man Ray.) In these films the much increased number of insert shots mostly appeared in continuous strings, either with dissolves between them, or more rarely cut straight together, so making up the newly-fashionable "montage sequences".

But when Fritz Lang too began to use more inserts, from *Spione* (1928) onwards, he did not put most of them in montage sequences, but introduced them, as had been the earlier custom, as single shots into the middle of scenes, at a more or less relevant point. In *Spione* 17 percent of the shots are inserts, and from any ordinary conception of film narration many of them are gratuitous; isolating objects whose function is already obvious and of no great interest.

With the coming of sound the use of inserts

decreased sharply in nearly all films, since they had largely been used as a roundabout way of conveying information that it is possible to convey more quickly and subtly by the combination of dialogue and behaviour. But Fritz Lang's first sound film, *M* (1931), is quite exceptional in having even more inserts (19 percent) than he had used in his last silent film. And in this particular case they are all well applied. Not content with this, in his next film, *Das Testament des Dr. Mabuse* (1933*)*, he went even further, and more than a quarter of the shots in this film are of things rather than people. This was some kind of record for mainstream cinema, and again Lang had reached a situation where a substantial proportion of the insert shots were non-functional, this time irretrievably. On the evidence available it seems to me that the proportion of inserts used in an ordinary narrative film cannot rise above 20 percent without some them holding up the movement of the film, while at the same time not contributing anything extra to it. While I do not know if Lang consciously drew this conclusion as well, it is quite certain that he retreated from this extreme, and all of his subsequent films have less than 15 percent inserts.

However, to have inserts making up even 15 percent of the shots is quite exceptional for a sound film, the usual upper limit being about 10 percent, and to get so many into a film in a meaningful way requires some special construction of the script at the writing stage. This was one of the main features of Lang's involvement in the scripting of his films, as is proved by the fact that in *The Ministry of Fear* (1944), the only one of his Hollywood films for which he was forced to accept the script as already written without his participation, the proportion of inserts quite exceptionally falls as low as 5 percent. So we can say that, with respect to this dimension of film form, and taking their context into account, Lang's sound films are more unusual than his silent films. Nevertheless, the actual way Lang used inserts in his sound films was till completely in the silent film tradition, leaving aside the purely decorative use of some inserts which I have already illustrated. Even the more complex examples in Lang's films, which have often been discussed, such as the arrow brooch belonging to the murdered prostitute which the hero in *Manhunt* turns into a weapon to kill her murderer, have their models in silent cinema. One such example of the dual-function object featured in insert shots in silent films, just the latest of many I have seen, occurs in Tod Browning's *Outside the Law* (1921). In this film the criminal protagonist

You Only Live Once

M

Die Spinnen II

Der Müde Tod

Secret Beyond the Door

Der Tiger von Eschnapur

makes a kite for a little child, and later the crossed sticks of the frame of the now-broken kite cast the shadow of a crucifix on the floor to recall him from his wrongful ways. Such devices were already the aim of the smartest American film-makers as early as 1917, but Fritz Lang's diagonal decorations of the frame were all his own.

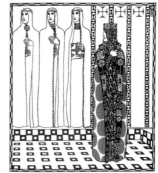

The frame enlargements used in this article are just a sample of those I have collected from Fritz Lang's films, so if you watch his films looking out for this special visual patterning you have many little pleasures in store. And I insist that it is a matter of design on the flat surface of the screen, or indeed on the ground glass of a Mitchell camera viewfinder, like the one he is looking through in the illustration. For those who have not used a Mitchell viewfinder, I should point out that the experience of looking at the image in it is not like that of looking through the reflex viewfinder of more recent cameras, both still and movie, because with the Mitchell finder you are looking directly at the image apparently fixed in the ground glass, not seen indirectly through an extended system of lenses. It is rather like looking at the image on the ground glass of an old-style double lens reflex still camera – another experience now being lost to the world. It is there to be inspected, unchanging even if you move your head, like a painting on the wall.

Fritz Lang wanted to be an artist, a painter, and that is what he did after studying art and design, in Vienna and elsewhere. He did *not* want to be a builder like his father, and although he went to the Technische Hochschule in Vienna briefly, this was not a possible preparation for being an architect. So

talking about architecture in relation to the style of his films is fundamentally misguided. In Vienna in 1910, the hot new art was from the Klimt group, which had broken away from the Secession movement a few years previously. Besides Klimt, now in the most decorative phase of his career with the famous "gold" paintings, the best-known figures in this group who exhibited together were Josef Hoffman, the architect, Kolo Moser, and Oskar Kokoschka. Egon Schiele, although also in this grouping, was still working out his style by combining features of Klimt and Kokoschka's graphic work of the time, and did not make a real impression till a few years later. There is no question that Schiele became Lang's favourite artist, but that must have happened later than 1910 when Lang set out on his travels.

The Klimt group also had strong connections with the Wiener Werkstätte, whose artists and craftsmen were producing objects intended to make interiors that were total works of art. Geometrical simplicity was of course characteristic of the work of Josef Hoffman and the artists of the Werkstätte, like Carl Otto Czeschka. Lang later claimed to have performed and done posters for the Café Fledermaus, where a number of these artists just mentioned were also involved in the shows. Czeschka is particularly important in this story, because the designs he did in 1907 for an unachieved stage production of Hebbel's *Die Nibelungen*, and adapted as book illustrations in 1908, were ripped off by Hunte, Kettelhut, and Vollbrecht for Lang's *Siegfried* in 1923. This has been well-known to Viennese art historians, but has escaped the attention of those interested in Lang's films, including Lotte Eisner. Czeschka went to to teach in Hamburg in 1908, but retained his connection with the Werkstätte. In 1910 he designed the Max Reinhardt production of *King Lear*, and it was seeing the designs for this

in 1982 that alerted me to the connection with Lang's *Siegfried*. The thing about working art directors (or production designers, as they are now known) is that they have to be, and are, adaptable. If you want Gothic, they'll give you Gothic. And if you want Czeschka, they'll give you Czeschka.

As for Lotte Eisner, although her book on Murnau is particularly valuable for the new information it contained, her other books, *The Haunted Screen* and *Fritz Lang,* miss out on may important connections between their subjects and German art of the early twentieth century. The reason for this is that Lotte Eisner was too young to have seen Max Reinhardt's most important and innovative productions, and for that matter any real Expressionist art when it was being produced. This is how she missed major connections between Reinhardt's productions and Lubitsch's films, and all the other things I have drawn attention to in the above pieces.

Another aspect of Fritz Lang's style is investigated in the following newly written piece.

"LES YEUX PAR ICI!"

"Look over here!" is what the photographer is saying to her subject in Fritz Lang's *Liliom* (1934). In other words, look at my finger, and not into the camera lens. Could this be an in-joke?

For elsewhere in this film, on a number of occasions, the director has made the actors look straight into the lens of the film camera. For instance, in an early scene in the film, when there is a three-way encounter between Liliom, Julie, and Mme. Muskat at night in a park, we get the series of shots illustrated. An objective shot gives way to this series of reverse

angles, with the characters looking straight into the lens in all of them. This is the technique that Lang was talking about in the caption for the production still in the previous article, which shows him with a viewfinder when filming *You and Me*. Having the actors look into the camera lens in this sort of situation went against the standard film industry convention in the United State, and indeed in Europe, in the 'thirties.

Whether Fritz Lang actually invented the idea of having characters looking straight into the lens on a series of reverse-angles is another matter.

Allowing actors to look into the camera lens has quite a history in the movies. In general, actors did not look straight into the lens right from the beginning, at any rate in dramas. This is not very surprising, since in the theatre actors in dramas did not fix their gaze at one spot straight to the front either. Comedies were always a different matter, with various amounts of recognition of the cinema audience, from the odd wink in their direction, to long passages of mugging, mostly in European comedies, in the period before the First World War. In dramas the look straight into the camera was explicitly forbidden by the Selig company, according to the instructions they published for actors in 1909 (reproduced on pages 63-64 of *Motion Picture Pioneer* by Kalton S. Lahue, 1973). I remember Noël Burch getting quite excited about this piece of information after he came across it, and using it to prop up a highly questionable Marxist generalisation about the nature of cinema and its relation to society. This was that the standard form of movies (the IMR, or Institutional Mode of Representation, as he put it) demanded the spectator's *invulnerability*, or the freedom not to be looked at by the characters on the screen. That is, he could not be treated as a voyeur, according to the laws of Capitalism, as seen by Marxism and Noël Burch. I was not particularly impressed, partly because I had a very low opinion of the quality of Selig production and hence the Selig management's grip on what they were doing (see *The Best of the Rest* later on in this book). But more importantly, if there was any such rule at the other American studios at this date, it was often broken, particularly by D.W. Griffith. His films regularly feature what might be called a "mute soliloquy". When one of the characters is faced with a difficult decision about their situation at a climactic point in the plot, Griffith has them look intensely straight into the camera for quite a long time, no doubt with the actor concerned struggling to convey what might be going on in their mind, though usually without really changing their expression. This trick only draws attention to itself strongly when the actor is shown in a close shot, so it is most significant

A "mute soliloquy" directed straight into the camera lens in D.W. Griffith's Friends *(1913).*

when there first began to be a certain number of close shots in films; in other words, in America after 1910. Although Griffith was the director most fond of this device, it can be found elsewhere in American films, and in Europe as well. For example, Asta Nielsen does it in *Afgrunden* (1911), and a few years later, Mosjoukine made it a fixed and frequent feature of his film performances in Russian films during the First World War.

However, American film-makers other than D.W. Griffith did eventually drop the device after the War, which was more or less the same time that the use of reverse-angle cutting became common.

Fritz Lang used the look into the lens in his early films of the early 'twenties, like many other European directors. For instance, in *Dr. Mabuse, der Spieler* (1922), Dr. Mabuse is shown in close shots staring straight into the lens when he is putting the 'fluence on his victims. However, when the victim is shown in a reverse-angle in the adjoining shot, they are looking off the lens. It is the same in *Die Nibelungen* (1924). Various principal characters get to look straight into the lens in these two films, but the looks of those they are looking at are still off-lens. However, in two cases in *Kriemhilds Rache*, the looks of both characters involved in a highly emotional confrontation are very close to the lens. These two instances are the first meeting of Etzel, the King of the Huns, with Kriemhild, his betrothed. She is looking very slightly above the lens, and he, very slightly below. The same happens when her brother Gishelder (the blonde one) appeals to Kriemhild outside the hall in which the Burgundians are trapped, towards the end of the film. Although *Die Nibelungen* has 17 percent reverse-angle cuts, a large part of these are really reverse scenes, with the camera far from the characters, and the number of standard reverse-angles close in to the actors is small. But Lang's next film, *Metropolis* (1927), has 37 percent reverse angle cuts, and they are often closer in. Despite now working closer to the standard American form, Lang is still having trouble getting the screen directions for looks, and for entrances and exits from the shot, correct. The scene in Joh Fredersen's office, when his son brings news of the explosion, is a good study in how confusing for the audience bad directions can be. With this increase in reverse angle cutting, Lang now finally has characters looking absolutely straight into the lens on both angle and reverse. This happens at two particularly emotional moments, when Freder meets Maria for the first and second times. Of course, there are a few other looks into the lens by other principal characters, but only in isolated shots.

It seems that Lang was not the first with this device of having two characters look straight into the lens in succeeding shots, since Alfred Hitchcock did it in *The Lodger* (1926). If there was a common source for this device for both directors, it remains to be discovered. After this, Hitchcock pushed the use of the device much further in his succeeding films, and much further than Fritz Lang ever did, reaching a peak in *The Manxman* (1929), in which most of the looks of the characters are directed straight into the lens on reverse angles. The

A POV-reverse angle pair of shots in The Lodger, *with the two characters looking straight into the lens and each others eyes.*

constraints of early sound film-making reduced Hitchcock's use of the device, and there are only a couple of short passages of it at peak moments in *Blackmail* (1929), and none at all in *Juno and the Paycock* (1930). Some of his subsequent films have a single alternation of Close Up reverse-angles with the characters looking straight into the lens at a particularly fraught moment, and he also continued to use the isolated shot of a character looking straight into the lens at one or two points in many of his films for the rest of his career. Because of the placement of these into-the-lens shots in the narrative, it is possible to miss them if you are swept up into the story.

Interestingly, at the same time that Fritz Lang was making *Liliom* in France, John Cromwell was making *Of Human Bondage* in Hollywood. In this film, which has many extended dialogue scenes, Cromwell has the characters looking closer and closer to the lens axis as the scene goes on, at the same time as he works closer and closer in to the actors on a series of reverse angles. At the climax of these scenes, when the actors are in Big Close Up, they are looking straight into the lens, and there are more such shots in total in *Of Human Bondage* than in *Liliom*. Because of the way Cromwell sneaks up to the straight into the lens reverse angles, they are less noticeable than in *Liliom*, where Lang just bangs straight into them from the objective wide shot, as illustrated. It is quite possible that Lang did not see *Of Human Bondage* and the Hitchcock films I have mentioned, which left him free to imagine, and claim — via the publicity department of Paramount Studios — the origination and ownership of this technique.

But in the long run, it is really Alfred Hitchcock who was its master.

When I was taking frame enlargements from Fritz Lang films with a view to writing about his particular visual style, I noticed what was said and done in the photographer's studio in *Liliom*, and thought of writing an article about it, probably for *Sight & Sound*. But I could not see how to expand the idea, and so dropped it. It was only when laying out this book that I saw the connection with what was said on the back of the Paramount publicity photograph relating to *You and Me*, and realised how to go on from my original starting point.

By 1990 the interest in silent film history in Italy was becoming really competitive. Another festival, the *Mostra Internazionale del Nuovo Cinema* at Pesaro included sections on early cinema in 1989 and 1990, and Ricardo Redi asked me for pieces to put in associated books he was editing for Di Giacomo Editore entitled *Da Edison a Griffith* (1988) and *Il Primo Cinema Inglese: 1896-1914* (1990). My articles were published under the titles *Si è conservato il meglio?* and *Le scoperte dei pionieri (e di altri)* respectively. Although they repeat things I have said elsewhere, they also include some new points, and approach their subjects from a different angle; that of the production of individual studios. The Italian versions of these two pieces were illustrated by stills which were not provided by me, so here I have put in some frame enlargements from my own collection.

THE BEST OF THE REST 1906-1916

Before the first World War, the American film company with the largest presence in Europe was the Vitagraph Co. The films of this company, which survive in quite large numbers, have now received a fair amount of attention, as have those of the Biograph company, which was far less well represented in the European market. Other American producers who have left enough traces of their activities in Europe up to 1916 to make them worth investigating are Edison, Lubin, Selig, Essanay, and Kalem, which were all members of the Motion Picture Patents Corporation ("the Trust"), and amongst the independents outside the Trust, Thanhouser, the American Film Manufacturing Co., and the New York Motion Picture Co. are also worth considering. All of these companies had sales offices or representatives in London, and sold many prints of their entire production in Britain, so an appreciable proportion of their films still survive there. The following notes about the interesting features of these surviving films are mostly based on the examination of about three hundred prints of films from the above-mentioned companies which happen to be preserved in the National Film Archive, London. I have tried to make my comments complementary to the general description of filmic developments from 1906 to 1916 that I have already given in my *Film Style and Technology: History and Analysis*.

Edison

Although the Edison Co. was one of the major members of the Motion Picture Patents Corporation, its films apparently did less well in Europe than those from the other companies.

Easily the most striking one that I have seen is still *The Passer By* (1912), which was discovered by Kevin Brownlow long ago. The story in this film is told in flash-back (in the true modern sense of the word), using what was to become one of the standard ways of entering the scenes set in the past, namely a dissolve from a close shot of a person remembering the past events, straight into the scene remembered. In the case of *The Passer By*, there is the extra subtlety of a track in to a true Close Up prior to the dissolve to the past, and at the end of the film the exit from the flash-back is by the reverse procedure. Elsewhere in this film there are also a couple of cuts to closer shots made straight down the lens axis, and in this respect too it seems fairly exceptional for Edison films. However, in *The Test of Friendship* from 1911 there are also some well-handled

In the cut straight back from this Medium Shot to the Long Shot below in The Passer By*, there is a mis-match in both actor position and in lighting.*

cuts within scenes, again straight in and out, and this latter film, a melodrama about skyscraper construction workers, also includes documentary background shots of this work. This is not the first film on this subject, as American Mutoscope & Biograph had done the same sort of thing in 1906 in *The Skyscrapers*. The other surviving Edison films are not in general notable for such advanced technique, and even at the time they were made it was recognized that the cutting was slower in them, and that they were shot with a more distant camera, than films from most of the other American companies. (See George Pratt's

Spellbound in Darkness (New York Graphic Society Ltd., 1973) p. 102). This is particularly evident in the series of films J. Searle Dawley directed for Edison in 1912 based on true stories of the British Empire, such as *The Charge of the Light Brigade* and *The Relief of Lucknow*, which are almost entirely carried out in scenes done in one shot, with the camera well back from the action. In the case of the first there seems to be a real attempt at an authentic reproduction of the actual events, even down to the appearance of the location chosen, according to Ben Brewster, and this is possibly the case in the second as well, but because of the way they are shot they are both lacking in dramatic force by American standards of the time. Even as late as 1913 there are Edison films like *Leonie* in which there are no cuts within scenes, and consequently only 32 shots in one full reel (951 ft.) of film, though by now the playing of the actors is finally up to the nine-foot line as in the Vitagraph films, but without the low Vitagraph camera position.

Lubin

Lubin, like the other studios, employed more than one director after 1908, but there is mostly no visible indication of this in the style of their films. The surviving Lubin films that I have seen are in general not particularly interesting, though their technique and style are near the norms for American films of the particular date in question. As early as 1910 *The Dream Pill* has a cut straight in to Medium Close Shot, and in 1911 *The Substitute* use cross-cutting between parallel actions, but these techniques are absent from the subsequent Lubin films until 1913. The only film from this company in the National Film Archive which is really striking is *When the Earth Trembled* (1913), a two-reeler which twines an involved story around the great San Francisco earthquake of 1906. Just after that event, Sigmund Lubin had sent James Frawley, who made the films for him at the time, to San Francisco to get footage of the devastation, and then this was used as part of a fictional story in a short film. According to Fred Balshofer (*Two Reels a Week* by Fred Balshofer and Arthur Miller, page 9), the result was very crude, with cardboard models collapsed and burned to recreate the moment of disaster. Some of the same actuality footage was re-used in *When the Earth Trembled*, but in this case the collapsing sets built in the studio were much more convincing, and the effect was enhanced with skilful editing to suggest more violent destruction than was actually shown, so presaging the way the earthquake sequence was handled in the 1936 film *San Francisco*. Elsewhere in *When the Earth Trembled* cross-cutting is also used to handle the separate strands of the story in what was quite an up-to-date way for 1913.

Selig

There seems to be a tendency in the Selig films for there to be a marked difference in the appearance of the films made at the company's original large Chicago studios, and those made in California at the Selig Zoo. As with Vitagraph, the Eastern studios seem to have produced more polished films, while the West coast outfit produced roughly made work with more exciting contents. In fact some of these West Coast Selig films are the worst directed of any American films from the 1910 to 1914 period that I have seen. They are carried out almost entirely with the camera further back even than the French foreground (4 metres), and the action is staged entirely within one plane perpendicular to the lens just in front of the back of the sets. However not all of their directors were quite as incompetent as this, and there are occasionally interesting features in Selig films. *The Trade Gun Bullet* (1911) has quite a lot of realistic detail of ranch life, which one does not ordinarily get in the films of this period, but the story this documentary footage is decorating is very perfunctory. Indeed, thin stories are characteristic of the general run of Selig films. Some of the guilty men at the West Coast studio included Hobart Bosworth, Fred Huntley, and Colin Campbell, and later E.A. Martin and Lem Parker. Colin Campbell was famous for directing the long films *The Coming of Columbus* (1912) and *The Spoilers* (1914), both of which are rather stodgily made for their dates, but Campbell could do worse than that.

His *A Wild Ride* (1913) has the British besieged by black savages somewhere in Africa, and rescued in the nick of time by the heroine riding to get help on an ostrich, but the action scenes are staged with a total lack of conviction, and the acting and sets are awful. Some of the other Selig films featuring the lions, elephants and divers "wild" animals from the Selig Zoo are not quite as bad, though they basically rely on wild beasts appearing in the same shot as the actors to make up for the most trivial and perfunctory stories. Unlike both earlier and later wild animal films, this series does not in general use cutting to different angles within the scenes to produce the effect that the cast are in danger from the beasts, but it is not clear whether this is just lack of imagination, or a desire to make the events seem more authentic. However in the case of *Sallie's Sure Shot* (1913), Point-of-View shots *are* occasionally used to heighten the drama of mother and child being menaced by carnivores, and the leading actress here is clearly an Action Woman skilled with guns. Even when Selig directors tried something new, the others features of the film tended to be on the crude side. An instance of this is *The Family Record* (1914), which tells a story of two young lovers who are separated, then reunited in old age through a family Bible. What has happened to them in between is recounted in two separate flashbacks shown in sequence, one for him, and the other for her, which is an interesting variant in the use of this device that became so popular at this time. But the few cuts within scenes in this film are mishandled, and the acting is still directed to the front, which is just not good enough for an

American film made in 1914.

The films starring Tom Mix were always made by a unit separate from the other parts of the company from 1913 to 1917, and they are as crudely slapped together as the worst of the Selig production. But this did not prevent them from being very popular with the public because of their content, which was essentially the antics and personality of their star. Despite the fact that these Tom Mix films have been well-known for a long time, I do not think it has been remarked how much of the style of their action derives from the Wild West shows which had been touring America for decades. The way the cowboys spend so much time in them riding to and fro shooting their guns into the air and twirling them round their fingers, the lassooing of people and then dragging them behind horses, and other similar tricks were all standard features of these Wild West shows, as was the wearing of elaborate cowboy costumes, and it was this type of material which, through Tom Mix, came to dominate popular film Westerns in the 'twenties. (On the other hand, the William S. Hart Westerns made by the Thomas Ince organization were no more realistic, for Hart's performance, with the way he freezes into intense poses, with or without guns drawn, was completely based on the way these things had earlier been done in many popular stage dramas on Western subjects such as *The Squaw Man* and *The Girl of the Golden West*.)

Although Colin Campbell continued to be the main director for Selig through the First World War, even making the feature length *The Crisis* from a story by Winston Churchill (Yes!) in 1916, he didn't get much better. However, various younger men passed through the company on their way to greater heights, for example Marshall Neilan. His *The Country God Forgot* (1916) shows that some people had mastered the latest techniques like flashbacks, cross-cutting between parallel actions, high angle shots, and point of view shots, and could use them in moving a story along in an interesting way.

Essanay

Essanay is ordinarily thought of the studio that made G.M. (Broncho Billy) Anderson's films, and later some Chaplin films, and indeed these form the largest part of the surviving films. The Broncho Billy films start in 1910, and were directed by G.M. Anderson himself, but they are not particularly well-made for their date, and the character he played in them, the "good-bad man", was not particularly original either. Such "mixed" characters, who are presented initially as wrong-doers, but who then have a change of heart in the course of the action, had been introduced into the cinema by D.W. Griffith almost as soon as he started directing in 1908. He in turn got the idea from the popular drama of the turn of the century, where such characters occur frequently in the plays David Belasco staged, for instance, not to mention elsewhere. However,

as played by Anderson, the character appealed greatly to the public because of Anderson's personality, rather than because of his action exploits, and by 1911 Essanay had expanded enough to have two other directors also making films for them which did not star Broncho Billy One of these directors was Arthur Mackley, who made *The Loafer* at the end of 1911. After fifteen years of searching, this is still the earliest film that includes a series of close shots of two characters interacting, shot from opposite directions in the way that was eventually to become standard, and to be known later as "reverse-angle" cutting. At this date the technique and name of the "reverse scene" was already known, though infrequently used, but this latter device involved shots taken at a distance from the characters, and it did not happen during a dialogue scene, as in *The Loafer*. That the reverse-angle cutting in *The Loafer* was no accident is shown by *The Shotgun Ranchman*, which Mackley made several months later, which has even more reverse-angle cutting, and better-than-average acting for the period.

Another curious experiment at Essanay, but of a retrograde kind, is *Episode at Cloudy Canyon* (1913). Though made at a date when titling had just developed to the point where the use of dialogue titles was becoming standard practice, this film has no intertitles at all of any kind. This approach had been systematically tried out once before, in 1908, and by D.W. Griffith. At that date narrative (or descriptive) titles were already regularly used at Biograph, as elsewhere, but Griffith consistently made films without any intertitles at all for nearly a year. As a result, those of his films of this date which had complicated stories were impossible to follow in every intended detail, so he dropped the practice in 1909, and never returned to it. The same limitation of the narrative to very simple plots was later apparent in the 'twenties when the idea of using no intertitles at all surfaced again. In the case of *The Episode at Cloudy Canyon*, the story the film tells has clearly been worked out to make the omission of titles possible. This appears particularly regressive because in 1913 the use of dialogue titles as well as descriptive titles had just appeared, so allowing faster and more subtle narratives than had been possible before.

The Hour and the Man of 1914 can stand as one indication of the way that the basic features of mainstream cinema (or "classical cinema") developed independently of each other, for it is in general very smoothly put together, with the use of small pans and tilts to keep actors well framed when they move, dialogue titles cut in at the moment when the characters speak them, cuts straight in to closer shots with good action matching, and non-frontal staging, but it nevertheless lacks any use of true Point of View and reverse angle shots. Contrariwise, there are other films of the period which use reverse angle Point of View cutting, but have no dialogue titles and still use acting to the "front", and so on.

Kalem

Kalem films are mostly rather middle-of-the-road from a formal and stylistic point of view, but they often have a little extra interest in their setting and subject. The best known aspect of this is the overseas tours that the director Sidney Olcott and his company made to shoot films in exotic locations. The various trips to Ireland made by production units from the Kalem company has been described by Anthony Slide in *Aspects of American Film History Prior to 1920* (Scarecrow Press, 1978) (p.87 et seq.), but the company also did the same sort of thing inside America. Examples include *The Face at the Window* (1913), which was shot down near Florida, and *The Railroad Raiders of '62*, a civil war drama made on something like the authentic locations by Sidney Olcott in 1911. One drawback to these films made entirely on location was that the interiors were shot on improvised stages solely under sunlight, sometimes softened by a diffusing screen, but often hitting the set directly, which left their visual appearance well short of the best standards of those years. Another drawback to the practice of total location filming was that the scripts for these films were frequently flimsy and not well worked out, though in some cases good pre-existing stories such as *The Colleen Bawn* and *Rory O'More*, which were adapted from the Dion Boucicault plays, ensured that the film had a certain dramatic power. Nevertheless, there were occasionally features in these films which put them in the forefront of developments in film construction. Examples include the 270 degree pan round the deck of an ocean liner following the actors as they play a scene in *Captured by Bedouins* (1912), which was made on a trip to Egypt, and the use of a kind of reverse-angle cutting (though not on close shots), and also cutting to a closer shot with angle change "on action" in the middle of a scene in *The Railroad Raiders of '62*. In at least some of these cases, and perhaps all of them, the mind behind the camera was that of Sidney Olcott.

IMP – The Independent Moving Picture Company

In 1909 Carl Laemmle, who was at the centre of the resistance to the Motion Picture Patents Company's attempt to control the whole American motion picture business, set up his own production company, IMP, to supply the independent exchanges and exhibitors. Its first film, *Hiawatha*, directed by William Ranous, is a crude piece of work. The National Film Archive does not have many IMP films, but some of the later ones are a bit better than *Hiawatha*. Their principal director was George Loane Tucker, but his films are mostly not particularly distinguished in the context of their time. The one exception to this is the well-known *Traffic in Souls* (1913), the first real American feature film on a contemporary subject. Like his other films around this date, this is mostly conducted in Long Shot or Full Shot, with only a few cuts in to a closer shot within a scene. In studio interiors

it tends to use side-by-side rooms seen from the "front", with action moving between them, as D.W. Griffith did, though there is less cross-cutting between parallel actions. *Traffic in Souls* also has a small number of Point of View shots, though no reverse angles. However the cutting rate is even a bit above the Griffith level, with an Average Shot Length of 7 seconds. Griffith had not got below an ASL of 8 seconds in 1913. (Jack Cohn later claimed that it was he who cut *Traffic in Souls* down for speed, and it looks as though he was speaking the truth.)

At this point, the IMP films started to be released with the Universal badge on them, and the company was assimilated into the master organization.

Thanhouser

The Thanhouser Co. was one of the first group of independent film producing companies set up outside the Motion Picture Patents Corporation in 1910, when a number of American businessmen correctly recognized that the MPPC would not be able to produce enough films to supply the whole market. Its creator was Edwin Thanhouser, a successful theatrical manager in Milwaukee for 25 years, and the first to produce Ibsen's *Pillars of Society* in the United States. (for more details on the company organization, see Anthony Slide's *Aspects of American Film History prior to 1920*, page 68 et seq.). Its studio was a converted ice skating rink in New Rochelle, one of the up-and-coming new outer suburbs of New York. Up until 1912 the Thanhouser Co. did not have proper representation in London, so only one of their films from before 1911 survives in the National Film Archive collection, though there are quite a lot from after that date.

In the context of the time, the Thanhouser films show a real ambition towards quality in their choice of subjects and the care put into sets and costumes. This is evident in their Dickens adaptations, but is also quite general. Unfortunately, most of the surviving films are not particularly interesting in other respects. *Treasure Trove* (1912) does take up some of the latest ideas, having many reverse angle Point of View shots, and is generally shot close in to the actors throughout, but this is exceptional. Another exception is *Just a Shabby Doll* of 1913. This advances the new fashion for flashback construction by having a flashback inside the flashback that makes up the main body of the film. As was common in 1913, the main flashback, which was entered and left by fades in and out, was introduced and motivated by the discovery in the first scene of an object with associations with the past, in this case a doll that had belonged to one of the parents of a child.

Yet another exception to the general lack of sparkle in Thanhouser productions is *The Center of the Web*, a crime thriller with a fairly corny story, but pushed along very fast by its unknown director.

A shot in The Monogrammed Cigarette *(Yankee, 1910).*

The next frame, with the reverse-angle on the kidnapping.

Yankee

This was another company set up in 1910 to provide films for the independent distributors and exhibitors resisting the Motion Picture Patents Corporation cartel. Their only film preserved in the National Film Archive is *The Monogrammed Cigarette* (1910), which is about the doings of a resourceful girl detective. It is noteworthy for a series of repeated "reverse scene" cuts, which show an action from opposite directions, with such exact action matches that it was probably shot with two cameras. This was both very rare, and also very enterprising at that date.

American Film Manufacturing Company

This company, which was usually known as "Flying A" inside the film industry, was founded in 1910 in Chicago, with personnel hired away from Essanay. It was renamed the American Film Co. in 1916, and ceased production in 1921. (For background on the company organization see *The Silent Partner: The History of the American Film Manufacturing Company 1910-1921* by Timothy James Lyon (Arno Press, 1974)).

The principal claim to fame of "Flying A" was that Allan Dwan was the director of all of its films made in 1911 and 1912, and then half of them for the first six months of 1913. Unfortunately only a fairly small number of films made by "Flying A" survive, most of which seem to be in England, both in the NFTVA, and also in private hands. Because he had more talent and brains than most of the competition, Dwan's films usually have at least one interesting feature, and besides those things I have mentioned before in *The Early Development of Film Form* (p.24), there is a pro-Indian Western called *The Vanishing Tribe* (1912), which shows the American Indians being brutally treated by the white man, without even the kind of partial justification for this that one finds in the films of other directors of the period. After Dwan and his team,

which included Wallace Reid, Marshall Neilan and Victor Fleming, left the company, the subsequent remaining films suggest that there was a considerable drop in quality of the "Flying A" product.

For instance, *In the Shuffle* (1916), directed by Thomas Ricketts, who had been the company's first director in 1910, before being displaced by Dwan, and who was then re-hired when Dwan left, displays incompetence in almost every department -- narrative construction, scene dissection, and direction of actors. However *To Rent Furnished* (1915) is a fairly amusing light comedy, rather in the style of the comedies like *The Right Girl* that Ralph Ince made at Vitagraph with Anita Stewart, though the handling of reverse-angle and action cutting in it is appreciably rougher. This was one of the first directorial efforts of B. Reeves Eason, who had joined the American Film Co. in 1913, and then worked his way up to director. "Breezy" Eason later became famous as a director of serials and action sequences for major Hollywood companies, and indeed this film already shows an obsession with making a film move as fast as possible by cutting the lengths of shots to the bone, and even deeper.

Rex Motion Picture Company

Rex evolved out of the Defender Film Company, which was set up in 1910 by Edwin Porter, Joseph Engel and William Swanson to feed the independent market. In 1911 it transformed into the Rex Motion Picture Company. At first its films followed Porter's rejection of cutting within the scene, and shooting everything in Long Shot, but this began to change after he left. Then the main creative team became Phillips Smalley and his wife, the actress Lois Weber. Their work was mostly average for the period, with just one surviving title, *Suspense* (1913), which draws attention to itself for its use of cross-cutting between parallel actions to deliver the suspense of the

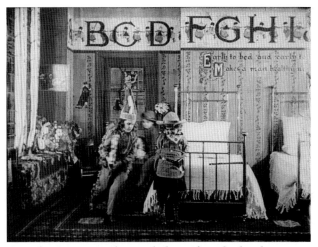

A studio interior with cross-lighting from both sides in
The Faith of a Child *(Weber & Smalley, 1911), for Rex.*

title, plus a flashy triptych screen effect for a combination of telephone conversation and action at the climax. Kevin Brownlow drew attention to it in his *The Parade's Gone By* (1968), and published stills illustrating the triptych screen on pages 26 and 27. It is worth adding that *Suspense* is essentially another remake of the now well-known Pathé film *The Physician of the Castle*, with more bells and whistles added. These include a Point of View shot taken straight down from an upstairs window onto the burglar trying to break into the house, and a shot taken from one car that shows a pursuing car visible in the rear-view mirror. It is an exception in the surviving Rex production, which otherwise completely lacks forward-looking features. When Lois Weber and Phillips Smalley moved on to full-length features a few years later, their films such as *Hypocrites* (1915) and *The Dumb Girl of Portici* (1916) are likewise retarded stylistically. A minor peculiarity of a number of Rex films at this time is the lighting of the sets with the basic illumination coming from groups of arc floodlights on floorstands straight out to the left and right, with nothing much coming from the front.

Solax

Solax was built from the New York branch of the French Gaumont company, which was run by Herbert Blaché and his wife Alice Guy. They joined up with the independents as well, with the only distinguishing feature of some of their films, presumably directed by Alice Guy, being a deliberate attempt to make films with resolutely theatrical-type light comedy playing, which went against the trend towards filmic restraint already visible in what were called "polite" comedies from other companies. Examples from Solax are *The Comedy of Errors* (1912) and *A House Divided* (1913), and the latter even includes characters repeatedly talking to the film audience.

Bison, Kay-Bee, Broncho, etcetera

Kessel and Baumann's *New York Motion Picture Company*, another of the first independent companies outside the Trust, produced under various labels over the years, starting with the Bison trademark. In this first period, from 1909 to 1911, the films were directed by Fred Balshofer, a partner in the enterprise, and a few of them have survived. *A Cowboy for Love* is typical in the frontal orientation of the acting, complete absence of cutting within scenes, and general lack of interest. After Thomas Ince took charge of production at the end of 1911 there was no technical advance whatsoever, as demonstrated by *Cowboy's Day Off* (1912), but the films did become a bit sharper dramatically, and the production values improved slightly. But the few really distinctive touches in some of the films from the company such as *The Indian Massacre* (1912), with its Red Indian burial ceremony played in silhouette against the skyline, were clearly due to Francis Ford, who directed it, and not Thomas Ince. The commercial success of Kay-Bee and Broncho films at the time was mostly due to the fact that they were longer than Westerns from other companies, and had slightly better scripts and production values, rather than to any special aesthetic or technical virtues inspired by Thomas Ince himself, though he *did* hire good directors to make them.

THE ACHIEVEMENTS OF THE EARLY BRITISH FILM-MAKERS

In the years up to 1905, before the world-wide film boom, the main British film-makers played the major part in establishing the basics of film construction as we still know them. But after 1906 they failed to quickly and fully industrialize their methods of production, and they soon lost their place in the now world-wide film industry. This is a brief outline of what they did up to 1915, principally in the area of film form, based on the viewing of about 300 British films made before 1915 which exist as viewing copies in the National Film Archive.

Robert W. Paul

R.W. Paul was a scientific instrument maker who became involved with the beginnings of cinematography through being asked to make copies of the Edison Kinetoscope towards the end of 1894, and as a result of this involvement was then asked to design a movie camera by Birt Acres. Acres was a well-established professional photographer, and already had the basic idea for a film transport mechanism that would be suitable for a motion picture camera. Paul put this idea into actual form, and with the camera R.W. Paul built, in February 1895 Birt Acres began making films suitable for use in the Edison Kinetoscopes, and more importantly, for use in Paul's copies of these. At this date no-one had, of course, succeeded in projecting moving pictures satisfactorily. The first camera built by Paul had, by the nature of its mechanism, much less than perfect registration of successive images, as can be seen from surviving fragments of film shot with it, and when Paul and Acres fell out in the middle of 1895 over who owned the patent to the camera, and then parted company, Acres kept the original design. Some of the films made in 1895 by Acres for Paul, and later for himself, survive, but none were fictional subjects. It was only in the middle of 1896, after the showings of Lumière films in London, that Acres produced a staged film entitled *Arrest of a Pickpocket*. In succeeding years Birt Acres made very few films, and quickly faded from the film production scene, though he continued to have some importance as a manufacturer of cameras and film stock for a short time.

On the other hand, Robert Paul designed and made a successful film projector at the beginning of 1896, which used a Maltese Cross (or Geneva) type of intermittent movement, and then several months later he produced a new type of film camera using the same principle. With this camera Paul plunged into production; mostly of actuality films. A few of these films survive, and as far as I can tell from them, and from the catalogue descriptions

The first scene of Come Along, Do! *(R.W. Paul, 1898) shown above in a frame from the surviving material, was ended by the old couple going through the door into the second scene, shown below in a frame enlargement reproduced in Paul's sales material printed at the time.*

of the others, none contributed anything new to the development of film construction until *Come Along, Do!*, made around April 1898. This film was undoubtedly made up of two scenes, each a single shot, and was filmed on constructed sets. So far it seems that only the first shot, which shows an old couple lunching outside an art gallery, and then following other people in through its doorway, survives. However, there also exist stills showing both the two scenes, and it is clear that the second scene was shot on a set representing the interior of the gallery, where the old man closely examines a nude statue, until removed by his wife. The probability is that these two shots were joined by a simple splice, since there is no sign of the beginning of a dissolve after the actors exit the frame in the first scene, but the exact nature of the transition still remains to be determined. This film was preceded by Méliès' *Sauvetage en Riviere* from early in 1896, which was twice as long as the standard length, and sold in two separate parts, but we have no way of telling whether it was really in two different scenes, or the nature of any action continuity between the two parts. In any case, the available evidence still says that Paul's *Come Along, Do!* was the first film made up of more than one scene joined together, and sold as such.

About July 1898 Paul also produced a series of four films, each made up of one scene done in one shot of 80 feet length, under the general heading of *The Servant Difficulty*. These films were sold separately, but dealt with a series of incidents involving the same characters. But such things were exceptional in R.W. Paul's output, which both before and after 1900 was mostly actualities, or single shot knockabout comedies.

Paul clearly had a casual approach to getting films made, and in many of these one-shot films little imagination has been expended on the action included in them, and their maker has been concerned with little more than filling up the standard length per title, which was 40 feet at first, and later 80 feet. For instance, his *Railway Collision* of 1900 is no more than a one shot record of two model toy trains colliding with each other on a track on a miniature set. But occasionally Paul tried harder, and then produced a few notably original efforts. One of these is *Upside Down; or, The Human Flies* made before September 1899. This shows people walking up the wall onto the ceiling by using trick cuts on action for the moves from one surface to the

This shot from Paul's The Cheese Mites (1901) *was done by filming the right half of the picture as a second exposure on a giant set representing the table and window with the human figures on it.*

next, with the actual floor of the set painted to look like a ceiling, and the camera inverted, for the final stage when the actors appear to be upside down. This idea was copied, with variations, by the Pathé company and Georges Méliès in 1902 in *La Soubrette géniale* and *L'Homme-Mouche* respectively.

Another of Paul's bright ideas that resulted in a whole string of imitations was *The Cheese Mites; or, Lilliputians in a London Restaurant*, made before August 1901, which shows tiny human figures appearing out of the cheese on a diner's table. This was done in the obvious way by superimposing a second exposure with actors shot on a giant set showing part of the table onto the original scene, and although there are a number of Méliès examples previously using this general technique, none of these feature two different sizes of human figures interacting until *La Danseuse microscopique*, made at the end of 1901. The idea was subsequently thoroughly exploited by the Pathé film-makers in films such as *Les Pantins de Miss Hold* (1908) and many others. Paul also demonstrated that he too could produce very smoothly executed trick films in the manner of Méliès in *The Haunted Curiosity Shop* (1901) and *Artistic Creation* (1901) when he wanted to take the trouble, but he was not obsessed with trick effects like Georges Méliès.

Another of Paul's films which produced a better-known imitation by another film-maker was *The Countryman and the Cinematograph*, made before October 1901. This shows an unsophisticated viewer of a film show of the period, who takes what he sees for reality, and then tries to get into the action on the screen, which he demolishes at the end of the film. Edwin Porter imitated this film exactly in his *Uncle Josh at the Moving Picture Show* of January 1902, even reproducing the same scenes used as the films within the film, namely a dancer, a train, and a courting couple.

As the demand for longer multi-shot films increased, Paul's lack of real talent for dramatic narrative told on his work, and he made things like *Buy Your Own Cherries* (1904), which is a scene for scene reproduction of one of the lantern slide shows on temperance subjects so popular at the end of the nineteenth century, and shows no filmic invention at all. By 1910 Robert Paul had given up film-making completely, and once more devoted all his attention to his scientific instrument-making business.

G.A. Smith

George Albert Smith had scientific and technical inclinations, being a Fellow of the Royal Astronomical Society, and he also gave popular lantern slide lectures on scientific subjects. Most importantly, he also had some leanings towards show-business, having become the lessee of St. Anne's Well Gardens in the town of Hove (next to Brighton) in 1894. This was a small pleasure garden which featured a mineral spring, a gipsy fortune teller, a cave with resident "hermit", light teas, and other small-scale and refined attractions.

Smith seems to have been directed towards cinematography by A. Esmé Collings, an associate of William Friese Green, the latter being famous for what we now know were unsuccessful attempts to produce satisfactory moving pictures. Collings had a camera made for him in 1896 by the Brighton engineer Alfred Darling, and shot a small number of films with it, all of which are now lost. Although Collings immediately vanished from the early film scene without producing anything of importance, Smith went on to make a major contribution to the development of the basics of film form over the next several years.

At first, his films were single shot actualities and knockabout comedies, the latter starting with *Hanging Out the Clothes; or, Master, Mistress, and Maid* (1897). Then in 1898, he began to invent novel techniques for special effects, demonstrated in *The Corsican Brothers*, which was made before July of that year. The Warwick Trading Company, which took up the distribution of Smith's films in 1900, gave this description of the film in their catalogue:-

'One of the twin brothers returns home from shooting in the Corsican mountains, and is visited by the ghost of the other twin. By extremely careful photography the ghost appears *quite transparent*. After indicating that he has been killed by a sword-thrust, and appealing for vengeance, he disappears. A "vision" then appears showing the fatal duel in the snow. To the Corsican's amazement, the duel and death of his brother are vividly depicted in the vision, and finally, overcome by his feelings, he falls to the floor just as his mother enters the room.'

The accompanying frame enlargements in the catalogue show frames including the two main effects. The ghost effect was simply done by draping the set in black velvet after the main action had been shot, and then re-exposing the negative with the actor playing the ghost going through the actions at the appropriate point, which was already a well-known technique in still photography, and referred to as "spirit photography". Likewise, the vision, which appeared within a circular vignette, was similarly superimposed over a black area in the backdrop to the scene, rather than over a part of the set with detail in it, so that nothing appeared through the image, which seemed quite solid. This idea too was already used in lantern slide shows and graphic illustrations to suggest visions, and also sometimes parallel action. Nevertheless, Smith applied for a provisional patent on these techniques as they applied to film, but this did not prevent other film-makers subsequently using these ideas when they felt

inclined. Although at this date Georges Méliès had been making trick films for more than a year, his films seem to have used the "stop camera and substitution of objects" technique exclusively, and his first films depending on superimposition on a dark ground, which were *La Caverne maudite* and *L'Homme de Têtes* were made just after *The Corsican Brothers*.

The only surviving film of this kind made by Smith is *Santa Claus*, made later in 1898. Here the "dream vision" of Santa Claus on the roof getting down the chimney, as the catalogue again describes it, appears to two small children asleep in bed on Christmas Eve. In this case, the circular inset vignette could also be taken as a depiction of parallel action, even though not described as such, since when it vanishes after Santa has disappeared down the chimney, he then appears out of the fireplace on the set, and fills the children's stockings with presents.

Another technique that Smith developed in 1899 was reverse action, the earliest surviving example of which is *The House That Jack Built*, made before September 1900. Here, a small boy is shown knocking down a castle just constructed by a little girl out of children's building blocks. Then a title appears, saying "Reversed", and the action is repeated in reverse, so that the castle re-erects itself under the blows of the little boy's hand. Previous to this, the same effect of reverse motion, which had already proved very popular with audiences, could only be achieved by running a film backwards through a film projector. However, by 1900 there were a number of makes of movie projector which would only run forwards, and the owners of these formed a market for films like *The House That Jack Built*, which achieved the effect in ordinary forwards projection. In the first examples from G.A. Smith, the trick was done by repeating the action a second time, while filming it with an inverted camera, and then joining the tail of the second negative to that of the first, but later Cecil Hepworth built an optical or projection printer that could be used to make a second print with the frames printed one at a time in reverse order.

Yet another of Smith's bright ideas was the use of a focus-pull transition in *Let Me Dream Again* (1900). In the first shot of this two-shot film a man is seen kissing a beautiful woman in Medium Shot, then the lens focus is changed to reduce the image to an out-of-focus blur, followed by a cut to another shot similarly out of focus, which then pulls into focus to show the same man in bed kissing his ugly wife, from whom he recoils in revulsion. When this film was remade by Pathé in 1902 as *Rêve et Réalité*, the focus pulls were replaced by a simple dissolve. This gives just one instance of the superior technical skill of the English film-makers at this date.

In the light of history, trick effects like these proved to be of relatively little importance in comparison with Smith's inventions that relate to the basics of film construction. His *The Kiss in the Tunnel*, made before November 1899,

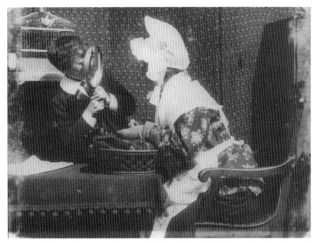

One of the shots making up G.A. Smith's Grandma's Reading Glass, *with "Willy" looking at his grandma's eye through a magnifying glass.*

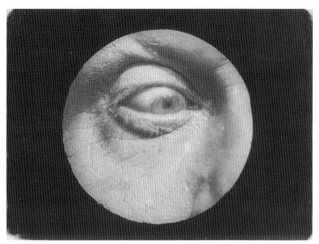

The next shot shows his simulated point of view, with the eye filmed through a circular vignette in front of the camera lens, not an actual magnifying glass.

advanced the idea of action continuity from one shot to the next a half step beyond what had already been achieved in R.W. Paul's *Come Along, Do!*. The Smith film shows a set representing the interior of a railway carriage compartment, with blackness visible through the window, and a man kissing a woman. The Warwick Trading Company catalogue instructs that it should be joined into a film of a "phantom ride" between the points at which the train enters and leaves a tunnel, an event which many "phantom rides" included, and this is indeed the case with the surviving copy of this film. (G.A. Smith had made a "phantom ride" film, which was the result of fixing a film camera on the front of a train, the year before, as had other film-makers, but it is difficult to tell which "phantom ride" is which amongst the few that still remain out of the many that were made in the first decade of cinema.) In any case, the catalogue instruction as to the point at which the cut should be made shows that the concept of action continuity was understood by Smith. A few months later, the Bamforth company made an imitation of Smith's film with the same title, which developed the idea even further. However Smith himself contributed little more towards the development of action continuity going out of one scene into the next, leaving that to Méliès in France and James Williamson in England, who established the rest of the conventions in the next couple of years.

Smith also invented the practice of dividing a continuous scene shot in the one place up into a number of shots, in a series of films beginning with *Grandma's Reading Glass* of 1900. In this film, a small boy is shown looking at various objects with a magnifying glass in the first shot, and then Big Close Ups of the objects seen from his Point of View (POV) are cut in in succession. As the Warwick Trading Company catalogue put it at the time: 'The conception is to produce on the screen the various objects as they

appeared to Willy while looking through the glass in their enormously enlarged form.' In the Big Close Ups of the objects the view through the actual magnifying glass is not used, but its field of view is simulated by photographing the object of interest inside a black circular mask fixed in front of the camera lens. Smith repeated this device in *As Seen Through the Telescope* (September 1900), which shows a man with a telescope spying on another man who is taking advantage of the act of helping a woman onto a bicycle to fondle her ankle. Into the Long Shot incorporating all this action is inserted the ostensible view through the telescope, which is represented by another Big Close Up showing the lady's foot inside a black circular mask. Unlike the previous film, there is only one cut-in P.O.V. Close Up rather than several, but in the development of *As Seen Through the Telescope* made later in the next year by the Pathé company, *Ce que Je vois de mon Sixième*, the man uses his telescope to spy through a number of different windows in succession, so combining the structures of both earlier Smith films.

Also in 1901, G.A. Smith initiated the other major form of scene dissection with *The Little Doctor*. In this film, which now only exists in the essentially identical restaged version of 1903, *The Sick Kitten*, there is a cut straight in down the lens axis from a Medium Long Shot of a child administering a spoon of medicine to a kitten, to a Big Close Up Insert of the kitten with the spoon in its mouth, and then back to the Medium Long Shot again. As this is an objective shot of the kitten there is no masking as in the other films, and the matching of the position of the kitten across the two cuts is not perfect, as is hardly surprising given the nature of kittens, but it could be worse.

An interesting example of the evolution of filmic devices through copying and modification is given by Edwin S. Porter's *Gay Shoe Clerk* (1903), which combines, as often with Porter, features from two or more previous films made by other people to give something a little different. This film, which shows a shoe salesman taking the opportunity to fondle a female customer's ankle in a Big Close Up Insert cut into the main scene, combines the general construction of *The Little Doctor* with the subject matter of *As Seen Through the Telescope*.

Apart from his own talent, ingenuity, and sense of humour, another of G.A. Smith's assets was his wife, who had formerly been on the stage in variety. She played the leading female part in most of his films, and makes a vivid impression on the screen. I personally would give her the highest star rating of any actor or actress in the first several years of the cinema. She plays the lead in a number of fairy tale subjects that Smith knocked out quickly after 1900 in competition with Méliès' long fantasy films. The only one of these that survives is *Robinson Crusoe*. This features Mrs. Smith in the name part, playing in travesty in the "principal boy" manner of English pantomime. Indeed the general impression this film gives, shot entirely with one Long Shot to each scene, is of an English pantomime done on a very small scale with a very small cast. Later in his life, Smith boasted that he could make one of these pantomime films in a day.

In 1903 Smith summed up and concentrated most of his technical achievements in his master-work, *Mary Jane's Mishap; or, Don't Fool with the Paraffin*. In the first scene of this film there is repeated three times a pair of cuts in, and then out again, from a Long Shot of Mary Jane lighting the fire to a Medium Close Shot of her. The matching of the position of the actress (Mrs. Smith) across the cuts is not perfect, but careful examination shows that she is taking trouble to hold an exact position at the end of the first shot, which she also assumes within a couple of frames as the camera starts turning at the beginning of the closer shot joined to it, and so on for succeeding cuts. In other words, the idea of position matching across a cut within a scene had already been arrived at by G.A. Smith. *Mary Jane's Mishap* also includes an example of "spirit photography", and even more remarkably, the use of vertical wipe to make the transition to the final scene, which is introduced by a close shot of Mary Jane's tombstone, and then another wipe from the close shot to the general shot of the graveyard. After this George Albert Smith gave up making films, and invented Kinemacolor, a system of colour cinematography which was very successful up to the First World War.

Bamforth and Company Ltd.

Bamforth & Co. were a well-established firm making and selling lantern slides and postcards in Holmfirth, Yorkshire, before the owner, James Bamforth, took them into film-making. Their version of G.A. Smith's *The Kiss in the Tunnel*, made at the end of 1899 has already been mentioned, and this film developed the idea of filmic continuity a little further, by putting the scene inside the railway carriage between two specially shot scenes of a train going into a tunnel, and then coming out the other end. Since these shots in the Bamforth film were objective shots, with the camera beside the track, rather than "phantom ride" shots, they made the point of the continuity of the action quite clear, rather than forcing the viewer to work it out by logical deduction.

Bamforth also made a contribution to the development of cutting from one camera angle to another on a continuous scene. This occurs in *Women's Rights* (1901), in which the second shot is taken at 180 degrees to the first from the other side of the fence with time continuity. This was obviously done to make the action of the film clear. Interestingly, this cut is achieved by an ingenious cheat which depends on moving the actors to the other side of the same symmetrical fence, without moving the camera, for the second shot. The model for this idea pretty certainly came from already existing examples of story telling with a series of lantern slides, where at least one example has a comic sequence showing action on both sides of a fence in successive slides.

Most of Bamforth's film production entirely lacked this kind of special interest, being actualities or one shot knockabouts just like those made by many other early film-makers, and they quickly dropped from view as film producers until 1913, when a comedy series featuring the character "Winky" made a certain impression on the British market.

James Williamson

James A. Williamson had a chemist's shop and photographic business in Hove quite near G.A. Smith's pleasure gardens. As a dedicated photographer, and also occasional lantern-slide showman, he was fairly inevitably drawn into the new medium of cinematography. He started shooting a few films at the end of 1897, and also undertook film processing for other amateur cinematographers. At first, most of the films he projected in his shows were made by G.A. Smith and others, but his own involvement rapidly increased through 1898, though the vast bulk of his films were still actualities at this date. The earliest Williamson film to survive is part of his *Attack on a Chinese Mission - Bluejackets to the Rescue* (1900), which was a fictionalised reconstruction of an incident during the recent Boxer rebellion in China. At one time claims were made for the importance of this film in terms of the development of film construction, but a careful examination of the remaining section and the catalogue description suggest that it was actually of little significance in this respect. Much more important were several of the films Williamson made during 1901.

Leading on from the two versions of *The Kiss in the Tunnel* previously mentioned, James Williamson continued the development of action continuity through shots cut

directly together in *Stop Thief!* (1901) and *Fire!* (1901).
The first of these films is the source of the subsequent
development of "chase" films, and is made up of three
shots. In the first shot the thief is chased out of the side
of the frame, and then in the second shot set in a different
place he runs in one side of the frame and is chased
towards the camera and out of the other side of the frame,
and then he runs into the third shot, where he is finally
caught; all of these shots being joined by simple cuts. *Fire!*
introduces this feature into a more complex construction.
In this film an actor moves from a scene outside a burning
building by exiting from the side of the frame and into a
shot outside a fire station, then the fire cart moves out of
this shot and next appears in the distant background of a
shot of a street, advancing forward and out of frame past
the camera. From this point the film moves back to the
burning house, though not to the real exterior as before,
but rather to a set showing a room inside the house. A
fireman comes into the room from the top of a ladder
outside the window, picks up the helpless occupant, and
starts to lift him through the window. At this point there
is a cut to the real exterior again, with the victim being
lifted through the window and carried down the ladder.
In the absolute sense the continuity of action across the
cut from inside to outside is imperfect, as there is a second
or so of movement across the window sill missing, but
even to the modern eye, the cut *looks* smooth, in the same
way that contemporary editing often elides small parts of
movement invisibly. The film ends with more movement
towards the camera and out of frame past it.

It must be mentioned that at the same time that
Williamson was making these films, Georges Méliès was
also beginning to use action moving out of one shot into
another, but in his case the shots were always joined by
a dissolve. The first Méliès film in which this happens is
Barbe-Bleue, made in the middle of 1901. Here there is a

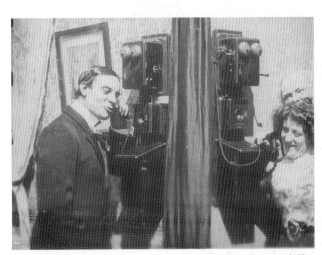

A telephone conversation between parties in two different places represented by a split set in Are You There? *(Williamson, 1901).*

scene in which Bluebeard's last wife unlocks and enters
the door to his secret room at frame right, and then there
is a dissolve to a shot of the inside of this room with the
wife coming through the door at frame left. In this film, as
in other films that Méliès made subsequently in his studio,
the directions of entrance and exit are what we would
nowadays think of as "correct", which is not always the
case in films made partly or wholly on real locations by
Williamson and other English film-makers.

The other striking Williamson production from 1901
was *The Big Swallow*. The catalogue description of this
reads:-

> '"I won't! I won't! I'll eat the camera first."
> Gentleman reading, finds a camera fiend with
> his head under a cloth, focussing him up. He
> orders him off, approaching nearer and nearer,
> gesticulating and ordering the photographer off,
> until his head fills the picture, and finally his mouth
> only occupies the screen. He opens it, and first the
> camera, and then the operator disappear inside. He
> retires munching him up and expressing his great
> satisfaction.'

In fact, not quite all of this is represented in the film,
and it is an example, of which there a number of others,
of films from the first ten years which are not completely
understandable without the commentary which would
have been supplied at the time by the showman projecting
the film. What the film actually shows begins with the
man advancing straight into the lens of the movie camera
actually taking the shot, followed by what is meant to be an
invisible trick cut to the still photographer and his camera
against a black background matching the black hole of
the giant mouth, and then falling below the bottom of the
frame, followed by another trick cut to the man backing
off munching.

Are You There? is again not completely intelligible from
what is shown on the screen. It is the first attempt to deal with
the problem of representing a telephone conversation on
film, which it does by a split screen effect. This was created
by building a split set, with a division down the centre of
the frame separating the two telephones. What is said over
the phone is vital to understanding the second scene of
the film, but again this would have to be supplied by the
showman's commentary when the film was projected. The
split screen treatment of telephone conversations became
the first standard method of dealing with this situation in
films, and it has never completely been replaced by the
cross-cutting method which appeared in 1908.

Williamson used a structure very similar to that of *Fire!*
again in 1902 in *The Soldier's Return*, although here the
suspense element is a bit weaker. This film is also notable
for the naturalism of the acting, which was advertised as
such in the contemporary Warwick Trading Company

catalogue, along with the fact that the parts were played by people who actually *were* what they were representing; the old ladies by old ladies, the returning soldier by an actual long-term serving soldier.

Looking at the surviving films, it seems to me that there is a real difference in the aspects of film construction that interested James Williamson and G.A. Smith. Williamson's films developed the basics of continuity of action moving from shot to shot in different locations, whereas Smith's films were concerned with breaking a scene down into a number of shots taken from different camera positions. When interviewed late in life, Smith said that although he knew Williamson quite well, and saw most of his films when they were exhibited locally, they did not work together in any way. This was an implicit rejection of the notion of a "Brighton school" of film-making, which I can only agree with. Although not as misleading as some other favourite mindless journalistic terms used in writing about film such as "Expressionism", it would be better if "Brighton school" was dropped in favour of an accurate description of what Smith and Williamson actually did independently in their different ways.

Although Williamson did not give up film making after 1903 like Smith, it would not have made a lot of difference if he had, because there are no specially interesting features in his later production up to 1910, when he concentrated very successfully on his other business of manufacturing cameras and other film equipment.

Sheffield Photographic Company

So far no other films repeating the continuous shot-to-shot movement of Williamson's films are known before early 1903, and the appearance of *Daring Daylight Burglary*, made by the Sheffield Photo Company. This company was a photographic business run by Frank Mottershaw in Sheffield, and he took up film-making about 1900. The eldest son of the family, F.S. Mottershaw, then spent a year in London working for R.W. Paul and

Desperate Poaching Affray *(Haggar, 1903).*

learning the craft, and after he came back, the company made its most celebrated films. *Daring Daylight Burglary* was released before April 1903, and starts with a high-angle shot of a burglar breaking into the back of a house. He is observed by a small boy looking over the side fence, who then runs off into the next shot of a street elsewhere in which he alerts the police. Then there is another straight cut back to the original scene, as the police arrive and enter the house after the burglar. The next scene shows a fight on the roof between a policeman and the burglar, who throws the policeman off the roof after a trick cut replacing the live performer with a dummy. After the badly hurt policeman has been removed in an ambulance, a chase develops that is carried through several shots, which gives an overall structure to the film that is a combination of *Fire!* and *Stop Thief!*. *Daring Daylight Burglary* was one of the most commercially successful films made up to that date, and it was distributed in America by the Edison Company under the title *Daylight Robbery* some months before their employee Edwin S. Porter made *The Great Train Robbery* for them. The Sheffield Photo Co. continued this tradition with *Robbery of the Mail Coach*, made a few months later, and released in October 1903. This repeated a very similar structure, but in a period setting, with added violence. Near the beginning of the film highwaymen hold up a mail coach, and then shoot the driver and guard, and then after an elaborated chase through five scenes they are shot down in their turn by the Kingsmen (i.e. period police) at the end of the film. It was undoubtedly these two films that inspired Porter's *The Great Train Robbery*, made in December 1903, which has the content of the American stage melodrama of the same name poured into the Sheffield Photo Co. structure, though Porter was unable to handle the chase element in it satisfactorily.

The Sheffield Photo Company's final big success in this style was a film of *The Life of Charles Peace, the Notorious Burglar*, which was very similar to the film of the same name made a few months earlier in 1905 by the Haggar family. After this the company gradually faded out of film production over the next several years.

Haggar and Sons

Walter Haggar was a showman with a travelling tent cinematograph show touring the fairgrounds in Wales and the west of England at the beginning of the century. Like a number of other travelling showmen, he started shooting his own films, but unlike the others, he made better films, and had them distributed internationally by the Gaumont company, amongst others. He took up the criminal chase idea from the Sheffield Photo Company, and applied it to a film about poachers made before July 1903, when it was already listed in the sales catalogue. This film was *Desperate Poaching Affray*, and it was one of the most successful films of the pre-nickelodeon period, having a fame not far below that of Méliès' *Le voyage dans la lune* and Porter's *The Great Train Robbery*. The reason for its success was that, on the screen, it was effectively the most violent film of the period, because the extensive shooting and realistic fighting that goes on between the poachers and their pursuers takes place much closer to the camera than in any other films of the time. The film probably also had a lot to do with firmly establishing the idea that in chase films the actors should run from the background towards the camera and quite close past one side of it out of frame for the maximum visual impact. It also uses, for the first time, the reverse arrangement, with the actors then running into the next shot, past the camera now turned to the opposite direction, and then away into the distance. This extra subtlety took a while to catch on generally, with most film-makers being content, when they were making chase films, to just repeat the same staging in series in successive locations, with the actors always appearing tiny in the background and always running towards the camera and past it. *Desperate Poaching Affray* includes a number of panning shots to follow the movement of the characters, which also contribute to its relatively modern look compared to other films of the same date.

Alf Collins and the Gaumont Company

A branch of the French Gaumont company was opened in England at the end of 1898, and at first sold film equipment and films imported from France. However, they shortly started to sell films made by independent English makers, and eventually, in 1903, they began producing their own films in England. These were all directed by Alf Collins, a well-known variety artist, and he often acted in them as well. Although his productions were in general roughly finished, with obvious signs of some scenes being shot without any rehearsal at all, Collins was one of the most inventive film-makers of the period, and introduced a number of original and important ideas for film construction.

The most important of these was the idea of cutting to different angles on a scene, rather than cutting to a closer shot straight down the lens axis. This occurs in *The Pickpocket - A Chase Through London* (1903), and in *The Runaway Match* (1903). In the latter film the cuts are in fact reverse-angle cuts, from the pursuing car to the one pursued. These cuts within the scene are reproduced and elaborated in an American copy of this film made a year or two later, *Marriage by Motor-Car*. Other Alf Collins films which show that this use of shots at different angles to a scene was not just a lucky accident include *When Extremes Meet* (1905). This begins by covering action on a park bench in Very Long Shot, and then cuts in closer to Long Shot with a simultaneous change of camera direction of 60 degrees, so covering slight discrepancies in actor position between the two shots and ensuring a smooth transition (as seen in subsequent terms). Despite the existence of

these films, and also a few others which use cuts to the opposite angle on the other side of a wall during comedy chases, there was no general adoption of the use of cuts to a different angle during this period in any way comparable to the common use of cuts straight in to a close shot. *The Runaway Match* and *The Pickpocket* are also notable for being among the first films that established the idea of "chase" construction, in which a person is chased by others through a series of shots cut straight together. They were both distributed in America by the American Mutoscope and Biograph Company from the beginning of December 1903, and were among the British films that inspired American (and French) film-makers to take up the chase idea. After a comparatively short career in films, Alf Collins returned to the stage, and the British branch of the Gaumont company returned to being just an agency for their French films and those made by other independent producers.

Cecil M. Hepworth

Cecil Hepworth was the son of a lantern lecturer, and began touring with his own film show in 1896 when he was only 22. He published the first technical manual on film-making and film exhibition in 1897, and in 1898 he began making films for Charles Urban, who was just turning the London agency of the American firm of Maguire and Baucus into the Warwick Trading Company Ltd. Besides shooting actuality films for Urban, Hepworth also made various improvements to the projectors the firm was selling, and designed special continuous film developing machines for them too. In 1899 Hepworth set up his own film laboratory at Walton-on-Thames in partnership with H.V. Lawley. At the beginning of this century, Hepworth's company was producing about 100 films a year, and he was delegating much of the directing to other people, principally Percy Stow. The early Hepworth films made no great contributions to the basics of film technique, but some of them have interesting features.

Examples of this include *How It Feels To Be Run Over* made in 1900, in which we see a motor car driving straight at the camera, with its occupants gesticulating, presumably at the unseen camera operator, to get out of the way. Then as the car is right up at the camera there is a cut to black screen covered with stars, flashes, and exclamation marks, and then another cut to a title, "Oh, mother will be pleased!" Even more interesting is *The Indian Chief and the Seidlitz Powder* of 1901. This shows a man dressed as an American Indian Chief stealing into a chemist's shop, and rifling it. He comes upon a crate of Seidlitz powders, and drinks a large quantity of them, after which his stomach blows up like a balloon, and he starts leaping about as though lifted up by the gas in his stomach. This last part of the film was shot with the camera cranked very fast; somewhere between 50 and 100 frames per second, which gives a very suitably balloon-like appearance to the man's movements. Given Hepworth's command of the technical side of film-making, it is not surprising that he built an optical or projection printer as early as 1900. With this he made *The Bathers*, which shows two men undressing and diving into a river. The action then reverses, they shoot backwards out of the water onto the bank, and their clothes fly back onto them. Unlike G.A. Smith's earlier reversing films, where the action was staged twice, and the second time shot upside down after which the negative was reversed end for end, in the Hepworth film the same negative was used, and printed frame by frame in reverse order on his projection printer. This was simply a projector holding the negative with the lens pulled out far enough to project a same-sized image into the gate of a camera from which the lens had been removed, and then the film was advanced one frame at a time in each machine to produce a series of single exposures onto the positive film in the camera in reverse order. Although this involved a lot of work to make each print of the film, it did mean that the action seen in reverse was absolutely identical to that forwards, and this made possible more remarkable effects, as in Hepworth's *A Frustrated Elopement* of 1902. Here the young couple escaping down a ladder from the girl's bedroom are trapped in mid-flight, and then they slide rapidly up and down the ladder with the aid of reverse printing, during the middle section of the single shot which makes up the film.

One of Hepworth's most interesting productions of this period is *Alice in Wonderland* (1903), which depicts some of the Lewis Carroll story in several minutes. In this film, going against the now standard British practice of joining shots with straight cuts, Hepworth took up the Méliès idea of joining all the shots by dissolves. This method of joining shots had been tentatively adopted after 1901 by some other foreign film-makers such as Edwin Porter. Since *Alice in Wonderland* has very advanced *découpage*, with some of the scenes broken down into shots taken from different angles, and with action from shot to shot matching across the dissolves, this produces a rather curious effect to the modern eye. As we know, the idea of using dissolves between every shot in a film did not really catch on, despite the prestige of Georges Méliès, and *Alice* is the only film of Hepworth's known to use the technique.

At first, like all the other British film-makers, Hepworth shot interior scenes for his pictures on a temporary open-air stage, but in 1903 he built a proper fully enclosed studio on the pattern of the one Méliès had built four years before, with muranese glass to diffuse the sunlight, and also with arc floodlights for subsidiary lighting. In 1904 H.V. Lawley and Percy Stow left Hepworth to set up the Clarendon film company, and the man who directed most of the Hepworth films for the next several years was Lewin Fitzhamon.

The results of the use of arc lighting at the Hepworth

A scene in the Hepworth company film Falsely Accused *(1905) shot under direct sunlight, with a cut in to an Insert shot of the money in the man's hand.*

studios can be seen in a number of films made in 1905. One extremely interesting example is in *Falsely Accused*, in which a man searching a totally dark room by lantern light is photographed doing just that, the sole illumination of the scene coming from a tiny electric arc concealed in his lantern! (illustrated in *Film Style and Technology*) It was several years before this technique turned up in films again. There would seem to have been someone at Hepworth aware of the possibilities of available-light photography, because in the same year *Stolen Guy* includes a bonfire scene lit solely by the light from the bonfire. And the famous *Rescued by Rover* (1905) includes an interior studio scene in the gipsy's attic in which the effect of light coming through the window is simulated by a couple of arc lights coming in from that side of the set. *Rescued by Rover* builds on the continuity construction of the best British films of the previous few years, which were of course world leaders in this area, with the cuts between each shot in *Rover* sharpened to the point where there is no time lost in waiting for the actors who have left one shot to appear in the next. This approach was followed by films from Pathé over the next few years, and so became the general standard. *The ? Motorist* (1905) was likewise very sharply edited, though its basic content was a combination Méliès' *Le Voyage dans la Lune* (1902) and Hepworth's own *The Jonah Man* (1904).

When the world-wide film boom began in 1906, largely led by the establishment of large numbers of "nickelodeons" in the United States, the British producers failed to increase the amount and quality of their production to take advantage of the new conditions in the industry. This was just as true of the Hepworth company, which was now the largest British film company, as it was of the other British producers. By 1908, the reel of film, understood as containing nearly 1000 feet of picture, was the standard unit of merchandise in the film industry. But Hepworth, along with the other British manufacturers, was still producing dramatic subjects that were only 500 to 600 feet long in 1910, and indeed even later than that. In fact in that year, of the 137 films Hepworth made, only about 20 were longer than 600 feet. Worse than that, these Hepworth films lacked some of the newest technical features that were now usual in American films, and even to some extent in French and Italian films of the time.

For instance, *A Woman's Treachery* of 1910 was only 570 feet long, and in it the actors talk to the camera, and generally indulge in melodramatic acting, and the next year, *Jim of the Mounted Police*, directed by Lewin Fitzhamon, was only 500 feet in length, and was filmed entirely in Long Shot. The only thing that could be said for it was that it contained a lot of conventionally pretty pictures of the countryside. This last feature was fairly typical of the Hepworth company's films, and was just about their only positive selling point. Remember that by 1911 the major American companies such as Vitagraph and Biograph were providing three or more full reels a week, each of which contained an interesting and complex story lasting from twelve to fifteen minutes, and in them this story was conveyed with fairly naturalistic acting done fairly close up to the camera, frequently as close as Medium Shot. The best Hepworth films from this period are no more than mediocre by American standards, not to mention their brevity.

Basically the problem was due to lack of investment to build up the quantity of films made, and also their production values, during the crucial years around 1908. Everyone concerned was aware of the fact that British films were losing out in the home market, let alone overseas, but in the main their response was just to increase the publicity for what were alleged to be the various company's "top-liner" pictures, rather than increasing their quality. Even as late as 1915, the Hepworth Company could still put out *The Midnight Mail*, which was still only 600 feet long, contained no cutting within scenes, had no dialogue titles, and had nearly every scene joined to the next by

a fade-out followed by a fade-in. This was not just lack of progress, this was regress. However, there were a few Hepworth films made in 1913 that achieved a decent European standard, even if they were not up to that of the better American films of that date. The most striking of these is *At the Foot of the Scaffold*, which includes a tracking shot through a wall to show the action on the other side, which was a very new idea at the time, and has well-modelled arc lighting of the sets, and also reasonably good acting with free occasional use of dialogue titles to convey the narrative with greater smoothness. For the climax, it also features cross-cutting between parallel action, which was still very rare in European films.

Cricks and Sharp — Cricks and Martin

After a year working for Hepworth, G.H. Cricks set up a film company at Mitcham on the outskirts of London with H.M. Sharp in 1901. Sharp left the company in 1908, and was replaced by J. H. Martin, who had been working for Robert Paul for several years, and was a specialist in trick films. The twenty or so fiction films made by this firm that survive give little reason to regret all the others that have now vanished, since those remaining are undistinguished even by British standards of the time. The only interesting Cricks and Sharp film is the actuality *A Visit to Peek Frean's Biscuit Works* (1906), which was commissioned as a publicity film by the large biscuit firm for publicity purposes. This film is really a documentary which shows in fair detail the process of making and shipping biscuits, with arc lighting specially brought in to illuminate the large work rooms.

Alpha Trading Company

Alpha was the name used for his films by the young independent film-maker Arthur Melbourne-Cooper when he started making films about 1903. Like most early film-makers he started with actualities and one shot films depicting knockabout action, or children paying with puppies, or the like. He also produced imitations of other film-maker's more successful ideas, and the earliest film certainly made by him is *Lost — A Leg of Mutton* of 1904, which is a slightly elaborated version of Williamson's *Stop Thief!* (1901). His films occasionally had a touch of the bizarre, and his greatest claim to fame is that he was the first British film-maker to master the technique of object animation. Like Segundo de Chomon and Emil Cohl in France, Melbourne-Cooper worked out how the trick of photographing objects or drawings one frame at a time, and moving them in between each exposure, was done in the Vitagraph films *Work Made Easy* and *The Haunted Hotel* which appeared in Europe in 1907. Using this technique, Melbourne-Cooper produced *Dreams of Toyland* (1908), which has more different toys moving simultaneously in different ways within one shot than anyone else attempted before or since. When the film gets going it has a manic quality that makes one quite dizzy. Like so many early film-makers, Arthur Melbourne-Cooper did not have what it takes to make interesting longer films.

Clarendon Film Company

The Clarendon Film Company was set up with a studio in Croydon by H.V. Lawley and Percy Stow after they left Hepworth in 1904. Their films at first were mostly comedies of no particular distinction, but Percy Stow did pick up the idea of using dialogue titles very early in the evolution of the regular use of this device. *Where's Baby* of 1908 uses dialogue representing a character's thoughts, and *Never Late* (1909), a slightly amusing comedy about office clerks playing tricks on each other, has an example of ordinary dialogue given in an intertitle. Their series built around the exploits of the character "Lieutenant Rose" were quite successful in England at the time, and gave rise to imitations from other studios, but were basically at the children's comic strip level in their content. Stow had some idea about the value of using Point of View shots and Insert shots of objects for film narration, but the way he used them was slightly clumsy, as can be seen in *Lieutenant Rose and the Robbers of Fingall's Creek* (1910).

Barker Motion Photography Ltd.

This was one of the most conspicuous of the firms that opened up after 1908, when most of the pioneering companies faded away, and was founded by William George Barker in 1909. Barker had been in the business since the beginning of the century, first making topicals, then also making acted films for his Autoscope company from 1904 onwards, though without producing anything of great importance. After that, he was managing director of Urban's Warwick Trading Company for a while, establishing it as pre-eminent in instant films on immediate news subjects. Barker's approach with his new company was to make fairly spectacular films that tried to rival the more impressive foreign production now taking over British screens, and he did this by making longer films of well-known stage works, particularly melodramas, and sometimes with well-known stage actors playing in them. The first example of this was his film of *Henry VIII* with Sir Herbert Tree and his London stage company, which was made in 1911. The best known surviving example of his work is *East Lynne* (1913), which is a version of the popular Victorian novel (and stage play) of the same name. As a piece of cinema this is again very undistinguished by the best American standards of that date, with no real cutting within the scenes, which all go on for ages, no dialogue titles, and with only a few shots as close as Medium Long Shot.

British and Colonial Kinematograph Company

British and Colonial was also set up in 1909, but the heads of the new company, A.H. Bloomfield and

J.B. McDowell, were not already important figures in the film business like George Barker. Their films were imitative of other people's successes, such as Clarendon's "Lieutenant Rose" adventure series, which they rivalled with their "Lieutenant Daring" and "Three-fingered Kate" series. These were quite popular in Britain, but had the same flaws when compared with the best American product of the time. *The Mountaineer's Romance* of 1912 is quite clearly an attempt to make something that would be saleable in the United States, with the leading male character quite unnecessarily alleged to be American by the intertitles, and with the action set in some of the more spectacular British scenery in the north, rather than in the more convenient area round London, as was still usual. But like the other British and Colonial films of this late date, the interiors were still being shot on an open stage under direct sunlight.

London Film Company

This was the one company that showed much sign of making films in a way that might make them capable of competing with the American product, and the founder of the firm, Dr. R.T. Jupp, did this by hiring American talent. In 1912, Jupp was the manager of one of the largest cinema circuits in the country, and a major figure in that side of the business. In 1913 he brought over George Loane Tucker, who had just directed the famous *Traffic in Souls*, and Harold Shaw, who had likewise been working for IMP in the United States, to direct his company's films, and also the actress Edna Flugrath, and the writers Anne and Bannister Merwin, all from the Edison company. The only London Film Co. films to survive are several made by Harold Shaw in 1914, and titles like *The Two Columbines* do finally begin to match at least the average American standards in finish, speed, and use of the latest narrative techniques such as flash-backs. But this initiative to put British production back into competition internationally was scuttled by the beginning of the First World War.

BACKGROUND INFORMATION

The first few years of the British cinema up to 1898 are carefully covered in detail in John Barnes' series of books *The Beginnings of the Cinema in England* (David & Charles, 1976), *The Rise of the Cinema in Great Britain* (Bishopgate Press, 1983), and *Pioneers of the British Film* (Bishopgate Press, 1983). The first volume of *The History of the British Film (1896-1906)* (Allen & Unwin, 1948), by Rachael Low and Roger Manvell, is a little more sketchy than subsequent volumes of that excellent series, and in particular than the next volume covering 1906-1914, written by Rachael Low on her own. Vastly more films from the first twenty years have become available in the forty years since Rachael Low started her work, so I have been able to give a more accurate account of the important formal developments in cinema.

Many of the films mentioned in this article are now available on the DVD *Early Cinema — Primitives and Pioneers*, selected by myself, and put out by the British Film Institute. From the DVD you can see that I was really right off beam in 1990 with my assessment of the *Attack on a Chinese Mission* in the preceding piece. My only excuse is that this was before the almost complete copy of the film turned up, and I was tired of all the fuss that had been made about the film on the basis of the one shot fragment and the catalogue description. Anyway, I made up for it later, as you can see on pages 292 to 298.

More importantly, after the Pordenone *Giornate* had established itself, Bologna had started a section in 1986 in its long-running *Mostra Internazionale del Cinema Libero* called "Il Cinema Ritrovato", which was devoted to film history. All this was funded by the Comune di Bologna, who also set up a laboratory for the restoration of old films in the city. The historical Italian phenomenon of *campanilismo* (...our bell-tower is bigger than yours...) has its useful side. Niccola Mazzanti at Bologna invited me to contribute to one of the themes of the 1991 Bologna *Mostra*, which was Italian silent cinema. I wrote a piece on the stylistics of early Italian cinema which appeared as *Il cinema italiano dalla nascita alla Grande Guerra: un analisa stilistica* in the book *Sperduto nel buio* edited by Renzo Renzi (Capelli editore 1991).

The illustrations to this English version of the article are not quite the same as those in the book *Sperduti nel buio*, and I have also modified the section on the history of flash-backs in Italian cinema to include a mention of the film *Le Fiabe della nonna* (1908). *Sperduti nel buio* was set with Baskerville as the body text, and here I have used the Berthold version.

THE STYLE OF EARLY ITALIAN PICTURES

As more and more old films see the light of the projector, the story of what exactly happened in the first twenty-five years of the movies becomes more complicated. In particular, Italian films now seem to me to be more involved in some aspects of the progressive developments of film form before the First World War than I originally thought when I wrote the first edition of my *Film Style and Technology: History and Analysis* a decade or more ago. The following comments are based on viewing about 200 Italian films made before 1921, and these in their turn are considered against a background of about 2500 films of the same period made elsewhere. Most of the Italian films I shall be writing about are in the National Film Archive in London, which already had quite a good collection of around 100 early Italian fictional films even before acquiring the Joseph Joye collection,

Daylight coming from the left through the glass studio wall in the Cines film Antro funesto

which itself includes about 50 Italian fictional movies. These collections are heavily biased towards films on historical subjects and comedies, which exaggerates, by the preferences of the foreign market and the tastes of film collectors, a bias towards these genres which already existed in Italian film production in the early years.

Lighting

Once continuous production was well under way, the major Italian companies built studios on the standard model, with walls and ceilings of diffusing glass, plus extra diffusion by cotton blinds on sunny days, but they tended to be rather bigger than comparable studios elsewhere. There is in general far less use of supplementary artificial lighting in studio scenes in Italian films than there is in French or American films of the pre-war period; indeed very few of the surviving Italian films show any visible effect of artificial lighting at all. In the case of the films from the Cines studio, the diffuse sunlight or daylight coming through the studio walls gives an idiosyncratic look to their lighting, as it is very frequently directly from the side, rather than from

the high front direction usual elsewhere. In 1909 we do find a little arc floodlighting supplementing the general diffuse daylight in one of the studio scenes in the Itala company's *I due sargenti*, and by 1910 all the major Italian studios did have arc lights, as can be seen for instance in the arc fill light applied to some studio scenes in the Cines film *Tontolini si batte in duello*, but in general they were little used for ordinary studio lighting.

Notable instances of the use of artificial lighting include Guazzoni's *Quo vadis?* (1912), where the scene of Nero playing the harp while Rome burns has lighting applied to him from a low angle with arc floodlights. This usage was then carried further in *Cabiria* (1914), where the effect was similarly naturalistically motivated by a large-scale fire out of shot. In another scene in *Cabiria* the source of this low-angle lighting was actually in the shot, and the aim was apparently to suggest a weird atmosphere. Finally, the most massive general use of arc floodlights up to this date took place on some of the giant sets of *Cabiria* for the night scenes. By 1913 there was beginning to be fairly good simulation of the light from lamps actually appearing in shot in a few Italian films,

Low arc floodlights lighting Nero in Guazzoni's Quo Vadis?
(1912)

Contre-jour scene in Patrizia e schiava (Cines, 1909)

and this was done by sneaking the light from an arc light outside the frame into the appropriate part of the image. This followed the practice standard years before in films from other countries. As might be expected, *La lampada della nonna* (1913) contains a number of fairly good examples of this. A series of low-key scenes are carried through even better in *L'antro funesto* (Itala, 1913), which has a number of scenes in a cave, and climaxes with an attempt to escape from it with the aid of a hand-held lantern. The simulation of the lamp light is very well handled, and almost comparable with the best in this manner from America, France, or Denmark. In fact, when I first saw this film in an English-language print with no company identification on it, I thought it was a Gaumont film, because of its resemblance to some of Léonce Perret's works such as *Les rochers de Kador* (1912) and *Roman d'un mousse* (1913), not only in its lighting, but also in its stagings.

Silhouette Effects

The exact way that silhouette effects came to be intentionally used in an integrated way in film stories is still not clear, nor for that matter is priority in introducing the device. At the moment, 1909 seems to be the crucial year, with a striking *contre-jour* shot of a boat on the sea in the Cines *Patrizia e schiava*. Also in 1909 the Italian Aquila company also made a film including a shot done along these lines, *Floriana de Lys*, this time with the figures in semi-silhouette against window lighting. I have seen nothing from the United States using silhouette effects in an integrated way earlier than 1909, when there were two Griffith films from late in the year which have silhouettes used purely pictorially, without expressive connotations. *In Old Kentucky* has a skyline silhouette showing a sentry at his post, and there are semi-silhouette figures in *Lines of White on a Sullen Sea*, though after this date this photographic feature never

Silhouette effect in L'Inferno (Milano Films, 1911)

Semi-silhouette scene in Jone (Enrico Vidali, 1913)

The significant action in this scene is shown as a shadow on the wall in Il pellegrino *(Ambrosio, 1913)*

recurs in Griffith's films as far as I can tell. Other later Italian films also used contre-jour shots showing figures near the mouth of a cave, including the Cines *Il Cid* (Mario Caserini, 1910), and *Quo vadis?* (1912), but by the latter date it is not unusual to see semi-silhouette effects in doorways and windows in films from a number of countries.

Another interesting expressive device which Italian movies helped carry on was the use of shadow effects. In the Ambrosio company's *Il pellegrino* (1913), the scourging of Christ is represented solely by the shadow of the action on the wall. This is presumably inspired by the way this scene was handled in the 1906 Gaumont *La vie de Jésus*, but in that case the action was taking place behind a pillar, and the shadow was part of a larger scene, whereas in the Ambrosio version all we get is a close shot of part of the shadow on the wall. This is the

sort of thing that Cecil B. DeMille and others became famous for a few years later.

The use of the kind of *contre-jour* effects mentioned above carried through into the War years as an aspect of the pursuit of "pictorialism" in Italian films, particularly in exterior scenes, regardless of its relevance to the narrative. In short, the story stopped while the leading characters stood around in a beautiful landscape picture. This can be readily seen in the Eleanora Duse vehicle, *Cenere* (1916), but it touched even the best Italian films of the period, such as *Assunta Spina* (1915).

The Staging of the Shot

At first theatrical tradition provided the model for the staging of the acting within the film shot, but by 1910 other influences had begun to appear, particularly in Italy. In that country the effect of the graphic art of the recent past can be seen in *L'inferno* (Milano, 1909) and *La caduta di Troia* (Giovanni Pastrone, 1911), and others. Many of the compositions in the Milano film *L'inferno* are modelled on Gustave Doré's engravings for *La divina commedia*, and in *La caduta di Troia* the influence is from the Alma-Tadema type of 'Salon' history painting. However, mixed in with the more derivative approaches to large-scale staging, the emergence of a more purely filmic approach can also be seen in some films. Sometimes this is just a matter of the conjunction of the topography of the location and the relatively unorganized enthusiasm of the extras, and sometimes it is the result of camera placement, as in other examples from *La caduta di Troia*. As is well-known, the Italians pushed the staging of large-scale scenes much further in the next few years, and both the Salon Painting strain in staging and the purely filmic approach developed side by side in such films as *Gli ultimi giorni di Pompei* (Vidali, 1913) and *Quo vadis?* (Enrico Guazzoni, 1912). The kind of composition that is sometimes used to

The bottom of the pit of Hell in L'Inferno *(Milano, 1913)*

The Gustave Doré illustration which inspired the film frame.

Purely filmic staging in La caduta di Troia *(Giovanni Pastrone, 1911)*

La sposa del Nilo *(Guazzoni, 1911)*

combine principal figures with massed extras in D.W. Griffith's films from 1913 onwards is anticipated in *La sposa del Nilo* (Cines, 1911), though this may not be a matter of influence, but rather of directors with similar backgrounds producing a similar solution to the same filmic problem.

Influences from the film scenography in other countries can sometimes be definitely picked out, and one instance of this is the building of sets representing the interior of a house which have a large doorway or other opening at the back of the room leading to another room visible through it. Some of the action in the film usually takes place in this space behind the main set, within the length of the shot which covers the whole scene. This idea was developed in France from 1909, but it only really makes its appearance in Italian films from 1913 with the Itala company's *L'antro funesto*.

The film *Thais* made in 1916 by the Italian Futurist

Bragaglia is usually mentioned as the first instance of decor fully stylized beyond any connection with reality, but this only applies to one set used in the last few scenes. This set had the walls covered with sets of black and white rectangles and triangles nesting inside each other, but contrary to some suggestions, the geometric

A scene in Jone *(1913), directed by Enrico Vidali*

The Oleander, *painted by Lawrence Alma-Tadema in 1882*

regularity of these designs sets them apart from true Expressionist art. The rest of this film seems to me to be a tedious and inept entry in the "diva" genre, played out in what are, in film terms, perfectly ordinary sets.

Acting

The acting in Italian films before the First World War was widely regarded in the United States as exaggerated, and it still seems to me that this is true when they are compared with American films of the same date. However, the fact that it was comedies and films on historical subjects which were most shown abroad does distort the picture somewhat, because in the films made in any country during the silent period the acting was mostly less restrained or naturalistic in these genres than in contemporary dramas. To make a fairer comparison, the acting in Italian comedies and historical dramas was not much worse than that in French ones of the same date. In films from both countries you will find talking to the audience in the comedies, and frontal direction of the acting in historical dramas. But in some Italian films the frontal direction is more blatant and the miming wilder than in just about any films from elsewhere. As is well known, the one truly original contribution of the Italian cinema in the area of performance was the result of the exaggeration of acting into a new dimension in the "diva" films. The first really distinctive one of these was *Ma l'amor mio non muore* (Mario Caserini, 1913). Within a succession of scenes in this film, Lyda Borelli moves slowly from one Art Nouveau pose to another as she is racked by love anguish of various kinds.

The furthest development of this idea that I have seen is in *La Contessa Sara* (1919), in which Francesca Bertini manages some remarkable moves between two to three "artistic" poses per shot, frequently through sitting and reclining positions, and mostly within a close framing. In this case the style of the poses has moved on from Art Nouveau to the sort of thing one would see in "artistic" photographic portraits of the time. I presume the invention in the poses and movement is due to the actress herself, though the study of more Roberto Roberti films should provide the conclusive answer.

Scene Dissection

When film production in Italy really got going in 1907, with other companies besides Ambrosio entering the competition, the model for really filmic construction had to be that of French films, and in particular films from the Pathé company, which dominated the market everywhere at that date. This shows up in the simplest way, in the adoption by the major Italian companies such as Cines, Ambrosio, Aquila, and Itala, of the Pathé habit of filming with the camera at waist level. These Italian film-makers persisted with this camera position till around 1912, and such a camera height was consistent

with the filming of all scenes in Long Shot, as was mostly the case in all Italian films made up to 1911. The Pathé film-makers had been using the occasional close shot of people in a few films from 1906 onwards, but for some reason this practice did not become really popular till years later in any of the film-making countries, including France. (I am not talking about cuts in to an Insert Shot of a letter or other object, which are a quite different matter, and as in all countries, these were sometimes used in Italian films when appropriate, almost from the beginning). Nevertheless, there are a few rare examples of shots of actors taken closer than the full length figure, and cut into the middle of a scene, in surviving Italian films, and these should be mentioned for the sake of completeness. *Floriana de Lys* (Aquila, 1909), *La maschera di ferro* (Itala, 1909), and *L'inferno* (Helios, 1911) all have Medium Long Shots cut into the middle of a scene, though in all cases the matching across the cut is poor. (A Medium Long Shot cuts the actor off at the thighs, by my definition.) After 1911 there begin to be a fair number of Italian films with one or two cuts in to a closer shot, though when they do occur, the matching of the actor's position across the cut continues to be bad in most cases. In this practice the Italian film-makers were keeping up fairly well with the latest developments in the United States. Another minor enthusiasm of the earliest period was the "emblematic" shot, which is a shot separate from the film narrative proper put at the beginning or end of the film, and containing an arrangement of things which indicates the general nature of the film. In the USA, Britain, and France this notion was developed long before, from the example of Edwin Porter's *The Great Train Robbery* (1903), and it later appears in a few Italian films such as *Luigi XI, re di Francia* (Ambrosio, 1909), which starts with a posed Medium Shot of Louis XI in front of a background of hanged men.

Around 1908, it was the standard practice everywhere to film all scenes with the actors shown full-length, but from 1910 onwards, there began a competition between film-makers at the major American companies to shoot more of the scenes in their films from closer in. This led in the first place to reducing the closest distance the actors could come to the camera to nine feet. This "nine foot line" was marked out on the stage floor or the ground with a plank, or rope, or chalk line, and by 1912 films made at Vitagraph and Biograph had most of their scenes played out by the actors right up to this line. But in Europe, including Italy, the forward limit for the actors in a general scene in a film was at best 4 metres. The numerous Italian films on historical subjects were conducted basically in Long Shot, whereas in the United States costume films were shot in pretty much the same way as contemporary subjects. In America, by 1914, many film-makers were cutting true Close Ups, showing head and shoulders only, into their scenes, and doing it with good matches of action across the cuts as well, whereas the Italian "primo piano" on the limited occasions when it occurred, was a Medium Shot, or at best a Medium Close Up, cutting the actor off at the waist. More to the point, in American films of 1914, there was an increasing tendency to break a continuous scene down into more than one shot.

Cutting Rates

The other major development in American film-making from 1910 onwards was the increase in the number of shots per reel, and this development was led by D.W. Griffith alone, with the rest trailing behind. Here again, European film-makers did not pick up this development to any great extent. As far as Italian films are concerned, the position can be briefly indicated by quoting some figures. For instance, *Patrizia e schiava* has 31 shots in a 936 foot reel, while *La morte di Socrate*, also made at Cines in the same year has only 7 shots in 430 feet, and *Floriana de Lys* from Aquila on the other hand contains many more scenes, with 30 shots in 584 feet. These examples indicate the range in cutting rate in Italian films at that date, which is not so different from that in other countries. But four years later, the number of shots used to tell the story had hardly increased, with *Ma l'amore mio non muore* (Gloria, 1913) having only 86 shots in 1734 feet, and *Mano accusatrice* (Milano, 1913) having 89 shots in 2600 feet. This contrasts strongly with American cutting which by this date was reaching figures of twice this on the average. For example, *Now I Lay Me Down To Sleep* from IMP has 62 shots on only 906 feet, and even companies which did not go in for fast cutting like Vitagraph had many films like *The Spirit of Christmas* which has 52 shots in 885 feet, not to mention what D.W. Griffith and the makers of Westerns were up to by this time. For instance, Griffith's *Fate*, made at the very end of 1912, and released at the beginning of 1913, has 119 shots in 1012 feet.

In Griffith's case this cutting speed was usually helped by the use of cross-cutting between parallel actions, but this was not the only reason for such a large number of shots per reel. Another was the fact that American films got the same amount of story into one reel of film as would be spread across two, or even three reels of film in an Italian movie, and hence more scenes and more shots were needed per reel. As far as the use of cross-cutting was concerned, American film-makers other than D.W. Griffith were using it when appropriate before 1913, but the first Italian films that use the technique, as far as I know, are *L'antro funesto* (Itala) and *Il fascino dell'innocenza* (Pasquali), both of 1913. In the first case there are two or three cutaways to parallel action at the climax, and likewise between both sides of a telephone conversation in the second. The unease that the makers of *Il fascino dell'innocenza* felt about the use of the device is indicated by the fact that the person who is revealed speaking at the other end of the telephone line is always enclosed in a hard circular vignette, presumably in reminiscence of the primitive way of dealing with telephone conversations by the use of a split screen.

Camera Angles

In general, the Italian films made before 1920 which I have seen show little or nothing of the development of the use of different camera angles on the scenes filmed, which technique was being slowly developed from 1910 onwards in the American cinema. On those very rare occasions when there is a cut to a closer shot in the course of a scene in an Italian picture, the change in camera position goes down the line of the established lens direction, and shots taken from a high or low angle to the scene are hardly to be found. The only significant exception to this that I have come across is the Ambrosio company's *La nave dei leoni* of 1912. This made quite an impression in the United States for an Italian film on a contemporary subject, as is shown by these excerpts from the review by G.F. Blaisdell in *The Moving Picture World* (26 October 1912, p.323)

> "Among the many lion pictures which the public has recently been privileged to see, probably none has had more thrilling situations than are contained in this latest production of the Ambrosio. Adding to the effectiveness of the film is the superb photography. Good photography these days is a common thing. Poor photography is the unusual thing. So when we see pictures that strike us forcibly, pictures that strike us in such unquestioned manner as to make us sit up in our chairs, we know we have something out of the ordinary. In "The Ship with the Lions" there are many good scenes -- and great discretion has been used in the tinting of them. There is one picture that particularly stands out. This is when the man at the masthead sights San Blas Bay. It is a night scene. The sailor, with flag in hand is shown in the masthead signalling the shore. It is close camera work, and the man and the mast are most effectively silhouetted against the sky."

In fact, the following shot to the low angle of the man at the masthead, which is another low angle shot of a man on land on a cliff-top signalling back, is even better pictorially, though not mentioned by Blaisdell. Neither shot is actually any kind of close shot, contrary to Blaisdell. The scenes taken of the lions on deck after their release are shot from a high angle, which is again a first for the surviving Italian films, though again this kind of shot had started appearing in American and Danish films over the previous couple of years.

Low angle shot in La nave dei leoni *(1912).*

The following shot, also low angle, but NOT a reverse angle.

Reverse Angle Cutting and Point of View Shots

Like other European film-makers, the Italians did not take up the other important new ideas coming from America, which were the use of Point of View (POV) shots and reverse angle cutting. I have only seen a couple of true reverse angle shots in Italian films made up to 1920, and the very few POV shots in a few films made during the war years are badly handled. Although this is again not untypical of European films, there were some European film-makers in other countries who did a bit better than this. Excepting reverse cuts between members of a theatre audience and what they are watching, which was a simpler concept for film-makers to cope with, the first true reverse angle cuts I have seen in an Italian film are in *Eva nemica* (Ambrosio, 1916), and even in 1919, there are only a handful of reverse angle cuts, and one POV shot, within the two hour running time of Guazzoni's *Clemento VII e il sacco di Roma*.

It seems that there was a quite conscious rejection of the major new developments in scene dissection or *découpage* that I have been describing by major figures in the Italian film industry, to judge by events in 1915 related on page 78 of Maria Adriana Prolo's *Storia del cinema muto Italiano - Vol.1*. Apparently Charles Pathé, as part of his plans to take advantage of Italian production facilities, had had published a *Manuale per uso dei direttori di scena italiani* written by Louis Gasnier, who was a very experienced director who worked at the New York studios of the Pathé company from 1912 onwards. This manual recommended greater use of Close Ups, and hence implicitly greater scene dissection along the lines of the latest American trends which I have just described. Arturo Ambrosio and Count Baldassare Negroni rejected this on the grounds that Italian film-makers had a refined artistic sensibility that could make its effects without American technique. As far as the mass audience response to films is concerned,

they were of course wrong, but they weren't the only Europeans to fail to understand that more angles on a scene, POV shots, cross cutting to parallel actions, and so on, not only make it possible to speed up the story by leaving out the boring bits, but also effectively put the audience right into the middle of the narrative.

Flash-Back Construction

However, there was one aspect of the development of the large-scale construction of film narrative in which Italian film-makers *were* strongly involved, and this was in the use of flash-backs. An Italian film made by Cines in 1908 titled *Le fiabe della nonna* has the grandmother of the title shown telling a legend to a group of children. There is a dissolve from this scene to the first of a series of scenes representing the story, and then a dissolve straight back to the scene of the grandmother telling the story. This is not strictly what was to become the standard flashback, and there are no dialogue titles conveying the grandmother's narration.

As is well known now, the Vitagraph's *Napoleon – Man of Destiny*, made in 1909, is the first film with someone remembering past events while awake. In this film, Napoleon is shown sitting in his palace in 1815 after the battle of Waterloo, awake and remembering his past life, scenes of which are cut directly into the framing scene after a superimposed title has appeared naming the event to come. The film ends with a *flash-forward* to what is, in the context of the film story, the future scene of his imprisonment on St. Helena.

The variety of narrated flashback, in which a character in the film starts telling a story to other characters, and the flashback scenes which follow are supported and explained by dialogue titles cut into the film is fully developed in the Milano company's version of *L'inferno*, made in 1911. Here, the titles are taken from the verses of Dante's poem, which run throughout the whole course of the film, and these introduce various filmed episodes told by some of the damned souls, starting with Paolo and Francesca. In the National Film Archive print the flashback is entered by a straight cut after the explanatory title, but since this print has been abbreviated, it is possible that the transition may have been marked by fades. Certainly, in the 1911 Helios company version of *L'inferno*, the beginning and ending of the Paolo and Francesca flash-back is marked by fade-outs and fade-ins. I think it highly likely that there is more to the development of true flashback construction, for there is an example from 1910 in the Swedish film, *Fanrik Stals sagner*, in which the story is presented as a flashback inside a scene showing Runeberg, the actual author of the story on which it is based, relating the events. The narrated flashback, rather than the "thought" flashback, remained the more popular for the next few years, and can next be seen in a surviving film in Luigi Maggi's *Nozze d'oro* made in 1911. In this film a couple on their golden wedding anniversary tell their children that they will describe how they met, and immediately after the intertitle conveying this information there is a straight cut to a series of scenes continuously depicting those past events, which form the main body of the film. At the end the framing scene is returned to by means of a fade-out and a fade-in. Other later Italian examples of flashback construction include *La lampada della nonna*, made by Luigi Maggi at Ambrosio in 1913, but these are less remarkable, since the use of flashback construction was starting to catch on more generally by 1913.

Using Insert Shots

There were just two other special forms of film construction in which Italian film-makers took an equal part with the Americans in advancing technique, both to do with the use of Insert Shots. (By "Insert Shot" I understand the later meaning it acquired in film-making, which is a shot which shows an object or part of an actors body other than the face, and hence can be taken without the participation of the leading performers in the film.)

The first of these was a highly specialised form, where the entire film story is carried in close shots showing only part of the actors. This idea appeared very early, with G.A. Smith's *As Seen Through an Area Window* (1901), which related an incident revolving round a man making advances to a woman, done in just one shot showing the feet of the people involved. I have seen no sign of this technique reappearing until the Ambrosio company made *La storia di Lulu* in 1909, though Vitagraph's *The Story the Boots Told* of 1908 *does* use some close-ups of feet doing this and that as part of a moralising story, but most of its narrative is carried on in ordinary shots of the characters. *La storia di Lulu* on the other hand tells a story in several scenes by using nothing but insert shots of

the feet of the actors. Unfortunately the narrative organization of this film is rather confused, at least in the print from the Joseph Joye collection in the National Film Archive. Later on the American Vitagraph company returned to the idea, with variations, in *Over the Chafing Dish* (1911) and *Extremities* (1913), which in their turn may have had something to do with Ambrosio having another more extended try at the same idea in *L'amore pedestre* of 1914.

"Symbolism" and the Insert Shot

As a result of the increasing artistic ambitions of film-makers in all the major film producing countries during this period, poems and other "literary" subjects began to be transposed directly into films. Griffith's filming of Browning's *Pippa Passes* in 1909 is well-known, but the same impulse can be seen at work in the Italian Cines company's film *La Campana* of the same year, which is based on Schiller's poem *Die Glocke*. These films are mostly no more than live illustrated versions of the verses of the poems, which precede the various scenes in them, but Griffith was capable of moving on from this to an adaptation of the poetic refrain to its purely visual equivalent in an original film subject, *The Way of the World*, made a year later. Although this featured repeated Insert Shots of bells again, it was more than a simple illustration of a poem. However it took some years for Griffith to develop the Insert Shot further as a force in its own right, as a way of drawing attention to narrative objects with significant connotations. In his other 1910 films the Insert Shots were still just used to show things clearly, as had been a long established usage. Later in 1910 Griffith made a couple of films that make explicit claims to "symbolism" in their titles, namely *The Two Paths – A Symbolism* and *A Modern Prodigal – A Story in Symbolism*, but neither contain any special new filmic usages in this area. However, by 1913 there were the first signs of the special use of the Insert which was to prove so important from that date onwards. One of the still very rare examples is in Griffith's *The Massacre*, which was made at the end of 1912, and this was an Insert Shot of a candle at a sick man's bedside flickering out to indicate his death. Another is in the Ambrosio company version of *Gli ultimi giorni di Pompei* (1913). In this film there is a scene, preceded by the title "The thorns of jealousy", in which a rejected woman overhears the man she loves with another woman, and this is followed by a fade to a shot of a pair of doves, which then dissolves into a shot of a bird of prey. Unfortunately this is about the only point of interest in this film, which is otherwise much cruder than the contemporary Pasquali version, titled *Jone*, and directed by Enrico Vidali. The inspiration for the use of the symbolic effects in this film may have come from the original novel by Bulwer Lytton on which it is based. This has a couple of chapter headings such as "A Wasp

Ventures into the Spider's Web", which feature the same kind of metaphor.

Gli ultimi giorni di Pompei was of course widely shown in the United States, and it may have been an influence on D.W. Griffith's *The Avenging Conscience* (1914). In this latter film the title, "The birth of the evil thought" precedes a series of three shots of the protagonist looking at a spider, and at ants eating an insect, though at a later point in the film when he prepares to kill someone these shots are cut straight in without explanation.

Giovanni Pastrone's *Il fuoco* (1916) represents a further advance to some extent, in that the symbolic effects, though admittedly extremely obvious, are not explained in this way. *Il fuoco* was an entry in the already established "vampire" genre, of which the best-known example is Frank Powell's *A Fool There Was* (1915), but in fact these tales of a man enticed and destroyed by an evilly seductive woman had been developing in European cinema for years before that, probably starting with the Danish *Vampyrdanserinden* of 1912. The central figures of *Il fuoco* are introduced as "He - The Unknown Painter" and "She - The Famous Poetess", and the three stages of the affair are introduced by illustrated titles showing **The Lightning Flash, The Flame**, and **The Ashes**. Throughout the early stages of the film her dress and poses are arranged so as to suggest a bird of prey, and at a key moment a shot of one is cut in without explanation. A further Italian development along these lines is *Le Chat noir* of 1920, from the Lombardo film company, with its neurasthenic protagonist and symbolic black cat.

Although it only concerns a minor part of Italian production, this transfer into films of a "decadent" Symbolist aesthetic derived from that worked out in the high arts around the turn of the century in many European countries is remarkable, and has an interesting close parallel with trends in the Russian cinema of those same war years, as everyone interested is probably aware by now. I am particularly thinking of some of the Yevgeni Bauer films, of course. There is really nothing comparable in the films from elsewhere in Europe or the United States that I am aware of, with the rather weak exception of parts of Robert Reinert's *Opium*, made in Germany in 1918.

Second Edition

All this time I had been working on updating *Film Style and Technology*, to take account of developments in cinema during the years since 1970, which was when my original survey terminated. There had also been developments in publishing, as there were now proper computer programmes for book and magazine publishing that produced exact facsimiles of the layout of the work, ready to be typeset. I had moved up to a more powerful personal computer, and now obtained a copy of Ventura Publisher, the first desk-top publishing programmes for IBM-type personal computers. This time I did a proper search for the best deal from printers, rather than accepting the first printer suggested to me, which had been a big mistake for the first edition. I selected a large page size, calculating the most efficient usage of the printing press sheet size used by Hobbs the Printers down in Southampton, and this time did double column setting of the text. I changed the typeface I used to Adobe Garamond, which was available cheaply, and has some interesting and useful properties. It has a set smaller than Times Roman, but avoids the black colour of a page full of Times text, which I dislike. It achieves these two things by having a slightly smaller x-height than usual for a given point size, and slightly narrower strokes. The italic is also quite sharply distinguished from the regular faces by the broad curvature of its serifs. It has lots of swash, as Stephen Miller of the Oxford University Computing Service, who output my computer files to the page on their photo-typesetter, put it.

The second edition of *Film Style and Technology* was a lot bigger than the first, not only because of the new chapters on the nineteen-seventies and 'eighties, but also because I had seen thousands more films from the silent period, and in particular from the first twenty years of cinema, since writing the first edition. Hence the chapter on 1907-1913 in particular was more than twice as long as before. I think that my treatment in it of the major stylistic developments of the first twenty years is now definitive, as there are not enough films from the period left unseen to significantly change my analysis of what happened during those years.

The most recent alternative account of these early years is contained in the History of the American Cinema published by Charles Scribner's Sons from 1990 onwards. I wrote a review of the first four volumes of this series that had come out so far at the invitation from one of the editorial board members for publication in *Screen*. Although *Screen* had moved up to Scotland, and was run by an different crowd of people, their inclinations had not changed that much, so that when I supplied the 2,000 words requested, the editorial board turned my review down, without giving any explanation. They never did review the books in this American film history series. Since the new *Sight & Sound* had not reviewed the series either, I offered my review to them, but they too were not interested. In fact I believe there has been no review of these books in any other serious periodical in Britain. That is how much real film history matters to most of the film critics and academics in this country.

History of the American Cinema

Charles Musser, *The Emergence of Cinema: The American Screen to 1907*. New York: Charles Scribner's Sons, 1991, 613 pp.

Eileen Bowser *The Transformation of Cinema: 1907-1915*. New York: Charles Scribner's Sons, 1991, 337 pp.

Richard Koszarski *An Evening's Entertainment: the Age of the Silent Feature Picture, 1915-1928*. New York: Charles Scribner's Sons, 1991, 395 pp.

Tino Balio *Grand Design: Hollywood as a Modern Business Enterprise, 1930-1939*. New York: Charles Scribner's Sons, 1993, 483 pp.

The project of a *History of the American Cinema* was initiated decades ago, and the first volumes of it are now appearing. To attempt a fully adequate description of the silent period in American film means a lot of new research, and this is indeed what we have in the first three of these books, though to a decreasing extent as one moves towards the coming of sound.

The first volume in the series is by Charles Musser, and titled *The Emergence of Cinema: The American Screen to 1907*. This book is largely based on a vast amount of invaluable original work by the author in American public archives and newspapers, and reveals some significant new information, as well as filling up the gaps in the standard ideas about the period. For instance, Musser describes a scattering of small permanent cinemas existing before the opening of the original Nickelodeon, the production organization at Vitagraph in 1905-07, and the production of specially staged prizefight films in the last years of the nineteenth century.

However, despite the immense quantity of useful information it contains, this volume has a major flaw, which is likely to mislead the readers (i.e. most of them) who have no familiarity with the actual films of the period. Musser claims in his introduction and elsewhere that there was no real development of film continuity before 1907 and the nickelodeon boom, which is his adaptation of Noël Burch's notion of a "Primitive Mode of Representation" or PMR, and how it was suddenly replaced by the recognizable basic elements of standard "classical" continuity with the coming of the nickelodeons, through some unexplained magic Marxist mechanism. Musser does not mention his source for these ideas, which is just as well, as Burch himself has since become equivocal on this point, because it is not sustainable in the face of the evidence.

Musser renames Burch's "Primitive Mode of Representation" the "presentational style", and the main components of this "style", which actually do not have any necessary or intentional connection with each other, are -- according to Musser -- recognition of the camera by the performers, "bad" continuity as this would later be understood, and the use of obviously painted sets. The source of the first of these features is the fact that the very short films made before

1903, and consisting of only one or two shots, were inevitably mostly based on vaudeville acts or other popular comic material from the stage and elsewhere, in which acknowledgement of the existence of the audience was standard. "Bad" continuity obviously arises through chance because most American film-makers of the period gave no thought to how they joined shots together, and in any case its importance has been much exaggerated, since audiences then and now do not notice it. Indeed some aspects of "bad" continuity continued extensively into the 'thirties in European cinema. In other words, films can be successful with audiences despite "bad" continuity if they are attractive enough in other respects. And likewise with painted sets in the early period, at least.

Musser is able to delude himself on this point because the bulk of his book is devoted to American production before 1904, when, compared to European cinema, American films were noticeably more "primitive" in their features, and after that he rushes through the description of American production of 1905-1907, when the length and number of films was much increased. When he does describe some of these films, he confines himself to drawing attention to only a few special instances of "incorrect" continuity, and ignoring the increasing amount of better cutting, particularly in the films from Vitagraph, which was the major American production company by the end of this period.

In the second volume in the series, *The Transformation of Cinema: 1907-1915*, Eileen Bowser makes excellent use of her long study of the trade press. Most of the major aspects of film production in these years, such as the brief reign of the Motion Picture Patents Corporation, have recently come to be more accurately treated in other places, and Bowser is up to date here, often with her own valuable detail in quotation. Her treatment of the beginning of the film star system is more detailed and accurate than previous attempts, and as elsewhere she introduces fascinating new details, such as the sale of star photos on cushion covers. She has a more difficult task in surveying the nature of the actual films of the period, since most of the surviving prints are in Europe rather than the United States. Bowser's coverage of the stylistic developments in these years, which continued to be very rapid, is satisfactory up to a point, but there are major developments, particularly after 1911, such as the use of reverse-angle cutting, flashbacks, Point of View shots, and the development of low-key lighting, not to mention the peculiarities of D.W. Griffith's style, where she is quite inadequate. Returning to the positive side, Bowser includes many relevant and previously unseen photographs, and this volume, along with the next by Richard Koszarski, is also the best written of the series. Throughout, Bowser follows the soundest art historical principles, in seeking out evidence for what the film-makers of the time thought they were doing, rather than indulging in interpretations of the "meaning" of the films as seen from some dubious present-day standpoint.

The general editor of the series has not imposed a completely uniform approach on the contributors, and Richard Koszarski's *An Evening's Entertainment: the Age of the Silent*

Feature Picture, 1915-1928 is the most idiosyncratic of the volumes so far published. It avowedly approaches American film production of 1915-1928 from the point of view of the audience – what one might call a sophisticated film fan's perspective. This means that anyone who has not seen a lot of the surviving films of the period will not be able to get much of a feel of what they are like; indeed in this respect William Everson's *American Silent Film* (Oxford: Oxford University Press, 1978) is a lot better, despite its many serious flaws. However, in his treatment of subjects such as film exhibition Koszarski supplies solid coverage, including the kind of figures for audience attendance and box-office returns which are conspicuously lacking in Douglas Gomery's recent *Shared Pleasures* (London: BFI Publishing, 1992). Here, and elsewhere in the chapters on production procedures, industry organization, the stars, and the film-makers, there are many valuable and previously unseen illustrations. The chapter "Watching the Screen" also contains good material on film journalism and censorship that was not available before.

Koszarski includes a chapter on film technology which starts very badly, by defining orthochromatic film as being sensitive only to ultraviolet, violet, and blue light, whereas of course it gets it name by also being sensitive to green light, and to some extent yellow light as well. Most of the rest of the facts in this chapter are correct, but Koszarski shows very limited understanding of what the technology *does*. For instance, there is no proper discussion of the major changes in lighting style through the period, such as the reduction in depth of field, and the introduction of double back lighting at the beginning of the 'twenties, and so on. In fact, this is an aspect of the major weakness of this volume, which gives no idea of the significant changes in film style from 1915 to 1928, and in particular how during 1915-1920 standard dramatic construction from the theatre was fitted together with the still emerging "classical" film construction to give the perfected American Intercontinental Filmic Missile (AICFM). There are also other curious aspects of those turbulent war-time years which do not figure at all here, such as the mini-genre of films from 1915 like *Ambition, Purity, Youth, The Primrose Path*, and so on, which included "symbolic" effects to go with their titles.

The weakest chapters are those on "The Stars and The Filmmakers", where about a page each is devoted to a selection of figures who were highly regarded at the time, though not necessarily nowadays. I have no objection to this approach in principle, but these sections contain hardly anything that could not be got from say Ephraim Katz's *The International Film Encyclopedia* (New York: Macmillan Press, 1980), with Koszarski showing a lack of penetration in cases where there *is* something new to be said about the person discussed. An obvious example is Mary Pickford, who was a central figure in the development of standard film dramatic structure mentioned above. And having introduced Lois Weber, he fails to note that her career failure was obviously due to the tediousness of her films.

(Although you would not discover it from these books, there is fortunately already a work that remedies most of the serious deficiencies that I have mentioned above, but modesty forbids me to say more.)

Volume 4 of the series, on the period of the transition to sound, is not to appear for some years, but Volume 5, *Grand Design: Hollywood as a Modern Business Enterprise, 1930-1939* has just been published. The key difference from the previous volumes is immediately signalled visually. Whereas they were all illustrated with novel, striking, and highly relevant production stills and frame enlargements, this volume mostly uses the dullest of production stills, which do not illuminate the points being made. Likewise the text processes steadily through mostly well-known material, with only a small amount new findings scattered here and there. The treatment of industry organization and financing is heavily dependent on such well-known sources as the *Fortune* reports on the Hollywood majors, Michael Conant's *Anti-trust in the Motion Picture Industry* (University of California Press, 1960), and Leo Rosten's *Hollywood: the Movie colony, the Movie Makers* (Harcourt, Brace, 1941). To be fair, it may have been Tino Balio himself who first drew attention to some of these sources long ago, in his *The American Film Industry* (Wisconsin University Press, 1976). There *are* a few minor revisions to accepted ideas, due to the incorporation of recent research by people concerned to be more objective and quantitative in defining trends and their causes, such as Robert Gustafson on script source material at Warners, and Moya Luckett on "fallen woman" films.

Although Balio is listed on the cover as the sole author, actually more than a third of the book is made up of chapters by other writers such as Richard Maltby on censorship, Brian Taves on the B film, and so on. The chapter on Avant-garde film by Jan-Christopher Horak takes the subject, which was not treated in Koszarski's volume, through from its beginning in the 'twenties. Although mostly devoted to well-known people such as Watson and Webber, Paul Steiner and Mary-Ellen Bute, it does contain more information than usual about their work and that of such forgotten figures as Henwar Rodakiewicz. On the other hand, Charles Wolfe's treatment of American documentary film only deals with the best known films from the Pare Lorentz group and the Film and Photo League, and can only look inadequate when compared with Rachael Low's two volume study of factual film in Britain during the same period.

In the chapter on "Technological Change and Classical Film Style" David Bordwell and Kristin Thompson continue to push their obviously mistaken idea that film industry institutions such as the Society of Motion Picture Engineers and the American Society of Cinematographers played a major part in producing technological development, and they also make various mistaken observations about particular features of cinematography in the early 'thirties. Strangely, they say nothing about the major stylistic trends during this period which *do* intersect with technological development, such as cutting rate. Altogether the most noticeable omissions overall in this volume are proper industry statistics, and any discussion of one of the American cinema's glories, the animated cartoon.

There is a great deal more that should be said about these books, particularly since, inevitably, they have been uncritically praised in the United States, but the interim judgement is that you *have* to read the first three volumes (with caution), but not the fifth.

In 1993 Peter Lehmann asked me for a piece on film lighting in 1913 for a number of Davide Turconi's long-running magazine *Griffithiana,* which was to be devoted to cinema in 1913. This magazine had been associated with the Pordenone *Giornate del Cinema Muto* for many years, and included articles related to the Giornate, and since I was eager to push the new edition of *Film Style and Technology*, I readily agreed. It appeared in No. 50 of May 1994, and was set in ITC Century.

FILM LIGHTING IN 1913

In 1913 the evolution of film form was still continuing rapidly, particularly in the United States, with the use of the Point of View shot and reverse-angle cutting spreading amongst the most adventurous film-makers, and there was also quite a lot going on in the field of studio set lighting. This was mostly to do with the use of low-key lighting, but also with the beginning of applying special lighting to the figures of the actors. But before treating these important matters, it is necessary that I survey the standard methods of film lighting, as a background to these developments. My comments are based on viewings of more than 300 films released in 1913.

Standard Studio Lighting

The vast majority of scenes shot in film studios in 1913 were lit in the same way as they had been for years before; with most of the light falling on the sets coming from diffused sunlight shining through the glass studio roof. The sunlight was diffused in the first place by the type of glass making up the studio walls and ceilings, for this was not ordinary flat window glass, but sheets of glass with a ripple surface, usually referred to at the time as "Florentine glass". If the sun was exceptionally bright in the middle of a clear day, further diffusion was applied to it by drawing thin cotton sheets across under the glass roof. In general, film studios were constructed with only one solid wall, against which the sets were built, facing north, so that the sun could shine onto the set from the "front" (i.e. the filming direction) for as much as possible of the day. However, filming during the hours just before sunset, and just after sunrise was usually avoided, even though the sun would still be shining into the studio. This was because at these hours the diffused sunlight was both weakened and reddened, to the point at which it was difficult to get an exposure with the slow orthochromatic film and slowish lenses in use at the time. In any case, cameramen wanted to work at a standard aperture for studio filming, which in those days was still in the region of f5.6 to f8. Such an aperture was required with the usual 50 mm. lens to give sharp focus all the way from nine feet to the back of the set at up to 30 feet from the camera. All of this meant that in general during this period the sunlight fell onto the scene from a high direction, and more or less from the front. There are a few exceptions

to this, and they are fairly conspicuous when one comes across them. In American films, the well-known *Traffic in Souls* (1913) has scenes in one of the office sets which were filmed under different light coming through the glass studio walls on different occasions. There was also a tendency for films from the Italian

An office set in Traffic in Souls *mostly lit by daylight diffused through the studio walls during the brighter part of the day.*

The same set when the outside light level was reduced, with the sun lower and more to the left. The lens aperture has been opened up to compensate, and extra artificial light has been added from out left, and particularly on the woman standing on the right of the frame.

Cines company to have studio scenes basically lit by sunlight coming from the side, though in the case the sun was fairly high. This may have been because the Cines studio was not aligned directly south, as most were. There were certainly some studios elsewhere which did not face directly south, but shooting in them was arranged so that the sunlight came from the front quarter rather than the side

At the beginning of the century it had been very common to build sets in the open, and to film scenes in them under direct, undiffused sunlight, and this was still sometimes happening in 1913. The most common occasion was when a film unit was working on location, far away from the main studio of the company, and wanted to shoot interior scenes to go with the exterior scenes they had already shot. In America, the Kalem company made a regular practice of this sort of production, and it had units moving round the south of the United States, shooting stories with local connections in the appropriate locations. Examples of interior scenes shot on open, improvised stages can be seen in many of their 1913 films, such as *The Face at*

the Window, made by their Florida unit, and many of the railroad films made by their California unit, such as *The Railroad Inspector's Peril*. Although shooting on open sets lit by direct sunlight without diffusion could still be found in Europe a year or two before, by 1913 this had practically vanished. In California, although the increasing number of film companies working there were still almost entirely shooting on open semi-improvised stages, they nearly always stretched cotton diffusing sheets over these stages while filming was in progress.

As well as the modified natural light falling on the scene in film studios, there was very frequently some extra artificial light applied to the set and the actors, either from arc lights, or from banks of mercury vapour tubes arranged in wooden frames, or from both. Just how this extra artificial light was arranged varied from film company to film company, and it was in this area that development was still proceeding quite rapidly in 1913.

The original technique for adding artificial light to the scene in the United States was with rows of

An Edison company studio scene in 1912, with street lighting arcs with added reflectors hanging above the set and on floorstands.

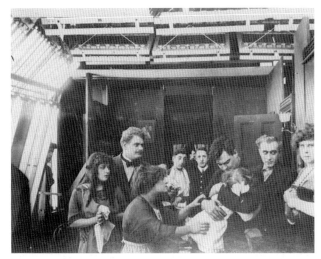

A scene being shot in the Biograph studio around 1913. It is lit exclusively by mercury vapour tube racks, some of which can be seen at the left.

floodlights of the kind used for street-lighting hung over the set on wooden beams. These were referred to as "Aristo" arcs, after the name of their principal manufacturer in the United States, and the light from them was slightly restricted and concentrated by curved reflectors of bright sheet metal added to the side of them facing towards the camera. Well before 1913, the film companies also used this type of arc light unit mounted on floor stands to provide extra lighting in a horizontal direction, rather than in the downwards oblique direction supplied by the hanging overhead arc floodlights. As more of these floor units came to be used closer in to the actors, they began to change the appearance of the film image, as they were now supplying the largest part of the lighting on the actors, and were becoming what would later be termed "key" and "fill" lights.

Some years earlier, around 1908, when lights on floor stands were already in use at major companies like Pathé, they only acted to lighten the shadows cast by the diffused sunlight, and hence were really what we now call "fill" light. In such cases we would now say that the diffused sunlight was the "key" (or brightest) light falling on the scene, and it fell evenly over the whole scene. But in 1913, there was just beginning to be something like a special lighting for the figures of the actors, and this special lighting was just beginning to become something separate from the general lighting of the set.

Lighting in the American Studios

In the home studios of most of the major American companies, be they in New York (Vitagraph, Edison, Kalem, Thanhouser), or Chicago (Selig, Essanay),

or Philadelphia (Lubin), the lighting arrangements were almost exactly the same. This was, as already described, diffused sunlight through the studio roof and walls, plus arc floodlights suspended overhead, and on floorstands. All studios had racks of Cooper-Hewitt mercury vapour tubes as well, but these seem to have been less used, and presumably only to give a boost to the diffused sunlight when this was weaker than usual.

However at Biograph, the home studio on Manhattan was almost completely dark, with effectively no natural light coming into it. Here the usual diffuse sunlight was replaced by its almost exact equivalent coming from many racks of Cooper-Hewitts lined up close to each other along one side of the set, along the front on either side of the camera, and suspended overhead shining straight down. Although in most cases the effect on the screen was almost the same as the diffuse sun lighting at other studios, there were some sorts of sets where the Biograph arrangement created difficulties. If a set had to have two side walls rather than one, because doors were necessary on both sides of the room, as often happened with D.W. Griffith's peculiar methods of scene dissection using movement of the action through side-by-side spaces, it was difficult to get the full amount of light onto the back wall and the area near it. A partial solution to this used at Biograph around 1912 was to build one of the side walls only coming half the way forward towards the camera, but even if this was done the back of the set remained rather dark. Biograph did have arc floodlights, and indeed had them from very early on, but these were rarely used in this situation for some reason. It is possible that this may have been because the conscious idea of separating the actors from the background was already being applied in 1912. Certainly this kind of weak separation effect, with the back of the set being much less brightly lit, was common at Vitagraph from about 1911.

European Lighting

In Europe there was also some increase in the use of artificial lighting around 1913, particularly in the more northern countries. This increase is most noticeable in films from the British Hepworth company, where by 1913 most of the lighting in many of their productions is coming from arc floodlights. And it is put on quite well by later standards, too, as in *At the Foot of the Scaffold* and *Sally in Our Alley*. Of course, in France the Gaumont company had been using heavy arc lighting from 1906. Gaumont lighting had been rather unsubtly applied most of the time, just being poured on from clusters of arc floodlights on either side of the camera and overhead, but by 1913 it was sometimes used more selectively. Again, *Roman d'un mousse* gives some good examples, as do other Léonce Perret

Sally in our Alley, *made by the Hepworth company in* 1913.

Simple Simon Stays at the Royal Hotel (Gaumont 1913), *lit by arc floodlights on floor stands ranged across the front of the scene.*

films. Gaumont films were quite influential models, and the Italian *L'antro funesto* could be mistaken for a Gaumont movie, as could the German *Das Geheimnis von Chateau Richmond* (1914). The lighting at Pathé and Eclair was quite like the standard American pattern, and arcs were not used as much as in Gaumont films. In Italy, the standard lighting relied even less on arcs, but they usually, but not always, provided weak fill from the front to lighten the faces.

The New Floodlights

At some time around 1912, the American studios began to use a new type of arc floodlight on floor stands. Instead of the street lighting type of arc, another type made principally by the Wohl company for graphic arts purposes was taken up for film use. These arc floodlights had the arc formed between a pair of carbons incorporating rare earth minerals, so that they produced a more nearly white light, like sunlight, rather than the long blue electric spark produced by the older street-lighting arcs. The arc was contained in a more or less rectangular metal box with an open front, and this was mounted between two tall upright rods, with a mechanism for raising or lowering the reflector unit as desired. They were often referred to as "guillotine arcs", from the resemblance of the stand to the structure of a guillotine. The European equivalent, often called "Jupiter lights", seem to have come into use slightly earlier.

The exact kind of light or lighting unit used on studio scenes could have a noticeable visual effect on the image, and one aspect of this that has not been discussed so far is to do with the different spectra of light emitted by the various light sources. Most films in 1913 were shot with Eastman Kodak negative,

whatever positive stock they ended up being printed on. Eastman film negative had been "orthochromatic" from the beginning, which meant that it was sensitive to blue and green light, and to some extent to yellow light as well. To slightly over-simplify, ordinary daylight contains a full range of the spectral colours, in fairly equal amounts, but the old style street lighting arcs emitted mostly blue light, and Cooper-Hewitt mercury vapour tubes only blue and green light. In this they were almost perfectly matched to film negative. However, under such light, things in the real world that were coloured bright red, orange, or yellow reproduced as either black or dark grey. This did not matter too much, since there were very few things in the real world prior to the First World War, other than flowers and some fruit, that were those colours. The few obvious things that were bright red, etc., such as British Post Boxes, could usually be repainted for film purposes. However, the colour of light did have an effect on blonde hair, and under the old type of arc light, or mercury vapour-tube light, average blonde hair reproduced as dark grey, and was not recognizably blonde, whereas under daylight or white flame arc light it reproduced as a light grey, and was recognizable as blonde hair. This meant that in some films a leading actresses' hair could change tone between exteriors and interiors, when the latter were lit mostly by "Aristo" arcs or Cooper-Hewitts, rather than by diffuse daylight. It is doubtful if anyone worried about this much, but if they did, it was confined to East Coast film-making in America, since in California the interiors were still lit mostly by diffuse daylight.

Figure Lighting

In 1913 most studio lighting was still done in a standardized way, with the exact arrangement of the

Back sunlight and reflector fill from the front on the foreground figures in The Massacre.

lighting differing somewhat from studio to studio, as has been described above. But a new development was just beginning, which would eventually lead to each studio lighting set-up being considered in its own right when the lighting was applied, and hence to a reduction of the amount of standardization in lighting set-ups. This trend was associated with a number of developments in scene dissection, and in particular the use of more close shots, and also of the use of cuts to different angles on the scene, rather than taking all the shots from the "front", as had previously been the case. This new development can best be approached by looking at it in terms of the way the figures of the actors were lit. To exaggerate a little, if no special effect lighting was being used, such as the simulation of the light from a window, or a fire, or a lamp, then actors were ordinarily lit as being part of the scene, no

Weak backlight on the figures in an interior in The Massacre. *General light from sunlight through cotton diffusers on an open-air stage.*

Three-quarter backlight from left, and key light from arc floodlights at front in A Soul in Bondage.

different to any part of the set.

The first step on the path away from this had happened on some exterior scenes from about 1909. A few film-makers, particularly D.W. Griffith, began to shoot some exterior scenes with the sun coming towards the camera from behind the actors. In the average scene, this meant that the actors were outlined with a bright line on one side and on top of their head. If the exposure was taken as for scenes shot in the same conditions with the sun behind the cameraman, which was the usual case, then the actor's faces would have come out almost completely black. On the other hand, it was possible to open the camera aperture to increase the exposure, and so make the actor's features visible. But this tended to overexpose the background, and so was avoided in general, though examples of this approach can be seen in some Eclair films. The preferred method in using backlighting, basically established by Billy Bitzer and D.W. Griffith in their 1910 California films, was to bounce light back onto the front of the actors with a reflecting sheet placed below the camera lens, and out of shot. This procedure had become fairly general by 1913 for exterior scenes shot under bright sunlight in American films, and was also starting to be used in European films by that date.

In 1913, Griffith and Bitzer were just starting to use backlighting in the same way on studio sets in some of their films, for instance in *The Massacre*. In this case the backlight was also provided by the sun, with the set arranged so that the sun was behind the actors, and diffused by the cotton scrims over the set. This notion became fairly common in studio film-making in California over the next couple of years. Meanwhile, on the East Coast, some cameramen had started to put a different sort of backlight onto the figures in studio scenes. Vitagraph was the leader here, and an example

Low-key lighting done with controlled daylight in Victorin Jasset's Zigomar, peau d'anguille.

from 1913 can be seen in *A Soul in Bondage*, where there are arc floodlights on floor stands out of shot to one side shining onto the backs of the actors from what has come to be referred to as the "three-quarter back" direction, or "cross-back lighting". That is, the light comes from about 135 degrees to the camera lens axis. Another example of this sort of figure backlighting from arc floods can be seen in Thanhouser's *Just a Shabby Doll*, and here there is also a weak backlight from behind and above the figures as well. Eventually these harbingers were to develop into the lighting of the figures almost completely separately from the lighting of the set, but that did not happen till after the American studios were blacked-out around 1917.

Yet another factor contributing towards the move towards the lighting of the actor's figures as a separate thing from the lighting of the set was the move towards

taking the shots from closer in, particularly in the United States, and also to taking close shots of the actors separately from the master shot of the scene, and then cutting them into it. When this was done, it was sometimes the practice to reposition arc lights nearer the actor for the close shot, so that the lighting was more flattering to the actor. Although such relighting of close shots had been occasionally happening from before 1908, it was only now that close shots were being cut in with any frequency, and so only now was relighting for the close shots beginning to become standard technique.

Low-Key Lighting

The previous discussion of figure lighting refers to what was being done in ordinary studio scenes, and not to what was being done in low-key scenes. (`low-key lighting' is the term eventually coined for scenes in which most of the film image is dark, or to put it another way, in which there is a preponderance of dark greys in the image. Such scenes were still fairly rare, and most lighting was what would be called `high-key', with fairly even light, and hence full exposure, over the whole image, or `mid-key', which is of course mid-way between the two extremes. It is most important to note that `key' has a quite different meaning here to that in the phrase `key light'.) The full development and application of low-key lighting depended on the transition to filming in dark studios, even more than did the development of figure lighting, but examples were nevertheless increasing in 1913. It seems clear to me that this was as a result of a desire to inject more expression into film scenes, and this was enough to persuade film-makers to film at night, or to take extra measures to keep daylight out of the studios, so that they could achieve such effects.

Low key lighting done essentially with a single high arc at right front in Vitagaph's The Mystery of the Silver Skull

Semi-silhouette effect in Enrico Vidali's Jone.

Thrillers of one kind of another were obvious places to use low-key lighting, and the European genre of "master criminal" stories got such scenes, notably in the sewer in Jasset's *Zigomar Peau d'anguille*. In this case the low-key effect is done by shading the daylight off the scene, as it is in an American example such as Vitagraph's *The Mystery of the Silver Skull*. There are a few cases in which low key effects were done in a completely dark studio, with the light provided by arc floodlights confined to small areas of the set, and one such is in the cave scene in *L'antro funesto* (Itala). Nevertheless, given the well established production line techniques for turning out as many films as possible, particularly in the United States, there was a reluctance to take such special measures, and so low-key lighting was mostly not done in all the cases where it would be appropriate.

Silhouette and Contre-jour Effects

Silhouette effects had been developing from around 1909. D.W. Griffith's *In Old Kentucky* has a skyline silhouette showing a sentry at his post, and there are semi-silhouette figures in *Lines of White on a Sullen Sea*, though in both cases they are used purely pictorially, without strong expressive connotations. The only example after this date of this feature in Griffith's Biograph films that I am aware of is a shot of figures silhouetted against the sunset in *The Yaqui Cur* (1913). Italian film-makers had developed the contre-jour technique further in films like *Patrizia e schiava* (Cines, 1909), *Il Cid* (Cines, 1910), *L'Inferno* (Milano, 1911), and by this date a number of other film-makers had taken up the idea, principally in Europe. Most used it for pictorial purposes, but there was a gradual move over to more expressive ends. By 1913 the technique was becoming fairly standard, though still infrequently used. Many examples can be found from Italy (*L'antro funesto*, *Jone* and *La lampada della nonna*), but the idea had even got as far as Russia (*Sumerki zhenskoi dushi*). Léonce Perret's *Roman d'un mousse* (1913) makes a special feature of silhouette shots, and the influence of this was carried over into one of the films inspired by it, Benjamin Christensen's *Det Hemmelighedsfulde X* (1914), in which silhouette effects done both with daylight and artificial light, as well as with all sorts of extreme

chiaroscuro of other kinds, are used throughout its entire length. Here these effects are definitely used to contribute to the atmosphere implied by the title.

Effect Lighting

The simulation of special kinds of natural light, such as that coming from a fire or through a window, or from a lamp, had long been occasionally done on film sets. In 1913 this practice continued, and there was slightly more of it than there had been before. In the case of a fire effect, the usual way of doing this was to put an arc light in the fire place out of sight of the camera, and if the cameraman was especially conscientious, to make a flame-like flicker by waving a board in front of the arc. A lamp light effect was still sometimes created by a floodlight just outside the frame, when the light was supposed to come from a table lamp near the edge of the frame, but it was becoming more usual to put small arcs inside oil lamps to produce a practical light source. Examples are numerous in films from most countries, but well-done European instances from 1913 include *Ingeborg Holm* (Victor Sjöström) and *Roman d'un mousse* (Léonce Perret). A variant of this lamp light effect has the arc light source above the top of the frame casting light straight down onto a small area of the scene beneath, without there being any ostensible source of light within the shot. A German example is in *Der Student von Prag* (Stellan Rye). Another Danish interest was in light changes within the duration of the shot ostensibly caused by the actors switching the room lights on and off. This technique had first appeared in American films earlier than 1909, and was done with a stop-camera effect and an almost invisible cut in the shot while the lighting change was being made. The incessant use of this effect came to be a feature of Benjamin Christensen's films. However, one can still see many films from 1913 where this effect is very clumsily done.

Spotlighting

Although theatrical-type spotlights had been appearing as props in some American films with back-stage stories for a couple of years (a 1913 example is Lubin's *The Gift of the Storm*), no-one has yet identified a case of their use for actual film lighting in 1913. Keep looking.

This is also a good place to put in a piece on early German cinema that was commissioned a few years later by Thomas Elsaesser. It appeared in 1996 in *A Second Life: German Cinema's First Decades* published by Amsterdam University Press, and edited by Thomas Elsaesser and Michael Wedel. It was made possible by a season of early German films shown at the National Film Theatre and the Goethe Institute in 1995. With their co-operation, and that of the National Film Archive, which I had many times before, I was able to use to do the analysis and get the frame enlargements. But this was the last time that it was possible for me to do this.

This article was also eventually published in German in *Kino der Kaiserzeit: Zwischen Tradition und Moderne*. That book was published in 2002 by edition text + kritik, and again edited by Thomas Elsaesser and Michael Wedel. The contributions from other writers included in the two volumes are partly the same, but partly not, I am not sure why. It is set in ITC Garamond Book.

EARLY GERMAN FILM

THE STYLISTICS IN COMPARATIVE CONTEXT

Far more American films than German films were shown in Germany in 1912, as can be seen on page 10 of Emilie Altenloh's *Zur Soziologie des Kino*. This was not the case in France in the same year, for instance, though that was about to change. So why did German audiences in 1912 watch more American films than German films, and indeed more than those from any other European country? Of course, there were more American films available, but I think that there was more to the matter than that. I think American films were already more attractive to audiences, even before the First World War. There were certainly some marked differences between American films and European films, as can be shown objectively by a stylistic analysis of the kind I introduced long ago. (see the 2nd. edition of my *Film Style and Technology: History and Analysis*, Starword 1993)

The Method

The correct basis for the formal analysis of any art work, including films, is to use the analytical terms that the makers used in creating them. For films, this starts with the components of the script, with scenes forming the basic unit, and then extends through the variables about which decisions have to be made during filming, such as camera placement, type of staging within the shot, control of the nature of the actor's performances, the lighting and framing of the scene, and then on to the lengths of shots and the use of intertitles in the finished film.

The Sample

Although I have seen scores of German films made before 1917, only nine multi-reel films were immediately available for close analysis. This is a rather small sample, but the indications from these samples accord with my subjective memories of a much larger number of films of all lengths.

Shot Length

This is the most obvious stylistic variable, and I am not the first to investigate it. One of my predecessors is Herbert Birett, and he gives a list of even earlier investigations in an article in issue No.2 of *Diskurs Film* (Munich, 1988). The first person to look into this matter was the Reverend Dr. Stockton in 1912, whose investigations are reported in an article on page 542 of *The Moving Picture World* of August 10, 1912, which has been republished in George Pratt's *Spellbound in Darkness* (New York Graphic Society, 1973). The figures Dr. Stockton gives are for the number of shots, intertitles and inserts in a series of one reel films. Since most of the films on his list are now lost, and their exact length unknown, it is impossible to derive exact figures for their Average Shot Lengths (ASL). However, I myself have gathered a number of figures for this period, and typical examples from 1913 are 81 shots in 1737 feet in the French Gaumont film *Panther's Prey*, while the American Thanhouser Company's *Just a Shabby Doll* includes 60 shots in 871 feet. But in the same year D.W. Griffith's *The Coming of Angelo* has 116 shots in 967 feet.

TITLE	DIRECTOR	YEAR	ASL
DANISH FILMS			
Fire Djævle, de	Dinesen, R. & Lind, A.	1911	21
Ekspeditricen	Blom, August	1911	43
Dödspringet til Hest fra Cirkuskuplen	Schnedler-Sørensen, E.	1912	17
Mystike Fremmende, den	Holger-Madsen	1914	17

TITLE	DIRECTOR	YEAR	ASL
DANISH FILMS			
Hemmelighedsfulde X, det	Christensen, Benjamin	1914	12
Fremmende, den	Gluckstadt, Vilhelm	1914	16
Ekspressens Mysterium	Davidsen, Hjalmar	1914	21
Verdens Undergang	Blom, August	1916	13
Klovnen	Sandberg, Anders W.	1917	18
FRENCH FILMS			
Zigomar - Peau d'anguille	Jasset, Victorin	1913	13
1793	Capellani, Albert	1914	12.5
Barberousse	Gance, Abel	1916	13.5
Alsace	Pouctal, Henri	1916	18.5
GERMAN FILMS			
Zweimal gelebt	Mack, Max	1912	27
Schwarze Kugel, die	Hofer, Franz	1913	16
Sumpfblume, die	Larsen, Viggo	1913	27.5
Dämonit		1914	19.4
Kinder des Majors, die		1914	23.5
Geheimnis von Chateau Richmond, der		1914	26.5
Tirol in Waffen	Froelich, Carl	1914	27.8
Und das Licht erloscht	Bernhardt, Fritz	1914	25
Stolz der Firma, der	Wilhelm, Carl	1914	14
Schuhpalast Pinkus	Lubitsch, Ernst	1916	13
Wenn Vier dasselbe tun	Lubitsch, Ernst	1917	8.5
ITALIAN FILMS			
Pellegrino, Il	Caserini, Mario	1912	27.5
Ma l'amor mio non muore	Caserini, Mario	1913	67
Tragedia alla corte di Spagna		1914	22
Tigre Reale	Pastrone, Giovanni	1916	13
Fuoco, Il	Pastrone, Giovanni	1916	18
SWEDISH FILMS			
Trägardmästaren	Sjöström, Victor	1912	24
Havsgamar	Sjöström, Victor	1916	14
Minnenans Band	Klercker, Georg af	1916	14

TITLE	DIRECTOR	YEAR	ASL
SWEDISH FILMS			
Ministerpresidenten	Klercker, Georg af	1916	17
Karleken Segrar	Klercker, Georg af	1916	18
Vingarna	Stiller, Mauritz	1917	13
Vem sköt?	Tallroth, Konrad	1917	14
Tösen fra Stormyrtorpet	Sjöström, Victor	1917	6
Thomas Graals bästa Film	Stiller, Mauritz	1917	9
Revelj	Klercker, Georg af	1917	11.5
Mysteriet Natten till den 25:e	Klercker, Georg af	1917	13
I Moerkrets Bojor	Klercker, Georg af	1917	13
Forstadsprästen	Klercker, Georg af	1917	15
For Hjem och Hard	Klercker, Georg af	1917	11
Allt hamnar sig	Tallroth, Konrad	1917	13
AMERICAN FILMS			
Traffic in Souls	Tucker, George Loane	1913	7
Wishing Ring, The	Tourneur, Maurice	1914	11.5
What's-His-Name	DeMille, Cecil B.	1914	24
Three Musketeers, The	Henkel, Charles V.	1914	11.2
Squaw Man, The	DeMille, C.B. & Apfel, O.	1914	11.5
Spoilers, The	Campbell, Colin	1914	13
Florida Enchantment, A	Drew, Sidney	1914	8
Avenging Conscience, The	Griffith, D.W.	1914	7.5
Young Romance	Melford, George	1915	15
Royal Family, The	Frohman, Charles	1915	7.2
Playing Dead	Drew, Sidney	1915	9
Martyrs of the Alamo	Cabanne, W.C.	1915	6
Madame Butterfly	Olcott, Sidney	1915	16
Italian, The	Barker, Reginald	1915	10
Coward, The	Barker, Reginald	1915	11
Hypocrites	Weber, Lois	1915	16.5
Warrens of Virginia, The	DeMille, Cecil B.	1915	11
Kindling	DeMille, Cecil B.	1915	13
Golden Chance, The	DeMille, Cecil B.	1915	15
Girl of the Golden West, The	DeMille, Cecil B.	1915	13
Cheat, The	DeMille, Cecil B.	1915	12.5
Carmen	DeMille, Cecil B.	1915	11.5
Ghosts	Nichols, George	1915	12

TITLE	DIRECTOR	YEAR	ASL
AMERICAN FILMS			
David Harum	Dwan, Allan	1915	20
Case of Becky, The	Reicher, Frank	1915	13
Birth of a Nation	Griffith, D.W.	1915	7
Good Bad Man, The	Dwan, Allan	1916	5.8
Vie de Bohéme, La	Capellani, A.	1916	8.5
Vagabond, The	Chaplin, Charles	1916	14
Sunshine Dad	Dillon, Ed	1916	8
Poor Little Peppina	Olcott, Sidney	1916	9.6
Less Than the Dust	Emerson, John	1916	11
Hoodoo Ann	Ingraham, Lloyd	1916	7.5
Happiness	Barker, Reginald	1916	5.8
Going Straight	Franklin, Chester & Sidney	1916	7.5
Female of the Species, The	West, Raymond	1916	10
Crisis, The	Campbell, Colin	1916	8.5
Country God Forgot, The	Neilan, Marshall	1916	9
Child of the Streets, A	Ingraham, Lloyd	1916	7.5
Argonauts of Cailfornia, The	Kabierske, Henry	1916	6.9
Woman God Forgot, The	DeMille, Cecil B.	1917	10
Romance of the Redwoods	DeMille, Cecil B.	1917	10
Whip, The	Tourneur, Maurice	1917	6
Until They Get Me	Borzage, Frank	1917	6.8
Truthful Tulliver	Hart, William S.	1917	7
Tom Sawyer	Taylor, William D.	1917	6.4
Sawdust Ring, The	Miller, Charles	1917	7
Rebecca of Sunnybrook Farm	Neilan, Marshall	1917	5
Poor Little Rich Girl	Tourneur, Maurice	1917	10
Narrow Trail, The	Hillyer, Lambert	1917	4.5
Modern Musketeer, A	Dwan, Allan	1917	4
Little Lost Sister	Green, A.E.	1917	6.5
Kidnapped	Crosland, Alan	1917	8
Iced Bullet, The	Barker, Reginald	1917	6.4
Heart of Texas Ryan, The	Martin, E.A.	1917	9.5
Haunted Pajamas	Balshofer, Fred	1917	5.7
Girl Without a Soul, The	Collins, John H.	1917	5.3
Forbidden Paths	Thornby, Robert S.	1917	7.5
Castles for Two	Reicher, Frank	1917	9
Apple Tree Girl, The	Crosland, Alan	1917	4

These figures, and a number of others like them, show clearly that the move towards faster cutting was led from the United States, and within the American film industry it was undoubtedly led by D.W. Griffith from 1908 onwards.

As far as long feature films are concerned, the state of things for the products of the major industries are indicated by the samples above showing the various ASLs..

You might ask what is the point of all these boring figures. Well, the cutting rate (or ASL) is generally fairly closely connected with the apparent speed of the film narrative. This happens in various ways. The most obvious of these is that the more scenes there are within a given length, the more cuts there will be from one scene to the next, and hence the shorter the ASL. And in general, the faster the plot advances, the more scenes there will be. A greater number of scenes is also connected with the use of technique of cross-cutting between parallel actions. This was particularly developed by D.W. Griffith in the United States, though he did not invent it in the first place. By 1913 a number of other American film-makers were starting to take up this idea, and it is a feature of *Traffic in Souls*, the 90 minute American feature film tabulated above. However, amongst more than 2,000 European films made before 1914, none use fully developed cross-cutting in the Griffith manner, and only a dozen or so use it in to show both sides of a telephone conversation, or action inside and outside a house.

Despite the fact that there are some German films from this period, particularly thrillers, which contain a situation that could have been developed into a cross-cut race to the rescue, the only German example I have seen that even begins to use the device is Urban Gad's *Die Verräterin* (1912), where there are a couple of cuts between the hero hurrying to save the heroine from execution, and the execution itself. But this kind of embryonic cross-cutting dates back to 1907, before Griffith fully developed the notion.

By 1914 it was widely held in the American film industry that cross-cutting was most generally useful because it made possible the elimination of uninteresting parts of the action that play no part in advancing the drama, even if no suspense was involved. The introduction of crosscutting into a film requires special thought at the script stage, and this of course requires special training of the writers, which was far from being the norm in Europe, and especially in Germany.

The other technique that introduces more cuts into a given length of film is the use of cutting within a scene, and in particular cutting in to a closer shot of the actors, and then back again. Like all noticeable cuts, I believe this has some sort of dynamic psychological effect, and in any case the introduction of closer shots

in themselves can act to produce intensification of the dramatic situation. Although there was not vastly more cutting to closer shots in American than in European film up to 1914, when such cuts *were* used in American films, they tended to be from a general shot of the scene that was already closer to the actors than its European equivalent, and the close shot itself was likely to be closer too. But during the war years there certainly was more scene dissection in American film than European films, and this is brought out in the statistics for scale or closeness of shot given later in this article.

A German film that illustrates the effect of lack of cutting, combined with very poor staging of the action, is *Zweimal gelebt* (1912). The plot of this film revolves around a doctor who falls in love with a seriously ill woman whom he is treating in hospital. After she apparently dies in hospital, he pays a last visit to see her body in an open coffin lying in a church before burial, with no one else present. He discovers that she is not actually dead, and picks her up and carries her to his car outside the church. Every foot of his travel during this process is shown in its complete detail in three shots, one inside the church, the next showing him taking her out the door, and the third taken from the street showing him carrying her about 20 metres from the side of the church out to his car and dragging her passive form into it. All this has taken the better part of a minute, and then we are taken all the way back through the same series of shots as the doctor goes back to the church to get his top hat, which he left behind, and to put the lid on the coffin. Now this is an extreme case, but nearly all other German films of the period have at least a little of this kind of failure to think out how the simple progress of the action could be easily speeded up with better selection of shots, and more cuts between them. This is a great pity, because a very interesting situation is now set up in this film, but the director fails completely to exploit it. The doctor takes the revived woman away to another country and lives with her there, but the woman's little daughter turns up in the same town, and the woman sees her. The inevitable scene in which the woman spies on her daughter without daring to approach her is also staged in an incredibly crude way, with the woman lurking behind a tree at one side of the scene, in such a way that she would be clearly visible to anyone glancing her way. It is done like an incredibly bad nineteenth century melodrama on the stage.

In European cinema, I have found no films with an ASL shorter than 11 seconds before 1917, by which date a few clever and perceptive directors had finally begun to understand the new American methods of film construction. In Sweden, Victor Sjöström had all the devices of continuity cinema working properly in *Tösen fra Stormyrtorpet* (1917), with an ASL of 6 seconds. (His other films of this time, in which he acted as well as directed, unlike the one just mentioned, are slightly more retarded stylistically.) Mauritz Stiller also went some of the way down the same path in *Thomas Graals bästa Film* (ASL=9 sec.), but this was not typical for the Nordic region, as figures for films made by Georg af Klerker and others show. The long scenes and very slow cutting in German films is clearly indicated in the figures given above. Ernst Lubitsch seems to have been the first to get a grip on American methods, as is indicated by the ASL for *Wenn Vier dasselbe tun* (1917) of 8.5 seconds, while his *Die Puppe* of 1919 has an ASL of 5.5 seconds, not to mention the fact that he was already using a lot of reverse-angle shots by this date. His *Carmen* of 1918 has 14% of such cuts, and *Die Puppe* includes 19% reverse-angle cuts. On the other hand, there are many American films with an ASL shorter than 10 seconds *before* 1915.

Scale or Closeness of Shot

Another filmic variable about which conscious decisions have to be made when a film is being shot is Scale (or Closeness) of Shot, and even before 1919 distinctions were already being drawn by American film-makers between the categories of "Bust" or Close Up, American Foreground, French Foreground, Long Shot, and Distance Shot. Although there was already a small amount of disagreement about precisely what shot scale corresponded to each of these descriptive terms, it is sufficient for the purposes of analysis to define carefully what one means by each category, and then stick to it. I will in fact use categories of Scale of Shot more like those used in the nineteen-forties and later, as follows: Big Close Up (BCU) shows head only, Close Up (CU) shows head and shoulders, Medium Close Up (MCU) includes body from the waist up, Medium Shot (MS) includes from just below the hip to above the head of upright actors, Medium Long Shot (MLS) shows the body from the knee upwards, Long Shot (LS) shows at least the full height of the body, and Very Long Shot (VLS) shows the actor small in the frame. It must be appreciated that the closer categories of shot are understood to allow only a fairly small amount of space above the actor's head, so that the kind of situation where just the head and shoulders of a distant actor are sticking up into the bottom of the frame with vast amounts of space above him would *not* be classed as a Close Up. Although all the analyses in this book are done with the above categories, it might be preferable for future work to subdivide the category of Long Shot into Full Shot, which just shows the full height of the actor, and Long Shot showing the actor so distant that the frame height is two or three times the actor height, and still reserving Very Long Shot for those shots in which the actors are very small in the frame.

Since there is very little camera movement in the films made in the period we are dealing with at the moment, and since the actors also tend to stay mostly at the same distance from the camera in them, it is not difficult to assign the shots to the appropriate category. However, if a shot does include extensive actor movement towards, or away from, the camera, it is always possible to carry out an averaging process for actor closeness within the length of the shot to any desired degree of accuracy, if one takes enough time and care over it. Also it should be noted that since we are considering films with 200 or more shots in them, there is a tendency for occasional errors in the assignments of shots to their correct category to cancel out.

The exact scales of shot that lie at the centre of the categories I have been using up to now in my work are not entirely satisfactory for films made up to the end of the First World War, because two of the standardized distances that were fairly strictly used during this period both lie within one of my categories of Scale of Shot. The usual working distance for European films up to the First World War was the four metre line, and if actors play at this distance from the camera they are cut off at the shins when photographed with a standard 50 mm. lens, so giving what was called "the French foreground" in the USA. On the other hand, the usual shooting distance in America was the "nine foot line", with the actors working right up to a line laid on the floor at that distance from the camera. Under these conditions this cut the actors off just below the hips when they were framed with their heads a reasonable distance from the top of the frame. This was called the "American foreground". Although the "American foreground" corresponds with the centre of the later standard category, the Medium Shot, that I use, the "French foreground" falls towards the point where Medium Long Shot changes into Full Shot. It would be possible to introduce a new category for this, but for consistency with my earlier work, I have included French foreground shots under Medium Long Shot in these new figures. In any case, they are closer to being a Medium Long Shot (as it is nowadays understood) than to being a Full Shot, let alone a Long Shot.

The Technique

Although in the first place I record the total number of Close Ups, etc. in a film, for the purpose of the comparison between one particular film and other films which will include different numbers of shots in total, it is preferable to multiply the number of shots in each category by 500 divided by the total number of shots in the film, so that one then has the number of each type of shot per 500 shots. This 'standardization' or 'normalization' not only enables one to easily compare one film with another, but also gives a direct measure of the relative probability of a director choosing any particular closeness of shot.

A kind of crude summary of the results for the purposes of comparison can be given by quoting the

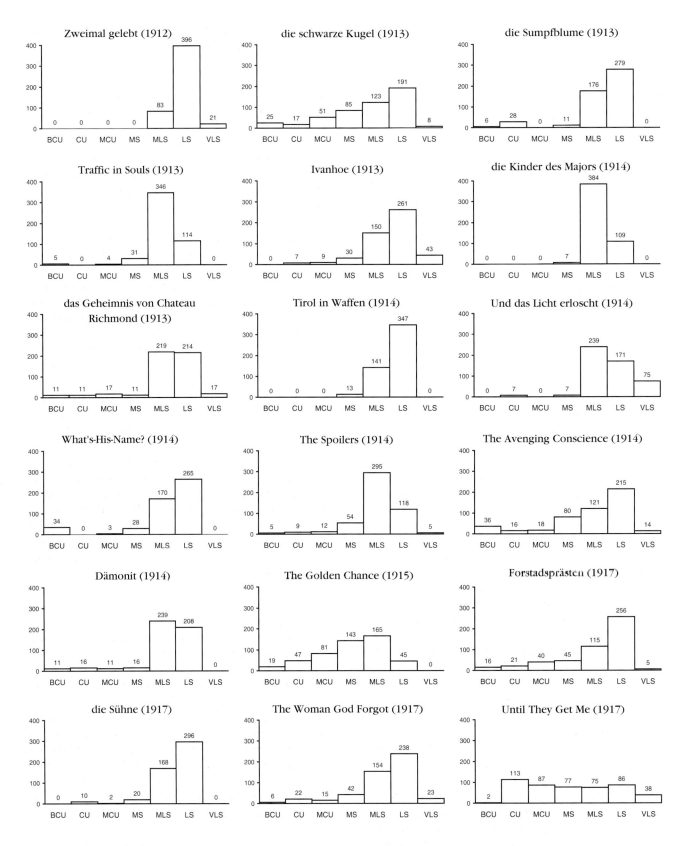

Number of shots with given Scale of Shot per 500 shots for the named films

percentages of shots closer than Medium Long Shot for the groups of German and American films.

Zweimal gelebt	1912	0%
Die Sumpfblume	1913	9%
Die schwarze Kugel	1913	28%
Der Geheimnis von Chateau Richmond	1913	10%
Dämonit	1914	11%
Die Kinder des Majors	1914	1%
Tirol in Waffen	1914	3%
Und das Licht erloscht	1914	3%
Die Sühne	1917	7%
Traffic in Souls	1913	8%
Ivanhoe	1913	9%
What's-His-Name?	1914	13%
The Spoilers	1914	16%
The Avenging Conscience	1914	30%
Until They Get Me	1917	56%

The most striking thing about these results is the high proportion of close shots in Franz Hofer's *Die schwarze Kugel*. This reaches a Griffith-like level. All the BCUs and CUs in this film are insert shots of objects, more or less relevant to the action. Taking this together with other features of this film, it looks to me as though Hofer had noticed some features of contemporary American film-making, without completely realizing their significance. The situations in which they are used would not bring forth such inserts in American films of this period or later, for they do not add extra clarity or force to what can already be clearly seen in the preceding shots in the film. The same is true of Hofer's use of masked Point of View shots (see below). Unfortunately, I have not been able to analyse any German films from 1915 and 1916 in detail, but *Die Sühne*, made in 1917, though not released till the following year, gives an indication of what is visible in other films I have seen, but not listed here. This is that there seems to have been very little progressive stylistic development in German films during the war years.

Reverse Angle Shots

As in the rest of Europe, it was not till after the war that German film-makers took the use of the fully developed technique of reverse-angle cutting which had begun to appear in American films from 1911. The one exception to this was the use of cuts to the opposite angle to show the audience watching a stage show, as well as the show itself seen in Long Shot from the audiences direction and point of view. It seems that many film-makers all over the world had difficulty generalizing from this situation to the general one. In fact even in theatrical scenes many European film-makers were unable to get their heads around this idea, even though they must have seen it in other people's films. For instance, Franz Hofer in *die schwarze Kugel* repeatedly tries to include the spectators of the stage show central to his plot in the foreground of the same shot as what they are watching. Unfortunately, his cameraman does not have sufficient depth of field to cover the audience, and either they or the show are out badly out of focus in successive shots. This is an extreme case of the technical ineptitude generally visible to some extent in all German films of the period.

Point of View Shots

The only true examples of Point of View (POV) shots in German films made before are the masked variety, where the scene looked at is shown inside a vignette shaped to represent the aperture of whatever is being looked through by the character in the film – telescope, keyhole, or whatever. e.g. *Die Sumpfblume*, and *Der Schirm mit dem Schwan* (1916).

The true Point of View shot, which shows what a character in the film is looking at without any mask, and *from a camera position along his line of sight*, began to appear in some quantities in American films from 1912. There are one or two examples of what might appear to be POV shots in German films made before 1918, such as *Die Suffragette* (1913), but closer inspection shows that the scene that the characters are looking at is not actually taken in the direction they are looking, but from a quite different direction. Indeed, such was the mental difficulty that German film-makers had with the concept of the true POV shot that a shot of an important thing that one character is looking at in Joseph Delmont's *Auf einsamer Insel* is shown inside a circular mask, even though neither he nor anyone else in the scene is using a telescope.

Staging within the shot

Given the great length of the takes in German films, there is inevitably a fair amount of staging with the actors moving between positions up near the four metre line and deeper in the set, and for the same reason the actors tend to face towards the "front" in a fairly obvious way. It was possible to stage scenes in one long take and avoid obvious frontality, as most Danish film dramas of the period show, and it was possible to go beyond this, as in Sjöström's *Ingeborg Holm* (1913), and use great subtlety in the placing of the actors with respect to each other, but you won't find anything like that in German films of the same date.

There is also a certain amount of use of deep sets including a space behind visible through a doorway or arch, in which parts of the action can take place. This is

A staging including a 'scene behind' in Und das Licht erloscht *(1914).*

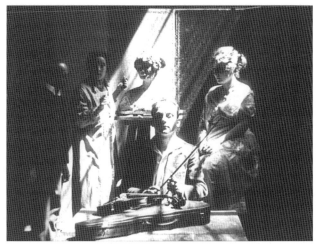

Low key lighting from available light in scene in a real artist's studio in Die Liebe der Maria Bonde *(1918).*

something that appears occasionally in European films made in the 'teens, but more rarely in American films, where action moves to adjoining spaces and back with a cut and a change of camera position.

Lighting

The lighting in German films of the period before 1918 is in general like that in other European films of the period, though the amount of lighting applied from arc floodlights on floor stands to the front and sides of the sets is a little heavier than the European average. In this respect it approaches the lighting in French Gaumont films, which used an exceptionally large number of arc floodlights. Combining this with the sort of staging used, I have been struck by the way that many German films, such as *Die Geheimnis von Chateau Richmond*, do indeed look like Gaumont films. Apart from the fact

Gaumont style lighting in Das Geheimnis von Chateau Richmond *(1913). The Foreground figure is almost up the the nine foot line, or 'American foreground'.*

that French films were probably the principal models for German films, the somewhat lower light levels of the sunlight through the studio roofs at Berlin's more northerly latitude may have had something to do with this. As in the rest of Europe, the old style glass studios continued to be used until after the war, whereas the Americans moved over to shooting solely with artificial light in dark studios during the war. And also as in the rest of Europe, there is no backlighting of the figures with spotlights in studio scenes. However, none of the German films made before 1917 that I have seen have the subtlety of the lighting of the best Gaumont films; the precision with which the light is applied to the figures and particular areas of the scene. Indeed the lighting can be downright crude, as in the attempts at low-key lighting in *Und das Licht erloscht* and *Homunculus*. Things began to change a little after the war, and a harbinger of this is the lighting in *Die Liebe der Maria Bonde* (1918), which does interesting things with available light in an artist's studio.

Script Construction

The basic problem with German films stems from their poor scripting, and this can be illustrated in its most extreme form by *Die Sumpfblume* (1913), where it takes the first ten minutes of the film for the hero to get to know the heroine and the story of the film to start at all, and another seven minutes to get the other components of the plot into place, so that something interesting can happen at last! In more action oriented films there are chases that have no goal, and indeed even return to the point of origin, and utterly irrelevant pieces of action, as in *Die schwarze Kugel*. Here much is made of the mechanism of a secret entrance through a staircase to a cellar, but this reputed cellar plays no part in the plot, and we never even see it. And so on. Even the best German films from before the war, which are undoubtedly the Asta Nielsen films directed by Urban Gad, are not quite completely free from these kinds of defects.

Miscellanea

There seems to be a notion that Joseph Delmont worked for the Vitagraph company in the United States in their wild animal films in 1902, and was also a circus acrobat before making films in Germany. The first of these is certainly untrue, as Vitagraph made no films in the year 1902, with wild animals or otherwise, and the latter is highly unlikely, as his physique, when revealed by a doctor's examination in *Das Recht aus Dasein* (1913), is one of the weediest I have ever seen on an actor of the period. Not to mention the fact that his attempts at stunts in that film are likewise feeble, even when compared to the 'action women' of other countries, let alone their male stunt players. More show business lying, I am afraid.

Conclusion

This is simply that foreign audiences preferred American films when they were put before them. And this was because American films were in general more exciting, gripping, and entertaining, for the reasons indicated above.

My usual thanks to the National Film Archive and National Film Theatre for their usual extensive cooperation in making films available for analysis, and this time the Goethe Institute also deserves a full share of my appreciation for their help.

After the new edition of *Film Style and Technology* had been out for a while, I finally got an American distributor for it. Samuel French, a long-established firm famous for publishing large numbers of stage plays, had added a catalogue of practically oriented books on film subjects from other small publishers to their own distribution list, and Gwen Feldman, the manager of the Samuel French Trade division, accepted my book. They were very good people to deal with, and sold thousands of copies over the next few years, until the bosses who ran the whole Samuel French business decided that they were not making enough money from distributing other people's books, and closed the division down.

In 1993, Paolo Cherchi Usai asked me for an article for a special number of the journal *Film History* that he was editing on the philosophy of film history. He was no more specific than that. This was an opportunity to make quite clear my opinion as to what real film history was, and with examples that illustrate how to do it properly. I had thought of writing about all of Alfred Hitchcock's films quite some time before, and had collected statistics and frame enlargements from all the viewing copies that the National Film Archive had, which was pretty well all of them up to the 'fifties. I could not use all of this material for a short piece cogently illustrating my general points about how to do film history, so besides using a selection of the films to illustrate what one could do with style analysis, I felt I had to tackle other aspects of doing film history properly. This amounted to a few words on how to do economic analysis, and more importantly, how to do thematic analysis properly. I practically knew the contents of my old, well-thumbed paperback copy of *Hitchcock* by Francois Truffaut by heart, so Hitchcock's identification of a "psychological" genre came quickly to me. Then I thought about doing another variation on the trick of connected sectional headings for the piece, as in some of my previous articles about German cinema. And the relevant section of the interview on *Lifeboat* provided the necessary material.

These procedures accord with my conception of how to do creative research, which I had elaborated to myself long ago when working in theoretical physics. I pictured what went on in my mind when trying to solve an intellectual problem as being like shaking a kaleidoscope around to get the right pattern. If repeated shaking was not doing the trick, the thing to do was to add some more pieces of coloured glass, and shake some more. Eventually, provided one added the right pieces, which one picks up here and there, the correct pattern will come out. Like most people engaged in such intellectual activities, I find extended periods of silence and solitude necessary for this.

...film in a lifeboat?

Truffaut: **Wasn't it pretty daring to undertake to shoot a whole film in a lifeboat?**

Hitchcock: **That's right, it was a challenge, but it was also because I wanted to prove a theory that I had then. Analysing the psychological pictures that were being turned out, it seemed to me that, visually, eighty per cent of the footage was shot in close-ups or semi-close shots. Most likely it wasn't a conscious thing with most of the directors, but rather an instinctive need to come closer to the action. In a sense this treatment was an anticipation of what was to become television technique.**

Truffaut: **That's an interesting point**.

(*Hitchcock by Francois Truffaut*, Panther, 1969, p.183-4).

...a challenge...

To describe the basic nature of film history, with some interesting new illustrations.

...theory...

The task of film history, like all proper history, is to describe what happened in the past, and the causal reasons for this. It is about films, otherwise it would be some other sort of history, so the films are central to it. In other words, what were the films like, how did they relate to other films, why were they like that, and what else happened in relation to the films?

In investigating the causal relations between features in films and other events in film history, only commonsense derivations should be allowed, and of course also the extensions to commonsense provided by well-established science. This approach certainly does not allow the use of speculative and unproven theories in establishing generalizations about features and events in film history, particularly theories like psychoanalysis and Marxism, which have already been demonstrated to have failed in their practical application. More than that, it excludes what is called "culture criticism" or "cultural history". These things are always practised by taking no more than a handful of films, and then picking out a few features of them which are claimed to support some large-scale generalization about the nature of society, which has itself been arrived at by equally insubstantial and unsound methods. And film history does not include interpretation of the "meaning" of films either.

Principles like mine, though not usually expressed, doubtless because they are obvious, have guided the fruitful development of musicology and art history during this century. An important aspect of my approach is that only as much theory as is necessary to deal with the matter in hand is used; there is no point in the pursuit of totally unnecessary and unobtainable rigour and generality. In other words, there is no point in making the general theoretical problem too difficult, and then failing to solve it after a lot of huffing and puffing.

Analysing...

At the lowest level, the films describe themselves, but to understand them, we need to get some truly significant patterns from them, and to relate their features one to another. This means first of all identifying their significant features, and here the terms are supplied by the people who made the films. For instance, in analysing the large-scale patterns in film production, the first classifications to use are those used by the film-makers themselves. As far as subject matter goes, film-makers have always had their own classifications, from the distinctions between ordinary commercial films, factual films and `art films', through the next level, which makes distinctions between `A' films and `B' films, and then on to distinctions of genre. Most people now accept and use this terminology, though there is some tendency amongst commentators to invent new genres unknown to the industry. And then there are sub-genres, series, and cycles, which come and go over time.

...psychological pictures...

The film reviews in *Variety*, which give a film industry view of such matters, show that already in 1939 there were a few films, mostly foreign, to which the `psychological' label was being applied. However, the native industry produced *Blind Alley*, in which "... Bellamy proceeds to uncover the subconscious basis Morris's killing mania." and ".. psychoanalysis of a criminal provides a new twist to what would otherwise become another crime picture of general trend.", as the issue of Variety for 26 April 1939 put it. *Le Jour se lève* was described as "... another of the series of psychological studies..." and *A Woman's Face* (Gustaf Molander's *en Kvinnas Ansikte*, released in 1938 in Sweden) as "... a study of psycho-physics...". In 1940 the foreign entries were tailing off, though the British picture *Gaslight*, made by Thorold Dickinson, was called a "...psychological drama..." by *Variety*, and there were now American films, such as Hitchcock's own *Rebecca*, described as "...too tragic and deeply psychological...", and *Street of Memories* from Twentieth Century-Fox was called "...arty and psychological preachment..." In 1941 there were also *Rage in Heaven* (Robert Sinclair & W.S. VanDyke, MGM), which drew the description "... psychopathic studies...", and *Flight from Destiny* (Vincent Sherman, Warners), which was called a "psychological drama". In 1942 only *Cat People* from the Val Lewton team earned the label "psychological" from *Variety*, though that journal did mention "mental emotions" as central in Hitchcock's own *Suspicion*. The real wave of psychological pictures from Hollywood only started in 1944, as was registered at the time, and not only in *Variety*. Films from that year which were described in a way that suggests they were seen as part of this trend include *The Lodger*, *Shadows in the Night*, *Dark Waters*, *End of the Road*, *When Strangers Marry*, *Guest in the House*, and *Destiny*.

Although in the interview I quoted above, Hitchcock suggested that he was thinking about making *Lifeboat* around 1940-41, actually at the end of 1941 he was still shooting *Saboteur* (see p.183 of *Hitch* by John Russell Taylor (Faber and Faber, 1978)), and it is unlikely that he was that far ahead in his thinking, since his next film was to be *Shadow of a Doubt*, shot in

1942. Given that the initial planning of *Lifeboat* was more probably done in 1942, the `psychological films' Hitchcock might have been thinking about could not be much more than the titles made before 1943 that I have just mentioned.

...close-ups...

As it happens, mainstream film construction has been fairly stable for so long that it is possible to safely use present day terms to describe the features of films as far back as the 'teens of the century. Before the First World War there were few standard terms, and these were nearly all different from those used later. Examples include "bust" for a close shot showing the head and shoulders of a person, rather than the later `Close Up', which became standard around 1914, and "French Foreground", which has no exact equivalent in later practice. "French Foreground" corresponded in American parlance to the closest framing usual in European films in the 1909-1913 period, with the actors playing at a line laid down 4 metres from the camera. This closeness of shot left the actor's legs cut off at the shins, and was defined in contradistinction to the "American foreground", which cut the actors off at the thighs, resulting from them playing up to a line nine feet from the camera. Although the term "insert" already existed at this time, it was used with a more general sense than it was later. Before the First World War "insert" referred to any material interrupting a continuous scene done in one shot taken from a fair distance. Thus it included what we would now call intertitles, as well as close shots of actor's faces and of objects. Such interruptions of the continuous scene were rare at that time, but after it became usual to break a scene down into a number of shots, the word "insert" came to be restricted to just close shots of objects, which is still the case today.

Occasionally there is no film industry term for what nevertheless seems to be a significant feature of many films, and in this case it seems to me that the best thing to do is to invent a descriptive name for the feature concerned. This is obviously much more likely to be necessary when dealing with the early period. A case in point is what I called the "emblematic shot" (see *The Early Development of Film Form* in *Film Form*, Vol.1, No.1, 1976). Having noticed that there were quite a group of films from different film-makers from 1903 onwards that started or ended with a close shot which was not part of the continuous narrative of the film,

The different scales of shot (or Closeness of Shot) – Long Shot (LS), Full Shot (FS), Medium Long Shot (MLS), Medium Shot (MS), Medium Close Up (MCU), Close Up (CU), and Big Close Up (BCU) – as used in this article.

[Frame enlargement from *Suspicion* (1941).]

though it might contain characters who appeared in the main narrative, I felt that this was such a striking phenomenon that it needed a name to describe it. Since the people and things in this special kind of shot seemed to be such as to summarize the nature of the film to which it was attached, I called it the "emblematic shot". The instance which particularly suggested the name to me was *Raid on a Coiner's Den* (British Gaumont, 1904), in which the first shot is a Close Up of hands holding a revolver, a fistful of money, and handcuffs, the last hand belonging to an arm inside the sleeve of a British policeman's coat. It seemed fairly probable that the source of this feature was the opening (or closing) shot of *The Great Train Robbery*, but afterwards I noticed that the last shot of Edwin Porter's *Rube and Mandy at Coney Island* might be considered

in the same light, though in this case the action of the film is so discontinuous that the final Medium Shot of Rube and Mandy eating hot dogs and grimacing at the camera is not so markedly outside the main narrative as the later examples. Recently Charles Musser has noted in *The Emergence of Cinema* (Charles Scribner's Sons, 1991, p.351), that the first of the two shots making up the Edison Company's *Laura Comstock's Bag-Punching Dog*, copyrighted on 6 May 1901, might be counted as the beginning of the use of the device.

In a case like this, it is desirable to find out if film-makers at the time developed their own name for the feature in question, and even more importantly, what they thought about its function in their films. By my principles, if we knew the term used at the time, we should use that in discussing it, rather than create a neologism, as I have with the "emblematic shot". For this reason, I am less happy with another of my inventions that also seems to have caught on a little. This is what I called "scene dissection", and it stands for a description of the kinds of shots into which a continuous film scene shot in one place is broken down. In this case, there is an existing film industry term that more or less corresponds, and that is "shot breakdown". In the United States it is now probably more usual to refer to the "shot list", but both the "shot list" and "shot breakdown" tend to include only a rough description of the shots. For instance, since they are only an approximate guide for the director, the scale of shot is not specified closely in them. So there does seem to be some place for a term that describes how one analyses a film precisely into shots *after* it is made.

In general, I see no point in inventing new names for film devices that already have a quite specific and standard name, as has become fashionable in recent years. Unfortunate examples include "diegetic music", for what is actually called in the industry "source music"; i.e. music whose source is apparent within the film scene, as opposed to ordinary background music, which comes from outside the represented scene. Another term that is even more common amongst academics without much knowledge of film-making is the "180 degree line", invented by Edward Branigan. This is an unnecessary replacement for the standard industry term "the eyeline", (often abbreviated to just "the line"), and the term "180 degree line" has demonstrably confused people in film studies who know even less about film-making than Branigan.

In areas of film history other than film technique, the participants at the time usually also had names to describe what they were doing. For instance, in the economics of the film industry, the standard terms of the science have long been used, such as "appreciation of site values", "long term credits", "film inventory values", and so on.

Film-makers do not often use large-scale classifications to describe the differences between films with respect to their form, for the obvious reason that at any particular time most fiction films are rather like each other in style, and were intended to be so. Nevertheless, deviations from the norm are sometimes commented on by people in the industry, and when they do, it is in terms of things like speed of cutting, i.e. the number of shots per unit time, or the types of lenses mostly used, i.e. whether wide-angle or long focal length, or how close in the film is shot, and so on.

...eighty per cent of the footage...

It is not as easy to determine the total footage devoted to each scale of shot (or closeness of shot) as it is to extract the total numbers of shots with any particular scale in a film, and so it is the latter that I have usually dealt with in my work. However, the two things are fairly closely related, as I will show later. The only "psychological films" of the early 'forties that I have been able to get my hands on, with the usual assistance from the National Film and Television Archive, are those made by Hitchcock, together with *Cat People* and *Gaslight*, but their analysis still produces suggestive results. I reproduce the Scale of Shot distributions for them here.

If we take semi-close shots (a somewhat vague and non-standard expression) to include what I define as Medium Shot (i.e. shots showing the figures from the hips to the usual height just above their heads), we get the table showing the percentage of shots with scale (or closeness) from Big Close Up (shows head only) up to and including Medium Shot for most Hitchcock films from *Jamaica Inn* to *Notorious*, plus some other relevant films.

Film	% of shots MS or closer
Jamaica Inn (1939)	55%
Rebecca (1940)	65%
Foreign Correspondent (1940)	66%
Suspicion (1942)	75%
Saboteur (1942)	53%
Shadow of a Doubt (1943)	65%
Lifeboat (1944)	76%
Notorious (1947)	71%
Gaslight (1939)	63%
Cat People (1942)	62%
Back Street (1941)	71%
Sergeant Madden (1939)	71%

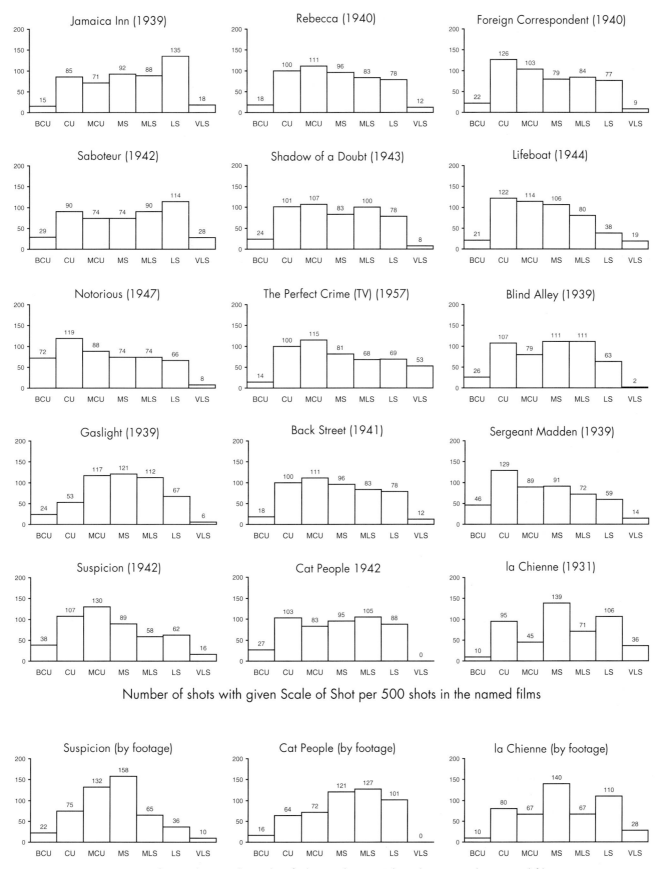

Number of shots with given Scale of Shot per 500 shots in the named films

Footage devoted to each Scale of Shot within 500 length units in the named films

As you can see, this percentage of shots at Medium Shot or closer rises from 55% for *Jamaica Inn* to 75% for *Suspicion*, then drops back to 53% for *Saboteur*, which is certainly not a 'psychological film', before moving back up again to 76% for *Lifeboat*, the result of Hitchcock's quoted thoughts about film technique. On the other hand, the distributions for *Cat People* and *Gaslight* have appreciably lower values, 62% and 63%, which are like those for Hitchcock's non-psychological films. It is also worth remarking that distributions of shot scale with heavy emphasis on close shots, though not common, were not restricted to "psychological films" in American cinema at the beginning of the 'forties, as can be seen for the distributions for the 1941 version of *Back Street* and von Sternberg's *Sergeant Madden* (1939). There are some qualifications to be made about these results, the most obvious of which is that I have been dealing with the numbers of shots of different kinds in the film, rather than their total footage. In general, given the fairly random distribution of shot lengths for films *as a whole*, the two things are roughly equivalent, as can be seen from the distributions for *Suspicion*, *Cat People*, and Renoir's *la Chienne* (1931), which give respectively the numbers of shots of each scale per 500 shots, and the length (i.e. footage equivalent) devoted to each shot scale within 500 arbitrary length units. In the case of *Suspicion*, the percentage of shots at Medium Shot or closer (75%) is very close to that for the percentage of footage devoted to Medium Shot or closer (77%). (for more on the statistical analysis of films see my *Film Style and Technology: History and Analysis* (2nd Edition), Starword, 1993.)

To sum up, though Hitchcock was fairly correct about his claim for the closeness of filming in his own psychological pictures, he was certainly not for all those made by other people before 1944. Even the statements of someone with an analytical turn of mind and a good memory like Alfred Hitchcock are not to be relied upon completely. In this case he may well have been shifting his memories of other people's psychological films made after 1943 back in time, and combining them with his intimate knowledge of his own psychological films made before 1943. The other possibility is that Hitchcock was being arch in his reply, and was well aware that he was the only maker of 'psychological films' before 1944 who was shooting them from very close in. (The matter might be resolved by studying the original tapes of the Hitchcock-Truffaut interviews.) This is one of the reasons that I introduced the statistical methods I have just been demonstrating again here.

They provide a more objective basis for doing film history, and this is important, because otherwise mistakes will be copied from one historian to another, and false arguments will be built upon them, and then further diffused. It is *not* sufficient to say that Hitchcock is a filmmaker, so whatever he says about film-making must be correct, and just give a reference to where he said it, as some people seem to think. One needs to know as much as possible about the situation one is researching and writing about, and all its ramifications. In the case of the technical aspects of film-making, this is particularly true, otherwise one gets things like the statement that the shooting of a 'thin' (low density) negative by some cameramen in the 'twenties produced a low contrast print that was also sharp. Thin negatives certainly give low contrast prints, but they equally certainly have less sharpness than correctly exposed and developed prints. I am not claiming that encyclopaedic and extensive practical knowledge of film-making guarantees correctness, just that it gives one a much better chance of being right. Lots of footnotes and references are not enough on their own, I am afraid.

...a conscious thing with most of the directors...

Although Hitchcock was more reflective and communicative about his work than most film-makers, there have been sufficient comments from others to enable us to fairly safely deduce what most film-makers thought they were doing in most situations over the last eighty years. This is essentially because of the large degree of uniformity in ordinary commercial film-making over this period. Good historians give some idea about this topic by quoting film-makers' opinions on their craft, as Rachael Low does in her *History of the British Film*, and there is some of this too in the earlier volumes of the *History of American Cinema* that have recently appeared. I am a little ashamed that there has not been as much of this in my own work as there should be.

However, care is still necessary on this point, since there are a small proportion of ordinary commercial films that deviate from the norms, and also film-makers can change their ideas about film-making. Hitchcock is an example of this, with his exploration of 'long-take' filming in *Rope* and *Under Capricorn*.

...come closer to the action...

Actually most of Hitchcock's later films are shot in

the same way as *Rebecca* and *Suspicion*, with the exception of the more lighthearted of his thrillers, such as *The Trouble With Harry*, *To Catch a Thief*, *North by North West*, and also the technically constrained *Dial M for Murder*.

...television technique...

As you can see for the distribution of shot scale for two of the short television programs directed by Hitchcock himself in the *Alfred Hitchcock Presents* series, *Mr. Blanchard's Secret* (1956) and *The Perfect Crime* (1957), his own television technique only roughly matched his prescription, but then standard television technique has continued changing over the last forty years. Perhaps someone will do a thorough analysis of that topic one day.

...an interesting point.

The basic principle behind my approach to film history is to look at it from the perspective of the filmmakers, and the beauty of this is that it will handle everything about film history that matters, including the relation of films to their audience at the time that they appeared. The only kind of artistic evaluation it allows is based on what people in the past thought about this point, and it excludes the *subjective* value judgements of people in the present, including film historians. Nevertheless, I do consider it legitimate to include the very occasional subjective comment when writing about film history, as long as it is clear to any intelligent and informed reader, as well as to one's self, that that is what it is, and as long as one's historical arguments do not depend on it. The same is true for speculation, and I consider that it is permissible to include a little bit of speculation about where one's results might lead at the end of a substantial piece of objective work, again if it is clearly marked out. I am not certain what the general position amongst historians is about this matter, but this is certainly the position taken in the scientific community when writing a paper for publication in one of the major scientific journals.

I think my principles of film history agree with what I observe of the practice of most people working in film history nowadays, so perhaps other film historians also believe in these principles already, even though they haven't stated them. And they don't need a lifeboat.

The journal *Film History* uses Futura Book as a body text font, and it has the usual defect of sans serif fonts, from my point of view, which is that the oblique face does not stand out enough when used for film titles.

Since 1962 I had been living in a couple of small cheap rented rooms in Shepherds Bush in west London, sometimes putting up visiting relations and indigent friends. My cousin Bill Brown (the one looking really tough at the right of the photo on page 2) and his wife Rosemary led the influx from Australia, though all the Salt cousins turned up eventually. It got quite crowded in there on a few occasions. But in 1993 I bought a standard inner-London terrace house in behind the north side of Shepherds Bush Green. It was only about a hundred and twenty years old, and dated from the period when the last sheep were driven out of Shepherds Bush. Contrary to the naïve Colonial's first thoughts and impressions, the vast majority of the structures in this country are not that old, and indeed have been built within the last two hundred years.

Inside my piece of recent English history I now wallowed in space, peace and quiet, and the pride of ownership. Equally importantly, I could spread my tools out. I turned to constructing my own computers out of new and old components, and networked them across two floors. I also acquired a row of television sets, and VHS recorders to go with them, and got down to collecting ASLs for everything that passed across their screens. Previously to this I had only had television sets for a couple of short periods, and I acquired all my data from film prints viewed on Steenbecks or on the screen at the National Film Theatre.

In 1993 Ray Durgnat generously passed on another invitation to me. He had taught at the Radio and Television Institute belonging to the national Finnish broadcasting company, Oy Yleisradio AB, and they had invited him again for 1994. He did not want to go for some reason, so he suggested me to Sakari Salko, who was organizing the event. I took the offer up, and proposed to apply my style analysis to TV shows. I had already analysed a collection of American television shows from around 1960 back in the 'seventies, using films prints of them that the British Film Institute had been distributing, though I had not published the results. Now I used my new facilities to record and analyse a lot of recent TV crime shows and soap operas, etc. from Britain and the USA before leaving for Finland, and added these to my data.

In Finland, Sakari Salko looked after me well, but it was the hardest week of teaching I have ever done. I was doing six hours lecturing a day continuously, and by the end I was running out of relevant material. This was despite my obtaining new results to feed into my lectures by working each evening analysing some Finnish TV shows. The one they were most proud of was *Milkshake*, a soap aimed at the young Finnish audience. The students were quite interested in what I did with statistical style analysis, but I got the best response to an impromptu analysis of the cutting in Hitchcock's *Lifeboat*. The other thing they were particularly interested in were episodes of *NYPD Blue* and *Homicide: Life on the Streets*, which had not been shown in Finland at that point. I rather hope this did not trigger an epidemic of wildly waving cameras on Finnish TV over the next few years. Sakari Salko also sprang on me a quick dash up to Lahti one afternoon to address a large training conference of Finnish TV designers. I had noticed that some Finnish television lighting cameramen were starting to use coloured light on their shows, copying something that had been going on in Britain for some time, though they were not doing it that well. So I shuffled through the film tapes that Sakari had available, and gave a brief illustrated history of content co-ordinated colour design in film, from *Bambi* to *Gremlins 2*. This was not a big success, probably because they were exhausted by the previous days of being talked at, plus a lot of them not understanding English that well. Or maybe they knew it all already.

I managed to fit in my usual dash around the national art galleries in Helsinki, and Sakari Salko and his friends gave me a lightning tour of the modern architecture by the Saarinens etc. around the city, plus a taste of smoked lamb, a delicious local treat, before I jetted out again.

Writing up the mass of data I had acquired did not take long, and since I thought my analysis of TV style was rather important, I sought somewhere to publish it. There are no significant British journals dealing seriously with television, and so the only possibilities were the American academic journals devoted to broadcasting matters. These appeared less averse to statistical empirical enquiry than academic film journals. But submission to the *Journal of Film and Video* and the *Journal of Communication* proved as usual that they wanted to keep out stuff that showed up their own lack of enterprise in this area.

THE STYLISTIC ANALYSIS OF TELEVISION DRAMA PROGRAMS

Although there have been occasional brief attempts to analyse shot lengths in films from early in this century, full-scale quantitative analysis of film style really began in 1974 with my article *Statistical Style Analysis of Motion Pictures* in Film Quarterly (v 28 n 1). The theoretical framework intended to deal with all audio-visual media (including television) which lies behind this work was first outlined in *Film Form, Style, and Aesthetics* in Sight & Sound (v 43 n 2) the same year. My research program into the nature and history of film style gave rise to a series of further articles in Film Quarterly and elsewhere, and then a book called *Film Style and Technology: History and Analysis,* of which the first edition was published in 1983 by Starword. Some of my ideas and methods were taken up by a few other people, including David Bordwell and Kristin Thompson, with results included in their *The Classical American Cinema* (Routledge, 1984). I only took the step of extending my analyses to television programs in a substantial way in 1994 (though I had done some much earlier work in this area), as the result of an invitation from Sakari Salko to teach at the Radio-Television Institute of the Finnish national broadcasting organization, Yleisradio Oy. Only after writing the first draft of this article did I discover that a somewhat more limited form of quantitative style analysis had begun to appear in television studies in the 1980s. The significant names here are David Barker with *Television Production Techniques as Communication* in Critical Studies in Mass Communication (1985 No. 2. Pp 234-246), and more importantly Michael J. Porter, with his *A Comparative Analysis of Directing Styles in Hill Street Blues*, published in The Journal of Broadcasting and Electronic Media (V. 31 No. 3, Summer 1987), and also Barbatsis and Guy, likewise in The Journal of Broadcasting and Electronic Media (Volume 35 No. 1, Winter 1991)

The essence of my own theoretical ideas about the analysis of film and television (and indeed other media) is that the process should reverse the process of the composition of the work. This commonsense idea means that the terms used for the analysis should be those used by the maker (or makers) of the work, and as far as possible not new terms invented by the analyst. This approach also means that useful communication is then possible with the makers of the works, without whom academic analysts and other commentators would have nothing to justify their own existence.

Like movies, the production of television drama programs starts with a script describing the action to take place in front of the cameras. Detailed analysis of the dramatic structure of television scripts is outside my concern at the moment, so I will just remark that not only ordinary single episode dramas and comedies, but also most episodic dramas and comedies, follow the standard dramatic structures established in American movies when they reached their standard form during the First World War. This in its turn was exactly based on the standard dramatic structure used in American commercial theatre towards the end of the nineteenth century. Quite a lot of people make a good living these days by teaching film and television scriptwriting, but all the basic principles of dramatic construction clearly expounded in Alfred Hennequin's *The Art of Playwriting* (Houghton-Mifflin Co., 1890) are still those in use. The only partial exception to this is the dramatic construction of television serials or "soap operas". The dramatic structure of these is of course directly derived from the serial radio plays developed in US during the 1920s and 1930s. Each episode of a soap opera can be simply described as part of an incomplete play, or better as like an endless string of Second Acts which involve a whole group of protagonists of equal importance, rather than the standard one or two leading characters animating traditional feature films, and indeed television "one-off" dramas.

The essential mechanism of standard commercial play construction was the conflict between one character striving to accomplish some purpose in which he is thwarted by another character. This initial situation is developed purely by a logical process of realistic cause and effect.

Although these ideas were ancient, the nineteenth century playwrights added refinements to them. Variation of mood was most important, both from scene to scene, and also within scenes. To quote Alfred Hennequin, who was the first to give a complete exposition of these ideas: 'Pathos must be followed by humour, wit by eloquence, talky passages by quick-succeeding scenes of incident, soliloquies by the rapid give-and-take of dialogue. The entire act should be a rapidly shifting kaleidoscope, presenting new features at every turn'. This alternation of mood was associated with the device of suspense - 'In some form or another, it must exist throughout the entire progress of the story. At various points of the play, generally at the close of each act, it may be partially relieved, but it must always be done in such a way as to give rise to new suspense, or to leave one or two particulars still unsettled, etc.' Associated with this was a progression of climaxes – 'A dramatic story should be full of climaxes from beginning to end. Every act should have several lesser ones scattered through it, and should invariably end with one of greater importance. Toward the end of the play should occur the great climax in the technical sense of the word, i.e. the point at which the interest of the play reaches its highest stage.' The final major constituent of the standard stage and film plot was the 'heart interest' as it was called before World War I. (Later this came to be called 'the love interest'.) This required that the hero, as well as solving his problem, or defeating the villain, should also get the girl. (The reversal of sexual roles was also possible, though quite rare.) The vast majority of American feature films have always had this double plot action. (See Chapter XI of *The Content of Motion Pictures* by Edgar Dale. (The Macmillan Company, 1935))

The complete creation of a script before a program is staged and recorded demands a simple "old-fashioned" separation between content and form as the first stage for any rational analysis of television, just as it is in dealing with the cinema.

Production continues with the script being rehearsed and staged, and then recorded by cameras as a series of shots taken at different distances from the actors who are making the moves as required and rehearsed. The different scale or closeness of the shots – Close Up, Medium Shot, etc. are chosen as the director of the program thinks appropriate, as are the camera angles and moves, and of course the length of the shots also. There are various conventional ideas of long standing about such choices, in television exactly as in the movies. The standard ideas about choice of shots, their lengths, and so on, solidified in the United States around the time of the First World War, when the new ideas about scene dissection were aligned with the standard dramatic structure taken from commercial play scripts as previously mentioned. I give some examples of the way that the scale of shot chosen and the lengths of shots vary within a film depending on the subject matter of successive scenes in *Film Style and Technology* (on p. 177 and in Chapter 22), but I will briefly demonstrate the way that the same is true, as far as cutting rate goes, for an episode of *Star Trek*.

I have used the standard film and television division into script scenes for the very first episode of the *Star Trek* series that was transmitted in 1966, *Man Trap*. The starting point of this story is that the USS *Enterprise* has arrived at an isolated planet, and Captain Kirk, Dr. McCoy, and another crewman are beamed down onto it to give a routine medical examination to the two archaeologists who are alone on the planet, researching the relics of a vanished civilization. They are Professor Crater and his wife Nancy, who had been a girl-friend of McCoy years before. I give the basic dramatic events of each scene, followed by the average length of the shots (ASL) making up each scene. For instance, the first scene lasts 60 seconds, and contains 7 shots. This gives an ASL of 8.9 seconds for the scene, whereas the whole episode contains 527 shots in a total length of 47 minutes 14 seconds (excluding front and end titles), which gives an overall ASL of 5.5 seconds. (For this programme, as well as all the other American shows originally made on film, and which I recorded for analysis off-air from British television, the timings have been corrected to allow for the different frame rates of telecine recording in the US and Europe.)

Shot	Action	ASL
1	The Captain Kirk, Dr. McCoy and a crewman from the *Enterprise* land on the planet.	8.9
2	They go inside a building and meet Professor Crater and his wife. McCoy thinks she looks exactly as she did many years ago. She appears to the crewman as a quite different girl he knew once on a pleasure planet.	3.6
3	The crewman goes outside, and Nancy Crater, appearing as the girl, follows him.	7.1
4	MAIN TITLE.	
5	Prof. Crater resists the medical examination, but eventually gives in. A scream is heard from outside.	9.0
6	The men rush outside and find the body of the crewman with weird scars on his face.	4.1
7	A shot of the *Enterprise* with a captain's log entry read over on the sound track.	
8	On the ship Spock and Uhura tease each other verbally.	7.6
9	Kirk and McCoy puzzle about the cause of death in the medical room on the ship.	7.6
10	Exterior shot of the ship in space.	

Shot	Action	ASL
12	Spock Kirk and McCoy in the medical room puzzling about the complete absence of salt in the body.	11.7
13	Inside buildings down on the planet the Prof. resists investigation of the death by Kirk and McCoy, then runs off. Two crewmen follow him out.	12.9
14	Outside on the planet Nancy, the shape shifter, assumes the appearance of another dead crewman. Kirk and McCoy discover the body of the other crewman.	5.9
15	A shot of the ship.	
16	Kirk and McCoy beam back to the ship with the false crewman. It roams the corridors of the ship.	8.0
17	Spock etc. puzzle over why their detectors only register one human down on planet.	20.8
18	The shape shifter roams the corridors, where it observes crewmen engaging in banter with a pretty crewgirl carrying a meal.	8.5
19	The crewgirl brings the meal to Sulu in the Biology lab. They engage in banter.	5.7
20	The false crewman investigates the corridor and comes to the Biology lab.	15.6
21	He enters, looks around, frightens Sulu's sensitive plant, disturbing Sulu and crewgirl, and leaves.	4.4
22	The false crewman sees Uhura in the corridors, and, unobserved, changes into a black man. It then makes a pass at her, but is disturbed before it can attack her.	5.7
23	McCoy's in his cabin is told to take a sleeping draught to calm himself down.	6.9
24	The shape shifter stalks yet another crewman.	6.2
25	On the bridge Kirk, Spock and Uhura are still puzzling about why there is only one person down on the planet.	34.3
26	In the corridor the shape shifter changes back into Nancy, enters McCoy's room, and smooches up to him.	12.9
27	The body of another crewman is discovered in the corridor.	10.9
28	Exterior shot of the *Enterprise.*	
29	In his cabin, the shape shifter continues to smooch up to McCoy. When there is a warning on the intercom it hypnotizes him to sleep, and changes into his likeness.	10.9
30	Shot of ship.	
31	Down on the planet Kirk and Spock find the body of the other crewman who was killed earlier, and who Nancy had impersonated. Professor Crater refuses to come back to the *Enterprise* and runs off.	5.1
32	Intruder alert on ship.	4.4
33	On the planet, Crater shoots at Kirk and Spock. They start to hunt him.	9.7
34	On the ship the false McCoy joins the crew on the bridge monitoring the situation.	4.2
35	Kirk and McCoy hunt and capture Crater. Under pressure he partially explains about the shape-shifter.	3.3
36	Shot of the ship.	

Shot	**Action**	**ASL**
37	Shot of the real McCoy in his cabin sleeping. Crew searching corridors.	6.8
38	Everyone, including the false McCoy, in the conference room arguing about how to catch the shape-shifter. Crater tries to defend it.	4.0
39	Shot of the ship.	
40	In the dispensary, Spock is treated after being attacked by the shape-shifter.	4.7
41	The shape-shifter is cornered in McCoy's cabin. The real McCoy stops it being shot, and then it starts to suck the juices out of Kirk. Spock hits it, causing it to reveal its true monstrous appearance, and McCoy shoots it.	3.5
42	On the bridge the matter is summed up, and the ship sets off on its voyages again.	5.4

It should be obvious that the level of dramatic excitement alternates from one scene to the next, just as recommended a hundred years ago by Alfred Hennequin, and just as is still standard in ordinary feature film construction. Corresponding to these alternations in the intensity of the drama, the cutting rate is also varied, with faster cutting than the norm (i.e. shorter ASL) in the scenes involving more dramatic tension and/or action, and slower in the more relaxed scenes.

But as I have demonstrated in *Film Style and Technology*, there is still quite a lot of acceptable room for variation around the norms as far as movie making is concerned. There are undoubtedly variations between film-makers regarding these choices, and there are also group aspects of style that change with time, linking together by their formal resemblance works produced by different people. The question is, how far is this true for television?

The Early Days

Little material is readily available from the early days of 100 percent live television, when programs were transmitted to the viewing audience in real time direct from the studio floor. The only programs I have been able to obtain are those few American television shows of the 'fifties still held by the Distribution Division of the British Film Institute.

In the nineteen-fifties there were two basic production methods, firstly the use of multiple television cameras recording a series of scenes staged in front of them, and transmitted in real time, with a breakdown into shots by switching between the cameras in the instant, and secondly by recording scenes with film cameras, and then editing the processed film from them in the standard way that is used in the production of cinema films. This second method had two variants. In one the scenes were filmed with a single camera, with each shot made separately, and the camera moved between set-ups, and in the other method the scene was filmed continuously with multiple film cameras shooting from different angles to the scene. The first method produced what was essentially a film made specially for television, whereas the second, and most common, was peculiar to television. This multiple camera method was of course the most used because it was the fastest, and hence the cheapest; for then, as now, television production worked under very severe financial constraints compared to feature film production.

The earliest show I have been able to analyse is a drama from the CBS series *Schlitz Playhouse of the Stars* entitled *So Help Me*, and dating from 1952. It was directed by Phil Brown, shot on 35 mm. film (though probably not with multiple cameras throughout), and began with an introduction by Irene Dunne. I have excluded this introduction from my analysis of the numbers of different kinds of shots making up of the program. In the main remaining part of the show with a total running time of 24 minutes, I counted 8 Big Close Ups, 31 Close Ups, 34 Medium Close Ups, 38 Medium Shots, 10 Medium Long Shots, and 1 Long Shot.

Although there is a small amount of disagreement about precisely what shot scale corresponds to each descriptive term, it is sufficient for the purposes of analysis to define carefully what one means by each category, and then stick to it. I am using categories of Scale of Shot like those commonly used in the film industry from the nineteen-forties, as follows: Big Close Up (BCU) shows head only, Close Up (CU) shows head and shoulders, Medium Close Up (MCU) includes body from the waist up, Medium Shot (MS) includes from just below the hip to above the head of upright actors, Medium Long Shot (MLS) shows the body from the knee upwards, Long Shot (LS) shows at least the full height of the body, and Very Long Shot

(VLS) shows the actor small in the frame. In recent decades in film and television the vaguer term 'Wide Shot' has come to replace the various kinds of Long Shot described above, but I am keeping to the more finely graded terminology used when I first became involved with film-making nearly fifty years ago.

For comparative purposes, so as to give an obvious relative measure of the likelihood of a director choosing a particular scale of shot in a program, I have taken the actual number of shots of each scale in *So Help Me*, and then normalized the number to correspond to the number that would have occurred if the program was longer and made up of 500 shots, rather than the actual 122 shots. (The normalization to 500 shots, rather than to some other fixed standard number, is for consistency with my extensive previous work on feature films.) The results are displayed as a graph below, along with other distributions of shot scale for other TV programs.

The next program in chronological order that was available is *How the Books Were Balanced* from the NBC series *Wonderful John Acton*, a drama produced and staged by Edward A. Byron, and directed by Grey Lockwood, according to the credits on the film. It dates from around 1953. This show was made live for direct transmission, and was shot with multiple television cameras on a series of sets in the one studio in real time. The advertising break in the middle of the show was used for set changes. For this analysis I was working with a 16 mm. kinescope recording taken on film from a special monitor as the show was being transmitted. In this case there were only 72 shots in the 27 minute running time, and the normalized distribution of types of shots can be seen below. The effect of live television presentation can be seen in the Average Shot Length (ASL), which is 23.2 seconds, which compares with the value for *So Help Me*, which is 12.2 seconds. In their turn, both these values may be compared with typical Average Shot Lengths for American cinema films of the 'fifties, which are nearly all in the range 6 to 12 seconds. There are a very small number of American cinema films with ASLs longer than 20 seconds from the 'fifties, but they are highly untypical. In general, the longer the takes, the shorter the production time, both in film and in television. The other way that the production technique shows up in the statistics is that whereas in *So Help Me* there are 77 cuts from a shot to a reverse angle shot (i.e. 63% of the cuts are of this nature), in *How the Books Were Balanced* there are only 26 such cuts, (i.e. 36% of the cuts). Reverse angle cuts are defined here as changes of camera direction of more than 90 degrees. The point of this observation is that with multiple camera shooting, it is difficult to

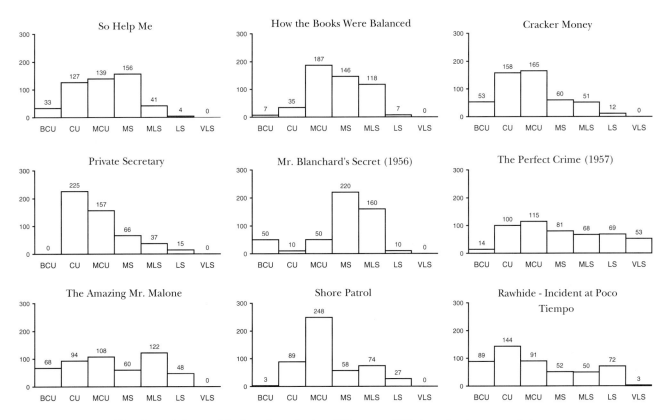

Number of shots with the given Scale of Shot per 500 shots in the named shows

avoid getting one of the other cameras into shot if the cameras are shooting in almost opposite directions. Thus there is a pressure against using such shots in multiple camera use, but with tricks such as shooting through doors andwindows and even concealed apertures in the walls, as in *How the Books Were Balanced*, it was possible. Also, many of the reverse angles I have counted in *How the Books Were Balanced* only just qualify as reverse angles, as they all involve angle changes of only a little more than 90 degrees, whereas in *So Help Me* the changes of angle are more like the 120 degree-plus changes usual in ordinary film-making. Another feature of the statistics that shows the same constraint is the number of cuts to or from a Point of View (POV) shot in the two films. Such shots are those taken from the position of one of the participants in the scene, and hence require the camera which is taking such a shot to be put in front of the person. In ordinary filming, where the shots are taken one at a time, this presents no great problem, but in multiple camera filming it is extremely difficult to arrange, though not absolutely impossible. So in *So Help Me* there are 8 Point of View shots, or to put it another way, 7% of the cuts in this program were to or from a POV shot. On the other hand, in *How the Books Were Balanced*, there were no POV shots at all.

Another live television production from about the same date is *Cracker Money* from the Kaiser Aluminium Hour series of 1956 on NBC. This show was produced and directed by Fielder Cook, and was again viewed in a 16 mm. kinescope recording. This is one of those serious dramas that are celebrated as part of the 'Golden Age' of live television. It deals in a fairly realistic way with the small dramas of middle-class family life at home and at work.

Again, the continuous filming with multiple cameras pushes the Average Shot Length to 12.8 seconds, whereas a cinema feature film directed by Fielder Cook in 1966, *Big Hand for a Little Lady*, has an ASL of 6.3 seconds. The Scale of Shot distribution shows rather closer shooting on the whole than the two previous shows, as can be seen by comparing the numbers of shots closer than Medium Shot in the three cases. I would say that this is mostly a matter of the director's attitude to the material in the script, but since a number of scenes take place in the corridor of a house, the naturalistic dimensions of the sets have something to do with the matter as well. (The two previous shows have sets built larger than life, following the usual manner of traditional film design.) The production team manage to get quite a lot of reverse angle shooting (73% of the cuts) by going to a lot of effort to get the cameras into position to shoot them despite the confined spaces of the sets. Again, I would say that this is related to a desire to get head-on as well as close in to the faces, so as to register subtle detail of reaction to what are clearly intended to be like real life situations. However, the production circumstances still helped to prevent any Point of View shots being used.

An entry from the series comedy genre, *Private Secretary*, and which is also from 1956, was shot on 35 mm. film, again mostly with multiple cameras like *So Help Me*. I don't know on which American TV channel this was originally shown, but it is a Jack Chertok production starring Ann Sothern and directed by Oscar Rudolph. As you can see from the Scale of Shot distribution, this is much more like the present-day image of television style in general, with very heavy emphasis on Close Ups, and the ASL of 6.5 seconds, not to mention 57% reverse angle cuts.

Shore Patrol, from the *Hennessy* series, is another comedy shot on 35 mm. film, and shown on CBS in

Program Title	Year	ASL	RA	POV	Inserts
Playhouse of the Stars - So Help Me	1952	12.2	63	7	0
How the Books Were Balanced	1955	23.2	36	0	7
Cracker Money	1956	12.8	73	0	2
Private Secretary	1956	6.5	57	0	3
Alfred Hitchcock Presents - Mr. Blanchard's Secret	1956	13.7	24	28	11
Alfred Hitchcock Presents - The Perfect Crime	1957	27.5	58	9	12
The Amazing Mr. Malone - The Squealer	1959	43.7	6	0	15
Hennessy - Shore Patrol	1959	8.1	53	1	1

1959. Like the previous show, it may well have been filmed in front of an audience. It also has a laugh track, though this has been constructed in the editing. The Scale of Shot distribution is again markedly different from any of the other shows studied here, with its very heavy emphasis on Medium Close Up. This can be reasonably interpreted as sheer lack of imagination in staging from the writer/director, Don McGuire.

Videotape recording for television production began to be introduced from about 1957, but it was at first used in a limited way. This is exemplified by the fact that my next example, though from 1959, was still clearly shot live in real time. *The Squealer* is a self-contained episode from the *Amazing Mr. Malone* series shown on the ABC network in 1959. This show is a fairly extreme case of the long-take method of shooting live television, with an Average Shot Length of 43.7 seconds. In fact there are only 34 shots in the 23 minute length of the whole program. In this case many shots range over a series of scales as the camera and actors both move to change their relative positions during their length. In the works studied here, and indeed for films in general, you may be surprised to learn that there is not usually much change in shot scale during the length of shots, even in films that have a lot of camera movement. In such cases I apply an averaging process to get the value of shot scale assigned to each shot. This averaging process can have varying degrees of refinement, as seems appropriate.

However, in the long takes of *The Squealer* nearly all the shots range over most of the Scale of Shot during their length, so another method of getting an impression of the overall closeness of shot is appropriate. The method was originally suggested to me in another context by Elaine Burrows of the National Film and Television Archive. It involves making a determination of the Scale of Shot at fixed time interval increments over the whole length of the program. I chose to use an interval of five feet, (i.e. approximately 8 seconds)

for the 16 mm. print under examination. The result as tabulated shows that much less time is spent in closer shots than in the previous shows. In a few instances during the length of the drama the director keeps the long and complex shots going by having a character manage to reappear by going round the back of the camera after having walked out of the other side of the shot. The constraints of the method of shooting also mean that there are only two cuts from a camera angle to its reverse in this show. However, the makers did manage, against all odds, to create a montage sequence in real time. This was done by alternating shots from two cameras focussed on a series of changing objects in front of them, with the traditional joining dissolves made electronically.

Finally for the 1950s, I introduce two shows directed by the master himself from the *Alfred Hitchcock Presents* series, namely *Mr. Blanchard's Secret* (1956) and *The Perfect Crime* (1957). Both were shot on film, and both work with long takes, particularly *Mr. Blanchard's Secret*, which only has 50 shots in its 23 minute length. Although the bare statistics for camera movement are quite like those for the other long take shows from the 1950s, *The Squealer* and *How the Books Were Balanced*, the Scale of Shot distributions reveal differences, particularly in *Mr. Blanchard's Secret*, with its very heavy emphasis on Medium Shot and Medium Long Shot. Looked at in more detail, a good deal of the dialogue in *Mr. Blanchard's Secret* is covered in profile two-shots during the "camera holds" in the middle of the long takes. (A "camera hold" is when the camera is stationary during a shot that otherwise involves tracking or panning.) This is a rather unusual way of shooting for film or TV, though not completely unknown. On the other hand, in *The Perfect Crime* the long takes are panning shots interspersed between a series of faster reverse-angle sequences of shots. In this latter program, the camera is kept much lower than usual, and so the shots are angled upwards. Another noticeable way that it differs

Program Title	Year	Pan	Tilt	Pan with Tilt	Track	Track with Pan	Crane	Zoom	Zoom with Pan
Playhouse of the Stars - So Help Me	1952	37		25	20	16			
How the Books Were Balanced	1955		2	9	30	44	5		
Private Secretary	1956	44	2	4	28	20			
Alfred Hitchcock - Mr. Blanchard's Secret	1956	70		50	40	100			
Alfred Hitchcock - The Perfect Crime	1957	23		68	23	34			
The Amazing Mr. Malone - The Squealer	1959			59	59	147			
Hennessy - Shore Patrol	1959	37	3	9	3	28			

from the earlier Hitchcock show is in the lighting, which is beginning to go in the low key direction. I would guess that this, together with the low angle shots, is meant to be expressive, since the story is more of a straight sinister drama, whereas *Mr. Blanchard's Secret* is a comedy-drama. The uniquely large number of POV shots in this film is completely untypical for television, but is not unusual for Hitchcock's theatrical films. (A single straight-through viewing of some other Hitchcock-directed shows from the *Alfred Hitchcock Presents* series suggests that the special styles of the two programmes analysed here are untypical of his work for the series, which seems to be otherwise much more conventionally shot.)

I handle the objective treatment of camera movement by tabulating the numbers of shots with the different kinds of camera movement in each show, and again normalizing to the number that would be expected if the program in question contained 500 shots. The categories I use are Panning, Tilting, Panning and Tilting simultaneously, Tracking both without and with panning movements, movement involving the use of a camera crane, Zooming straight in or out, and Zooming with panning and/or tilting. Only panning or tilting movements of more than 10 degrees are counted, as small movements to keep the actors well framed as they change their position slightly are made automatically by camera operators, and in general need no special thought about their relation to the director's ideas of staging. The same applies to small movements of a foot or so in the position of the rolling camera pedestal or dolly during the shot, and also of the height of the camera.

The 'sixties, 'seventies and 'eighties

I only have a few samples of dramatic programs from the period between the end of the 'sixties and recent years. During this period videotape recording came to be more and more used in television production, but for most of this time American programs intended for the widest audience, both nationally and internationally, and hence having larger production budgets, continued to be made on film. This is the case for all my examples, which are from the old American shows thought sufficiently popular to be re-run on British television after I began this work in 1994.

In order, they are an episode from the *Burke's Law* series, *Who Killed the Paper Dragon?* (Marc Daniels, 1964), one from *Rawhide* entitled *Incident at Poco Tiempo* (Ted Post, 1960), one from *Gunsmoke* identified as *Fandango*, (James Landis, 1967), and one from *Columbo*, entitled *Blueprint for Murder* (Peter Falk, 1972). When after writing the first version of this piece I discovered that a few American researchers had also carried out work on the quantitative analysis of style in television

drama, I added the analysis of some programmes from *Hill Street Blues*, which have just been re-run on British television, for comparison with the results of Barbatsis and Guy. There are also two episodes of *Star Trek*, one being the first ever transmitted when the series started in 1966, *Man Trap*, which was directed by Marc Daniels, and the other *Turnabout Intruder* of 1969, directed by Herb Wallenstein. Apart from being made on film, all these shows were basically shot in the standard feature film manner, with most of the coverage coming from a single camera moved from set-up to set-up. This is indicated by the many shots in them that would have revealed the second and third cameras if they had been used, not to mention the fact that the lighting on the closer shots is adjusted for each set-up.

Looking at the tables and graphs, one can readily see clear differences between the styles of many of the programs. The statistics for the two Westerns are fairly similar. The Scale of Shot distributions cover the range more evenly than most of my examples, though both are shot rather closer in on balance than traditional cinema Westerns, and in particular lack Very Long Shots. The reason for this should be obvious. Both are cut reasonably fast, with ASL's of 6.2 seconds and 6.9 seconds. Both have fairly extensive use of reverse angle construction (50% and 56%), and some use of Point of View shots (4% of the shots in both). A possibly significant difference in the statistics is the emphasis on Medium Shots in the *Gunsmoke* episode, and their relative absence in the *Rawhide* episode, and another significant difference is connected with the use of camera movement, with the *Gunsmoke* episode using much more tracking with panning than the *Rawhide* episode.

The *Burke's Law* episode is closer to my earlier examples of television programmes shot on film in its Shot Scale distribution, and also in the proportion of reverse angles and POV shots used. (44% and 3% respectively). On the other hand, the episode of *Columbo* (1972), which happens to have been directed by its regular star, Peter Falk, has very obvious differences from the other shows. Although its ASL of 7.8 seconds is not much longer than the other dramas from this period, it is shot with more and different camera movement, with the action sometimes followed by panning and zooming. This corresponds to a fashion that developed in feature films in the 'seventies, led by such notable examples as Altman's film *M.A.S.H.* (1970). This style did not last into the 'eighties in any significant way in feature film making, and its inevitable fairly heavy emphasis on the more distant shots is not to be seen in any of my other examples, which are all from other decades.

The first two *Star Trek* episodes have a very close resemblance to each other in all respects, with the

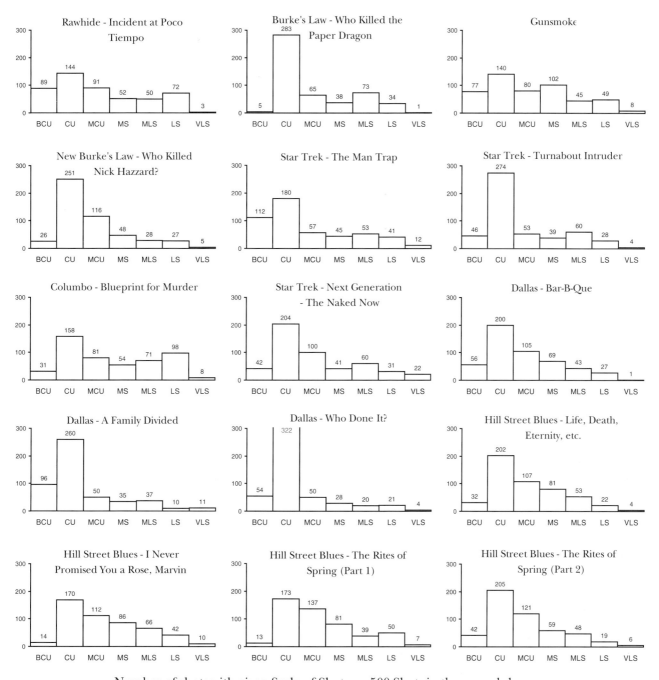

Number of shots with given Scale of Shot per 500 Shots in the named shows

small exception of the handling of the Close Ups. *Man Trap* has quite a lot more Big Close Ups than *Turnabout Intruder,* though lumping both kinds of Close Ups together in one category for the two episodes removes this anomaly. Since *Turnabout Intruder* was made two years later as the final episode from the third series, it may be simply a matter of different camera operators having different ideas about what is appropriate when a Close Up is called for. In the dialogue interchanges both episodes have many strings of successive shots with the same shot scale, which is something that the

better film-makers tend to avoid. The third episode is from much later, indeed from the revival of the series in 1987 as *Star Trek - The Next Generation*, with new actors, new sets, and no mini-skirts for the women. It is entitled *The Naked Now*, and directed by Paul Lynch. However, the cutting rate is pretty much the same, and the Scale of Shot used is not that different as well. You will also notice that there is a marked increase in the number of Insert shots and Point of View shots. This reflects a greater use of images on computer screens which are being watched by the actors than in the earlier programs. To some extent this change is also due to the particular plot of this episode, which involves another space ship and a star going nova. These last points are also responsible for the increase in the number of Very Long Shots. The style of staging has also changed a bit, with some play with staging in depth, which was largely absent from the earlier programs. The other change in the scene dissection is the reduction in camera movement, particularly panning and tracking with panning. This is fairly obvious to the technically informed eye even without the statistics, as is often the case for camera movement. Another aspect of this that does not show up in the statistics, because of the definition of panning I am using, is that there are less small framing movements, not only with respect to earlier episodes of *Star Trek*, but also compared to the other 1960s programs.

The *Hill Street Blues* episodes from 1981 that I have been able to analyse were three episodes directed by Gregory Hoblit, one of the producers of the series, namely *I Never Promised You a Rose, Marvin,* and *The Rites of Spring*, Parts 1 and 2, and *Life, Death, Eternity, etc.*, which was directed by Robert C. Thompson. As was remarked at the time by intelligent and perceptive people in the American TV profession, the essence of this innovative series was that it was the first soap opera set in a police station, and as was also remarked, many of its features, particularly the visual ones, were heavily influenced by the feature film *Fort Apache, the Bronx* (1981), which the producers of *Hill Street Blues* saw in preview.

The Scale of Shot distributions for the *Hill Street Blues* episodes bear a very close resemblance to each other, and the camera movement statistics, though not quite so close, are about as close to each other as is usual for films by the same director, even though there are two different directors involved. The same is almost as true for the three episodes of *Dallas*, which were made by three different directors. This corresponds to a generally held idea of the anonymity of television series direction, but it does not apply to some of the British series that we will come to shortly. The relative absence of Big Close Ups in *Hill Street Blues* when compared with other cop shows of the 'eighties is related to the extra amount of camera movement in the episodes of this series, though not absolutely determined by it. (My experience shows that generally each of the stylistic variables do not change by more than around 10% for films made by the same director around the same time. See my *Film Style and Technology*).

Program Title	Year	ASL	RA	POV	Inserts
Rawhide - Incident at Poco Tiempo	1960	6.5	50	4	2
Burke's Law - Who Killed the Paper Dragon?	1964	7.2	44	3	1
Gunsmoke - Fandango	1967	7.2	56	4	4
Columbo - Blueprint for Murder	1972	8.1	55	9	8
Dallas - Bar-B-Que	1978	6.4	57	3	1
Dallas - A Family Divided	1980	5.8	66	4	4
Dallas - Who Done It?	1980	6.0	70	2	2
Hill Street Blues - Life, Death, Eternity, etc.	1981	8.5	66	2	8
Hill Street Blues - I Never Promised You a Rose, Marvin	1981	6.5	64	3	12
Hill Street Blues - The Rites of Spring, Pt.1	1981	7.2	58	4	6
Hill Street Blues - The Rites of Spring, Pt.2	1981	8.3	40	9	2
Star Trek - Man Trap	1966	5.5	55	7	5
Star Trek - Turnabout Intruder	1969	4.8	40	1	1
Star Trek - Next Generation - The Naked Now	1987	5.2	41	11	11

Program Title	Year	Pan	Tilt	Pan with Tilt	Track	Track with Pan	Crane	Zoom	Zoom with Pan
Rawhide - Incident at Poco Tiempo	1960	32	1	22	1	4			
Burke's Law - Who Killed the Paper Dragon?	1964	18		8	20	29			
Gunsmoke - Fandango	1967	14	4	15	8	26	5		
Star Trek - Man Trap	1966	21	1	1	12	23			
Star Trek - Turnabout Intruder	1969	23	2	4	9	20		1	
Star Trek - Next Generation - The Naked Now	1987	9	1	11	8	12		1	
Columbo - Blueprint for Murder	1972	23	2	18	4	15		8	26
Dallas - Bar-B-Que	1978	18	2	5	14	23	1	9	2
Dallas - A Family Divided	1980	9	2	5	11	17		10	3
Dallas - Who Done It?	1980	23	1	12	13	22		14	13
Hill Street Blues - Life, Death, Eternity, etc.	1981	22		4	3	25		2	3
Hill Street Blues - I Never Promised You ...	1981	17		13	2	10		6	1
Hill Street Blues - The Rites of Spring, Pt.1	1981	26	5	11	5	13	1	5	11
Hill Street Blues - The Rites of Spring, Pt.2	1981	14		8	4	10		7	6

It is unfortunately not possible to make a direct comparison between my Scale of Shot results and those of Barbatsis and Guy for *Hill Street Blues*, as they do not specify where the dividing lines between their three categories of camera closeness lie. If they had, I could have made an approximate conversion from my categories to the ones they use.

Some of the other variables used by Barbatsis and Guy in their analyses are derived from the ideas of Herbert Zettl expounded in his book *Sight, Sound, Motion: Applied Media Aesthetics.* (Belmont, CA: Wadsworth, 1973), and these are obviously confusing, particularly those he uses in his own peculiar way, such as 'vectors'. The way Zettl uses his idea of 'z-axis' has also confused Barbatsis and Guy, and they indeed periodically drop this to return to the generally understood description of action being staged (or blocked) in depth, and of movement in depth towards and away from the camera. Although Zettl has apparently worked in television, he seems not to understand or know the standard technical terminology, and invents his own terms, such as 'fast fall-off lighting' to replace the standard 'soft lighting', and 'literal sounds' to replace 'sync. sounds'.

Television Style in the 'Nineties

Actually, the rather larger sample of television programs with which I am now going to deal are mostly from around 1994. Although I had already done the analysis of ancient television programs included above long ago, it was only in that year that I really turned my attention from films to TV, following an invitation from Sakari Salko of the Radio and Television Institute, which is part of the Finnish National Broadcasting Company (Oy Yleisradio AB), to give a series of classes on my work in style analysis. As preparation for this I analysed a number of British and American television programs of various kinds, and when in Finland I also analysed a few examples of their own production for comparison. The Finnish examples I analyse were shot on tape, with one exception, and so were the British programs, but all the American examples considered below were still shot on film.

To start with the American shows, *New Burke's Law* was an attempt at a revival of the old series, though now shot in colour, and featuring the eponymous principal character's son as his assistant, who now does all the running around. It was not popular in Britain any more than it was in the US, and is only included because it gave the opportunity for a direct comparison with the old original series. As the title of the episode under consideration, *Who Killed Nick Hazzard?* indicates, the format was otherwise intended to be the same. The Scale of Shot may be rather similar to that for the old series, (this is shown on page 267) but the ASL of 4.3

seconds shows that at least one thing has changed over the intervening thirty years. There has indeed been a general speeding up of the cutting rate in American television shows over this time, just as there has been in American feature films. However, this speeding up has *not* been led by television, as many people think. This is evident from comparison with the thousands of Average Shot Lengths I have collected for American films made since the Second World War. It is clear that the process was already under way in movies by the 1950s, and as mentioned above, the television shows I have studied from the 1950s are on the average cut slower than American films from the same period. It

appears that television cutting more or less caught up to film in the 1960s, when the most common ASL had decreased to about 6 seconds. Since then the process has continued fairly equally in both film and television. However, there are no signs so far of any television programs with ASLs below 3 seconds, whereas this is quite common with the more mindless action films of the present day, and even can be found in many comedies and ordinary dramas.

Although I have concentrated on crime shows throughout this work to provide a more meaningful comparison, I could not resist including an episode of *Baywatch*. This programme was so much more

Program Title	Year	ASL	RA	POV	Inserts
New Burke's Law - Who Killed Nick Hazzard?	1994	4.5	65	8	7
Baywatch - Skyrider	1994	3.5	36	11	6
NYPD Blue	1993	4.9	48	1	2
Homicide	1993	12.0	34	4	8
Roseanne	1993	8.0	11	0	3
Friends - The One Where Ross and Rachel...You Know	1996	5.8	37	0	5
The Bill - Mix and Match	1994	5.2	53	9	5
The Bill - Dealer Wins	1994	4.3	66	0	1
The Bill - No Job for an Amateur	1994	6.5	53	2	1
Coronation Street - David Penn	1994	9.8	49	0	2
Coronation Street - Romey Allison	1994	5.6	36	1	0
Coronation Street - Jeremy Summers	1994	7.7	50	3	1
EastEnders - Garth Tucker 25 & 27/1/94	1994	5.7	57	2	1
EastEnders - Bill Hays 1 & 3/2/94	1994	6.7	55	1	1
EastEnders - Brian Stirner 8 & 10/2/94	1994	6.0	65	1	0
Melrose Place	1999	4.0	70	3	5
Neighbours	1999	5.7	59	1	3
Brookside - Jeremy Summers	2000	4.0	66	3	1
Brookside - Tim Holloway 7&8/3/00	2000	6.8	68	8	2
Hirveä juttu	1993	5.3	39	2	2
Milkshake	1994	5.0	59	4	5
Tapulikylä	1992	10.8	28	0	3
Seven Brothers	1989	13.3	5	0	17

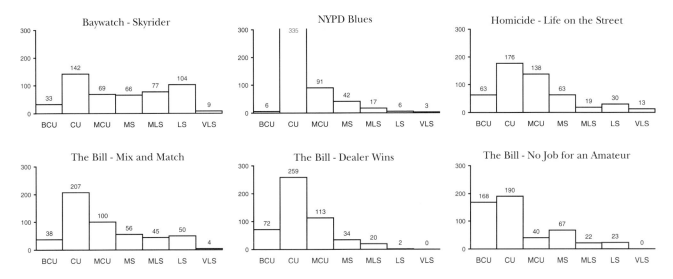

Number of shots with given Scale of Shot per 500 shots in the named shows

popular in Australia and Britain than in the US that our television companies were able to back a new series when the original show was about to be cancelled in the US. This new series is often titled "*New Baywatch*" to make the distinction. You will see that the Scale of Shot distribution for this is quite different from the police dramas, with a fairly even spread of types of shot across the range. This is not altogether surprising, given its outdoors setting. In other respects *Baywatch* is also different. It is the only present-day show that includes a fair number of crane shots, though these are confined to the scenes around the lifesaver's watch tower. Other types of camera movement are also used more in this *Baywatch* episode. In all these respects its statistics are more like those for the television Westerns, which is not all that surprising, given its setting in the wide outdoors. The cutting of *Baywatch* is also very distinctive, being appreciably faster than any other television program I have studied, with an ASL of 3.4 seconds.

In all the previous programs analysed, although most of the characters are taken over from previous episodes, in any specific episode there is one story, or dramatic chain of events, that begins during the episode, independent of any events in previous episodes, and then concludes by the end of the episode. This is reflected in the fact that each episode has its own separate title which identifies it. On the other hand, in a soap opera, or continuing serial, most plot events depend strongly on what has happened in previous episodes, and no major plots both begin and end within a single episode. Hence the episodes in a true serial are only identified by the date of their first transmission on television, and also by a production number used internally by the production company.

The two American police shows from the 1990s are of course a continuation of the *Hill Street Blues* model, in which although there is always one plot that begins and ends within the episode, the actions of the continuing characters in the series are affected by what has happened in previous episodes, and their own conflicts and problems are not necessarily resolved within the episode.

Everyone is vaguely aware of the stylistic peculiarities of *NYPD Blue* and *Homicide - Life on the Street*, though I have never seen a really accurate description of what those peculiarities are. The "agitated camera" effect often mentioned is produced in different ways in the two shows. In the case of *NYPD Blue*, most of the filming is done with the camera on a fixed support – either a dolly or rolling pedestal, and small pans and tilts are made by the operator that are not related to the movements of the characters. Ordinarily, as mentioned above, camera operators make small panning and tilting adjustments when the characters move a bit within the frame, and these are referred to as framing movements or framing adjustments. Camera operators are taught to make them automatically, so as to follow the standard ideas about good composition for the image. These framing movements naturally tend to move more or less in the same direction as the actor who moves within the frame. But in the case of *NYPD Blue*, the small panning and tilting movements are made when the characters are not moving, or they go the wrong way, like the sort of thing one might expect from an untrained camera operator with brain damage. They might be called "anti-framing movements". The other strange thing about their application, at any rate in the episode studied, is that although they are going on most of the time, regardless of the dramatic context, they stop during the most intense dramatic scene in the program. The general stylistic effect is analogous to delivering all the dialogue in a play at a shout. Since these anti-framings in *NYPD Blue* are only rotations of several degrees, just like ordinary framing movements, they are excluded from my tabulation of camera movements.

In the case of *Homicide*, the agitated effect springs from two sources. One is that nearly all the shooting is done with the camera moving in hand-held long takes around the participants in the scene. The fact that *Homicide* is shot in this way shows up in the Average Shot Length of 11.5 seconds, which is much greater than any of the other contemporary television programs include here. It is also shown by the excessive numbers of tracks, either with or without panning, that are indicated in my tabulation of camera movements. The hand-held camera produces a certain amount of wobble in the image, but the other source of agitation is that alternate takes shot in this way are often joined

together in the middle of their duration without regard for any matching in the position of the actors across the cut. Inevitably, with two or more actors moving within the shot as well as the cameraman moving, no-one is in exactly the same position at the same point within successive takes, so when a cut is made to go over to the continuation of the scene in the second take at a specific instant in the action, there is a noticeable jump of the actor's positions within the frame. This is exactly the kind of discontinuity editors ordinarily seek to avoid when they are following the standard principles of keeping the cuts "invisible", so it is a kind of "anti-editing", and adds on to the general agitated effect of the constantly moving camera.

The British police series, *The Bill*, which was the third most popular continuing series program on British TV in 1995, has probably been influenced by the recent American examples, but it is more conservative in its methods. Like all modern cop shows, it includes a fair amount of location work, though about half the action takes place in the police station, which is a

Program Title	Year	Pan	Tilt	Pan with Tilt	Track	Track with Pan	Crane	Zoom	Zoom with Pan
New Burke's Law - Who Killed Nick Hazzard?	1994	9	2	8	8	19			2
Baywatch - Skyrider	1994	47	12	11	19	26	8	4	3
NYPD Blue	1994	61	2	42	1	6		4	4
Homicide	1994	44	10	44	17	117	2		
The Bill - Mix and Match	1994	28		26	11	38			
The Bill - Dealer Wins	1994	17		6	5	16			
The Bill - No Job for an Amateur	1994	20		22	2	59	2		
Coronation Street - David Penn	1994	29	2		24	47			4
Coronation Street - Romey Allison	1994	10		6	2	7			
Coronation Street - Jeremy Summers	1994	11		11	10	27			8
Eastenders - Garth Tucker 25 & 27/1/94	1994	10	1	9	4	14			1
EastEnders - Bill Hays 1 & 3/2/94	1994	12		4	19	22			1
Eastenders - Brian Stirner 8 & 10/2/94	1994	12		3	19	18		1	
Neighbours	1999	10	1	6	3	27	1		
Melrose Place	1999	4	1	3	11	6	4	2	2
Brookside - Jeremy Summers	2000	14	1	4	1	7		1	
Brookside - Tim Holloway	2000	34	4	17	5	18			

series of standing sets in the studio. Of all the programs analysed, the statistics of this show seems to me to be the most influenced by its subject matter and by the preferences of its different directors. The studio scenes include some sections shot with multiple cameras, but a good deal of the location shooting is done with a single camera, and indeed with hand-held camera moves, but not in the obtrusive way used in *Homicide*. That is, the tracking shots are used to follow the characters, rather than circling round them. Just how much hand-held camera is used appears to vary with the director. The first two episodes, *Mix and Match* and *Dealer Wins*, were directed by Charles Beeson, and *No Job for an Amateur* was directed by Riita Leena Lynn. You can see that there is a strong degree of resemblance between the first two episodes in most respects. The small differences can be attributed to the different content of the stories. *Mix and Match* involves a fair amount of surveillance of

suspects, and hence the POV shots, whereas most of the location time in *Dealer Wins* is spent in court scenes. This also explains the fact that the Scale of Shot distribution is skewed towards more close shots in *Dealer Wins*. As you can see from the camera movement tabulation, *No Job for an Amateur* contains much more tracking with panning than the other two episodes. However, this is still much less than that in *Homicide*, and in any case is used for following moving people. These long tracking shots are also the reason for the longer ASL. The other significant difference in the direction of this episode is the large number of Big Close Ups.

The power of my methods to reveal individual directorial style meets its strongest challenge in dealing with soap operas. These are the only sort of television drama which derives their form from radio programmes rather than from movies. They do not have real action scenes, and also largely lack true love

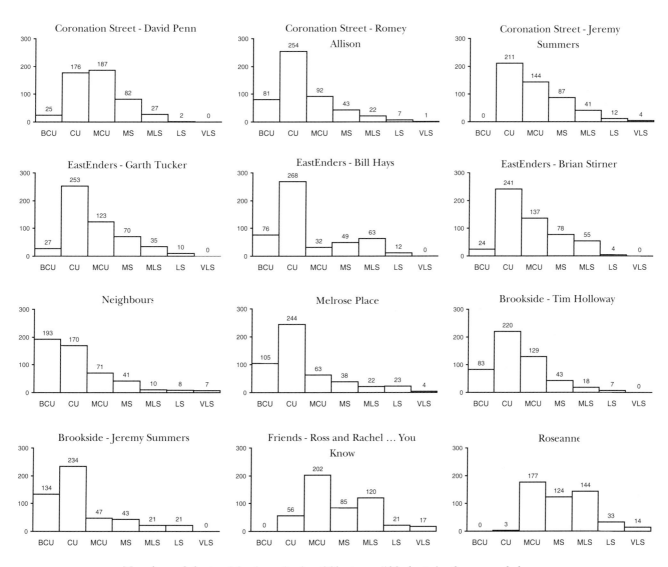

Number of shots with given Scale of Shot per 500 shots in the named shows

scenes and comic scenes. Thus the full alternation of type of scene found in ordinary films and TV drama is absent, though there is still some variation in tension depending on whether the scenes show a confrontation or simply a communication of information between two characters. The basic dramatic content of most scenes involves the interaction of only two characters, though other characters may be present and say things. This gives TV soap operas a very simple and uniform dramatic structure. The producers and editors of British soap operas are aware of this feature of the basic construction of their shows, and do their best to make the scenes more complex, but they mostly fail in this endeavour.

Of the British examples I have chosen to analyse, *EastEnders,* and *Coronation Street*, were, and still are, the most popular programmes on British TV. Like all TV soap operas, they are shot under great constraints from the standing sets which are used for all the episodes, the speed of production, and the general uniformity of characters and stories involved. In these shows, the sets are also of realistic size, which puts a further limitation on camera placement. In 1994 *EastEnders* was being made and shown on the basis of two half hour episodes a week. These were shot back to back, with the same director, and usually with the same scriptwriter for both. The shooting took roughly four days, which in the old Hollywood days would represent the kind of schedule in force at the lowest end of B-movie production. For the next week's episodes there would be a different director and scriptwriter, but the various plot lines would be continued into the new episodes. A similar procedure was followed in the production of *Coronation Street* and *Brookside*. Because of this, I have lumped the two weekly episodes of these programs together as one unit in my analysis.

The basic difference between the work of the three directors who made the episodes of *EastEnders* that I have analysed is that Tucker's work is appreciably more static, with less camera movement, and rather more reverse angle cutting. On the other hand, Bill Hays and Brian Stirner have far more camera movement. Although the figures for their camera movement are almost identical, the way they use panning and tracking is slightly different. The longer ASL in Bill Hays' episodes largely arises from his use of a number of very long takes on exteriors covered with tracking and panning. His way of staging when using fixed camera setups is somewhat more complex than those of the other directors too, and there is a greater sense of variation in scale and arrangement from shot to shot in his work. In fact, his scene dissection is beginning to be like the work of a good film director from the High Hollywood period of the 1930s and 1940s. The scale of shot distributions for Tucker and Stirner are very

similar, and more like the usual TV kind of distribution for dramas on city subjects. Hays has a slightly more peculiar distribution, with a peak at MLS instead of the smooth fall away from CU towards the more distant shots. This corresponds to the complexity of his groupings of the actors in a proportion of his shots. Nevertheless, like the others, most of his episodes are conducted in strings of alternating Close Ups of the two participants in a dialogue.

Coronation Street has been running for 30 years, but even so there is some stylistic variation visible between directors. As you can see from the Scale of Shot distributions, the two episodes directed by David Penn are shot a little further back on the average, departing from the standard TV drama profile with more Medium Close Ups than usual. Connected with this is his use of quite a lot of camera movement, though this is done in a rather dull way, with most of the tracks straight in and out. However, Penn does revive a trick with seventy years of history behind it in the cinema. This is to start some scenes with a close Insert shot of an object, and then pull the camera back to reveal the whole scene, rather than showing all or most of the scene at the very beginning. The episodes directed by Romey Allison have the most static and fixed camera of any program studied here, though to go with this they have the fastest cutting of any of the *Coronation Street* episodes. On the other hand, although the Jeremy Summers episodes have less camera movement than the Penn episodes, the individual camera moves he does call for sometimes have more complexity when examined in detail. For instance, he has the camera track round a static group of actors seated around a table, which is the kind of noticeable flourish that none of the other soap directors in this sample try.

A subtle but clear difference in house style between *Coronation Street* and *EastEnders* lies in camera height, which tends to be more around chest and head height in *Coronation Street*, whereas the camera is often down towards waist height in *EastEnders*. Also, *EastEnders* episodes, whoever the director, have more adjustments of camera pedestal position (i.e. short tracks of three or four feet) than *Coronation Street*. In this, the style of *EastEnders* is more closely related to a camera usage which started in 1940s Hollywood, and continued into the other TV programs from the 1960s that I have analysed.

My most recent analyses are of episodes from *Brookside*, which has ben running on Channel 4 in Britain from 1992. Initially this production was unique in that even the interiors were shot on location, in a precinct of small new suburban houses specially bought for the purpose by the producers. This produced special features in the style of shooting, but nowadays some interiors for this series are shot on studio sets, and its uniqueness in this respect has seriously weakened. The other peculiarity in the shooting of this soap opera is that multiple camera shooting is not in general used, though it is shot on videotape. The most obvious feature in the style of this show when compared to the other British series is that there has been a substantial increase in the use of Big Close Ups. This is made particularly evident, since the pair of episodes from 7 and 8 March 2000, which I have lumped together as usual, were directed by Jeremy Summers, who had previously worked on *Coronation Street*. His shooting of the episodes from *Coronation Street* that I have analysed included no Big Close Ups whatever, while on *Brookside* he has 83 BCUs per 500 shots. On the other hand, Summers has developed his use of camera movement even further, to some of the highest levels for television, and beyond this (which is not picked up by my statistics), he also uses much staging in depth within the shots, in a way that neither he nor anyone else had been doing previously in soaps. Both these stylistic features help to push up his shot lengths to a somewhat higher level than seen in TV made during the last year or so by other directors. These comparisons between the styles of the British soaps show the value of using more finely graded steps in the Scale of Shot analysis, as differences like the peak at Medium Close Up in David Penn's episodes of *Coronation Street* and differences within the range of Close Up and Big Close Up in some of the others would have been lost if I had used just a tri-partite division of Scale of Shot.

Foreign comparisons in the soap opera genre are provided by episodes from the Australian *Neighbours* and the American *Melrose Place*, both first shown in 1998 on their native TV channels. For *Neighbours*, two

successive 23 minute episodes, both directed by the same director, Tony Osicka, though written by different writers, Margaret Wilson and John Upton, are lumped together to make up the unit of analysis, just as with the British programmes. The fifty minute *Melrose Place* episode was written by Frank South and Darren Star, and directed by Richard Lang.

I also present figures for three standard Finnish television programs, *Hirveä juttu*, *Milkshake*, and *Tapulikylä*, all made for YLE. (There are also a commercial broadcast channel and a Swedish language channel in Finland besides the two state-funded channels run by YLE.) *Hirveä juttu* (1993) was a family comedy series, which uses the not completely unknown format of a slightly eccentric family sardonically observed by their daughter. *Milkshake* (1994) was a series involving the doings of a group of young people working in a hamburger bar. All shows conform fairly closely to contemporary international standards in nearly all their formal aspects, though *Tapulikylä* is cut a lot slower, and indeed is a cruder piece of work than the other two. This last series deals with family dramas in one of the new housing estates in big Finnish cities, as indicated by its title, which is the local term for such places, and I have analysed episode No. 7, which was first transmitted on 21 December 1992. For interest's sake I have also included the first episode of a twelve part adaptation of a novel made on film for YLE. This is *Seitsemän veljestä (Seven Brothers)* (12 December 1989), taken from the great Finnish national classic by Aleksis Kivi, which was first published in 1870. The novel deals with the life and passions of a large rural family in what was at that time a newly realistic manner. As you can see from my figures for the first hour long section of

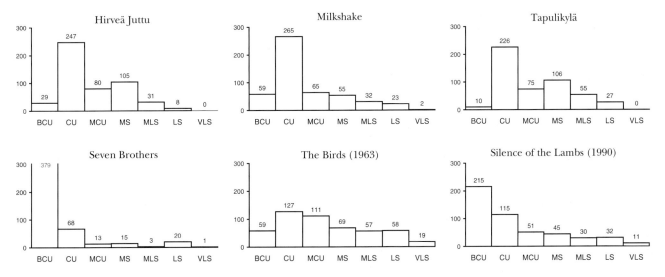

Number of shots with given Scale of Shot per 500 shots in the named shows

this version, it is shot in an extremely unusual manner, almost entirely in long sequences of Big Close Ups. The result of this is of course that it is very difficult to tell where the various characters are at any point in the film, or indeed who or what they are looking at. Since the actors also spend most of their time glowering rather than talking, I would say that this is a unique experiment that is unlikely to be repeated.

Conclusions

On the basis of the objective information so far available, it does indeed seem that the style of television series drama with an urban setting is more stereotyped than that of cinema films of the same kind. This is obvious if you contrast the wide variation amongst Scale of Shot distributions and Average Shot Lengths, not to mention the figures for feature films displayed in my book showing the use of reverse angle cutting, inserts, and POV shots, with the information for TV programmes given here. The close resemblance between the British soap opera episodes in this respect is not surprising, but these in their turn resemble a far-flung example like *NYPD Blue*, and indeed also the Finnish series *Milkshake, Tapulikylä,* and *Hirveä Juttu*. The resemblance even extends back to the comedy episode of *Private Secretary* from 1956. The main variations in Scale of Shot seem to depend on genre, with the Westerns resembling each other in this respect. The very small usage of Point of View shots and inserts is also general, though as already remarked, both are due to the production pressure of TV, which affects even those series which were shot on film. Since all television cameras have been fitted with zoom lenses as standard from the 1970s to the present it is surprising that there are hardly any zoom shots in the episodes considered. The only exception to this is the episode of *Columbo* from 1972. I would say that in this case the makers were responding to the short-lived

fashion for the use of the zoom to cover action which started in the late 1960s in cinema films. Nowadays, as in cinema films, the zoom lens is only used in television as a convenient variable focus lens, so that the framing can be changed quickly *between* shots, not during them. However, there *is* occasional use of the zoom to make a very small tightening of the framing during the shot in some contemporary television drama and comedy, but I ignore this in my statistics, just as I ignore small panning movements to reframe.

Nevertheless, as I have demonstrated, if you dig deep enough there are some more subtle differences in style between the work of some directors in television who are working in the same area at the same time. And there appears to be a little more differentiation in directorial style in British examples than in the American series for which I have examples showing the work of more than one director.

In general, television drama style has followed behind the changes in cinema film style, such as the general increase in cutting rate, up to just before the present. The sole exceptions to this are the special shooting style developed in *NYPD Blue* and *Homicide - Life on the Street*. Here for the first time TV leads film, as the peculiar combination of hand-held tracking combined with mis-matched cuts used in *Homicide* was adopted by Lars von Trier for his cinema feature *Breaking the Waves* (1996), and Bertolucci's *Besieged* (1998) also shows traces of influence from this source.

Despite some exceptions, there is probably also a tendency for comedy series to be shot from further back than drama programs, and I have included figures for an episode from *Roseanne* (the 1993 Thanksgiving Day episode) and a 1996 *Friends* (The One Where Ross and Rachel ...You Know) to justify this suggestion. Comedy is always cut a bit slower on the average than drama, whatever the period, though of course comedy shot on film for TV in the 1950s will obviously be cut a lot faster than live TV drama of the same period.

In 2001 the London International Film School acquired a new director, Ben Gibson, who re-branded the institution as the London Film School, and was eager to raise the school's visibility. As one result of this, the film school sent me to a conference of the Association of Media Practitioners in Education being held over a weekend in Southampton. This was the first and only time the school funded my attendance at a conference. I presented some of my work on television, and was asked to submit an article based on it the association's periodical, the *Journal of Media Practice*. I cut the preceding piece in half, eliminating the material on old television programs. This appeared in Volume 2, Number 2 of 2001. The full-length original which you have just read is set in ITC New Baskerville, as in the magazine.

The most revelatory of the Pordenone *Giornate* had been in 1989, when the subject was Russian cinema from before the revolution. These films, most of which survived as original negatives, had been kept hidden in the Soviet archives. A group of film historians in Moscow had been getting them printed up, with new intertitles, and Yuri Tsivian, who was involved in this, organized the Pordenone screenings. One might surmise that the motive of the Communist authorities for keeping them out of sight was to conceal the fact that there had been a substantial Russian film industry before Communism, but seeing the films suggested another possibility as well. The streets of Moscow in these old films are shiny and clean, with neatly dressed people circulating in them, in sharp comparison with the run-down, dirty, decayed and scruffy streets, buildings, and people visible in Russian films of the 'twenties such as *Mr. West in the Land of the Bolsheviks*. My other thoughts about these pre-revolutionary films can be read in *Film Style and Technology*. And Yuri Tsivian's truly excellent presentation of them can be read in *Silent Witnesses: Russian Films 1908-1919*, published by the British Film Institute and Edizioni Biblioteca dell' Immagine in 1989.

Yuri Tsivian is actually a Latvian, and some years later, after the fall of Communism, in 1995, he organized a summer school on acting in the silent cinema back home in Riga. The event was run with the help of other enthusiastic young people centered on the Riga Film Museum, and it recruited, as the speakers at the conference, the usual small gang from the English-speaking world who were really interested in researching early cinema, plus some not-so-usual others.

I put in a couple of weeks thought on how one could best analyse acting, and this led to the following notes and quotations, which I took with me to extemporize on.

How I think about acting.

Broader and less broad.

Comparisons with specific kinds of movement.

Dance of various kinds and mime.

Actors directed by 3 classes of instructions.

     1. "More" or "Less"

     2. "Don't do that" or "Do this".

     3. "Feel this emotion."

This approach has been used since early times, e.g. Gish on Griffith.

Examples: *Physician of the Castle*, *The Mill Girl*

Melodrama poses. Slides.

Naturalism. Quotes.

1913 films. *The Substitute Stenographer*, *Good For Evil*.

The Movies, Mr. Griffith, and Me

p.36

    "Gentlemen," he said in a courtly manner that we were to discover was characteristic, "These are the Gish sisters, Miss Lillian and Miss Dorothy. We will rehearse the story of two girls trapped in an isolated house while thieves are trying to get in and rob the safe." He stared at us. "You're not twins, are you? I can't tell you apart." He strode out of the room and returned with two ribbons, one red and the other blue: "Take off your black bows, and tie these on. Blue for Lillian, red for Dorothy. Now, Red, you hear a strange noise. Run to your sister. Blue, you're scared, too. Look toward me, where the camera is. Show your fear. You hear something. What is it? You're two frightened children, trapped in a lonely house by these brutes. They're in the next room"

Griffith turned to one of the men: "Elmer, pry open a window. Climb into the house. Kick down the door to the room that holds the safe. You are mean! These girls are hiding thousands of dollars. Think of what *that* will buy! Let your avarice show – *Blue*, you hear the door breaking. You run in panic to bolt it."

"What door," I stammered.

"Right in front of you! I know there is no door, but pretend there is. Run to the telephone. Start to use it. No one answers. You realize the wires have been cut. Tell the camera what you feel. Fear, *more fear*. Look into the lens! Now you see a gun coming through the hole as he knocks the stovepipe to the floor. Look scared, I tell you."

 It was not difficult to obey, We were practically paralyzed with fright.

"No, that's not enough! Girls, hold each other. Cower in the corner".

Whereupon he pulled a real gun from his pocket and began chasing us around the room, shooting it off. We did not realize that he was aiming at the ceiling.

 "He's gone mad!" I thought as we scurried around the room, looking frantically for an exit.

Suddenly the noise died. Mr. Griffith put away his gun. He was smiling, evidently pleased with the results. "That will make a wonderful scene," he said. "You have expressive bodies. I can use you. Do you want to work for me? Would you like to make the picture we just rehearsed?"

p.86

 Although Griffith had a tendency to exhort and exaggerate during rehearsals, he grew quiet when filming started. He usually put his head as close as possible to the lens to view the angle of each shot. Then he would sit down on his wooden chair and nervously twirl his ring or jingle a handful of coins in his pocket. He would shift the coins from one hand to the other. It reminded me, after I had travelled through the Near East, of the amber prayer beads men there use to keep their hands occupied.

Sometimes he would suggest in that beautiful commanding voice

"Not so much, not so much. Less, less – simple, simple, *true*. Don't act it, feel it; feel it, don't act it" And then, "more, more, we need *more*!"

And we knew what *more* meant, just as we knew what *less* meant. As the scene unfolded, we were always fearful lest the camera catch us acting.

If the actors were especially good, he would relax in his chair, his smile benevolent, and say in that resonant voice: "Now, that's what I call acting! Did you see that, all of you? Did you learn something?"

He had various ways of coping when the actor could not project a mood. Once when Mary Pickford was still with the company, he wanted her to register anger. But Mary was in a sunny mood; it was evident to him that the camera would not get the desired result. In the cast was a handsome young Irishman named Owen Moore. He was a good actor, but Griffith began to cast aspersions on both his acting and his character. Mary had a quick temper and great loyalty. She turned the torrent of her actor against Mr. Griffith.

"Shoot it, Billy," Mr. Griffith ordered

Later he apologized to her. When he singled out this man for criticism he knew that Mary and Owen Moore were secretly engaged to be married.

The two pairs of films mentioned in my notes were intended to illustrate the range of acting styles in silent cinema in 1907-8 and 1913. In the event, I could not get them all to the conference, and made do with *The Mill Girl*, a Vitagraph film from 1907, and *The Substitute Stenographer*, which was an Edison film from 1913. Although I had also collected extracts from the thoughts of stage actors and directors of the latter part of the nineteenth century on acting, I did not use them in the end.

It seems to me that the whole matter can be treated very simply, as follows on the next page:

ACTING IN THE MOVIES — AND ELSEWHERE

Acting is based on real human behaviour, but the movements of body, face, and voice are exaggerated to a greater or lesser degree. Actors are trained to control these degrees of exaggeration, and it is indeed not particularly difficult to control a more or less continuous range of movement and distortion of the face and body to represents degrees of intensity of emotion. Hence the primary method of directing actors, telling them to give "more" or "less".

As the movements and positions of the body become more extreme, and hence further removed from natural movements and positions, they can be stylized in various ways. The most obvious of these stylizations of movement relates to actual ritualistic movement, or dance of various kinds, principally ballet. In formal dance the limbs tend to be fully stretched and extended, in a way that does not happen in natural movement. Ballet adds to this a simple geometricalization of positions,

Mr. O. Smith as the Wolf of the Sea

and stylized forms. These can be seen in illustrations of the period, which would seem to fairly accurately represent what actors actually did.

The Factory Lad
Surrey 1834

For instance, this photograph from 1871 of a scene in *The Bells* shows that the great Henry Irving really did that kind of thing in the nineteenth century.

Bells, Act II and Act III (Lyceum, 1871)

with attempts to make movements and positions straight forward and back, and straight out to each side, insofar as the human body is capable of it. Since training in dance has long been part of the education of actors, this style has long ago got into the poses of legitimate stage acting. In particular, nineteenth century melodrama, which had the aim of affecting the emotions of the audience to the greatest extent, by any means possible, inevitably pushed acting poses into extreme

An 1890 production of Blue Jeans, *with the villain in dark clothes and the hero wearing standard hero dress.*

1890

These melodrama poses were standardized, and can be seen in many early films from all countries. The film *The Mill Girl* was based on a very successful American stage melodrama from the turn of the century of the same title, and contains quite a number of these melodrama poses executed by the hero. The villain also gets in one or two, including the notorious moustache-curling gesture when eyeing his

female prey, but everyone else in the film gives fairly standard naturalistic performances, particularly the heroine. By the way, the hero wears the standard melodrama hero's costume, with light-coloured trousers and brief jacket and neckerchief, as established long before in the early nineteenth century, while everyone else in the film wears standard 1907 work clothes.

The second method of directing actors, which is to show them by example exactly what is wanted, or not wanted, is not much used, as actors dislike being instructed in this way. Nevertheless, sometimes it is necessary, and most actors will put up with it. Ernst Lubitsch was famous for demonstrating exactly what to do to all his actors, all of the time, but he was fairly exceptional in that respect.

The third method, which is to convey to actors what they should be feeling, is more acceptable, and has become vastly elaborated in the last seventy years as "the Method"; the American derivative of Stanislavsky's directing technique. Stanislavsky's original intention was to achieve greater naturalism, but nowadays the result is something well removed from average human behaviour. Actors clearly identify themselves as Method actors, or otherwise. My advice, for what it is worth, is to avoid Method actors, unless you need out-of-control semi-psychotic intensity in a particular role.

All of the above three methods I have laid out are being used by D.W. Griffith in Lillian Gish's description of him at work, but of course he did not invent them. They were used in the theatre from long, long ago.

You may notice that there is actually a fourth method described in Gish's anecdotes. This involves tricking the actor into feeling an emotion. Although it makes for a good story, of the kind actors love, it is not much use when you have to get a second take. Nevertheless, it may be necessary when directing non-actors, and in particular, children.

That's all there is to it.

As it turned out, it was just as well that I had not fixed exactly what I was going to say, as the previous speakers at the conference on the day I delivered my piece over-ran their allotted time, and I was asked, not for the first, or indeed last time, to cut my address down. I don't remember exactly what I said, and I didn't get quite all the above points in, but the version printed here is near enough. There were plans to publish a collection of the contributions from the speakers, but nothing came of it.

The most important feature of the event was descriptions of systems used for training actors in movement in the early twentieth century. As well as being described, these were also demonstrated with actors. The Delsarte system and Dalcroze's Eurythmics were shown, though my opinion is that these had no significant *visible* effect on film acting. But much the most important was an exposition of Meyerhold's method of body training for his Biomechanics system of movement, given by Mel Gordon, an experienced actor and director who teaches drama at the University of California. He has also researched and published articles about other forms of stylized movement used in the theatre over the last few centuries. At the Riga summer school he trained up a group of local actors to demonstrate the exercises used in this technique, which was quite an achievement, as some of them had rather poor movement ability. The Meyerhold exercises are based on miming cycles of natural movement, such as swinging a sledge-hammer around, up, and down onto its target. Four poses through the cycle are fixed and given the numbers 1 to 4. Then the instructor calls out the numbers in non-sequential order, and the student has to go immediately from one position to another as ordered. This creates a very unnatural sequence of movements, and certainly exercises some different muscles. These exercises were performed to music in the same way that ballet exercises are. Strangely, these Meyerhold exercises somehow have become attached to the Stanislavsky method in the United States, though not as an essential part of it.

In *Film Style and Technology* I mentioned the connection between Meyerhold's stage work and some features of Ei-

senstein's silent films, but I did not illustrate this point. So here are some pictures to make quite clear what I was talking about. In his production of Crommelynck's play *le Cocu magnifique* in 1922, Meyerhold had his cast give stylized perform-

ances that entwined them into the stylized set, and Eisenstein took some of this approach into his first feature film, *Strike*. In it, real industrial structures neatly substituted for Popova's constructivist set used in the production of the play.

*On the left is a fight scene from Meyerhold's
production of* The Magnificent Cuckold, *and
above is a shot from Eisenstein's* Strike.

*Traces of Meyerholdian
contortions occasionally surface
in Eisenstein's subsequent silent
films, for instance in the scene of
the tractor driver dealing with
a breakdown towards the end of*
The Old and the New, *but then
disappear from his subsequent
output.*

Eisenstein has so thoroughly analysed his own work that there is not a great deal more to be usefully said about it, but there are still a few new points to be brought out about the idiosyncrasies of his visual style. One is his taste for bilaterally symmetrical compositions, and as a corollary to that, his use of three similar figures or objects that line up evenly across the frame. The first example on the left is from *Strike*, and the next four are all from *Que viva Mexico!*

You may notice that the contents of these frame enlargements from *Que viva Mexico!* are not perfectly symmetrical. This is because they were shot with a Debrie camera with the full silent aperture, but with the expectation that they would be used to make a sound film with the sound track running down a narrow area on the left of the frame.

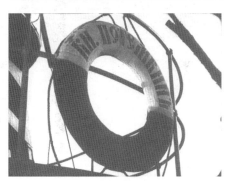

Eisenstein did not put such laterally symmetrical shots one after another in his editing, because the basic principle of his construction was, as he said himself, a strong contrast (or conflict) between successive images. This comes out well in the sequence of shots at the right from *Battleship Potemkin*, where the basic geometricality of the main shapes is evident. This sequence is also an early example of what Eisenstein later called "intellectual montage", but that is another matter.

UP AND DOWN AND BACK AND FORTH

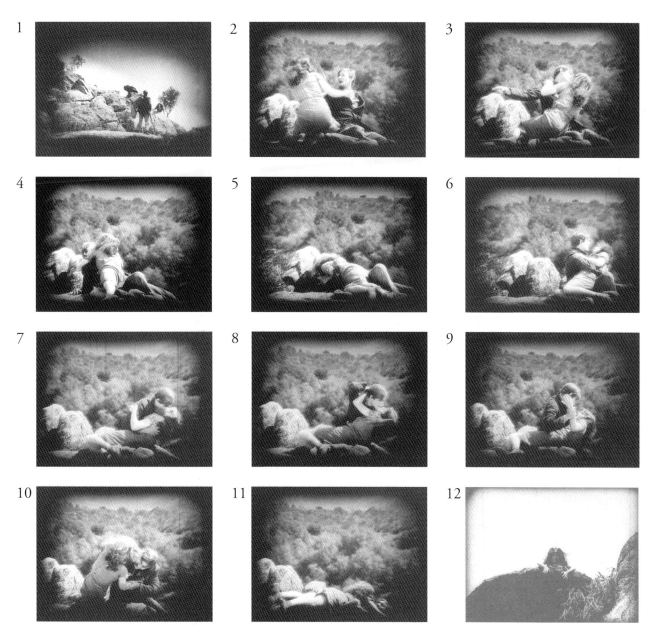

Edmund Goulding was the first American master of the long take whose stagings derived from the theatrical tradition. On the stage, a whole scene is one long take, and the art of staging is to make certain that the audience's attention is directed to the right actor at the right moment. Goulding who was born in 1891, became a child actor on the London stage, and then rapidly made a career as actor, writer, and director. He joined the army in 1914, was wounded, and invalided out. He then went to the United States, and got into movies by selling film companies some of his plays. After more

work as a screenwriter, he first directed in 1925, adapting a 1924 Broadway success, *Sun-Up*. The most notable scene in this film is illustrated above. Set amongst hill-billies, the story has Rufus (Conrad Nagel) being called up for service in World War I. As he leaves down the mountain, his girl-friend Emmy (Pauline Starke) runs after him to try to prevent him leaving. She catches up with him (Frame 1), and clasps him to her. Shown in a new angle, they collapse onto the rocks, and flow through a series of embraces in various positions as lust and duty struggle for the upper hand. (Frames 2-11) This goes on in one continuous shot for about a minute, till Rufus slips free down the rock face, leaving Emmy hanging despairingly over the edge seen in a new shot (Frame 12). This scene is exceptional for its length in the film taken as a whole, for *Sun-Up* has an Average Shot Length (ASL) of 7.5 seconds. At the end of his career, Goulding created an a pair of even more virtuosic horizontal scenes in *Teenage Rebel* (1956)

However, in the 'thirties, when he was directing at MGM, Goulding really developed his long takes, and set a world record for the decade with *The Flame Within* (1935), which has an ASL of 46 seconds. The nearest rival from Europe is Sacha Guitry's *Faisons un rêve* (1936), with an ASL of 36 seconds. His only real competition in Hollywood was from John Stahl, until Cukor and other joined the long take craze at the end of the 'thirties. In comparison with Stahl, my impression is that Goulding kept his takes going rather more by moving the actors around with respect to the camera, whereas Stahl

was more inclined to keep the take going with the actors in profile two-shot.

Goulding went to Warners in 1937, and there the producers and editors put a damper on his long take inclinations, though his films were on the slower side of the Warners cutting norm. However, when he moved over to Twentieth Century-Fox in 1943, he returned to the long take, despite efforts by Daryl Zanuck, the studio boss, to restrain him.

A good example of how this sort of long take is carried out can be given from *The Razor's Edge* (1946), which has an ASL of 28.0 seconds. The story of the film starts in 1920, and concerns Larry Darrell, who has returned from serving in the American Air Force in the First World War, and is reluctant to settle back into his wealthy milieu and marry his fianceé Isabel. Trying to find more meaning in life, he goes to Paris, where Isabel follows him, to try to persuade him to come home. She goes with him to his room above a cheap restaurant.

Shot 1.

(Seen from outside looking at the window of Larry's room. Larry opens the window from the inside, and he and Isabel look out through it.)

(They turn to face each other as the camera tracks in.)

ISABEL: This is where you live?
LARRY: You don't like it?
ISABEL: No.
LARRY: It's alright. It's convenient. How about a cup of coffee?

(He walks towards the back, she crosses from right to left and looks out of the window.)

ISABEL: How can you bear to sit here in this backwash? When America's living through the most glorious adventure the world has ever known.

(Track in)
Isabel: You have been away a year now. A whole year out of your life. You just can't go on moping forever. Or can you?
LARRY: It's possible. (he smiles)
ISABEL: And what about me? Am I of no importance to you at all?
LARRY: You are of great importance to me, I said I love you, and I want you to marry me.
ISABEL: When, in ten years?
LARRY: No, now, as soon as possible.
ISABEL: On what?
LARRY: I've got 3000 dollars a year.

ISABEL: Oh, Larry. (he backs away into the room)
LARRY: Lots of people live on a great deal less.
ISABEL: But I don't want to live on 3000 dollars a year. I never have, and I don't see why I should.

(She walks to back of room)

CUT TO:
Shot 2
LARRY: (voice over) We could go down to Capri for our honeymoon, and then in the Fall we could go down to Greece.

CUT TO:
Shot 3
LARRY: Remember how we used to talk about travelling all over the world together.

CUT TO:
Shot 4

ISABEL: Of course I want to travel, *(moves towards him and speaks affectionately)* but not like that. Cheap restaurants, third rate hotels.

ISABEL: Besides, I want to have babies, darling.
LARRY: (laughingly) Alright, darling, we'll take them along with us.
ISABEL: Larry, your so impractical. You don't know what you're asking me to do. I'm young, I want to have fun. Do all the things people do. We wouldn't have a friend in the world.
LARRY: Isabel, stop exaggerating.

(He turns away from her and walks towards the camera, crossing over from left to right.)

5

6

7

8

9

10

(He turns to face her.)

LARRY: We'll do everything you want to do, and we'll do it together.

ISABEL: *(lunges towards him)* Oh, listen, Darling, if you didn't have a cent to your name, and got a job that brought you in 3000 a year, I'd marry you without a minutes hesitation. I'd cook for you. (low and breathy) I'd make beds.
I wouldn't care what I wore, I'd think it was fun, because it was only a question of time before you'd make good.
But this would mean living like this all out lives, with nothing to look forward to. It's asking too much!

(He turns away from her towards camera.)
ISABEL: Oh, Larry, you've had your fling now. For your own sake, I beg you to come home with us.

(He turns to face her.)
LARRY: I wouldn't make you happy. What you forget is that I want to learn, as passionately as — as Gray for example, wants to make a lot of money.

(Pause. He walks away from her to the back of the room, and then turns to face her, then walks forwards towards her)

LARRY: I came over here because I was restless, and because my mind was muddled. I came looking for the answer to a lot of questions. Some of them I found, others I may never find. But I can't stop now.

(He walks away to back, and then turns while speaking.)
LARRY: Oh, I know its sounds vague and trivial compared with --- well, compared with what's happening at home today, and I know I'm being very difficult,

(walks towards her and the camera)
LARRY: ... but I can't stop now, I just can't.
ISABEL: But what would happen to America if everyone did as you are doing?
LARRY: The answer to that is that everyone doesn't feel as I do. Fortunately for themselves, everyone is content to follow the normal course, and take things as they are.
Oh, I wish I could too, but I know if I tries, I would just make a mess of your life, and of mine too.

(She turns to camera)

(She turns back to him)
ISABEL: But – what's this all going to lead to?
(she recoils from him)
LARRY: I don't know. It may be that when I'm through, I will have found something to give that people will be glad to take.
(pause)
It's just a chance, but even if I fail, I shan't be any worse off than a fellow who has gone into business, and hasn't made a go of it.

(pause. She turns towards camera)

ISABEL: Then there is nothing more to be said. *(taking glove off, then ring)*

ISABEL: Here you are.
(hands him ring,.)

(She walks to back of room and turns to face him and the camera)

LARRY: Isabel!

LARRY: Wear this on another finger, please.*(pause. He looks at her)*
We're still friends?

ISABEL: Of course.

(As she starts walking past him to door)
ISABEL: Shall we go?

(He turns back to camera to watch her. She exits. He picks up hat and follows her. Camera pulls back.)

FADE-OUT

The first shot in this scene lasts 1 minute 10 seconds, then shots 2 and 3 last about ten seconds, and the fourth and final shot making up the scene runs 3 minutes 4 seconds. It would have been possible, using Goulding's sort of scene dissection, to have done the whole scene in one shot. It might be that repeated fluffs by the actors and crew on a series of takes discouraged this, or that Goulding wanted to get the camera inside the room set from outside the window to give more freedom to his subsequent moves. Certainly the pair of reverse angles making up shots 2 and 3 do not give extra emphasis to the content at a crucial point in the scene. There are other points in the scene where the drama could be pointed up more.

In the part of the scene covered by frames 1 to 4, most of the dialogue is covered in profile two-shot, which shows both the actor's faces all the time, though not in the ideal way. The exception is the moment when Isabel looks out the window in frame 3. This indicates the scene outside that she is talking about, and also gives the conventional frontal view to show her feelings on her face. (Gene Tierney's face lacks mobility, but it is still possible to read her expressions, as you can see in these frame enlargements.)

Then follows Shot 2 represented in frame 6, which shows Isabel's reaction to Larry's speech. This is the only place in this scene where the staging seems wrong to me. This is my subjective feeling, of course, but it is sharpened by watching thousands of feature films for such technical features, not to mention decades spent advising students on the editing of

their work, where one can immediately see the results of different cutting points in a scene. In fact, I would say that it would be much better if this first part of Larry's plea to her had been on him, with the bed in the background as he mentions the honeymoon, and then going to the reverse on her for her reaction to his second line, "Remember how we used to talk about travelling the world together?" and then holding on her for her reply in Frame 8.

At Frame 10, Larry is directed to look towards the camera, to pick up his expression as he tries to josh her, but the look is naturalised as part of his walk across to the other side of the frame. More noticeable turns side-on to the camera to reveal the face, and hence give the equivalent of a reaction shot occur at Frames 13, 19 and 21. At Frames 14 and 15, Larry Darrell walks past Isabel to give an effective reverse angle favouring him, and the opposite happens in Frames 22 and 23, to take the frontal view to Isabel from Larry, where it has been for quite a while in the scene.

Overall, the camera direction vastly favours Larry in this scene, but this makes sense, because his search for his soul is the subject of the film, and the love interest is decidedly secondary. As indicated in the description of the action, there are a few camera moves in and out in this scene, but this is obviously much less important than the movements of the actors relative to the camera, which is Goulding's principal method of prolonging the takes and directing the audience's attention.

Back around the beginning of the nineteen-eighties when I saw Goulding's *Sun Up* at the National Film Theatre, I was very struck by the scene illustrated here, and also by other clever directorial touches, so I took frame enlargements from it, as well as getting the usual statistics. The material in the second part of this piece was part of an attempt to find a rule for when to go to a reaction shot in shooting and editing a film. With enough experience one can sense this, but an explicit rule, or set of rules, would be nice to have, particularly for film students who have to make films on very low shooting ratios. Of course, with plenty of resources, this is not a problem, as a scene can be covered all the way through from both directions, and the choices about where to use a reaction shot can be made by trial and error in the cutting room.

Returning to my time-line, in 1996 there was a small celebration of 100 years of cinema in England. Part of this was a small symposium organized in the Polytechnic building in Regent Street where the Lumières gave their first show in the country. The University of Westminster, which the Polytechnic has now become, published a book of articles related to the event; *Cinema: the Beginnings and the Future*, and this was edited by Christopher Williams. My contribution was an attempt to straddle the divide proposed in the title of the book, and at the same time draw attention to my recent reconstruction of Williamson's *Attack on a China Mission*.

On the verso of the title page of the book, the University of Westminster Press thoughtfully specified that they had set the body text of the book in 8.5 point ITC Bookman, with 12 point leading, so for once I did not have to deduce the typographic details myself. Presumably they did not use the standard arrangement of 10 point type with 12 point leading because Bookman is on the heavy side and has a very large x-height. I have followed them in this, though I do not use their Argo sans serif font for headings. In the text I have corrected the date of first showing of *Attack on a China Mission* to 1900, as established by John Barnes and Denis Gifford.

CUT AND SHUFFLE

Films are made up of shots, and to make the films you shuffle the shots around and cut them together.

FIRST SHUFFLE

But in the beginning, films consisted of only one shot, which showed only one scene, and ran continuously from the beginning of a standard roll of film negative to its end (65-80 feet). These films could be shown in any order by the showmen who bought them, and this was usually done without much regard for the content of the individual films. The spoken commentary which usually accompanied the projection of films in the early years could support any assemblage.

FIRST CUT

The first known cut from one shot to another was in the Edison Company's *The Execution of Mary, Queen of Scots*, which was made by Alfred Clark in 1895 for exhibition in the company's Kinetoscope peepshow machines. In this film, the actor playing Mary, Queen of Scots is brought up to the execution block, and his head laid down on it. At this point, the camera was stopped, the actor removed, a dummy in the same clothes substituted, the camera was restarted, and the headsman brought his axe down, cutting off the head. Afterwards the negatives of the two sections of the scene were joined (or 'cut') together to give a complete negative from which prints could be made. This cut was meant to be invisible, so as to create the illusion that the character had actually had her head cut off, but actually the cut was evident on close inspection, since the bystanders watching within the scene moved their positions while the camera was stopped and the substitution made. When Georges Méliès took up this 'stop-camera' technique in 1896 after Edison Kinetoscopes and their films had reached Europe, he did a much better job in making such trick cuts invisible in his *Escamotage d'une dame chez Robert-Houdin*, and many other subsequent films.

SECOND SHUFFLE

However, exhibitors did sometimes show the first one-shot films in an order that made sense. Francis Doublier, one of Lumiere's travelling cameramen/exhibitors, claimed that in 1898 he showed a series of actuality shots of soldiers, a battleship, the Palais de Justice, anal grey-haired man, as a film of the Dreyfus case. If this event actually happened, rather than just being a good story, it happened no earlier than the first film actually made up of more than one shot, and sold as such.

SECOND CUT

The first real step in film construction was the use of a cut from shot to another different one, and in this case the cut was meant seen. This first happened in R.W. Paul's *Come Along, Do!* shot around April 1898. This film was undoubtedly made up of two scenes, each consisting of a single shot, and was filmed on constructed sets. Only the first shot, which shows an old couple lunching outside gallery, and then following other people in through its door survives. However, there also exist stills showing frames from both of the scenes, and it is clear that the second scene was shot on a set representing the interior of the gallery, where the old man examines a nude statue, until removed by his wife. Later in 1898 Méliès made a film entitled *La Lune à un mètre* was closely based on one of the miniature fantastic shows that previously staged in his theatre. *La Lune à un mètre* was made three scenes, representing first 'The Observatory', in which an aged astronomer looks at the moon through a telescope and then falls asleep; next 'The Moon at One Metre,' in which the moon descends from the sky and swallows him up; and lastly 'Phoebe', in which he meets the goddess of the moon. The second scene and the beginning of the third were intended to be understood as the dream of the astronomer, who wakes up in the middle of the final scene when goddess he is chasing vanishes by a stop-camera effect.

This was the first of a long line of films made over the next couple of decades which used the device of a dream story turning back to at the crucial moment, but the most important thing about *La lune à un mètre* was that this whole concept was not immediately apparent from the film itself. This was because there were only small change made in the decor between one scene and the next, so that there was no way for the viewer to instantly notice the transition between what took place when the astronomer was awake and what took place when he was asleep. Since films in those years were nearly always with an accompanying commentary by the showman who projected them (just as in the earlier lantern-slide shows), this was not such a great handicap, but Méliès must have felt that the way he had treated the matter was not ideal, for in his next fantasy film, *Cendrillon* (1899), he joined all the scenes by dissolves, just as was the practice in most slide shows. In this and all subsequent long films made by Méliès during the next seven years, dissolves were used indiscriminately between every shot, even when the action was continuous from one shot to the next - that is, when there was no time lapse between shots. The dissolve was used in the same indiscriminate way in the slide shows which pre-existed the cinema, and hence in both cases the dissolve definitely did not signify a time lapse.

THIRD CUT WITH SHUFFLE

The next film after *Come Along, Do!* developing action continuity from shot to shot, was G.A. Smith's *The Kiss in the Tunnel*, made before November 1899. The Smith film shows a set representing the interior of a railway carriage compartment, with blackness visible through the window, and a man kissing a woman. The Warwick Trading Company catalogue instructs that it should be joined into a film of a 'phantom ride' between the points at which the train enters and leaves a tunnel, an event which many 'phantom rides' included, and this is indeed the case with the surviving copy of this film. (G.A. Smith had made a 'phantom ride' film, which was the result of fixing a film camera on the front of a train, the year before, as had other film-makers, but it is difficult to tell which 'phantom ride' is which amongst the few that still remain out of the many that were made in the first decade of cinema.) In any case, the catalogue instruction as to the point at which the cut should be made shows that the concept of action continuity was understood by Smith. A few months later, the Bamforth company made an imitation of Smith's film with the same title, which developed the idea even further. Bamforth & Co. were a well-established film making and selling lantern slides and postcards in Holmfirth, Yorkshire, before the owner, James Bamforth, took them into film-making. Their version of G.A. Smith's *The Kiss in the Tunnel* was made at the very end of 1899. This put their restaging of the scene inside the railway carriage between two specially shot scenes of a train going into a tunnel, and then coming out the other end. Since these shots in the Bamforth film were objective shots, with the camera beside the track, rather than 'phantom ride' shots, they made the point of the continuity of the action quite clear, rather than forcing the viewer to work it out by logical deduction.

STACKING THE DECK

The further development of movement from one shot to the next was carried out by James Williamson in films like *Attack on a China Mission*, which was made and first shown 1900. For a long time it seemed that this famous film, which originally consisted of four scenes according to the Williamson sales catalogue of 1902, only survived as a single shot, but a more complete version turned up several years ago at the Imperial War Museum.

Attack on a China Mission: *according to the Williamson catalogue, the first scene shows the outer gate of the China Mission Station, with Chinese Boxer rebels breaking through it. In the Imperial War Museum print, this scene occurs second, and the last frame of it shows the jagged splice across the middle of the frame — a tear really — where the alteration was made.*

The second scene was originally the garden in front of the house, with the mission and family attacked by the Boxers. Again, the last frame of the shot from the Imperial War Museum copy shows another rather crude splice made to put this scene first, rather than second as it should have been.

This version contained the four scenes described in the sales catalogue, but two of them were spliced together in an order different from that in the catalogue. Close examination of the National Film Archive viewing copy print made from the master preservation material showed a cut or splice from one shot to another which was quite different from, and much cruder than the ones joining the other shots. This made it clear that at some time after the shots of the film were first joined together, someone had recut the film. It was also clear that the single shot form of the film was, as various people had conjectured, an uncut print of the unedited camera negative for what was eventually edited by Williamson into shots two and four of the film. That is, he was doing what G.A. Smith recommended the buyer of his *Kiss in the Tunnel* to do: to cut a shot into two parts and join another shot in

The third scene shows the reverse angle through the gate, with the British bluejackets coming to the rescue, kneeling and firing, and then rushing past the camera to engage with the Boxers.

The fourth scene reverts to the same camera set-up as the first, and is actually filmed continuously with it as one shot It shows the bluejackets rushing past the camera (shooting in the opposite direction), and engaging with the rebels hand to hand

between so as to construct a multi-shot film. This was real film editing in its fullest possible sense, and done long before Edwin Porter had any idea about it. I regret to say that Americans are still publishing books saying Porter invented film editing.

As my examination of the unedited single shot from the film showed it was longer, and contained more action at its beginning and end than the material in the Imperial War Museum version (which had been shortened through the wear and tear of repeated projection, as usually happens with prints of very old films), I used it to make a reconstructed version of the film. This contains the shots in the original order, and by using the unedited material combined with the rest of the Imperial War Museum version, creates a more nearly complete version. But this reconstructed version is still not complete, because the original film had five shots in it, not the four remaining. The fifth shot, about 80 feet long (i.e. a full reel of camera negative) continued the fourth scene, and originally was joined onto the fourth shot by an 'invisible' splice, since it was shot with exactly the same camera position and direction as the fourth shot, and at a brief break in the action, when the scene had been briefly cleared of actors by their exit off-screen. I very much hope this shot will eventually turn up as well.

FOURTH CUT

G.A. Smith also invented the practice of dividing a continuous scene shot in the one place up into a number of shots, in a series of films beginning with *Grandma's Reading Glass* of 1900. In this film, a small boy is shown looking at various objects with a magnifying glass in the first shot, and then Big Close Ups of the objects seen from his Point of View (POV) are cut in in succession. As the Warwick Trading Company catalogue put it at the time: 'The conception is to produce on the screen the various objects as they appeared to Willy while looking through the glass in their enormously enlarged form'. In the Big Close Ups of the objects the view through the actual magnifying glass is not used, but its field of view is simulated by photographing the object of interest inside a black circular mask fixed in front of the camera lens. Smith repeated this device in *As Seen Through the Telescope* (September 1900), which shows a man with a telescope spying on another man who is taking advantage of the act of helping a woman onto a bicycle to fondle her ankle. Into the Long Shot incorporating all this action is inserted the ostensible view through the telescope, which is represented by another Big Close Up showing the lady's foot inside a black circular mask. Unlike the previous film, there is only one cut-in POV Close Up rather than several, but in the development of *As Seen Through the Telescope* made in 1901 by the French Pathé company, *Ce que je vois de mon sixième*, the man uses his telescope to spy through a number of different windows in succession, so combining the structures of both earlier Smith films.

Also in 1901, G.A. Smith initiated the other major form of scene dissection with *The Little Doctor*. In this film, which now only exists in the essentially identical restaged version he made in 1903, *The Sick Kitten*, there is a cut straight in down the lens axis from a Medium Long Shot of a child administering a spoon of medicine to a kitten, to a Big Close Up Insert of the kitten with the spoon in its mouth, and then back to the Medium Long Shot again. As this is an objective shot of the kitten there is no masking as in the other films, and the matching of the position of the kitten across the two cuts is not perfect, as is hardly surprising given the nature of kittens, but it could be worse.

ANOTHER LITTLE SHUFFLE

The last sign of the variable film for a long time was *The Great Train Robbery* that Edwin Porter made for the Edison company towards the end of 1903. As the sales catalogue announced, the close shot of the bandit Barnes firing straight into the camera could be placed at either the beginning or the end of the film. This shot was not part of the story, and I say it was handled thus because Porter did not know what to do with the kind of Close Ups he had seen in the films of other filmmakers in the previous two years.

FINAL CUT

By 1901 all the basic techniques for joining individual shots to construct a film had been introduced by the leading English filmmakers, and it remained only to add the final refinements of the way cuts related to the shots on either sides of them. For instance, the only kind of Point of View shots which were used in the early years was those in which the watcher in the film looked through something that had an aperture in it, and his view was then shown with a black mask round its edges of the same shape as the hole through which he was looking. The more usual kind of Point of View shot nowadays is that in which a watcher looks at something with his unobstructed vision, and his view is then shown with ordinary full film frame. The use of this sort of POV shot apparently represented some kind of conceptual problem to early film-makers, and did not really begin to develop till about 19 10.

TRACK LAYING

Around 1910, another major development for film construction was the introduction of 'spoken titles' between shots, which gave the text of some of the crucial things that the characters in the film would say in the succeeding shots. When these spoken titles came to be cut into the middle of a shot at exactly the point at which they were spoken, which happened around 1913, the result was equivalent to a modern film with sound track.

MARRIED PRINT

Theories about how the film screenplay should be structured began to be articulated at least as early as 1908, when film production and exhibition had standardised into programmes of single reel films. All of these theories were variants and adaptations of the basic ideas that had

developed in the nineteenth century about writing stage plays. These ideas about play construction were in their turn a development of the original Aristotelian conception of what drama should be, and were well known to, and thoroughly internalised by, most writers of plays.

The essential mechanism was the conflict between one character striving to accomplish some purpose in which he is thwarted by another character. This initial situation is developed purely by a logical process of cause and effect. Further than this, there were other essential ideas which can be found in most of the American manuals on play construction and film script writing from the end of the nineteenth century through the early twentieth century.

Variation of mood was most important, both from scene to scene, and also within scenes. To quote Alfred Hennequin's *The Art of Playwriting* (Houghton Mifflin & Co., 1890), which was the first complete exposition of these ideas: 'Pathos must be followed by humour, wit by eloquence, talky passages by quick-succeeding scenes of incident, soliloquies by the rapid give-and-take of dialogue. The entire act should be a rapidly shifting kaleidoscope, presenting new features at every turn'. This alternation of mood was associated with the device of suspense - 'In some form or another, it must exist throughout the entire progress of the story. At various points of the play, generally at the close of each act, it may be partially relieved, but it must always be done in such a way as to give rise to new suspense, or to leave one or two particulars still unsettled, etc.'- and a progression of climaxes – 'A dramatic story should be full of climaxes from beginning to end. Every act should have several lesser ones scattered through it, and should invariably end with one of greater importance. Toward the end of the play should occur the great climax in the technical sense of the word, i.e. the point at which the interest of the play reaches its highest stage.' The final major constituent of the standard stage and film plot was the 'heart interest' as it was called before World War I. (Later this came to be called 'the love interest'.) This required that the hero, as well as solving his problem, or defeating the villain, should also get the girl. (The reversal of sexual roles was also possible, though quite rare.) By the 1930s the vast majority of American films had this double plot action.

In the American one reel film the requirement that the character or mood of succeeding incidents be varied was usually not met, though it is actually possible for really skilled film-makers to do this with a certain amount of effort. Some of D.W. Griffith's Biograph films do contain one or two lighter incidents, verging on comedy, among the more dramatic scenes that make up the bulk of his films, and he and other people also made some comedies that involved suspenseful scenes amid the more usual fooling.

Then, once films became several reels long, and had

their dialogue rendered in inter titles, it became fairly easy for them to accommodate all the desirable dramatic features just mentioned. The full assumption of theatrical methods of dramatic construction by American motion pictures took place at the same time that the final features of continuity cinema were being generally polished and diffused, during the First World War. The perfection of standard film dramatic construction particularly involved people like Mary Pickford, who had starred in Belasco plays in New York, and who worked to incorporate features from such plays into her films when she became an independent producer. 1917 was really a crucial year for some of the new leaders of the American film industry, because, besides Pickford finally getting these things right from *Rebecca of Sunnybrook Farm* onwards, Chaplin began to introduce pathetic scenes into his comedies, and Douglas Fairbanks moved beyond his stodgy early works like *His Picture in the Papers* to better shaped constructions.

The proven success of this formula for ordinary commercial filmmaking has meant that it has been the standard ever since, even if some film-makers, particularly outside the U.S, have not always completely adhered to it.

SHUFFLING ALONG

Alternative versions of films have been produced for commercial reasons from before the First World War, but nearly always this was just a matter of changing the ending from happy to unhappy (or vice versa), or of shortening the film. Both of these practices were most common in the silent period, with the American market demanding a happy ending, and the pre-Communist Russian market an unhappy one. Film-making for export could produce both endings for the one film. In general, the small number of European films imported into America tended to be cut, and not just for censorship reasons, but because American audiences considered them slow and boring. This sort of cutting was usually done by omitting whole scenes, but occasionally there were cases like the British distribution print of Fritz Lang's *Kriemhilds Rache* (1924), which was shortened by cutting the beginning and end off every shot. It has been claimed that some Western films were completely re-edited for the Soviet market in the 1920s, but since no-one has ever produced a print of these films as evidence, this may just be more show-business exaggeration.

Inevitably, the practices in other advanced art during the 1960s had an effect on avant-garde film-making, and films made up of sections which could be shown in any order appeared. The best-known example is Andy Warhol's *Chelsea Girls* (1967), but this is not really a narrative film, and I think my own *Six Reels of Film to be Shown in any Order* (1971) was the first truly variable film with a story, or rather 120 stories. Five of the reels each contained a couple of scenes involving a selection of four principal characters in which a few dramatic interactions took place between them, and one or two facts about their past were disclosed. (One of the reels was neutral with respect to any possible narrative.) The interactions, which involved such dramatic favourites as sex, marital infidelity, nervous breakdown, and suicide, were selected so that they might give rise to some of the events in some of the other reels. I checked the plausibility of the different stories arising from the different possible orders of the scenes by writing them on five cards and shuffling these into a substantial proportion of the total possible number of permutations. Since this produced satisfactory results, I trusted that the rest of the permutations would also produce convincing sequences of events.

My miscalculation was to think that other people enjoyed this sort of thing as much as I did. So the film was not much of a success, partly because, as one critic suggested, people like himself preferred to do their own inventing of interpretations of the films they saw. In other words, your average critic with intellectual pretensions preferred to do his or her own shuffling of the content, and didn't want the maker doing it for them. Another way of approaching my creation was to suggest that the film in fact had only one story, and all the 120 alternative versions were just the same story told through different arrangements of flashbacks (and maybe flashforwards). It hadn't occurred to me that anyone would take this attitude either. Part of the lesson of this incident is that most members of the cinema audience prefer films the way they are, with the scenes in a fixed order.

However, there have been a few recent indications that the wisdom of ages about the best approach to script construction may not be completely correct. The idea of alternating scenes with greater dramatic tension, such as action scenes, with scenes with a more relaxed tone, such as romantic or comedy scenes, seems to have been dropped in some action films that have been extremely successful at the box office. They might be thought of as 'robotic action movies'. The one of these which most caught my attention was *Total Recall* (1990), though an earlier Schwarzenegger film, *Commando* (1985), is pretty much the same. Incidentally, both of these films have only the most perfunctory hint of a love interest. On the other hand, other recent films which break the ancient commandments of script construction in other ways, for instance *Henry and June* (1990), which has effectively no plot at all, have been commercial failures.

THE NEW DEAL

So what does all this presage for the multi-media creations of the future, be they on CD-ROM, or some other medium?

Factual multi-media works are already truly variable in the way they can be used, but I think those which involve a narrative element are generally not. Many current computer games have a plot, or narrative, or story aspect, but so far as I am aware they usually have only one end to the game, and only one way of reaching it, with no truly alternative paths through them. Those games which are basically a matter of puzzle-solving, such as *Lemmings* or *The Incredible Machine* sometimes have more than one way of solving their earlier, simpler stages (or 'levels', as they are called), but as the puzzles grow more complex, there is usually only one way to solve them. So-called adventure games also include puzzle elements at various points, and these puzzle elements require a unique solution to an even greater extent. Games which might appear to be strategy games, with a large number of possible solutions, such as *Populous*, usually turn out to respond to a fairly simple-minded brute force solution. (In this last case, raise as much flat land around your populations as fast as possible.) Only games which are really simulations rather than games, such as the Maxis 'Sim-' series. are truly infinitely variable in their progress. And they are not going towards any particular goal, and have no story at all in the conventional sense. Their mass appeal is also far less.

The games with the greatest mass appeal are of course 'shoot 'em ups', 'beat 'em ups' and the related driving games ('crash 'em ups'), Here brute force and speed are of the essence, and these are of course very similar to the new trend in action films noted above, with more or less continuous action, explosions, and noise, without relief.

One recent variety of the 'shoot 'em up' is the kind of game that presents a three-dimensional representation of a world that the player sees, apparently from the his point of view, as he moves around inside it. The point of the game is to blast as many as possible of the moving figures which appear before one, as well as solving the occasional puzzle to enable one to get from one area of the labyrinth that makes up the game's world to another of its three dimensional areas. In general, such games,

of which *Doom* is currently the best known example, are only seen from what is referred to as 'the first person perspective', though in film terms this means that they are one long POV shot, like Robert Montgomery's *The Lady in the Lake* (1947). As that film proved, continuous Point of View presentation of a dramatic narrative slows it down considerably, and negates one of the major virtues of film cutting. POV shoot 'em ups like *Doom* offer continuous blasting at any moving thing that appears as a way retaining the participant's interest.

There has recently been an attempt to make it possible to switch between an objective view of the action and the player's POV in one of these games, *Bioforge*, but this still falls a long way short of the true 'interactive movie' that some computer game creators dream about This hypothetical form, which would involve not only different objective angles on the scene as well as Point of View presentations and also variable reactions to the actions of the player's persona from the other figures appearing in them, is theoretically possible, but requires a vast increase in the computing power available to any ordinary person playing them. Sometime, but not yet.

The most recently developed computer games, which involve scenes digitised from filmed live-action sequences, have the same kind of narrative mechanisms underneath them as the games I have discussed earlier. The economic imperative says that money spent on creating expensive alternative scenes of this kind is wasted if the scenes might not ever be seen by someone working their way through the game by alternative paths.

From all this I make the prediction that the older form of audiovisual creation, with its fixed structure varied in the ways established long ago, will continue to be the favourite for audiences large and small, whatever medium it is delivered on, but that the 'shoot 'em up', in its direct, disguised, or developed forms, may take a larger share of the recreational market. But I could be wrong, so deal your own hand from the cards on the table.

The reconstructed version of *Attack on a China Mission* is available on the DVD *Early Cinema — Primitives and Pioneers* from the British Film Institute.

My remarks about the nature of computer games as they were in 1996 had a small error of fact. Actually, in some sports simulations, such as soccer games, it was already possible in 1996 to view the action from a limited number of different camera angles. Most of the development in computer games since then has been in increasing the realism of the moving images, and this has in its turn depended on a great increase in the available computer power. However, there has been little innovation in the nature of the games themselves, basically because there has been little innovation in the psychology of young male humans. The Maxis company has introduced a version of real human interaction with its *The Sims,* but that is about it.

My comments on computer games in the preceding piece also led to me being invited to address a small conference on the future of multimedia applications, which in turn led to an invitation to advise and write for a new version of the well-known Microsoft multimedia encyclopaedia, *Encarta.* In typical Microsoft fashion, *Encarta* had been created by buying the contents of *Funk and Wagnall's Encyclopaedia,* a rather low-brow work of reference that sells well in the United States, but nowhere else, and adding multi-media elements to it. When it was released in Britain, *Encarta* was very successful, but there was endless local criticism of the totally American bias of its contents. After a couple of years, Microsoft hired the English branch of Webster's to produce a revised version that was at first called the "World English Edition". Microsoft's plan was to add articles on matters of local interest, but also to undertake a gradual rewrite of all the contents, so that Microsoft would own it completely, and not have to pay anything to Funk and Wagnall. The new local editor asked me to rewrite most of the film material, and to supply other people to fill in the gaps. The original film history sections were the usual tired old recycled clichés and errors, so although the pay was not really worth my time, I undertook the job to give the public something better. My contributions continued for many years, including even short technical pieces on video and related subjects. Eventually the editorial staff started adding to my pieces, then changing bits of some articles, and also taking my name off them. When I looked at the fine print of the contracts I had signed for the work, I found that I had apparently signed away my moral right to be recognized as the author of the pieces. By this time I had come to realise the true nature of American capitalism, so although my feelings were hurt, I was not surprised.

Another project that I was sucked into in 1997 was a book on 100 years of great European cinematography. This project had been put together by Roger Sears, who is a book packager specialising in books on art and photography. The packager conceives of a book for which they think there is a certain market, and which requires the collaboration of a number of specialists to create, and then gets a publisher to put up the money to fund the project. In this particular case, Roger Sears was inspired by the centenary of cinematography to suggest a book on 100 years of European cinematography to the association of European cinematographers, which goes under the name of Imago. He engaged Michael Leitch as editor and writer of the section on the history of film lighting in Europe, Cathy Greenhalgh to write on theories of cinematography, and Zoë Bicât to write about the photography of 100 important European films spanning the century. As you should be able to tell from the book you are holding in your hand, this is not the way I would go about such a project.

When they started work, they found that they were having to constantly refer to my *Film Style and Technology* for help, so Roger Sears asked me to take part in the project. I did so reluctantly, as I really needed all my time for my own research, and I did not need the money. But as with Encarta, I thought that the work would be markedly better with my collaboration, so I agreed, with some private misgivings. My work was mostly on the 100 films, which were selected by a committee from Imago (bad move number two). The 100 exemplary films were now parcelled out between Zoë Bicât and myself, with Zoë doing roughly the first 50 chronologically, and myself the more recent ones. I looked at Zoë's films with her, and told her what was going on technically in them. We had to work mostly from videotapes, which makes it difficult to see the fine detail in the image necessary to get a precise idea about where and what the lights illuminating the scene actually were. Roger Sears' idea was that the book should be illustrated by frame enlargements of the best possible quality, and it was here that the serious problems really began.

I naturally selected frames that were best suited to illustrating the points I was making about the lighting, but the Imago people overseeing the publication could not see that, and often insisted on choosing their own. But the main problem was with British films for which the rights had passed to the major American film companies. These companies, like Disney and Warner Bros., had no interest in anyone illustrating the particular beauties of the works they now owned. They were only motivated by limitless greed. In the end, we had to use production stills for some of the films, which, for instance, completely destroyed the careful compositions of David Watkin and Hugh Hudson in *Chariots of Fire.* The book finally came out in 2003 as *Making Pictures: A Century of European Cinematography,* under the imprint of the Aurum Press.

Sometimes on Friday and Saturday nights around the end of the Twentieth Century I had all my three TVs going simultaneously, and was still not able to capture every film being broadcast that was new to me. This work gave me a broad and complete view of film production in the nineteen-nineties, to an extent that was not possible for my considerations of previous decades. This information fed into a survey of the development of film style and technology in the 'nineties, which carried on from the point I left off in the second edition of *Film Style and Technology: History and Analysis.* Ideally, it should be added to a third edition of that book, but since I still have about 500 copies of the third printing of the second edition on hand, I am including it here.

FILM STYLE AND TECHNOLOGY IN THE NINETIES

The generally rising prosperity in most of the world ensured that film production in most countries held up in quantity during the nineteen-nineties. However, the collapse of Communism in the Soviet Union caused a massive shrinkage in Russian film production, and the same effect was noticeable to some extent in the rest of Eastern Europe. The positive side of these events was that amongst the films that *did* get made in Eastern Europe, there were a number that were innovative in subject matter and style, and also a number of previously banned films were released. Also, many more film productions originating from America and Western Europe came to be made on location and in the studios of the former Eastern Bloc. In the West, German film production weakened as the local audience continued to turn away from the films made by the local subsidised art film sector.

In the United States, on the other hand, the continuing rise in wealth for most of the population, and in particular the middle classes, meant that American art films were made in increasing numbers. It is not too difficult to get hold of a half a million dollars if you have enough push, and dangle the glamour of film-making in front of Americans with more money than they really need. This trend was institutionalized by the Sundance Institute and Film Festival, created by Robert Redford in 1981 to encourage the production of artistically adventurous independent films. By the nineties, this festival was very successful, and the existing American film distribution companies were competing to buy the most commercially appealing products from the movement. There was a fairly successful attempt in the United States to usurp the title "independent film" purely for what had been called up to this point, "art films". The Independent Feature Project, which was an organization founded in 1979 at the New York Film Festival to market American art films, defined "independent films" as having their financing put together by the film-maker. This financing could include studio money, but the film could not be a genre film, an action thriller, or be "canned Hollywood product". Admittedly, this would exclude an art film set up and funded by a studio, but these were not common.

For ordinary commercial production in the United States, the movement away from shooting in the Hollywood studios continued, and was so pervasive that the derogatory term "runaway production" was no longer used as often as it had been. In particular, shooting American films in Canada was now common.

In the nineteen-nineties, the content of independent films became increasingly misanthropic, reflecting the way social attitudes have become more and more cynical and nihilistic in recent times, and some of these films contained only stupid or despicable characters in the main parts, which was unthinkable a few decades ago. Leading film-makers in this respect are Neil LaBute (*In the Company of Men*, 1997), and Todd Solondz (*Happiness*, 1998). Similar cynical and nihilistic attitudes are also evident in ordinary commercial American cinema, and were even quite conscious amongst some film-makers. For instance, John Carpenter said in an interview in the *American Cinematographer* (p.70 September 1988) "I must tell you that my criticisms of society and the film business are not entirely serious. I've made a lot of money out of the film business the way it is run today, and I am a complete capitalist. I'm just advocating a little humanity in the world. In order to do that, you have to go strong in the other direction, be a little outrageous. It's fun to attack the status quo." And in September 1996 about his *Escape from L.A.*, "But I wanted to do to L.A. what we did to New York, which was to have a great time with it in a cynical and sarcastic way,...".

Nevertheless, there has been a somewhat countervailing trend in American commercial film-making through the latter part of the 'nineties, which was towards a reduction in the amount of extreme violence and sexuality. This is apparently due to a public backlash against the handling of such matters in ordinary Hollywood films, and was given expression in a book by Michael Medved, *Hollywood vs. America: Popular Culture and the War on Traditional Values* (1992), and the following discussion of the matter in the American media. Unlike the backlash against the content of Hollywood films in the early thirties, this was not orchestrated by the Roman Catholic church, but it equally represented a real public concern about the content of Hollywood films. Another connected factor is the economic ramifications of the content rating system used by the MPAA, in which a new category, NC-17, was introduced in 1990.

In the nineteen-nineties, film technology conclusively lost its autonomy. Developments in lighting for television had been taken over into film lighting in the previous decade, but now developments in computer technology joined together with developments which had happened first in television and music recording, and these were taken over into film use. European equipment makers continued to make a strong showing in these areas, and also in more purely traditional film technology, with lighting equipment from Arriflex and Dedo Weigert in Germany, and LTM in France, and cameras from Fritz Bauer in Austria all selling well in the American and other markets.

Production Procedures

The tendency in American film production towards using multiple cameras on all scenes, already noted for the nineteen-eighties in *Film Style and Technology: History and Analysis*, continued to grow, to the point where it was exceptional for only a single camera to be used on ordinary scenes in big film productions. For some directors, the practice was to use the two cameras from the same direction, with a longer lens on one of them to get closer shots, and for others to use one of them on the reverse angle in dialogue scenes. On action scenes, there was a tendency to use even more cameras than had been habitually used in these situations. An extreme was reached by John Woo in *Hard Target* (1993), in which the big action scenes were shot with seven or more cameras from every possible direction, rather than with them only placed on one side of the scene, as was usual. Independent films, and also productions in other countries, did not have the budgets to pursue the multi-camera method. The amount of scenes shot with Steadicam mounts also continued to increase on American films, to the point where many had around half their footage filmed in this way.

Film Stock

Eastman Kodak film stock continued to dominate the market, particularly in the United States, where little else was used in ordinary commercial film-making. In television, Fuji stocks had a certain share, as the Fuji materials continued to be cheaper than Kodak. In Europe, Fuji did rather better, and some cameramen continued to prefer it, because of its less saturated colours and lower definition. Sometimes American cameramen also chose Fuji negative for these reasons. Agfa stocks were fading away through the nineties, although new negatives balanced for tungsten light were introduced in 1991 (XT100) and 1992 (XT320 and XT400).

The slow Kodak EXR stocks 5245 (EI 50 and daylight balanced), which was introduced in 1989, and 5248 (EI 100 and tungsten light balanced), which was introduced in 1990, continued to be used extensively when filming under high light levels throughout the 'nineties, and were neither upgraded nor replaced. All the development in Kodak emulsions in this decade was confined to the fast negatives. In 1994 Eastman Color 5298 (7298 for 16mm.), which was rated 500 ISO (or EI), replaced the 5296 negative, and in 1996 the introduction of a whole new range of negatives was begun with the release of the first in the "Vision" series, namely Vision 500T and 320T negatives. The first of these competed with the still new 5298, and the second with Eastman Color 5287. These new negatives had reduced grain size, and were claimed to have greater latitude than their predecessors, and were also said by some cameramen to be warmer in colour response. Despite Kodak's claim of greater latitude for these new stocks, many cameramen considered that they were more contrasty, and continued to use the older fast stocks which remained available for some years, particularly 5298, when they thought it was appropriate. The new Vision negatives were also more expensive than the older stocks, and this deterred cinematographers from using them on cheap productions.

Kodak said that these new stocks had their colour response adjusted to what cameramen wanted, which was in its turn influenced by their ever greater use of HMI and fluorescent lights for film lighting purposes. Both of these sources, and particularly the latter, had uneven emission of wavelengths across the visible spectrum, and hence generated some slightly incorrect colour reproduction. This was a major turning point, for up to this point, the effort of Eastman Kodak scientists had always been to create film stocks that approached as nearly as possible to perfect colour reproduction under the even spectral light of daylight or tungsten light.

Later additions in 1997 to the Vision series included a 200 EI tungsten balanced negative, type number 5274, and a 250 EI daylight balanced negative, Type 5246. The latter was little used for feature cinematography, but was popular for actuality filming, where difficult available light situations were common. Its daylight colour balance meant that existing light could be economically reinforced with HMI lights, which have a natural daylight balance. In 1998 we had Vision 800T film (Type 5289/7289), which became the fastest film so far available, and Kodak SFX 200T negative for special effects green and blue screen filming, to replace the older 5293 negative previously used for this purpose. This was last was modified in 1999 to make it less contrasty. A special low contrast Vision Color Teleprint positive (Type 2395) for use in telecine transfers was added to the range at the end of 1999. The point of this stock was that, although the telecine-ing of films was usually done from a negative, sometimes prints were needed of a new film for export to other countries that had different television systems.

In 1995, Eastman Kodak also produced the first of a new series of negatives purely for television purposes, called Primetime 640T, which had an exposure index (EI) of 640 under tungsten light. This had even less contrastiness than their other fast motion picture negatives, and was not intended for making prints, but had its colour response optimized for direct transfer to videotape in telecine machines. Eastman Kodak also upgraded its intermediate film stocks with EXR intermediate 5244 in 1992, and then in 1998 there was 2383 and 2393, all of which could be used either as intermediate positive, or intermediate negative in the duplicating process. The 2393 stock had more contrast and more colour saturation than the 2383 material, which was useful for cinematographers who wanted to get brighter colours than normal.

The Fuji company introduced some new or improved film stocks throughout the decade, with the new Fuji F-250D (a fast daylight negative identified as Type 8570) and the fast tungsten-balanced stock F-500 improved in 1991. The latter was replaced by the new Super F series F-500, with type numbers 8571 for 35 mm and 8671 for 16 mm in 1997. There was also a new Fuji intermediate stock introduced in 1995. These new Fuji stocks did not gain the company any ground in the competition.

Throughout the 'nineties, the trend continued towards shooting more and more films mostly, or sometimes entirely, on the fastest stock, no doubt encouraged by the continually improving Kodak fast negatives. This had some influence on the look of the film image, as the use of lower light levels on the scene that follows from the use of faster camera negative changes the behaviour of light within a film scene. With 500 EI (or ISO) negative, a light intensity of 10 foot-candles gives an aperture of f2 for correct exposure, and many cameramen were working down towards this sort of level in the 'nineties. Under these conditions, the light emitted by the sources lighting the scene, not just the film lights, but also any practical lights on the set, is reflected and re-emitted by the surfaces it hits, and after bouncing around further, adds up to a general undirected wash of light that gives an intensity of a foot-candle or so, and creates the effect of uncontrolled and non-directional fill light. At higher levels of the light from film lights, this does not happen proportionally to the same extent. The result of this wash of multiply reflected light at low light levels does not resemble the effect of fill light intentionally put directly onto the figures, etc. from film light sources, even the softest ones.

The only new black and white film introduced during this period was an Ilford negative intended for special effects work, called Ilford SFX 200, which had extended sensitivity into the infra-red region of the spectrum, and had an Exposure Index of 200 under tungsten light and 100 under daylight. This was the reverse of the usual order of things with black and white negative.

The professional use of Super 8 mm. film continued, particularly with the trend to include sections shot in 8 mm. in feature films, as described below. This encouraged the American firm Super 8 Sound to buy 35 mm. negative from Eastman Kodak in 1996, and have it slit and perforated to the Super 8 gauge, and then re-sell it to professional film-makers. Super 8 Sound also provided processing and telecine facilities for 8 mm. film.

Laboratory Work and Special Treatment Techniques

The kind of special film processing techniques that had appeared in the 'eighties, starting with the Technicolor ENR process (which was mentioned in *Film Style and Technology*), were used more widely in many countries. To give a concise and more accurate description of them, they all involved omitting, or reducing the duration of the bleach bath which comes after the colour development bath in the development of colour film. The colour development bath, which is the first stage of the active processing of colour film, produces a silver image in each of the three layers of the emulsion, just as in ordinary black and white film, but also a colour image made up of varying amounts of dye, which surrounds the developed silver grains. The function of the bleach bath is to remove the silver image, and just leave the colour image, so if it is omitted, or the bleaching chemicals are reduced in strength, all or some of the black silver image will be retained. All film laboratories can carry out this process if they wish to, and some that do so give it a proprietary name, e.g. CFI's "Silver Tint" and LTC's "NEC". If the process is used in producing a positive print, the most intense colours in the image will be darkened by the silver, and the blacks will become very black. If the process is

used in negative developing, it will reduce the colour saturation in the brightest parts of the image, and also make the overall image more contrasty. One of the first notable uses of this simple bleach bypass process, colloquially called "skip bleach", was the film *1984*, directed in England in 1984 by Michael Radford, and processed by Kays Laboratories in London. The desaturation of colour in this film, together with the added black, gave a powerful amplification to the picture of Orwell's run-down alternative future under totalitarian rule. As in all the most effective uses of silver retention techniques, the effect was aided by the colours used in the sets. In the 'nineties, these silver retention processes were in general used for this kind of effect; that is, for the creation of a depressing atmosphere, as in *Seven* (1995) And *Fight Club* (1999). The silver retention process works slightly differently in the most visually novel part of *Delicatessen* (1990), where Darius Khondji lit the sewer scenes in the mid-key and high key range, instead of working towards low key as is usual in this sort of situation. The sewer sets contain so much black metal and dark walls, not to mention hordes of Troglodists wearing black rubber wet suits, that the heavy dose of added silver in these images emphasises the shiny blackness and the highlights from the film lighting units scattered over the curved wet black surfaces, and creates a truly distinctive look.

However, Technicolor's ENR process was the first silver retention process, and was first used by Vittorio Storaro for a complete film with *Reds* (1981). It involved an extra developing stage as well as the omission of the bleach bath. This extra bath developed more of the undeveloped silver remaining in the emulsion after the colour development. This produces the same kind of effect as simple bleach bath bypassing, but with more degrees of control, and the possibility of even stronger effect, if desired. The CCE process offered by Deluxe laboratories is carried out in much the same sort of way as the ENR process, but other film laboratories do not provide an equivalent, as it involves introducing an extra development tank into the standard machinery.

All the silver retention processes are usually used on the final prints of the film, which increases the cost of the printing process, since the silver in the film stock is not recovered from the processing solutions in the usual way for resale by the film laboratory. This means that the producing company may only have the process used on some of the prints of the film that are released, and not on all the extra prints made. Nevertheless, the use of these processes increased in the 'nineties, but still only on a minority of films. It must be noted that since video cassettes and DVDs are usually produced from a film negative, the exact equivalent effect may not be visible on copies of the film released in these ways. The silver retention processes are not usually used on the negative, though they can be.

In this decade silver retention processes have often been used in conjunction with flashing the film stock, particularly with the Arri Lightcon, and also with the Panaflasher, both adding white or coloured light to the exposure in the camera, and both of them introduced in the previous decade. In the case of *Saving Private Ryan* (1998), the strongly desaturated colours were due at least as much to flashing the film as to the ENR silver enhancement process that was also used.

A new idea that appeared in the 'nineties is the use of reversal colour film stock as though it was negative film. So the reversal stock (usually Kodak Ektachrome) is exposed in the camera in the usual way, and then given ordinary negative developing. This treatment is commonly referred to as "cross processing". The resulting image has higher contrast and increased grain, and can give some alteration of the colours or hues in the scene, particularly in the highlights and shadows. The increased contrast and colour alteration was visible in the first film to use this technique, Spike Lee's *Clockers* (1995)

There were attempts to revive the Technicolor dye imbibition printing process in the United States in this decade, but they did not get anywhere much.

Lighting Equipment

European companies making lighting units, such as France's LTM and Germany's Arri companies, continued to became more important internationally in the 'nineties, particularly in the United States, and they did this partly by introducing new types of lighting units. The most significant new types of lighting equipment in the 'nineties had actually first appeared at the end of the previous decade. These were the Kino Flo system using fluorescent lights, and HMI PAR lights, which were lampheads with parabolic reflectors and open fronts that used a new type of single-ended HMI bulb.

The Kino Flo system was the result of the use by the cameraman Robby Mueller and his gaffers of ordinary fluorescent tubes powered by special high frequency ballasts on the film *Barfly* (1987). Ordinary fluorescent tubes powered in the standard way from the mains suffer from a stroboscopic effect caused by the difference between the mains frequency and the frequency of opening and closing of the shutter of a film camera. This shows as a visible fluctuation or pulsing in the brightness of the film scene lit by ordinary fluorescent lights. This was solved by the use of a ballast unit generating high frequency alternating current, just as in the electronic ballasts that were starting to be used for HMI lights to solve the same problem. The second defect of fluorescent lights for colour photography is the uneven intensity of the wavelengths they emit across the visible spectrum, when compared to sunlight and tungsten lights. In particular, they show large peaks of emission at certain blue and green wavelengths from the ionised mercury vapour inside them. When the Kino Flo company put a commercial product on the market in the 'nineties, they solved this, up to a point, by having special phosphors made for their fluorescent tubes. In fact, the peaks in the emission spectrum of Kino Flo tubes were not eliminated, only reduced to the point where they did not have too obvious an effect on the reproduction of colour in film scenes. I regret to say that the Kino Flo company sought to obfuscate the shortcomings of the colour spectrum of their lights by publishing their own specially devised type of spectral

Kino Flo lampheads

graph for their lights, and an accompanying specially devised colour reproduction index (CRI).

In the Kino Flo system, their special fluorescent tubes are put in units as racks of various sizes, containing various numbers of tubes. Standard sizes of fluorescent tubes of lengths from 8 feet to 2 feet can be used, and the units held from one to eight tubes. Effectively, their lampheads are shallow trays, with a metal reflective surface behind, and large barn doors at the sides in the longitudinal direction. This gives a certain amount of directionality to the light, as does the optional addition of "egg crate" baffles (a grid of open cells made of black plastic) that can be clipped on the front of the units. Some models could be dimmed, up to a point. Very small units called Mini-flos taking 12 inch tubes were added to the range, and these could run from 12 volt DC as well as normal AC power sources. In 1993 a new range of even smaller units called "Micro-flos", taking 5 inch long tubes were produced for the system. These could run also from 12 volt DC batteries or 120 volt AC. Kino Flo units essentially act as soft sources, just like the old softlight and northlight units containing incandescent bulbs. Kino Flos saw rapidly increasing use by film cameramen throughout the 'nineties.

New HMI type lamps continued to be developed in this decade, and they were used more and more. HMI bulbs in Fresnel lens lampheads increasingly displaced Fresnel lens tungsten spotlights in standard use, particularly for daylight use, but even on studio sets. HMI tubes were improved with a shorter gap between the electrodes, which increased the light output. A new type of bulb was created at the end of the eighties, when HMI tubes were put inside large PAR type bulbs. (PAR bulbs had existed for many decades, in the first place for car headlights and aircraft landing lights, and then taken over for film purposes, as described in *Film Style and Technology*.) PAR bulbs were moulded of heavy glass with a parabolic reflector making up the back half, and a sort of prismatic lens sealed onto the front. The HMI variant had an inner HMI tube sealed inside the envelope instead of the bare tungsten filament in the older types. They were being made in sizes up to 1200 watts at the beginning of the 'nineties, and like all HMI lights produced a spectrum that approximated to daylight. Also like all HMI lights, they needed a special ballast unit to power them, and now these were all of the high frequency square wave electronic type that removed the problems with stroboscopic effects from the camera shutter frequency.

However, another newly important kind of light confusingly referred to as a HMI PAR light had a different construction. These units had a deep parabolic reflector that was independent of the actual HMI lamp or globe. In fact it was somewhat like the first quartz-iodine (or tungsten-halogen) film lights of the nineteen-sixties, called first Multibcams, then various other names as they were made by different makers, e.g. LowelQuartz or Redheads, etc. These all had rough surfaced parabolic metal reflectors that could be focussed over a certain middle flood range. The new lights had deeper parabolic reflectors with a polished surface, and a new type of single-ended HMI lamp bulb projecting through a hole in the centre of the bottom of the reflector. Up to this point, HMI lamp tubes were all made with the two contacts for the electric current at opposite ends of the tube, which was referred to as "double-ended" construction. The new type of lamps had the actual HMI tube inside another larger tube with two electrical contact pins on its base, which was referred to as "single-ended" construction. The complete HMI PAR

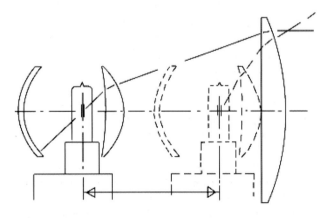

A diagram of the focussing system of a Dedolight, with the bulb, reflector, and internal lens shown at the left (spot) positions, and in dashed outline in the right (flood) position.

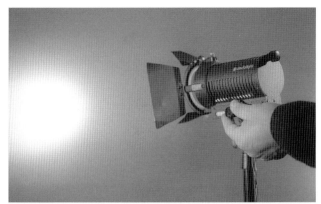

A Dedolight and the area it illuminates at the semi-spot focus position.

lamp unit produced a very narrow spot beam with a spread of only about 6 degrees that could scarcely be varied by moving the lamp back and forth inside the reflector. However they could be converted to give flood beams of various width by putting accessory lenses of various kinds over the open front of the lamp. These included a Fresnel lens, which could vary the beam spread from around 40 degrees to 60 degrees.

The power and size of these units gradually moved upward over the 'nineties from 2.5 Kw in 1990, to 4Kw around 1994, to 6 Kw in 1995, and so on to 12 Kw at the end of the decade, and they were extensively used from their introduction for location and set lighting, but not for lighting the actors directly.

A new type of small lighting unit appeared at the beginning of the decade, designed by the German cameraman Dedo Weigert, and called "Dedolights". These had a new and efficient focussing system, involving a moving section with a 12 volt 100 watt tungsten halide bulb with a spherical reflector behind it, and a convex lens in front. This moved inside the tubular body with respect to another larger convex lens fixed to the front of the unit. This double lens system gave a beam angle from 4.5 degrees to 46 degrees, and also a very even intensity across the width of the beam in the middle focussing range (around medium flood beam), dropping very quickly to zero once past the edge. This was unlike all the standard film lighting units of the past, which had a soft edge to their beams; a penumbra of at least several degrees. The sharp edge to the Dedolight beam was not actually a great advantage, as in general it is preferable that the beam of light from any lighting unit melts into the surrounding illumination, in the way that light does from real world sources. In fact, the light from Dedolights would have been even harder if the front surface of the front lens had not been made with a rough surface, creating a built-in diffusion filter. However, the optical efficiency of Dedolights was an advantage, as was their small size and light weight – they were about 160 mm. long and 100 mm. wide, and weighed about 700 gram. The type of construction used, with a lens very close to the lamp, meant that the design could not be used for large lights, though the Dedo company eventually produced a 300 watt model. Another factor in their success, as was also the case for the Kinoflo lights, was that cameramen were using the new fast film stocks more and more in photographing films, and hence tended to use small lighting units more. Nevertheless, Dedolights were only used as supplementary lights, not for general set lighting. Their lack of sensitivity to vibration was another factor in their adoption in certain situations, such as moving car and plane interiors.

Another newcomer in 1993 was a device called a Chimera. This was an accessory that could be attached to the front of spotlights, and was a sort of diffuser that softened the beam very considerably. It was in fact not a new idea, but a commercial version of the "Croniecone" invented by the cameraman Jordan Cronenweth in the 'eighties. This was a truncated cone about a metre long made of light rigid opaque sheet, which had its narrow end fixed to the front of a spotlight, and had the wider end covered with a sheet of translucent diffusing material. The point of this device was that it diffused the spot beam more than would a sheet of diffusing material fixed just in front of the lens of a spotlight, but less than a larger sheet of diffusing material held several metres in front of a spotlight on stands. This latter device needed more setting up, and also acted as a completely soft (non-directional) source. To put it another way, the light from a Croniecone still had a certain amount of directionality in it. The Chimera, which was marketed in the United States by a company of that name, had a rectangular frame held out from the attachment on front of a spotlight by curved struts to each corner, and covered with black fabric, except at the front, which was covered with white translucent sheet. A further advantage that the Chimera had over the original Croniecone was that it was collapsible. Other companies produced similar diffusing devices, for instance Lowellight designed a "Rifalite" with built-in light source and such things were classified under the general title "lightbanks". These devices caught on fairly rapidly in the 'nineties, and spread to other countries quite quickly.

Although it had been previously used on *The River* (1984), it was only during this decade that a new type of soft light became really important. These were helium-filled balloons made of white translucent material, which had a light source suspended inside them near their centre. They had first been developed for the lighting of large scale construction sites, but in films their main use was to light very large and high interior spaces where it was difficult or impossible to rig ordinary film lighting above the action being filmed. Leading companies in the introduction of these lighting balloons for film purposes were LTM, Publux, and Lee Lighting. The balloons were usually about 2 metres in diameter, and the lights inside were 4 Kw or 8 Kw tungsten bulbs, though HMI lamps were also used. In America, an alternative idea for the same purpose was to use white weather balloons, without lights inside them, as reflectors over a large indoor area, with powerful spots shone up onto them from the floor.

A smaller and simpler spherical soft light source had first been used in the previous decade, but became more prominent in the 'nineties. This was the Chinese lantern. These were widely available as a domestic lighting device, and they consist of a sphere of thin white paper kept in shape by a series of circular rings on the inside, about half a metre in diameter, and with openings at the top and bottom. For film purposes, a more powerful lamp of some hundreds of watts might be used, and this radiated soft light in all directions that falls off quite rapidly in intensity. A standard technique was to hang one from the end of a fishpole so that a grip could move it about to give a bit of extra light on a moving actor as the scene developed.

Traditional Fresnel lens spotlights continued to be used most overall in lighting sets, and the main development in this area was that most makes were redesigned to be a bit smaller and lighter, though essentially the same. Many of the lighting manufacturing companies gave their smaller units individual names, such as "Bambino", "Mizar", and "Pepper", instead of just using the traditional nicknames such a "Dinky" and "Pup" for those with powers in the 100 to 500 watt region. No doubt this was connected with the marketing obsession with "branding" and "intellectual property" which has become so dominant in recent times. At the more powerful end of the Fresnel spotlight range, development had centered on creating units with ever more powerful HMI lamps inside, and maximum wattages reached 18 Kw in 1990, where they stayed for the rest of the decade.

A quite new accessory material for film lighting appeared early in the 'nineties, and was much used. This was "Blackwrap", which was a sheet of very thick aluminium foil with a black coating on both sides. This proved very useful for moulding around the front of lighting units to add extra control and delimitation of the light beam coming from them, with an extra degree of precision beyond that given by the traditional "barn doors", "snoots", and so on.

Lighting Styles

Foreign cameramen were used more and more on American films during the 'nineties. One reason was that it was easier to get away with this, as more production took place outside the reach of the Hollywood unions, and another was that good foreign cameramen were cheaper than American cameramen, and yet another was that they were faster. This last was because their lighting was on the whole simpler, though remaining good-looking. British television drama was a particularly good training ground for these qualities. American made-for-television films were not so useful for developing high quality lighting technique, as the producers continued to insist on low lighting ratios being used on them, which tends to produce a bland flatness in their visual appearance.

Although television commercials and pop music promo shorts had an increasing influence on film style, and began to contribute more new directors to feature film-making, very few new film cameraman came up solely through lighting

them, the only obvious examples of this career structure being Bill Pope and Ken Kelsch.

A major topic in the professional discussion of film lighting in this decade was the search for a special "look" for a film, and how this might be achieved. It was acknowledged that the production design of a film was important in this respect (as indeed it is very important indeed), but cameramen and camerawomen were very eager to put their own mark on a film. The special treatment techniques described above were very important in this respect, and these were used rather more than in the previous decade, though still not on the majority of films, because of their extra cost, particularly when applied to the final distribution prints of a film.

The continuing collaboration of Robert Richardson with the director Oliver Stone led to some of the most distinctive and influential pictures in American film-making during the 'nineties. The peak of their efforts was *Natural Born Killers* (1994), which used many different techniques to produce obviously noticeable disjunctions in the image flow, to go with the very aggressive content of this film. The film was shot on a mixture of 35 mm. colour, Super 8 colour, 16 mm. black and white and 35 mm. black and white, and on colour video as well. Although the experienced eye could make out the visual difference between these different media, the only major noticeable distinction for general audiences was between the colour material and the black and white material. This is because the 35 mm. colour cinematography was entirely done with diffusion filters on the lens, and this, combined with Robert Richardson's trick of letting parts of the image flare out, made most of the 35 mm. material not much less fuzzy than the Super 8 footage blown up to 35 mm.

Oliver Stone had an expressive program for the use of all the different effects in the film, as can be read in *American Cinematographer* (November 1994, Vol.75 No. 11, p.36-56), but as usual in this area, the relation between the visual effects and the content was not completely consistent. To start at the beginning, the introduction of the black and white footage into the narrative starts before the aggression in the café scene develops, and not at the same time, as Stone claimed. On the lighting side, there is the occasional use of top and backlight on the actors that goes far into over-exposure, and again the application of this strays from a strong connection with the moods of the principal characters. This over-exposure is further accentuated by the flare around the over-exposed areas generated by the fairly heavy diffusion filters on the camera lens used throughout the film. Other exaggerated lighting effects include colour scenes totally in red light and green light. There are three of the latter, and these are particularly striking, as they are done by having nearly all the light sources giving off the same strong green light contrasted with some tiny areas in the image lit with white light. Throw in wide angle lens cinematography combined with swaying hand-held camera and speed changes, not to mention scenes in front of back projection showing archive film footage, and you have a peak in visual aggression that has not been exceeded since. And there are drawn animation scenes cut in suddenly as well.

The use of over-exposure in parts of the image was developed to an extreme in Robert Richardson's work for another inherently aggressive film-maker, Martin Scorsese, in *Bringing Out the Dead* (1999). This film is a symphony of burn-out and flare, particularly in the driving scenes. This is due in the first place to the inherent contrastiness of the scenes being filmed, with the white of medical uniforms and ambulances, plus lots of white street lights against the dark of night inside the shot. Then this contrastiness is accentuated by the bleach bypass treatment given to the prints, and on top of that is the sheer overexposure of the white areas allowed by Richardson. The colours in the image are desaturated by the bleach bypass, which together with the predominance of white and black in the image, takes the look of the film a long way

A strong spotlight coming straight down burns out the areas where it strikes, and the lens diffusion puts a flare around these over-exposed areas in Natural Born Killers.

A production still showing a set-up in Interview with the Vampire *lit by Philippe Rousselot with Chinese lanterns.*

towards high contrast monochrome. The flare from the burnt out whites is accentuated by diffusion filters on the lens of the camera throughout the whole film. (Richardson claimed that this lens diffusion was intended to reduce the extra contrast in the image produced by the bleach bypass process, but with the contrast already so extreme, due to the factors listed, there is no visible effect in the opposite direction.)

The major dimension in the general description of lighting style is that between the use soft and hard light. This is a manner of description taken from the practitioners — to quote Bryan England in *American Cinematographer* (Vol. 71 No.1 Jan. 1990 p.29), talking of his recent work on *I, Madman*, "The general lighting style for the film involved very direct sources, but it was not what I would call a 'hard light' show. I wince when people say 'Was it a hard light show or a soft light show?' It's a 'both' show, depending on what was right for the scene. We have direct source lighting, hard and soft, as the case called for it." This is a fairly typical sort of middle of the road approach. The claim to be using only 'source' lighting, meaning only putting film lights onto the scene from the directions of the ostensible real sources within the scene, which was so common in the previous decade, was a bit less obsessive with cameramen in the 'nineties, but didn't go away, even when it was not completely true. Indeed, there was even the case of Frederick Elmes saying that he didn't use source lighting on *The Ice Storm* (1997). Incidentally, it is a contradiction in terms to call any sort of truly soft lighting "direct", but although the discussion by cameramen of what

The shot resulting from the arrangement of Chinese lanterns shown in the production still above. This lighting style loses its magic when reduced from the actual colour in the film to monochrome,

Philippe Rousselot's "overcast moonlight" type of lighting on an exterior of Interview with the Vampire.

they were doing became both more precise and more detailed in the 'nineties, they could still say muddled and contradictory things sometimes when being interviewed.

At one extreme of the hard/soft spectrum, we find the ultimate in soft lighting from the Old Master David Watkin in *Critical Care* (1997). The sets of this hospital-based film are lit in a high key entirely with large area soft sources that produces the ultimate in creamy beauty. An outstanding piece of work with soft light in low key is *Interview with the Vampire* (1995), in which Philippe Rousselot did most of the lighting with soft sources, working at low light levels around 10-20 foot candles with fast film stock (Kodak 5296). The more intimate scenes are lit with a small number of Chinese lanterns from the directions of the apparent practical sources within the scene, such as candles or fires, and with no backlight. The larger scale night exteriors are lit with bunches of 10 spacelights hung from big cranes over the scene, with only a weak bias in the blue direction in the colour of the light. Rousselot characterised this look as "overcast moonlight", and it was completely different to the usual hard blue directional light from Musco lights or the like which is commonly used,

and utterly distinctive.

At the other extreme, one could mention Anthony Richmond's work on *Candyman* (1992), which is mostly done with hard light, without the intervention of much diffusion to speak of on the lights or on the lens. Another accomplished hard light show was *The Hot Spot*, lit by Ueli Steiger in 1990.

The hard and soft light distinction was used as part of the expressive program on *Dead Again* (1991) — hard light and a black and white picture for the past scenes, and soft light and colour film for the present day scenes. More elaborate expressive programmes worked out over the length of the film narrative, and involving various aspects of cinematography, were quite frequent during the 'nineties.

The use of smoke on film scenes continued to increase in this decade, though it was not all pervasive. Synthetic smoke is not obviously noticeable if used very lightly, but some cameramen used it very heavily and visibly in circumstances where it was implausible. Notable in this respect was Peter Hyams, who sustained his double career as lighting cameraman as well as director of his films by the relentless use of smoke on interiors. The thing about smoke is that it scatters and spreads the light

A typical shot in The Last Boy Scout, *with background brighter than the faces of the actors. Smoke plus lens diffusion spreads the light in this shot, as it does throughout the film.*

around in all directions, so eliminating what would otherwise be visible failures in getting the light into particular areas of the film scene. Heavy lens diffusion works in somewhat the same way, and both can fool most people into thinking the lighting is better than it is.

The increasing use of smoke is also implicated in a new style in lighting that became widely adopted in the 'nineties. One of the most influential pieces of lighting of the 'eighties was Jordan Cronenweth's work on *Blade Runner* (Ridley Scott, 1982). This used smoke relentlessly on both interiors and exteriors, and these scenes were frequently backlit with very strong beams of light or with sources of light within the shot. This produces what is effectively a blurred wall of light behind the actors which is brighter than their faces. Letting large area windows behind the actors go overexposed on interior scenes produces much the same kind of effect, and this also became more common as the 'eighties turned into the 'nineties. Cameramen had always avoided having this happen in the past, as they had also always kept any background less brightly lit than the actors, even in high key scenes – that is, scenes that are mostly bright all over. The most extreme development of this new style, which used all these three kinds of bright backgrounds behind actors pretty well continuously throughout, was *The Last Boy Scout*, photographed by Ward Russell for Tony Scott in 1991. Nothing has since matched this, to my knowledge, but many films now use this style a good deal of the time, particularly big action and science-fiction films.

Another lighting theme carried over from the previous decade, though it has maybe even weakened a bit, is the use of coloured light. This is perhaps more important in Britain than in the United States, for making British city locations, both interior and exterior, less boring than they really are. Examples can be seen in many films, both famous, like *Trainspotting* (1995), and less so, with the work of Ashley Rowe showing a particular inclination in this direction.

Cameras

No new camera companies emerged to challenge the world-wide dominance of Arri, Panavision, and the Fritz Bauer company making the Moviecam. The Arnold & Richter company took to using "Arri" as their company name, and new Arri cameras continued to emerge from Munich. The Arriflex 535 was first shown in 1989, and was described in *Film Style and Technology*, but it was not actually available until 1990. To repeat its major features, it was in general layout and basic construction and features based on the 35 BL4. However, it had redesigned body castings, and more built-in electronics. The most important of the electronics was an electrical interlinking of the variable shutter and the camera speed (frame rate), so that changes in either one of these during the course of the shot would change the other to keep the exposure automatically constant. The Arriflex 535 also had a built-in SMPTE time code and Kodak Keycode generators. The data from the internal electronic controls regulating all the functions of the camera could be read out through a serial data port on the body. This was almost immediately made use of by Marc Shipman-Mueller to connect to a laptop computer running a program to read out the data and control the camera. This did not have that much effect at the time, but it was eventually developed into the Data Capture System used on the *Star Wars Episode One: The Phantom Menace* in 1999.

The other important feature of the Arriflex 535 was a modification to the view-finder system so that it could be swung over from the left to the right side of the camera if desired, and also angled out sideways, as previously available on the Arriflex 16SR. The viewfinder also included a set of illuminated frame markings on the ground glass viewing screen, which made it much easier for the camera operator to see what he was including in the picture under low light levels. In fact these improvements were designed to keep the Arri 35 mm. sync. sound camera competitive with the Panaflex.

All of these new features were taken over into the 16

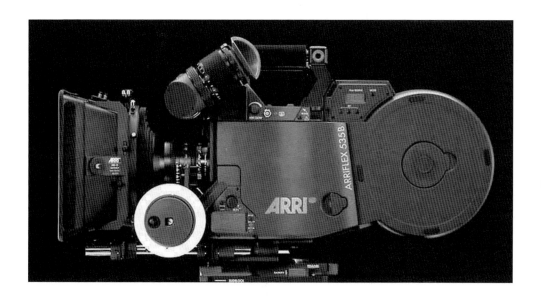

The Arriflex 535. The later B model is illustrated, but the first version was essentially the same.

mm. Arri 16 SR3, which came out in 1993. Otherwise, this camera was very similar to the preceding Arri 16 SR2, and it continued the Arri domination of the world market for 16 mm. cameras.

Arriflex introduced a new 35 mm. camera called the 435 in 1996. This was intended solely for non-synch filming, and would run at speeds up to 150 fps. It weighed 6.5 Kg without the magazine, and had the traditional layout of the old Arriflex 35 mm. cameras, with a slanting displacement magazine on top of the body, rather than the coaxial magazine directly behind the body of the BL series and the 535 camera. There was also a new Arriflex 65 mm. camera called the 765 introduced in 1990. This also had the old Arriflex layout with mirror reflex shutter. However, it was much heavier at 32 Kg., and also appreciably noisier than the other contemporary Arriflex cameras, with noise of 25 dBA at 1 metre from the camera. It would run up to 100 fps.

There was a new model of the Moviecam in 1991, replacing the SuperAmerica model. This was called the "Compact", and it was indeed a bit smaller and lighter than the previous model, weighing only 6.3 Kg with lens and film, but it contained no significant new features. The lighter weight and smaller size gave it a real advantage for use on a Steadicam mount, which was very important given the increasing use of this device.

Panavision brought out a new high speed model in 1991 called the Panastar. This was just like the existing models, but could be run at up to 120 fps (frames per second) in forward and reverse. The major Panaflex camera through the 'nineties continued to be the Platinum model, until Panavision introduced the Millennium Panaflex in 1999. Although this latter camera had a reworked body that was a bit smaller and lighter (39.4 lb.) than the previous model, it was basically the same as far as general layout and mechanics and film movement. There were more internal electronics for speed and shutter control, and some improvements in the viewfinder system and the video assist, all the kind of things that the competition from Arriflex had been doing earlier. Its top film speed remained at 50 fps.

The French Aäton camera company dropped the pretentious dieresis on the second letter of their name at the beginning of the decade, and from this point on their cameras were just Aatons. (Both forms of the name meant nothing, but the double "a"s were intended to put the company at the head of any alphabetical listing, before Arriflex and other camera makers.) Their new 35 mm. camera, which had a similar construction to the 16 mm. model, had some use during the decade in Europe, but in general made little headway in the feature film industry, as although it had a lower physical profile than other cameras, it was no lighter than the Moviecam Compact, and also it was rather noisier than the competition. However, the 16 mm Aaton, now called the XTR model, was used by many cinéma vérité practitioners such as Frederick Wiseman. In 1992 a model called the X-Prod was introduced which took Panavision PL mount lenses, and in 1999 Aaton came out with a new 16mm. camera called

the A-Minima. This used the same movement as the other Aaton cameras, but it had a new body that was much smaller than the others, being 9.7 inches long, 5.5 inches high, and 4.4 inches wide. This was possible because it only took 200 foot daylight loading spools in its magazine. It weighed only 4 lbs. all up, including an onboard battery that would take through 1 hour's worth of film. The motor would run from 2 to 50 fps, and it also had a built-in intervalometer for time lapse photography. It was cheap, too, at around $15,000.

There was some activity amongst special purpose cameras, with a new small 35 mm. camera called the Robings SL, which only weighed 6 lbs when fully loaded, and was used on *Strange Days* (1995) for the long POV takes which were basic to that film's plot. The Clairmont Camera Co. adapted some Mitchell GC cameras from the late 'fifties giving them a mirror reflex shutter. The point about these was there extremely low height of 6 3/4 inches, which was useful for getting them into small spaces or for having cars drive over them.

In 1990 there was a new high speed 35 mm. camera from the General Camera Corporation – the Image 300 and then in 1992 the Wilcam company made the Wilcam 12 for Clairmont Camera. Both had pin registration, and both would go up to 300 fps. In this area the competition was the Photosonics 4ER from the previous decade, which would do 360 fps. The really significant use of these cameras came later in the decade, when science fiction films like *The Matrix* made much play with slow motion acrobatics.

Photosonics, the longest established firm in slow-motion cameras, also introduced a new extreme high speed reflex camera in 1992, the 4B/4C, which would run at 2,500 fps, though without pin registration, and with of course a rotating prism shutter.

In 1993 the Wilcam company also made some new VistaVision cameras for hire by the Clairmont Camera Co. These were the W7 and the W9, which were for shooting without sound, and would run at speeds from 2 to 200 fps in the case of the first, and 2 to 100 fps in the case of the second. There was also the W11 for synch. sound shooting, which would run at 24,25 or 30 fps, and was not as quiet as it might have been, producing 24 dBA at 3 metres. All these cameras were provided with a range of lenses from 28 mm. to 135 mm.

Messing with the Camera

The internal interconnection between camera speed and shutter angle in the Arri 535 and subsequent models of the Arri cameras made it easier to compensate for the change in exposure resulting from speed changes of the camera during a shot. Such changes in camera speed, from normal motion to slow motion or accelerated motion, or vice versa, became increasingly fashionable during the 'nineties. As a result, the technique acquired a special name in the United States, and came to be described as "ramping" the camera speed. However, this new internal electronic control was not necessary to this technique, as the first famous and intentionally noticeable use of it occurred in *Raging Bull* in 1980, before such advanced camera features were available. The change in aperture to compensate for the camera speed change could still be done by hand, as it was then. And these internal electronic controls of speed and shutter angle, etc. were not foolproof, as a lag in the reaction of the system to changes made to the speed sometimes occurred under certain conditions.

Another new camera trick involved shooting scenes with the shutter angle reduced from its usual 180 degree opening to 90 or 45 degrees. The effect of this is that fast moving objects appear as a series of sharply defined shapes on the film frame, instead of having a certain amount of blurring out in the direction of their motion. In other words, the illusion of smooth movement of fast moving objects across the screen is disrupted for the film audience. The first notable use of this technique in feature films occurred in *Saving Private Ryan* (1998), where it was applied to some battle scenes. The intention, as described by the cameraman Janusz Kaminski in *American Cinematographer* (August 1998), was to create "... a definite sense of urgency and reality." Now, this technique possibly creates something like a sense of urgency, but it has nothing to do with a sense of reality, since all the cameras used to film the World War II all had shutters fixed at 180 degrees (or nearby), so the effect does not occur in footage from the Normandy landings or anywhere else. The technique was purely expressive, like other things that Spielberg and Kaminski did on this film, and which had already been used by others. These include shooting some of the footage with uncoated lenses, as done by David Watkin in *The Charge of the Light Brigade* (1968), and adding extra vibration mechanically and optically to the cameras in the battle scenes, as had been previously done in *The Rock* (1996). Another technique Spielberg used was to have the camera shutters put slightly out of synchronism with the film pull-down mechanism, so that there was a vertical streaking of the highlights in the image, as done in *Full Metal Jacket* (1987). So Spielberg piled them all up, and audiences seemed to like it. Actually, defective footage that was taken with a shaking or out-of-focus camera was in general not included in newsreels during World War II, so there is no sense of reality in such methods from this point of view either. An "illusion of reality" for present-day audiences, maybe.

Although it is strictly outside my concerns here, I can't help remarking on another aspect of the way this and other recent war films treat of reality. This is that the troops on the beach, the parachutists dropping, the planes flying overhead, and so on, are shown as packed far more closely together than they were in reality back in World War II. This tendency was by no means so marked in the war films made in the 'fifties and 'sixties, presumably because so many of the film-makers then had actually been around during World War II. Careful inspection of the archive newsreel footage does show how it actually was in those days, but this kind of realism is quite incompatible with the main stylistic development of entertainment film-making in recent times. What is desired

is more jolts per millisecond for the audience, and excess in every possible way.

Camera Lenses

There were no major developments in ordinary lenses for cinematography in the decade, but a certain amount of updating of designs from the major firms. Cooke zoom lenses continued to be made by Taylor-Hobson, with a new 18-100 mm. Varotal model appearing in 1992 and a new 25-250 mm. Cinetal model in 1993. But in 1998 Cooke Optics Ltd. became an independent company, so going against the general trend of industrial consolidation into larger and larger companies, and they marked this occasion with a return to making fixed focal length prime lenses. Cooke Optics also took over the continued production of the zoom lenses. The new S4 series had a maximum aperture of T2, and focal lengths of 18 mm., 25 mm., 32 mm., 50 mm., 75 mm., and 100 mm. The company also continued to design and make lenses for others over this decade. For instance, they produced a new series of anamorphic zoom lenses for the Technovision brand in 1992; specifically 18-90 mm T2.3, 25-250 mm. T2.3, and 18.5-55.5 mm T2.4 lenses.

Arri cameras were supplied only with Carl Zeiss lenses, and in 1995 Zeiss added a series of what they called variable prime lenses to their range. These had focal lengths that could be varied over a very short 2:1 range, so could not reasonably be described as "zoom" lenses. The advantage to this was that they could be almost the same size, and have almost as little distortion, as ordinary fixed focus lenses, and also have a larger maximum aperture of T2.2. The focal length range of the three lenses in this group went in three steps from 16 mm. to 105 mm.

Super 16 filming became more important in the 'nineties, and there was little point now in an optical company producing new lenses that just covered the ordinary 16 mm. frame area. Super 16 lenses from the Russian Optica company were being imported into other countries from 1995. The range ran from 8 mm. to 50 mm. with a maximum aperture of T1.3, and also included a rather unadventurous 25-80 mm. zoom with a maximum aperture of T3.3. Century Precision Optics in the United States made a better contribution to covering the extreme wide-angle end of Super 16 filming with their 6mm. T1.9 lens in 1995. In 1999 Optex did even better, with a range of Super 16 wide-angle lenses of focal lengths 4mm., 5.5 mm., and 8 mm., all with maximum aperture of T1.9.

As before, video camera zoom lenses continued to be adapted for 16 mm. filming, with a conversion of a Canon zoom that had a focal length of 7 mm. to 56 mm. being specially popular. This was improved upon by a purpose-built new zoom from Angénieux in 1998, labelled the HR for Super 16 filming. It had a focal length from 7-81 mm and a maximum aperture of T2.4.

Russia was also involved in a new range of Anamorphic lenses for 35 mm. filming marketed under the name Hawk in 1997. The design for these was done in Russia, but the lenses were actually made in Germany by the Rodenstock optical company. Focal lengths ran from 25 mm. to 100 mm. with a maximum aperture of T2.2, and then with some longer lenses going the rest of the way to 250 mm. with a maximum aperture of T3. These were well received, and used on *Star Wars: The Phantom Menace,* amongst other films.

There was a flurry of development in the area of specialised lenses, with the introduction of a new group of lenses with swivelling mounts. It is not clear what caused the revival of this idea, which had been used in the late 'thirties as part of the interest in getting greater depth of field, as described in *Film Style and Technology*. With 500 EI film stock widely used, and good wide angle lenses readily available, Gregg Toland type deep focus would be no problem in the 'nineties. Perhaps the contemporary habit of working near maximum aperture was so ingrained that this approach was not considered. In any case, the Clairmont Camera company announced in 1992 what they called "swing/shift" lenses with 24mm., 28mm., and 35 mm. lenses in special mounts in which the lens could be rotated off its axis. Focussing was by moving the front part of the lens on tracks. Panavision also came out with its own lenses of this type, which they called "slant focus" lenses, which term gives a better idea of how the idea worked. They had a 45 mm T2.8 for ordinary 35 mm. filming, and a 90 mm. T4.5 for anamorphic use. Possibly provoked by the independent Bergerson company putting a series of Nikon still camera lenses in tilt mounts with an Arri PL fitting, Arri eventually produced its own "shift and tilt" lens system in 1996. One common situation where the staggered depth of field of tilting lenses was useful is when filming two people sitting side by side in a car. Frequently one wants to get a shot from about 45 degrees to the line joining them – it would be an over the shoulder shot if they were facing each other – and keep them both in focus. Using a very wide angle lens to get greater depth of field to achieve this brings with it a certain amount of perspective distortion, and a swinging or tilting lens of normal focal length avoids this. Certainly this is one of the ways that swing/shift lenses were used when they became available again in this decade, though it was not how they were used when they were first invented in the 'thirties.

There was new activity in another area of specialized lens design. This was in the production of what were called in the 'sixties "snorkel", or probe, or periscope lenses. These lenses were mounted on the end of a long tube, either in line with the tube axis, or at right angles to it. In the latter case there was a prism or mirror included to turn the image through ninety degrees. The extension tube has to include extra relay or field lenses inside itself to maintain the focus of the lens used. The point of this device was to film inside very constricted spaces, particularly small-scale three-dimensional models, as desired in the production of some commercials. It was customary to use a wide angle lens on the device, and this produces an even more striking wide angle deep focus visual effect than if the same lens was mounted directly on the camera. These lenses had a restricted maximum aperture of T11 at best.

As the competition to spice up feature films with ever more striking shots increased, this sort of lens moved into feature film production. So in 1995 Panavision introduced a new version of this kind of lens, called the Frazier lens system, after the Australian wild-life cameraman Jim Frazier, who had worked it out for his own filming of insects and the like. His design had the main lens mounted on two swivelling joints that could rotate independently of each other through 360 degrees at the tip of the extension tube. This could put the taking lens at any desired angle relative to the camera body. Any rotation of these joints inevitably produced a rotation of the image, and this was compensated for by a special prism at the back end of the system which rotated the image back to vertical. The adapted still camera lenses used on the device gave a maximum aperture of T7, which was another significant advance. Eventually all the movements of the system were motorized, so it could be used when motion control was required for special effects compositing. The Frazier system was used on *Titanic*, *Men in Black*, *Saving Private Ryan*, and *Love is the Devil*, amongst other features made in the late 'nineties. The success of the Frazier system prompted other manufacturers to produce very similar lens systems at the end of the decade.

Love is the Devil (John Maybury, 1998) also tried a few other kinds of camera tricks to produce a film equivalent to the distortions in the paintings of Francis Bacon, who was the subject of this fiction feature. The former British avant-garde film-maker John Maybury borrowed from his more famous avant-garde predecessors such devices as removing the camera shutter, and replacing it with rotating vanes on an electric drill held in front of the lens, and shooting through the bottom of a glass ashtray, as the great Brakhage had done long before. But actually most of the quasi-Baconian visual stylings of *Love is the Devil* were done by lighting the scenes with a well-placed top light, plus a fair amount of lens diffusion.

The movements of the *zeitgeist* had the Clairmont Camera Company in the United States producing a commercial method for creating the "through an ashtray" or fun-house mirror kind of effect, simultaneously with the production of *Love is the Devil*. This was their "squishy lens", which produced a wobbly image surrounding a clear undistorted area. The distorted shapes it produced could be altered and moved around, up to a point, by controls mounted on the lens. Of course this kind of device was becoming fairly pointless, as it is much easier to do this sort of thing by computer graphics manipulation.

Camera Supports

The only really new idea in devices for supporting a movie camera was the Cinesaddle, a cheap Australian invention that became available in other countries in 1990. This was a canvas bag about 40 cm. each way, loosely filled with plastic granules, rather like a small version of the "bean bag" chairs of the 'sixties. It could be placed on any surface, irregular or not, and then a camera could be plumped down into it to point in the appropriate direction. It allowed smooth rotations of the camera over small angles, and could also be tied down with the supplied ropes to make a quick car hood mount for car shots. Other related tricks were also possible with the device.

Otherwise there were no major developments in camera supports in the 'nineties, just somewhat improved versions of existing devices. The Steadicam patents expired around 1994 in the United States, and in 1997 a copy of the concept was marketed as the Glide-Cam. At first only a lightweight version taking small cameras was sold, though heavy duty models were announced. It does not seem to have been taken up for feature film-making to any great extent in the 'nineties. In 1991 a device called the Pogocam was produced, which was very like the central support post and gimbal section of the Steadicam. That is, it was a vertical rod with a pivoted hand grip in the middle, to which the camera attached at the top with a small video assist on it, and a long dumbbell shaped counterweight at the bottom of the rod. Other similar devices also appeared, but unlike the original Steadicam, they did not prove very important.

Dollies made by the German Panther company were already made with digital control of their movements, and were preferred for motion control use. There was a fair amount of activity amongst smaller manufacturers producing new and improved hot heads, though the only significant innovation was adding an extra degree of rotation. This could be of some use occasionally, but not in general. New jib arms to carry cameras on hot heads also appeared, and the most successful of these was the Technocrane made by the Technovision company, and introduced at the beginning of the decade in Europe. This had a jib arm which could extend out to 21 feet. This and other similar cranes were an improvement on the Louma crane in that they were more rigid, and that their movement could be more precisely controlled, which made them more suitable for use with electronic motion control, which was being used more and more for special effects on films as the years went by. In 1999 even bigger cranes for use with cameras on hotheads appeared with an even greater reach. These were the SuperAero crane which could extend to 40 ft carrying a hot head, and the Swissjib which went out to 43 ft. The use of a jib arm with hot head became standard, and it was mostly used fairly discretely, but it gave opportunity for showing-off with complicated crane movements close-in to things, for those directors so inclined.

Elaborate methods of getting aerial travelling shots continued to be devised, with the camera suspended on a moving platform on cables between pylons, as in the Skyman and Cablecam systems invented at the beginning of the decade. Helicopter mounts like the Wescam and the very similar Spacecam continued to be frequently used, particularly in the United States, and in 1994 Cine-Hovercam came out with a small Pegasus remote-controlled helicopter to do the same kind of job.

70mm. and Special Formats

There was very little use of shooting on 65/70 mm. film for ordinary feature film-making during the 'nineties. The only examples were, firstly, *Far and Away* (1992), which was not completely shot on 65 mm. negative, but incorporated sections shot on 35mm. anamorphic negative which were then blown up to 70mm. for the prime show prints. There were some complaints about the quality of this, and even more so about the quality of the 6 track sound for the film. The second example was Kenneth Branagh's *Hamlet* (1996), which was completely shot on 65 mm., and which was much more satisfactory. Despite using a certain amount of long take moving camera, Branagh kept the Average Shot Length down to 6 seconds by fast cutting in many of the dialogue scenes.

The main use for 70 mm. film was in film-making for what were called the special format venues. These cinemas had one form or another of very large screens, were often part of museums or theme parks, and had films made exclusively for them. The most numerous of them used the IMAX format, established in 1970, which shot on 65 mm. negative moving sideways through the special cameras for the process, which had 15 perforation pull-down. The resulting size of the film frame is 50 mm by 70 mm., and the finished film was projected by an entirely novel form of projector which used a rolling loop system without pull-down claws or sprockets. This type of movement greatly reduced the wear and scratching on the film prints. The kind of wear and scratching produced by ordinary projector mechanisms would have been very noticeable when images are being shown with such large viewing angle and such magnification to the audiences in the special theatres used for the process. The IMAX company also had another process called OMNIMAX, which used the same large film, but was filmed with a 180 degree fish-eye lens, and then the image was projected onto a hemispherical domed screen in a special auditorium. Other processes included Showscan, which used 70 mm. film shot at 60 frames per second rather than 24 fps., and various forms of 360 degree projection. These latter either used multiple cameras photographing adjoining sectors of the full circle, or a special lens taking a single image ring shaped image of the surrounding scene within a square frame on 70 mm. film with 10 perforation pull down. The image was projected back onto a circular screen by a special lens pointing straight down into the centre of the circle, but only emitting the image around the edge of the lens. Although invented by Ernst Heiniger as "Swissorama", this process was manufactured and marketed by the Iwerks company in the United States as Imagine 360.

Most films made for these special formats were non-fiction, just like the original Cinerama, and the few that *were* fiction films were only about 30 minutes in length. Unlike the special format films that appeared at the Montreal Expo in 1967, these more recent special formats had no effect on ordinary film-making.

Motion Control

The increased use of elaborate composite shots, done either the old way in the optical printer, or in a computer as was happening more and more, meant that motion control of camera movements became more and more important. A desire to show off this technique, and also the virtuosity of actor Michael Keaton, resulted in *Multiplicity* in 1996. At the peak of this, Michael Keaton acted with three copies of himself within the one frame, in shots that included a fair amount of camera movement. The technology had advanced to the point that, by recording the images from the video assist on the camera, a composite showing the potential final result from the combined takes could be played back almost immediately. This indicated whether further attempts would be needed to get perfect interplay within the shot between the versions of Keaton's character. Of course, the final composite shot actually used for the film was created afterwards in the usual way from the separate film negatives that had been shot. This technique did have production costs, as about 60 technicians were on set to run the motion control for all of this. But on the other hand, in this particular case you were getting four actors for the price of one.

By 1999, in *Star Wars Episode One: The Phantom Menace*, motion control was used on almost all the shots, regardless of whether particular special effects were planned for them or not. The idea was that if it seemed appropriate to add unplanned special effects afterwards, it could be easily done. This total motion control was based on features of the Arri 535 and 435 cameras that have been mentioned above. That is, the camera speed in fps, the shutter-angle, time-code and footage information could be output through the camera's serial data port. The Arri Controlled Lens Motors being used already had encoders in them to note their positions, and simple encoders were attached to the tripod head and the dolly, along the lines already used for motion control of these devices. All this data was fed into a central Universal Data Capture (UDC) box. Inside the UDC, the separate pieces of information were combined and correlated to the camera shutter pulse. For each frame exposed by the camera, the UDC sends out a message which includes the following information: frame number, time-code number, userbits number, feet-per-second, shutter angle, tripod pan, tripod tilt, tripod roll, dolly track, dolly height, and dolly spare. This data was translated then into a format that Industrial Light and Magic computers could deal with when the special effects, including the CGI characters in the scene, were created.

All the footage of *Star Wars Episode One: The Phantom Menace* was digitized.

Computer Digital Effects

At the beginning of the 'nineties, special effects compositing was still being done almost entirely in the traditional manner in optical printers. In 1990, a successful film that absolutely depended on special effects, like *Ghost*, could still be entirely done with the old methods, and very well, at that. The leading edge of the use of computer graphics in film in this year was *The Abyss*, which had a few shots including a computer generated creature that consisted of a fairly simple

moving watery amoeboid form with simulated reflections in it. The very small number of other examples in this year also consisted of dropping a three-dimensional computer graphic into an ordinary scene. Otherwise, there was a small amount of wire removal from shots of suspended models and the like, which had already been done with computer methods for a year or so.

Further development of computer manipulation of scenes shot on film had to wait for the development of devices to sequentially scan and digitize the images on motion picture film at a high enough resolution to capture most of the visual information in them. This happened in 1993, with the introduction of Kodak's Cineon scanner, which scanned at 4,000 lines per inch, and Quantel's Domino system, which included a scanner and recorder working at 2,900 lines per inch. However the actual compositing in the Domino system works at 2880 by 2048 pixels.

The scanning speed of the Kodak device was about 2 seconds per frame. It should be pointed out that there is information involving very fine detail in the image on film negative that even scanning at 4,000 lines per inch does not pick up, but it was judged that this was not essential to the entertainment version of reality used in fiction films. There was also a problem in handling the immense amounts of computer data generated by scanning at even 4,000 lines per inch. (Up to 9.4 Megabytes per film frame.) In fact as things developed over the next several years, there was a general tendency to only work at 2,000 lines per inch for film purposes. The film recorder (dubbed the Lightning) for the Cineon system took 10 seconds to record one frame back to film.

There were already other high resolution film recorders available to take the results of computer generation and manipulation of imagery back onto film, so from 1993 onwards the use of CGI (Computer Generated Imagery) in feature film increased fairly quickly, even though the price of these systems was in the region of 1 to 2 million dollars, and the charges for using them correspondingly high. As other makes of film scanners and recorders became available over the next several years, and as the cost of faster and faster computers to do the digital work dropped, the amount of computer graphics work done on feature films increased. By 1998, the first telecine working in real time at a resolution of 2000 lines per inch (the Philips Spirit) became available, and it was now possible to digitize the entire footage of a film (*Pleasantville*) for computer treatment, and then record it back to film, which was certainly not practical five years before.

Time Stands Still

These new methods for the computer treatment of film images made another development possible. This was the simultaneous photography of a scene with a linear array of closely spaced still cameras, and then the turning these images into a sequence of frames on film. With about 100 still cameras, which was common for this technique, one obtains 4 seconds of screen time, which shows a fairly fast track along or around what appears as a frozen moment in time. If the scene includes what would be fast moving objects in real time, such as people running, or pigeons taking off, the effect is extremely striking. The duration of the effect can be extended and manipulated by making a computer graphics interpolation of more intermediate frames between the actual frames from the still cameras. The possibility of doing this was created by the recent advances in computer digital graphics. The technique was dubbed "time slice", and was used in many commercials and pop videos from 1995 onwards by people who worked in this area, such as Tim McMillan, Emmanuel Carlier, and Michel Gondry. A refinement of this technique was to have a motion picture camera at the beginning and end of the array, so that normal motion in the scene could be made to lead seamlessly into the effect. For feature films, the first significant outing for these methods was in *The Matrix* (1999). This film also used an extension of the technique, which was to have the still cameras fired in very rapid sequence, rather than simultaneously. If a row of 96 cameras are fired successively at 1 thousandth of a second intervals, the resulting sequence of frames at 24 frames per second runs 4 seconds, and is the same as if it had been filmed by a camera running at 1000 frames per second while it travelled down the length of the array of cameras. This effect is exactly the same as extreme slow motion shot with a very rapidly moving camera, though actually doing it that way would be extremely impractical. This latter technique was eventually called "flo-mo".

A further refinement in this particular film was to shoot these effects with a circular array of cameras shooting the action going on at their centre, through holes in a surrounding circular green screen, rather than filming with a linear array of cameras on a real location or set. The film resulting from the shoot was combined with the image of a synthetic set created with three dimensional computer graphics, and which matched the movement of the apparent camera filming the scene. More of the details of this can be read in the article "TechnoBabel" on pages 46 to 55 in *American Cinematographer* (April 1999, Vol. 80, No. 4)

Motion Capture

Motion capture, as a means of getting realistic movement into computer generated and animated figures, was only just starting in 1990. As a guide to the computer animators, this technique uses actual humans to perform the movements that are going to be done by the figures to be created by three-dimensional computer animation. In the early development of this technique, the actors wore black tights with white ping-pong balls attached to them at key points such as their joints and extremities, and their movements were recorded on video from several angles. From these recordings, the co-ordinates of their key points could be transferred into the three-dimensional computer animation program as a guide to the animation of synthetic figures. One could view it as the equivalent of the rotoscoping process which has long been used as a guide for animators working in two-dimensional

drawn animation. A primitive version of this technique was used in *Total Recall* for the only scene in the film involving computer graphics, but it was rapidly refined, and used more and more as the decade went on.

Straight Out of the Funny Pages

Live-action films based on comic strips date way back, at least to the nineteen-twenties, but it was only during the 'nineties that a conscious attempt was made to base the design of films on the design of the images in the comic books which provided their source material. The important year was 1989, when *Batman* was an immense commercial success. Less successful was the lower budget *Captain America*, directed by Albert Pyun, though it also did its best to reproduce the look of its source comic strip. The next major entry, *Dick Tracy* (Warren Beatty, 1990) was less close to its inspiration. The original Dick Tracy comic strip was a poor model for pictorial design, since its frames were packed with dialogue balloons which overpowered the composition. The only significant visual feature that stood out was that Dick Tracy himself was frequently drawn in profile in foreground Close Up. In fact, back in the early days of the strip, he was *only* drawn in profile. Much more recently, Chester Gould was still drawing Tracy in profile Close Up about once every six frames, and the speech balloons were still fairly dense. But in contrast, the film only manages six profile Close Ups of Dick Tracy in approximately 1,500 shots, and this is an index of how little it owes to the comic strip as far as design is concerned. Of course, Warren Beatty does not really have the right nose (a broken hawk-nose) for the part, and would hardly want to spend all his time side-on to the camera anyway. The impossibly grotesque heads of the various villains, which tended to be geometrically aligned with the frame in the comic strip, lose some of that quality in the film. Actually the design of the film *Dick Tracy* is more about the *idea* of comic strip design. The film compositions rely on large simply shaped areas of primary colour applied to the sets and costumes, either directly, or with coloured lighting, in a way that does not occur in the source strip.

When Tim Burton came to make *Batman Returns* (1992), he inevitably used his new production power to turn it away from the original comic strip towards his own visual style as much as possible. The production design for the sections dealing with the world of "The Penguin" are very visibly based on Burton's own illustrative style, and indeed the component of his own personal monochrome drawing style derived from the art of Edward Gorey comes through very strongly in these parts of the film.

Younger directors were more concerned to get the real look of "graphic novels", as comic books with pretensions are called in recent times. Alex Proyas with his 1992 film based on *The Crow* comic book series, and Danny Cannon, with the 1995 *Judge Dredd*, were obviously concerned to get a close reproduction of the look of their original sources, and Proyas later produced *Dark City* in 1998, which managed to look like a graphic novel that had not yet been written and drawn.

Then there were the live-action movies derived from the cheap TV animation of the 'fifties and 'sixties such as *Boris and Natasha* (1992) and *The Flintstones* (1994), of which the less said, the better.

Film Sound

During the nineteen-nineties digital methods took over the treatment of sound in films even more completely than on the visual side. This was inevitable, as the amount of information in the sound track is vastly less than that in the film, or even video, picture. Hence it is far easier to store sound and manipulate it in digital form in a computer. The music industry had already been working with digital sound as standard from the beginning of the 'eighties, when Compact Discs were introduced, so much of the technology was available for use in film with minimal modification. There was some use of digital recording and mixing of music for American feature film sound from 1982, and in 1984 digital recording was used in the treatment of sound effects for *Indiana Jones and the Temple of Doom*, using what was described as a "computer-controlled digital sound work station" at Lucasfilm.

Another important 'eighties development that was left out of the second edition of *Film Style and Technology* was the use of computer controlled motorized fader controls on film sound mixing desks. Previous to this, when a dubbing mixer was adjusting the levels of the various sound tracks being re-recorded to produce the mixed sound track, he had to remember where he had set the volume control faders at each instant when another pass was being made to get the relative sound levels just right. The first mixing desks to use computer systems to memorize the settings of the faders at every instant were introduced for film purposes at the very beginning of the nineteen-eighties. These made a substantial improvement to the efficiency of the sound mixing process, but since they were extremely expensive to buy, they were only slowly introduced into the top end of the film industry through the 'eighties.

In the 'nineties the situation in the film dubbing theatres completely changed. Computer industry developments meant that the latest hard disks and magneto-optical disks had sufficient storage capacity to hold a workable amount of digital sound. This meant that proprietary systems using a computer-controlled disk recorder, used in conjunction with a mixing desk, began to replace working from sprocketed magnetic film on multiple replay machines when mixing film sound tracks. As in most of these areas in the last couple of decades, television practice led film practice. The first company in the field was AMS with their Audiofile system, but others such as Fairlight and the DAR SoundStation II joined in quickly at the end of the 'eighties. The SoundStation incorporated the "Wordfit" program for automatic dialogue replacement (ADR) mentioned in *Film Style and Technology* in the chapter on the 'eighties. This computer program could mould specially recorded replacement dialogue or dialogue from alternative takes to exactly fit with the unsatisfactory sync. dialogue originally recorded with the picture. This was much

faster than the traditional trial and error method of having an actor record the replacement dialogue over and over again till it approximately fitted the lip movements in the picture.

Digital Audio Workstations (DAWs) like those mentioned basically comprised a computer controlling their functions, a hard disk or magneto-optical disk carrying the digital sound recording, and extra electronics to provide the processing power to handle operations on the digital sound files. These were essentially printed circuit boards with extra microchips; in particular digital signal processing chips (DSPs). In the 'nineties, the processor in the computer was not powerful enough to carry out signal processing as well as control functions. DAWs were being extensively used in Hollywood and elsewhere for sound mixing and editing by 1993. These DAWs were sold as complete turnkey systems by their manufacturers, but computer developments meant that the circuit boards and dedicated software could be sold separately to be fitted into standard PCs and Macintoshes, so turning them into digital audio workstations that were completely equivalent to the turnkey systems, and much cheaper. The company that was most successful at this in the 'nineties was Digidesign with their ProTools board and software packages, and indeed their system became the film industry standard for laying and editing sound tracks by the end of the decade.

Mixing desks also shifted to become completely digital in operation during the 'nineties, to go with the developments in the ancillary equipment just mentioned.

Microphones

The largest producers of quality microphones for film sound recording, namely Sennheiser and AKG, introduced new versions of their capacitor microphones in the 'eighties. This was necessary because their best microphones had also been used for music recording, and the adoption of digital music recording, with its ability to record a greater dynamic range of sound, required microphones that likewise could capture a greater dynamic range. AKG, with its CMS system of microphones in 1983, was first off the mark. These followed the established AKG practice of having separate capsules containing the diaphragm units with different directional responses, which could be screwed on to the base tube that contained the pre-amplifier. Sennheiser also followed its own practice of keeping its top quality models with integral construction, with the pre-amplifier inside a single tube below the capsule, though they did copy the AKG approach for a cheaper range as well. Their new cardioid response pattern microphone, the MKH-40, came out in 1985, followed by the MKH-20 omni-directional and MKH-30 figure of eight, through to the MKH-50 supercardioid in 1989. These microphones all had the same frequency range as before, but had lower self-noise generated internally, and could handle a greater sound pressure level (SPL), so extending the dynamic range of sound with which they could effectively cope. In the 'nineties, AKG introduced a new modular system of microphones, the Blue Line, and then a replacement for their top CMS system mentioned above in 1997, which was made up of the C480B body and the CK61, CK62, CK63 and CK69 capsules, which had respectively cardioid, omni-directional, hypercardioid, and ultra-directional (shotgun) responses.

However, as the 'nineties moved on, smaller manufacturers of microphones became more important in the film and television market. The German Schoeps company had existed since the late 'forties, but it was only with their new CCM range of small condenser microphones introduced in 1994 that they made a real impression on the film industry, particularly in the United States. Their microphones did not have quite as flat a response as the Sennheiser and AKG microphones, whose cardioid response pattern type of microphones were flat all the way from 20 Hz to 20 kHz. In contrast, the Schoeps cardioid fell off in its response by a few decibels below 100 Hz.

Lapel or lavalier microphones, for concealing about the person of actors when it was impossible to get a microphone on a boom in close, were also improved. They were now usually described as "body microphones", and almost exclusively used the electret type of capacitor diaphragm unit. The performance of pre-polarised (electret) microphones had been continually improved over the decades, and the best were now comparable with the standard capacitor microphones which had their polarising voltage applied from a power supply, like the traditional film recording models from Sennheiser and AKG. The leader in this area was the Danish firm of Brüel & Kjaer, which had long specialised in high quality electrical measuring equipment. Their 4000 series of high quality electret microphones had established a place in music recording through the nineteen-eighties, as they had a response that was flat from 20 Hz to 20 kHz within one dB. In 1992 their division producing these was spun off, and eventually renamed as DPA Microphones. Their best seller was the 4011, which was a cardioid microphone weighing only 30 gramme. Although DPA microphones were a bit more expensive than the other brands, their 4011 series, and its successor, the 4022, were used for ordinary film recording by many recordists. The 4022 series also had a slight advantage over the competition in that their response to higher frequencies held up better from the side-on direction, and hence they slightly reduced the "off-mike" effect characteristic of directional microphones, in which sounds from the side of the microphone are reduced in level, and have the highest frequencies particularly cut.

In 1996 DPA began making the 4060 series of miniature microphones, which immediately made a big impression as body microphones for film recording as well as for stage work. Their particular virtue was that they suffered less from handling noise on their cables than the competition. They were also very small, being about 5 mm. in diameter. In 1998 Sennheiser responded with very similar body mikes, the MKE 102 and 104, which were only 5 mm. in diameter and 10 mm. long. The other major manufacturers also produced similar microphones for these purposes, but film recordists did not necessarily go for the smallest possible size. For instance, the TRAM TR-50 lavalier was quite often used in the early part

of the decade. This was a flat unit about 7 mm. by 13 mm. and 4 mm. thick. The extra size of its diaphragm gave it a slightly greater frequency range than the others, from 40 Hz to 16 KHz.

The radio transmitters which were nearly always needed for use with these microphones were also improved, with a switch to diversity or multiple channel operation, and eventually to using UHF rather than VHF transmission. The main driving force in this area was television and stage work. By the nineties all stage musicals used amplification with radio mikes on all their singers, and this that drove the production of smaller and smaller units.

Stereophonic and Multi-channel Sound

The standard practice for the creation of stereophonic and multi-channel sound for motion pictures continued to be to record dialogue as monophonic tracks, and then to place them with respect to the position of the actors on the screen by panning them electrically during the sound track mixing for the finished film. However, music and background sound atmospheres were recorded stereophonically, as these could not be given a satisfactory imitation of stereophony during dubbing. True stereophonic recording of music was ordinarily done with a crossed stereophonic pair of microphones – usually two identical microphones with a cardioid response pattern set at 90 degrees (X-Y stereo) to each other to give the left and right stereo channels. However, there were other possibilities, and a "mid-side" (MS) arrangement was sometimes used, particularly for field recording of atmospheres. This method used a cardioid microphone pointing straight forward, and a figure of eight response pattern aligned so that its two response lobes pointed straight out to each side. The output of the two microphones could be combined electrically to recreate the simple left and right channel stereo effect. This arrangement was particularly favoured for television, even for single voice recording, as it fitted well with the way the NICAM stereo sound system used for television worked. However, it did not work well with the Dolby matrix (the base of the Dolby encoding system), so was not taken up for film purposes, which stayed with the X-Y microphone arrangement.

Recording Machines

At the beginning of the 'nineties film sound was still being recorded with the existing analogue recorders, principally the Nagra IV, but a new small form of digital audio recorder had appeared at the end of the 'eighties using the Digital Audio Tape (DAT) standard. DAT recorders are like a miniature version of a video cassette recorder, with special metal particle coated tape 3.81 mm. wide carried in a very small cassette. The tape runs past two rotating heads on a small drum of 30 mm. diameter which is inclined at a small angle to the tape travel, like a helical scan video recorder. However, unlike video recorders, the tape is only in contact with the scanning heads and drum through an angle of 90 degrees. The analogue audio signal coming into the recorder was sampled and quantized

Fostex PD-4 DAT recorder

in the usual way, with sampling rates of 32 kHz, 44.1 kHz, and 48 kHz. These DAT recorders were not suitable for film synchronised recording, as they lacked any built-in form of time code.

The first DAT recorder suitable for film recording was the Fostex PD-2, which was used for feature film recording from 1993. This was a version of the Fostex D-20 made by the Japanese Fostex company, which had appeared in 1990, but with added provision for recording film-type time code along with the sound signal. The PD-2 had dimensions 96 by 307 by 216 mm. (3.75 by 12 by 8.5 inches), weighed 10 lbs. and cost a bit under $10,000. At the same time, another DAT recorder suitable for film recording was introduced by the Swiss company Stellavox, which had a long history of making quality sound recorders. Their Stelladat was smaller, but more expensive, at $12,000-15,000, depending on how many extra modules were installed. The Swiss Nagra company, makers of the analogue Nagra IV machine, which had dominated film recording up to this point, more or less simultaneously came out with their own unique digital recorder, the Nagra-D. This was heavier, larger, and more expensive, weighing 20 lbs., and costing $29,000. It did not follow the DAT standard and tape drive mechanism, but one devised by the Nagra company itself, using 1/4 inch tape, and it had a large head drum with 180 degree wrap of the tape. It weighed 20 lbs, which was heavier than the Nagra IV, and since it was also a bit bigger than the older machine, it could not be used slung on the shoulder in the traditional way for *verité*-type filming. It recorded 4 tracks of sound, unlike the other portable DAT recorders, which could only record two tracks, and it used a 20 bit word length, also unlike the DAT recorders, which had 16 bit sound. This meant that it could record a larger dynamic range of sound levels than the DAT recorders, although these in their turn could record a larger dynamic range than the older analogue recorders.

Another new portable DAT recorder was introduced at the end of 1993 by the English HHB company, which specialised in digital recording equipment for the music industry. This was called the Portadat, and was a bit smaller and lighter than

the Fostex PD-2. In fact, 240 mm. by 177 mm. by 86 mm., and weighing 2.5 Kg. The Portadat model with time code built in, the PDR 1000TC, was substantially cheaper than the Fostex machine, and immediately made a big impression on the lower end of the film and TV market. In response to this, in 1995 the Fostex DAT recorder was upgraded to the PD-4 model, which was basically the same as the PD-2, though it had a 3 channel built-in mixer, and was cheaper at £4,295. This was the most successful of the DAT recorders used for film purposes, particularly in the United States.

Problems with DAT recorders were the fragility of the tape, and tape and head misalignment, which meant that recordings made on one machine could often not be played back on another. Nevertheless, the digital machines took over, though film sound recordists all used a back-up analogue machine as well for a year or two, till the new medium had proved itself.

In the latter end of the 'nineties, many big films were recorded on non-portable 8-track digital recorders of the kind long used in music recording, such as the Tascam DA-88.

Having lost their dominant position in the industry to Fostex, Nagra tried again in 1997 with a completely new approach, the Nagra ARES-C recorder. This used 64 Mb PCMCIA computer flash memory cards as recording medium, instead of tape, and the recording was digitally compressed to get a sufficient amount onto a memory card. It could give 2 hrs. of mono recording. It was modelled after earlier Nagras in general physical layout, but the cost of the memory cards and the digital compression meant that it was not generally used for feature film production.

Quite another approach to sound recording technology also emerged in 1997 from the small American Zaxcom company. This was to record the digital sound signal onto a removable computer hard disk slotted into the recorder. This had become possible because hard disks for computers had now reached a storage capacity of a couple of Gigabytes, which meant that it could contain an hour or two of recorded sound. Even more importantly for this application, hard disks had also been made more shock resistant by this date, so that it was now possible to bang them about without damaging their internal mechanisms. Zaxcom called their recorder the DEVA, and it was quite small, being about 20 mm. by 75 mm. by 180 mm. and weighing 2.25 Kg. It had a built-in 4 channel mixer and could record to 4 channels of 20 bit sound. It cost about $10,000, and was slowly taken up by film sound recordists from 1999 onwards. This approach to digital sound recording was copied by the Nagra company in the next decade.

Cinema Digital Sound Systems

The CDS (Cinema Digital Sound) sound system which was introduced in 1990 has already been described in *Film Style and Technology*. This system required separate distribution prints with the digital track replacing the standard analogue sound track, and so film distribution organizations would need to stock a double inventory of prints for each film title, as most cinemas did not have their projection converted to the special digital playback system required. This was fatal, as predicted, and it was displaced when Dolby Laboratories introduced their own system of digital sound recording on film prints, which they already had under development. This system, called Dolby Digital, recorded the digital information for 5 separate full frequency sound channels plus a channel for very low frequency sound information as a series of blocks made up of a matrix of microscopic dots between each sprocket hole on 35 mm. film. This meant that the film print could retain the ordinary soundtrack for theatres not equipped to play digital sound. The first film using this system was *Batman Returns*, released in 1992. The Sony company immediately joined in with their own digital sound system for cinemas, called SDDS. This carried the digital information on the film print in two new tracks lying between the outer edge of the sprocket holes and the edge of the film, on both sides. If desired by the production company, film prints could carry these tracks as well as that for the Dolby digital system, and films using the SDDS system started with *The Last Action Hero* in 1993. The final competitor so far in this area was DTS (Digital Theatre Sound), which carried the digital sound tracks on a compact disc (a CD), which was played in a special CD player in synchronism with the picture. The synchronism was maintained by a very narrow synchronizing track squeezed into a small part of the area of the film print containing the standard analogue sound track. As the CD sound was read a couple of seconds ahead of the corresponding frame on the film, and stored briefly in digital memory, any missing frames resulting from print damage could be compensated for. This was an improvement on the original 1926 Warner Bros. sound-on-disc system, which this new system resembled in a very general sort of way. The first film using this system was *Jurassic Park* in 1994. Obviously prints used for this system could also carry the other two systems if desired, and this is what has happened subsequently, though the Dolby Digital system is probably the most used.

Editing

During the nineteen-nineties, digital video methods also took over in film editing from the traditional editing machines. These machines were called in general "Non-Linear Editors" or NLEs. Since 1985, a small number of feature films had been edited on systems like Laseredit and Editdroid, which worked with telecine recordings of the film rushes transferred to laser video discs, which were put in video disc players controlled by a computer program. These systems were an improvement on the even earlier systems that used multiple video recorders carrying the rushes, but were still not handy enough to displace traditional editing methods. They were also much more costly to buy and to run, as the laser video discs had to be specially made, and the rushes for a complete film needed multiple laser players running simultaneously to contain them all.

Alternatives which recorded the video stream onto hard

discs controlled by a standard computer had appeared in television production. The leader here was Avid Technologies, whose machines, called Media Composers, were introduced in 1989. They comprised purpose-built boxes of electronic circuitry for digitizing the input video, and for playing it back on a computer screen, which were attached to an ordinary Apple Macintosh computer. The system was controlled by a special program running on the computer. This program used the Macintosh computer's graphic interface to represent the sections or "clips" of video being edited, and where they were with respect to each other in the sequence of the edit. Operations on them used the kind of "cut and paste" and "drag and drop" operations controlled by a mouse which had become standard in computer word processing programs running on computers using graphical interfaces like the Macintosh. The Avid system was initially limited by the amount of video running time that could be stored, but this was solved, up to a point, by the company's development in 1991 of a standard method of compressing digital video, called Quicktime. The problem with using the Avid system for film editing, rather than the video editing for which it was designed, was that it intrinsically worked with 30 frames per second video on the American television standard, and would not work at the 24 frames per second need for film editing. In 1993 a 24 fps film option on the system was introduced, and Avid entered the film editing machine competition, with one or two feature films edited using the system in that year.

The general problem of storing reasonable amounts of video or film footage as digital data was solved with the development by the computer industry of improved methods of recording large quantities of data with effectively instantaneous random access. Computer hard discs had been rapidly increasing in capacity and speed, and a new NLE system called Lightworks was introduced in 1991 to take advantage of this. The Lightworks system would hold 100 minutes of digitized footage on internal hard discs in a computer, and was set up to work in a fairly analogous way to the procedures used by film editors working on traditional flat-bed editing machines, down to having a manual jog-shuttle control like that on a Steenbeck. This recommended it to many film editors, and it was the major competitor to Avid till the end of the decade, when it rather faded.

For a short time at the beginning of the 'nineties, it seemed that magneto-optical (M-O) disc recorders might be a solution, as this was a brief period when they had a greater capacity than removable hard drives, and Pioneer and others introduced M-O drives with a capacity of around 6 Gb in 1992. This was large enough to hold about 30 minutes of uncompressed standard video footage. A company called Editing Machines Corporation used them in their EMC² system which came out the next year. Other companies such as Montage and D-Vision had similar systems that had some success too, but by the end of the decade the Avid system had practically swept the board. There were some film editors and directors who insisted on staying with film, but producers preferred NLE systems, as they opened the possibility of not printing the rushes, but just taking the processed negative straight through telecine to the NLE, and so saving money. It was also possible to cut down on the assistant editors who did much of the film handling in the traditional method of film editing.

Once editors had mastered the non-linear editing systems, it was evident that one could edit faster with them, though many older editors were never happy with them.

Time Code

To function in the fullest way, non-linear editing systems need time code incorporated in the picture and sound tracks and this was available from the beginning of the decade. The current models of all the major cameras used in the film industry generated time code which was imprinted onto the negative inside the camera as the picture was being taken. The code was generated by microchip oscillator circuits, and printed onto the negative between the sprocket holes by very small LED (light emitting diode) arrays. If multiple cameras were being used on a shoot, their time code generators, and that of the sound recorder, were synchronized to a master clock (a small electronic unit) at the beginning of the day by taking it around the cameras and plugging it in to them for a short period. This synchronization process, which was referred to as "jamming", would hold for about four hours, after which it had to be done again. The importance of time code can be illustrated by Panavision's purchase of half of the French Aaton company so that they could use their time code system in Panavision cameras.

The next stage in the process was the transfer of the picture rushes to video in a telecine. Here the time code on the film was read by an extra sensor which was added to the standard telecine machines, such as the Rank Cintel, from the end of the 'eighties. A sensor to read the Kodak barcodes printed onto the edge of the film was also added to the major makes of telecine around the beginning of the decade.

Editing Style

The main trend in film editing was towards ever shorter shot lengths, as it had been over previous decades. This process was led from the top, and was now definitely a matter of conscious choice by many film directors. The cameraman Bill Pope, who had begun his career photographing pop music videos and television commercials, said to *American Cinematographer* in February 1992 on page 88 (Music Video Cinematography: A New Film Grammar) "When I did my first feature, *Darkman* (1990), the director said, 'I want one cut for every three seconds of film.' Compared to what I was used to, that was kind of luxurious. But that was three times more than most movies had up to that point." As it happens, the ASL of *Darkman* is only 5.5 seconds, so the director Sam Raimi got nowhere near his aim. And this figure is in its turn quite close to the mean ASL of 5.85 seconds for American films of the 1988-93 period, so Bill Pope's notion that the movies preceding *Darkman* had an ASL of about 9 seconds

was also quite wrong. This is by no means unusual, and there are many other examples of the subjective judgements of those professionally involved in film-making being wrong in such areas.

As shown in the following article, "The Shape of 1999", the cutting rate in American films has been increasing fairly continuously since about 1950. The figures, which are derived from about 5,400 American films, give mean Average Shot Lengths in seconds for a succession of six year periods as above right. You can see that although the cutting rate continuously increases over the 50 year period, the *rate* of increase in the cutting rate through the same period varies. In particular, there was a rapid increase in the cutting rate during the 'sixties.

Period	Mean ASL
1946-51	10.47 sec.
1952-57	10.13 sec.
1958-63	8.80 sec.
1964-69	7.11 sec.
1970-75	6.63 sec.
1976-81	6.55 sec.
1982-87	6.12 sec.
1988-93	5.85 sec.
1994-99	4.92 sec.

Inspecting the actual list of the films involved suggests that this was the result of the exit of older directors like Billy Wilder and Otto Preminger who had been devoted to long takes, and their replacement by younger directors who had their training in the 'fifties or later. In a sound-bite, you could characterise the change as that from John Ford to Andrew V. McLagen, who had a cutting rate two-thirds of that of the master, while working in the same genres. There was also a slowdown in the 'seventies, as many directors took to using shots that followed characters around with simultaneous zooming and panning. There wasn't enough of this to actually reverse the trend towards faster cutting, just enough to almost halt the increase. Then in the latter part of the 'nineties there was another sudden increase.

In the general matter of the decrease in ASLs over the last two decades, it has been suggested that this is due to the introduction of non-linear editing systems in the middle of the 'eighties. The first thing to be said about this idea is that directors and editors have been able to use very fast cutting long before these devices were invented. *Bronenosets Potyomkin* has an ASL of 3 seconds, for instance (at 16 frames per second, which is the speed at which it was shot). And in the 'seventies, Russ Meyer's films had ASLs under 3 seconds. In the 'eighties, there was an appreciable increase in the number of American films with ASLs less than 3 seconds, with Sylvester Stallone action subjects like *Rambo: First Blood Part II* (ASL = 2.7 sec.) and *Rocky IV* (ASL = 2.5 sec.) leading the way in 1985. These were still being cut in the traditional manner, as the first use of a true non-linear editing system to cut a feature was for *The Patriot* (Frank Harris), which came out in 1986, and this had an ASL of only 5.2 seconds. But it *is* possible that the sudden large increase in the numbers of fast-cut films around 1995 was facilitated by the fairly general use of NLEs which began at that time. However, the desire of many directors to cut as fast as possible existed before that, as indicated by the quote about Sam Raimi's attitude to cutting rates at the beginning of this section. Incidentally, at the last count, Sam Raimi has *still* not got down to an ASL of 3 seconds. The best he has done to my knowledge is *Army of Darkness* in 1993, which has an ASL of 3.8 seconds. And his *The Gift* of 2000 has an ASL of 4.7 seconds, which is still only a bit below the mean for American films of the late 'nineties. Raimi is a director with a good visual sense, as can be seen in *Darkman*, and making individual shots look good takes time, which conflicts with getting a lot of set-ups per day. Also, once you have created a good-looking shot, there is a natural tendency to want to give the audience time to appreciate it.

Another possible influence on cutting rates are television commercials and pop music videos, as referred to by Bill Pope in the quotation. It is true that commercials tend to be cut faster than feature films, and also that some narrative commercials get down to one cut a second nowadays. But such commercials are either completely free of dialogue, or close to it. Commercials containing real dialogue exchanges have an ASL in the 2 to 3 second range, at any rate in England.

A 100 minute film with an ASL of 2 seconds is a film with 3,000 shots in it, and creating one like that involves a decision to do so beforehand by the director and producer. It is not possible for an editor to satisfactorily create more and more shots by cutting the ones supplied into smaller and smaller bits, and scattering them about a film scene. (This is called "double cutting".) The number of shots in a film *is* usually greater than the number of set-ups — that is, shots taken from different camera positions — but not more than about 50 percent greater. As I have remarked before, there is also a restriction to the amount that lines of dialogue can be sensibly cut up into separate shots, which has probably been reached in some films. The increase over the last couple of decades in the number of reaction shots (shots showing someone else listening to the speaker) in scenes involving a group of more than two people should be quite obvious to any one who has been looking carefully at American films for a long time. And filming those reaction shots has to be decided on by the director. Action scenes give the greatest opportunity for increasing the cutting rate, as breaking an action down into a number of separate shots taken with good continuity is not particularly obtrusive. The fastest cut American film so far known is *The End of Days* (Peter Hyams, 1999), with an

ASL of 1.74 seconds, and looking at it carefully suggests to me that it is possible to go further in this direction. In one respect, faster cutting is *necessary* for some present-day action films, although I do not think this is what has been powering the increase in cutting rate. Films that involve a lot of acrobatics, of the kind only possible with the actors suspended on wires, have to be broken down into a series of shots showing separate parts of a particular move, as otherwise the movement would not be convincing as something apparently done by the performer without any extra help. This is particularly true of a film like *The Matrix*, and you can see what happens when the principals do a complete sequence of movement without cuts in the rehearsals which are included in the ancillary material on DVD copies of the film. Nobody would pay money to see a film with that sort of ragged beginning and ending to the movements left in the shot. (In many of the Hong Kong movies that inspired this American interest in action acrobatics, such as *Jing wu ying xiong (Fist of Legend)* (Gordon Chan, 1994), the movements are more complete within the shots, as the actors performing them, such as Jet Li, are trained acrobats, unlike Keanu Reeves, etc.)

As was already the case twenty years ago, most films use a mixture of jump cuts, dissolves and fades for time lapses both between scenes and within scenes. But there is a tendency for action films and comedies to advance the story largely with jump cuts. On the other hand, the use of fades, particularly slow ones, tends to occur in films with artistic pretensions. The use of one of the hardest (i.e. most conspicuous) forms of jump cut has finally become a cliché thirty years after it was introduced by Jean-Luc Godard. This involves shooting a scene with a camera fixed in front of it while one or more characters bustle about doing something, for instance getting ready to go out, and then cutting out chunks of the action, so that the actor repeatedly jumps from one part of the scene to another.

In ordinary films nowadays occasionally one finds all sorts of small flourishes that would have only appeared in art films in the past, such as lines of dialogue carried across series of jump cut scenes set in different places in *X-Men*.

American Style

The norms for American film-making in 1999 are demonstrated in the following article, "The Shape of 1999". I believe that although there has been some change over the decade, there is no reason to think that similar results for 1990 would be utterly different, though obviously the cutting rates would be slightly slower. It remains to make some comments on the departures from these norms in other American films of the 'nineties.

To give an idea of what one finds for American films with much longer Average Shot Lengths than the norm, I have listed those with ASLs longer than 15 seconds amongst the 1728 films I have looked at from the years 1990 to 1999. There are just 28 of them.

A film with an ASL of 15 seconds will have about 10% of

TITLE	DIRECTOR	YEAR	ASL
Sweet and Lowdown	Allen, Woody	1999	16.1
Everyone Says I Love You	Allen, Woody	1996	33.1
Mighty Aphrodite	Allen, Woody	1995	34.5
Shadows and Fog	Allen, Woody	1991	30.9
Bullets Over Broadway	Allen, Woody	1994	51.9
Alice	Allen, Woody	1990	38.9
Manhattan Murder Mystery	Allen, Woody	1993	34.5
Husbands and Wives	Allen, Woody	1992	28
Living End, The	Araki, Greg	1992	15.7
Without You I'm Nothing	Boskovich, John	1990	16
Addiction, The	Ferrara, Abel	1994	20
Dangerous Game	Ferrara, Abel	1993	24.1
Miami Rhapsody	Frankel, David	1995	21.8
Mother Night	Gordon, Keith	1996	17.2
Rhythm Thief	Harrison, Matthew	1994	17.1
All the Vermeers in New York	Jost, Jon	1990	42.8
In the Company of Men	LaBute, Neil	1997	17.4
Slacker	Linklater, Richard	1991	34.5
Small Time	Loftis, Norman	1990	15.8
Vanya on 42nd Street	Malle, Louis	1994	15.2
Hours and Times, The	Münch, Christopher	1992	22.8
Blair Witch Project, The	Myrick, D. & Sanchez, E.	1999	15.8
Jerry and Tom	Rubinek, Saul	1998	17
Mrs. Parker and the Vicious Circle	Rudolph, Alan	1994	16.5
Light Sleeper	Schrader, Paul	1992	15.2
Sling Blade	Thornton, Billy Bob	1995	23.7
Smoke	Wang, Wayne	1995	22.6
Blue in the Face	Wang, Wayne & Auster, P.	1995	25.5

its shots longer than 30 seconds. As we approach an ASL of 1 minute, the films concerned are close to having one shot per scene, or to use the industry terminology, the scenes are only covered with a master shot. This is particularly the case with most of the Woody Allen films from this period, though as you might expect, *Sweet and Lowdown* has a small amount of scene dissection. As a corollary of this, the shots are in general back a bit from the actors, and in the case of *Bullets Over Broadway*, mostly in Medium Long Shot and Long Shot. I hope you will agree that nearly all the films listed below could reasonably be described as art films, with the obvious exception of *The Blair Witch Project*, which comes into the "exploitation film" category.

Widening the net to American films with an ASL greater than 10 seconds, which I have half-seriously suggested forms a dividing line between art and commerce for films made in the last twenty years, still only collects another forty titles, some of which are also by the directors listed above, some of which are by other art film makers like Edward Burns and Hal Hartley, but which also include several that are not art films, but are made by older directors like Mike Nicholls and Sidney Lumet, who date back to the period when it was not so exceptional to make long-take films. It also includes the films of Paul Thomas Anderson, the new Hollywood auteur of the period. These have developed an increasingly idiosyncratic style, as exemplified in *Magnolia* (1999), which has an ASL of

12.1 seconds. This film contains more tracks straight in onto quasi-static scenes than I have ever seen anywhere else, and these tracks in are in general neither functional nor dramatically motivated. There is also a just hint in this film of the choice of the wrong closeness of shot with respect to what is going on dramatically from time to time — for instance going further back from an actor when the intensity of the scene is holding up, or even increasing.

The other long-take films I have been discussing keep the takes going in general either by following the action around with a moving camera (*Manhattan Murder Mystery*), or by using long static takes (*In the Company of Men*), or by doing nothing special, just not cutting around as much as usual. The *Citizen Kane* option, which involves long takes staged in depth with a wide-angle lens, is not used in a thorough-going way. Many of the movies I have mentioned have some shots with a certain amount of staging in depth, but it is done with ordinary lenses, and without stopping down for extreme depth of field. Those films that do use a lot of very wide angle lens filming don't use it to keep the shots going, but just as a visual flourish. Some of the moving camera films tend to use a slightly wide angle lens, but otherwise the use of really wide-angle lenses in the 'nineties is as a shock effect when put in amongst more normal focal length shots.

As mentioned in "The Shape of 1999", there was an influence from television on the type of camera movements used in film-making. The small panning and tilting movements used in the American *NYPD Blue* television series inspired film-makers to use wobbly camera moves to create extra "excitement". Examples include *The Rock* (1996), *GI Jane* (1997) and *Any Given Sunday* (1999), and the combination of hand-held tracking combined with mis-matched cuts used in *Homicide – Life on the Street* was adopted by Lars von Trier for his cinema feature *Breaking the Waves* (1996). Bertolucci's *Besieged* (1998) also shows traces of influence from this source, though all this may prove to be a passing fancy.

Steven Spielberg is by far the most commercially successful film-maker of the last two decades, but he is not quite a typical American director. He has nearly always been a little on the longer side of the mean ASL for American films. This corresponds to his evident desire to keep the scene dissection interesting, and in particular in doing interesting camera moves that are relevant to the narrative. There is one exception to this, and that is his "Indiana Jones" films, which are right on the ASL norms for when they were made. This seems to be the result of a decision to make pure mindless entertainment with these movies, which after all are part of George Lucas' project, not Spielberg's. So why are *Jurassic Park* (1993) and *The Lost World: Jurassic Park* (1997) cut markedly slower than the norm for American movies (ASL 6.1 and 7.6), and even more so than the norm for American action movies? Presumably because the director considered there were one or two serious points being made in their stories. On the other hand, *Jurassic Park III* (2001), directed by Joe Johnston, is conventional in every way, including the cutting rate of 3.6 seconds.

Indeed, Spielberg is one of those directors who appears to adapt his scene dissection to the task in hand, and there was a major change in his style when he made *Schindler's List* (1993). Here many of the scenes are covered with long takes by a moving camera, sometimes with a wide-angle lens. This pushes the overall ASL of the film up to 9.1 seconds. I would guess the inspiration for this style change comes from Andrzej Wajda's film *Pokolenie* (1954), which is about the Polish resistance, and goes much further than Spielberg in using moving master shots with a wide-angle lens, as do Wajda's other films in his World War II trilogy.

European Style

The major distinction between American film style and European film style that was made over and over in *Film Style and Technology* has persisted into the nineteen-nineties. This is that European films are shot with the camera further back on the average, and their shots go on longer. On this last point, I have sufficient data to again fairly conclusively demonstrate it with distributions of Average Shot Lengths for samples of French and British films for the six year periods 1988-93 and 1994-99.

The startling difference between the French and British samples illustrated by the graphs on the next page pretty certainly exaggerates the contrast, as the British sample constitutes a large part of British production for the period, whereas the French selection is only a small part (48 and 74 films respectively) of the industry's output, and highly skewed towards the more serious and artistic productions that are considered most suitable for English exhibition.

Although at first sight, it might seem that French cinema has been unaffected by the speed up in cutting rate in American cinema, this is not completely true. There are French films from the 'nineties in these samples with an ASL shorter than 5 seconds, whereas I have found none from the nineteen-eighties. They are:

Mon père, ce héros (Gérard Lauzier, 1991)	4.7 seconds
les Visiteurs (Jean-Marie Poir, 1993)	2.9 seconds
Léon (Luc Besson, 1994)	4.6 seconds
The Fifth Element (Luc Besson, 1997)	2.9 seconds
Jeanne d'Arc (Luc Besson, 1999)	3.5 seconds
Dobermann (Jan Kounen, 1997)	3.5 seconds
le Dinêr des cons (Francois Veber, 1998)	4.4 seconds

and all were big box office in France. *Les Visiteurs* is peculiar in that it is not shot nearly as close in to the actors as an American film with the same cutting rate would be, so a lot of cuts are between shots in the middle range of closeness, which gives it a clumsy feel to the connoisseur of film direction, but that does not seem to have bothered the French audience. *Dobermann* is a conscious attempt to put even more of the "amusing" violence and viciousness of *Natural Born Killers* into its own source material, and obviously succeeds for

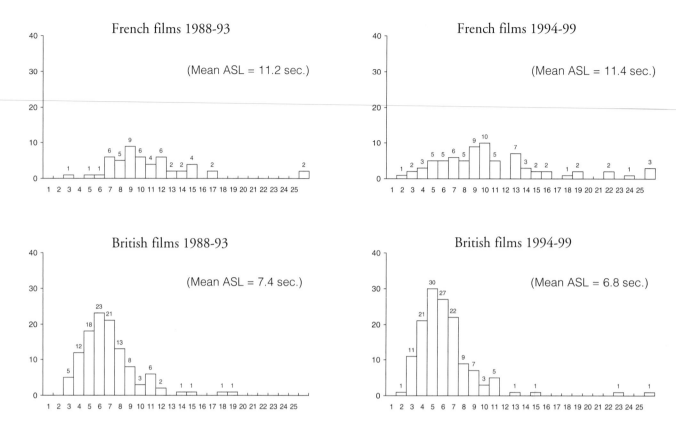

Number of films with Average Shot Length (ASL) in the given ranges

those prepared to ignore the mindlessness of it. However, it is noticeable that despite the relatively fast cutting rate, the action within most of the scenes in *Dobermann* does not move along as quickly as in the contemporary American style, and many shots are occupied solely by the actors doing some desultory 'acting tough' in a posy way. It is not the only example from outside the United States which shows that a fast cutting rate does not necessarily imply a fast moving narrative. As for Francis Veber, he had been over in Hollywood, and directed two films there at the beginning of the decade, and had picked up the current American style. Beyond this, if one looks carefully at the French films with rather longer ASLs, one often finds that the first ten or fifteen minutes of them has much faster cutting than the rest of the film, and it definitely looks to me like the director attempting to go faster in the current American manner, before collapsing under the strain.

There are more interesting things at the other end of the spectrum, where directors work with very long takes. Raul Ruiz had another of his truly new ideas when he filmed Proust's *le Temps retrouvé* (1999). Taking his cue from Proust's description of the way the church steeple at Combray seemed to change its position with respect to other parts of the landscape, Ruiz has the furniture and walls of the rooms subtly slide around with respect to each other during moving camera shots at some key points in this mélange of memories. At the opposite pole of content, there have appeared a number of

French exercises in miserabilism treated in *cinéma vérité* style with long takes and zoom lens or hand-held camera. This approach seems to be partly inspired by the films of Ken Loach, who is highly regarded in Europe, as well as by the makers' real concern for the lives of those at the bottom of the pile. The extreme so far has been reached by Jean-Paul and Luc Dardenne's *Rosetta* (1999) (ASL = 38.9 sec.), which continuously follows hand-held along *behind* the protagonist for minutes at a time as she drags herself round from one demeaning low of her existence to the next.

As for British films of the 'nineties, although they had been pretty much up with American contemporary cinema in the 'sixties in terms of cutting rates, in the interim they have almost remained where they were.

The slowing down in the cutting rate in British films in the 'eighties is probably a real effect, as the number of films in the sample for 1982-87 is large enough, at 111 films, against a total British production for the six years of about 200 films, to give a pretty accurate figure. You can see that the difference in ASLs for the two period is that there is a marked increase in the in the numbers of films with ASLs of 9 seconds and above in the 1982-87 period when compared to the previous six year period, and it is this that increases the mean ASL a little. An examination of the actual films concerned in the two periods shows that the names of the directors making these films with ASLs greater than 8 seconds are almost completely different

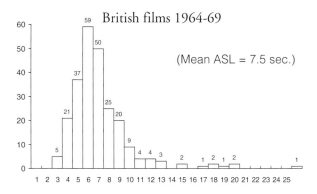

British films 1964-69

(Mean ASL = 7.5 sec.)

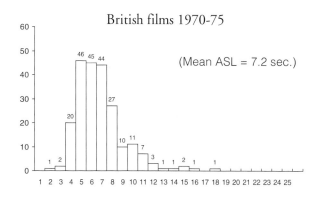

British films 1970-75

(Mean ASL = 7.2 sec.)

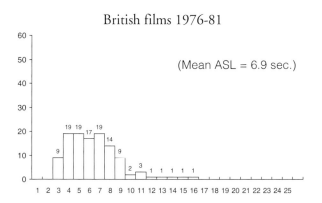

British films 1976-81

(Mean ASL = 6.9 sec.)

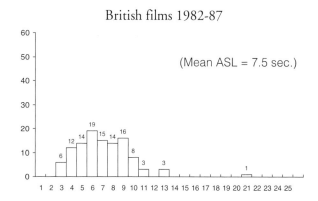

British films 1982-87

(Mean ASL = 7.5 sec.)

Number of films with Average Shot Length (ASL) in the given ranges

for the two periods. Only Kubrick, Frears, and John MacKenzie made films in both periods. The other 38 directors concerned only got a go in one of the two periods. So it appears that in a medium-sized film industry the lack of continuity in production can cause noticeable stylistic fluctuations.

Moving on to the 'nineties, we do get a speeding up in the 1994-99 period corresponding to the marked speed up in the United States at the same time, though the cutting rate is still well behind that obtaining in the United States. (See the American ASL distributions illustrated in the following article, *The Shape of 1999*.) At least we got the first British film ever to get down under 3 seconds, which was *Spice World* (Bob Spiers, 1997), a tribute to the artistry of the Spice Girls pop group. The sole British big action film of the decade, *Goldeneye* (1995), only managed an ASL of 3.1 seconds. At the other end of the spectrum we find the usual suspects, Terence Davies and Peter Greenaway, doing their usual thing. Terence Davies was working for the first time with someone else's material in *The Neon Bible* (1995) (ASL = 23.9 sec.), but he treated it much the same way he had memories of his own youth in his films made earlier, such as *The Long Day Closes* (1992) (ASL = 15.8 sec.). That is, mostly long static takes varied with slow simple camera moves, not a lot happening, and old popular numbers on the sound track. Peter Greenaway had began to use funding from across Europe for his films during the 'eighties, but his centre of operations was still England, and some of

his films had a British co-production element, so I will mention them here. In 1991, he added a new component to his repertoire of theatrical-style settings and long takes. In *Prospero's Books*, extra images were inset within the frame of the shot using high definition video compositing, and this continued more extensively in *The Pillow Book* (1995). In both films a large proportion of the setups were, as usual for Greenaway, flat-on to the walls of the sets, with a strong tendency to symmetrical composition, and the succession of static shots was relieved with occasional sideways tracks.

The local trend-setter in hymning feckless youth was Danny Boyle. His *Trainspotting* was a determined effort to make heroin addiction stylish. Apart from the unrealistic colourful set design applied to the interiors of the Edinburgh slums, and the application of coloured light to them as well, his basic approach was continuous wide-angle lens photography from extreme angles. What variation there was in this was down to whether the lens was very short focal length (10 mm.), or just short focal length (say, 15 mm.) for a bit of a change.

Dominion over Palm and Pine

The former pink bits on the map still went along with the home country in the 'nineties, as the ASL distributions for Australia, Canada, and India illustrate. Here I have changed the period covered to 1990-99, to get better-sized samples. Apart from the 208 British films from the decade, there are 62

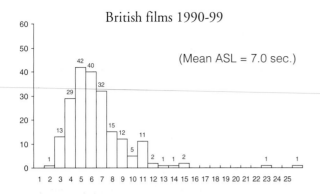

British films 1990-99

(Mean ASL = 7.0 sec.)

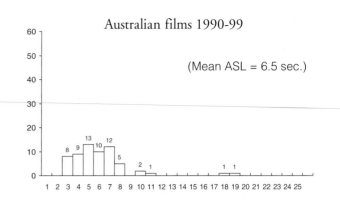

Australian films 1990-99

(Mean ASL = 6.5 sec.)

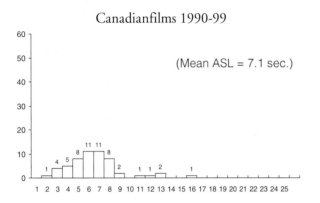

Canadianfilms 1990-99

(Mean ASL = 7.1 sec.)

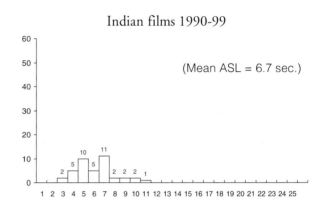

Indian films 1990-99

(Mean ASL = 6.7 sec.)

Number of films with Average Shot Length (ASL) in the given ranges

Australian films, 55 Canadian ones, and 40 from India.

As you can see, after allowing for the larger size of the British collection, the shapes of the distributions are very similar. When actually looked at, rather than just counted, the Australian films can be seen to be more distinctive for their content than their form. The only long-take movies in this Australian sample are due to Australia's original art movie director, Paul Cox, and his films continue to apply fairly ordinary scene dissection, though with the shots kept going longer than usual, to his characteristic very muted and recessive stories.

Canada has its own art movie stars, and one of them shows up on the long-take radar here. Atom Egoyan specializes in just slightly less than believable character psychology and situation treated in a restrained way, but there is again nothing special about his scene dissection, though his compositions are interesting. In this collection, *The Adjuster* (1991), *Exotica* (1994), and *The Sweet Hereafter* (1997) have Average Shot Lengths of 16.7 seconds, 12.9 and 13 seconds respectively. The other Canadian who has to be mentioned is Guy Maddin, who has made a success out of far-fetched stories done in an amateurish way, in a style that is supposed to be inspired by silent movies. He has apparently seen a few well-known 'twenties films in tenth generation 16 mm. dupes, and manages to approximate that high contrast, fuzzed-out look fairly well. What the point of this is, other than being Canadian, I don't know.

The Indian film industry is often said to be the largest in

the world. As the figure usually quoted for the yearly Indian production is about 800 films, this appears to be yet another myth. As mentioned in "The Shape of 1999", and as you can check yourself by using the advanced search facility at *IMDb.com*, the American production of fictional feature films, *excluding* made-for-television features and straight-to-video features, is over 1000 films a year. Apart from the well-known distinctive feature of ordinary Indian films, which is the regular insertion of musical numbers down the length of the story, they use exactly the same structures, both filmic and dramatic, as Western films. This has always been the case, and the only difference is the competence of the craftsmanship in following these norms. One aspect of this is that the pace of the story in Indian films tends to be slow, as quite often too little plot is stretched out to cover too much time. The acting is also a little bit broader in general than in Western films. Another noticeable peculiarity of some directors' work nowadays is sudden short bursts of extremely fast cutting at peak moments, in a way that would not happen in a Western film, where the faster bits of cutting are prepared for by moving into them in a graded way. The cutting rates of Indian films have increased over past decades in the same sort of way as in other countries, and at present they are pretty much exactly the same as the other "dominion" films in this respect. Although there is a very small Indian art film sector, none of its film-makers go in for really long-take filming. And the in-your-face ultra wide-angle lens shock stuff has not reached India yet, as far as I know.

As for the notorious Indian musical numbers, the weakness of these from a Western point of view is that in recent times the songs they feature are always about love, either requited, about to be requited, or unrequited. This was not always quite as true of older Indian films, and it is quite different to the Western tradition of musicals, where the songs frequently stem from other aspects of the developing story of the film, and hence can keep the drama moving forward while the songs are going on. Some young Indian directors are well aware of this, but whether there will be any change is another matter. In former times, the dancing that went on in these musical numbers was mostly straightforwardly folk-dance based, but in recent decades a style that is a new hybrid of folk dance steps and Western disco dancing has almost completely taken hold. The stage patterns used have got less subtle as well, with mostly massed lines of dancers dancing in unison, with the stars prancing in the centre of these lines. Once upon a time the musical numbers in a film would occasionally be varied by having a skilled professional dancer, such as the famous Helen, featured in some of the dance numbers, but now the dancing is entirely simplified to what the big stars can do. The filming of these song and dance numbers now relies almost entirely on jump cuts from one background to another every eight bars in an attempt to keep the interest going in the minimal proceedings, though shock zooms are still used as well, once in a while.

Other Places, Other Ideas

In Denmark, the man with ideas was Lars Trier, or Lars von Trier, as he styled himself. He attracted international attention with his first film *The Tooth of Crime* (1989), and moved on to more unconventional territory with *Europa* (1991). Not only is the vision of this film peculiarly personal, but, as in his other films, Lars von Trier exploits a whole bag of technical tricks to produce a very distinctive product. In the case of *Europa*, the main device is the extensive use of front projection, but employed in a way that draws attention to itself at key moments. The film begins with black and white photography, and most of the time the front projection is used in the standard way, to produce a seamless combination of actors and background. However, at various points people and objects in full colour appear in front of a black and white scene, while at other key moments, during what was apparently a simple shot showing a person standing within a room, the background starts rotating behind them. This film was followed by *Breaking the Waves* (1996), which has already been mentioned in connection with its use of the discontinuous cutting of hand-held camera moves. As well as this feature, the lighting of the interiors in the film by Robby Müller was quite close to using available light, even though the interiors were shot on sets. That is, most of the light on the sets came from practical lights integral to the sets, and the 5298 stock was pushed two stops to 2000 EI to get an exposure. These features of *Breaking the Waves* were endorsed by a film-making manifesto issued in 1995 by Lars von Trier and Thomas Vinterberg as *Dogme 95*.

This "Vow of Chastity" stated:

I swear to submit to the following set of rules drawn up and confirmed by DOGMA 95:

1. Shooting must be done on location. Props and sets must not be brought in (if a particular prop is necessary for the story, a location must be chosen where this prop is to be found).

2. The sound must never be produced apart from the images or vice versa. (Music must not be used unless it occurs where the scene is being shot).

3. The camera must be hand-held. Any movement or immobility attainable in the hand is permitted. (The film must not take place where the camera is standing; shooting must take place where the film takes place).

4. The film must be in colour. Special lighting is not acceptable. (If there is too little light for exposure the scene must be cut or a single lamp be attached to the camera).

5. Optical work and filters are forbidden.

6. The film must not contain superficial action. (Murders, weapons, etc. must not occur.)

7. Temporal and geographical alienation are forbidden. (That is to say that the film takes place here and now.)

8. Genre movies are not acceptable.

9. The film format must be Academy 35 mm.

10. The director must not be credited.

Furthermore I swear as a director to refrain from personal taste! I am no longer an artist. I swear to refrain from creating a "work", as I regard the instant as more important than the whole. My supreme goal is to force the truth out of my characters and settings. I swear to do so by all the means available and at the cost of any good taste and any aesthetic considerations.

Nobody took much notice of this manifesto at the time, but eventually, after *Breaking the Waves* was commercially successful (for an art movie), Vinterberg and von Trier made films that were publicised under the Dogme label. These were *Festen* (1998) and *Idioterna* (1998). These films conformed to the principles of the movement in most respects, but most importantly, they were shot and edited on video, not film, to save money, and only when finished were they transferred to 35 mm. film. There was also a little bit of cheating with respect to lighting in *Idioterna*, and some of the subsequent films allegedly made in conformity with the Dogma principles also do not fully conform to these principles in one way or another. After *Festen* was also well received, a number of people outside the Lars von Trier circle, such as Harmony Korine, wanted to join in, and altogether 35 films were licensed to use the Dogme designation, the last of these being released in 2003. But well before this, the instigators, having got a lot of publicity for themselves out of the enterprise, lost interest in the whole thing. Indeed Lars von Trier's subsequent films were not billed as Dogme 95 productions. However, I think the Dogme films did encourage others to shoot hand-held in video, though this is something that only really took hold in the twenty-first century.

Acting

There has been a marked change in acting style in American films, and this has inevitably moved through into acting in Britain and elsewhere to some extent. The amount of superfluous gesturing by film actors has vastly increased in the last decade or two, in both dramas and comedies. When this acting style is forced into Close Up we get director Tony Scott's speciality, the twisting of the head to one side, during the one second the shot lasts, even though there is no good reason for the actor to change his direction of look. For extra emphasis the head can be twisted to both sides quickly in succession. This cliché can be studied *in extenso* in *Crimson Tide* (1995), but it goes back at least to his *Top Gun* (1986). An even more annoying trick that is special to quite a lot of not-terribly-good young actors is a sharp and loud exhalation between sentences for extra emphasis. This is usually brought up more in the sound mix, but the actors are doing it themselves in the first place. Of course, if an actor is always shown in a shot that only lasts a couple of seconds, that gives barely enough time for him or her to assume even one expression, and the classic "double take", the delayed recognition that the situation is not what the character thought it was, becomes quite impossible. Is it any wonder that the best and most dedicated actors are willing to work for Woody Allen for peanuts?

Indeed, some of these best film actors are now capable of subtlety in performance far beyond the reach of those actors of former days. And some stars have on occasion got so far into a part that their normal persona has completely vanished — I am thinking of cases like Bruce Willis in *Death Becomes Her* (1992) and Cameron Diaz in *Being John Malkovitch* (1999).

The use of improvisation to develop all or part of a film increased in European films, and the 'nineties were the period in which Mike Leigh, who used this method exclusively, was most successful. In his case, his films were developed by improvisation over a long period of rehearsal, with strong guidance given by Leigh to the direction in which the story was going. However, once this was complete, and a final script had been arrived at, this was filmed in the standard way. This meant that the scene dissection could follow the standard patterns if desired, and hence after *Life is Sweet* (1990), which had an ASL of 15.3, the Average Shot Lengths of his films went down towards the British norm. For example, the ASL of *Career Girls* (1997) is 5.2 seconds, and *Topsy-Turvy* (1999) is 6 seconds. But this is strictly more a matter of production than of acting style. Mike Leigh's method of script construction tends to produce some deviations from the conventional form, reducing the usual alternation and variation of mood and content of the scenes down the length of the film, but the other interesting qualities of his films make up for that.

Script Construction

In the 'nineties there was an increase in the number of films containing multiple stories happening in the same place at the same time. Robert Altman, who had been the only film-maker specialising in this approach to script construction, continued the line with *The Player* (1992) and *Short Cuts* (1993), which seem to have encouraged others to join in. These included Quentin Tarantino with *Pulp Fiction* (1994) and Paul Thomas Anderson with *Magnolia* (1999). With this form, the major variable is how interconnected the stories turn out to be. It is easy to have most of them unconnected, but still give the appearance of connection by having a character from one strand merely walk though a scene from another strand, as in Altman's *Nashville* (1975), and this is more or less the case in *Short Cuts* too. Or one can have the connection between the stories revealed gradually, as in *Pulp Fiction* and *Magnolia*.

Lola rennt (1998), the German entry in the series of flashy filmic presentations of the lives of young criminals that started with *Natural Born Killers*, uses another approach, with three variations on the same story, with different outcomes for each, presented in succession. It is further decorated with brief montage sequences showing what subsequently happens to by-standers along the path of Lola's run.

The opposite extreme, which is to have no story at all, also continued in a mild way, for *Henry and June* (1990) was succeeded by Harmony Korine's *Gummo* (1997) and Terry Gilliam's *Fear and Loathing in Las Vegas* (1998). *Gummo* is the most completely unmotivated series of incidents so far put together into a film that has got commercial distribution. Another golden oldie; the film in which its makers discuss the possible plot, interleaved with a representation of their alternative suggestions, made a reappearance. *Wes Craven's New Nightmare* (1994) took this to a new level of cheek, as the director Wes Craven used his own appearances in the framing action to give dubious justifications for the illogical and implausible events occurring in the narrative of the film being made, and which we see realised on the screen.

In the middle of the narrative spectrum, the so-called "character based" film continued. In these, there is no causal link between the series of things that happen to the protagonist: they are just things that might conceivably happen to someone like him or her. Such films are by their very nature art films, and the principal perpetrator of them continued to be Lasse Hallström, as in *Who's Eating Gilbert Grape?* (1993). Other notable workers in this area included Richard Linklater, with *Slacker* (1991).

As remarked in "The Shape of 1999", the use of voice-over narration to power the story has become more common in the last couple of decades, and some films even have multiple voices giving their individual way of looking at what is going on, as in *Election* (Alexander Payne, 1999). Another feature of recent films is the large number of them that use shots and sequences representing mental images in the minds of their characters cut into the narrative, in a way that was last common in the nineteen-twenties.

After I wrote up this chapter, since it deals with recent features of film technology, I asked some of my colleagues at the London Film School to check it for errors and omissions. The helpful people who made comments included Terry Hopkins, Howard Thompson, and Wojciech Wrzesniewski. Nigel Woodford of Richmond Film Services also looked at the section on sound recording, and I am very grateful for the corrections they suggested.

You may notice the reduced definition of the frame enlargements in this chapter. This is because, unlike nearly all the others in this book, which are taken from 35 mm. prints, these are frame grabs from DVD copies of the films concerned. And of course they are all reduced to monochrome. However, I consider that this does not lessen their value for making my particular points about the lighting of these films, even if it detracts from their visual appeal.

While I was still contemplating extending my coverage of film style and technology into the 'nineties, I was asked for a contribution to a new academic periodical called the *New Review of Film and Television Studies*. This journal was set up and edited by Warren Buckland, and he wanted something on "Contemporary American Cinema" for issue Number 1 in Volume 2 (May 2004). This gave me the opportunity to conclusively demonstrate the major changes in film style over the last 50 years. The more specific details of how the research was done are included within my paper.

Routledge, the publishers of the journal, did not want to include the frame enlargements illustrating the important change in the conventions of film framing I mentioned within the article, but I have put these back in this version here. I have also added a frame enlargement from *Angela's Ashes* to illustrate a point I make about its lighting.

The *New Review of Film and Television Studies* uses Perpetua for body text; a face that is a pleasure to look at, and one of Eric Gill's triumphs. However, it needs the application of InDesign's optical kerning to appear at its very best.

THE SHAPE OF 1999

THE STYLISTICS OF AMERICAN MOVIES AT THE END OF THE CENTURY

Why does it matter whether or not there is an objective description of the standard form of American commercial cinema in the here and now? Well, just for a start, there is surely something wrong when none of the reviews of Paul Thomas Anderson's *Magnolia* mention one of its major formal features, which is that it is conducted in very long takes by the standards of 1999. Amongst the hundreds of other films backed in one way or another by Hollywood studios appearing in that year, there is only one other film, Woody Allen's *Sweet and Lowdown*, which is filmed with long takes. That nobody mentioned the long take style in connection with *Sweet and Lowdown* is just slightly more excusable, as Woody Allen has been shooting films that way for many years. The fundamental principle of aesthetic judgement that is important in this context is that deviations from the norms of the period are important, and indeed potentially of artistic worth. If you can't handle this, then you are off in the egomaniacal world where nothing but "critical intuition" is used in dealing with art.

So how does one deal with establishing objective descriptive standards for dealing with the mass arts of film and television?

How To Do It

It should be obvious that the terms used for analysing movies are those used by their makers in putting them together, and indeed that the only rational approach in general terms is for the analysis to reverse the construction process used in creating the work. Fortunately for my task, the basic components of film form have been constant for most of the past century, once they had been established in American cinema around the time of the First World War. In fact the American cinema has drawn the commercial cinema in the rest of the world along behind it stylistically ever since, up to the present.

The easiest basic variable in film construction to obtain is what I call the Average Shot Length (ASL). The lengths of the shots making up films has been discussed from time to time by film-makers since at least 1912, though they have invariably done it in terms of the number of shots in particular individual films. This would be perfectly satisfactory if all films were exactly the same length, but they are not. All films are not even approximately the same length. Hence my introduction of the ASL, which has since been taken up by other people interested in this matter.

Another obvious variable used in film construction is the Scale of Shot, or Closeness of Shot. This is measured by how much of the height of the actors in the foreground of the shot is visible within the frame. Again, this has been discussed by film-makers from at least as early as 1912. The descriptive terms used then were "French foreground" and "American foreground", followed shortly afterwards by the still-used term "close up". The terms I use are those current in the 'forties, and to be found in *The Five C's of Cinematography*, written by a Hollywood cameraman of the period, Joseph V. Mascelli. They are as follows: Big Close Up (BCU) shows head only, Close Up (CU) shows head and shoulders, Medium Close Up (MCU) includes body from the waist up, Medium Shot (MS) includes from just below the hip to above the head of upright actors, Medium Long Shot (MLS) shows the body from the knee upwards, Long Shot (LS) shows at least the full height of the body, and Very Long Shot (VLS) shows the actor small in the frame. (A shot which shows the head and shoulders of an actor sticking into the lower part of the frame with a yard of air above them does not count as a Close Up.) In recent decades in film and television the vaguer term 'Wide Shot' has come to replace the various kinds of Long Shot described above, but I am keeping to the earlier, more finely graded, terminology which was in use when I first became involved with film-making more than fifty years ago. If one wishes to use a different system of Scale of Shot in making a similar analysis to the one here, the results can still be compared with mine, as long as a definition is given of what each gradation of scale of shot corresponds to against the actor's height.

After counting the total number of shots in each category in a film, I then normalize or standardize the number to be the relative proportion there would be in an average 500 shots in the film. I round to the nearest integer in this operation. This is done to make an easy and clear comparison between the relative tendencies of different film makers to use different Closeness of Shot. It would be possible to express the relative frequency of each type of shot as a percentage of the total number, but I am loath to go back and alter thirty years worth of results to do this. (Also, you can easily convert to percentages if you wish, by dividing by five.) Incidentally, the use of percentages almost demands that one begin to use decimal fractions in the results, which I think is unnecessarily messy.

Other basic units of film construction refer to the relation of shots to each other within scenes. These are reverse angles, which describe a shot taken in approximately the opposite direction to the preceding shot in the scene, and Point of View shots, which are shots taken exactly in the direction a character is looking in the preceding or succeeding shot. (The term originally used in the United States for what are now called "reverse angles", or often just "reverses", was "reverse scene", after such things began to appear in 1908. At that time they were always shot at a distance from the actors, but as the camera moved closer in, and was applied at more varied angles, and indeed the term "camera angle" itself came to be used, the expression shifted to "reverse angle". "Reverse shot" was occasionally, but far less frequently, used.) In my work, I count a cut as being one to a reverse angle (RA) when it changes the camera direction by more than 90 degrees. In other words, not all cuts between "singles" of two actors facing each other in the scene count as reverse angle cuts. The other basic quantity that I collect is the number of inserts used. That is, shots of objects, or distant scenes, either of which do not show an actor featured in the film story. I also include in this category such shots as a Big Close Up of an actor's hand going into their pocket, for these can be, and frequently are, shot with a stand-in. I express these three quantities as percentages of the total number of shots or cuts in a film.

As for camera movement, the categories I use are pan, tilt, pan with tilt, track, track with pan, track with pan and tilt, crane, and zoom. All of these are fairly self-explanatory, but it is worth remarking that my category of simple tracking shot includes only camera dolly movements in a straight line, including those sideways to the camera direction and subject, which is sometimes referred to as "crabbing". Any tracking on a curved path invariably contains panning movements as well. The zoom category, admittedly not strictly a camera movement, includes zooms made with simultaneous panning or tilting. Camera movements of small extent which are made to keep the actors well-framed as they move about a little are not counted, as these have been done effectively automatically by camera operators for the last eighty years at least, and are hence without significance. The same applies to small dolly adjustments of a foot or so made for the same reason. Camera movements are also normalized to the number per 500 shots for the film in question.

A few other people have taken up these methods over the last thirty years, first Harv Bishop (1985) in a stylistic comparison of the films of Peter Bogdanovitch and certain other directors, then Michael J. Porter (1987) has applied similar methods in television analysis, and most recently, Warren Buckland (2001) has tested them on a couple of recent Hollywood films.

What To Do It To

For this survey, I chose to work with films from 1999 because this is the most recent year for which I have been able to see large numbers of American films on British free-to-air television. (British television companies have an agreement with the major American film distributors only to show films that were released in the cinema in the UK at least three years previously.) According to the International Movie Database (which seems to have fairly reliable data for recent years), there were more than 1000 American feature films released in 1999. (I am including films that are listed as American co-productions with another country by the IMDb, but I am excluding made for TV feature films, and also "straight to video" features, not to mention feature-length documentaries and animated features.) Ideally, in the search for a representative sample, one would make a random selection from these 1000 or so films, but not all of them are available on VHS cassettes or DVDs even in the USA. A rough check shows that those films that are available in these formats correspond fairly exactly to those for which at least 10 people have registered a vote

on the IMDb. This reduces the number to be considered to 671. A random selection of 20 films from this corpus using a random number generator produced the following list:-

The Underground Comedy Movie
The Storytellers
Music of the Heart
Heart to Heart.com
Money Buys Happiness
The Curse
The Treasure of Pirate's Point
Hot Wax Zombies on Wheels
Point Doom
Palmer's Pick Up
Playthings
Coming Soon
Outside Providence
Cremaster 2
Storm
An Invited Guest
Scar City
Jesus' Son
Raw Nerve
The Distraction

How many of these have you seen, or even heard of? With titles like *The Storytellers* and *An Invited Guest*, some of these films are longing to be ignored. And would you really want to read my analysis of them? In any case, only *Jesus' Son* and *Music of the Heart* have been released in the UK. So I decided to limit myself to a selection from a smaller group of films about which rather more people had been interested in expressing an opinion. So I narrowed the corpus to those films for which at least 500 people had put in an opinion and vote on the IMDb. (As you can check for yourself, such opinions and votes are far from always being complimentary to the film concerned.) This gave me 179 films to select from, and these usefully happened to have a rough correspondence with the body of the American films from 1999 released on VHS or DVD in Britain. Making another random selection of 20 films from these produced the following list:-

10 Things I Hate About You (Gil Junger)
Angela's Ashes (Alan Parker)
The Blair Witch Project (Myrick & Sanchez)
Brokedown Palace (Jonathan Kaplan)
Crazy in Alabama (Antonio Banderas)
Deep Blue Sea (Renny Harlin)
Detroit Rock City (Adam Rifkin)
Edtv (Ron Howard)
The Insider (Michael Mann)
Jakob the Liar (Peter Kassovitz)
Life (Ted Demme)
Love Stinks (Jeff Franklin)
Man on the Moon (Milos Forman)
The Mating Habits of the Earthbound Human (Jeff Abugov)

The Minus Man (Hampton Fancher)
The Sixth Sense (M. Night Shyamalan)
SLC Punk! (James Merendino)
Snow Falling on Cedars (Scott Hicks)
The Talented Mr. Ripley (Anthony Minghella)
Three to Tango (Damon Santostefano)

This seems to me to be a convincingly varied collection, though naturally, given the method of sampling, it contains no proper representation of the rather large amount of absolute rubbish in the original list of all US features from 1999. However, it does include representatives from the cheap end of production, with *The Mating Habits of the Earthbound Human* and *SLC Punk!* being clearly made for just a few hundred thousand dollars, not to mention *The Blair Witch Project*. The quite representative balance of genres in the final sample also reminds us that extremely expensive mindless action films like *Deep Blue Sea* only form a very small part of American production, however much attention they attract, and however much money they take at the box-office. Well, actually not that much in the case of *Deep Blue Sea*. Minor points I discovered in this sample is that none of them contains a real car chase sequence, though *Detroit Rock City*, which is a very conventional teen rock-music comedy, does have a short highway car-bumping duel. There is no genuine "art film" in my sample, though such things do exist in the total American production for the year, but *The Minus Man* and *SLC Punk!* are nudging the edge of this category. The other thing I notice in the sample is the relative absence of nudity and explicit sexual activity, even though such scenes could be justified by many of the scripts. In fact the only real nudity in the sample is in *Angela's Ashes*, and it is very brief at that. I think this may actually represent a trend which has been underway for a few years, with representation of sexual activity now being increasingly exiled to the very bottom end of production, and in Britain, to television.

I have also included in the results the figures for two additional shows. These are the film *Dark City* (Alex Proyas) from 1998, because this has, as far as I know, the fastest cutting in American film up to the present, and a piece of television drama from 1999, namely an episode from the soap opera *Melrose Place* (Richard Lang).

What We Get

The first thing to look at is Average Shot Length (ASL). To put this in context, I present a historical survey of the trends in this variable in American commercial cinema since 1940, including all the latest figures I have collected. Over the last decade I have obtained many thousands more values for this variable, so the figures represented in the histograms here supersede those in my *Film Style and Technology: History and Analysis* (Starword, 1992). The graphs cover the same six year periods used in that source, and as in the earlier survey, the class intervals are defined so that the height of the column or bar above the number five, say, represents the number of films with ASLs between 5.0 seconds and 5.9999... seconds. In the case of the 1994-99 period, for instance, this is 192 films. Any films with ASLs greater than 25

seconds are lumped together in the column after the 25 second column. The total number of films recorded in the 1994-99 sample is 1035, whereas the period 1970-75 is represented by only 373 films. The other periods are represented by numbers of films between these two figures, and for the whole sixty years I am dealing with 5,893 films altogether. The number of films covered by each graph is proportional to the total area inside the columns (bars) of the histograms of that graph. The majority of these ASLs are taken for the complete length of the films concerned. My initial practice of being satisfied in some cases with the ASL for the first 40 minutes of a film was abandoned ten years ago.

The first observation about the general trend of change over this sixty years of American cinema is obvious. The cutting rate or number of shots has increased fairly steady over the period, and the measure of this, the ASL, has decreased. The position of the modal (or most common) value of the ASL can easily be seen to be moving leftwards from 9 seconds in 1946-51 to 3 seconds in 1994-99. Although it stands out clearly, the modal value is not the most accurate way of measuring the general trend, because its value is susceptible to the size of the class interval chosen. Preferable is the mean ASL for each period. This can be seen to be decreasing continuously from the high value of 10.47 seconds in 1946-51 to 4.92 seconds in 1994-99. The period 1946-51 was the peak of the adoption of the long take way of shooting films by a select group of Hollywood directors, though not by the majority. (Any film with an ASL of greater than 11 seconds will contain many long takes; that is, shots having durations of 30 seconds and above.) The long take school of directors were still hard at work in Hollywood through the 'fifties, but then they began to be displaced by newer entrants to the profession in the late 'fifties, and the mean ASL started to go down. The continual decrease was held up for a while in the 'seventies by a bit of a return to shooting long takes, now using the zoom lens as well as tracking and panning as a means of keeping a shot going beyond the normal length.

At the other extreme, the first appearance of ASLs of less than 3 seconds in American sound cinema appears to be in 1968, with Daniel Haller's *The Wild Racers*, followed by Russ Meyer's *Cherry, Harry, and Raquel* in 1969. Through the 'seventies there were a few more Russ Meyer films, and also a handful from Sam Peckinpah and George A. Romero. In the nineteen-eighties, there were slightly more action films such as the later "Rambo" and "Rocky" films, and also a few action horror films, that also had ASLs below 3 seconds. Then suddenly in the 1994-99 period the number of films with ASLs less than 3 seconds leapt to 72 films out of the sample of 1035. This development is accurately represented by two films in the twenty film sample for 1999 that I am analysing in detail. These are *Deep Blue Sea* and *Detroit Rock City*, as you can see in the table below.

Incidentally, the move towards faster and faster cutting in American cinema over the last fifty years has not been led by American television practice. I believe the pressure on time and expenditure in TV production militates against the larger number of camera set-ups necessary to get a shorter ASL. In any case, I have a collection of results for TV drama and comedy for the

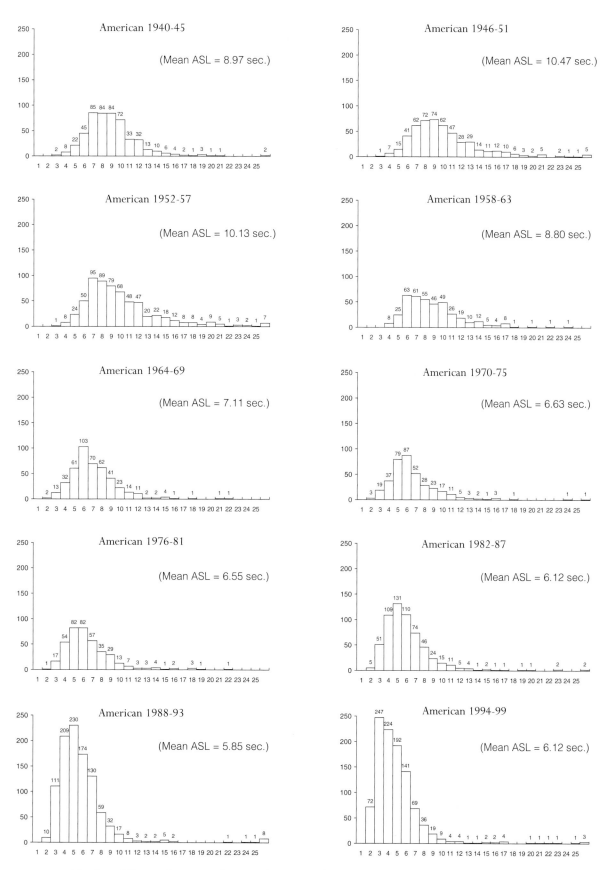

Number of films with Average Shot Length (ASL) in the given ranges for periods from 1940 to 1999

last fifty years, and these show that film cutting rates have always been faster than those in television. This research is in "The Stylistic Analysis of Television Drama Programs" in this book.

Going back to the slow end of cutting, you can see from the distributions that in the 'nineties there are now very few films indeed with an ASL greater than 11 seconds. I have previously suggested that for American films made after 1990, any having an ASL greater than 9 seconds falls into the "art film" category, though I now think that 10 seconds is a better dividing line. For the 1994-99 sample of 1035 films there are only 26 features with ASLs longer than 10 seconds. The only ones from 1999 amongst the 140 odd that I have so far seen, and having an ASL greater than 10 seconds, are *Sweet and Lowdown*, *Magnolia*, and *The Blair Witch Project*. Inside the sample, *The Sixth Sense* is flirting with the idea of being an art film, according to this criterion, with an ASL of 8.6 seconds. Otherwise, the majority of films in the sample (16 of them) have ASLs between 3 and 7 seconds, just like the vast majority of the films in my much larger sample for 1994-99.

One would think that eventually a limit will be reached in cutting rate, and we may be near it now. This limit is presumably imposed by the minimum length of comprehensible sentences in dialogue scenes, together with just how many reaction shots a dialogue scene will stand without looking ridiculous. There is no limit to how many shots a scene of pure action may be broken down into, but even the most mindless action film needs a certain amount of explanation in the dialogue as to the reason for all the bashes, crashes and explosions. However, we may already be seeing a new way of getting the effect of a cut without actually making one within a shot. For the last several years, many action films have scenes in which the lights that are ostensibly lighting the scene are flashing on and off during the course of the shots, which, particularly if these lighting changes are extreme, gives the effect of virtual cuts within the shot, because successive lengths of footage look so different to each other under the lighting changes. There are a number of examples of scenes with this technique in *Deep Blue Sea*, *Detroit Rock City*, and *Dark City*.

The complete tabulation of Average Shot Lengths, percentage of Reverse Angle cuts, percentage of POV shots, and percentage of Insert shots for my 20 film sample from 1999 is given below.

There is not a great deal to be said about the percentages of reverse angle cuts in the films under consideration – they range from 21% to 70%, ignoring *The Blair Witch Project*, and all these values could have been found forty years ago. However, there are probably more films with RA percentages above 40% than there would have been forty years ago. In the very special case of *The Blair Witch Project*, its basic feature that all its shots were taken

TITLE	DIRECTOR	ASL	RA	POV	INS
10 Things I Hate About You	Junger, Gil	6.7	58	4	2
Angela's Ashes	Parker, Alan	3.9	31	4	10
Blair Witch Project, The	Myrick, D & Sanchez, E.	15.8	1	2	44
Brokedown Palace	Kaplan, Jonathan	5.8	50	6	6
Crazy in Alabama	Banderas, Antonio	5.4	45	8	8
Deep Blue Sea	Harlin, Renny	2.6	24	10	23
Detroit Rock City	Rifkin, Adam	2.2	25	5	11
EDtv	Howard, Ron	5.5	31	8	12
Insider, The	Mann, Michael	5.4	33	6	6
Jakob the Liar	Kassovitz, Peter	5.7	37	10	4
Life	Demme, Ted	4.5	55	6	2
Love Stinks	Franklin, Jeff	4.6	49	7	6
Man on the Moon	Forman, Milos	3.9	46	18	4
Mating Habits of the Earthbound Human, The	Abugov, Jeff	5.6	35	6	9
Minus Man, The	Fancher, Hampton	5.5	50	10	15
Sixth Sense, The	Shyamalam, M. Night	8.6	57	21	15
SLC Punk!	Merendino, James	4.2	38	3	7
Snow Falling on Cedars	Hicks, Scott	5.3	23	6	13
Talented Mr. Ripley, The	Minghella, Anthony	5.0	45	6	6
Three to Tango	Santostefano, Damon	3.7	61	5	6
Melrose Place	Lang, Richard	4.0	70	3	5
Dark City	Proyas, Alex	2.0	26	7	14

by the two cameras used by the characters in it eliminates the possibility of reverse angles and POV shots, except under very special circumstances. That is, one of the characters has to be shown filming one of the others, and then there has to be a cut to the footage from their camera. This does happen a couple of times in the introductory scenes, but not thereafter. You might say that the fact that since all the shots in the movie are filmed by characters in the film, then that should make all of them POV shots, but my definition of a POV shot is one that represents what one of the characters shown in an adjoining shot sees, which accords with ordinary film nomenclature, and it is this definition that gives the result above.

The percentage of POV shots is in general below 10% for the sample, with the exception of two films. In *Man on the Moon* a great deal of the film is occupied with the protagonist performing on stage or television, watched by people who know him, so *The Sixth Sense* is the only truly exceptional case. Here, a proportion of the POV shots are assigned to the psychiatrist character after the prologue near the beginning of the main story, and also at its end. Those near the beginning seem to me misleading about the physical existence of the psychiatrist, since if we see his POV shots just like those of the real people in the film, this tends to imply that he exists, just like them. You might say that this goes with the treatment of the restaurant scene, in which his wife appears to reply to what he says, and which is equally deceiving of the film audience. But at least there are no shots of him done as POV shots from the viewpoint of the other characters. And it must be pointed out that the handling of "subjective" effects,

including POV shots, has frequently been logically inconsistent, ever since such things first appeared in movies a hundred years ago. Also striking, in a negative way, is the low proportion of POV shots in *The Talented Mr. Ripley*, particularly if we contrast it with Alfred Hitchcock's treatment of a not dissimilar Patricia Highsmith novel, *Strangers on a Train*, fifty years before. In that case, 18% of the cuts are between one of a character and their POV, and, boy, are they working dramatically!

Insert shots are another aspect of "pure cinema", as Alfred was wont to put it, (or basic filmic narration, if you want to be pretentious about it), and these are given due emphasis in some of the films. They are of course performing their suspense/thriller function in *Deep Blue Sea, The Minus Man*, and *The Sixth Sense*. *The Blair Witch Project* takes this kind of thing to what must be a new world record, eclipsing Fritz Lang's efforts of long ago, which peaked at 27% Insert shots in *Das Testament des Dr. Mabuse* (1933) (see *Fritz Lang's Diagonal Symphony* earlier in this book). Whether they would have worked just as well if there were rather less of them in *The Blair Witch Project* is an interesting question. In *Snow Falling on Cedars* the inserts mostly occur in the numerous arty "mental image" sequences.

How Close We Are

The proportions of shots of different scale (or closeness) for the films in my sample are presented in a series of graphs of the histogram variety. I have grouped them on the page according to the degree of resemblance between their profiles. The degree of close resemblance between the Scale of Shot profiles for the first

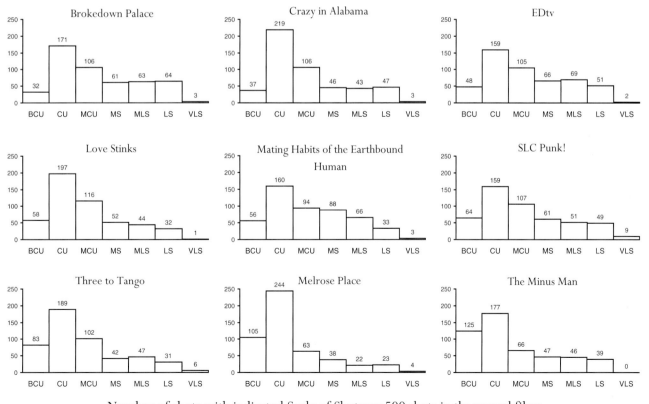

Number of shots with indicated Scale of Shot per 500 shots in the named films

eight of the films, and also their resemblance to that for the *Melrose Place* television show is rather scary, particularly in contrast to the variety to be seen in the many results for the 'twenties through the "High Hollywood" period of the 'thirties and 'forties presented in Film Style and Technology: History and Analysis. And of course this very heavy emphasis on the use of close shots is unparalleled in the past. The first variant on what is clearly now a standard profile is represented by the group made up of *10 Things I Hate About You, Angela's Ashes, Detroit Rock City, Jakob the Liar*, and *The Talented Mr. Ripley*. In these films the large number of Close Ups (CUs) stand out above a more even background of the other

scales of shot. One interpretation of this sort of profile is that the directors concerned are reluctantly paying lip service to the notion of "more Close Ups" by just going for that pure category alone. And it is noticeable that there are three un-American directors in this group – Alan Parker, Peter Kassovitz, and Anthony Minghella. On the other hand, Gil Junger and Adam Rifkin are purely American film-makers, the former having directed a large amount of commercial television before making *10 Things*, and Adam Rifkin having been involved with making low budget film junk for quite a while before getting a bit more money to make this film celebrating the band Kiss. So perhaps there is nothing

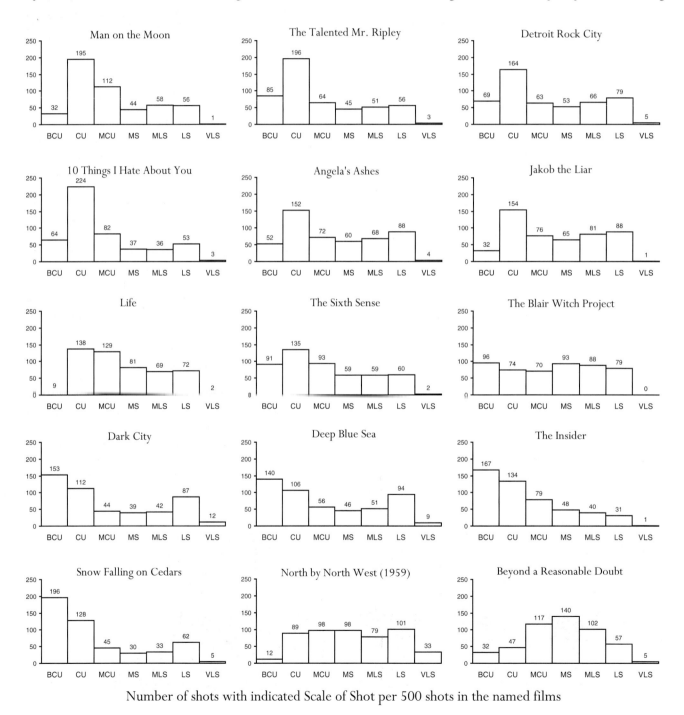

Number of shots with indicated Scale of Shot per 500 shots in the named films

in my interpretation. Milos Forman's *Man on the Moon* also has a fairly similar Scale of Shot profile.

Ted Demme's *Life* is the only film in the sample that has the kind of fairly even distribution across the Scale of Shot from CU to LS that was quite common once upon a time. *The Sixth Sense* and *The Blair Witch Project* also have a pretty even distribution across the Scales of Shot, but in this case they have the equally heavy emphasis on Big Close Up so characteristic of recent times. *Deep Blue Sea* and *Dark City* push the emphasis even further onto Big Close Up, and at the other end of the scale onto LS. They are both science fiction spectaculars, and the extra proportion of Long Shots against the middle range of closeness is to contain the spectacular sets and their destruction and transformation that is so essential to these films' being. I wouldn't be surprised if further work showed that this profile was characteristic of other similar big budget films.

Incidentally, *The Blair Witch Project* has a number of peculiarities in framing, which are due to the desire of the makers to give the impression that it is the rushes of a real cinéma vérité film that were shot by the characters in it. As their fear and anguish grows, the framings become compositionally unbalanced, and indeed go so far as to be a crude sort of Dutch tilt framing even when they put the camera down onto some fixed surface to get a shot with themselves in it. These devices probably work in the usual expressive way for an unsophisticated audience, but a microsecond's thought should tell you that someone who can conquer their fear

sufficiently to pick up a camera and film what is going on, will be certain to also get the shot reasonably well framed.

Finally we have two films which have the most extreme use of Big Close Up, *The Insider* and *Snow Falling on Cedars*, both of which have relatively intimate stories, which makes possible such large numbers of BCUs, and both of which are intentionally pushing the envelope of commercially acceptable style. They also show the way that film leads television, for TV shows do not get quite this close on the average, as indicated by the Scale of Shot distribution for the *Melrose Place* episode. (The pressure against TV shows using very large amounts of BCUs is that under the fast shooting regime of TV, there is a considerable danger of producing ugly looking pictures of the actor's heads in BCU if a slight error is made in framing by the operator. In looser framings, slight framing errors do not draw attention to themselves quite so much.)

In the process of analysing these films with respect to Closeness of Shot, I realised that there has been a change in the standard framing of a head in Big Close Up, and also to some of extent of ordinary Close Ups, over the last decade or two. Whereas Big Close Ups used to be framed cutting the figure at the neck at the bottom of the frame, and just above the head at the top of the frame, now it is common to include a bit of the shoulders, and cut through the forehead at the top, so leaving the closeness the same, but substantially changing the look of the shot. (See illustrations from *Casablanca* above, and *The Minus Man* below.)

That this change had passed me by up to the point of making this analysis is yet another illustration of the usefulness of these methods.

Moving Around the Scene

There are characteristic variations in the use of camera movement amongst film directors, and I deal with this by counting the number of camera movements of various types in the films. These are tilts, pans, panning and tilting simultaneously, tracking, tracking with panning, tracking with panning and tilting, crane movements, and zooming. (Yes, I know the last of these is not actually a camera movement, but it changes the content of the frame during the shot, and I have to get it in somewhere.) Although I actually collect all these categories, in this case I will consolidate some of them, so as to bring out the similarities and differences between the films more clearly. So I put both pans and tilts together in the category of Pans, and put the Tracks with Pans together with the Tracks with both Panning and Tilting. The films are ordered in terms of the total number of shots with

camera movement per 500 shots. I do not distinguish the different methods of supporting the camera, so that hand-held tracking and Steadicam tracking go in together with the traditional tracking with the camera on a dolly.

One curiosity that leaps to the eye is the relatively uniform use of simple pans and tilts, which range between 15 and 27, with the exception of *The Sixth Sense* and *Three To Tango*. Apart from this, *The Blair Witch Project* is totally unique with respect to camera movement, as it is in other respects. Nevertheless, we can see that the different combinations of kinds of movement do make some distinctions amongst some of the films. It is possible to distinguish a definite low camera movement class, made up of *Angela's Ashes, Man on the Moon, Three to Tango*, and *The Mating Habits of the Earthbound Human*. The noticeably small use of camera movements in the first three of these is undoubtedly intentional, since their directors are all very experienced, but it is likely that *The Mating Habits of the Earthbound Human* has little camera movement because of the sheer lack of talent of its director, as well as his inexperience. (Proven by some dubious eye-line matches.)

Title	Pan	Pan with Tilt	Track	Track with Pan & Tilt	Crane	Zoom	Total
Blair Witch Project, The	24	79	24	152	0	31	310
Jakob the Liar	24	17	24	47	3	0	115
Brokedown Palace	22	23	19	30	10	0	104
Snow Falling on Cedars	28	30	22	18	5	0	103
10 Things I Hate About You	15	6	20	50	10	1	102
Dark City	25	11	22	7	35	0	100
Sixth Sense, The	9	11	46	26	5	0	97
Insider, The	26	11	21	34	2	2	96
Detroit Rock City	22	15	21	23	2	7	96
Crazy in Alabama	22	12	27	28	6	0	93
SLC Punk!	17	13	31	21	10	0	92
EDtv	18	11	29	20	3	5	86
Minus Man, The	26	21	13	20	3	0	79
Talented Mr. Ripley, The	17	15	19	25	3	0	79
Love Stinks	23	7	14	29	4	0	77
Deep Blue Sea	21	8	27	16	2	0	74
Life	16	3	19	24	4	0	66
Angela's Ashes	24	14	9	5	0	1	53
Man on the Moon	27	7	6	9	2	0	51
Three to Tango	10	7	15	14	2	0	48
Mating Habits of the Earthbound Human	28	5	9	4	1	0	47

Perhaps *Life* should be included in this group. Other things that stand out are the very large proportion of crane shots in *Dark City*, though this is not strictly part of our main sample, and the particularly large amount of tracking with a free head in *Jakob the Liar* and *10 Things I Hate About You*. In both of these cases, most of the tracking is actually done with a Steadicam, as it has to be nowadays when there is a lot of it, since laying tracks for a dolly is very expensive in terms of time and labour. No doubt Gil Junger was relishing the opportunity to set his camera free, for lots of tracking of any kind, and the Steadicam kind in particular, are not used in TV studio work.

The other stand-out figure is the amount of straight-line tracking in *The Sixth Sense*. These movements are in general short in range, and slow, and a lot of them are also sideways tracks or crabbing movements, and most of them are done on quasi-static scenes. That is, they are not following the characters as they move around. The characters are sitting down, say, and the camera tracks slowly across behind one of them sitting on a sofa. This trick does not originate with M. Night Shyamalan, but he does it a bit more in *The Sixth Sense* than his contemporaries. Indeed, there is a smaller amount of this kind of short and slow tracking in *Snow Falling On Cedars* and *The Talented Mr. Ripley* in our sample. It could be claimed that it produces an expressive sense of unease in *The Sixth Sense*, but it just irritates me, here and elsewhere. The most adventurous of these films stylistically is *The Insider*, which uses a high amount of camera movement, with both moves on a dolly, and on a Steadicam, and also old-style hand shooting. There seems to be an expressively graded use of these techniques, from dolly to Steadicam to hand-held shots having an extra bit of wobble put on, and so intentionally producing a more and more agitated effect as we go through to the last of these.

Incidentally, there are some other films from 1999 and thereabouts which show the influence of the camera operating in the TV show *NYPD Blue*. Waving the camera around for extra excitement is to be found extensively in *GI Jane* (1997), and in *Any Given Sunday* (1999) a new optical device was used in front of the lens on some shots to give the effect with a camera that was not being moved at all.

But the most striking device in *The Insider* is the use of out-of-focus effects. For instance, when Russell Crowe enters the room where the bosses of the tobacco company are meeting near the beginning of the film, the shot is a CU of the back of the head of the big boss, which is in sharp focus. Crowe is distant in the background and well out of focus, and he stays that way for the rest of the shot, even though he is the object of principal interest. There are also brutal focus pulls all the way from BCU to VLS, and much play with messy bits of out-of-focus hair etc. obscuring parts of the frame in the foreground, in a thoroughly unconventional way.

Zooming is in general not used in our sample films, at least in any noticeable way. (Some of these movies were filmed with a zoom lens on the camera to give a quick adjustment of the focal length when changing from set-up to set-up, and sometimes they have an occasional slight tightening or loosening of the framing due to a small change in the focal length within the shot, but I do not count that as a zoom, any more than I count a small pan or tilt for re-framing purposes.) Otherwise, we have a small number of zooms in *Detroit Rock City* in the final rock concert, where they naturally belong, and a similarly a small number in *Edtv*, which is about actuality TV, another natural habitat of the zoom. Otherwise, real zooming is mostly out nowadays, with one exception. This is a repetition of the "Vertigo" effect or contra-zoom; that is, a simultaneous zoom and track in the reverse direction, so that the framing stays the same, but the internal perspective of the shot changes. This expressive device is used for comedy near the beginning of *10 Things I Hate About You*, and also almost invisibly near the beginning of *The Sixth Sense*, when the psychiatrist is staking out his prospective child patient. And I have seen this device used in these sorts of ways in other recent films. Even "Salman Pax" (the Bagdad Blogger), used it to round off one of his video diaries recently! It has become a cliché.

The Look of the Picture

My casual impression of films from the last decade was that a large proportion of them had colour bias applied to all their scenes for expressive or stylistic purposes. But careful examination of the films in my sample just goes to show how wrong intuitive impressions can be, even for the expert eye. In fact, most of the twenty films have their shots fairly correctly balanced to white light, with the exception of the night exteriors, which are generally given the traditional bluish bias. The minor exceptions to this generalization are *Brokedown Palace* and *Life*, which have an orange or amber bias given to many day exteriors, presumably to suggest the heat of the Far East or the Deep South, and *The Insider*, which has a number of night interiors with a slightly warm tone. The major exceptions are *Angela's Ashes*, *Jakob the Liar*, and *Snow Falling on Cedars*, all of which have had desaturation applied to the all colours throughout. In the first two, this has presumably been done to emphasize the miserable conditions under which their characters exist, and in the case of the latter, to emphasize the pastness of the story, with a touch of the miserables as well. At a more technical level, there is a just noticeable variation in lighting style across the sample, with in the first place a varying degree of hardness (directionality) in the light applied to the interior scenes. This ranges from hard lighting on the figures in *Love Stinks* and *Life* through to very soft lighting on the figures in *The Minus Man* and *Man on the Moon*. Another variable is the amount of backlight used on the figures. This tends to be low, as usual nowadays, and is largely absent in *Jakob the Liar*, and completely absent in *Angela's Ashes*, which is truly exceptional in this respect. This film has much the most realistic lighting, with its poverty-stricken interiors lit by one or two fairly small soft sources just out of shot, with the level of light falling rapidly away to the walls of the sets, so that there is little conventional separation of the figures from the background.

Telling the Story

Fourteen of these films tell their stories in the basic straightforward way that was standard fifty, and more, years ago. Of the rest, *Angela's Ashes*, *SLC Punk!*, and *Crazy in Alabama* are narrated

A typical scene in Angela's Ashes, *lit by Michael Seresin with a large area soft source out right, probably a Kinoflo bank, and nothing else.*

in voice over by someone who appears in the film as their younger self, while *Life* is presented as a series of flashbacks told to an audience within the framing scenes by an old participant in the past events. *The Talented Mr. Ripley* is begun with a voice over by the protagonist regretting what he had done to initiate the action, but this does not reappear, so it doesn't really count as a narrated film. *The Mating Habits of the Earthbound Human* is presented as a documentary, with personal narration, made by some kind of extra-terrestrial being, about the subject of the title. *Snow Falling on Cedars* is a mixture of flashback narration and memories framed by a trial scene. My impression is that the use of voice-over narration to power the story has become more common in the last couple of decades than it was fifty years ago, since a quick check on a list of films from 1946-51 shows less than 5% with narrated stories.

The other feature that I have noticed in these and many other recent films is the large number of them that use shots and sequences representing mental images in the minds of their characters. In *The Minus Man* scenes representing the imaginings of the protagonist are cut straight into the action, and *Life* has a sequence in which the verbally expressed fantasies of the leading characters are followed by a depiction of these fantasies, with the dialogue carrying back and forth between fantasy and reality in a fairly ingenious way. *SLC Punk!* has a couple of scenes in which the background behind the characters changes within the shot to represent their fantasies. In *The Mating Habits of the Earthbound Human* there are fantasy scenes belonging to the human characters who are the subject of the film, which doesn't

make much logical sense, and in *The Sixth Sense* the psychiatrist also has his mental images represented visually. *Crazy in Alabama* does not have any visual mental images, but it does have a voice inside the head of the female lead coming through on the sound track at times, presumably to convey her insanity. As for *Snow Falling on Cedars*, throughout this film, besides the conventional flashback sequences, there are also many brief flashes of images of objects from the characters' past cutting in unexpectedly. The combination of all this, together with the lack of much dramatic development in the framing trial scene of this film, come close to reducing its narrative drive to zero, and sufficiently explains its commercial failure.

Single shots of unexpected content suddenly cut into the narrative have begun appearing in quite a number of films recently, and other notable examples from 1999 include the skies with lightning flash appearing gratuitously in the latter parts of Oliver Stone's *Any Given Sunday*. (Oliver Stone has had quite a bit of influence on the work of other directors, including in particular *Snow Falling on Cedars*, in this sample.) The most outlandish of the cut-ins from 1999 is the viewpoint of a spent bullet inside the guts of a wounded soldier in David O. Russell's *Three Kings*. Apart from showing-off, the point of these memory flashes and inserts is that they are another way of increasing the cutting rate a bit.

How Good Are They?

The most rational and objective criteria for evaluating aesthetic worth are, in order of their importance: 1. Originality, 2. Influence, 3. Success in carrying out the maker's intentions.

Here, as in other respects, *The Blair Witch Project* stands out for its originality from conception to execution, and also its great commercial success scores some points under Criterion No. 3. The degree of commercial success counts for all these films, since none of them are art films, let alone avant-garde films, and their makers undoubtedly had commercial success in mind. The runner-up in originality is *Snow Falling On Cedars*, with its heavily worked mixture of flashbacks and mental images, closely followed by *The Insider*, with its novel play with focus, and then *SLC Punk!*. This last film uses a small array of New Wave style tricks, such as freeze frames, peculiar shots, jokey fake documentary sequences, and talking to the audience, besides the matted-in background transformations that I have already mentioned. *The Sixth Sense* is also a possible contender for innovation, since it appears to go further than other ordinary films in the avoidance of the standard dialogue cutting point. That is, in cutting from speaker to speaker, there is very frequently a pause of several frames, or more, after the first person has finished speaking, before the cut to the other person who is going to reply, and then another pause before they actually say anything. Although this occurs to the greatest extent in the conversations between the boy and the psychiatrist, others are also favoured with this treatment to some extent. Shyamalan's use of this technique is something that needs further investigation.

Evaluating Criterion 3, success in carrying out the maker's intentions, depends on knowing what the maker's intentions are, and for recent films this is mostly fairly easy to find out if you want to. Indeed, statements on this usually form part of the press pack at the film's release. For instance, in the case of *Snow Falling on Cedars*, according to a conversation recorded by Chrisopher Probst (2000) in the *American Cinematographer* (p. 98), Scott Hicks said,

> "The whole film is about the process of revealing. Nothing is quite what it appears to be; therefore, you never give it all away at once, but instead gradually. That was our guiding principle in the overall design of the film. The story is told through the gradual unravelling of several different mysteries: what happened at sea, in the war, [and between] Hatsue and Ishmael. I wanted the film to move seamlessly through its different time frames, like a knife through a slice of cake."

He more or less achieves this, but obviously the idea was pushed too far, for the audience rejection of it upset its makers, which shows that they were indeed concerned with audience response. This is unlike the directors of real art films, who tend to shrug off such reactions.

Something similar is the case with *The Talented Mr. Ripley*. Anthony Minghella is quoted by Jay Holben (2000) on p. 57 as saying that,

> "The film is lit with warm hues that serve to collect what is innately gorgeous about the landscape, and completely contradict the rather purgatorial journey that

we are being led on. Rather than present Mr. Ripley as a collection of monochrome and increasingly moody images full of presentiment, we decided it would be much more interesting to do absolutely the reverse, and lend the film a romantic look that would stand in counterpoint to the action."

As I have noted above, there are other aspects of the form of this film that avoid the standard filmic expressive methods, so Minghella's approach, like that of Hicks, is surprisingly perverse for the maker of an expensive commercial film. It occurs to me that this is another tendency that has appeared in recent decades, along with various changes in subject matter that are outside my immediate concerns, such as the marked increase in cynicism and nihilism in film scripts. Incidentally, the previous film adaptation of this novel, René Clément's *Plein soleil* (1959), was equally photographed in high key throughout.

One can reasonably assume that the makers of the more ordinary of these films were intending to comply with the ordinary craft standards, and evaluating their success in doing this makes up part of the calculus of Criterion 3. So one can definitely mark down *The Mating Habits of the Earthbound Human* in this area. The quality of script construction by conventional standards also counts under the craft part of Criterion 3, and here it is worth commenting on a feature of *Jakob the Liar* which I have not seen mentioned in the reviews. This is that there are no dramatic developments stemming from the basic situation established at the beginning until about half-way through the film. This is of course a serious deficiency for most audiences. The rest of the films not discussed here are fairly equal with respect to script construction.

Discovering the influence of a film has to wait for at least several years, and so it cannot be applied to the evaluation of these movies. A film's influence depends, of course, on the interest other film-makers have in it, both immediately, and in the longer term.

Tricks of the Trade

Ideally, the analysis should be done by recording the complete characteristics of each shot (scale, movement, length, etc.) in succession down the length of the film. This permits the most complete analysis of all the possible interrelationships between the variables. But although I initially tried this out thirty odd years ago, I found that it took about three times longer than the method I have since used. This gives sufficient information for the general comparisons you see made above. My method collects each quantity sequentially over the length of the film, and even this took about 35 twelve-hour days to analyse the twenty-one films dealt with in this article.

Up to this piece of research, I have always worked with prints of the films I was analysing, and indeed almost exclusively with 35 mm. prints, and I worked with them on Steenbecks and other flat-bed editing machines. It would have been possible for me to get 35 mm. prints of most of these films, but the costs to me of educational hire and transport would have been around £2,000, not to mention the labour of then lugging the cans up five floors of stairs to the editing department of the London Film School. So the analysis was done from DVDs and VHS tapes. I fed these into a non-linear editing system (NLE), in fact Adobe Premiere on an ordinary PC (though a cheaper NLE would do just as well), and while they were being digitized in real time, I recorded the camera moves from the window in the digitizing programme screen. For the experienced analyst, this is just possible to do in real time, even for the fastest cut films. Then I went more slowly through the film in the NLE programme, recording the Scale of Shot, which usually requires some stopping and starting and going back, particularly for the films with very short ASLs. I also recorded the Inserts on this pass. Two more passes are necessary to get the numbers of reverse angles and POV shots. If I have a VHS tape I usually do these last things on a VHS recorder with a jog-shuttle control, as I can usually manage recording these last two quantities at high speed for most films. Alternatively, it is possible to do the complete analytical process entirely on a VHS recorder with a jog-shuttle control, as I have done when analysing television programmes in the past. For my analytical procedure the standard control system for DVD players is awkward to use when trying to work directly with the DVD disc.

There are important cautions to be made about the analytical process when working from tape recordings or DVDs of films. The first of these relates purely to the use of recordings made for the PAL television system. These are initially created from film prints that were shot at 24 frames per second when the original film were made, but are always transferred to the consumer medium at 25 frames per second. This means that their running time when played on PAL system devices is shortened by 4% of the original running time. This means that a correction factor has to be applied to the ASL has to be applied by multiplying it by a factor of 25/24. I have applied this correction in the above results. No correction is necessary for NTSC recordings. More important is the question of Scale of Shot determination from video and DVD copies of films. For old Academy screen ratio films, both 16 mm. copies and, even more so, video copies are cropped in all around the frame on transfer to a greater extent than the screen masking when they are shown in the cinema, or on a Steenbeck. The effect of this on the Scale of Shot is fairly slight, as it shifts a very small proportion of the CUs into the BCU category, and an even smaller proportion of the more distant Shot Scales into the next closer category. Since all American feature films made since 1954 are intended to be masked to widescreen on projection, or are shot in one of the anamorphic 'Scope systems, or in a wide film system, the difficulty does not exist in quite this form for wide screen films. The problem is that films made since then which are shot "flat", i.e. with spherical lenses on the camera, may have the full Academy image, that was invariably recorded on the negative for American films, transferred to video, and not masked in to the widescreen proportions that were intended to be seen in the cinema. Despite the fact that DVD transfers are virtually always given the correct masking, and there is an increasing trend to releasing VHS copies properly masked in to wide screen, this problem has received a new boost

from the shooting of many films in Super 35. In this process, the camera exposes what is called the "full" aperture in the gate of the camera, which is equivalent to the old silent period aperture. This image on the original film is masked in to widescreen or even to 'Scope proportions by optical printing when making the release prints of the film.

Where possible, I used DVD copies when analysing the sample, and I also check with the VHS copy of the same film where possible. This check showed that in the case of *Deep Blue Sea*, which was shot in Super 35, the VHS copy had been taken from the full frame, and the DVD copy, like the cinema prints, was taken from the middle of the original frame in 'Scope proportions. This meant that for any shot much more could be seen of the scene vertically in the VHS frame than could be seen in the DVD copy. That is, if I had analysed the VHS copy, I would have found that the film was shot from much further back than it really was, with respect to the intended cinema release framing. Another difficulty that can occur with films shots in Panavision, or other 'Scope systems, (as opposed to merely being filmed with a Panavision camera with ordinary spherical lenses), is that full frame VHS copies can be made by "scanning and panning" the 1:2.35 'Scope frame. A pan made across the 'Scope frame during the video transfer will show almost the true height of the frame, so creating no more of a problem than a video copy of an old Academy ratio film, but a scanning cut from one end of the 'Scope frame to the other, which sometimes happens, introduces an apparent extra cut into the film which wasn't there before. If there are a substantial number of these, this will affect the ASL slightly. Fortunately, the expert eye can detect most of them, but even I find I have missed some scanning cuts on re-examining a film. But to repeat, as long as you stick to DVD copies most of these difficulties can be avoided.

The Last Word

I believe this research has identified an increasingly restricted stylistic norm that has gripped most ordinary American commercial feature film making, which uses extremely fast cutting, and continuous close shooting, and I have described its essential nature. Substantial deviations from this stylistic norm are mostly, but fortunately not quite entirely, restricted to low budget film-making. And a number of other interesting and unexpected points have turned up along the way.

Stop Press

A new winner in the fast cutting stakes has just been identified from the corpus of American films of 1999 shown in England. It is *End of Days*, directed by Peter Hyams. It contains 3875 shots in its 112.5 minutes running time, which is an Average Shot Length of 1.74 seconds. After studying it, I believe this record can and will be broken in later years.

Bibliography

Bishop, H.J. (1985) *A Medium Variable Analysis in Film: A Comparison of Bogdanovich with Ford, Hawks, Hitchcock and Welles* (M.A., Journalism) University of Colorado at Boulder

Buckland, W. (2001) *Mise en scène Criticism and Statistical Style Analysis* in: Thomas Elsaesser and Warren Buckland *Studying Contemporary American Films – A Guide to Movie Analysis* London: Edward Arnold 80-116

Holben, J. (2000) *Alter Ego* in American Cinematographer 81 (1) 56-71

Porter, M.J. (1987) *A Comparative Analysis of Directing Styles in Hill Street Blues*, in The Journal of Broadcasting and Electronic Media 31 (30) 323-334

Probst, C. (2000) *Impeccable Images* in American Cinematographer 81 (6) 97-105

Salt, B. (1974a) *Film Form, Style, and Aesthetics* in Sight & Sound 43 (2) 108-109

Salt, B. (1974b) *Statistical Style Analysis of Motion Pictures* in Film Quarterly 28 (1) 13-22

Salt, B. (1992) *Film Style and Technology: History and Analysis* 2nd ed. London: Starword.

Salt, B. (2001) *Practical Film Theory and its Application to TV Series Drama* in Journal of Media Practice 2 (2) 98-113

Salt, B. (2002) *Fritz Lang's Diagonal Symphony* under "New Book" at *www.starword.com*

If you check the latest results for the cutting rate in American films in this article against those in *Film Style and Technology*, you will notice some discrepancies. This is inevitable, given the relatively small samples that I had in 1992. To illustrate the effect of sample size, I reproduce a graph for the ASLs of American films released between 1982 and 1987, inclusive

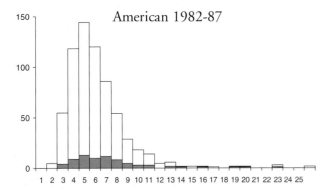

American 1982-87

of those years. This is based on the relevant histogram you can see on page 333 of this book, but also includes the data from the histogram for the same period on page 283 of *Film Style and Technology*, recorded as short dark bars on the above graph. They are short because the sample size was only 75 films in 1992, whereas the latest results are for a sample of 596 films. You can see that there is a general resemblance between the shapes of the two distributions, allowing for the difference in scale, and the modal (most common) values are about the same, in the range of 5 to 6 seconds. However, the early results give a mean ASL for the period of 8.4 seconds, whereas the mean ASL for the period from the vastly larger present sample is 6.12 seconds. Closer inspection shows that the early small sample has relatively too many films in the range 7 to 9 seconds, which accounts for the error.

All this illustrates a basic fact about the reliability of estimating a variable (ASL in this case) characteristic of a popula-

tion (the films) by selecting a sample from the population. My initial sample was not only small given the size of the population, which is in the area of 2,000 to 3,000 feature films for the period, but also it was definitely non-random. That is, it is taken from films that I *wanted* to see in those days. If it had been completely randomly selected, it would probably have got closer to the true value for the mean ASL, but not certainly, since there is an appreciable chance of even a random sample dragging in too many non-typical films, according to statistical sampling theory. Even though my much larger present sample is strictly speaking non-random, it results from my getting the ASL of every film I could possibly see on TV over the last dozen years. In other words, it includes lots of rubbish. And given that it represents about a quarter of the population of American films for the period, it is probably pretty close to the correct value of the mean ASL.

Inevitably, within a year of the previous article, there was a new fast cutting champion. It was *Derailed* (2002), directed by Bob Misiorowski, and starring Jean-Claude Van Damme, and it has an ASL of 1.63 seconds. This film was clearly not a really big budget production, but Misiorowski got quite a lot of bang for his bucks by shooting in eastern Europe. A great deal of the film was set on a train, and much of this was shot hand-held, which would have speeded up production considerably. Unlike the previous champions, there was not much attention to visual elegance in the shooting of this film, nor to tidy shot transitions; another casualty of budget restrictions.

As part of my work on the films of Max Ophuls for the Warwick University conference of 1978, I studied the lighting of some his films, and wrote up my conclusions afterwards. I was going to include this with my examination of other aspects of Ophuls' films in the first edition of *Film Style and Technology*, but I decided it would interfere with the coherence of that chapter. So it has lain around unpublished till now.

Apart from demonstrating a stylistic analysis of film lighting, I was also trying to deal with the evaluation of the quality of a lighting cameraman's work, as you may notice.

HOW TO LIGHT A MAX OPHULS FILM

Franz Planer's lighting of *Liebelei* is quite typical of the style used in German films in the 'thirties, and rather different from the various approaches used in Hollywood at that time. The major part of the difference lay in the greater simplicity of German lighting, and the frame enlargements show this if one looks at them carefully. The first shot shows the scene in which Fritz visits the Baron and Baroness at their home after the Baron's suspicions of Fritz's liaison with his wife have been fully aroused. The whole scene is lit by just three sources; a key spotlight from almost straight above illuminating just the Baroness and nothing more, general weak fill light from a flood light placed left front covering the whole scene, and a back light from behind and overhead picking up quite strongly on Fritz and the Baroness's hair, and also falling on

the forward part of the scene including the Baron. The closer shot immediately following shows only the very slightest adjustment of the positions of the lights, and this opposition to the usual Hollywood practice of largely re-lighting the closer shots was to remain characteristic of Planer throughout his career. The lighting of the men in this scene would be regarded as inadequate by the Hollywood standards of 1932 and later. Despite the small number of lights used, some extra complexity is introduced into the chiaroscuro by the diffuse patches of weak shadow cast on the wall by a cookalorous or similar opaque piece of tracery put just in front of the backlight. Another feature of the lighting of this scene that would never be seen in Hollywood films, but which can sometimes be seen in German films of the 'thirties lit by other cameramen, is the way the almost overhead key light casts the Baroness's eyes into two pools of total shadow. This is just another of the small differences which add up to define the overall difference between American and German lighting in the 'thirties and 'forties. Incidentally, this shot shows quite clearly the complete lack of period authenticity in the Baroness's dress, hairdo, and room decor; quite the equal of similar lacks of authenticity in similar circumstances in Hollywood films.

The same simplicity of approach can also be seen in the lighting of the two night exterior scenes (shot in the studio) which are reproduced. The nocturnal walk through the streets after Christine and Frantz have first met is lit so that there are at most two lights at any particular time on the two actors; at the instant shown there is a strong backlight and a weak fill from the front. This can be contrasted with a night exterior from *Letter From an Unknown Woman* which shows Planer's adaptation to that aspect of American practice which requires anyone speaking lines in a scene to be "properly" lit. The central group in this shot is lit by three sources; namely spotlights at the side right above, at the back above, and front right. The central part of the beam of the front right spotlight illuminates only the small boy with the central part of its beam, but the outer edges of the beam also provides weak fill light on the other characters. This lighting is considerably adjusted for the following closer shot of this group of actors, even though nothing of any importance to the narrative is taking place there, despite the amount of lighting lavished on it. The background in the Long Shot is also separately lit by a number of other lights, and the general key (average brightness) is higher in this and similar scenes in *Letter From an Unknown Woman* than in the comparable scenes in *Liebelei*. In the earlier film the principals are sometimes left very underlit even in dialogue scenes. Of course by the 'forties very different kinds of lighting units were being used most of the time, but this does not in itself account for the major difference in lighting of the two films.

If he so desired, Planer could work in a way much closer to his German style, as indicated by the still from the scene in *Letter* in which Lisa says goodnight to her

son in his bedroom before attending the opera. In this case the basic lighting inside the room is done with floodlights on floor stands below camera level to the left and right, as one can see from the shadows of the bedhead they cast on the wall. There is also a small spotlight from to one side doing no more than putting a gleam into Lisa's hair and casting some extra light onto her son. The second set of weaker, blurred shadows on the wall come from the lights outside the window of the room. In fact this frame still is just one static point in a one-take scene in which the actress and camera move from the door to the bed to the window, and then all the way back again, during which movement the disposition of light and shade remains equally striking all the way. This passage could be considered to be the high point in the lighting of this film.

The reasoned justification for my claim that this scene is indeed an outstanding piece of lighting is not easy to give. I could say that the lights are not put in the conventional places, which is certainly true, and demonstrate this subsidiary assertion by comparison with other similar scenes lit by other cameramen, and indeed I will do this a

little later. One important point here is that it is not usual to put the key light on a female star below eye-level in a tender scene. But beyond such comparisons, my personal response is undoubtedly influenced by memories of an immense number of other composed images in photographs, films, and even paintings, even though in the latter there is never represented the kind of multiple-source lighting usual in films. And I have to admit that there is no way of analysing that completely.

Some interest has been expressed by other commentators in the visual presentation of Joan Fontaine in the role of Lisa in *Letter From an Unknown Woman*, and there is indeed a special "glowing" quality to the closer shots of her. This is achieved in part by always lighting these close shots with an absolutely frontal spotlight. Well, strictly speaking this spotlight is a bit above eye-level, as is shown by a couple of millimetres of shadow below the nose in the frame enlargement. This spot illuminates the area of Lisa's face only, and the rest of the foreground is lit only by another spot behind and overhead, which also acts as a backlight on Lisa. The highlights from this backlight make the actress's

average brightness. Hence the "glowing" effect. There is no fill light used in these shots of Lisa, and altogether this is an unparalleled approach to the lighting of a female star, not to be confused, for instance, with the high single light style used on Dietrich and others. The overall bright effect on Joan Fontaine in this film is helped by the flat, pale facial make-up used on her, and altogether it throws a lot of weight onto her intrinsic looks. Nearly all the closer shots of Lisa in the rest of the film are lit in the way I have described. In the instance of this particular scene there is absolutely no change in the lighting with the cut into a

hair appear a lighter colour than it actually was, as also is the case elsewhere in the film where she represents the adult Lisa, and the flatness of the key light on her face means that there are no shadows cast by the protuberant parts of the face onto itself to produce any decrease in its overall

Close Up as the scene proceeds, and here as elsewhere in this film there is only the very slightest and nearly invisible lens diffusion ("soft focus") is used on Close Ups of Lisa, though this general level of image sharpness and reduction in the use of lens diffusion is quite typical of late 'forties

films. Interestingly, the only heavy diffusion in *Letter* occurs on the Close Ups of Stefan when Lisa meets him again at the opera, which can obviously be considered a standard "expression of her subjective feelings" effect.

Despite the individual spot used to light Lisa, in a very general way Frantz Planer's lighting in this film does still have some of the long-established European tendency to apply lights to the image as a whole, and not to light the background and then the actors separately as was more usual in Hollywood. This difference can be seen if we look at Burnett Guffey's lighting of a scene in *The*

Reckless Moment which in content is not too different to the bedroom scene in *Letter From an Unknown Woman* just discussed. In the scene the mother comes into her daughter's bedroom in the morning, raises the blinds on the windows, and then talks to her daughter while she is still lying in bed. This scene is intrinsically more complex in terms of lighting than that in *Letter*, since extra light has to be brought in when the blinds are raised, but this still leaves quite a bit of latitude as to exactly how the lighting of this scene should be done. Guffey opts for the conventional way, lighting it almost entirely from above with a series of small spotlights providing a front- and back-light inside a series of isolated small areas through which the mother walks as she goes from window to window raising the blinds, and then finally to her daughter's bedside. Three of these positions where the lighting falls in the standard way on the mother are illustrated in the order in which they occur, while in

between them, in the positions not illustrated, the mother is only dimly lit by spill light. When the real dialogue in the scene starts, and there are cut-ins to Medium Close Shots of the mother, these are relit with changed position of the key light on her, and fairly heavy fill light put onto her face from the right in the conventional way, and also medium-heavy lens diffusion is applied. This standard "glamour" approach is not particularly appropriate at this point in this scene, but is just an unthinking cameraman's reflex when faced with a "star" Close Up. There is nothing outstandingly elegant about the patterns the lighting creates in this scene and elsewhere in this film, it is mostly just good standard stuff, which fits well with the natural location footage scattered throughout the film, and indeed with the general style of the film as a whole, for *The Reckless Moment* gets a lot closer to the realities of a particular time and place than any other Max Ophuls film.

The mother has just opened the blind on this window in her daughter's bedroom. She is lit by a flooded spot high back left. The impression of sunlight coming through the net curtain is created by a spot outside the window shining through and hitting the base of the artist's easel.

The camera begins to pan with the mother as she walks out of the alcove and into the main part of her daughter's bedroom. She has left the beam of the overhead spot there, and is just walking into the edge of the beam from another overhead spot lighting the main part of her daughter's bedroom. She is also backlit by the spot through the window.

The camera has panned further left with
the mother as she walks into the main
part of her daughter's bedroom, and away
towards the other window. The mother is
lit by a spotlight, set with a flood beam,
and almost overhead, but slightly to
her right. The daughter in bed is lit by
an overhead spot almost straight down,
centered on her hips. The spot beam coming through the other window now out
right has been adjusted so that it comes
flat across the room and hits the wall and
bedside lamp behind the daughter. There
is also a light out in the hall falling on
the half-open door behind the daughter.

The mother has now opened the blinds
on the other window. The only change
to the lighting is the addition of fill
light from the front to the whole room,
brought up on a dimmer as the mother
opened the blinds.

The mother walks forward towards
her daughter's bed, passing through the
same high right spot beam evident in
the frame enlargement before the last
one.

The mother is now lit by the high spot from the front above the camera that is also the main light on her daughter.

The shot now ends, and there is a cut to a Medium Close Up of the daughter from almost the same angle. A small spotlight on the daughter from right front has been added to the exisitng lighting, and a medium diffusion filter has been put on the camera lens.

Next there is a cut to a Medium Close Up of the mother, also with medium heavy lens diffusion. The spot providing the key light on her has been moved slightly to the right and extra diffusion put on it, and extra fill light has been on from a soft floodlight from right front.

A daytime scene in Philip Marlowe's office in The Big Sleep. *Note the similarity of the lighting on the walls and the rear figure in both scenes.*

A night scene in Philip Marlowe's office. The desk has been cheated forward towards the camera in this shot.

For comparison with Burnett Guffey's work on *The Reckless Moment,* I can give an example of truly mediocre lighting of a room set by Sid Hickox in *The Big Sleep* (1946). These two frame stills are from two scenes in Philip Marlowe's office. The first takes place in daylight, and the second at night. As you can see, the lighting inside the room is almost exactly the same, for day or night, with just the practical desk lamp lit on the table visible between the actors indicating that it is intended to be night in one of them. The only significant difference between the two shots is the way the backdrop representing the street outside the window is lit. This is why Sid Hickox was never nominated for an Academy Award over his long career working for major studios.

The adjustments to the lighting between shots in the scenes illustrated from the Max Ophuls films are fairly small, largely because the camera stays shooting pretty much in the same direction. In this respect they are not typical of a good deal of the lighting adjustments in Hollywood films, because many of them accompany large changes of angle between shots.

The following piece, written down completely for the first time here, is based on a study of the lighting of Alfred Hitchcock's *Notorious* that I made back in the nineteen-seventies. However, I have used this material for teaching purposes a few times in the interim.

SOME NOTORIOUS CHEATING

Cheating is a very important word in professional film-making. Essentially it means deceiving the audience by giving the impression that nothing has changed in the world appearing on the screen during the change from one shot to the next, when in actual fact things on the set have been altered to produce a better visual effect on the screen in the succeeding shot. The case that everyone knows about is when a short leading man is stood on a box so that he is at least equal in height to a tall leading lady. Alfred Hitchcock's film *Notorious* does indeed contain this sort of thing in a few of the shots of Claude Rains acting with Ingrid Bergman, mostly done by having him walk up onto planks laid on the floor below the bottom edge of the film frame. However, that is not what I am concerned with here. I want to talk about cheating with film lighting, which is at work in creating what is called "lighting continuity". This is something that is not discussed properly in textbooks on film lighting, as far as I am aware.

The picture to the right shows the first scene on the balcony of Ingrid Bergman's apartment in Rio de Janeiro. At this point in the story she and Cary Grant are starting to fall in love. It shows the general layout of furniture and so on for this set. The door in the French windows of her living room

is open on the right. For some reason the background showing the sea front of Rio is done with a travelling matte, rather than using background projection as is done in all the other shots in this and the other balcony scene. You can just see the "minus", or black line, around the curve of the hand rail on the wall, where the edges of the background and foreground images fail to coincide. The second balcony scene takes place at dusk, when Cary Grant has to return to the apartment to tell Ingrid Bergman of the new orders from the American spymaster for her to seduce Claude Rains, who is part of the German spy ring they are trying to penetrate. Unaware of this, she is cooking a love meal for Cary Grant. The scene starts inside the apartment at a point in the film 26 minutes 18 seconds after the director's credit. There follow four shots of Ingrid Bergman cutting up a chicken while conversing with Cary Grant, who has walked out onto the balcony, all taken from inside the apartment. A flashing lighthouse is visible on the horizon behind Ingrid Bergman's back after she has joined him on the balcony in Shot No. 4 of the scene, as illustrated. Then the rest of the scene is shot from outside on the set representing the terrace.

Shot 5. The Cary Grant is lit by a spotlight from the left of the camera which has its beam focussed so that it only hits the upper part of his body, and misses Ingrid Bergman. She is lit by another spot coming down very steeply from the right over Grant's shoulder, and centered on her right shoulder and arm. There is a small backlight spot high and slightly right behind the actors outlining just the top of their heads, and also some weak fill-light on their faces from almost straight to the front. The background is lit by a floodlight shining from inside the apartment through the window onto the wall of the balcony.

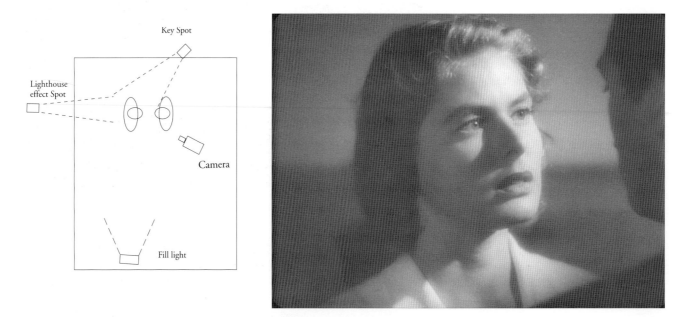

Shot 6. There is then a cut to a Close Up of Ingrid Bergman, for which the lighting on her is completely changed. The camera has been moved around about 75 degrees, and her face is now lit by a moderately high spot hitting her face obliquely. Now there is only a very weak fill light on her and on the side of Cary Grant's face, coming from a floodlight to the left of the camera. The large change in camera angle helps conceal the change in the lighting from the previous shot to this one. The lighthouse effect spot is not switched on at this moment.

Shot 6A. During this shot, the lighthouse effect light flashes intermittently onto the back of Bergman's head. The actors have been "cheated" (moved) away from the window so that the camera can be got into position without having to take out the French windows on the set. This cheat is completely invisible because the wall to the balcony is out of shot.

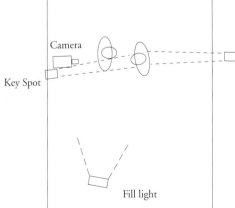

Shot 7. The reverse-angle Close Up of Cary Grant follows, lit by a very small spot confined to the lower part of the face, plus a small backlight creating a rim of brightness on his shoulder and the right of his head. There is also a very low level of fill lighting barely illuminating the rest of his body.

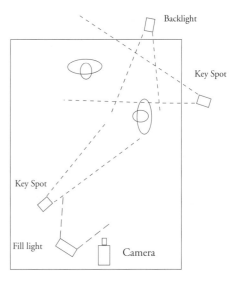

Shot 17. The two previous set-ups are repeated five times each as Cary Grant breaks the news of her distasteful assignment to Ingrid Bergman. There is a cut back to the first angle illustrated on the previous page, and then the camera pulls back to a Medium Long Shot as shown here, as Ingrid Bergman walks away from Cary Grant and sits down. The lighting set up is essentially the same as in the first shot illustrated on the previous page. Bergman is lit by the spot through the window and nothing else, while Cary Grant is lit in exactly the same way as in frame enlargement from shot No. 5.

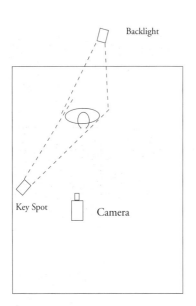

Shot 18. There is now a cut in closer from the same direction to a Medium Close Up of Ingrid Bergman, taken from the same direction as the previous shot. But there is now a candle on the table, which had not been visible before. And the light on Bergman has switched sides, though coming downwards from about the same height. And if you look at the balcony wall behind her, you can see that she has been cheated sideways to screen left.

One of the reasons that the lighting change is not noticed is that the cut is made in the standard place with respect to the dialogue; that is, right at the end of a line spoken by Cary Grant, so that we are unconcsiously expecting a cut to the other person. Also, there is a cut on action at the same instant as Ingrid Bergman folds her serviette.

Shot 18A. As Shot 18 continues, Cary Grant walks into shot and around behind Bergman into the beam of a spot already in place, but with its beam going invisibly over the balcony wall until Grant stands in its path. (It was omitted from the previous lighting plan for the earlier part of this shot.) The camera tilts and pans a little as Grant walks in to give this modified framing.

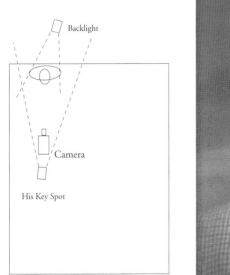

Shot 19. A cut to a Close Up of Grant, with another fairly substantial change of the lighting on him, with the moved to an almost frontal direction, and lowered in height as well. However, to my eye, the most noticeably discontinuity is in Cary Grant's head position across this cut.

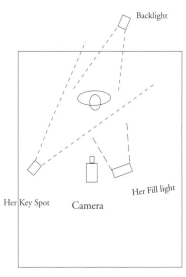

Shot 20. The next shot is a Close Up of Bergman, only a very small adjustment in the lighting from that in Shot 18. Her key spot has been moved slightly more oblique to her, and her backlight lowered and moved a bit more to the right. The fill light stays the same. This and the previous Close Up of Cary Grant are alternated three times as the dialogue continues.

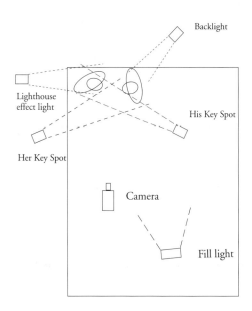

Shot 26 starts as a repetition of Shot 18, and then Bergman gets up and joins Grant by the wall of the balcony. They are lit by the spot for him coming down from high right, which also acts as a cross-backlight on her, when she moves into the position. She also walks in the beam of her new key spot which comes from a bit above eye level from the left, but flagged off so that it passes in front of him, without hitting him. The beam of this light was again invisible until she walked into it. A spot pretending to be from the lighhouse intermittently strikes him from the left side, as in this frame.

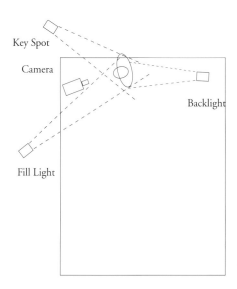

Shot 27. There is next a cut to a Close Up of Ingrid Bergman, with her spot now coming in from the other side of her face. This lighting change is quite invisible because of the large change in the camera angle on her.

Shot 28. The next shot of Cary Grant has his key coming in from the same direction as in Shot 26, but with its beam much more tightly focussed, so that it only lights his face and right shoulder.

Subjectively speaking, I am aware that I notice the slight changes in position across the cut from Shot 17 to Shot 18, but not the change in lighting. Indeed, I had spent quite a lot of time looking at this scene before I noticed this particular lighting discontinuity. Is this to because the eye-brain system gives primacy to outline detection?

The use of the standard dialogue cutting point is also most important in smoothing over discontinuities across cuts, like this one. This is something that has been completely unrecognized in any discussions of editing technique that I have seen. In this particular case, the cut is made right under the end of Cary Grant's speech "... You have to work on him and land him.", in fact in the middle of the word "him". After the cut there is a pause of a second before Ingrid Bergman says "Mata Hari". This is what is nowadays known as an "L" edit, from the way it appears on the picture and sound tracks as represented on the computer screen in modern non-linear digital editing systems; i.e. Avids and the like. But this cut has long been used by many editors as the smoothest, least noticeable way to make a cut between two speakers in a dialogue scene. Another notable use of this kind of dialogue cut to cover up a peculiar visual transition is in Hitchcock's *The Birds*. The peculiarity of this cut is discussed at length by Noël Burch in his *Theory of Film Practice*, without him recognizing what it is that smoothes it over.

Principles of Lighting Continuity

It is not the preservation of lighting directions on the set from one shot to the next in a scene that gives good lighting continuity on the cinema screen. This can be easily illustrated, as here. This specially arranged studio scene is lit solely by a spotlight behind and a little to the right of the camera.

But if the light and actors are left where they were, and the camera is moved round to the reverse angle, we get the next picture, which bears no relation in tonalities to the previous angle. There is almost zero lighting continuity. If the studio floor had been covered with a dark carpet, the difference would be even more marked, as the small amount of diffuse underlight reflected onto the Stacey Bertrand's face from the painted floor would have been eliminated. Incidentally, if I were lighting this set-up in a real film, I would not do it like this on either angle. On the angle favouring Ahmed Hassan, I would at least shade off the light a bit on the back of Stacey Bertrand's head, and adjust the depth of field so that the background behind Ahmed Hassan was out of focus, not to mention down a bit in exposure. And so on.

To how to ensure lighting continuity from one shot to the next in a scene? The best answer is to keep the same *sort* of general pattern of light and dark on the figures, and in particular on their faces, though it does not have to be in the same places on them. Which is what Ted Tetzlaff does in the shots making up the scene in *Notorious* that I have just discussed.

When I published my piece "The Early Development of Film Form", which you have read on page 24 of this book, in Tony Harrild's magazine *Film Form* in 1976, the same issue contained a piece by Peter Wollen, called "North by North West: A Morphological Analysis". This sought to apply a system invented by Vladimir Propp in 1928 for the analysis of Russian fairy tales to Hitchcock's film *North by North West*. Propp himself explicitly rejected the idea that his system could be applied to any other sort of story, which Wollen failed to mention. Propp's idea was that all Russian fairy tales had the same structure because they all had been evolved from an initial "*ur*-tale", and they all contained a series of standard events or functions that occurred in a fixed order, though Wollen mentioned neither of these points in his analysis. He could not fit all of Propp's functions onto the story of *North by North West*, nor did they occur in the standard fairy tale order. He didn't draw attention to this either. Nor that some of Propp's functions had to interpreted in a metaphorical sense to get them to fit the film. Given these shortcomings, it is impossible to see any useful point in applying Propp's ideas to *North by North West*.

What also annoyed me was Wollen's claim that the Hitchcock suspense thrillers formed a "tranformation group". He clearly used this mathematical term without understanding what it means; just as a piece of charlatanry. (In each instance making up the representation of a mathematical group, all the elements of the group have to occur once, and once only.) This is clearly not true of the Hitchcock films. However, it is obvious that there is relation in the plot elements used in many Hitchcock films, and instances of this have been remarked at various times by various people. I took up the challenge to do better than than Wollen on this problem. I tried breaking the films down using a more general series of elementary actions, but this proved unwieldy. I also investigated other ideas that were current in the 'seventies about the analysis of stories in general. There was quite a bit of this, mostly deriving from the new interest in generative grammar in linguistics. In particular, I remember checking out the work David Rumelhart and his collaborators based on the "cognitive science" they were inventing. This involved speculative ideas about how the human mind functioned, using models derived from the current computer science. None of this helped, and I dropped the subject.

Quite recently, I came back to the matter, and this time, I managed to get hold of a copy of the book *Plotto*, which I had been aware that Hitcock possessed and valued. After trying to use the plot elements (or "conflicts") in this book to recreate a Hitchcock plot, I saw the solution, as you can now read it.

PLOTTO

A New Method of Plot Suggestion
for Writers of Creative Fiction

By
William Wallace Cook

ELLIS PUBLISHING COMPANY
BATTLE CREEK, MICHIGAN
U.S.A.

INTRODUCTION

THE PLOTTO METHOD. Plotto achieves creative art in fiction by a new Method of plot suggestion. Suggestion is based on Themes (or Masterplots) and Conflicts.

THEME. Every story has a Theme, or an underlying proposition that indicates its type. The Theme may be clear-cut and distinct, or shadowy and vague; it is always in evidence, and differentiates one type of story from all the other types. Around each Theme any number of distinctly different stories may be written.

A story may be constructed with, or without, a certain Theme in mind. Rarely perhaps does a writer begin a story with a set Theme in front of him. He may develop his plot from a situation, or Conflict; nevertheless, as the plot develops the Theme develops with it. The writer will **feel** the Theme and, consciously or unconsciously, combine his Conflicts to a certain pattern. This pattern, plain in the finished work, will conform to a Theme. When a story is built around a Theme, the Theme becomes a Masterplot.

The Plotto Method enables the Plottoist to begin his story with a Masterplot and marshal his situations or Conflicts in conformity to it; or, it enables him to begin with a situation or Conflict and consciously to watch the particular Theme as the plot unfolds.

MASTERPLOTS WITH INTERCHANGEABLE CLAUSES. Each Plotto Masterplot classifies in general terms and in a single terse sentence a certain type of story. Each Masterplot consists of three Clauses: An initial Clause defining the protagonist in general terms, a middle Clause initiating and carrying on the action, and a final Clause carrying on and terminating the action. Suggestions for exemplifying the action with concrete situations are offered by the Conflicts.

THE CONFLICTS. Desire, in some one of its many forms, is responsible for the awakening of Purpose. Something from without, impinging upon something within, excites a feeling or an emotion, and the soul flows into Purpose, and Purpose into action. Then, somewhere on the path of rising action, Purpose encounters Obstacle. At this point, and at this point only, do we establish what writers of creative fiction call a **situation.** Purpose alone never made a situation; Obstacle alone never made one; but strike the flint of Obstacle with the steel of Purpose and sparks of situation begin to fly.

Plotto, as a Method of plot **suggestion** for writers of **creative** fiction, is founded upon this law: **Purpose, expressed or implied, opposing Obstacle, expressed or implied, yields Conflict.**

PURPOSES AND OBSTACLES. How many Purposes are there in the world? Not many, although their variations are infinite, Perhaps, in the last analysis one General Purpose would comprehend all the Purposes: TO ACHIEVE HAPPINESS. That is the end and aim of life on this planet. But happiness has a different meaning for most of us. There is the happiness of love and courtship, of married life, of achieving wealth or power by all the many methods, good or evil. that may be contrived by the thinking mind. Religion may be the road to happiness for some, and revenge the road to a doubtful happiness for others. The virtues or the faults of a human soul set the pattern of Purpose for that soul.

Plotto concerns itself with but one General Purpose in its application to three general goals of endeavor:
1. To Achieve Happiness in Love and Courtship.
2. To Achieve Happiness in Married Life.
3. To Achieve Happiness (Success) in Enterprise.

The Conflicts in Plotto are brief statements of Purpose in active opposition with Obstacle—situations which are to he combined with other situations. For instance: "A, in love with B, is not favored by F-B. father of B." Here is the implied Purpose, "To Achieve Happiness in Love," meeting an Obstacle bluntly expressed.

Purpose and Obstacle give concrete exemplification of the Theme in every form of fictional narrative, whether short story, novelette, or novel,

THE SHORT STORY. Purpose and Obstacle at grips in one dramatic situation will define the short story, since it is calculated to leave a single dominant impression upon the reader's mind. Ordinarily, this form of narrative fiction will be woven about a plot of the simplest construction. There will be the main situation as suggested by a chosen Conflict, the Conflict leading up to it and the Conflict carrying on and terminating the action. These three Conflicts may be reduced to two, if the main Conflict should in itself possess the qualities of a terminal Conflict. Conflicts too long, or too involved, for short story purposes will usually be found to be broken Conflicts, When such a Conflict is selected for the main situation, it is possible to use only that part of it which contains the most dramatic appeal.

THE NOVELETTE. This form of narrative fiction may be considered as a long short story, or as **a** short novel. If the former, the Conflict suggesting the situation will be elaborated with dramatic material concerned with the Purpose and Obstacle. If, on the other hand, the novelette partakes of the character of a short novel, the Paramount Purpose and Obstacle will involve subordinate Purposes and Obstacles all cumulative in power and bearing upon the story's climax or crisis. Here, as everywhere, the imagination must exercise constructive judgment.

THE NOVEL. The full-fledged novel may be considered as consisting of several short stories all leading up to, and intimately bound up with, the Paramount Purpose and Obstacle that give the complete story its unity. Construction here plays its most discriminating role, for the subordinate situations must grow toward a single, decisive crisis, The effect must he cumulative. If the main Conflict shall involve the crisis—and it should—all the subordinate situations dealing with the Theme will be so selected as to grow naturally in dramatic strength toward the climax, Here no rules of construction will take the place of taste and discrimination. The constructive imagination, properly exercised, will deal capably with the situations, and the creative imagination will work a miracle of dramaturgic power.

ORIGINALITY. The Conflicts all come from the vast storehouse of Human Nature. They are there, millions upon millions of them, waiting for the imagination to select them and group them in an original combination. For there is "nothing new under the sun." Originality in creative work comes from our own individual use of the tools so bountifully provided by the Divine Creator. All that is possible to a mortal craftsman is the combining of old material into something new and different.

Originality is the ideal of the Plotto Method; and it is realized by disregarding the references prefixed and affixed to the Conflicts and (or) interpreting the Specific as well as the General. Conflicts in terms of the Plottoist's own experience. Nothing in the Specific Conflicts will be used literally, but the concrete exemplification in such Conflicts will serve as a suggestion, lending wings to the creative imagination for its own high flight.

For original combinations of Conflicts the Classification by Symbols will be found a treasure-trove of suggestions. If the main Conflict selected is built around A, or B, alone, the A or B group should be scanned; if around A and B alone, the A and B group will yield suggestions, or the A or B group may be found to serve; or, if several characters are involved in the main Conflict, reference may be had to that particular group of symbols. If a certain group of symbols proves too limited, drop one of the lesser character symbols and consult the group represented by those remaining. This course may be followed, in the search for original combinations, until only the protagonist remains in the situation. Somewhere along the line of search the imagination is certain to find exactly what it is looking for.

CONFLICT GROUPS AND SUB-GROUPS. The Conflicts in Plotto are classified in three main groups:
1. Conflicts in Love and Courtship.
2. Conflicts in Married Life,
3. Conflicts in Enterprise.

The Conflicts in Love and Courtship are re-grouped as follows:

Conflicts in Love's Beginnings.
Conflicts in Love's Misadventures.
Conflicts of the Marriage Proposal.
Conflicts in Love's Rejection.
Conflicts of Marriage.

All the sub-groups are classified, for convenience of reference, under the middle, or "B," Clauses of the Masterplots; and these form the only subdivisions of the main group, "Married Life." Conflicts of the third group, "Enterprise," fall into the following general classifications:

Conflicts in Misfortune.
Conflicts in Mistaken Judgment.
Conflicts in Helpfulness.
Conflicts in Deliverance.
Conflicts in Idealism.
Conflicts in Obligation.
Conflicts in Necessity.
Conflicts in Chance.
Conflicts in Personal Limitations.

Conflicts in Simulation.
Conflicts in Craftiness.
Conflicts in Transgression.
Conflicts in Revenge.
Conflicts in Mystery.
Conflicts in Revelation,

Inasmuch as dramatic situations are a product of the emotions, and the emotions, by reason of their complexity, have defied a hard and fast classification, it follows naturally that the Conflicts themselves will defy a rigid classification. The groupings noted above are more or less arbitrary, yet they will be bound to serve. Some Conflicts in Misfortune might easily fall into the subgroups. Mistaken Judgment, Simulation, etc., and Conflicts in other sub-groups might logically be reclassified. Nevertheless, the classification in each case will exemplify in the Conflict the particular sub-group in which it has' been placed.

MECHANICAL STRUCTURE. There is, of course, a mechanical structure underlying every properly constructed story. There are some very intelligent people who believe in the "divine afflatus" as something apart from hard, consistent, carefully calculated effort. Overlooking the old adage that "Genius is an infinite capacity for taking pains," these wise ones will have their back-handed slap at anything mechanical in its application to Art.

It remains, however, that a good story must have a carefully developed plot for its framework; and the plot in itself, is purely mechanical. It is the logical devising of means to an end, a motivating of all the parts into a harmonious whole. A plot may be simple, or it may he complex, but an interesting story without some sort of plot is inconceivable. This machinery must not creak or complain as the story advances. A discriminating imagination must oil it so well with logic and plausibility that the god in the machine shall not be ruffled by the turning wheels. Plausibility is attained when fine discrimination, true judgment and a facility with words so cover the necessary mechanism that it does not intrude at any point upon the completed work. And therein lies the art of the story teller. Plotto, at least, holds this to be true; and, as a corollary of the position thus taken, exalts the **imagination** as the greatest force in the world.

IMAGINATION, If a story is a skeleton structure of plot, overlaid with a felicity of thought and phrase that may be called the flesh, then the pulsing heart of the creation, the one factor that gives it life and beauty, is the imagination. But this imagination must be rightly controlled.

The demands of fictional narrative would seem to predicate an imagination of three types: Mediocre. Constructive and Creative. A mind positively brilliant in its mastery of scientific research, or of the pursuit of trade, might be hopeless in meeting the demands of fictional narrative. Nevertheless. Plotto believes sincerely that a **desire** to write successful fiction is predicated upon the ability to write successful fiction; and that, given the technical requirements of experience and a fair education, not often will the mediocre imagination be found hopeless. Intensive training should develop constructive power; and it is but a step, in the interpretation of suggestion, from the constructive to the creative. Originality is the soul of creative art, and originality is nothing more than the interpretation of suggestion in terms of individual experience.

Each life is the sum of many experiences, and character indicates the reaction of those experiences upon the soul, In other words, life is a combination of situations, or Conflicts, with a spiritual signification drawn from the Conflicts themselves. So a story plot, which holds the mirror up to life, is a combination of Conflicts, selected to the pattern of a single Theme, or Masterplot. Life, with its multitude of experiences, is general; the imagination, dealing with a cross-section of life, makes the story plot particular. And imagination does this through the interpretation of suggestion.

SUGGESTION. The ideal of the Plotto Method, as stated elsewhere, is the interpretation of Conflict suggestions in terms of individual experience. Some of the Conflicts are General. Thus. Conflict No. 31 reads:

"B, rescued from an accident by A, whom she does not know, falls in love with him." The nature of the accident, and the character of B and of A, are circumstances left to the constructive imagination. In dealing with these circumstances, references to other Conflicts, prefixed and affixed to this general suggestion, will offer further suggestions for inventing the circumstances.

Many of the Conflicts are Specific. Thus, to quote Conflict No. 647: "B, a respectable working girl seeking employment, follows the advice of a supposed friend, A-5, and finds herself in an immoral dance ball where she is compelled to dance with patrons and serve drinks." References to other Conflicts will suggest the cause of B's necessity for seeking employment, and other references will suggest a finale for B's unhappy plight. The constructive imagination might use Conflict No. 647 literally, but Plotto would not approve of such literal use. The ideal method is for the imagination to use the dance hall merely as a suggestion for something equally pertinent to the situation; in other words, use the concrete example in interpreting an equivalent for this specific suggestion as to B's misfortune. Herein lies the opportunity for originality, and the way to creative work.

CONFLICT MANIPULATIONS.

Characters in the Plotto Conflicts are represented by symbols. These symbols indicate the relationship of the auxiliary characters .to the protagonist. This relationship is invariably explained in the text of the Conflicts, with the exception of the symbols A and B — these being the symbols of the male, and the female, protagonists. These symbols give a certain uniformity to the characters and facilitate character changes or transpositions. Protagonist A, or B, might be a criminal, an officer of the law, an employer. etc., but the numeral is never used in connection with the protagonist symbol — the explanation is given in the text.

A, male protagonist	B. female protagonist
A-2, male friend of A	B-2. female friend of B
A-3, male rival or enemy of A	B-3, female rival or enemy of B
A-4. male stranger	B-4. female stranger
A-5. male criminal	B-5. female criminal
A-6. male officer of the law	B-6, female officer of the law
A-7, male inferior. employee	B-7, female inferior. employee
A-8, male utility symbol	B-8. female utility symbol
A-9. male superior, employer, one in authority	B-9, female superior, employer, one in authority
F-A. father of A	F-B. father of B
M-A, mother of A	M-B. mother of B
BR-A, brother of A	BR-B. brother of B
SR-A, sister of A	SR-B, sister of B
SN-A, son of A	SN-B, son of B
D-A, daughter of A	D-B, daughter of B
U-A, uncle of A	U-B, uncle of B
AU-A, aunt of A	AU-B, aunt of B
CN-A, male cousin of A	CN-B, female cousin of B
NW-A, nephew of A	NW-B. nephew of B
NC-A, niece of A	NC-B, niece of B
GF-A, grandfather of A	GF-B, grandfather of B
GM-A, grandmother of A	GM-B, grandmother of B
SF-A, stepfather of A	SF-B, stepfather of B
SM-A, stepmother of A	SM-B, stepmother of B
GCH-A. grandchild of A	GCH-B, grandchild of B
CH, a child	

AX, a mysterious male person, or one of unusual character

BX, a mysterious female person. or one of unusual character

X, inanimate object, an object of mystery, an uncertain quantity

X added to any character gives to the character a suggestion of mystery.

These symbols may be readily changed or transposed, as an aid in manipulating the Conflict suggestions, Thus, "261 ch A-3 to A," indicates that A-3 in the Conflict is to he changed to A; and, "578b tr B & B-3." indicates a transposition in which B-3 takes the place of B and B of B-S.

The character symbols are changed, or transposed, in the auxiliary Conflicts to agree with the character symbols of the Conflict whose ramifications are being studied.

In many instances the Conflicts are "broken—that is, divided into two or more parts. The end of the first part is marked with a star (*), of the second part, with a double star (**), of the third part with a triple star (***), etc, Thus,"-*" indicates that the Conflict is to be used up to the first star; "*-**" indicates that the first part of the Conflict is not to be used, but only that part between the first star and the double star; "-**" indicates that all of the Conflict is to be used up to the double star, etc.

DEVELOPING THE PLOT FROM A SELECTED SITUATION. The most practical way to illustrate the Plotto Method of developing a plot from a single situation, or Conflict, will he to select a Conflict and follow the Method through, step by step. For this purpose, one of the Conflicts from the sub-group (54). "Becoming Involved in a Puzzling Complication that Has to do with an Object Possessing Mysterious Powers" is selected, namely No. 1383.

1383

(1389b) (1427b) A, proceeding about his business and caught in a crowd, is confronted suddenly by a strange woman, BX, who thrusts a mysterious object, X, into his hand and, without a word disappears. (541) (561) (1343) (1367a)

Selecting from the numbers in brackets at the end of Conflict 1383 to get a carry-on Conflict, we pick No. 1343

1343

(1380) (1282a-*) (1383) A carries in his pocket a queer object of mystery, X* A, apparently as the result of carrying in his pocket a queer object of mystery, X, experiences all sorts of misfortunes. ** (595) (596) (597) (1352) (1377b) (1382*-**)

and repeating the process twice more we add to the sequence

596

(612) (646 ch B to A & AX to A-5) (1114) A secures knowledge of a closely guarded secret.* A, securing knowledge of a closely-guarded secret, is hounded by a guilty persecutor, A-5, until his life is made miserable.** (705) (854 ch A-9 to A-5) (884a)

854

(1346 ch A to A-9; 596 ch A-5 to A-9) (1303) (1290a ch A to A-9; 596 ch A-5 to A-9) A discovers a fateful secret of his rich and powerful employer, A-9.* A, because he has knowledge of A-9's guilty secret, is persecuted, spied upon and thrown into prison on a trumped up charge.** (884a ch A-5 to A-9) (887a ch A-3 to A-9)

If this sequence faintly suggests the beginning of a well-known film, that is no accident, for I have created my own example following William Wallace Cook's technique. (The example he actually gives for developing a plot from a selected situation stems from his Conflict 1a, namely "A, poor, is in love with wealthy and aristocratic B.")

THE GREAT PLOTTOIST

The great Plottoist was Alfred Hitchcock. Ivor Montagu, who was the producer on Hitchcock's films made at Gaumont-British from 1934 to 1936, tells us in his article "Working with Hitchcock" in *Sight & Sound* (Summer 1980), that Hitchcock had been given a copy of *Plotto*, and regarded it highly. The *Plotto* situations or conflicts are largely derived from a collection of the better known and more successful short stories from the late nineteenth into the early twentieth century. In Cook's list of 1462 situations, there are hardly any which correspond to the sort of situations characteristic of Hitchcock's major series of suspense films from *The Man Who Knew Too Much* onwards. However, Cook's character symbols AX and BX for a man or woman of mystery, combined with his symbol X for an object of mystery are powerfully suggestive in the Hitchcock context. MacGuffins, anyone? The example of plot development I gave above is the best of mere a handful that I have been able to create having some resemblance to a Hitchcock plot, out of all the situations or conflicts listed in *Plotto*. So Hitchcock did not use that book crudely and directly, but it does seem to me that he took over its method for his plotting, using his own collection of conflicts or situations. And he began by assembling his collection of situations out of various works of popular fiction, most importantly the Bulldog Drummond novels, and John Buchan's series of thrillers featuring the character Richard Hannay.

An analysis of Hitchcock's spy thrillers from this point of view will reveal the usefulness of the method, how he developed it, and even how to generate new Hitchcock-type film scripts.

The first Hitchcock film that began to use this method was *The Man Who Knew Too Much* (1934). This was an original story developed by Hitchcock and Charles Bennett under the title *Bulldog Drummond's Baby*. I suspect that the impulse for this came from the announcement by "Sapper" in 1929 that he was not going to write any more Bulldog

Drummond stories, which was a great shock to his immense number of fans in England. The main novelty of Hitchcock and Bennett's story is that Bulldog Drummond's baby is kidnapped by the conspiratorial foreign master criminal gang, rather than his wife, Phyllis, who was the victim of such abductions more than once in the novels. In the story as filmed, Bulldog Drummond's band of supporters is reduced to just one, Clive, the equivalent of his "silly-ass" right-hand man Algy Longworth in the novels. In any case, copyright law demanded the removal of any extremely obvious relation between Hitchcock's film script and Sapper's work. Incidentally, in Sapper's novels, Phyllis was quite capable of initiative, resistance, and action when trapped by Carl Peterson and his minions, so the spirited defence of her child by Jill Lawrence in Hitchcock's film is not that surprising. The ambiguous relation between Carl Peterson and his constant female companion Irma in the novels is also reproduced (and accentuated) in the film. And the first Bulldog Drummond novel includes a scene in which Bulldog Drummond is trapped on the roof of a house by a villain with a gun, while the police watch from ground level. But the apparent source for more of the elements in the script appears to be the Buchan thrillers, of which *The Three Hostages* also contains an even more peculiar relation between the master criminal and his mother, as well as being centered on the kidnapping of three teenagers by the villains. The situation which really starts the plot of *The Man Who Knew Too Much*, with a cryptic clue being passed on to the hero by a spy who has been killed by the villains, of course comes from Buchan's *The Thirty-Nine Steps*, though Buchan also uses it in *Greenmantle*. It is not a device that occurs in the "Sapper" novels. Another element that comes from *The Three Hostages* is the use of hypnotism, which is a major technique used by the villain to control his hostages, and yet another feature of this novel is the cover provided for the villains by an Eastern religious cult.

So here is the plot of Hitchcock's film version of *The Man Who Knew Too Much* written down as a series of actions using William Wallace Cook's character symbols in the central column, and these actions are grouped into conflicts or situations on the *Plotto* model, which are listed in the right-hand column, though I use descriptive titles rather than numbers to identify them. In the left-hand column are the sequential index numbers for the conflicts making up each film.

A1	A, B, D-A are on holiday. They are friends with AX. At dinner, AX flirts with B. A plays a trick on AX.	INTRO
A2	AX is shot by A-5, and tells A of X. A goes to get X	START (A-5: A, AX, X)
A3	A-5 traps A in room. A gets X. A escapes.	TRAP/ESC (A-5: A)
A4	A-6 ask A and B about X. A threatens A-6. A-6 release A and B	NOTHELP (A: A-6)
A5	A-3 kidnaps D-A. A-3 threatens A with D-A's death	THREAT (A-3: A)
A6	A-6 question A about missing daughter. A-6 want X.	EXPLANATION (A-6: A, B)
A7	A rejects A-6 A-3 tell A and B that D-A is still alive. A-6 tell A and B that the call was from Wapping.	NOTHELP (A: A-6)
A8	A and A-2 go to Wapping. A and A-2 find A-5 from X. A enters A-5 headquarters. A sees A-3. A-7 traps A. A incapacitates A-7. A impersonates A-7. A-5 and A-3 arrange assassination. A overhears this.	BASETRAP/ESC (A-5:A) [ATTACK (A: A-7) IMPERSONATION (A: A-7)]
A9	A and A-2 follow A-3 and A-5 to base.	PURSUIT (A, A-2: A-5)
A10	M-A-3 recognizes A. M-A-3 incapacitates A-2. A and A-2 trapped in base. A fights A, A-5. A finds ticket clue. A tells A-2. A helps A-2 to escape. A is trapped. A-2 tells B to go to Albert Hall	BASETRAP/ESC (A-5: A, A-2)
A11	A-2 bring A-6 to base. A-3 and M-A-3 fool A-6. A-3 tells A-5 to threaten B with death of A and D-A	DECEPTION (A-5: A-6)
A12	B goes to Albert Hall. A-5 threatens B	THREAT (A-5: B)
A13	B stops assassination.	HELP (B: A-6)
A14	A-6 and B pursue A-5	PURSUIT (A-6: A-5)
A15	A-5 comes to base. A-6 trap A-3, A-5, M-A-3. A-3. A-5 shoot at A-6. A escapes and gets D-A. A-6 kill M-A-3. A-3 sends A-5 to get D-A. A-5 injures A. A-5 traps D-A on roof. B kills A-5. A-3 kills himself. A, B, D-A are reunited.	FINALTRAP (A-6, A, B: A-5)

As you can see, the plot of this film is fairly simple. In my named identification of the types of situations, I don't count the cover identity of the villains as a religious sect as impersonation, since it was already in place before the film starts. The IMPERSONATION situation in my analysis is when a false identity is assumed and then discarded in the service of an immediate problem. Although impersonation can be considered a kind of deception, I think it is useful to distinguish a separate DECEPTION situation. IMPERSONATION by both sides had long been a standard component of spy thrillers, as was also the case for the situation of the hero being trapped in the villain's headquarters and then escaping — (BASETRAP/ESC), and also pursuit by both sides of the other — (PURSUIT). Requests by the hero for help can be either satisfied — (HELP), or more frequently refused — (NOTHELP).

Ordinary TRAP/ESC situations can be simple, with no more than that happening, or can include other situations between the trapping and the escape, usually the granting or refusal of HELP, but also IMPERSONATION and yet other situations. The FINALTRAP sequence here and elsewhere almost invariably involves a shoot-out, as well as the final union of the hero and heroine, which again was already common in spy and master-criminal novels.

In *The Man Who Knew Too Much*, Hitchcock borrowed the notion of the mysterious figure passing on a secret to the hero to start the real action of the plot from one of his favourite novels, *The Thirty-Nine Steps*, and when he was in a position to actually film this story, he naturally left this START situation in.

B1	A watches a memorist A-7 at a Music Hall. A rescues BX from a fight at the Music Hall. BX tells A she started the fight to escape spies A-5.	TRAP/ESC (A-5:BX) [HELP (A: BX)]
B2	BX wants to save X for England. A-5 trap BX. A-5 kill BX. A finds where X is.	START (A-5: BX, A, X)
B3	A-5 trap A in flat. A escapes by a trick.	TRAP/ESC (A-5: A)
B4	A takes train to Scotland to get X. A-5 pursue A.	PURSUIT (A-5: A)
B5	A-6 believe A killed BX. A-6 pursue A.	PURSUIT (A-6: A)
B6	A trapped on train by A-6. A appeals to B for help. B rejects him and gives him away to A-6. A escapes from train by a trick.	TRAP/ESC (A-6: A) [NOTHELP (B: A)]
B7	A asks A-8 for help. A-8 gives him help. B-8 tells A she is unhappy. B-8 warns A of A-6 coming. A-8 suspects A and B-8 of making love.	HELP (A-8, B-8: A)
B8	A-6 trap A. A bribes A-8 to help him. A-8 tricks A. B-8 helps A escape.	TRAP/ESC (A-6: A) [HELP (B-8: A)]
B9	A-6 pursue A.	PURSUIT (A-6: A)
B10	A comes to A-3 house. A tells A-3 of BX. A-3 protects A from A-6. A-3 reveals he is A-3 to A. A-3 shoots A. A escapes by luck.	BASETRAP/ESC (A-5: A)
B11	A tells A-6 of A-5 threat, but they don't believe him.	NOTHELP (A-6: A)
B12	A-6 traps A. A-5 posing as police arrive. A escapes.	TRAP/ESC (A-6: A)
B13	A-6 pursue A. A hides in parade.	PURSUIT (A-6:A)
B14	A hides in political meeting. A is mistaken for politician. A impersonates politician.	IMPERSONATION (A: politician)
B15	A-5 impersonating A-6 trap A. B arrives and accuses A of killing BX. A-5 take A and B away in car. A reveals A-5 as impersonators. A-5 handcuff A to B (trap B). A escapes with B.	TRAP/ESC (A-5: A, B) [IMPERSONATION (A-5: A-6)]
B16	A tries to convince B of his innocence. B does not believe A.	NOTHELP (B: A)
B17	A threatens B into submission.	THREAT (A: B)
B18	A and B travel to hotel. A pretends to be eloping with B. A gets more friendly with B.	IMPERSONATION (A, B: newlyweds)
B19	B gets out of handcuffs. B finds A tricked her.	INFO (falsegun: B)
B20	A-5 trap A and B in hotel. B hears A-5 ringing A-3. A-5 ask hotel for A and B. Hotel conceals A and B.	TRAP/ESC (A-5,A,B) [HELP (hotel: A, B)]
B21	B tells A about A-5 coming to hotel and A-3 going to Palladium. A and B quarrel.	QUARREL (A: B)
B22	B tells A-6 about A-5. A-6 do not believe B.	NOTHELP (A-6: B)
B23	A-6 ask B to give them A for murder. B rejects A-6.	NOTHELP (B: A-6)
B24	A-6 pursue B.	PURSUIT (A-6: B)
B25	B meets A at Palladium. A-6 trap A and B. A sees A-3. Memorist contacts A-3. A tricks Memorist A-7 into exposing A-3. A-3 shoots Memorist A-7. A-6 capture A-3. A-7 reveals X. A-7 dies. A and B are united.	FINALTRAP (A-6: A,B, A-3)

The most important innovation here is that the hero is menaced throughout the film by both the villains and the police, and not just the villains. This powerful mechanism for generating extra suspense is taken directly from the Buchan novel, which may have introduced it for the first time. In previous literary thrillers, the hero usually has at least the grudging support of the police in his struggles with the villains.

However, Hitchcock and Charles Bennett's script for *The Thirty-Nine Steps* includes situations that are not found in John Buchan's original novel, mostly provided to fulfil the requirements of a commercial film in the nineteen-thirties. The most basic of these was the "love interest", which was entirely absent in the novel. The way to introduce this element was probably suggested by the scene in which Richard Hannay hijacks a car driven by Marmaduke Jopley, a "blood stockbroker". (This period use of the adjective indicated a fashionable young man.) This person is characterized in the novel by the comment, "I asked afterwards why nobody kicked him, and was told it was because the English reverenced the weaker sex." Later Hannay runs into Jopley again, and the latter gives him away to the police. So Jopley becomes Pamela, whose part is then further elaborated. Likewise, one of the functions of the scenes with the crofter and his wife is to put a touch more sex into the film.

From a structural point of view, the film is much more tightly organized than the novel. The only reason for Hannay's excursion to Scotland in the novel is to hide out in countryside that he knows well until a set period has passed, whereas in the film, he goes there following a clue to the whereabouts of the secret plans. (Incidentally, the final reference to the secret in the novel is "They want our naval dispositions for their collection at the Marinamt; but they will be pigeonholed – nothing more.", which shows that their MacGuffin nature was already present in Buchan.) In the novel they have been stolen by one of the spy gang memorizing them.

Hannay's trip to Scotland in the novel contains little threat to him, and when he gets in touch with the authorities some way before the end, they readily accept his story and lack of involvement in the murder. The repeated bickering between Hannay and Pamela in the film reflects a fashion in film script-writing that was becoming standard for attractive couples in Hollywood screwball comedies at the time, although in this case it may equally have come straight from the original source for this sort of thing, which was Noel Coward's plays.

IMPERSONATION appears in the novel – the spies do a perfect impersonation of ordinary English people, and Hannay masquerades as a road-mender, not to mention a parliamentary candidate, though as the latter he is not menaced by villains or police at all. In the original novel of *The Thirty-Nine Steps*, the spies are trapped in one of their bases at the end, but there is no shooting. The way I analyse these films, the BASETRAP and FINALTRAP situations are usually complex, being made up of more actions than the other situations.

This is the way things continued, as Hitchcock and his collaborators exploited their success with these two films. For the next film after *The Thirty-Nine Steps*, which was titled *Secret Agent* (1936), Hitchcock and Bennett used as source material the "Ashenden" short stories by Somerset Maugham. These were based on Maugham's own experiences as a spy during the First World War, and they provided the following material used in the film script:

In *The Hairless Mexican,* Ashenden is given an associate who is hairless and a Mexican, and who talks a lot, chases women, and likes to be called "General".

In *The Greek* a message for Ashenden in code comes to the hotel desk and has to be decoded. Meanwhile the Mexican gets off with a woman in a sordid café. The cable when decoded reveals that the Mexican has killed the wrong man.

In *The Traitor*, an English traitor has a very patriotic German wife and dog. Ashenden inveigles himself into their confidence, and they go walking on the Alps. Ashenden gets her to give him German lessons. Ashenden then sets the traitor up to go to England to do some spying. Information comes from R., Ashenden's boss, that the traitor has been caught, and his dog howls, and his wife realizes his fate.

In *Giulia Lazzari* Ashenden has to accompany the mistress of an Indian subversive on a train to Switzerland to decoy him out.

A Chance Acquaintance describes a train journey across Russia with the American business representative Mr. Harrington. (But he is not a spy.)

And finally *Miss King* contains the detail that secret messages are passed when buying butter.

It appears that the play by Campbell Dixon based on the same material contributed the love interest to the film script, according to Ivor Montagu's interviews with John Russell Taylor summarised in his *Hitchcock: The Authorised Biography*. (p.135). The part of Robert Marvin was written in to use Robert Young, who had been contracted to Gainsborough for two films to assist American sales. Just how his part was elaborated during the script-writing process is still unclear.

The action and situations in the film script are as follows:-

C1 A is told he is dead by secret service boss A-9. IMPERSONATION (A: civilian)

C2 A-9 sends A to Switzerland to locate German agent and kill him. A is to take A-2 with him as assistant. A is to conceal his mission from A-6. In Swiss hotel A finds he has "wife" B already there. MISSION (A-9: A, B, A-2)

C3	A finds A-3 flirting with B. A-2 arrives.	LOVE (A-3: B)
C4	A and A-2 get message to go to church nearby and find an organist with information. A-5 try to stop A getting information X. A and A-2 come to church to find organist dead with coat button gripped in his hand.	START (A-5: A, A-2, Organist)
C5	A-3 and B go to casino. A-3 flirts with B. A and A-2 get message that spy is leaving tomorrow and must be eliminated.	INFO (A-9: A, A-2)
C6	A and A-2 arrive at casino. Coat button held by dead organist is dropped on roulette table by A. A-4 picks up coat button and says it is his. A-4 says he was near church. A and A-2 suspect A-4.	SUSPICION (A, A-2: A-4)
C7	A and A-2 get A-4 to climb mountain with them the next day.	DECEPTION (A, A-2: A-4)
C8	Next day B is having a German lesson from W-A-4. B and W-A-4 are joined by A-3. A-3 flirts with B.	LOVE (A-3: B)
C9	On mountain, A refuses to kill A-4. A-2 kills A-4.	NOTHELP (A: A-2) [KILL (A-2: A-4)]
C10	A and B are at caf, and depressed. A-2 tells them they are not suspected of the killing. A shows A-2 and B telegram from London that proves they got wrong man. A-2 is amused and B is upset.	DECEPTION (A, A-2: A-6)
C11	B tells A that she loved him but now she doesn't because of his job. A says he doesn't like it either. They are reconciled.	XLOVE (B: A) LOVE (B: A)
C12	Next morning A-3 rings up with more flirting with B.	LOVE (A-3: B)
C13	A and B tell A-2 that they are quitting. A-2 is angry and takes A off on new lead. A-2 has made friends with B-4. B-4's boyfriend works in chocolate factory which is German spy centre. A tells B that he is going there with A-2. B is upset at this.	NOTHELP (A, B: A-2)
C14	In chocolate factory A-2 sees man send message to another man that English spies are in factory. A-6 are tipped off, and tell manager. A and A-2 get information from B-4's boyfriend that shows A-3 to be German spy. A and A-2 trapped in factory by A-6. A-2 and A escape by trick.	BASETRAP/ESC (A-5: A, A-2)
C15	B leaves with A-3. A and A-2 find out and follow. At railway station A and A-2 tell B about A-3. B refuses to believe them, but comes with them.	PURSUIT (A, A-2: A-3)
C16	On train B tries to prevent them killing A-3. B meets A-3 on train and says she wants to go with him. Alone in compartment A-3 pulls gun on B and says he knows she is British spy. A-3 tells B that if A and A-2 are on train they are dead men. B pretends A and A-2 are not on train. B says she is in love with A-3. A-3 doesn't altogether believe her. Allied planes attack train. A-3 tells B that he doesn't love her, but kisses her. A and A-2 come in, and A-2 is going to kill A-3. B pulls gun on A and A-2 to stop them killing A-3. Bomb hits train. In wreckage, A-3 is pinned under beam. A-2 puts gun down and A-3 shoots him and then dies. Shots of desert campaign. A and B are shown married.	FINALTRAP (A, A-2, B: A-3)

The major innovation here is the character of Robert Marvin, the antagonist A-3 in the above plot analysis. His initial principal function is to compete with the hero for the affections of the heroine – LOVE (A-3:B), but he is revealed as a German spy near the end of the film. The most obvious thing about the situations in this film is the small number of TRAP/ ESCAPE situations and of PURSUITS, contrasted with the increased numbers of DECEPTIONS. The last feature arises because all the principals are spies, and this in its turn reduces the amount of simple-minded thrills when compared to the previous films. This may have been part of the point for the makers – for the original stories put emphasis on the dubious moral grounds of the spy's business, and this is carried through into the film. This extra moral depth was appropriate for a film with the leading role played by England's best Hamlet of the period, John Gielgud.

The seriousness of the basic material being used was continued into Hitchcock's next film, *Sabotage* (1936). Here the relative respect shown for the original source, Joseph Conrad's *The Secret Agent*, meant that there was little place for what were now the standard Hitchcock situations, although he did make some strained attempts to get them in. For this reason, I will omit it, and continue on to *Young and Innocent*, which on the other hand shows little respect for the source novel, Josephine Tey's *A Shilling for Candles*. It is clear from the preliminary announcements of the project in the trade press that the studio made the film as a vehicle for their young star Nova Pilbeam, and the adaptation reflects this.

D1	Man with twitching eye (A-3) accuses film star former wife (W-A-3) of infidelity. A-3 storms out.	QUARREL (A-3: W-A-3)
D2	Body of W-A-3 strangled with belt washed up on beach and found by A. A runs off, seen by B-8. A and B-8 and A-6 are on beach. B-8 accuse A of murder.	START (A-3: A, W-A-3)
D3	A-6 suspiciously interrogate A. A tells them he has known dead woman and sold her stories. His coat belt is missing. A says it was stolen. A faints. B, daughter of Chief Constable A-9, comes in and gives him first aid. A-8, defence lawyer, unhelpfully and unenthusiastically questions A. A-8 takes A's money. In courtroom, A walks away from A-6 by mistake. A disguises himself with glasses he has taken from A-8.	TRAP/ESC (A-6: A) [HELP (B: A) NOTHELP (A-8: A)]
D4	A-6 hunt him incompetently. B joins the hunt.	PURSUIT (A-6: B, A)
D5	B and A-6 in her car run out of petrol. A-6 leave and A appears. A helps B push car. At village petrol pump A has to pay for petrol as B has no money. B doesn't give him away. B orders A out of car. He proclaims his innocence and suggests she come back at night.	HELP (A: B)
D6	Hiding in mill A sees B meet A-6. B doesn't give him away.	HELP (B: A)
D7	B brings food to A in mill. B says she only came back to give him his money back. A asks for her help in getting to the transport caf, where he left his coat. A tells B he only did dead woman a good turn in Hollywood, and is not her lover.	HELP (B: A)
D8	A-6 see movement in mill and goes in. A and B escape out back. A-6 see them, but don't recognize B. A and B escape in her car, with B hiding.	TRAP/ESC (A-6: A)
D9	B objects to going with A to transport cafe. B wants to give him up to police. Roadworks block her taking A back to town.	HELP (B: A)
D10	B goes into transport cafe to find coat X. Truck driver tells her Old Will (A-2) has it and can be found at Nobby's lodging house in Dorchester. Other drivers try to stop him, and a fight breaks out.	NOTHELP (drivers: B)
D11	A is injured trying to rescue B, and she gives him first aid. A thanks her and sets off to find A-2.	HELP (A: B)
D12	B follows him and gives him a lift. B takes A to visit AU-B aunt, to provide a reason for her not going home. A poses as friend of B's family but Aunt-B is suspicious. A and B escape children's party, but aunt rings A-9.	TRAP/ESC (Aunt-B: A) [IMPERSONATION (B: famfriend)]
D13	A-9 telephones police to stop B, and get her to ring him.	INFO (A-9: A-6)
D14	A-6 stop car and recognize A. B and A escape and drive off.	TRAP/ESC (A-6: A, B)
D15	A-6 hunt them in forest.	PURSUIT (A-6: A, B)
D16	A and B hide in railway yard in Dorchester. A tells B that she will be free soon, and starts to leave. B falls asleep on his shoulder. He leaves.	LOVE (B: A)
D17	In Nobby's lodging house A waits for A-2, but falls asleep. Next morning A sees A-2's bed used but empty. A identifies A-2 by breaking crockery trick.	DECEPTION (A: A-2)
D18	A's identity is revealed to inmates, who try to capture him. A escapes the pursuit dragging A-2 with him. A and A-2 escape from railway yard with B in her car.	TRAP/ESC (inmates: A)

D19	A-6 pursue A and B by car.	PURSUIT (A-6: A: B)
D20	A and B find A-2 is wearing A's coat. There is no belt, but A-2 tells them there was none when A-3 gave it to him. B says they need better evidence.	INFO (A-2: A, B)
D21	They go to hide in mine, chased by A-6. Their car falls through the mine floor with B still in it. A grabs her hand and pulls her out. B goes back for her dog, and the A-6 catch her.	TRAP/ESC (A-6: A, B)
D22	B is interrogated by A-6, and says she believes A is innocent. This is overheard by A-9. A-9 tells B that because she is shielding A he has to resign his job. B runs crying to bedroom.	XLOVE (A-9: B)
D23	Later, A comes in B's bedroom window. A says he is going to give himself up because he can't prove his innocence. B finds Grand Hotel matches in his coat.	HELP (B: A)
D24	B and A-2 are at Grand Hotel. A-6 are suspicious of A-2 and B. A-2 and B go into ballroom. A-3 is drummer in band and recognizes A-2. A-3 tries to hide, but sees police surrounding ballroom, actually to catch B and A-2. A-3 gets anxious. A-9 arrives and A gives himself up. B, A-2, and A are being led away by police when A-3 collapses. B goes to give him first aid, and notices his twitch. A-2 recognizes him. A-3 confesses. A-9 is reconciled with B and A.	FINALTRAP (A-6: A,B, A-3)

There is nothing new in plot construction here, though the analysis helps the emerging notion that the standard situations can be put together in any order. The protagonist is only under threat from the police throughout the story, and not from the lone villain, who is absent from the screen for most of the film.

Hitchcock's next film, *The Lady Vanishes*, stays fairly close to the original novel by Ethel Lina White, and was given to him as a completed script. As can be read on page 89 of Geoff Brown's *Launder and Gilliat* (BFI, 1977), the only changes Hitchcock made were to the beginning and the end. The latter part was put more fully into his usual FINALTRAP sequence, and I presume that he introduced the killing of the informant passing on the X to the woman of mystery BX at the beginning, on the model of *The Man Who Knew Too Much* and *The Thirty-Nine Steps*.

The next entry in the suspense thriller sequence is *Foreign Correspondent*, which uses a completely original script for the first time since *The Man Who Knew Too Much*, and its story introduces some new situations into the collection.

E1	Proprietor, A-9, of NY newspaper sends A to London to get information on treaty negotiated by AX, the Dutch "strongman".	MISSION (A-9: A)
E2	In London, AX evades A 's questions about political situation.	NOTHELP (AX: A)
E3	At political meeting arranged by F-B for AX, A meets and is attracted to B, daughter of F-B.	LOVE (A: B)
E4	A is sent to Holland to cover an AX speech. A waits on steps of hall for AX, and meets F-B. A tries to talk to A-X, but AX does not recognize him. AX is shot by A-5 photographer.	START (A-5: AX, A, X)
E5	A chases A-5. A jumps into passing car in pursuit with A-2, and B.	PURSUIT (A, A-2, B: A-5)
E6	A-6 also chase A-5.	PURSUIT (A-6: A-5)
E7	A-5's getaway car vanishes near windmills. A-6 come up, then go on. A sees windmill running backwards and guesses A-5 is in mill. He sends A-2 and B off to get A-6 back, while he searches mill.	INFO (A: A-2, B)
E8	A goes into mill and sees A-5 talking to A-3. A is trapped in mill by more A-5 approaching mill and goes upstairs to hide. A finds AX in a room, and AX says he has been drugged. AX explains that a double has been shot, and he will be taken away. AX passes out. A escapes unseen as AX is removed.	BASETRAP/ESC (A-5: A) [EXPLANATION (AX: A)]

E9	A , A-2, B, and A-6 come back to mill and find it empty, with no trace of AX and A-5. A man claims he has been there alone all day. A-6 do not believe A . A-2 sees man in mill acting suspiciously.	NOTHELP (A-6: A)
E10	A is in Amsterdam hotel writing despatch to newspaper about the affair when A-5 posing as police come in and ask him to come to see Chief of Police. He asks A-5 if he can go into bathroom, and then sees A-5 through keyhole getting their guns out. A escapes out bathroom window into B's dressing room.	TRAP/ESC (A-5: A) [IMPERSONATION (A-5: A-6)]
E11	B refuses to believe A 's story. He insists on the danger he is in, and insults her peace movement. She is about to throw him out, but relents. A rings for services to be sent to his room to trap A-5. A and B leave the hotel in the confusion.	NOTHELP (B: A)
E12	A and B are pursued by A-5, but escape on boat.	PURSUIT (A-5: A, B)
E13	A declares his love for B, and B says she loves him.	LOVE (A: B)
E14	In London, A and B go to the F-B house, where A-3 is having breakfast with F-B. A tells F-B that A-3 is part of plot to capture AX. F-B speaks to A-3 in his study, and reveals that he is part of plot, but B is not. F-B tells A-3 to get assassin to dispose of A. F-B stops A from going to to A-6 by saying that AX will be kille if he does, and that A needs protection. F-B tells A he will investigate A-3. B tells F-B that she loves A, and F-B thinks of stopping A-5.	DECEPTION (F-B: A)
E15	A-5 tries to push A under truck, but A escapes. A-5 pretends that he pushed A to save him.	ATTACK/ESC (A-5: A)
E16	A-5 pretends that they are being followed, and gets A up tower to escape. A-5 tries to push A off, but falls off himself.	ATTACK/ESC (A-5: A)
E17	At newspaper office, A and A-2 realise that F-B is a villain associated with A-3. A-2 says AX has memorized secret clause, X, in peace treaty. A-2 suggests pretending to kidnap B to force F-B to give up AX.	EXPLANATION (A-2: A)
E18	B comes in and worries about A's safety. B, primed by A-2, suggests taking A to country.	DECEPTION (A-2: B)
E19	At country hotel A prevents B from going to London, and declares his love. A-2, who can't get in touch with F-B, rings A and insists he keep B there.	LOVE (A: B)
E20	A arranges a room for B, but she overhears this and leaves.	XLOVE (B: A)
E21	A-2 tells F-B that B has been kidnapped and she will be swapped for AX. A-3 rings F-B to tell him that he must come to help get AX to talk before F-B goes to America.	DECEPTION (A-2: F-B)
E22	F-B apparently writes down address of AX prison for A-2, but F-B has heard B come in, and A-2 finds there is no information.	DECEPTION (F-B: A-2)
E23	B unhappily tells F-B that A took her to the country to seduce her. B agrees to go to America with F-B.	XLOVE (B: A)
E24	F-B takes taxi, and A-2 hears address. A-2 tells A-7, who is with him, to wait and tell A when he comes to F-B house. B answers phone call from A-3 for F-B, and recognizes A-3's voice.	INFO (A-3: B)
E25	F-B goes to prison house where drugged AX is being tortured. AX asks F-B to help him. A-2 comes in and is caught by villains. F-B pretends that he is there to help AX, and asks him for X. A-2 tells AX that F-B is not his friend, and AX realises this, and makes a speech against A-5. A-5 torture him, and he is about to tell secret X when A-2 breaks loose and jumps out window. As A and A-7 come up. A-2, A , and A-7 break back into building, but villains have fled, leaving unconscious AX.	BASETRAP/ESC (A-5: A-2)

E26	At Scotland Yard, Head Policeman refuses to stop F-B leaving the country while AX is unconscious.	NOTHELP (A-6: A)
E27	A and A-2 get on plane, F-B intercepts message for A-2 saying AX is conscious, and F-B is to be caught on arrival. F-B tries to explain his treachery to B, who has realised the truth. F-B passes the message on to A-2. A goes to speak to B, who rejects him as having deceived her. Plane is shot down and all end up on floating wing. When wing is about to sink, F-B drops off it to save them. Rescued by US ship, A tell A-2 that he won't send despatch that implicates F-B because he saved them. B overhears this and is reconciled with A. A , A-2, and B trick captain of US ship into getting the news through to NY newspaper. Later in London, A makes inspirational broadcast to US in the middle of bombing raid.	FINALTRAP (A, A-2: F-B)

New in this film is the ATTACK on the hero by the villains as a separate situation. This has of course to be unsuccessful for the story to continue. There had been a few physical attacks on the hero before this as an internal part of the TRAP type of situations, for instance in the FINALTRAP sequence of *The Man Who Knew Too Much*, but here they are quite separate. There is a lot of DECEPTION, including another figure, F-B, who presents a false front throughout the entire length of the film, as does the Robert Marvin character in *Secret Agent*. That film is clearly the model for *Foreign Correspondent*, with the major change that the heroine is now the daughter of the antagonist, rather than just a stranger slightly enamoured of him. (Incidentally, in the first Bulldog Drummond novel, Phyllis, Drummond's future wife, is the daughter of one of the men involved in the political and criminal conspiracy that is the mainspring of the story.) And the FINALTRAP of *Secret Agent* is clearly the model for the FINALTRAP of the present example. There are also two situations in *Foreign Correspondent* to which I have not given identifying names, as I judge they are too special to this film to be of use for my immediate purposes.

There is a somewhat curious sequence in *Foreign Correspondent* resulting from A-2 persuading B to hide out with A in the country, so that he can blackmail F-B with her pretended kidnap, and hence get F-B to give up AX. Taken by itself, the involved mechanics of this sequence are like a stratagem taken from the middle of a nineteen-thirties sophisticated comedy, and it seems too elaborate for its function of turning B against A in the plot.

The next simple action suspense thriller, or "chase" film, as Hitchcock himself referred to them, is *Saboteur* (1942), and this is obviously closely derived from *The Thirty-Nine Steps*, as has been recognized even without the following analysis.

F1	At war plant, A sees AX's name on envelope he dropped. Fire breaks out, and A is given fire extinguisher by AX, and he then gives it to A's friend. A's friend is burned up in the fire.	START (AX: A)
F2	A describes events to A-6, and then tells the mother of A's friend.	INFO (A: A-6, mother)
F3	While A is out of room, the A-6 come to arrest A for sabotage. They tell A's friend's mother that the fire extinguisher was full of gasoline, and there is no AX working at the plant. Mother shields A.	TRAP/ESC (A-6: A) [HELP (mother: A)]
F4	A hitches a ride with Truck Driver to ranch whose address was on AX's letter. A-6 stops truck, but it is for something else.	HELP (driver: A)
F5	At ranch, the owner, A-3 denies knowledge of AX, but A sees telegram from AX saying job is done, and AX is going to Soda City. A accuses A-3, who says he recognized A and has sent for the A-6. A-3 says A-6 will not believe A, because A-3 is a good citizen. When A tries to leave, maid holds him with pistol, but A uses A-3's granddaughter as a shield and escapes on a horse.	BASETRAP/ESC (A-3, A-5: A)
F6	A is pursued and caught by ranch hands.	PURSUIT (A-5: A)
F7	A accuses A-3 again when the A-6 come, but they ignore him.	NOTHELP (A-6:A)
F8	When A-6 car is blocked on a bridge by Truck Driver's truck, A leaps off bridge in handcuffs and Truck Driver misdirects A-6.	TRAP/ESC (A-6:A) [HELP (driver: A)]

F9	A comes to an isolated cabin of a blind man (A-8), who makes him welcome. A gives a false name, but A-8 detects his handcuffs. A-8's niece B comes in, and says A-6 are looking for A. A tries to conceal handcuffs, but B sees them. B wants to give A up to A-6, but A-8 says he thinks A is innocent, and tells B to take A to blacksmith friend to get handcuffs off.	HELP (A-8: A)
F10	On way to blacksmith, B says she is taking A to A-6, and hooks the handcuffs round the steering wheel. A puts his foot on the accelerator, and manages to drive the car out into the desert. B escapes down the road and tries to stop passing cars, while A grinds through handcuff-chain with fan belt pulley. As passing car stops for B, A drags B into the car, and old couple in car assume they are quarrelling newly-weds.	TRAP/ESC (B: A) [NOTHELP (B: A)]
F11	A and B quarrel. A tries to convince her of his innocence, and she warms to him a little.	QUARREL (B: A)
F12	A train of circus wagons comes along, and after threatening B with desert snakes, A stops her calling to caravan, and then jumps on last wagon. B pleads to come too.	NOTHELP (B: A)
F13	Freaks in wagon discover them, and A tells them of his predicament. When A-6 stop caravan, the Freaks vote whether to give A away, and B by her silence has the casting vote in A's favour. Freaks hide them. Freaks drop them off at Soda City.	TRAP/ESC (A-6:A) [HELP (freaks: A)]
F14	A and B discover a room used for spying, and then A-5 come. A hides B in another room, then tells A-5 he is a wanted saboteur, and convinces them to help him get back to NY. A-5 hear noise, and look in next room, but it is empty. They all set off.	BASETRAP/ESC (A-5: A, B) [IMPERSONATION (A: A-5)]
F15	B tells story to A-6, who is actually A-5, and he tells her they want to keep in touch.	IMPERSONATION (A-5: A-6)
F16	In NY, A-5 and A go to Mrs. Sutton's (M-A-3) mansion. B is already there, captured because the A-6 she confided in was a spy. A-3 comes in, and says the A-6 are after him, and B and A are patriots. A-3 says tomorrow's sabotage must be carried out, and he is leaving country. A-5 are worried about their position. A-3 says A and B must be disposed of. A and B escape when an innocent guest of the charity event comes in.	BASETRAP/ESC (A-5: A, B)
F17	A and B find the exits from the ballroom guarded by A-5. A and B try to convince guests that the event is being run by A-5, but no-one believes them. A and B dance, and A says B must get out to warn authorities about sabotage tomorrow. A and B speak their love for each other. One of the A-5 takes over B on dance floor and waltzes her away. A starts to address the audience, but is shown gun pointing at him. He turns his speech into an auction of M-A-3's jewels. A is brought out of ballroom by a threat to B.	TRAP/ESC (A-5: A, B) [LOVE (A: B)]
F18	A-5 plan sabotage using pretend newsreel crew. B is held captive in newsreel office.	
F19	A is locked in storeroom, and gets out by setting off sprinkler system and escaping in the confusion.	ESC (A: A-5)
F20	Outside, A sees newspaper about battleship launch, and realises this is sabotage target. A rushes to launch site.	INFO (newspaper: A)
F21	In newsreel office, B throws message out window.	INFO (B: A-6)
F22	A gets to shipyard and sees AX in Newsreel van. A struggles with AX to stop him setting off explosion, and manages to delay him till ship is in water.	ATTACK/ESC (A: AX)
F23	AX holds A at gun point in van which escapes from shipyard. A-5 and AX take A to newsreel office, but A-6 are waiting there.	TRAP/ESC (A-5:A)

F24   A-5 and AX escape under fire, leaving A behind. AX escapes into cinema, and   TRAP/ESC (A-6: AX)
      shoots it out with A-6 in front of screen. As A and B are taken out of building, A
      sees AX escaping.

F25   A-6 hold A, who sends B in pursuit of AX.   PURSUIT (B: AX)

F26   AX goes to Statue of Liberty, followed by B. B rings FBI headquarters, where   FINALTRAP (B, A: AX)
      agent and A are sent after AX. B makes an approach to AX on top of Statue to try
      to detain him. A-6 arrive at Statue and AX is trapped at top. A goes up after him
      with gun AX dropped, and AX backs over the edge and falls onto hand. A goes
      down after him, and as he tries to pull AX up by his sleeve, the A-6 arrive, and AX
      promises to clear A. But AX's sleeve gives way and he falls to his death. B and A are
      reunited.

The plot is not identical to that of *The Thirty-Nine Steps*, since the order of the situations is changed, the role of B is enlarged, and she acts independently of A in the latter part of the film. This produces extra situations, and also greater complexity within some of them, particularly in the sequence in Mrs. Sutton's mansion. Another major change is that the hero and heroine trap the villain in the FINALTRAP situation, rather than the other way round. After this film, Hitchcock concentrated on what he called his "psychological" films, and although these do sometimes include some of the situations I have been dealing with, their structure is largely derived from other material. However, he returned to the chase thrillers with *North by North-West* (1959), which has the ultimate plot complexity of the series.

G1   A leaves advertising agency with secretary dictating notes to girlfriend, ex-wife,   INTRO
     mother (M-A), then steals taxi from another man.

G2   A mistaken for AX in hotel lobby. Two A-5 notice this, and abduct A with guns. In   BASETRAP/ESC (A-5: A)
     the A-5 car, A tries to get out, but fails. A-5 car takes A to Townsend mansion. A-3
     asks A what he knows about them, calling him AX. A says he knows nothing and is
     not AX. A-3 and Leonard (A-5) refuse to believe him, and threaten to kill him. A-5s
     force drink on A, put him in car on cliff road and start it towards edge with one of
     them driving. A pushes him out and steers away from edge and down road, narrowly
     missing oncoming cars. A-5s pursue. A-6 also chase A. A stops suddenly to avoid
     cyclist, and A-6 crash into A. A-5s see this and drive away.

G3   A-6 take A to Police station. A accuses A-5s of being responsible. A-6 don't believe   NOTHELP (A-6: A)
     him. They let him ring M-A, and he asks her to get lawyer. Next morning in court,
     lawyer tells A's story, but M-A and judge don't believe it. Judge sets local A-6 to
     investigate.

G4   A, A-M, and A-6 go to Townsend house. A tries to show A-6 traces of drunk-making   DECEPTION (A-5: A-6)
     assault, but they have been removed. A-5 pretend A is an old friend who got drunk
     and borrowed car. A-6 and M-A refuse to believe A's denials. They leave, and A-5
     watches them go.

G5   Back in NY, A takes M-A to hotel and rings AX's room. AX has not been there. A and   DECEPTION (A, M-A:
     M-A trick their way into AX's room, which has not been slept in. Servants have not   hotel)
     seen A before, but all call him AX. Phone rings, and it is A-5, who are in hotel.

G6   As A and M-A get into lift, A-5s follow them in, and M-A asks if they are trying to   TRAP/ESC (A-5: A)
     kill A. They laugh at this, and everyone joins in, including M-A. On ground floor, A
     pushes A-5s back into lift, and grabs taxi.

G7   A-5s grab next taxi. A orders driver to UN building, and gets him to shake off   PURSUIT (A-5: A)
     following taxi.

G8   In UN building, A asks for Townsend, saying he is AX. A-5 watches him. Townsend   START (A-5: Townsend, A)
     arrives. He is a different man. He owns the house, but has not been there. As A
     shows him photo of "Townsend", A-5 throws knife into his back. No one sees this.
     Townsend collapses in A's arms and crowd sees A with hand on knife, and he is
     photographed. A flees.

G9	At US Intelligence agency, A-9 and associates discuss how A has been mistaken by A-5s for the non-existent AX. AX has been created to draw attention away from their own agent working under A-3's nose. One associate worries what will happen to A with both the A-5s and A-6 after him, but A-9 says they will just have to let it go to protect their agent.	EXPLANATION (A-9:A-5)
G10	At station, A rings M-A and tells her that he is going to find AX in Chicago. A sees newspaper headlines saying he is hunted. A puts on dark glasses and tries to buy ticket. Clerk is suspicious and stalls him while he rings A-6 to get him. A bolts while clerk's back is turned. A pushes past ticket collector as he sees A-6 following, and gets onto train.	TRAP/ESC (A-6: A)
G11	On train, he runs into Eve (B), who shields him from A-6 by misdirecting them. A says they want him for parking tickets. Later, as ticket collector comes round, A hides in toilet.	HELP (B: A)
G12	In dining car, waiter seats him with B. She flirts with him, and says she had him seated with her. A says he lied about parking tickets, and flirts back. A lies about who he is, but B says she knows who he is. A asks why she doesn't turn him in. B says she likes the look of him and wants to spend the night with him. B offers A a bed in her compartment.	LOVE (B: A)
G13	B tells him that A-6 have just got on, and they leave dining car. In compartment, B hides him in bunk. A-6 come in, tell her A is a murderer. A-6 question B about what happened in dining car. B lies about this. A-6 leave after warning B to watch out for A.	TRAP/ESC (A-6: A) [HELP (B: A)]
G14	B lets A out and offers to get into bed with him. Slightly later, B offers to hide him in her Chicago hotel. They kiss, and B asks A more about himself. A jokes that he might be a murderer, and B offers to let him kill her. They kiss again. Attendant rings to come in and make up bed, and A hides in washroom. Attendant leaves, and A and B start kissing again.	LOVE (B: A)
G15	Attendant takes message from B to A-3 and A-5 in another compartment. Message asks what B should do with A in morning.	DECEPTION (B: A)
G16	Next morning, A disguised as a Redcap gets off train with B. A-6 stop her and ask if she has seen A. B lies about this. B tells A that he has to get changed while she rings AX.	HELP (B: A)
G17	A-3 and A-5 follow them unseen.	PURSUIT (A-5: A)
G18	A-6 find Redcap who has been bribed. He directs them after A. In hall, A-6 grab all Redcaps. In toilet A has his face covered with foam so A-6 don't recognize him.	TRAP/ESC (A-6: A)
G19	B gets message from A-5 in next phone booth. A comes out, and B tells A that AX will meet him at prairie stop. A wants to arrange another meeting with her, but she lies about the A-6 coming, and A leaves.	DECEPTION (B: A)
G20	Bus drops A at crossing on prairie. Cars pass, but they don't stop. A man is dropped off, and A asks him if he is AX. He says no, and points out crop dusting plane is dusting where there are no crops. He gets on next bus. The plane attacks A with gunfire, but he evades it. Plane crashes into oil truck and is destroyed. Other cars stop, and as people go to watch, A steals one.	ATTACK/ESC (A-5: A)
G21	A goes to hotel and asks for AX, and is told he left early in the morning for Rapid City. A is suspicious, and then sees B going up to her room. A goes into B's room angry. B is glad to see him and embraces him. A is still suspicious. B asks him about meeting. A questions her, but B lies. A is still suspicious. B gets phone call, and makes arrangement to see someone.	DECEPTION (B: A)
G22	B asks A to go away and never see her again. A resists this but finally agrees. B gets him to get his clothes cleaned and slips out while he is in shower. A is expecting this. He finds an impression of where she is going.	XLOVE (B: A)

G23   At auction rooms, A watches A-3 caressing B.   LOVE (A-3: B)

G24   A goes up to them and accuses them all of trying to kill him. A-3 asks B what she has   JEALOUSY (A: A-3)
       been doing with A, and B lies about A forcing his way into her room. A is jealous,
       and tells A-3 that B has slept with him.

G25   A-3 accuses A of being bad at his job as a spy, and threatens him with death. A-5 goes   THREAT (A-3: A)
       out, and A makes nasty remarks to B, who is angry. A-9 is secretly watching this. A
       realises that A-3 doesn't want him to go to A-6.

G26   A starts to go out, but is blocked by A-5s. A-3 and B leave. A makes crazy bids and   TRAP/ESC (A-5: A)
       disrupts auction, and A-6 take him away as A-9 makes a phone call.

G27   In A-6 car A identifies himself as a murderer. A-6 call in and are told to take A to   EXPLANATION (A-9: A)
       airport. A protests. At airport, A-9 explains that they know he is innocent, and that
       AX doesn't exist. They are to go to Mount Rushmore where A-3 has house and is
       about to leave country. A doesn't want to help, but A-9 says B is their agent, and A-
       3 must be prevented from realizing this, as she could be killed. At Mt. Rushmore,
       A and A-9 discuss the problem of A-3 knowing that B is in love with a government
       agent A. In restaurant, A offers to let A-3 get away in exchange for B

G28   B comes up and says she is leaving, and when A tries to stop her, she resists and   START (A-6, A, B: A-5)
       shoots him. B gets away in car. A-3 and A-5 watch as A is pronounced dead and body
       is taken away by A-9.

G29   A is taken to meeting with B in forest that she has asked for. B apologizes for the way   EXPLANATION (B, A-9: A)
       she has treated A. She explains that she fell in love with A-3, and was recruited by
       CIA. B is loving to A, but has to get back to A-3. She reveals that she has to leave the
       country with A-3. A-9 comes up and says the deception was to force A-3 to take B
       with him.

G30   A is angry, and when he tries to stop B, who is upset, leaving, A-9 has A-6 man knock   TRAP/ESC (A-6: A)
       him out. A is locked in hospital room, where radio reveals that he is supposed to be
       critically ill. A-9 comes in and says A will have to stay locked up, as B is about to
       leave. A escapes through window and into next room.

G31   A climbs up outside, and sees runaway ready, A-5 go in, and A-3 with B in lounge.   BASETRAP/ESC (A-5: B)
       B explains to A-3 why she had to shoot A.   A-3 says he will now be free to devote
       himself to her. A-5 asks for a word to A-3 in private, and B goes upstairs. A tries to
       get B's attention, but fails as A-5 hears noise. A-5 parades suspicions about B, and
       shoots A-3 with her gun. A-3 hits him, but covers up when B comes out of room
       momentarily. A-3 says to A-5 that they will take her on plane and throw her out,
       without B hearing.

G32   A explains how he got away, and A and B abandon car at locked gate.   PURSUIT (A-5: A, B)

G33   A and B are on top of monument with no way out. A-3 and A-5s are coming. A and   FINALTRAP (A-5: A,B)
       B climb down, pursued by A-5. As A and B hide, A proposes to B. A-5 jumps on A
       with knife, but A throws him over. A-5 grabs statue from B, who falls off. As A holds
       B's hand and tries to pull her up, A-5 steps on A's other hand. A-6 at top, who have
       captured A-3, shoot A-5, and A pulls B up into train berth as his wife. Train goes into
       tunnel.

In the wider film world, things had moved on since 1942. Although Hitchcock was early in the field with his "psychological" films, which became one of the components of *film noir*, that trend also had other new aspects, such as the treacherous female lead. A shade of this sort of character is present in the B (Eve Kendall) in *North by North-West*. The fact that the heroine appears to love the villain as well as the hero at various points is an added element, and this presumably derives from the plot of *Notorious* (1946). But the major innovation in the structure of this film is that the START situation is in the middle of the film. For the first part of the film, the hero is threatened by the villains, for reasons that neither he nor the audience knows. So this section is a variant of *The Man Who Knew Too Much* plot, or more closely that of *The Lady Vanishes*, in which the heroine, B, does not know why the mysterious woman, BX, has vanished. In

North by North-West the mysterious person AX does not exist, which is a quite new idea in Hitchcock's dramaturgy. After the START finally arrives, the general structure becomes that of the *Thirty-Nine Steps* type, with the protagonist threatened by both the villains and the police. Indeed, the film could have begun at that point. This switch necessitates a scene with an elaborate EXPLANATION after the START. Later, after what can be considered a second START, which is a variant of the START of *Foreign Correspondent*, the plot switches back to the simpler type in which the hero is under threat from the villains alone, and this switch again demands another EXPLANATION. These explanations involve the character called "The Professor", who largely stands outside the action and manipulates its events, in a way that almost demands the interpretation that he stands in for the creator of the film.

Torn Curtain is generally considered to be the weakest of the series, and the main reasons for this can be seen from by my analysis.

H1	Ostfjord, Norway. Frozen scientists on floating conference.	INTRO
H2	A is in bed making love with his assistant and mistress B.	LOVE (A: B)
H3	A and B then quarrel about getting married.	QUARREL (A: B)
H4	A telegram comes for A, but he pretends it is not for him. Later he secretly gets it, and send answer.	DECEPTION (A: B)
H5	In Copenhagen, B answers phone and gets message to pick up book. A-3 Scientist intercepts message and goes with B to get book. Bookshop owner cautions B. A goes into lav and decodes message.	MISSION (A-9: A)
H6	A tell B he has to go to Stockholm for science job. B is upset and suspicious. She wants to come. A gives her the brushoff.	XLOVE (A: B)
H7	B finds out A is going to East Germany. B follows him on same plane. A tells her to get out and go home.	PURSUIT (B: A)
H8	At Berlin airport A-3 is surprised by B's presence. A says she just followed him. A-3 welcomes A to East Germany as a defector. B is stunned. B is offered chance to stay with A. At Press Conference, American journalists ask A if he has defected because his AntiMissile project has been cancelled. A says that US does not want to prevent nuclear war. A has defected to produce ABM for Commies to abolish war.	DECEPTION (A: A-5, Journalists)
H9	In hotel B accuses A of treachery. B pledges love to A, and asks to be taken home.	QUARREL (B: A)
H10	Next morning, B gets letter from A telling her to go home.	XLOVE (A: B)
H11	A sneaks out, tracked by A-5. A gives A-5 the slip and takes taxi to farm house.	PURSUIT (A-5: A)
H12	A gives secret Pi sign to B-2 who directs him to A-2 in field. A-2 reveals that A's defection is fake. A tells A-2 that X is in head of Prof. Lindt in Leipzig. A arranges escape.	START (A: A-2, X)
H13	A-5 arrives and tells A he will report him. A-5 has noticed Pi sign, and questions him, saying he knows about the Pi organization. B-2 and A kill A-5.	TRAP/ESC (A-5: A, B-2) [KILL (B-2, A: A-5)]
H14	Back at hotel, B tells A and Minister that she wants to stay with A. Minister says A-5 is missing.	HELP (B: A, A-3)
H15	In Leipzig A gets new minder H. A is contacted by A-4, who is the escape expert. A tells A-4 that B does not know of the plan. A reveals his plan to get X out of Prof L.	EXPLANATION (A: A-4)
H16	Taxi driver tells A-5 about farm, A etc.	INFO (taxidriver: a-5)
H17	A is queried by Commie scientists, but H asks him about his visit to farm. A-3 wants to stop session, but ProfL insists on questioning B. B refuses to answer about ABM experiment, and denounces A's treachery, then leaves. Outside, A-3 pleads with B to answer, but she refuses.	NOTHELP (B: A-3)

H18	A goes apart to plead with B, and tells her of his plan. They kiss. A briefs her about what to ask Prof L.	EXPLANATION (A: B) [LOVE (B: A)]
H19	A-5 find clues at farm.	INFO (farm: A-5)
H20	B has talked to Prof L and got him interested. A updates A-4, and she tells him to be at her clinic tomorrow. ProfL arranges meeting with A next morning.	DECEPTION (B: ProfL)
H21	A-5 dig up farm.	INFO (farm: A-5)
H22	B is with A-4 who gets news about police find.	INFO (Pi: A-4)
H23	A is with Prof L and describes his work. Prof L corrects it, and so reveals X. Message comes in of hunt for A and B. Prof L realises he has been tricked, but A gets away.	DECEPTION (A: ProfL)
H24	A and B get to A-4, and all escape on bicycles.	PURSUIT (A-5: A, B, A-4)
H25	Pi puts them in fake regular bus for Berlin. They fool roadblock, and also bandit troops. The real bus comes up, but everyone gets away before the police realise it.	TRAP/ESC (A-5: A, B) [IMPERSONATION (A,B: A-5)
H26	A and B ask the way to meeting point, and are accosted by A-8 who wants to get to USA, and who recognizes them. A-8 gets them to contact in Post Office. They get it just before police come. A-8 stops police and is arrested. Pi representative meets them outside, and tells them they will go out with Czech ballet.	HELP (A-8: A, B)
H27	At theatre, Ballerina spots them as spies, and police trap come and trap them. A shouts "fire", and they get backstage to contact who hides them in baskets.	TRAP/ESC (A-5: A, B)
H28	As boat docks in Sweden, Ballerina sees contact talking to baskets, and stops the crane. Guards shoot baskets, but A and B were in other baskets, and swim ashore with contact. He explains that he noticed Ballerina was watching him and suspected them. A and B are united under blanket.	FINALTRAP/ESC (A-5: A, B)

The major defect of this plot is that the hero's motivations seem perverse for quite some distance into the film. This necessitates a fair amount of EXPLANATION, which is always best minimized. Secondly, he is only under threat from the villains, which, although not unique in the series, has been demonstrably less successful as a structure when tried on previous occasions. Outside the bounds of the present analysis, it is worth remarking that even in 1966 it was difficult to believe that East Germany was stuffed full of rebels against the Communist system.

Across this series of films, we can see new situations being added to the basic list from time to time, so the notion that their plots were obtained purely by rearranging situations that were all present in the first couple of them is quite mistaken.

The Larger View

Outside of the Plotto method, there are some other generalizations that can be made about the plots of these films. The first is that they differ as to whether the protagonist is being pursued by the police, or by the villains, or by both. In *The Man Who Knew Too Much*, *The Lady Vanishes*, *Foreign Correspondent*, and *Torn Curtain*, the hero is only really in danger from the villains, while in *Young and Innocent* he is

only in danger from the police. But in *The Thirty-Nine Steps*, *Saboteur*, *North by North-West*, and *Secret Agent*, he is menaced by both the villains and the police, though only in a weak kind of way in the last of these.

A somewhat less obvious classification is in terms of the person of mystery (AX or BX) who is at the heart of the intrigue, and who possesses the secret or MacGuffin, X. In the original models for the series, *The Man Who Knew Too Much*, and *The Thirty-Nine Steps*, these characters die at the beginning of the film. In *The Lady Vanishes* and *Foreign Correspondent*, BX and AX are on the side of good, and survive the picture, in *Torn Curtain* there is no AX, and in *North by North-West*, AX is a fiction. In *Saboteur*, *Young and Innocent*, and *Secret Agent*, there is also no AX in the simple sense, though the villain, A-3, does to some extent act as a mysterious person, since their true identity is unknown to the hero. A more subtle distinction is in how the heroine relates to the hero throughout the length of the plot, with degrees of acceptance and rejection varying over time, and also forming different patterns from film to film. In most of the films, the heroine is antagonistic to the hero when they first meet. Then there are fluctuations in their relationship until they are fully united at the end of the film. The exceptions to this are *The*

Man Who Knew Too Much, in which the hero and heroine are happily married at the beginning, and *Torn Curtain*, in which the heroine has a fairly settled relationship with the hero at the beginning. In the first of these films there is a small amount of tension between them at various points subsequently, and a great deal in the latter film.

These last considerations are important for the project of creating our own new Hitchcock plot. The most trivial method for creating an apparently new plot out of the Hitchcock examples is to change the sexes of the characters, and the details of the existing situations, and that has inevitably been done in recent times. Take *The Net* (1995). But for something

a really different, more manipulation is needed.

The simplest and crudest method is to make a series of random selections from the collection of Hitchcock situations, without creating a chain by the use of the carry-on or lead-up situations actually occurring in the films. Surprisingly, this can be made to work, as I will demonstrate. The following series of situations were selected successively by random choice from the complete corpus, but leaving out the FINALTRAP situations. Since some types of situation (e.g. TRAP/ESC) occur in greater total number than others, these are inevitably more likely to be selected. A series of 25 situations were chosen using a random number generator.

B6	A trapped on train by A-6. A appeals to B for help. B rejects him and gives him away to A-6. A escapes from train by a trick.	TRAP/ESC (A-6: A) [NOTHELP (B: A)]
D10	B goes into transport cafe to find coat. Truck driver tells her Old Will (A-2) has it and can be found at Nobby's lodging house in Dorchester. Other drivers try to stop him, and a fight breaks out.	NOTHELP (drivers: B)
G28	B comes up and says she is leaving, and when A tries to stop her, she resists and shoots him. B gets away in car. A-3 and A-5 watch as A is pronounced dead and body is taken away by A-9.	DECEPTION (A-6: A-5)
D15	A-6 hunt them in forest.	PURSUIT (A-6: A: B)
B14	A hides in political meeting. A is mistaken for politician. A impersonates politician.	IMPERSONATION (A: politician)
C7	A and A-2 get A-4 to climb mountain with them the next day.	DECEPTION (A, A-2: A-4)
G9	At US Intelligence agency, A-9 and associates discuss how A has been mistaken by A-5s for the non-existent AX. AX has been created to draw attention away from their own agent working under A-3's nose. One associate worries what will happen to A with both the A-5s and A-6 after him, but A-9 says they will just have to let it go to protect their agent.	EXPLANATION (A-9:A-5)
H16	Taxi driver tells police about farm, A etc.	INFO (taxidriver: a-5)
A8	A and A-2 go to Wapping. A and A-2 find A-5 from X. A enters A-5 headquarters. A sees A-3. A-7 traps A. A incapacitates A-7. A impersonates A-7. A-5 and A-3 arrange assassination. A overhears this.	BASETRAP/ESC (A-5: A) [ATTACK (A: A-7) IMPERSONATION (A: A-7)]
D7	B brings food to A in mill. B says she only came back to give him his money back. A asks for her help in getting to the transport caf, where he left his coat. A tells B he only did dead woman a good turn in Hollywood, and is not her lover.	HELP (B: A)
A4	A-6 ask A and B about X. A threatens A-6. A-6 release A and B.	NOTHELP (A: A-6)
G19	B gets message from A-5 in next phone booth. A comes out, and B tells A that AX will meet him at prairie stop. A wants to arrange another meeting with her, but she lies about the A-6 coming, and A leaves.	DECEPTION (B: A)
E9	A , A-2, B, and A-6 come back to mill and find it empty, with no trace of AX and A-5. A man claims he has been there alone all day. No-one believes A . A-2 sees man in mill acting suspiciously.	NOTHELP (A-6: A)
H21	A-5 dig up farm.	INFO (farm: A-5)

E21	A-2 tells F-B that B has been kidnapped and she will be swapped for AX. A-3 rings F-B to tell him that he must come to help get AX to talk before F-B goes to America.	DECEPTION (A-2: F-B)
D14	A-6 stop car and recognize A. B and A escape and drive off.	TRAP/ESC (A-6: A, B)
G29	A is taken to meeting with B in forest that she has asked for. B apologizes for the way she has treated A. She explains that she fell in love with A-3, and was recruited by CIA. B is loving to A, but has to get back to A-3. She reveals that she has to leave the country with A-3. A-9 comes up and says the deception was to force A-3 to take B with him.	EXPLANATION (B, A-9: A)
F9	A comes to the isolated cabin of a blind man (A-8), who makes him welcome. A gives a false name, but A-8 detects his handcuffs. A-8's niece B comes in, and says A-6 are looking for A. A tries to conceal handcuffs, but B sees them. B wants to give A up to A-6, but A-8 says he thinks A is innocent, and tells B to take A to blacksmith friend to get handcuffs off.	HELP (A-8: A)
E18	B comes in and worries about A's safety. B, primed by A-2, suggests taking A to country.	DECEPTION (A-2: B)
B10	A comes to A-3 house. A tells A-3 of BX. A-3 protects A from A-6. A-3 reveals he is A-3 to A. A-3 shoots A. A escapes by luck.	BASETRAP/ESC (A-5: A)
E3	At political meeting arranged by F-B for AX, A meets and is attracted to B, daughter of F-B.	LOVE (A: B)

Although there is not always consistency of characters across from one situation to the next, this can be easily adjusted, just as it is in William Wallace Cook's *Plotto* method. However, there are more serious inconsistencies in time sequence and causality towards the end of the selected series, and it is impossible to use the last four situations while making any sense of the plot. This will always tend to happen towards the latter part of any series of pre-existing situations put together by such a crude method. Even if one uses the next more sophisticated method, which involves chaining forwards (or backwards) from one initial situation by selecting one of the types of situation that is found to follow the initial type chosen from within the collection of Hitchcock "chase" situations, I can assure you that the same problem arises there.

Nevertheless, I will show that by dropping these last four situations in the sequence above, starting with F9 – "A comes to the isolated cabin of a blind man....", one can get a plausible plot. So making character changes for consistency, putting an INTRO at the beginning which indicates the background and

	A and B work in university biolaboratory under AX on supervirus. AX warns A that A-5 are after them both, because they want supervirus X.	INTRO
B6	A trapped in canteen by A-5. A appeals to B for help. B rejects him and gives him away to A-5. A escapes from canteen by a trick.	TRAP/ESC (A-6: A) [NOTHELP (B: A)]
D10	A goes into car park to look for X in AX's car. Attendant tells him B has it and can be found at B's flat. Other attendants try to stop attendant telling him, and a fight breaks out.	NOTHELP (drivers: B)
G28	B says she is going to US Military Bioweapons, and when AX tries to stop her, she resists and injects him with drug. B gets away. A-5 watch as AX is pronounced dead and body is taken away.	START (A-6, A, B: A-5)
D15	A-6 hunt B in subway.	PURSUIT (A-6: A, B)
B14	B hides in cosmetics show. B is mistaken for cosmetics demonstrator. B impersonates cosmetics demonstrator.	IMPERSONATION (A: politician)
C7	A tricks A-4 into giving him info on AX.	DECEPTION (A, A-2: A-4)

G9	At US Military Bioweapons, A-3 and associates discuss how B has been mistaken by A-6s for the killer of AX. AX has been abducted to get X out of him. One associate worries what will happen to B with A-6 after her, but A-3 says they will just have to let it go to protect themselves.	EXPLANATION (A-9:A-5)
H16	Taxi driver tells A-6 where B was going.	INFO (taxidriver: A-5)
A8	A goes to US Military Bioweapons. A finds A-5 from A-4 info. A enters A-5 headquarters. A sees A-3. A-7 traps A. A incapacitates A-7. A impersonates A-7. A-5 want to stage fake terrorist attack with X. A overhears this.	BASETRAP/ESC (A-5: A) [ATTACK (A: A-7) IMPERSONATION (A: A-7)]
D7	B brings food to A in B-2's flat. B says she accidentally gave AX the injection. A asks for her help in getting to the place where AX is.	HELP (B: A)
A4	A-6 ask A about B. A threatens A-6. A-6 release A.	NOTHELP (A: A-6)
G19	B gets message from A-5 in next phone booth. A comes out, and B tells A that AX is at industrial unit. A wants to arrange another meeting with her, but she lies about the A-5 coming, and A leaves.	DECEPTION (B: A)
E9	A and A-6 come to industrial unit and find it empty, with no trace of AX and A-5. A man claims he has been there alone all day. A-6 do not believe A. A realises that B tricked him.	NOTHELP (A-6: A)
H21	A-6 search B's flat.	INFO (farm: A-5)
E21	A tells A-5 that B has been kidnapped and she will be swapped for AX. A-5 rings A-3 to tell him that he must come to help get AX to talk so A-5 can get X to stage fake terrorist attack.	DECEPTION (A-2: A-3)
D14	A-5 stop car and recognize A. A escapes and drive off.	TRAP/ESC (A-6: A, B)
G29	A comes to meeting with B in forest that she has asked for. B apologizes for the way she has treated A. She explains that she fell in love with A-3, and was recruited by A-5. B is loving to A, but has to get back to A-3. She reveals that she has to go to US Military Bioweapons with A-3. A-3 comes up and says the deception was to allow A-3 to take AX with him.	EXPLANATION (B, A-9: A)
A15	A-5 comes to US Military Bioweapons. A-6 trap A-3, A-5. A-3, A-5 shoot at A-6. A escapes and gets AX. A-3 sends A-5 to get AX. A-5 injures A. A-5 traps AX in lab. B kills A-5. A-3 kills himself with supervirus. A, B, AX are reunited.	FINALTRAP (A-6, A, B: A-5)

At this point I have to admit that producing consistency in the plot by character shuffling and tweaking details of the action took several days, off and on, using my meat computer, but I hope you agree that the result is a workable plot. And it has the innovative feature that the hero and heroine are simultaneously, but separately, pursued from the beginning by the villains and the police respectively. Ideally, it would continue on from situation G29 for a bit longer with the police and the villains joining forces to pursue the now united trio of hero, heroine, and figure of mystery, before the latter emerge triumphant. This would also take care of the fact that, at the moment, the story would probably run for about 70 minutes of screen time.

Eliminating the constructional scaffolding, and presenting the story in more conventional form, I get the following:-

Arthur Todd and Betty Furan work in a New York university biolaboratory under Alex Cross on a potential supervirus. Alex Cross warns Arthur Todd that the CIA are after them both, because they want the supervirus.

Arthur Todd is trapped in the university canteen by CIA. Arthur Todd appeals to Betty Furan for help. Betty Furan rejects him and gives him away to CIA. Arthur Todd escapes from canteen behind a cloud of steam he creates by tipping water into a pan of hot oil.

Arthur Todd goes into car park to look for the supervirus in Alex Cross's car. Attendant tells him Betty Furan has it and it can be found at Betty's flat. Other attendants try to stop attendant telling him, and a fight breaks out.

Betty Furan says she is going to US Military Bioweapons, and when Alex Cross tries to stop her, she resists and in doing so injects him with a drug from a handy syringe. Betty Furan gets away. CIA watch as Alex Cross is pronounced dead and body is taken away.

The police hunt Betty Furan, who is still wearing her white lab coat, in subway.

Betty Furan gets out of subway into a big store. There is a special cosmetics event going on, and Betty Furan is mistaken for a cosmetics demonstrator. She successfully impersonates a cosmetics demonstrator, despite some amusing blunders, which she quickly corrects.

Arthur Todd tricks the head of the university virology department into giving him info on who has been in contact with Alex Cross.

At US Military Bioweapons, Thomas Malone and his associates in the Special Methods unit of the CIA discuss how Betty Furan has been mistaken by the police for the killer of Alex Cross. Alex Cross has been abducted to get the supervirus out of him. One associate worries what will happen to Betty Furan with the police after her, but Thomas Malone says they will just have to let it go to protect themselves.

A taxi driver tells the police where Betty Furan was going.

Arthur Todd goes to US Military Bioweapons. Arthur Todd finds CIA Special Methods unit with information he got. Arthur Todd enters CIA area of lab. Arthur Todd sees Thomas Malone. A lab technician traps Arthur. Arthur Todd incapacitates the lab technician by sticking his head in a fume cupboard containing noxious gas. Arthur Todd impersonates the lab technician. CIA discuss staging fake terrorist attack with the supervirus, and Arthur Todd overhears this.

Betty Furan brings food to Arthur Todd in her flat. Betty says she accidentally gave Alex Cross the injection. Arthur Todd asks for her help in getting to the place where Alex Cross is.

The police ask Arthur Todd about Betty Furan. Arthur Todd threatens the police with CIA, and the police release him.

Betty Furan gets message from CIA man in next public phone booth. Arthur Todd comes out, and Betty Furan tells Arthur Todd that Alex Cross is at an industrial unit in the suburbs. Arthur Todd wants to arrange another meeting with her, but she lies about the CIA coming, and Arthur Todd leaves.

Arthur Todd and the police come to industrial unit and find it empty, with no trace of Alex Cross and CIA. A man claims he has been there alone all day. The police do not believe Arthur Todd. Arthur Todd realises that Betty Furan tricked him.

The police search Betty's flat.

Arthur Todd tells CIA that Betty Furan has been kidnapped and she will be swapped for Alex Cross. CIA ring Thomas Malone to tell him that he must come to help to get Alex Cross to talk so CIA can get supervirus to stage fake terrorist attack.

CIA stop car and recognize Arthur driving it. Arthur Todd escapes and drive off.

Arthur Todd comes to meeting with Betty Furan in a theme park that she has asked for. Betty Furan apologizes for the way she has treated Arthur. She explains that she fell in love with Thomas Malone, and was recruited by CIA. Betty Furan is loving to Arthur, but has to get back to Thomas Malone. She reveals that she has to go to US Military Bioweapons with Thomas Malone. Thomas Malone comes up and says the deception was to allow Thomas Malone to take Alex Cross with him. They all go to US Military Bioweapons.

The CIA Special Methods Unit people comes to US Military Bioweapons. The police trap Thomas Malone and his CIA men. Thomas Malone and the CIA shoot at the police. Arthur Todd escapes and gets Alex Cross. Thomas Malone sends CIA man to get Alex Cross. CIA man injures Arthur. CIA man and Thomas Malone trap Alex Cross in lab. Betty Furan kills CIA man. Thomas Malone kills himself with supervirus. Arthur, Betty, and Alex Cross are reunited.

Plotto Out in the World

Plotto seems to have sold very well, and indeed there was a second edition published in 1942. In modern terms, the *Plotto* list of conflicts or situations represents a database, with the conflict, its serial number, and the serial numbers of the lead-up and follow-on conflicts associated with it forming one record in a database. The rules for joining the conflicts together to form a plot by forwards and backwards chaining are very simple indeed, and practically all that would be necessary to make a plot-generating program out of it is the tedious task of keying in the data. I don't think this is worthwhile, since in the first place its collection of conflicts or situations in *Plotto* is not sufficiently large and varied for contemporary use. There are also some errors in the *Plotto* data. A small number of the follow-on and lead-up numbers for the conflicts are wrong – that is, when they are used the resulting section of the new plot doesn't make any sense. Also, there are a fair number of sequences in which after several iterations of the chaining process, an infinite loop forms, with two or three conflicts being repeated indefinitely. These defects are even more marked in one of the computer programs to generate plots inspired by *Plotto* that appeared in the 'nineties. This was *Plots Unlimited*. In this program, even one of the examples of plots that it generates which is quoted in the manual doesn't make sense, and as well as that the program's database of conflicts is much more restricted than that of *Plotto*. *Plots Unlimited* has been updated and now goes under the name of *Storybase*, but I have no reason to think it is any more proficient at plot generation. My conclusion is that the best use of *Plotto* is as a

very general suggestion of methods for generating plots, as I have just done, and as I believe Hitchcock did.

In fact, whether they were influenced by *Plotto* or not, the general approach to plot construction by shuffling around situations from successful films is quite apparent in many Hollywood products. Just to mention some that I have come across recently, the series of "son of Robin Hood" films made by Columbia from the late forties into the fifties use many of the situations from the famous Warner Bros. film *The Adventures of Robin Hood* (1938). In particular, *Rogues of Sherwood Forest* (1950) contains most of the situations in the original, but in a different order, and bracketed between quite different starting and concluding situations.

Another investigation that started when I was at the Slade back in the nineteen-seventies was into shot length patterns.

When I found widely different distribution profiles for the amount of usage by different directors of the various scales of shot -- Close Up, Medium Close Up, Medium Shot, Medium Long Shot, and so on, the obvious thing to do was to investigate the amount of usage of different shot lengths within a film: i.e. to find how many shots there were with lengths less than one foot, with lengths between one foot and two feet, two feet and three feet, and so on. I knew that the Average Shot Length (ASL) for films varied a great deal, and so I expected that the shape of the distributions of shot lengths for individual films when graphed would also be quite varied, but I was surprised to find that they all had a general family resemblance. This would not have been so surprising if I had been aware of the work done long ago on sentence lengths in literary texts by G. Udny Yule (*On Sentence Length as a Statistical Characteristic of Style in Prose* Biometrika XXX 1938 p. 363) and subsequently others.

My initial guess, based on films with rather longer Average Shot Lengths (circa 15 seconds), was that the distributions were fairly close to the Poisson distribution, with some deviation from that for films with short average shot lengths. (The only statistical distributions that physicists automatically learn about are the Normal distribution and the Poisson distribution.) But I had the sense to consult the Statistics Department at University College, and they put me onto Lawrence Baxter, who was just completing his Ph.D. there. He was interested in films, and introduced me to other distributions such as the Lognormal and Weibull. There followed the most congenial and exciting collaboration I have ever had. After more investigation under Lawrence Baxter's guidance, my feeling was that the Lognormal distribution seemed to provide the best fit for most distributions of shot length. I passed some of my data on to Valerie Isham, a lecturer at University College, and she had Wai Ling Chang, one of her final year undergraduate students run it through their statistical computer packages. This more or less confirmed my conclusions. In the last twenty years, working on my own, I have collected tabulations of shot lengths for more films, giving results for 28 complete films altogether, plus results for sections of about 30 minutes length from 10 other films. I reanalysed everything myself, and started a piece on the subject several years ago, but dropped it because I could not get a really striking conclusion for it. I still haven't got that, but I think the work is quite important enough to publish, particularly given that there is a new interest from other people in shot length statistics.

THE NUMBERS SPEAK

16 3 6 21 4 21 11 27 13 10 9 9 15 10 21 7 5 7 13 6 8 9 5 7 6 5 3 5 2 9 3 9

9 8 3 4 2 3 3 3 2 2 2 4 3 4 6 4 4 1 2 1 2 3 2 1 2 4 2 6 2 10 4 6 3 7

11 26 73 5 2 3 2 6 8 11 7 16 2 3 1 14 8 6 6 8 4 2 12 19 3 7 6 2 3 7 3

4 2 9 3 10 4 5 2 3 14 15 3 7 9 2 10 4 12 116 3 16 9 4 2 3 3 6 21 7 14 5 10

This may look like a meaningless jumble of numbers at first sight, but look at it again. The numbers in the second row are nearly all appreciably smaller than those in the first row. There are also a few brief sequences of the same numbers, such as three threes and three twos in the second row. These latter are less significant than you might think. The numbers actually represent a series of shot lengths in the middle of *The Adventures of Robin Hood* (1938), and their lengths have been recorded to the nearest foot of 35 mm. film. In fact, the real lengths of the shots making up the sequence of three shots in the second row with nominal two foot length are 39 frames, 34 frames, and 33 frames. That is, two feet plus seven frames, two feet plus two frames, and two feet plus one frame, since there are 16 frames for each foot of 35 mm film. In films in general it is extremely rare to find two shots next to each other with exactly the same length, to the very frame.

Another point about the sequence of numbers at the beginning of this piece, which is less obvious, is that there are more small numbers that big numbers. There are only 28 shot lengths in double figures out of the total of 128. More importantly, there are only 52 shots greater in length than the average shot length (ASL) for the sequence, which is 6.4 feet, whereas there are 70 shots shorter than this average.

There is greater significance in this series of shot lengths if we look at the scenes in which they occur. The sequence

16 3 6 21 4 21 11 27 13 10 9 9

corresponds to the tavern scene in which Lady Marion goes to Robin Hood's men to organize an attempt to rescue him. The ASL for the scene is 13.3 feet, which is much longer than the overall ASL for the whole film of 7.15 feet.

The next section is:

15 10 21 7 5 7 13 6 8 9

which makes up the beginning of the execution scene. Here we see the VIP stand in the town square with the bad guys gloating over Robin's impending death. The ASL for this scene speeds up from the previous scene to 10.1 feet, though still longer than the average.

Then follows an increase in the excitement of the crowd and the dramatic tension accompanied by faster cutting as Robin is brought into the square and led onto the gallows:

5 7 6 5 3 5 2 9 3 9 9 8 3 4 2 3 3 3 2 2 2 4 3

4 6 4 4 1 2 1

The ASL here is 4.13 feet.

The next section of the scene starts with the first of the arrows fired by Robin's men to kill his executioners, and continues with his escape and the resulting chaos in the square. The shot lengths are

2   3   2   1   2   4   2   6   2   10   4   6

and the high speed of the action is accompanied by even faster cutting, with a sectional ASL of 3.66 feet.

The next section is, strictly speaking, a new scene, as it takes place in a different part of the town to the three previous sections, which are all set in the town square. So as Robin and his band flee through the town, and out the town gate, rather surprisingly the cutting rate slows down a bit, with these shot lengths:

6   2   3   7   3   4   2   9   3   10   4   5   2   3   14   15   3   7   9   3

which give a sectional ASL of 5.7 feet. This is still appreciably faster than the overall average for the film, but the longer shots are presumably left entire to show the real natural agility, strength, and grace of the movement of Robin Hood (or rather his double) in riding the end of the rope up the gatehouse, and over the top.

After a fade out and fade in, we come to the scene outside, and then inside, Lady Marion's chamber, as Robin Hood scales the castle wall, and Marion confides her love for Robin to her maid:

7   11   26   73   5   2   3   2   6   8   11   7   16   2   3   1   14   8   6   6   8   4

2   12   19   3   7   2   10   4   12

The ASL for this section of 10 feet, which is of course slower than the average.

Then the real love scene between Robin and Marion follows:

116   3   16   9   4   2   3   3   6   21   7   14   5   10

in which the cutting slows down even further, to an average length of 15 feet, so following the normal expressive pattern of film editing, in which cuts are not allowed to disturb the union of the lovers.

The same sort of expressive variation in cutting rate, depending on the nature of the scene, can also be studied in this book on pages 266-267 for the first episode of the Star Trek television series, and on pages 177, 303 and 308 of *Film Style and Technology* for *The Iron Horse, Liebelei,* and *Letter from an Unknown Woman*.

Turning to the general use of different lengths of shot for different films, this is best investigated by taking the complete sequence of shots in the film and counting the number of shots with lengths between zero and one foot, between one foot and two feet, two feet and three feet, and so on. These divisions of the quantity in question are properly called "class intervals", but the popular name for them is "bins". The handy way to display the results of this enumeration is as a graph of the histogram kind. Histograms are a particular type of bar chart in which the bars are in contact with each other, which signifies that the quantity being described covers a continuous range, and is not just measured in simple integers. For *The Adventures of Robin Hood* we get a graph like that following:

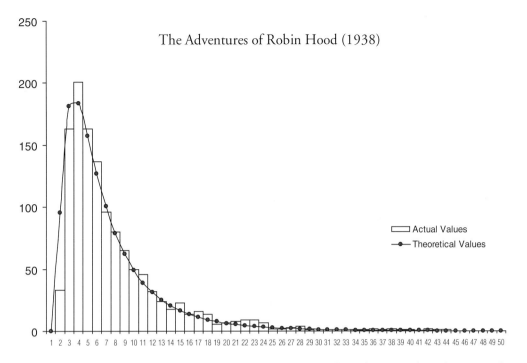

The Adventures of Robin Hood (1938)

Actual Values
Theoretical Values

Number of shots with lengths (in 35 mm. feet) within the given length intervals

The asymmetrical shape of the distribution of shot lengths for *The Adventures of Robin Hood* is described in a broad way by the difference between the mean or average value of length of the 1,254 shots making up the film, which is 7.15 feet, and the median value for the shot lengths; that is, the value that separates the 50% of the shots with larger values from the 50% with smaller values. The median shot length is 5 feet. In other words, most of the shots in the film are shorter than the average shot. (The mean or average only coincides with the median for symmetrical distributions, such as the well-known Normal or Gaussian distribution.) The actual or observed distribution of shot lengths for *the Adventures of Robin Hood* is well fitted by a standard theoretical statistical distribution called the Lognormal distribution. The probability density function $f(x)$ for a shot of any particular length x is given by:

$$f(x) = \frac{1}{x\,\sigma\,(2\pi)^{1/2}} \exp\left\{ \frac{-[\log(x/m)]^2}{2\sigma^2} \right\}$$

where σ is the shape factor, and m is the median value of the distribution.

$f(x)$ multiplied by the number of shots in the film is plotted on the graph above as a continuous line using the values of the median (the scale parameter) and the shape factor, which is the standard deviation of the logarithm of the shot lengths, both obtained from the actual values of the shot lengths for this film. You can see that it corresponds very closely to the actual values. There is a standard method of giving a value to the accuracy of fit between two sets of quantities; in this case the observed and theoretical values for the shot lengths, the latter assuming that the distribution is lognormal. It is called the correlation coefficient, and is best used with its value squared, written R^2, for comparison purposes. If the correspondence was perfect, its value would be 1, but in this case it is 0.956, which is still very good as these things go.

The Lognormal distribution is found to apply to many varied phenomena, particularly in economics. One example of this is the numbers of insurance claims for different amounts of money as a result of damage to motor cars in accidents. But more interestingly to us, it has also been found to apply in literary statistics, where the numbers of sentences of various given lengths in a stretch of prose conforms to the Lognormal distribution. Theoretically, the Lognormal distribution results when the quantity under consideration, in our case shot length, is determined as a result of the probabilities associated with a large number of independent causative factors being multiplied together. In films what is presumably concerned in determining the length of a shot is the simultaneous interaction of such factors in the scene being filmed as how the actor moves in the shot with respect to the closeness of the camera, the length of the lines he speaks, and how the other actors react, and so on. The fact that different individuals are usually responsible for these various components of a film, from the scriptwriter to the director to the editor, assists the independence of these causes.

The generality of the Lognormal distribution for shot lengths in movies is illustrated by some examples from films made between 1916 and 1998.

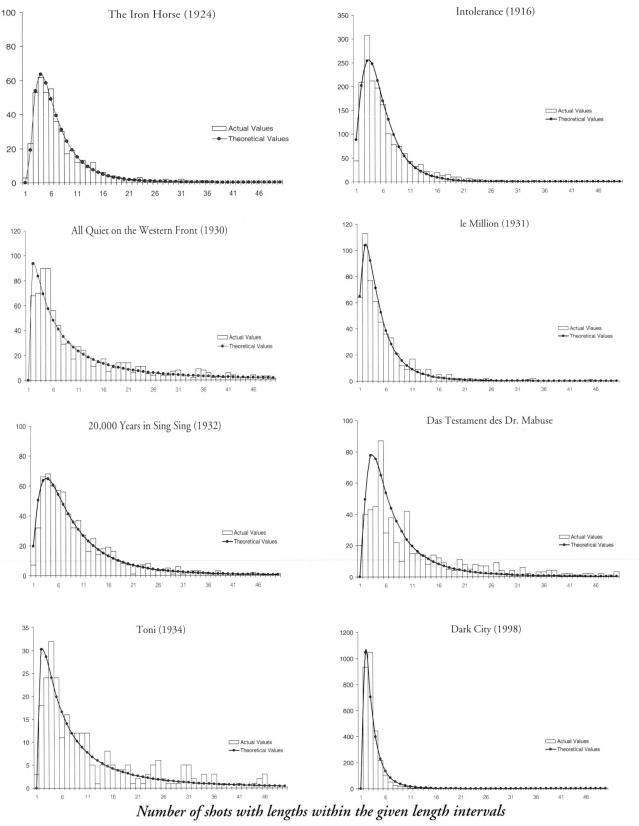

Number of shots with lengths within the given length intervals

These are all taken from the complete lengths of the films, with the exception of *The Iron Horse*, which covers the first 40 minutes of the film. You will notice that nearly all the lengths of shots are recorded either in 35 mm. feet or 16 mm. feet. This is because the prints that came my way in the nineteen-seventies were in both gauges.

More than that, some of the flat-bed editing machines I was using in those days had footage counters that did not indicate lengths to the exact frame, so in many cases I only took the shot lengths to the nearest half foot of film, either in 35 mm. or 16 mm. However, some of the 16 mm. films were measured on an Acmade picture synchronizer, which did have an indicator for frames as well as feet. It might occur to you that mathematical conversion is always possible between the lengths for the different film gauges, but if this is done when the results are only taken to the nearest foot, the consequent rounding introduces an extra unevenness when the resulting distribution is plotted. So I have left the footages in their original form. Finally, *Dark City* was analysed much more recently, using a DVD copy fed into a non-linear editing program on a computer, so the shot lengths are in seconds in that case.

As you can see, these observed results fit well with the Lognormal distribution, and the values for R^2 quoted in the table below confirm this. It is noticeable that the values for the shape factor for most of the films is in the region of 0.7 to 0.9. This is the reason for my assertion long ago in *Film Style and Technology* (p. 225) that given the ASL for a film, one can be fairly certain of the proportion of the shots that will be longer than a certain value, and so on. There are exceptions to this, as here in the case of *Toni* and *Good News,* with shape factors of 1.25 and 1.30, and *Intolerance* and *All Quiet on the Western Front,* where it is down near 0.5. This means that in the former case the distribution is not quite so skewed towards the left, and in the two latter case it is more skewed towards the left: that is, towards the y-axis. The first of these deviations seems to be connected with the long ASLs, around 20 seconds, of these two films. Though the reason for the deviation towards a low value of the shape factor in the case of *Intolerance* and *All Quiet on the Western Front* is obscure to me. So the shape factor seems to be fairly independent of the ASL up to around 20 seconds. The Godard films are in a world of their own.

Title	ASL	Shape Factor (σ)	R²
Intolerance (1916)	6.00	0.529	0.963
The Iron Horse (1924)	6.00	0.708	0.984
All Quiet on the Western Front (1930)	9.30	0.501	0.884
le Million (1931)	13.00	0.754	0.885
20,000 Years in Sing Sing (1933)	6.40	0.829	0.955
Das Testament des Dr. Mabuse (1933)	12.00	0.876	0.948
Toni (1934)	19.00	1.253	0.832
The Adventures of Robin Hood (1938)	5.00	0.783	0.956
Dark City (1998)	1.87	0.811	0.938
Good News (1947)	20.00	1.299	0.760
Carmen Jones (1954)	46.00	0.932	0.206
Black God, White Devil (1964)	21.08	1.670	0.955
Une femme mariée (1964)	21.00	1.309	0.945
Catherine the Great (1934)	8.50	0.792	0.950
The Scarlet Empress (1934)	10.00	0.916	0.728
Vivre sa vie (1962)	20.95	1.339	0.848
Vivre sa vie (reduced)	27.16	1.067	0.839
Week-end (1967)	26.50	2.037	0.898
Week-end (reduced)	38.12	1.847	0.573
Sauve qui peut (la vie) (1980)	6.30		
Sauve qui peut (la vie) (reduced)	19.40	1.642	0.82

For ASLs above 20 seconds, the fitting of the actual shot length distributions to the lognormal distribution is markedly less good, and an example of this is *Carmen Jones* (1954), which has an ASL of 46 seconds, as can be seen from the value of R^2 for goodness of fit in the table above, and the graph with comparative lognormal distribution on the next page.

For *Carmen Jones*, the Gamma distribution proves a slightly better fit (not illustrated), but is still not really good. In any case, films with very long ASLs are only a small minority of all films: in my collection of just over 12,000 Average Shot Lengths, only about 120 are greater than 25 seconds, which is around one film in one hundred.

It is possible to get quite good correlations of observed distributions with the theoretical distribution for films with ASLs of around 20 seconds, as the cases of *Black God, White Devil* (1964) and *Une femme mariée* (1964) demonstrate. The values of R^2 are 0.955 and 0.945 for these two films. Glauber Rocha's *Antonio das mortes* which was made immediately after his *Black God, White Devil*, is very similar indeed in style, and hence statistics, though I am not illustrating it here.

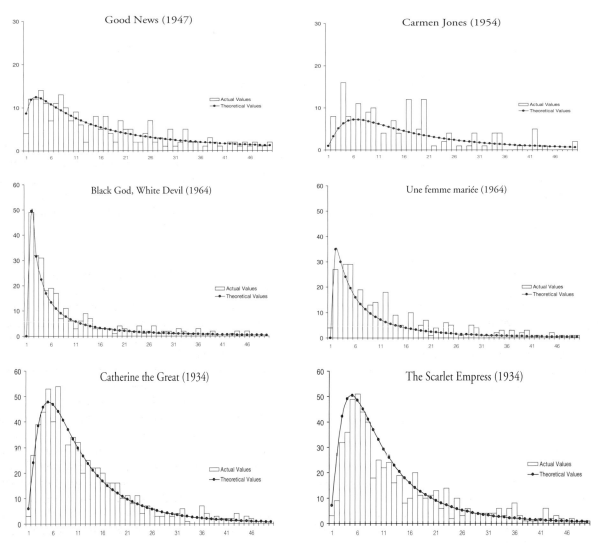

Number of shots with lengths within the given length intervals

The comparison between *The Scarlet Empress* (1934) and *Catherine the Great* (1934) is particularly interesting. These two films, made on the same subject almost simultaneously in the United States and England, have already been compared in other respects in the article *Sternberg's Heart Beats in Black and White* earlier in this book. As far as their shot length distributions are concerned, *Catherine the Great* is an appreciably better fit to the lognormal distribution, as is obvious from a glance at the two distributions, not to mention the values quoted in the table for R^2 on the previous page. Very noticeable in *The Scarlet Empress* graph is the way the numbers of shots of certain lengths are far below the expected value.

This is particularly true of shots of 9 feet, 11 feet, 14 feet, 16 feet, 24 feet, and 26 feet, though there are some other values that are rather low as well. I think this is very probably due to the lengths of the shots in the film being cut to accommodate the regular pulsation of light and dark at the centre of the frame, as is described in *Sternberg's Heart Beats in Black and White;* remember that the main frequency detected there was 160 frames (10 feet), with an occasional double frequency of 80 frames (5 feet), and also a section at 127 frames (7 feet 13 frames). The way this effect is observed in the shot length distribution is a confirmation of the remarkable phenomenon described in that previous article.

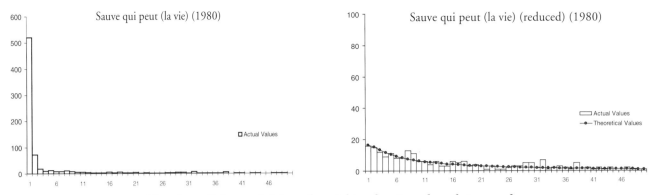

Number of shots with lengths within the given length intervals

Jean-Luc Godard's films mostly conform to the lognormal distribution, despite their peculiarities and large ASLs. The one exception to this is *Sauve qui peut (la vie)*, where the hic-cuping freeze frame effect applied to Nathalie Baye's periodic bicycle excursions are counted as shots. Each series of these has a different equal length for its constituent shots; 8 frames, 10 frames, 11 frames, and so on. The resulting distribution has a extremely large peak for shots of 0 to 1 foot in length, and certainly cannot be fitted by a Lognormal distribution, or indeed any other standard statistical distribution. However, if one does not count these freeze frames as separate shots, the resulting shot length distribution, which I call a "reduced" distribution, is then a pretty satisfactory Lognormal distribu-tion.

One might expect that the apparently random title cards announcing things like "Un film egaré dans le monde" and "Un film trouvé sur le ferroviaire" or more pointedly "???" etc. cut into *Week-end* might disturb its Lognormal purity, but this is not so. If one removes them from the listing of shot lengths, one still gets another Lognormal distribution. Strangely enough, the reverse happens if one removes the many inserts of images from women's magazines cut into *Une femme mariée*. This reduces the film's fit with the Lognormal distribution. For *Vivre sa vie*, which does not have lots of intertitles or insert shots extraneous to the story, but does have two sequences from Dreyer's *Passion of Joan of Arc* cut in when the heroine of the film watches it in the cinema, the fit with the Lognormal distribution is about as good without as with. That is Godard for you. Always perverse.

Inside the Atom

The patterning in shot lengths described in *The Adventures of Robin* Hood is undoubtedly due to a degree of standardization in the way that scenes in a film script are broken down into separate shots when the scene is filmed, and then standardization in the way it is later edited. The standard approach to film script-writing developed from the example of the "well-made play" of the late nineteenth century stage, and here the practice was to alternate sections involving much dramatic tension or action with sections of exposition or light

relief or romance. This happens both within scenes, and also from one scene to the next. Because film scenes are much shorter than play scenes, it often happens that the action in a whole film scene completely falls into one emotional category, but in such cases it is likely to be followed and preceded by a scene of the other kind. Starting from around the First World War, the standard practice in making films from film scripts was to break down scenes (or parts of scenes), involving dramatic tension, and also action scenes, into a large number of shots of short length, while the alternating romantic, or comic, or expository scenes (or parts of scenes), were shot with a smaller number of shots of longer duration. The intention here, which is quite consciously formulated by film-makers, is for an "expressive" intensification of the dramatic material in the film script being filmed.

The way in which there are long strings of shots of fairly similar length in *The Adventures of Robin* Hood, and indeed in other films is best measured by the autocorrelation coefficient, which computes a kind of average over the length of the series for the difference between the size of one value and that of the next in the series, or between one value and the value after the next, or between one value and that two values after the next, and so on. These different degrees of separation give autocorrelation coefficients of the 1st. order, 2nd. order, 3rd. order, and so on. (The terms lag 1, lag 2, lag 3, etc., are also used as alternative names to describe these orders). For sequences in which the successive values are very close indeed to each other, and hence to their average value, the autocorrelation coefficient approaches 1, while for sequences in which each successive value is as different as possible from the one before (i.e., a very large value is always followed by a very small value), the autocorrelation coefficient approaches -1, and for sequences in which the values are distributed completely at random, the autocorrelation coefficient is zero.

When the autocorrelation coefficient is computed it confirms what is usually visible to the experienced eye when it runs down the sequence of actual values of shot lengths in a film, which is that there are a few films which do not conform to the general pattern I have described and illustrated above for *The Adventures of Robin Hood*.

The usual value of the autocorrelation coefficient for films constructed on the standard pattern of shot breakdown ("classical cinema") is around 0.2, or as a statistician would put it, the shot lengths show weak autocorrelation, but there are a few groups of films in my sample for which there is very nearly no autocorrelation at all in shot lengths. Of these, the two Frederick Wiseman films, *Law and Order* and *Hospital* are not fiction features, but *cinéma vérité* documentaries, for which it is no surprise that the standard pattern for fictional films does not hold, as different considerations apply in the shooting and editing of such films. In particular, the notion of varying the cutting rate according to the nature of the scene cannot apply when a single camera is used running continuously all the way through the scene. If multiple cameras were used shooting simultaneously all the way through all the real events recorded in the documentary, it would be possible to impose different cutting rates on different scenes.

For *The Scarlet Empress*, the very peculiar structural principles being used, which I have previously described, have an effect on autocorrelation of shot lengths, but I can think of no reason for the anomalous value for *The Front Page* (1931).

Amongst Jean-Luc Godard's films in the sample, *le Petit soldat* and *Vivre sa vie* have about the usual degree of autocorrelation in their shots lengths, while *Pierrot le fou* is a bit on the low side at 0.110, but *Une femme mariée* and *Week-end* have close to zero autocorrelation. The latter instance is not surprising, given the way that fairly short title cards are stuck into the middle of the long takes that the action of *Week-end* is carried through. In *Une femme mariée*, there are not only the magazine page inserts, but also brief inserts of signs and details of posters making plays on words such as the famous "danger" -- "ange", etc. The result of removing these inserts from the statistics of these two films gives the autocorrelations for these "reduced" versions tabulated at the right. In *Sauve qui peut (la vie)*, the very high autocorrelation of 0.396 results from the chains of equal length freeze frames, but if we remove these, it goes back to a normal 0.146.

Glauber Rocha's *Black God, White Devil* and *Antonio das mortes* were consciously made in a variation of the latest advanced or "art film" style of the period, and to some extent influenced by Godard's work. However, their formal style is very different in the aspect I am considering, for they alternate shots of very long duration with long sequences of very short shots with very similar lengths indeed, and these latter are cut

Title	Auto-correlation
The Iron Horse (1924)	0.290
All Quiet on the Western Front (1930)	0.208
le Million (1931)	0.199
The Front Page (1931)	0.047
La chienne (1931)	0.251
Boudu sauvé des eaux (1932)	0.186
20,000 Years in Sing Sing (1932)	0.133
Das Testament des Dr. Mabuse (1933)	0.163
Toni (1934)	0.228
The Adventures of Robin Hood (1938)	0.174
Dark City (1998)	0.287
Good News (1947)	0.297
Carmen Jones (1954)	0.205
Black God, White Devil (1964)	0.347
Une femme mariée (1964)	0.013
Catherine the Great (1934)	0.116
The Scarlet Empress (1934)	0.052
Law and Order (1969)	0.022
Hospital (1970)	0.062
le Petit soldat (1960)	0.185
Vivre sa vie (1962)	0.169
Vivre sa vie (reduced)	0.164
Pierrot le fou (1965)	0.110
Week-end (1967)	-0.047
Week-end (reduced)	0.050
Sauve qui peut (la vie) (1980)	0.396
Sauve qui peut (la vie) (reduced)	0.146

to length without much regard for the action contained in each shot. It is these sequences with strings of equal length short shots which push the autocorrelation coefficient up to about 0.34 for the whole film, just as happens in Godard's *Sauve qui peut (la vie)*.

Autocorrelation statistics represent the lowest order of Markov chain analysis, which I mentioned as a means of analysis in *Let a Hundred Flowers Bloom*, long ago. The full development of this method requires a complete tabulation of the significant variables for each shot in a film, taken in order.

As noted in the preceding piece, most of my shot length distributions were obtained by examining films shot by shot on editing machines of one kind or another, but my recent results in this area, both for some of the TV programs described elsewhere in this book, and also for the film *Dark City*, have been obtained in a more modern way. This is to digitize the film from a tape or DVD recording into a non-linear editing (NLE) program on a computer, and then work with it there. I use Adobe Premiere, and I go through the film in it putting a marker on each cut or other transition. I then open up the "project file" relating to the film, and in the middle of it, amongst a list of other data relating to the editing of the project, one can find the progressive location of each marker, and hence each cut, measured in frames from the beginning of the film. This will probably work with some other non-linear editing programs, but not with all of them. Unfortunately the cheap NLEs such as U-Lead Video Studio and Pinnacle Studio have project files that are not in ASCII code, but partly in binary code, and in these cases it is impossible to see the values representing the positions of the cuts.

Recently, there has been a leap in interest in shot length patterns in films, and in 2005 Yuri Tsivian and Gunars Civjans set up a web site dedicated to film statistics at *www.cinemetrics.lv* Besides the researches and discussions following their ideas in this area, this site also contains nearly all my results for scale of shot distributions and camera movement. It will probably also contain my database of over 12,000 ASLs at some point in the near future.

Early in 2006, while I was reworking the preceding material, I received an invitation to speak at a conference on slapstick comedy organized by Tom Paulus in Brussels. This event was a follow-up to a conference on American slapstick comedy organized twenty years before in New York by Eileen Bowser, when she was head of the Museum of Modern Art film archive. I readily accepted, as I knew I could enlarge on a point made on page 138 of *Film Style and Technology* about the staging and scene dissection in American slapstick comedies during World War I. I refreshed my memory of the early Sennett films with a couple of hours in the National Film and Television Archive, and selected *A Healthy Neighborhood* to take with me to Brussels a couple of weeks later in the middle of May. Looking at the films again, I also realised that there was something new to be said about movement and gesture in early slapstick as well. I got hold of a pair of DVDs of Griffith Biograph films, and the DVDs of a programme on early cinema selected by myself and put out by the BFI, plus another DVD of Chaplin films. After a bit of frame grabbing and computerised drawing, I made up a Powerpoint slide sequence of stills and diagrams. Then on Friday afternoon I was out of the film school, under the river to Waterloo station, and on to the Eurostar train. This shot me under the Channel, through Lille station (the most sinister railway platforms in the world) and into Brussels in short order. This is the way to travel. The occasion was a kind of tribute to Eileen Bowser, and featured a couple of participants from the original occasion, as well as younger people. Exactly what I said and did around these films and graphic material was as usual impromptu, and when I came back I wrote it up into the following article.

D.W. GRIFFITH SHAPES SLAPSTICK

D.W. Griffith had a strong, and unrecognized, influence on the form of American film slapstick. He was a man lacking a real comic touch, but as everyone knows, Mack Sennett came out of his troupe at Biograph to set up Keystone Studios, and all those years of being in D.W. Griffith's films had an effect on what Sennett subsequently did.

But before Griffith made films, there were Pathé films, and he saw them before he started directing at Biograph. Besides *The Physician of the Castle*, amongst Pathé's biggest hits of 1907-1908 was *le Cheval emballé*.

I have written about this film before, but it is worth reminding you of the use of goings and comings on the Pathé staircase in it, and in other Pathé films. The delivery man goes up the staircase and into a room and back onto the staircase, while his horse is shown in a cross-cut sequence eating the contents of a bag of oats outside a grain shop on the street level. These scenes inside the house are all shot from the same frontal direction. *Le Cheval emballé* was so successful a film that it would have been difficult for film people to avoid seeing it in 1908 in New York, but in any case, Griffith made a version of it at the urging of Mack Sennett and Billy Bitzer under the title of *The Curtain Pole,* later in the year. At that point Griffith had not developed the idea of using side by side spaces shot from the same frontal direction. Ben Brewster has identified *An Awful Moment*, made about a month after *The Curtain Pole*, as the first use of the device, and the next example I know of was *A Wreath in Time,* made another month later, with Mack Sennett in the lead. After that, this layout became more and more frequent in Griffith's scenography.

I have illustrated Griffith's way of shooting scenes in adjoining spaces on page 99 of *Film Style and Technology* with an example from *The Battle,* but here is another example on the next page, from *The Sunbeam* (1912).

1

2

In shots 1 and 2, the little girl leaves her sick mother in their tenement room, and sets off downstairs looking for someone to play with.

In shots 3 and 4, she reaches the ground floor, and accosts a middle-aged spinster in the hallway. The spinster rejects her.

3

4

5

6

After more interaction with the spinster, the little girl approaches a man in the hall, and is rejected again. He goes into his room, shuts the door, and looks angrily back towards it.

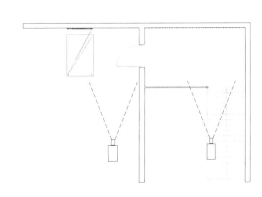

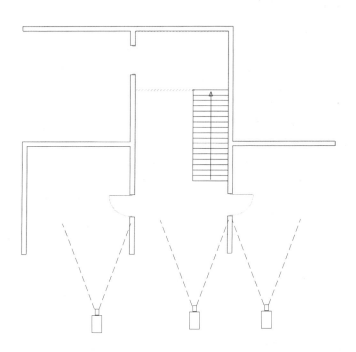

When Sennett, Dell Henderson, George Nichols, and other Griffith actors were allowed to direct at Biograph, it is not particularly surprising that they took up his use of room to room movement in side by side spaces filmed from the front. The only thing surprising about this is that no-one has remarked on it. In Sennett's case, he began directing comedies for Griffith in 1911, and the side by side room staging can be seen in films like *A Convenient Burglar* and *Too Many Burglars*. And then it became the usual way at Keystone of filming scenes taking place in a house with more than one room. A good example from 1913 is *A Healthy Neighborhood*, which Sennett personally directed.

In this film, the comically incompetent Dr. Noodles, played by Ford Sterling, has to give emergency treatment to a girl that his own medicine has made ill. She is in the dining room of her father's house, and then her father rushes out to the right into the adjoining kitchen to get water.

1

2

3

4

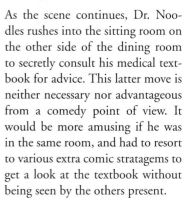

As the scene continues, Dr. Noodles rushes into the sitting room on the other side of the dining room to secretly consult his medical textbook for advice. This latter move is neither necessary nor advantageous from a comedy point of view. It would be more amusing if he was in the same room, and had to resort to various extra comic stratagems to get a look at the textbook without being seen by the others present.

Indeed, this would be the way such a scene would have been done on the stage, from whence the situation comes.

5

6

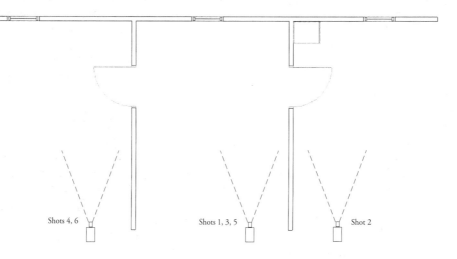

Shots 4, 6   Shots 1, 3, 5   Shot 2

Besides this rushing backwards and forwards several times though these three side-by-side rooms near the climax of the film, there are earlier scenes in Dr. Noodles' surgery, with the action going backwards and forwards from his consulting room to his waiting room, and vice-versa, which are also side-

by-side, and also shot from the same frontal direction. Sennett also throws in a little weak cross-cutting between parallel actions in this and some of his other films, but this is never particularly effective because it is not related to the drive of the plot.

Dr. Noodles' surgery on the left, and his waiting room on the right, are the location for more movement between adjoining spaces filmed from the "front". Dr. Noodles is engaged in a classic stethoscope routine with his pretty patient, but between them, Mack Sennett and Ford Sterling completely destroy the comedy in this routine by going through the moves so fast that the rationale for these moves is completely unrecognizable. And having put a dentist's chair in the doctor's surgery, they also fail to exploit it with some of the standard stage gags involving dentist's chairs.

The most obvious feature of *A Healthy Neighborhood* and *The Riot*, the only Sennett-directed films I have seen from the first two years of the company's existence, is the way they are relentlessly crammed with action and continual movement, so that the detail of the narrative is difficult to follow. It is a matter of "Why the hell is he doing that? " most of the time, to a degree that I have never seen anywhere else in a film. As I have indicated with one instance above, this represents a consistent failure by Sennett to develop and milk a number of viable comedy situations. It is just as well he left most of the directing to others at Keystone.

The Pathé comedies were not the only model available to Mack Sennett through the years from 1908 to 1912, before he developed his own sort of slapstick. The Gaumont company in France also had slapstick units making films from 1906 onwards, but its productions did not feature the use of side by side spaces, or indeed any other specific features that are to be found in the first few years of Keystone production. The Gaumont "Calino" series are mostly constructed from a discontinuous series of scenes each exploiting one basic gag, without the use of any moves or gestures that can be seen taken over into Keystone films. Both Pathé and Gaumont comedies

use undercranking (accelerated motion) to speed up their action at times, from 1909 onwards, but there is no accelerated motion used in the early Keystone period. The total destruction of interior sets, combined with acrobatic tumbling, that is so characteristic of the well-known Gaumont "Onésime" comedy series from 1912 onwards, likewise does not appear in Keystone films, where the violence is focussed on people rather than things.

When Charlie Chaplin came to Keystone at the beginning of 1914, he gradually moved towards a slower style of comedy, against Sennett's resistance. This was a matter of leaving space between the gags to give time for the characters' reactions, and hence their thought processes, to be savoured by the film audience. Not to mention giving the audience time to appreciate the cleverness of the gags, and also the idiosyncrasies of Chaplin's movement style, which also goes on in the spaces between gags. I think Chaplin's success also made it possible for Fatty Arbuckle to develop his own slower style of comedy. One can see Arbuckle trying to do things differently even in his first days at Keystone in 1913, when he was still one of the mob in films like *The Riot*. In this, while everybody else is throwing bombs and bricks in the usual frenetic Keystone way during the climax of the action, Arbuckle is using his own special sort of slowed down graceful pitches to launch his missiles.

When Chaplin started directing, he took up the use of side by side spaces shot from the front that was standard at Keystone, and he took this style with him when he moved to Essanay in 1915, and on to Mutual in 1916.

His New Job provides a good example of this. In this film, the row of side by side spaces are areas of the main stage of a large film studio, though some are separated by either the walls of sets, or actual walls.

402

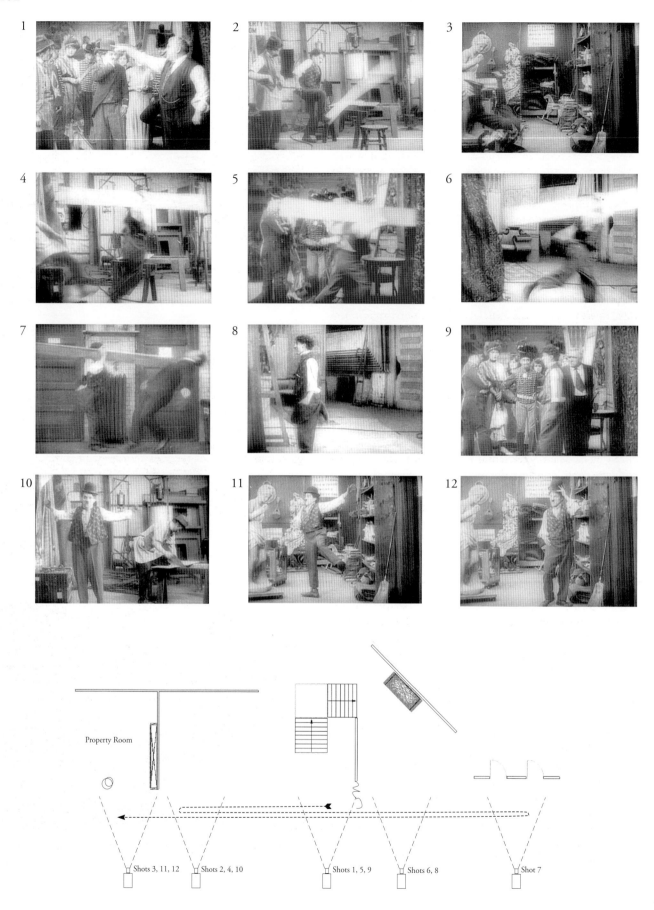

The sequence of events at this point in the film is that Charlie, after a misdemeanour in his new job at the film studio, is sent by the director (frame 1) to help the studio carpenter (frame 2). His attempt to saw a plank of wood flips it at the carpenter, knocking him through the door into the property room (frame 3). The carpenter retaliates by kicking him in the behind after he has picked up the plank (frame 4), which shoots him at high speed right through the shooting area, and then another intermediate space, before knocking down an actor in front of the dressing rooms in frame 7. Charlie then ambles back along his tracks and eventually into the property room, where he is startled by a life-sized female statue (frame 11). He tips his hat to her in frame 12, before his next misadventure starts.

The gag is the repercussions of Charlie's stupidity in handling wood, with the initial knocking over of the carpenter, topped by the exaggerated distance travelled by Charlie with the plank, culminating in the knocking over of another uninvolved person. The basic elements of this can be seen in my earlier examples (and of course hundreds of other films), but the new element is Charlie's leisurely and unconcerned walk back through the stages of his flight, embellished by funny gestures along the way. In frame 8 he does a silly high lift of his leg kicking himself in the behind, and in frame 10 he pauses to stretch as a relief from his exertions, before moving into the prop room and acting in frames 11 and 12 as though the statue was a real woman. The major traditional theories about humour are obviously relevant in this sequence. That is, Charlie's stupid actions giving rise to feelings of superiority in the audience, and the incongruity theory applies to his reaction to the statue, and also to his other unnatural gestures.

All the Right Moves

Chaplin's characteristic gestures of arm and leg had not appeared in other earlier film comedian's performances, though I wouldn't be surprised if they were acquired from other stage comedians. The main point is that he filled up so much screen time with them, in a way that other earlier film comedians did not. And there was more time available, because he was making two reel films, rather than the one-reelers or split reels of earlier film comedies.

In *A Healthy Neighborhood*, Ford Sterling uses a number of funny movements, but some of them are to be found in earlier films. He does a number of agitated runs in exterior scenes, and for these he runs with his legs turned out – with his knees rising to the sides rather than in front as in a normal run. And sometimes in the middle of these runs he does a jump rather than a step from one foot to the other, again with his legs turned out. The same jump can be seen interpolated in the runs of the gendarme in *le Cheval emballé*. The general point about this is that running and jumping with your legs turned out is intrinsically funny, because it is unnatural. This is the incongruity theory of comedy in action again.

Ford Sterling doing a funy turned-out jump while running in A Healthy Neighborhood *(above), and a gendarme doing likewise in* le Cheval emballé *(below).*

This Ford Sterling jump in A Healthy Neighborhood *could be funnier*

NOT FUNNY

FUNNY

A Healthy Neighborhood

Babes in Toyland

Amongst all Sterling's frenetic movement in his surgery, I notice a pose with a momentary position of his hands that later became one of Oliver Hardy's frequent characteristic gestures. There is plenty more analysis to be done in this area.

As Chaplin and others developed their comedy, the actual slapstick action became more and more subordinate to other elements. Besides separating the slapstick gags with charac-teristic perambulations, Chaplin put in more consistent plotting, with dramatic sentiment and love interest, and so did the others, adding real character to the personality of the leading comedians. By the 'twenties, the square-on stagings began to vanish as well, though Buster Keaton developed his own unique and sublime geometries of movement in space. Only Sennett kept the relentless kind of slapstick going.

Terry Hopkins took the photographs to illustrate funny and unfunny jumps after I got back to the London Film School and finished this piece.

So there I am, nearly seventy years later, back where I started, with *Babes in Toyland,* and so this is a good place to stop.

My aim has always been to try to solve the questions about the way the world is, and the way it works, to satisfy my own curiosity, and only after that to make the truth available for others, if they want it. That is what this book is for, and the structuring idea behind it lies somewhere in the wastelands between Jonathan Rosenbaum's *Moving Places*, and Benoit Mandelbrot's *Fractals*. The hardest part of making it has been getting the layout right. Keeping the large number of pictures that I need to make my points clearly in a close relation to the text that discusses them is very difficult, and occasionally it is impossible. It is also hard to do all this and keep the ensemble looking good. The previous piece, like some other parts of the book, has been written directly on to the page, rather than being written in a word-processing program, and then flowed through the pages, as is the usual way. This gave me a certain mild sense of power while doing it, but it does have a tendency to inhibit making small qualifications and additions to the text, for fear of upsetting the balance of the setting.

Having finished this book, I sent it to BFI Publishing and Routledge, just to see what would happen, but they did not even bother to write back. But now you have got it anyway.

A year or two ago, when I started putting this book together, I thought I was out of new ideas, but they are still coming occasionally. So onward and upward, whatever the obstacles.

TECHNICAL GLOSSARY AND INDEX

Art director Old name for the person in charge of all the design of a film. This position is now called the **Production Designer,** and the **Art Director** is his or her subordinate. 21, 58, 134, 135, 139, 196

Art film Film aimed at a more sophisticated section of the total film audience. 9, 18, 192, 251, 322, 326, 328, 332, 334, 341

ASL or **Average Shot Length** The length or running time of a film, excluding the front and end titles, divided by the number of shots, including intertitles, in it. Also the quantity arrived at in the same way for parts of a film. 32, 158, 240, 244, 245, 258, 261, 262, 265, 266, 270, 271, 272, 274, 276, 286, 320, 321, 323, 324, 325, 330, 332, 333, 334, 342, 388, 389, 390, 393, 394, 395

Aspect Ratio The ratio of the vertical to horizontal dimensions of the screen image.

Atmospheric montage sequence A **Montage Sequence (q.v.)** which only shows places, rather than people doing things. 55

Autocorrelation, Autocorrelation coefficient 395, 396

Available light The light ordinarily present in a location used for filming, without the addition of special film lighting. 25, 116, 125, 215, 301, 327

Avant-garde film Film derived in style or content from the most advanced art of the time. 19, 21, 60, 85, 102, 230, 297, 312, 341

Background image The scene to be put behind the film actors by some process of compositing. 353

Background music Old term for **Underscore (q.v.)** 69, 254

Background projection (or **Back Projection**) (Abbreviation - **BP**) The projection of a film image onto the back of a translucent screen in front of which the actors are filmed performing. 80, 137

Background screen Special screen for **Background Projection (q.v.)** 81

Background separation Making a clear visible distinction between the actors and the set by film lighting 234

Backlight Light shining onto actors from the opposite direction to that in which the camera is pointing. 21, 30, 31, 33, 115, 236, 248, 306, 308, 309, 339, 345, 346, 347, 348, 349, 354, 355, 358

Back sunlight Sunlight shining from behind the actors and towards the camera. 236

Ballast unit Electrical device that generates the special voltage needed to power and arc lights, a HMI lights, ot a fluorescent lights for film purposes. 303, 304

Big Close Up (BCU) Shot showing just the actor's head 74, 199, 210, 211, 247, 253, 254, 262, 267, 268, 275, 295, 296, 330, 337, 339, 342

Biomechanics System for training actors that treats the body as a machine. 282

Blackwrap Very thick aluminium foil with a matte black surface used to control film light. 305

Bleach bath Chemical bath through which colour film ordinarily passes during development to remove silver. 302

Bleach bypass Having the colour film not pass through the bleach bath during developing. 302, 306, 307

Body microphone Very small microphone for attaching to an actors clothes. Formerly called a **Neck Mike.** 317

Burn-out Removal of all image density in a restricted area of the film frame by over-exposure. 306

Bust Name for a **Close Up** used before World War I. 26, 245, 252

Camera angle 49, 129

Camera axis Conceptual line drawn forwards from the camera down its lens axis. 49

Camera blimp Casing put around a camera intended only for non-sound filming to silence its noise. 74

Camera booth Large soundproof box with a glass window to hold an unblimped camera or cameras and their operators for synchronous sound filming. 74

Camera height 94, 96, 111, 223, 274

Camera movement 64, 274, 341

Independent film A new name for **Art Films (q.v.)** 300

Insert shot A shot of an object or part of a person other than the face. (Before World War 1 this term was also used to describe anything cut into the main scene such as intertitles and close shots of faces.) 26, 33, 43, 90, 116, 163, 171, 192, 193, 210, 211, 217, 223, 226, 240, 247, 252, 267, 274, 276, 331, 335, 340, 395

Inset scene or **Inset Image** A small image with its own frame or boundary included within the scene occupying the full film frame. 31, 41, 90, 108

Intellectual montage A form of montage that generates ideas from a series of images that in themselves singly do not contain or represent the ideas. An invention of Sergei Eisenstein. 284

Intermediate negative (or **Internegative**) Special negative film with fine grain and low contrast used as the first stage in the duplication of a positive film. 301

Intermediate positive (or **Interpositive**) Special positive film with fine grain and low contrast used for the first stage in the duplication of a negative film. See also **Duplicating Stock**. 301

Intertitle The modern term for a shot including explanatory text or dialogue. In the silent period intertitles were called sub-titles or just titles. 58, 109, 110, 116, 117, 128, 168, 217, 240

Introductory cameo A very brief scene, not part of the story, introducing an actor at the beginning of a film. 169

Invisible cut A cut that is intended to be sufficiently smooth for the audience not to notice it. 292

Irising Use of an iris diaphragm in front of the lens to create a black mask (usually circular) whose edge moves to gradually obscure or reveal the film image within the frame.

Iris-in 129

Iris-out 129

Jamming The synchronization of the time-code generators in a recorder and camera (or cameras) before filming starts. 320

Jump Cut Cut which moves directly from one shot to another taking place at a later time. 321, 327

Keycode Very small images of a series of barcodes printed down the length of negative film between the sprocket holes when it is manufactured which indicate the length at any point from the beginning of the roll. 309

Key light The light producing the principal and most conspicuous illumination of set and/or actors, and which usually determines the photographic exposure of the shot. 29, 234, 237, 345, 347, 348, 349, 351, 358, 359

Key of lighting How generally bright or dark all over the film is. See **High-key, Mid-key** and **Low-key lighting (q.v.).** 346

Key spotlight The spotlight producing the **Key Light (q.v.)** on a scene. 345, 358

Kinemacolor Early form of colour cinematography reproducing only two primary colours with a special camera. 211

Kinescope recording A recording of a television show by filming it on a high intensity television monitor with a 16 mm. camera. 264

Kino Flo light A proprietary form of fluorescent light in which the ionizing gases and coating have been altered to produce a light which is closer to the regular spectrum produced by tungsten and arc lights, and hence more suitable for film and TV lighting purposes. 303, 305

Lamp light 220

Lamp light effect The effect of light froma lamp simulated with film lights. 30, 238

Lantern slide Image on a glass plate than can be projected by a special lantern onto a screen. 211

Lapel microphone Very small microphone clipped to the actor's clothes. Now called a **Body Microphone (q.v.)** 317

Laser video disc 12 inch plastic disc containing a digital recording of a film. The ancestor of the DVD. 319

Latitude The range of brightness that can be reproduced by any particular photographic film. 301

Matte Opaque black sheet of material (usually thin metal) placed in front of, or behind, a lens to to obscure part of the image it forms. See **Mask** and **Travelling Matte.** 24, 31, 171

Matte, gauze Semi-transparent matte made of gauze. 59

Matte artist 137

Matte painting A painting that fills part of the film frame with a scene that appears to continue realistically the scene in the other part of the frame. 138

Matting Anything that involves obscuring part of the film frame with a matte. 33

Medium Close Up (MCU) Shot that shows an actor from the waist up. 74, 128, 202, 211, 224, 245, 253, 262, 265, 274, 275, 330, 349, 351, 356, 388

Medium Long Shot (MLS) Shot that shows the actors from just below the knees upwards. 26, 74, 117, 210, 217, 223, 245, 247, 253, 262, 265, 274, 295, 322, 330, 356, 388

Medium Shot (MS) Shot that shows the actors from the hip upwards. 14, 26, 28, 31, 74, 120, 126, 201, 216, 224, 245, 253, 254, 260, 262, 265, 266, 330, 388

Melodrama Strictly speaking, a play that uses any means to create as much emotion in an audience as possible. Usually describes a drama that contains any exaggerated elements. 169, 213, 217, 244, 280, 281

Melodramatic acting 187, 216

Mental image The representation in a film shot of what a character in a film is thinking about. 335, 340, 341

Mercury Vapour Tube Light Form of lighting unit whose monochromatic blue light was produced by an electrical discharge through mercury vapour inside it. See also **Cooper-Hewitt.** 25, 29, 38, 233, 234, 235

Method acting 281

Mid-key lighting Form of lighting of a film shot which produces an image which has approximately equal total areas of light and dark distributed over it. 237, 302

Minus The dark line sometimes separating the things in the foreground scene from the background scene in **Travelling Matte** shots. 353

Objective shot (or angle) Any shot in a film that does not represent any character's **Point of View.** 199, 211, 293, 296, 298

Object animation **Animation (q.v.)** done by moving all, or part, of solid objects between the exposure of each frame. 107, 152, 216

Omni-directional microphone A microphone which responds equally to sounds coming from all directions. 316, 317

OMNIMAX Form of the **IMAX (q.v.)** large film exhibition system, im which the film is taken and then projected onto a hemispherical screen using **Fish Eye lenses (q.v.)** 23, 313

One-reel film, One-reeler Film whose length is approaching 1000 feet. 32, 89, 128, 296, 403

Ones (animating on) Animation with a change to every successive frame. 151, 153, 154, 155, 157, 158

Open set Set built on an open stage, i.e. a platform outdoors. 233

Optical Effects or **Opticals** Alterations to the ordinary filmed image such as **Fades**, **Wipes**, **Blow-Ups**, and **Freeze Frames** which can be produced by **Optical Printing.**

Optical printer Film printing machine for **Optical Printing (q.v.)** 209, 214, 215

Optical printing Printing of a film positive from a film negative in a special printer which forms the image from one film onto another by a lens system between them. See **Projection Printer.** 342

Optical sound track 74

Orthochromatic film Film whose emulsion responds strongly only to blue and green light, slightly to yellow light, and not at all to red and orange light. 230, 235

Out-of-focus effect 339

Super 8 mm. film   302, 306

Swept area **(Neologism)** The area of the frame covered by movement over the whole length of the shot.   156, 157

Swing/shift lens   Lens that can be rotated about its optical centre at an angle to its ordinary axial direction.   312

Switch-backs   D.W. Griffith's name for **cross-cutting between parallel actions (q.v.).**   108

Symbolism   Art movement at the end of the nineteenth century that depicted symbols for things and mental states, rather than the things themselves. 186, 226, 227, 230

Symbolist   Having to do with **Symbolism.**   181

Sync. sound or **Synch. sound**   Usual abbreviation of **Synchronized sound.**   269

Tableau   A static posed group creating the whole stage picture in a theatrical production.   50

Tableau films   25

Tank (Studio)   Large permanent hole containing water in a film studio, which is used for shooting scenes that take place on, or in, water.   133

Technicolor   The name of a film processing company, and also for its special patented methods of filming and printing colour films. These unique methods are no longer used by the company.   3

Technicolor dye imbibition   The name for the special process formerly used by the Technicolor company to print films.   303

Techniscope   System in which the film is only pulled down by two perforations in a camera with a special half-height aperture, then printed with vertical anamorphic expansion to give a result identical to CinemaScope.   12, 17

Telecine   Device for creating television pictures from a film run through it.   301, 314, 319, 320

Television commercial   305, 321

Television program   259, 269

Theatrical   26

Thin negative   Colloquial name for an under-exposed negative.   256

Tilting or **Tilt**   Rotating the camera about a horizontal axis at right angles to the lens.   29, 32, 128, 203, 266, 271, 323, 331, 338, 357

Time-code   Impression on the film when it is shot of markings at fixed intervals which contain precise information of the absolute time at which each frame was shot. This can be transferred into digital form for the purposes of **Non-linear editing (q.v.)**   314, 318, 320

Time-lapse   Single images taken with a period between them much longer than the 1/24 th. of a second for normal filming. 293

Time slice   A shot in which the camera appears to move around actors frozen in their movement.   315

Title   A shot that is only made up of text.   24, 26, 99

Title, explanatory   Another name for a **Narrative title (q.v.).**   25

Title card   The art work prepared to shoot a **Title (q.v.),** and loosely used for the title itself.   110

Top-light   Light shining straight down onto a scene.   306, 312

Track-laying   Editing the sound tracks for a film.   296

Tracking shot or **Track**   Movement of the camera on some sort of carriage with respect to its surroundings.   16, 33, 44, 91, 176, 216, 266, 268, 272, 273, 286, 323, 325, 331, 332, 338, 339

Travelling matte   Method of combining moving actors filmed in the studio in the foreground of a scene with a background filmed elsewhere separately, using black silhouettes on film (mattes) that exactly conform to the actors movements.   353

Trick film   Early film based on special effects rather than narrative.   38, 208, 209

Triptych screen   Film frame divided into three parts, each containing a different image.   34, 206

INDEX OF FILMS AND STAGE WORKS
(Stage works in Italic)

INDEX OF PEOPLE AND COMPANIES
(Names of companies in italic)